THE EVOLUTION OF
SOVIET POLITICS

THE DORSEY SERIES IN POLITICAL SCIENCE

THE
EVOLUTION
OF
SOVIET POLITICS

ROBERT J. OSBORN, Ph.D.
Associate Professor of Political Science
Temple University

1974

The Dorsey Press   Homewood, Illinois   60430
Irwin-Dorsey International, London, England   WC2H 9NJ
Irwin-Dorsey Limited, Georgetown, Ontario   L7G 4B3

66900

First printing, February 1974

ISBN 0-256-01533-3
Library of Congress Catalog Card No. 73-89118
Printed in the United States of America

For Edward and Barbara

PREFACE

I̲ₙ ᴛʜɪs ʙᴏᴏᴋ I have sought to show that the institutions that make up the Soviet Union's political system have been surprisingly durable over more than a half century of Soviet history, considering the great stresses placed on them. I also believe that the same can be said of the fundamental policy decisions that have shaped the lives of its 250 million people. In spite of much tinkering and adjusting, plus some experiments that at first seemed likely to change these decisions, many important economic and social policies retain the broad outlines they already possessed in the early 1930s.

Specialists on Soviet affairs, I should point out, remain divided over the question of stability in the Soviet political system. Is it likely to keep its present characteristics for another half century? Will it be unable to resist internal pressure for change? Is it undergoing the kind of planned evolution that is set forth in its ideological statements? Or have Soviet leaders discovered a formula that most political leaders seek and only a few have found, namely a technique for keeping the political system stable by somehow mastering the pressures generated from within? These and similar ideas have been the subject of numerous studies, and so far no one theory has proven satisfactory to the majority of specialists.

Rather than try to offer answers where specialized studies have failed, this volume is meant to introduce the problem of change and stability by looking at a number of major political decisions, and at the way each contributed to the Soviet system as it exists today. The three possible roots of each decision are examined: Soviet Marxist ideology, the situation that made a decision necessary, and improvisation in the face of crisis. Stress is laid on the different ways succeeding Soviet rulers have coped with the consequences of these decisions, and have changed or attempted to change some of them. I have examined the present-day Soviet system in terms of the appropriateness—or lack of it—of the major decisions in the light of the regime's present needs and challenges. These needs include both stability and adaptation to new social demands, plus the challenge of living up to Soviet Marxist prophecies of a transition to an entirely new form of society. Does the present Soviet regime confront major decisions on the scale of the decisions of the 1920s and 1930s? If so, what alternatives are open to it, and what is the regime's capacity for making well-considered choices?

For readers with little or no background in Soviet affairs and the pre-revolutionary Russian background, the economic components of political decisions need emphasis. Russian and Soviet history from the latter 19th century to the present show time after time the inseparability of politics and economics. Of the two areas, the chances are that the reader will have a harder time understanding the role of economics, the big questions of industrial growth and organization, and the crucial role of agriculture. For this reason, the book's opening chapters are devoted to the economic components of the big political decisions, with particular stress on the background of Russian economic development from the latter 19th century to World War I. Some writers on Soviet affairs have taken the point of view that political decisions have been a function of economic decisions, or even of a vaguely defined force called "economic necessity." The conclusion offered here is that Soviet leaders, far from being prisoners of economic forces, were attempting to solve economic and political problems simultaneously.

No account of Soviet politics is complete without a careful review of the major decisions that resulted in social transformations. The population's education, skills, geographical distribution, and social relations all had to be adapted to the regime's political and economic objectives. The final section deals with the major decisions in these and related areas. Here more than elsewhere in the Soviet system, the gap between the original intent of a decision and its later consequences may be great, and unanticipated side-effects are more likely than in decisions on political organization or economic policy. Soviet management of society has produced a mixture of successes and failures, and major policy problems could very well arise in this area during the 1970s and 1980s.

If this overview of the Soviet political system leaves question marks over a good many issues, it is because it necessarily reflects the current stage of our knowledge and ignorance about a very complex chapter in modern political history. This volume is meant both as a critical survey of some standard assumptions about the way the Soviet system has evolved, and as a framework of alternatives for future evolution.

January 1974   R. J. Osborn

CONTENTS

Policy: *Goals of Language Policy. Extent of the Use of Russian. Language Use in the Schools.* Demographic Developments and Policy: *Intermarriage. Mixing through Migration.* The Role of Economic Policy: *Equality and Disparities. Republics as Economic Units.* Religions: *Containment. Ideological Combat. The Publicity Use of Religion. Religions and National Identities.* Soviet Jews: A Special Case. Some Conclusions.

INTRODUCTION: REVOLUTION AND EVOLUTION

> Like a black river, filling all the street, without song
> or cheer we poured through the Red Arch, where the
> man just ahead of me said in a low voice: "Look out,
> comrades! Don't trust them. They will fire, surely!" In
> the open we began to run, stooping low and bunching to-
> gether, and jammed up suddenly behind the pedestal of the
> Alexander Column.
> "How many of you did they kill?" I asked.
> "I don't know. About ten . . . ."
> After a few minutes huddling there, some hundreds of
> men, the army seemed reassured and, without any orders,
> suddenly began again to flow forward. By this time, in
> the light that streamed out of all the Winter Palace win-
> dows, I could see that the first two or three hundred men
> were Red Guards, with only a few scattered soldiers. Over
> the barricade of firewood we clambered, and leaping down
> inside gave a triumphant shout as we stumbled on a heap
> of rifles thrown down by the *yunkers* who had stood
> there.[1]

This was the decisive stroke of the second Russian revolution of 1917,
the Bolshevik seizure of power in November (October by the old calen-
dar). It was hardly the heroic battle that later Soviet portrayals suggest.
At the Congress of Soviets, then in session not may blocks away, Leon

---

[1] John Reed, *Ten Days That Shook the World* (New York: Vintage Books,
1960), pp. 137–38.

1

Trotsky, the apostle of militant struggle, was stressing to the turbulent gathering that the coup thus far was entirely peaceful.[2] The last contingents guarding the Winter Palace in Petrograd, where ministers of the eight-month-old Provisional Government sat drafting futile appeals for support, offered no resistance to the Bolsheviks' Red Guards. The cruiser *Aurora's* "bombardment" of the Winter Palace from across the Neva River was carried on with blank shot. Still, there was plenty of drama for the coup's participants: At one stroke they were eradicating the last remnants of the two-century-old imperial rule founded by Peter the Great and of a legacy of harsh autocracy stretching several more centuries into the past. The insurgents were bent on building a type of government never before seen in history, and the prospect was intoxicating.

The coup's chief architect, Vladimir Ilyich Lenin, had struggled against improbable odds to attain this moment. He had overcome wide opposition not only among the Russian Social Democrats, but even among the leaders of his own Bolshevik wing of the Party. In the end his hard oratory, his ability to meet arguments head–on, his persuasive way of representing compromise as betrayal, all transformed him into a symbol of the revolutionary act. The Second Congress of Soviets, few of whose delegates could have foreseen that they would be called on to legitimize this act, was electrified by the supreme power which now was laid symbolically at its feet. Those opposed to the coup left the hall; the rest stayed to ride the wave of revolution with their new leader, a somewhat unlikely figure described here by an American admirer:

> It was just 8:40 [P.M., November 8] when a thundering wave of cheers announced the entrance of the presidium, with Lenin—great Lenin—among them. A short, stocky figure, with a big head set down in his shoulders, bald and bulging. Little eyes, a snubbish nose, wide, generous mouth, and heavy chin; clean-shaven now, but already beginning to bristle with the well-known beard of his past and future. Dressed in shabby clothes, his trousers much too long for him. Unimpressive, to be the idol of a mob, loved and revered as perhaps few leaders in history have been. A strange popular leader—a leader purely by virtue of intellect; colourless, humourless, uncompromising and detached, without picturesque idiosyncracies—but with the power of ex-plaining profound ideas in simple terms, of analysing a concrete situa-tion. And combined with shrewdness, the greatest intellectual audac-ity. . . . Now Lenin, gripping the edge of his reading stand, letting his little winking eyes travel over the crowd as he stood there waiting, apparently oblivious to the long-rolling ovation, which lasted several minutes. When it finished, he said simply, "We shall now proceed

[2] N. N. Sukhanov, *The Russian Revolution 1917*, vol. 2 (New York: Harper Torchbooks, 1962), pp. 627–28.

to construct the Socialist order!" Again that overwhelming human roar. . . .

His great mouth, seeming to smile, opened wide as he spoke; his voice was hoarse—not unpleasantly so, but as if it had hardened that way after years and years of speaking—and went on monotonously, with the effect of being able to go on forever. . . . For emphasis he bent forward slightly. No gestures. And before him, a thousand simple faces looking up in intent adoration.[3]

Lenin presented himself to his followers as history's supremely able servant, as the man who knew better than anyone else where the tide of war and revolution was leading, and hence as the man most qualified to chart Russia's predestined course into a new historical era. Probably most of Lenin's critics and enemies, whatever their political beliefs, were in agreement that nothing about the Bolshevik coup was predestined. Without Lenin himself, they argued, it would not have taken place at all; it was "adventurism" of a kind that even Lenin himself condemned in other contexts. This book makes no assumptions about history as an inexorable succession of events, or about history as the plaything of a few diabolically gifted individuals. It is quite simply an effort to describe certain important political choices, and to make them more comprehensible by looking at what the alternatives were at the time each choice was made.

While it is folly to try to "explain" these choices in the sense of proving that they had to be made the way they actually were made, at least one can attempt to define the limits within which the decision-makers worked. The limits are of different kinds: they include the limits of physical resources and space, the limits imposed at any given point by enemies both foreign and domestic, the limited capacities of the decision-makers themselves and of their staffs, the limits of information about the choices at hand, and—most intriguing of all—the limits imposed by beliefs, ideologies, and perceptions of the nation's people and culture. If one can draw a fair picture of these limits, then at least certain questions can be answered in rough fashion: Did a decision reflect an understanding of all the information available at the time? Did the decision-makers' beliefs appear to cloud their understanding of the facts? Was the actual principle of the decision in keeping with these beliefs, and with the principles which underlay other decisions? Were the major consequences of the decision foreseen at the time it was made?

If these and similar questions can be answered, then it may be possible to arrive at some conclusions about the way the Soviet Union's political system has been shaped up to now, and the way it may evolve in the future. The official Soviet view is that the present system was constructed according to a definite plan, which rested on a consistent group of princi-

---

[3] Reed, *Ten Days That Shook the World*, pp. 170–72.

ples and produced predictable results. Critics of various stripes maintain that other explanations must be sought: the decision-makers' principles, some say, were abandoned in favor of the sole principle of remaining in power at all costs; the consequences of decisions were not foreseen; facts were disregarded; and where decisions failed of their purpose, coercion and propaganda were used in order to convey the appearance oɪ success. The success or failure of decision-making may be judged according to just where the truth lies as between these extreme interpretations. As concerns the future development of the Soviet system, the decisions of the past, especially those of the recent past, may furnish some clues as to how the present leaders will react in given situations.

The major decisions that shaped the Soviet political system have a special fascination because they made dramatic changes that have endured. It is important to ask, among other things, whether the present Soviet leaders seem capable of making similarly sweeping decisions, when the need for them may arise. The early decisions, those of Lenin's time and of Stalin's early years of power, not only wrought drastic transformations, but appear to have placed narrow limits on the decisions that were made later on. Are the present Soviet leaders trapped within a narrow framework of perceptions that was fixed many years ago? Are they capable of responding creatively to changed circumstances? Or is the system that Lenin and Stalin built one that is best sustained by a certain narrowness and inflexibility on the part of the decision-makers?

Let us look at some overall theories about what factors set the limits for the two major groups of decisions that have shaped the present system: those that transformed Tsarist Russia into Stalin's system, and those that have modified Stalin's harsh rule over the last 20 years.

HOW DID BOLSHEVISM SUCCEED?

If one were to list the successful power seizures of the 20th century, they would certainly number many dozens. Of these power seizures many were started by movements which, like that of the Bolsheviks, were afire with the prospect of transforming their societies. One has only to think of Mexico in 1911, Turkey in 1919, Yugoslavia in 1941, China in both 1911 and 1946–49, Egypt in 1952, Iraq in 1958, and Cuba in 1959. Why, in retrospect, does the Bolshevik revolution still stand out among those which came before and after it? In part this was because of the suddenness of both the February and October revolutions of 1917; and in part it was because the regime which collapsed was legendary for its autocratic style of rule and for its massive system of control by bureaucracy and police. But even more, in the perspective of more than half a century, the Bolshevik coup cut a wide swath in history because what its leaders did then has proven so durable today. The extirpation

Lenin speaking on Red Square, May 1919. (*Sovfoto, Wide World*)

Stalin attending a gathering with Voroshilov (left) and Kalinin (right) in the 1930s. (*Bettmann Archive*)

Stalin and Molotov at a meeting marking the opening of the Moscow Metro (subway) in May 1935. (*Wide World*)

Left to right, President Voroshilov, First Secretary Khrushchev, Prime Minister Bulganin, and Defense Minister Zhukov, in conversation with a delegation from Afghanistan (not shown) in July 1957. Zhukov was removed from his post in October, Bulganin the following March. (*Wide World*)

Khrushchev viewing the corn crop at a collective farm in Kherson Province, September 1963. (*Sovfoto*)

Left to right, Prime
Minister Kosygin,
General Secretary
Brezhnev, and President
Podgorny at
Vnukovo Airport in
May 1973, as Brezhnev
departed to visit the
German Federal
Republic. (*Sovfoto*)

Brezhnev, in an expansive mood, gestures with a matchbox while conversing with American correspondents in his Kremlin office on the eve of his departure to visit the United States, June 1973. (*Wide World*)

of the old bourgeoisie and aristocracy as political forces, the building of the dual pyramid of Party and soviets, nationalization of the economy, central planning, propagation of an official ideology, transformation of a society of backward peasants into a modern industrial people—all the major domestic goals which Lenin announced to the Congress of Soviets have in one form or another been realized.

Why have the consequences of the Russian Revolution been so durable? There are three giant pieces to the puzzle, each of them built out of countless lesser pieces: (1) the Tsarist political system as it existed in the early 20th century; (2) the intentions and capacities of the Bolsheviks, who succeeded in inheriting this system; and (3) the Soviet system which emerged with the Stalin transformation of the 1930s, a system which in most of its important features has lasted up to the present. Whoever tries to build a theory about the emergence of the Soviet system must stress one or another kind of relationship among these three parts.

Theories of Continuity

One explanation stresses the continuity of Tsarism, Bolshevism, and the modern Soviet system. Nicholas Berdyayev, a noted Russian philosopher who emigrated after the Revolution, believed that the Soviet system was a reincarnation of the Tsarist system. "However paradoxical it may sound," he wrote in 1937, "Bolshevism is the third appearance of Russian autocratic imperialism, first presented by the Muscovite Tsardom and then by the Petrine Empire." Bolshevism triumphed, said Berdyayev, because it built the new system squarely on Russian traditions:

> It made use of the Russian traditions of government by imposition, and instead of an unfamiliar democracy of which they had no experience proclaimed a dictatorship which was more like the old rule of the Tsar. It made use of the characteristics of the Russian mind in all its incompatibility with the secularized bourgeois society. It made use of its religious instinct, its dogmatism and maximalism, its search after social justice and the kingdom of God upon earth, its capacity for sacrifice and the patient bearing of suffering, and also of its manifestations of coarseness and cruelty. It made use of Russian messianism and faith in Russia's own path of development.[4]

In a somewhat different version of this thesis, it was Stalin who in the 1930s reshaped the Soviet system in this fashion quite contrary to what Lenin had intended. That is, the modern system has returned to the

---

[4] Nicholas Berdyayev, *The Origin of Russian Communism* (1937), quoted in Hans Kohn (ed.), *The Mind of Modern Russia* (New Brunswick, N.J.: Rutgers University Press, 1955), p. 254.

Tsarist mold, while the Bolshevik Revolution as such was not, and could not possibly have been, a decisive event:

> As revolutionary leaders usually are Utopians, they do not recognize the natural limitations of human actions and strive for goals which cannot be attained. They succeed best in those phases where they continue historical trends which were temporarily inhibited before the outbreak of a revolution. But to achieve these successes, the nation has to pay a heavy price. Everybody knows that revolution means destruction of human lives, materials, and spiritual values. It is less well known that revolution, as shown by the Russian example, may mean retrogression. In any case, revolution is the most expensive mode of social change . . .[5]

Nicholas S. Timasheff, an American scholar who made this judgment after two decades of Stalin's rule, found that industry, population, and literacy had all grown in exactly the same way as they would have if prerevolutionary trends had continued undisturbed. Education and the arts had slipped backwards, and in political organization the nation had regressed to the latter 18th century. In his view, revolutions as factors in a nation's overall development seldom help and often hurt.

These two interpretations of Soviet development, if true, limit development of the present system to a fairly narrow path. The first suggests that the Brezhnev regime, like all its predecessors, still uses and reinforces the old Russian tradition of dictatorial rule. The second takes a dim view of any possibility of rapid forward strides: ". . . no Third Socialist Offensive will follow The Great Retreat."[6]

The American historian Theodore Von Laue found a different kind of linkage between Tsarism and the Soviet system under Stalin. While acknowledging the force of Russian tradition in shaping Bolshevik policies after the revolution, he places first emphasis on the imperatives of the "global power struggle." Russia in the 20th century had to catch up with the great powers industrially and militarily, or else decline to a second-rate power and be forever a prey of those which had become first-rate—Great Britain, the United States, France, Japan, and Germany. Already the great powers had humiliated Russia and thwarted its external ambitions, in the Crimean War (1854–55), the Berlin Conference of 1878, and the Russo-Japanese War (1904–05). The Bolshevik approach, in this view, had much in common with that of Peter the Great, who at great cost and by harsh rule had launched Russia on modernization of several kinds. Modernization at a forced pace and in directions set by other countries could be accomplished only by dictatorial means. "Overtaking the West," a constant theme of Soviet propaganda from the Revolution

---

[5] Nicholas S. Timasheff, *The Great Retreat* (New York: E. P. Dutton, 1946), p. 396.

[6] Ibid., p. 413.

to our day, not only ruled out the possibility of democratic evolution, but required the total mobilization of national resources through central command. It meant austerity and sacrifice, plus the uprooting of rural populations for industrial work. Even Britain, the United States, and the industrial West had used repression of some kinds to keep industry functioning and to quell protest movements. How much more did Russia, a nation now under severe pressure to modernize, have to use repression to meet its goals.[7]

Theories of Radical Change

A very different set of interpretations maintains that the Bolsheviks broke radically with Russian traditions. The Bolsheviks' coup in 1917 was the product of luck, and their victory in the subsequent civil war came about mainly because their enemies, domestic and foreign, worked at cross-purposes. These hazards once surmounted, the Bolsheviks then found themselves applying a highly unsuitable doctrine to Russian realities. The political system which emerged in Stalin's time was the not unsurprising result of imposing their utopian dogmas on an unwilling people. One variant stresses the content of Marxism, as reworked by Lenin; another stresses the problem of trying to use any kind of radical ideology as a chart for governing a nation. In both cases, Marxism is an alien product brought into Russia by a small fanatical group. That is to say, the Bolshevik Revolution did not grow out of Tsarism in the least, but stood in contradiction to it. The result, the Soviet system of Stalin and his successors, is the outcome of a strange historical accident. It will forever exist under high tension because Marxism was imposed from without, so to speak, and not cultivated from within. Professional anticommunists in the West have generally used this interpretation. It has enabled them to portray Soviet communism as a cancer which might some day be extirpated, possibly through a revolution like that of 1956 in Hungary. Once the props are knocked out from under a communist regime, they argue, a very different and hopefully democratic political system will emerge in reaction to what has gone before.

Theories of Totalitarianism

Some theories of Soviet political evolution stem from a definition of the Soviet system as totalitarian. Here the entire emphasis shifts to the way the modern structure is put together, and the Soviet system (or Stalin's system, at any rate) is put in the same category as Hitler's Germany and Mussolini's Italy. Totalitarian regimes, according to the best-

---

[7] Theodore Von Laue, *Why Lenin? Why Stalin?* (Philadelphia: J. B. Lippincott, 1964). See especially the Conclusion.

known definition of them, rest on six great pillars: an elaborate official ideology, a single mass party typically led by one man, a system of terror effected through party and secret-police control, a governmental monopoly of the means of mass communication, a monopoly of armed force, and tight central control of the economy. Carl J. Friedrich of Harvard University, who elaborated this definition, said that ". . . we cannot fully explain the rise of totalitarian dictatorship."[8] Therefore he refrained from attempting to find common roots for the Nazi and Soviet systems, and concentrated instead on the techniques by which they maintained themselves in power. From his writings on the subject, one gains the impression that totalitarian regimes depend on successful combination of the six elements enumerated above, and that a regime which achieves this combination can survive a long time unless it is destroyed from without.

The theory of totalitarianism in this version is attractive as a way of explaining Stalin's Russia, and perhaps also the Soviet Union of today. Its attractiveness is that it assumes only the most general sort of linkage between pre-revolution and post-revolution and can disregard the revolutionary act. If totalitarian regimes can emerge from systems as diverse as the Russia of Nicholas II and the Germany of Weimar, then one needs only to assume that each system displayed some kind of weakness which made it a prey to totalitarian movements. What Russia, Germany, and Italy shared during the first quarter of the 20th century was neither a common type of political system nor a common historical heritage, but internal weakness, an inability to cope with crises, whose origins could have been very different as among the three countries. As for totalitarianism, according to Friedrich, this was a unique product of the 20th century, a prescription for political order which could exploit and replace different types of systems caught in various kinds of crisis. It could subvert these systems by any means appropriate to the situation, from bloody uprisings to shrewd parliamentary maneuvers. Once established, it could either weave national traditions into its ruling ideology or reject traditions in favor of an invented set of doctrines. In any case, the emphasis of this analysis is on the success of the totalitarian technique as a successful and uniquely modern means of holding power, not on the setting from which totalitarianism emerged.

Still other versions of the theory of totalitarianism find it to be a product of 20th-century circumstances, regardless of how it arose or what techniques it employs. Modern dictatorships, in one version, need to find mass support if they are to survive for long; no longer is the support of the army and police enough, or the compliance of powerful privileged groups. To obtain mass support, there must be some kind

---

[8] Carl J. Friedrich and Zbigniew K. Brzezinski, *Totalitarian Dictatorship and Autocracy*, 2d ed. (New York: Praeger, 1966), pp. 7, 22, et passim.

of democratic ritual without the substance of democracy. In Hitler's Germany, an existing democracy had been subverted. In the Russia of Lenin and Stalin, controlled mass participation was held out as a lure to the peasants, who were then the vast majority of the population and largely hostile to the Bolsheviks. It was the failure of this effort that made necessary a full-blown totalitarian system.[9]

The concept of totalitarian rule reinforces the conspiracy notion of Western anticommunists only in some respects. It does indeed cast the Bolsheviks in the role of a conspiratorial minority. It does not, however, state that the Bolsheviks necessarily cut against the grain of Russian traditions. It posits differences in the mechanism of rule as between the Soviet system and Tsarism, but not necessarily in the purposes of rule. Quite definitely it does not mean that to destroy a totalitarian regime is to clear the way for a system agreeable to Western democratic tastes.

Was Democracy a Possibility?

Alas, decades of debates and an avalanche of literature from scholars, knowledgeable journalists, and professional Russia-watchers have produced no large areas of agreement on the foregoing questions. If there is consensus or near consensus on any one point, it is that the chances that a liberal constitutional political order would emerge were slim. This is not to say that the makings of a constitutional order were absent. On the contrary, the dozen years of the State Duma, Tsarist Russia's only parliament (1906–17), had seen some real gains in that direction.[10] Nevertheless, even the more optimistic observers have concluded that the miracles which might have coaxed the beginnings of modern democracy into full bloom simply could not have happened. Democracy appeared fated to be crushed under the triple pressure of Russia's long-unresolved internal problems, the chaos which the European powers brought down on their own heads in 1914, and the political forces which feed on weakness and chaos. Granted such a conclusion, we come back to our old problem: Who should have inherited Russia? Were Lenin and Stalin heirs mainly by accident?

Soviet Explanations of Change

The Soviet self-interpretation of the emergence of Soviet rule will be discussed in later chapters. Here it should be noted only that, by

---

[9] Such, in simplified form, is the argument of Franz Neumann, in *The Democratic and Authoritarian State* (Glencoe, Ill.: The Free Press, 1957).

[10] See, for example, the evaluation by Thomas Riha, "Constitutional Developments in Russia." in T. G. Stavrou (ed.), *Russia Under the Last Tsar* (Minneapolis: University of Minnesota Press, 1969) pp. 87–116.

the time Stalin's system had taken shape, ideological improvisations had been piled one on top of another. However, what at first seemed an awkward ideological problem later blossomed into a grand justification for some of the worst features of Stalin's rule. The fact that the proletarian revolution had occurred prematurely with reference to Russia's economic and social development was due to chance and luck. But this meant that the new regime, having taken power early, would be coping with great chunks of the old order at the same time that it was trying to hasten the growth of a radically new order.

As Marx had envisaged proletarian revolution in western Europe, it would happen when the old order had not only exhausted most of its possibilities for further development, but created the major components of the new order in its midst. There would be a fairly short period of birth pangs, of readjustment of the workers' habits and mentality to a society in which all men shared the rule, and the new socialist order would soon be well established.

Lenin used the premature occurrence of the Russian Revolution to justify his Party's monopoly of power, plus tight internal discipline within the Party. Under the rubric of "socialism in one country," from 1925 on, Stalin and others promoted the idea that this one nation could build a socialist economic order without waiting for the revolution to spread to the great industrial powers. Then Russia's economic isolation—the fact that there were no proletarian governments elsewhere to provide economic aid—was used as justification for the drastic belt-tightening which industrialization required. Both Lenin and Stalin justified political repression as made necessary by the fact that their domestic class enemies were likely to embark on subversion of the new regime. Finally, by way of justification for the Great Purge and the burgeoning labor camps of the 1930s, Stalin promoted the doctrine that the class enemies left over from the Tsarist era would increase their efforts at subversion right up to the point where the nation stood on the threshold of the new communist society. All these points except the last one—which was denounced in the Khrushchev era—are still part of the Soviet version of Marxism, and the increasingly severe measures taken against political dissidents during the Brezhnev period may be a step back in the direction of Stalin's doctrine. Among Marxists generally, there have been wide-ranging disputes about the validity of the other points as well.

HAS THE SOVIET SYSTEM CHANGED?

There is a second cluster of questions: Has the political system of Lenin and Stalin been evolving toward something fundamentally different? That Soviet society and the economy have undergone decisive changes can be seen in the statistics alone. But has the political system

accompanied these with changes of its own? If not, is the Soviet one-party
state under strong pressure to change, for the political survival of its
leaders if for no other reason?

From Lenin to Stalin

Here the puzzles begin with the differences between Lenin's system
and that of Stalin. Lenin had less than five years of active political leadership after the Bolshevik revolution; a stroke felled him in 1922, and he
died early in 1924. Much of his energies were absorbed by immediate
crises, the Civil War and Russia's disastrous economic condition. But
the formal structure of rule he built in this brief time has lasted over
a half century. The Communist Party had established its monopoly of
power within a few brief years, and all rival parties were now banned.
The dual administrative hierarchy of Party and soviets had been institutionalized with the Russian Republic's constitution of 1918. The multinational federation was made formal with the first constitution of the
whole Soviet Union in 1923. Public participation in the affairs of government was being promoted through the soviets and mass organizations
operating under the Party's guidance. A new Red Army had been organized, which featured a built-in hierarchy of political commissars from
top to bottom. The Cheka, or political police, forerunner of today's KGB,
had already been at work arresting the new regime's enemies a few
months after the October Revolution. Techniques of propaganda and
control of the mass media had assumed a shape familiar in the USSR
today.

While these features all remained constant, much else changed drastically within less than a decade after Lenin's death. By 1927, Stalin had
dealt mortal blows to his chief rivals for leadership. This was the fruit
of a titanic struggle within the Party, where the issues, on the face
of things, were the pace and character of economic development and
the relation of Soviet development to hoped-for proletarian revolutions
elsewhere. During this struggle Stalin steered a cautious middle course.
Then, in 1929, by launching an industrialization drive whose goals exceeded even the most optimistic economic plans then under debate, he
took up the cause of some of the men he had defeated. In the campaign
for collectivizing the farms, the surprise was even greater, since few
had suspected that Stalin or anyone else would risk the nation's all-important harvest by applying such swift, brutal pressure. There was similarly
brutal pressure on other elements of the Soviet population: suspect organizations were abolished, churches were attacked and many were closed
down, writers were herded into a single political fold, espionage and
sabotage trials warned the political waverers, former Mensheviks found
themselves once again under the axe, and the Ukrainians and other non-

Russian peoples suffered repression of various kinds. What followed is
well-known history: judicial murder of many of Stalin's own Party associates in the all-pervasive police terror, the Great Purge, and a labor
camp population of probably 10 million, which Stalin later left as a difficult legacy to his successors.

Did Stalin betray Lenin by perverting Lenin's political system and
forging his own Byzantine style of rule? Or had Lenin, perhaps in some
ways unwittingly, paved the way for the police-state barbarism which
Khrushchev was later to attack? Stalin had done everything to draw
Lenin's mantle over his shoulders. The names Marx-Engels-Lenin-Stalin
were linked, in that order, in countless propaganda devices of the Stalin
era. Officially, Stalin was continuing Lenin's work.

It is impossible to say how large a proportion of Russians shared the
opposite conviction of Leon Trotsky, since 1929 an exile, that Stalin
deliberately and purposefully turned Lenin's proletarian democracy into
"Caesarism" and "bureaucratic absolutism." In Trotsky's version of Soviet
political evolution, Stalin and his system were the product of sharp class
struggle; he and his lieutenants had appeared on the scene at the right
time to exploit class differences during a period of crisis following the
proletarian revolution:

> The Soviet bureaucracy is like all ruling classes in that it is ready
> to shut its eyes to the crudest mistakes of its leaders in the sphere
> of general politics, provided in return they show an unconditional fidel-
> ity in the defense of its privileges. The more alarmed becomes the
> mood of the new lords of the situation, the higher the value they
> set upon ruthlessness against the least threat to their so justly earned
> rights. It is from this point of view that the caste of parvenus selects
> its leaders. Therein lies the secret of Stalin's success.[11]

Trotsky traced the evils of Stalinism, in Marxist fashion, back to "the
dilatoriness of the world proletariat in solving the problems set for it
by history." The spread of revolution to other European countries, he
believed, would topple "Soviet Bonapartism" and set the Russian Revolution back on the right track.

Khrushchev's denunciation of Stalin at the 20th Party Congress (1956)
made no use of Marxism to explain the Stalin phenomenon. The real
root of Stalinism was Stalin himself, a man already corrupted by power
in Lenin's time, and roundly criticized in Lenin's political testament.
While Trotsky found that Stalin had done great damage to the building
of a socialist order, Khrushchev and his supporters stressed over and
over that Stalin's crimes had been against Party members rather than
against the new economic and social order.

---

[11] Leon Trotsky, *The Revolution Betrayed* (New York: Pathfinder Press, Inc.,
1972), p. 274.

The Khrushchev Era: What Kind of Reform?

Nikita S. Khrushchev, in denouncing the crimes of the Stalin era—in which he had played no small part—promised to restore "Leninist norms" in guiding the affairs of the Party, the government, and the whole nation. On the surface of things, Khrushchev did change some important characteristics of the system: the use of police terror was cut back greatly; deposed political leaders were no longer executed or imprisoned; many (if not all) labor camps were closed; there were important legal reforms; the business of Party and government bodies was regularized and opened to limited public scrutiny; writers worked for a time with fewer restraints; certain cultural contacts with foreign countries were again permitted; and for the first time the nation's resources were shifted somewhat away from heavy industry and defense, and toward more consumers' goods.

A considerable number of foreign observers were optimistic about these changes. Some went as far as to assert that the Soviet Union could no longer revert to the evils of the past, that Khrushchev had set irreversible processes in motion, which pointed in the direction of democracy. This enthusiasm cooled somewhat after 1960. While Khrushchev did not abandon his drive to maintain the policies of the latter 1950s, and even mounted some vigorous campaigns on behalf of certain ones, he accepted a number of compromises which were probably intended as props for his power. The demotion of some of his political protégés, a harder line in foreign policy in 1961–62, a shift of economic priorities in favor of higher outlays for defense and heavy industry, and renewed attacks on intellectual nonconformity were all part of a successful effort to cope with pressures from his increasingly restive Party associates. The fact that the latter conspired to remove him in 1964 does not necessarily detract from his success in keeping the political initiative in the years immediately preceding.

But even if Khrushchev's reforms had survived his rule in the form he originally sought, how many of them would have represented basic changes in the system that Stalin had built? Can it be argued that he was setting irreversible processes in motion? If the use of police terror had been cut back, still the KGB forces remained large, their files still bulged with data on potential dissidents, and they still enjoyed the protection of high Party figures who believed in rigorous police controls. Party organizations were once more operating in accordance with the Party Rules, but the full-time Party bureaucracy had changed little from Stalin's day: it remained full of Stalin-style conservatives, reluctant to relax their close grip on every important area of the nation's business. The Party showed no sign of a trend which might modify its absolute political monopoly, and Lenin's condemnation of factions and groupings within the Party remained in full force—note how Khrushchev revived this condemnation in labeling his defeated opponents of 1957 the "anti-Party group."

The Brezhnev Era: Stalinism Again?

The same kind of puzzles crop up when we try to assess changes in the Soviet political system since Khrushchev's removal in 1964. There is no consensus among the "Kremlin watchers" as to how the present system ought to be described. While few would go as far as to say that the Brezhnev era (1964 to the present) is simply Stalin's Russia all over again, a sizable group of experts and commentators argues that the present regime, in its most important political characteristics, remains within the same mold that Stalin gave it. The increasing political repression of the late 1960s and early 1970s, they say, is one kind of index which confirms this description.

Opponents of this view argue that, while in some ways today's political atmosphere does hark back to the 1930s and 1940s, fundamental changes have been taking place. Some see the most important changes in the realm of political decision-making, where a good deal of more or less open debate among the politically powerful has come to the fore. There has been a lively discussion among "Sovietologists" in the West as to whether something resembling interest groups has emerged. On the other hand, one may seek the differences first of all in the political culture of the Soviet population, the responses of people to the political system in which they live. It can be argued that today's Soviet citizens, compared with those of the Stalin era, are far better educated, politically better informed, and more skeptical of the demands made on them. As workers and consumers they have demonstrated to the Party leaders that they must be given an ever-increasing flow of material rewards; otherwise they will not keep up the kind of economic performance that the leadership needs. In their debates with Cuba, China, and other communist nations which preach consumer austerity, Soviet spokesmen have been very firm on this point. Thus, the argument goes, while the outward apparatus of Stalin's rule has survived its maker by two decades, its ability to exercise dictatorial rule is decidedly more limited today.

CONCEPTS OF CHANGE AND STABILITY

The "Industrial Society" and "Convergence"

The argument that Brezhnev's Russia is not Stalin's Russia raises the question of political change in a different form. If we use some definition of totalitarianism to describe the Stalin system, does this same model lend itself to hypotheses about change? We noted earlier the tempting hypothesis that the totalitarian system of the 1930s was first of all the result of a crash program of industrialization. It is equally tempting to assume that the prosperity which industrialization makes possible must sooner or later give rise to a different kind of political system. This need not be a system like those of the Western industrial democracies, but it could be a change in the direction of Western-style democracy. This particular line of thought is one version of the whole notion of "convergence." This is the idea that the political, economic, and social systems of the communist East and the capitalist West will all tend toward—though perhaps they will not fully arrive at—a common model. Some of the advocates of convergence call their model a form of social democracy, and some versions of it strike one as being a happy if improbable blend of Sweden and Yugoslavia. Prognoses about convergence in economic planning and management, or in the basic features of social structures, are on the whole more plausible than the expectation that political systems will follow in their wake.[12]

The critics of convergence have argued—and very effectively—that some characteristics of the industrial capitalist and socialist nations may converge, but without drawing other characteristics in their wake. Occupational, educational, and demographic similarity is inevitable, and some characteristics of economic management are likely to find a common ground. But it is possible to argue that, when this has happened, the potential for convergence has been exhausted as long as different systems continue to use their industrial economies and modernized societies for different ends. On a somewhat deeper plane of reasoning, the notion that economic change brings political change in its wake negates the role of ideas as actors in history. To this extent the proponents of convergence may be accused of having taken leave of one of the most widely held assumptions of Western intellectual culture.[13]

It is still possible to argue that political ideas themselves will arrive at a common denominator as between East and West, given sufficient communication between the two societies. At present, it is very hard to demonstrate that a trend of this kind is at work, attractive though

---

[12] The most outspoken proponent of convergence in all three fields has been Pitrim A. Sorokin. See his *Russia and the United States* (New York: Dutton, 1944), and *Basic Trends of Our Times* (New Haven: College and University Press, 1964). Qualified optimism was expressed by Talcott Parsons in "Communism and the West: The Sociology of the Conflict," in Amitai Etzioni and Eva Etzioni (eds.), *Social Change* (New York: Basic Books, 1964), pp. 390–99. The distinguished Soviet physicist Andrei D. Sakharov expressed optimism in his *Progress, Coexistence and Intellectual Freedom* (New York: Norton, 1968). For an example of a model for economic convergence, see Gunnar Adler-Karlsson, "Functional Socialism," *Peace Research Society: Papers*, vol. 6, 1966, pp. 87–100.

[13] See the strong case made in Raymond Aron, *The Industrial Society* (New York: Praeger, 1967).

the prospect is. The writings of some prominent dissident Soviet intellectuals, which have received so much attention abroad, argue strongly for
convergence on the plane of political and social ideas. At present it seems
unlikely that these speak for anything like a majority of the Soviet population. But we simply do not know enough about Soviet public opinion
to make an informed judgment here. It may turn out that these unorthodox thinkers, like their Russian predecessors a century ago, are the beginning of some sort of wave of the future.

The Idea of Stable Totalitarianism

Another area of argument has to do with the stability of totalitarian
systems. The fascist regimes in Germany and Italy were destroyed from
without; their appetite for foreign conquest was large, and their inflated
empires became vulnerable to powerful enemies. During the same two
decades that these empires flourished, Stalin's Russia pursued a fundamentally cautious foreign policy. There were some bad blunders and reverses,
but Stalin's basic caution was rewarded when, in the latter 1940s, in
the aftermath of World War II, he was able to bind most of Eastern
Europe into a sort of empire which the Western powers were not in
a position to challenge. But at home and abroad the whole emphasis
was on domestic strength and security rather than foreign conquest.
Stalin's political system survived where the others had blundered into
collapse. Its terror system and other excesses have been abolished or
curbed, but its other fundamental characteristics have persisted to this
day in spite of important social, economic, and organizational changes
within the system. Equally important, most of the communist regimes
which, by their own choice modelled themselves on the Soviet example
have shown hardly any indication of internal trends which could lead
towards their collapse.

The term totalitarianism is no longer considered appropriate by many
observers of Soviet affairs as a description of the present political system.
Other terms and definitions are used by those who stress its stability,
or its failure to evolve in the direction of Western-type democracy.
One specialist has called the Soviet system an "organizational society,"
based on command, as distinct from "market societies," based on contract,
and traditional societies, based on custom. The organizational form
reached its apex under Stalin. Since then an important development has
created pressure to introduce certain features of a market society: the
need to decentralize the command structure somewhat, both by splitting
this structure into different vertical segments and by devolving decisions
to lower levels.[14] In support of this idea, one may point to the post-Stalin

[14] T. H. Rigby, "Traditional, Market, and Organizational Societies and the USSR,"
World Politics, 16 (July 1964): 539–57.

phenomenon of interest groups in the form of bureaucratic alliances. The top policy-makers must reckon with these and often work through them in making their decisions. However, it is still a very long step from the politics of bureaucratic structures to the workings of interest groups in the noncommunist democracies.

A less optimistic view is the thesis that Stalin's totalitarianism has given way to the "administered society":

> The administered society can be defined as one in which an entrenched and extraordinarily powerful ruling group lays claim to ultimate and exclusive scientific knowledge of social and historical laws and is impelled by a belief not only in the practical desirability, but the moral necessity, of planning, direction, and coordination from above in the name of human welfare and progress.[15]

Terror has been dispensed with under this reformed system because it has been replaced by effective controls of other kinds. The driving force of the leadership is its belief that all of society must be coordinated; other goals are subordinated to this central belief. When reforms are carried out, no matter how "liberal" they may be in content, their prime objective is to bolster central administrative control. According to this theory, Stalin's Russia is very much alive, but its methods of rule have grown both more subtle and in the long run more effective.

One of the central purposes of this book is to describe the trends that might confirm or disprove these various theories of political change or lack of change. In order to do this, we shall look at the most important decisions which shaped the present-day Soviet system, the circumstances in which they occurred, their success or lack of it, and the likelihood that further major decisions will be made.

STUDYING THE BASIC DECISIONS

Several assumptions underlie the organization of this book. One is that the important decisions which shaped the Soviet political system as it exists today were made during the first 15 years of Soviet rule, that is, by the end of the First Five-Year Plan in 1932. Though all of these political decisions have been adjusted and readjusted countless times, the present Soviet political leadership has not moved to alter any of them fundamentally. Khrushchev sought some significant partial alterations, but was balked even while he was in power. Even those parts of Soviet Marxist ideology which call for change—i.e., the idea that "public self-administration" will replace state administration—have so far produced little but peripheral reforms.

---

[15] Allen Kassof, "The Administered Society: Totalitarianism Without Terror," *World Politics* 16 (July, 1964): 558. Copyright © 1964 by Princeton University Press; reprinted by permission of Princeton University Press.

A second assumption is that the content of these decisions was strongly influenced by the immediate crises which made some kind of decision necessary. Lenin, Stalin, and the other leading Bolsheviks clothed emergency measures in the language of ideology, and turned these measures into articles of faith which they and their successors were loath to alter later on.

An assumption closely related to this is that in seeking solutions to emergencies the Bolsheviks of the first 15 years frequently seized on devices which the Russian Empire had used to maintain itself in power. Rigid centralization of state administration, thoroughgoing censorship, restrictions on agricultural labor, promotion of an official ideology by means of tight limitations on competing beliefs, a conventional rather than revolutionary legal system, state manipulation of rewards and ranks—all these and others were quickly grasped as they were needed, and became cardinal features of the mature Soviet system. Some of these devices were prompted by Marxist ideology as well, to be sure, for example Marx's assumption that under communism the economy would continue to be centrally planned and directed. But the Bolsheviks turned out to have "very Russian reflexes" in choosing the components of their new system. This is not the same as saying that these decisions were fated to occur sooner or later because of the Russian political experience and political culture which formed their background. Others might have made very different decisions by rejecting the Russian political background. Here we can only note the fact that, in making ever so many important decisions within the limits imposed by their Soviet-style Marxism, the Bolsheviks often opted for the choice that was closest to the practices of the old Russian Empire.

There is little room within the confines of this book to characterize the political system of the Russian Empire in detail. Its economic development is described in chapter 1, and certain features of its administrative structure are noted in later chapters. Otherwise the pre–1917 political background is sketched in briefly wherever its relation to Soviet choices and practices are significant.

Another assumption is that the Soviet leaders have so far resisted—and have been well able to resist—changes in Soviet society and the economy which might be expected to produce serious pressures for change. For example, a society that has gone through a remarkable growth in educational level has produced demands by some elements for greater freedom of information and expression; but so far, in spite of periods of ferment among intellectuals—including the early 1970s—political measures have maintained the old system of censorship. Another example is the rising level of consumer welfare, which in the Western experience has been accompanied by a "privatization" of individual goals: concentration on individual well-being, resistance to demands of the state which might threaten this, and lack of response to ideological appeals which involve sacrifice, except for appeals which play on the theme of threats to individual welfare.

The history of the Soviet political system thus far is a success story. Its management of economic and social crises, and of its own internal political strife, has been such as to preserve one-party rule, oligarchic domination of the Party system, central state and economic administration, central direction of social organization, Party custodianship of the ruling ideology, and a monopoly of communications and of the important forms of expression. However, one cannot project the political success of the system's first half-century into its second half-century without considering the factors that could alter it. For one thing, the demands and pressures of Soviet society may after all increase to the point where the Soviet techniques of social management no longer suffice to contain them. Economic difficulties, especially under continuing international pressures to maintain economic strength, may force a drastic reordering of economic management, especially in agriculture. Finally, even the Party's very restrictive leadership recruitment pattern does not exclude the possibility that leaders chosen by the usual means will turn into reformers once they are in power. Until now, Soviet leaders have perceived their security, convenience, and power of control in preserving the system's existing characteristics. Future circumstances might suggest otherwise to leaders acute enough to realize the benefits of change.

FOR FURTHER READING

Until the 1960s, specialists in the Soviet political system and the politics of other communist nations pursued their studies apart from many of the important concepts and methods being used in other areas of political science. The following volumes are among those that have sought to bridge this gap in recent years: Frederic J. Fleron, Jr. (ed.), *Communist Studies and the Social Sciences: Essays on Methodology and Empirical Theory* (Chicago: Rand McNally, 1969); Roger E. Kanet (ed.), *The Behavioral Revolution and Communist Studies* (New York: The Free Press, 1969); Samuel P. Huntington and Clement H. Moore, *Authoritarian Politics in Modern Society: The Dynamics of Established One-Party Systems* (New York: Basic Books, 1970); Chalmers Johnson (ed.), *Change in Communist Systems* (Stanford, Calif.: Stanford University Press, 1970); and Jan Triska (ed.), *Communist Party-States: International and Comparative Studies* (Indianapolis: Bobbs-Merrill, 1969). Readings dealing with the specific questions raised in this Introduction are given at the end of the appropriate chapters.

Part I
COMMAND OF THE ECONOMY

1
THE RACE TO INDUSTRIALIZE

> It is sometimes asked whether it is not possible to slow down the tempo somewhat, to put a check on the movement. No, comrades, it is not possible! The tempo must not be reduced! On the contrary, we must increase it as much as is within our powers and possibilities. This is dictated to use by our obligations to the workers and peasants of the U.S.S.R. This is dictated to us by our obligation to the working class of the whole world.[1]

"It is sometimes asked . . ." Whoever is familiar with the official euphemisms of the communist world will note the acknowledgement of rumblings of dissatisfaction, probably in high political circles. And whoever is familiar with the writings of communist leaders individually will recognize the rhetorical questions and gnomic style of Joseph Stalin. The time was February 1931, the audience an assemblage of some 700 economic administrators, factory directors, and engineers.

If we try to imagine this scene, we must not picture the 52-year-old Stalin as a Hitler wooing the masses or thundering at his subordinates. His manner as speaker did not impress, nor did he seek an impressive style. To begin with, he stood only five feet six, his body somewhat too large for his legs. His voice, even in ripe manhood, was high-pitched and a trifle squeaky; a junior official who heard many of his speeches during this period remembered his "slow monotone which is tiresome to the ear." In his Russian speech the accent of his native Georgia, beyond the Caucasus, stayed with him to the end of his days. At public gatherings

---

[1] J. Stalin, *Works*, vol. 13 (Moscow: Foreign Languages Publishing House, 1955), pp. 40–41.

he preferred to sit at the side or back, smoking his famous pipe or a cigarette. Perhaps this was a habit from the rapid-fire intellectual discussions in which he was no match for the other Bolsheviks. He waved away applause as if annoyed, though in fact he probably enjoyed it. Impressive he was in many ways, but mainly to those who had the opportunity of conversing with him and observing at length his manner of dealing with people. The heroic figure who appeared on millions of portraits and posters came from the propaganda mills, not from reality.[2]

INDUSTRIALIZATION AND REPRESSION

The crash program of industrial investment which was the heart of the nation's First Five-Year Plan was about 18 months old at this point. The euphoria of Stalin's political lieutenants concerning this plan had given way to a sober anxiety. As for the industrial chiefs themselves, from project managers up to the leading lights of the Supreme Economic Council, probably few could still be convinced that their targets under the Plan could be reached on schedule. But Stalin kept up the pressure on all of them. At this same gathering, he was asking the economic administrators to meet the basic industrial goals of the Five-Year Plan in three years. He berated them caustically for not having fulfilled their pledges for the previous year.

Threats Spur Performance

A sort of threat hung about his report. During the whole previous year, those Party leaders who in the 1920s had argued for a moderate tempo of industrialization, and against laying the real cost of industrialization heavily on the peasantry, had been demoted, fired, and in some cases expelled from the Party. The key spokesman for what Stalin had branded the "Right Deviation" had been made to recant their views publicly. It was these who had argued for a balanced program of industrialization, for a program whose cost would not rest too oppressively on the shoulders of the peasants. One of this group, the former trade union chief Mikhail P. Tomsky, had been ousted from his union post as the Five-Year Plan got under way; henceforth the main task of unions was to help the state spur production and nip labor unrest in the bud, not to protect the rights and interests of workers. Yet even these recantations did not stop Stalin from making public whipping boys of his former associates at the 16th Party Congress in 1930.

---

[2] From Alexander Barmine, *One Who Survived*, cited in T. H. Rigby (ed.), *Stalin* (Englewood Cliffs, N.J.: Prentice-Hall, 1966), pp. 74–75.

Already matters had gone beyond demotions and Party expulsions. Stalin reminded his audience of two recent trials where industrial specialists had been convicted of sabotage and plots to overthrow the young socialist order: the Shakhty case of 1928 and the "Industrial Party" trial at the end of 1930. While both trials were directed against the bourgeois specialists whose services were so essential, they carried hints that the crime of "wrecking," as it was called, might be uncovered in other quarters too. In the very next month after Stalin's speech, a number of former Mensheviks would be brought to trial on charges of conspiring to restore capitalism.

The victims of this trial were Party members who, in spite of having belonged to the now shattered Menshevik wing of the Social Democrats, had thrown their lot with the Bolsheviks and gained important posts in the economy. Many of them had opposed a high tempo of industrialization.

Why Such a Risky Course?

Stalin had risked everything on maintaining a killing pace for his program. Had it failed, his political rivals from the 1920s were waiting on the sidelines to exploit the failure. It was precisely during these years, 1930 to 1933, that several high Party circles were uncovered which had been discussing plots against Stalin's rule. Unlike the fantastic plots charged against the leading victims of the Great Purge later in the decade, these plots were probably real. It would have been easy enough for Stalin to have avoided much of this risk by accepting one of the plan variants worked out by Soviet economists during the 1920s, making some concessions to those in disagreement with it, and starting the First Five-Year Plan with a more or less united team. Instead, he had thrown the reasoning of his planners to the winds; goals were now set that would be impossible to achieve within the time limits required; and Stalin was proceeding to tear the old team asunder.

Stalin's decision to do all this had such long-lasting consequences for the Soviet system that it needs a close look. To begin with, the issue was not whether to industrialize at a rapid tempo, or whether to collectivize the farmers, or whether to mobilize the resources of the entire nation to do all this, under the auspices of a one-party system. All these things were agreed on. What needs analysis is the possibility that Stalin, in his specific demands, displayed logic in his apparent illogic. Even at the height of Khrushchev's de-Stalinization campaign in the latter 1950s and early 1960s, one could meet Soviet citizens—mainly of the older generation—who defended Stalin's basic decisions, if not the excesses they led to.

If it is logic we are seeking, instead of psychopathic behavior, then we must look for economic, political, and social logic all at the same time. In any political system, major policy decisions are seldom devised as solutions to one problem alone, however serious. This is especially true of these decisions which cause a good deal of social disruption, or economic sacrifices, or serious political restrictions. As a reward for the risk that such decisions entail, the policy-makers contrive to benefit in as many separate areas as possible. It has been characteristic of Soviet policy-makers of every period that they have laid great stress on solving economic and political problems simultaneously.

With these warnings in mind, we can look at the circumstances which attended Stalin's decision of 1929, his resolve to carry on with it in 1931–32 in spite of grave risks, his plot of 1934 to do away with the men who sought to restrain his policy, and his measures to continue the basic features of his policy after World War II. First we shall look at the things that link these episodes to the recent Russian past: the resolution in the 1890s of a decades-long debate about whether Russia would embark on massive industrialization; and the dilemma at the turn of the century as to how fast a pace of investment could be maintained. Then we shall look at the economic situation the Bolshevik's inherited in the wake of World War I, the Revolution and the Civil War. This formed the background for the "Great Debate" of the 1920s concerning economic alternatives, which ended abruptly with Stalin's surprise decisions.

RUSSIA DEBATES THE INDUSTRIAL AGE

During much of the 19th century, some of the ablest minds in Russia's intellectual world were proclaiming that Russia would never follow the West's path of development. At least, even if Russia accepted technological advance, this would not lead its culture, society and national purposes down the same paths which the West followed. Never would industry become Russia's god; never would private property be the binding force of its social system. Many versions of this outlook rejected the idea of an industrialized Russia altogether.

Both friends and foes of Western-style modernization had something in common as Russians: their country was going to turn out differently. The notion of a special Russian destiny can be traced back at least to the 15th century monk Filofei who proclaimed Moscow—after the fall of Constantinople—to be the "Third Rome," the ultimate home of Orthodoxy and the world capital of Christianity. Today, one will encounter in the Soviet Union a good many ordinary Russians (though fewer non-Russians) who partake strongly of this feeling of uniqueness, sometimes in spite of their private criticisms of how the country is run.

The Populists and Agrarian Socialism

Serious debate about the prospect of an industrial and otherwise "Westernized" future for Russia began in the 1840s, among intellectuals who supported either a "Slavophile" or "Westernizer" point of view. ("Westernizer" was originally a term of contempt for those who urged that Russia follow the course of Western European civilization.) During this period Tsar Nicholas I (1825–55), the arch–conservative among the Romanov rulers, shared the Slavophiles' doubts about the wisdom of industrialization, and in particular feared its unsettling effect on Russian society. But it was during his rule that the first railways were built and government decrees promoted the practice of making serf labor available for factory work. The reforms of his successor, Alexander II (1855–81), spurred a second round of debate over the nation's future. The emancipation of the serfs (1861) provided the impetus for the birth of Russian Populism (not to be confused with American populism), which in different variants exalted the peasantry and saw Russia's future as that of a reformed agrarian order. Alexander's government was seriously interested in promoting industry, however, and welcomed foreign investment to this end.

By the beginning of the 1890s, the Russian government had committed itself to a major program of industrialization. It is at this point that the position of the Russian Populists becomes relevant to the story of how Russia became a major industrial power during the next four decades. Populism at this time was in great disarray, and not only because industrialization was surging forward with the government's blessing: in the 1880s the movement had become splintered, and the splinter groups had turned to terrorism. But important questions about the pace and purposes of industrialization remained unanswered, and it was these questions that provided the issues around which a new agrarian movement was founded at the turn of the century, the Social Revolutionary Party. Foremost was the issue of whether the Russian peasants should have to bear the main burden of industrial investment, through taxation. Related to this was the question of the pace of industrialization. The type of industrialization to be sought was of great importance: Would it benefit agriculture and the consumer directly in its early stages, or would Russia plunge immediately into the building of steel mills, power sources, and all the other equipment that now distinguished the industrial giants of the West? And finally, would the peasants' way of life have to change in order to satisfy the cities' demands for labor, food, and taxes? Would it be possible for Russia to enter the industrial age with caution, preserving the way of life and the institutions that Populists held to be unique and worth preserving?

Much Populist debate centered on the institution of the peasant commune or repartitional village. The commune was an old Russian form of common land ownership, in which village assemblies redistributed the land every few years so as to equalize the position of all the peasant households, each of which received (but did not own) a group of small and often widely scattered plots. The government had first promoted the commune after the emancipation of the serfs in the 1860s; two decades later it began removing the commune's legal underpinnings so as to free more rural labor for industrial work. What united the Populists was the belief that the commune embodied Russia's future. The writers Nicholas Chernyshevsky and Nicholas Mikhailovsky and other leading intellectuals saw it as socialism in embryo. Strengthening the commune would guarantee a future for Russia far different from what was happening in the West. While many Populists were prepared to accept technological advance, they proposed that it be used to strengthen agriculture rather than disrupt it by diverting people and resources into an urban-oriented industrial order.

Marx Considers Agrarian Socialism Possible

Karl Marx's contribution to the debate over the peasant commune and the future of Russian socialism may come as a shock to those who associate him (wrongly, actually) with a strict and all-encompassing brand of historical determinism. Russian intellectuals who during the 1870s had come across the first volume of *Capital* were understandably interested in knowing whether Russia, too, must pass through the purgatory of full-blown capitalism before it became eligible to enter the socialist era. Was not the commune already a socialist economic formation? Did it not offer Russia a direct route to socialist economic organization?

As yet there were no Russian Marxist organizations, or even any Russian Marxists of note. Nonetheless Marx, whose prodigious research had led him to learn Russian and study Russian economic developments, was impelled to intervene in a debate on the pages of *Fatherland Notes*, then the leading journal of Russian radical thought. Russia, said Marx, faces a critical choice between capitalist development and a direct transition to socialism, and only men and not History will make this choice. While capitalism in Russia had received quite an impetus in the wake of the Emancipation, Russia still confronted a unique choice. "If," wrote Marx, "Russia continues to pursue the path she has followed since 1861, she will lose the finest chance ever offered by history to a people and undergo all the fatal vicissitudes of the capitalist regime."[3] Several years later, in the preface to a Russian edition of the *Communist Manifesto*, Marx wrote that the "if" turned not so much on the choices made by the Russian government as on the timing of the Europe-wide proletarian

---

[3] Quoted in Lewis S. Feuer (ed.), *Marx and Engels: Basic Writings on Politics and Philosophy* (Garden City, N.Y.: Doubleday, 1959), p. 439.

revolution: an early revolution would find the commune still functioning, while a late revolution would find it in dissolution and unable to contribute to building a new socialist order.

Populist Views Shift

Russian radicals during the 1890s found themselves debating not the pros and cons of industrialization, but what their stance would be now that it was already happening. The idea of preserving the peasant commune died a slow death among the Populists, while the idea of agricultural cooperatives in a broader sense remained alive. Some foresaw a dynamic synthesis of industrial and agricultural production using large territorial units. That this was not a utopian dream was shown by the giant communes which China promoted during the "Great Leap Forward" of the latter 1950s.

Some Populists abandoned their views and became Marxian socialists. Others became supporters of rapid industrialization, while not renouncing their identity as Populists. Populists were just as alarmed as others over Russia's defeat at the hands of Japan in 1904–05, which was partly the result of the nation's technological lag. What remained of their Populism was an active concern for peasant welfare.

Concern for the lot of the peasant made an effective rallying point not only for the Populists, but for other groupings later on that were in a sense their spiritual descendants. The Social Revolutionary Party, founded in 1900, had grown to be Russia's majority party by 1917; it won a clear mandate in the national elections at the end of that year. Some of the adherents of the Bolshevik Right during the 1920s (described later), the doubtless many of those who protested the way collectivization was imposed in the early 1930s, shared the old Populist concern that the nation's peasant majority not be made the victim of industrial progress. From the 1890s to the early 1930s, Russian Marxists and Bolsheviks fought a series of ideological and political battles with the advocates of the peasantry, asserting the cause of the proleterian minority against that of the overwhelming peasant majority. When Stalin in 1931 spoke of those who would "slow down the tempo somewhat," much of the covert protest he referred to was peasant-oriented. And during those difficult years the debate ended—the peasantry was at last harnessed to the needs of high-tempo industrialization, and the protesters were dealt with by naked force.

Marxists Prophesy Capitalism and Industry

There was no permanently functioning Russian Marxist party in the 1890s—that was to come only in 1903—but there were many Marxist circles, and Marxist doctrines had gained wide currency among intellectuals and university students. The problem of importing Marxism to Russia was that the Russian economy, society, and government were nowhere near the historical point at which, according to Marx, a proletarian revolution would come about. Capitalism, the economic foundation of the bourgeois era of history, was only beginning to gather significant momentum.

During the first year of his Siberian exile, in 1896, Lenin wrote a well-documented study, *The Development of Capitalism in Russia*, prophesying Russia's continued rapid industrialization. Ever eager to push history forward, he foresaw that the rapid growth of the proletariat could give it a political weight which would transcend the handicap of its minority status in the population. The Russian proletariat had increased from 1.4 to 2.2 million during the 1890s, according to Lenin's calculations, but out of an overwhelmingly peasant population of over 100 million its proportion was still unimpressive by European standards. The political structure was still, by the Marxian definition, feudal; more precisely, it was the late absolutist stage of the feudal era. Feudal absolutism was thus presiding over an early capitalist economic formation, an anomaly if measured against Marx's periodization of history, yet still explicable in Marxian terms.

Russian Marxists were united in their prophecy that Russia must pass through the purgatory of capitalism before socialism could emerge. This meant that the countryside, too, must pass over to the control of capitalists small and great, from single-family farms to "agri-business" in huge holdings. In this Marxist conclusion lay the main battlefront between Marxists and Populists. There was no direct route to peasant socialism, said the Marxists, whether through the commune or by way of plans for integrating industry with agricultural progress.

Russian Marxism was born, so to speak, as the consequence of a debate over the future of the Russian peasantry and the prospects for rapid industrialization. The debate was kept alive because of the Social Revolutionaries' political success, particularly because they were dangerous (if also ill-organized) rivals of the Bolsheviks in 1917–18. Even in the 1920s there was still much "SR" sentiment in the villages which might have been mobilized had the Bolsheviks run into serious difficulties.

THE INDUSTRIAL AGE BEGINS

Russia's industrial boom of the 1890s was guided by Sergei Witte, the Minister of Finance and one of the most capable, interesting political figures produced by the Russian Empire. The son of a government official, he entered the railroad business as a government official himself, went over to private railroading in the 1870s when many lines were turned over to private hands, then went to the Finance Ministry in the 1880s, where he advanced to the ministerial chair in 1892. He shared the prevailing view in St. Petersburg that private enterprise was not a creed but a method, a method desirable under normal circumstances, but readily supplanted by state management where state interests required this. He brought to the Finance Ministry his businessman's intolerance of bureaucratic obstacles and a habit of riding roughshod over opposition. His love of autocracy as a form of government, though well established in his youth, was later reinforced by his realization that only a government untrammelled by constitutional obstacles could place its weight behind the drastic economic measures Russia now required to retain its great-power status.

Russia's Economic Lag

The Russia that Witte surveyed in 1892, the year he became Finance Minister, was a land of enormous natural resources for industrial growth, only some of which were being developed on a large scale. If one compares the use of known resources with the resource use of Europe's other great powers, Russian development was lagging well behind. Its economy was still heavily agricultural by any standard of measurement. Its population of 95 million, nearly twice the population of Germany and more than twice that of any other European power, was 85 percent rural. In industrial output Russia lagged far behind its major competitors. During the whole 18th century Russia had led Europe in pig iron production, thanks to Peter the Great's serf-manned enterprises in the Urals and elsewhere. In the 19th century, Western advances in metallurgy enabled the United States, Britain, and Europe to outstrip Russia many times over. By the time Witte took charge, Russia with its annual pig iron output of 900,000 tons was a third-rate producer beside Britain with 8 million tons and Germany with 4 million. Even France and Austria-Hungary, both well behind Britain and Germany industrially, were producing more than Russia. Russian coal production, for all the vast coal resources of the Ukraine, was negligible beside that of all the other great powers save Italy. The annual defense outlays had been running below those of France and Britain, and were about equal to Germany's outlays.

Considering the vastness of the Empire's territory, the length of its borders, and the locations of recently developed challenges to Russia's influence (from Japan in the Far East, from Britain in Persia and Afghanistan), the Russian outlays were dangerously low. While Germany had been perfecting its railroads in order to meet the crucial problem of shifting its armies between east and west, construction of the Trans-Siberian line to the Far East had not yet begun. Russian Central Asia, too, remained without effective modern transport. The disaster of the Crimean War, partly the result of Russian logistical impotence, might

easily be repeated in both those areas. The nation's manpower resources
were vast, but Russian arms expenditures per head of population were
less than those of any other European power, including Italy and
Austria-Hungary.[4]

The Witte System

The "Witte system," as it came to be called, took a number of programs and strategies that were already being used (or had been used)
and transformed them into a major drive which taxed the nation's financial resources to the limit. New railroads were built, mainly by the state;
these included most notably the Trans-Siberian Railroad, which had been
approved shortly before Witte took office in 1892. Railroads, according
to Witte, were the key to industrial investment. They would attract
both Russian and foreign capital from investors eager to have their share
of the nation's vast natural resources. While the vast bulk of this investment would be in private enterprises, the Ministry of Finance, using
the unique powers given to it decades before, actively promoted, regulated, and supervised the new undertakings. Subsidies and loans were
a favored means; officially recognized cartels parcelled out markets and
resources; a merchant fleet was promoted, commercial schools sponsored,
economic periodicals issued, and labor mobility regulated. To finance
these sweeping programs, Witte relied on large foreign loans (from
France, notably), import restrictions, aids to grain and raw material exports, higher taxes, and currency management culminating in a gold
standard and free convertibility for the ruble.[5]

The Industrial "Take-off"

The results of Witte's program were impressive, if one looks only
at the immediate, concrete achievements. In a bit more than a decade,
the railway network had been extended by almost 50 percent, not to
mention the double-tracking of many existing lines. Of all the other
modernizing nations, only the United States stood ahead of Russia in
the pace of railroad growth. The Russian rail system was being heavily
used, too. Most significantly, the bulk of its freight was now (1900)
nonagricultural goods.

The foreign investment which Witte hoped to attract with the new

---

[4] See the comparative figures in A. J. P. Taylor, *The Struggle for Mastery
in Europe, 1848–1918* (Oxford: Clarendon Press, 1954), ch. 1; and Alec Nove,
An Economic History of the U.S.S.R. (London: Penguin Press, 1969), chapter 1.

[5] For a full description of the Witte system, see Theodore Von Laue, *Sergei
Witte and the Industrialization of Russia* (New York: Columbia University Press,
1963), chapter 3.

railroads materialized in grand fashion. It was particularly the metallurgical industries of the Ukraine which attracted capital from the West, first of all from France and Belgium. These industries, in turn, thrived on orders from the railroads, which at the peak of the rail construction boom were consuming half of the nation's finished metallurgical products. Russia's output of iron and steel tripled during the decade, while coal output more than doubled. The Donets basin, which by 1900 was producing 70 percent of the nation's coal, had grown threefold in output. Oil production likewise tripled, the Baku area accounting for nearly all of it. Light industries rode the boom as well. The textile industry, Russia's largest single industry (by value of investment) at the beginning of the Witte period, came close to doubling its capital in the 1890s.

Economic Vulnerability Persists

It is important for understanding the debate over the Witte system to appreciate Russia's relatively low economic standing among the great powers even after this great industrial breakthrough. In its production of pig iron, the fundamental sinews of machinery, transport, armaments, and much else, Russia in 1900 had overtaken France and Austria-Hungary, but lagged well behind the other powers. Germany was producing more than twice what Russia produced, Britain more than three times, and the United States well over four times. Measured per capita of population, the Russian position was even worse. If one takes into account that Russia's vast territory made extraordinary demands on transportation and defense requirements, Russia remained a highly vulnerable nation. Russia's only major economic asset as against those of the other powers was its vast, unexploited subsoil resources.

Another point of vulnerability was Russia's great dependence on foreign investments, and the extent to which both industries and the national debt had passed into foreign hands. By 1900, foreign capital accounted for 70 percent of all mining capital; in the metallurgical industries, the proportion was 42 percent; and for corporations as a whole, the proportion was roughly half. Over a third of the national debt was held by foreign banks.

In the circumstances, it was not surprising that foreign capitals could bend St. Petersburg to their wishes in some matters, even to the point of humiliation and bribes. When some foreign-controlled metallurgical plants in the Ukraine experienced difficulties, French investors staged a press campaign against Witte. The latter had no choice but to increase the subsidies he had already been paying to the French press, and to bail out one of the biggest firms.[6] France had become Russia's ally against

---

[6] Ibid., pp. 296–98.

the Central Powers in 1894, and French loans to Russia during the 1890s
had been both a stimulus toward this alliance and a by-product of it.
But what if the alliance pattern later switched and the allies became
adversaries?

In Witte's time, there was no way to follow the West's industrial
path without first undergoing a period of dependence on the West for
many things: investments, long-term loans, and technological know-how.
Were Russia to reject this aid and the disadvantages it brought, it would
yield the race for industrialization to other nations at the very outset.
With the flow of aid once started, the foreign policy problem was to
minimize the impact of changing power alignments on economic relationships. This could be done first of all by avoiding risky steps that could
lead to war, and secondly by pursuing economic relations abroad which
would make Russia a power to be reckoned with in peacetime. Such
was the philosophy of Witte's program in China and the Far East, where
he was a vigorous promoter of Russian trade, investments, and
concessions.

What guarantee could Witte or anyone else offer that Russia would
not be carved into spheres of influence like China? Imperial Russia, unlike
the Manchu Dynasty, had been improving its highly centralized administration, begun under Peter the Great. For Witte, domination of the industrial growth process by the Ministry of Finance served to keep economic
initiative in St. Petersburg and prevented it from gravitating to Paris
or elsewhere. This in turn offered yet one more argument for Witte's
strong support of the autocracy principle: an autocracy is less susceptible
than a constitutional regime to being divided against itself through foreign
influence.

Protests against Witte's Program

The public debate over Witte's program was bitter and prolonged.
Opposition to his campaign for railroads and industries was by no means
limited to the Populists. The really significant opposition came from
high-ranking officials, influential landowners, and representatives of the
zemstvos, organs of local self-government set up in the 1860s and dominated by the liberal nobility. If one can identify a common denominator
of opposition, it was the charge that Witte was ruining Russian agriculture, worsening the lot of the peasant, and risking both peasant unrest
and fiscal disaster by what the opponents termed the artificial expansion
of industry.

Witte's most formidable opponent was Vyacheslav K. Plehve, twice
Russia's Minister of the Interior, the official who more than any other
answered for the country's internal security problems. Toward the end
of the Witte period, Plehve had become very alarmed at unrest among

both peasants and industrial workers. Witte, he contended, was promoting both types of unrest by oppressing the countryside with high taxes and by assembling a large urban proletariat. Factory legislation and other concessions on the part of the government had only stimulated strikes and labor agitation. "The Russian people are coming more and more to an oppressed, disastrous condition," he wrote in his diary in 1902. "Their patience weakens. The ground of anarchism becomes ever more fertile. . . . Russia is facing great calamities."[7]

Witte's Fall

Witte fell from power in 1903 as two of his predecessors in the Finance Ministry had fallen, the victim of an international emergency which required immediate military outlays and left economic development programs in ruins. Each of Russia's four last Tsars was persuaded at one point in his reign to risk Russia's military might in a foolhardy manner where the Imperial prestige appeared to be at stake: Nicholas I against the Ottoman Empire (1853), Alexander II once more against the Ottomans over Bulgaria (1876), Alexander III against Austria-Hungary, again over control of Bulgaria (1886), and Nicholas II against Japan, over control of Korea and Manchuria (1903). Each time, the result was not only national humiliation, but fiscal disaster of a kind which set back Russia's economic growth by years. And each time this happened, yet another Minister of Finance, the key man in mustering resources for economic growth, resigned or was removed: Reutern (1862–78), Bunge (1882–86), and Witte. Even the program of the one intervening Finance Minister, Vyshnegradsky (1887–92), came to ruin through a different kind of liability: the famine of 1891, symbol of the incapacity of Russian agriculture to compensate for the whims of the weather.

Comparisons are sometimes made between Stalin's economic program and that of Witte. The men themselves were very different, save perhaps for their common preference for autocratic governance. Stalin was his own master; Witte served at the pleasure of the Tsar, whose autocratic rule he sought to bolster, and he was under constant attack from his influential enemies. They were dealing with two somewhat different stages of industrial development, and in the context of quite different international situations. But both sought long-range industrial growth as the basis of national strength; both sought to avoid international contests of power which might jeopardize this goal; both were willing to sacrifice the welfare of agriculture in order to get resources for industrialization; both believed in concentrating on prime objectives at the expense of economic balance; and both evoked the specter of military disaster

---

[7] Ibid., p. 250.

in order to justify their harsh demands. Stalin, in a sense, had both the authority and the breathing space between international emergencies to solve the problems that Witte had only begun to solve.

Progress without Urgency

The war with Japan and the internal disorders of 1905 disrupted growth for several years, and it was not until 1908 that the economy was functioning normally once more. After 1908, while the nation's potential for a further industrial boom was good, the results were mixed but on the whole positive. Railroad construction fell off sharply, so that the pace of the years after 1908 was less than a quarter of the maximum tempo under Witte. There was a new emphasis on privately owned lines, especially on their being able to operate at a profit. Witte's huge subsidies were a thing of the past. No more of the loans which made these subsidies possible came from the capitals of Western Europe, though nearly 15 percent of the state budget went to service the debt on existing loans. Huge industrial syndicates were organized in nearly every major branch of production, which had the effect of maintaining high prices. Banking grew rapidly, reflecting the nation's growing capacity for internally generated savings, though the largest banks were on the whole controlled by Western European capital. Agriculture made great strides during this period, spurred on by the policies of Prime Minister Stolypin (1906–11), who was bent on breaking up the remaining communes in order to create a class of efficient peasant proprietors. Agricultural exports, so vital to the stability of the ruble and the nation's capacity to borrow and import, made especially good gains.[8]

Russia's economic progress after Witte would have been satisfactory for a nation that expected a half century of peace in which to reap the fruits of its vast, newly opened natural resources. What followed after 1914, during World War I and the Russian Civil War, was economic disaster of a kind which left the Bolshevik planners of the 1920s with an agonizingly narrow range of choices, worse than the choices that Witte had confronted so squarely in the 1890s.

The World War and Economic Ruin

For industrial and industrializing nations, wartime can also be boomtime. It helps, of course, if the war is a victorious one. The American Civil War, for example, played a large part in launching the spectacular

---

[8] See P. I. Lyashchenko, *History of the National Economy of Russia to the 1917 Revolution* (New York: Macmillan, 1949), chapters 23–25; and Hugh Seton-Watson, *The Decline of Imperial Russia* (New York: Praeger, 1952), pp. 280–92.

northern industrial boom of the latter 19th century. World War II gave Canadian industry an impetus which subsequently transformed that nation's whole economic profile. More common is the phenomenon of industrially advanced nations which are able to increase output to high levels as a result of both war-related contracts and the psychological impetus of wartime emergency. Even German industry during World War II displayed a performance of this kind, in spite of destruction from air raids and the impact of the post-1942 defeats on morale. In view of all this, it says a great deal about the state of the Russian economy, not to mention public morale, that Russia saw neither great expansion nor good utilization of capacity during World War I. The problems that plagued the economy during more than three years of war became even more acute during the ensuing three years of civil war and the Allied blockade.

Part of the trouble, a factor which would also plague the Bolshevik planners of the 1920s, was Russia's dependence on foreign machinery and parts. More than a third of the economy's machinery requirements had to be met by imports, and in heavy industry the proportion was over half. The textile industry's dependence on foreign cotton forced the closing of many mills as these supplies were shut off. Coal output was cut by the early loss of the Polish coal basin to the Germans, and an increased effort in the Donets basin never made this up. Transport quickly became an economic bottleneck. For all the frantic railroad building at the turn of the century, the lines were still inadequate. Unlike Germany, Russia had no advance plans for coping with transport problems in a national emergency. Agricultural output suffered most of all. Manpower and draft animals were drained off to the battlefronts, imports of fertilizers and agricultural equipment came to a halt, and domestic production of agricultural goods was throttled as well. The national income, according to a Soviet economist's reckonings, dropped by a quarter between 1913 and 1916.[9]

Russia's peculiar vulnerability lay in its vast distances, in the difficulty of making good its deficiencies with supplies from the West in wartime, and most of all in the smallness of the industrial sector as a whole as it is seen against the nation's needs in a protracted war. More than any other great power in the conflict, Russia was in need of economic planning to minimize the impact of its many shortages and bottlenecks. But at that early point in the 20th century, comprehensive economic planning was a complete unknown save in Germany; there a serious attempt at wartime planning was then in progress, watched with interest by Lenin from his Swiss refuge.

---

[9] Lyashchenko, *History of the National Economy of Russia to the 1917 Revolution*, p. 772.

WAR COMMUNISM

The Bolsheviks inherited an economy with seriously reduced capacity and drastically reduced production levels. Here are a few of the main indicators:[10]

	1913	*1921*
Industrial (factory) production (millions of 1926–27 rubles)	10,251	2,004
Pig iron (million tons)	4.2	0.1
Coal (million tons)	29.0	8.9
Railway tonnage carried (million tons)	132.4	39.4
Sown area (million hectares)	118.2	90.3
Grain harvest (million tons)	80.1	37.6

For two and one-half years the new Bolshevik regime attempted to cope with insuperable problems through a system that came to be known as "War Communism," or, in another translation, "Militant Communism." This had started in 1918 not with a grand concept of planning, but with two emergency measures: (1) Grain was requisitioned from the peasantry rather than purchased, very often by using the *Cheka* (security police) and brute force, in order to feed the cities and the new Red Army. (2) Almost all industries were nationalized in order to head off the economic chaos that Lenin feared would result from worker seizure and control, which had already happened in many industries. The nation's industries were placed under the Supreme Economic Council, known best by its Russian initials VSNKh. The government struggled, with varying success, to ban private trade, to replace money with state-directed allocations of goods, and to allocate critical supplies on a centrally coordinated basis. To make these measures effective, it sought to maintain discipline over workers and administrators through the combined use of Party controls, ideological exhortation, forced requisitions, and police terror.

The Bolsheviks later argued among themselves as to whether these measures had been a first attempt at building socialism, or simply a response to an emergency. At the time, during the years 1918–20, War Communism was regarded as both. When the military emergency had ended and there was hope of restoring economic ties with the major powers, War Communism's economic policies were greatly altered, and the "command economy" concept dropped. However, neither the basic nationalization laws nor the main economic agencies set up to administer War Communism were scrapped.

Emergency measure or not, it was the War Communism system that incorporated some basic decisions about Soviet economic management, decisions whose broad outlines are clearly visible today. War Communism

---

[10] Nove, *An Economic History of the U.S.S.R.*, p. 94.

was Lenin's creation and bore his ideological stamp of approval, while
the New Economic Policy (NEP) that replaced it was officially characterized as a temporary retreat. The structures, procedures, and policies
of 1918–20 were later translated into economic dogmas, and their impact
on succeeding decisions was great: total state control of the nonagricultural economy, subordination of agriculture to industry, detailed central
coordination of economic activity, and centralization in the form of vertical hierarchies of command were among the chief dogmas.

Syndicalism and Workers' Control

Syndicalism was strong among Russian industrial workers during 1917.
For many of them, the proletarian revolution meant nothing less than
worker-owned, worker-managed industries. It could also mean the freedom of these industries from any kind of outside control whatsoever.
In its extreme form, the vision of worker-run industries took the shape
of a utopia of cooperatives without the state. Doubtless Lenin's demand
for smashing the bourgeois state, plus Marx's prediction of the ultimate
stateless society, led some workers to imagine that these things would
come about immediately after the proletarian revolution. With this current of feeling went the urge to expel or shoot on the spot all the bourgeois directors and specialists who ran the industries, some of whom
continued to run them after the Bolsheviks took power.

Directly after his return to Russia in April 1917, Lenin urged workers'
control over the old management as a first step; nationalization of industry
would then be undertaken by deliberate stages. The large industrial
monopolies would be nationalized at once; other businesses would be
regulated through compulsory syndication, i.e., by becoming part of
state-sponsored trade associations. The banks would be taken over and
amalgamated into a single national bank—here Lenin remembered Marx's
despair over the failure of the Paris Commune of 1871 to seize the Bank
of France. Besides, this move had the explicit blessing of *The Communist
Manifesto*. The syndicalists certainly did not have Marx on their side.
In the *Manifesto* and elsewhere, Marx had called for centralization of
all means of production, transport, and communications under proletarian
rule. The new proletarian system would also have the responsibility for
economic growth according to an economic plan. As for the regulation
of consumption, Lenin had no guidelines from Marx save for the principle
of socialism—"to each according to his work." What he proposed before
the Bolshevik coup, then attempted to legislate afterwards, was the obligation of every citizen to join a consumers' cooperative; the cooperatives
would then serve as watchdogs for eliminating unequal consumption
norms.

Workers' control was a temporary political success in 1917–18, but it was a complete failure as an economic measure. In the circumstances, it would have been a miracle if the system had succeeded. The legislation, passed barely three weeks after the Bolsheviks assumed power, assigned to workers' control committees vast powers and subordinated them to the local soviets; it also assumed that the old managers would still be on hand to run their enterprises. Capitalists and managers had been ordered to stay on the job, while turning their stocks and securities over to the State Bank. In fact, workers had already seized many factories, or their management had fled, and production plummeted. Lenin admitted after several months that he had made little progress in "the fight to instill into the minds of the masses the idea of *Soviet* state control and accounting." Because syndicalism and anarchism were still strong among the workers, it would take a long struggle to change this mentality. Lenin likewise gave up his plan for enrolling everyone in consumer cooperatives, and conceded that his government had made some compromises with the bourgeois-dominated, 10-million-strong Russian cooperative movement.[11]

A System of Many Hierarchies

For industry Lenin now saw only centralized state management as a solution. Large industries had already been nationalized in a formal sense, and their securities seized. A supervisory mechanism already existed in the form of the Supreme Economic Council. In June 1918 nationalization was made final; small enterprises were eventually nationalized along with the large ones. To the VSNKh went the mind-boggling injunction "to regulate and organize all production and distribution and to manage every enterprise of the Republic."[12] A huge committee of some 70 commissars, trade union representatives, and economic officials, it presided over 40 directorates which often had to battle among themselves for resources.

Another characteristic of economic administration which outlasted the War Communism period was the practice of creating superagencies to deal with specific problems, often without regard for overlapping jurisdictions. The Revolutionary War Council, an emergency body separate from the VSNKh, was given control of "all forces and resources of the people that are needed for defense."[13] Toward the close of the Civil War, Trotsky was given charge of a new Central Transport Commission

[11] V. I. Lenin, *The Immediate Tasks of the Soviet Government* (Moscow: Foreign Languages Publishing House, 1951), pp. 31–36.

[12] James H. Meisel and Edward S. Kozera (eds.), *Materials for the Study of the Soviet System*, 2d ed. (Ann Arbor, Mich.: The George Wahr Publishing Co., 1953), p. 91.

[13] Ibid., p. 95. Shortly after this body was established, in October 1918, mobilization and resources were placed in a separate Council of Defense.

(*Tsektran*), which was endowed with sweeping powers of mobilizing people and resources in order to restore the all-important railway system. The early years of the New Economic Policy saw the founding of the State Planning Commission (Gosplan) and the Commissariat for Workers' and Peasants' Inspection (*Rabkrin*), each with a hierarchy that eventually reached down to the lowest levels of government. *Rabkrin* was given wide powers to investigate efficiency in government and the economy.

To meet each kind of emergency, the young Bolshevik regime improvised an administrative superweapon which inevitably came into conflict with other such superweapons; this is a fairly normal procedure for modern governments at war. But the extraordinary means that are used to deal with a crisis sometimes outlast the crisis and become part of the political system, as was the case here. While specific agencies were created, abolished, merged, and reorganized in bewildering fashion, the idea of central economic control through separate vertical structures was deeply imprinted on the outlook of Soviet leaders, beginning with War Communism. This system also enabled the leaders to use different agencies as vehicles for their policy struggles. For example, a profound difference in outlook arose between the Supreme Economic Council and the State Planning Commission (Gosplan). Each developed its "clientele" of powerful supporters in the Party. Both agencies were used politically by Stalin, who then rejected the economic projections of both in launching the First Five-Year Plan.

A related consequence was that the more important industrial branches began to develop into "fiefdoms" which were little disposed to cooperate among themselves or with local government agencies. They themselves could be controlled only through specialized hierarchies such as *Rabkrin*, each accountable only to a small circle of officials in Moscow. (The term "fiefdom" was actually used during the Khrushchev era in criticizing Stalin's economic administration.)

During 1918–20, relentless vertical control was a way of holding a badly shattered economic mechanism together in a crisis. In the First Five-Year Plan (1928–32), it helped achieve certain major industrial targets, though at the expense of many subordinate economic goals. But the dogmas and administrative outlook first generated during War Communism became a seemingly permanent fixture of the Soviet system, and a difficult legacy for the Khrushchev and Brezhnev periods.

THE "NEP": A BREATHING SPELL WITH PROBLEMS

War Communism's failure to set the Russian economy on the path to recovery is understandable. With the sole exception of the wartime German Empire, no country had attempted central economic direction on such a scale. While many histories of the Soviet Union treat the abandonment of War Communism as the demise of a whole system, it was economic policies that changed in 1921, rather than primarily structures. In the industrial sector particularly, an alternative would have been to introduce policy modifications rather than to proclaim a sharp change.

Several things impelled Lenin to make the change a decisive rather than gradual one. There were ominous political circumstances at the end of the Civil War, including an incipient peasant revolt and an anti-Bolshevik uprising on the Baltic island of Kronstadt, a major naval base not far from Petrograd (Leningrad). Famine threatened, and clearly steps had to be taken to gain peasant cooperation in producing and marketing grain. The possibility that foreign trade and investment could come to the assistance of the economy became real with the end of the Allied economic blockade in 1920 and signs of British interest in a trade deal.

Lenin's understanding of Marxian principles played its role, too, in making the policy change sudden and decisive. Marx had foreseen the proletariat's taking command of an economy thoroughly industrialized and modernized by profit-hungry capitalists; socialism could not be realized until the potential of the capitalist economy had been fully realized, according to Marx's application of the dialectic. Now, with no assistance likely from the proletariat of the advanced Western European countries, which might have helped a proletarian Russia to complete its half-finished industrialization, a proletarian government must itself finish the task by presiding over a capitalist economy. Only the "commanding heights" of the economy would remain socialized: the large industries, banks, foreign trade, and other crucial components. Thus Lenin justified the partial reintroduction of capitalism.

The reckless grain seizures in the countryside were halted; in their place a tax in kind was imposed, which at least had the merit of fixing the level of grain deliveries to the state. By law, the peasants were now assured proprietorship of the land; the great estates had been broken up, except for a small number which the new government had retained as state farms, so that 98 percent of the land now belonged to peasant households. While the government attempted to halt the buying and selling of land, this and other prerevolutionary practices persisted. There were millions of new peasant proprietors, thanks to the seizure of estate lands; the average size of the family holdings had diminished; and the peasant commune gained a new lease on life, so that by the middle of the 1920s over 90 percent of the agricultural lands once more belonged to the communes.[14] Stolypin's work had been undone. Harvests and the sown area quickly regained their prewar levels, but the amount of grain

[14] D. J. Male, *Russian Peasant Organisation Before Collectivisation: A Study of Commune and Gathering, 1925-1930* (Cambridge: At the University Press, 1971), p. 22.

delivered to the market lagged seriously. The smaller the plot, the less was the proportion of the crop marketed; and the more peasant proprietors there were, the easier it was to resist pressures to deliver produce to the market when prices were low. Bolshevik visions of rapid industrial growth hung in the balance as long as there was no answer to the problem of getting more grain from the villages.

The large industries, which under War Communism had lived on huge subsidies, were grouped into "trusts" which were obliged to show a profit in their operations, or at least to break even. For the time being, they did not have to adhere to any central plan. The trusts were free to deal with private suppliers in obtaining their raw materials and equipment. To market their output they often had to resort to bizarre methods, paying their workers in manufactured goods, which the workers then had to sell somehow for cash or barter for food and clothing.

In other sectors, private enterprise returned. Small-scale enterprises were formally denationalized and leased to private investors and cooperatives. Retail trade was almost wholly returned to private hands. The "Nepmen" who went into business under certain government restrictions—they could not, for example, hire more than 20 workers—loomed large in the Soviet economy of the 1920s, and a degree of prosperity returned. Lenin sought to invite foreign investors back into Russia to exploit its raw materials. But foreign investors were very wary of the Bolshevik regime and mindful of Russia's uncertain economic stability, so that foreign concessions were insignificant during this decade.

Even more important, the type of large foreign loans which Witte and others had negotiated simply was not to be had after the Revolution. Revolutionary propaganda, the Soviet government's refusal to assume any responsibility in principle for Tsarist debts, and its similar refusal to recognize the principle of compensation for nationalized property all combined to shut off this form of assistance. It is true that some major foreign powers were eager to promote trade with Soviet Russia after 1920. Foreign firms, which later included a number of American companies, were content to work in Russia under specific contracts (notably to build enterprises and install advanced equipment) as long as they were paid in hard Western currencies. As part of the price of these agreements, Moscow agreed to pay specific foreign debt claims. But the enormous loans from Paris and elsewhere which had enabled Witte to build up Russia's railroads were no longer attractive investments. Western governments were hostile to such loans even where private lenders may have been interested: In 1927, a police raid on the Soviet Trade Delegation in London was timed to put an end to negotiations for a large loan then in progress between Soviet officials and a London bank.[15]

---

[15] See the account in Louis Fischer, *The Soviets in World Affairs* (New York: Vintage Books, 1960), pp. 500–510.

The NEP period was a time of both economic recovery and political relaxation. Later on, many Soviet citizens were to look back on the NEP as a golden era: six years of war were over, the revolutionary government had ended its early tactics of repression, the peasants had their land, and food and consumer goods were available if not exactly abundant. The political storm that was brewing among the Bolshevik leaders did not affect or concern most of the population during these years. But it was the titanic debates at the Party congresses, in the Central Committee and Politburo, among the commissars and planning agencies, that was shaping the nation's economic destiny.

THE GREAT DEBATE

The Bolsheviks' sober look at the future, the "Great Debate" of 1924–28, was the product of crisis just as much as the NEP decisions had been. The main topic of the Great Debate was economic development, the strategy of industrial investment and socializing agriculture. But it was a number of other things too: a dispute over the uses of ideology, a clash of personalities, a struggle for rule, and a process of groping for a more workable method of governing the nation. It was also, as we shall see in chapter 2, a debate about the farmers, a difference of opinion as to what kind of cooperation could be expected from the villages.

A Triple Crisis

Three separate events during the fall and winter of 1923–24 touched off the bitter dispute in which Stalin was to emerge as sole victor. The first event was the defeat of a "last-gasp" attempt at fomenting a proletarian revolution in Germany. Though doomed at the outset, the short-lived uprising in Hamburg had carried with it the whole burden of Soviet hopes that Marx's prophecy of a European revolution was coming true at last. Germany, the Continent's most advanced industrial nation, which also possessed the largest and best-organized socialist party, was the key to this revolution. With the uprising's defeat, the Soviet leaders at last faced the reality that they could not reckon with a European revolution in terms of months, perhaps not even of years, and that it was more likely that they should think in terms of decades. The failure of the British General Strike in 1926, and the disaster of the young Chinese Communist Party in 1927, served to confirm this pessimism.

The second event was an unsettling economic trend. Because industrial production in the 1920s had recovered more slowly than agricultural production, manufactured goods remained scarce for a time, and their prices rose. For the peasants, whose agricultural prices had fallen in response, 1923 was a year of galloping inflation, when even a week's delay of getting into town to buy supplies meant higher prices the following week. The appearance of the two price indices on a graph, one rising and one falling, gave rise to the term "scissors crisis." A wave of wildcat strikes in August 1923 reduced industrial production still further and threatened political complications. By the spring of 1924 a variety of measures had succeeded in forcing down the prices on manufactures to a point much more favorable to the peasants. Now the opposite criticism arose: Was not the industrial sector paying too heavy a "tribute" to the countryside, which if prolonged would retard industrial growth seriously?

The third event was the death of Lenin in January 1924. A stroke in the spring of 1922 had made it difficult for him to use the great weight of his leadership in the Party's internecine disputes; nine months later a third stroke left him entirely helpless. Rivalry and differences among the top leaders, so characteristic of the Party during the whole 20 years of its existence, had reached a serious crisis point a year before Lenin's death. Had Lenin's final stroke not intervened at just the time it did, his next act would have been to remove Stalin from the post of General Secretary. (We know this from his "Testament"—see chapter 4.) As it turned out, it was Lenin's funeral that gave Stalin his chance to pull the dead leader's mantle about his own shoulders. Not only did he occupy the center of the stage in a week of elaborate ritual, but he promptly established himself as the chief custodian and codifier of Lenin's brand of Marxism. In so doing, he countered Trotsky's current interpretation of "permanent revolution" with his own "socialism in one country." It was this doctrine that set the stage for a massive debate over the country's economic future: Could the Soviet Union now proceed to build a complete socialist system within its own borders, unaided by the proletarians of other lands, or must it wait for assistance from future proletarian revolutions before completing its socialist edifice?

Karl Marx had written about the coming proletarian revolution as an international event, a political cataclysm embracing all of Europe. The proletariat itself, he believed, was international. Not only was its life under economic and political repression similar throughout the industrial areas of Europe, but it was cut off from national cultures and nationalism—these last were the product of the bourgeoisie. Moreover, a revolution victorious only in one country could very well be crushed by the reactionary regimes of surrounding countries, which had nearly happened during the French Revolution. The Soviet leaders had just seen, during the years of Allied intervention (1918–22), that the Russian Revolution, too, had barely escaped this fate.

Now the foreign troops were gone, the Allied blockade was lifted, trade relations were restored with Britain and other major powers. A diplomatically surprising accommodation with Germany (in 1922) helped protect both Russia and Germany against Allied claims. But from the Soviet perspective, the capitalist threat was still present. France had occupied German soil in 1923 to enforce its economic claims; what would stop the Western powers from returning to devastated Russia to do the same?

Trotsky versus Stalin

Several months after Lenin's death Stalin published a lengthy pamphlet entitled *The Foundations of Leninism*, which was an attempt both to appear as Lenin's most important heir and to strike a telling blow at Trotsky through the device of ideological debate. Stalin wrote that the political victory of the proletariat in one country alone was entirely possible according to Marxist theory, even if Marx had thought in terms of a revolution embracing all of Europe at once. Stalin conceded that the proletariat could not guarantee the "final victory" of socialism in the Soviet Union. But within less than a year after this he published a further pamphlet, *Problems of Leninism*, in which he specifically reversed this last judgment by terming it "inadequate." The socialist order could, he now wrote, be built in one country alone; but its "final victory" still could not be guaranteed before the revolution had spread elsewhere; until then, the danger of capitalist intervention would remain.

It seems at first glance that "socialism in one country" should have been the banner of those who, like Trotsky in the early 1920s, were calling for a campaign of rapid investment in heavy industry. But Stalin during this period supported a prolongation of the NEP and opposed the kind of measures against the peasantry which a massive industrialization drive would entail. Trotsky still linked the success of industrialization to the success of revolution elsewhere; but by the mid-1920s this constituted a very weak point in Trotsky's argument, vulnerable to Stalin's new slogan. Stalin quietly backed the notion that building a strong agricultural base at present, capitalist though it was, would provide the means of building socialism no matter how soon the Revolution spread abroad.

Trotsky had become alarmed at the swift inroads of capitalism under the NEP system. Like a good Marxist, he feared that the preponderant bourgeois influence in the economic "base" was endangering the proletarian political "superstructure." The industrial sector could be brought under a unified plan, he contended, even if such a plan could not embrace the 20 million petty capitalist farms. To do this, he urged first of all more sacrifices by the proletariat. From 1922 on, he advocated a policy of heavy taxation on the peasant proprietors, and on the whole private sector of the economy: "primitive socialist accumulation," he called it.

Stalin's adroit switch of theory was not prompted by the need to concede anything to Trotsky, who by this time (1924–25) was isolated among the Soviet leaders and politically vulnerable. Rather, it was because Stalin now realized what economists and industrial managers had known all along: the nation's capital equipment was on its last legs and in need of replacement on a massive scale, simply in order to keep the industries that Witte had built up. If this were not done, the output of manufactured goods would plummet again as it had in 1923, the "scissors crisis" would return, and the all-important supply of grain for the cities and for export might be choked off, with disastrous results.

The Debate on Strategy: Left versus Right

While there was no disagreement among the Bolsheviks that some kind of plan must be made for industrial growth, there was a very basic disagreement over the pace at which this could be accomplished. The variants in choice of pace depended, in turn, on differing views about the Soviet potential for industrial investment. Especially important was the relation of industrial growth to agricultural output, since from agriculture must come the bulk of the income available for investment. There was even disagreement about the possibility of having a national economic plan at all, in view of the large role played by capitalist producers. Lenin himself had been skeptical on this score. He did, however, launch the so-called GOELRO program for building up electrical output on a vast scale, an investment priority which later became virtually an article of faith.

While Soviet economists worked out a whole range of variants for future growth, the Soviet political leadership was becoming polarized in its attitudes toward the growth question. The "Right strategy" of growth stressed the need for building agriculture first as the basis for a future industrialization drive. Peasant demand for agricultural supplies and consumer goods would play an important role in stimulating the growth of light industry. The "Left strategy" stressed the key role of heavy industrial growth, especially the role of heavy industries as the main source of demand for industrial output generally. Industry, argued many supporters of the Left, was necessary in order to build a basis for modern agriculture. In the beginning, therefore, the terms of trade must be turned against agriculture. The Left's most articulate spokesman, whose views served to crystallize its position, was Yevgeny Preobrazhensky. It was he who in 1923 translated "primitive socialist accumulation" into economic terms. This meant squeezing savings from the agricultural sector, but without resorting either to forcible grain collections or to high agricultural taxes (which in practice could be one and the same thing). Instead, prices could be manipulated so as to give an advantage to manufactured goods.

The names of the political figures who occupied polar positions the reader will probably recognize: Nikolai I. Bukharin, the theoretical writer and editor, who began the 1920s as an advocate of the "Left," then switched to the "Right" after 1925; Georgi Zinoviev, the fiery orator who headed the Communist International, who began as a moderate "Rightist," then switched to the "Left" after 1925; Lev Kamenev, a capable Party administrator, Moscow Party boss, and the third member of Stalin's triumvirate, whose path paralleled that of Zinoviev; Alexei Rykov, who had moved into Lenin's post as Premier, a consistent Rightist and supporter of Stalin during the last years of the Great Debate; and Mikhail Tomsky, head of the Soviet trade unions, likewise a consistent Rightist.

The top economic managers and planners found themselves similarly polarized: Grigori Pyatakov, a commissar for heavy industry, and ardent supporter of the Left; Valerian Kuibyshev, head of the Supreme Economic Council after 1925, whose plans for industrial growth moved leftward while Stalin was still supporting the Right, before 1928; and Gleb Krzhizhanovsky, head of the State Planning Commission, an advocate of balanced growth and consequently on the Right. Professional economists joined the debate, including some men of real talent: Groman, Ginzburg, Feldman, Kovalevsky, Shanin, and others. A large number of them vanished in the purges of the 1930s, and this is significant in itself: Stalin after 1929 had little use for the kind of caution and balance the economic profession generally seeks.

Stalin Undermines the Left

The great zigzag in Stalin's economic course between 1925 and 1929 is a much-studied episode in Soviet political history. By 1925 the nation's economic alternatives had been studied and discussed; now choices were necessary. From this time on, the contest over economic policy was highly politicized. The artful Stalin chose economic policy as his central weapon for the political defeat, ultimately, of nearly all the leading participants in the Great Debate. Trotsky was formally condemned at a Central Committee meeting early in 1925. Then Stalin set about to undermine the position of both Zinoviev and Kamenev, the other two members (with Stalin) of the 1923 "triumvirate." This was quickly done: by early 1926, Kamenev had been removed from most of his posts, and Zinoviev's Party fiefdom—the important Leningrad Party organization—was snatched from under him. Too late, the two former triumvirs made common cause with Trotsky, their erstwhile foe. By the end of 1926, Trotsky and Kamenev were ousted from the Politburo, and Zinoviev was removed as head of the Communist International.

For the next year and a half, it seemed that the Right had triumphed. Stalin had not committed himself to either Right or Left; he had simply let Bukharin's views prevail, and Bukharin at this point was supporting a moderate Right position. The more extreme Rightists favored consumer- and agriculture-related industries; they opposed the transfer of savings from the agricultural sector to heavy industries. Bukharin maintained that such transfers could be made as long as a proper balance was struck. He contended that certain types of heavy industry were essential for building agricultural output. By the end of 1926, Party statements set an economic course in which agriculture, light industry, and heavy industry would all move forward in a measured relationship, a course favored by most of the professional economists. The farmers could now rest assured that no intolerable burdens would be laid on them, that their welfare would not be made a sacrifice to industrial growth.

The "Great Change"

Whatever Stalin may have intended during the latter 1920s, it was yet another crisis that precipitated his decisions and set the First Five-Year Plan in motion. There was the serious drop in grain procurements by the government during the winter of 1927–28. The reasons for this were evident. A second "goods famine" of manufactured products had turned the terms of trade once more against peasants, as in 1923; procurement prices were low; the kulaks (well-to-do peasants) and medium-sized peasant farms, the main source of grain for purchase, were withholding their grain from the market and had sown other crops. They concealed grain from state officials and threatened opposition by spreading the rumor that Moscow would order forcible collections, just as had been done ten years earlier. Force was being used in some areas already, in fact. Local Party leaders who balked at this policy were replaced by others who supported it.

For Stalin, this whole development spelled danger for any plan of rapid industrial growth. Even apart from the economic problem posed by peasant resistance, Stalin may have been equally concerned with the problem of political control over the peasantry, a majority of the population, whose loyalty to the new regime was still much in doubt. The leading spokesmen of the Right, who up to now had been helpful allies, were inclined to defend the farmers against the renewed pressures for grain procurement. By the end of 1928 Stalin had launched a vigorous public campaign against the economic strategy of the Right, and in the spring of 1929 he focused his fire on Bukharin and his supporters. Before the year was out, Bukharin, Tomsky and Rykov—the leaders of what was now branded the "Right deviation"—were removed from their posts.

THE FIVE-YEAR PLANS

The First Five-Year Plan had been in active preparation since mid-1927, and when the plan formally went into operation in September

1928, it still provided little indication of what was to follow. True, during 1928 Stalin had placed both Gosplan (the State Planning Commission) and the Supreme Economic Council under pressure to adopt higher industrial targets than the ones they had settled on. For the plan's first year, the projections and actual investment were as follows:[16]

Commissariat of Finance.	650 million rubles	
Gosplan	750 " "	
Supreme Economic Council	825 " "	
Central Committee Resolution of November 1928.	800 " "	
Actual Investment	1,300 " "	

The original plan had been drawn up in an initial variant and an optimal variant; a Party conference in April 1929 adopted the latter version. Already the strains of the investment program were making themselves felt in the form of heavier taxes on the whole capitalist sector, first of all on the kulaks. Bukharin and the Right were attacking the new policy as incompatible with NEP and as a danger to the alliance which the Party claimed existed between the proletariat and the peasants.

Then, without warning, the industrial investment figure for the second plan year was quadrupled over that of the first year, to 3,400 million rubles. The Politburo, its ranks so recently purged of the Right, had launched its projections far beyond what even the Left had been demanding. Production goals projected for the plan's final year were equally staggering, in that they assumed that a huge volume of industrial investment would have been completed, and that the new plants, mines and everything else would be in full operation (Table 1–1).

TABLE 1–1
Production Goals for Final Plan Year (1932)
(million tons)

Product	1927-28 Actual Output	1932-33 Optimal Plan Variant	1932 Amended Plan	1932 Actual Output
Coal	35.0	75.0	95–105	64.0
Oil	11.7	21.7	40–55	21.4
Iron ore	6.7	20.2	24–32	12.1
Pig iron.	3.2	10.0	15–16	6.2

Source: Nove, *An Economic History of the U.S.S.R.*, p. 188.

What the figures in the table say to an economist, including even the most dedicated Soviet economists of that time, is that economic policy

[16] Stalin, *Works*, vol. 11 (1954), p. 287; vol. 12 (1955), p. 128. Isaac Deutscher, *Stalin: A Political Biography* (New York: Oxford University Press, 1949), p. 321.

had abruptly taken leave of economics. Partly because of the good results of the first plan year, but for other reasons as well, Stalin and those remaining leaders who supported this new line worked themselves into a frenzy of optimism.

In chapter 2, we shall see how Stalin launched his sudden and devastating attack on private farming. The policy of collectivization on a crash basis was not announced until November 1929, that is, until somewhat after the incredible new industrialization tempo had been set. There had been almost no warning to the public or the Party about the *velíkii perelóm*, the "great turning-point" or "great change" that meant total collectivization by force.

The years of the First Five-Year Plan saw teams of workers and young people at work on huge industrial construction projects under the most severe conditions imaginable, usually making up in dedication what they lacked in training. The emphasis was on the gigantic and the highly visible: the iron and steel complex at Magnitogorsk, the Stalingrad tractor works, the great Dniepr dam, and the first lines of the ornate Moscow subway. These projects, by their very scope and the speed with which they were pushed forward, were meant to serve as testimony that miracles were possible under socialism. While many important goals of the first plan were not reached (statistically overblown Soviet figures notwithstanding), the psychological purposes of Stalin's sudden attack were attained. Attained, at least, for the key industries; for agriculture, as we shall see, the experience was a different one.

After the "Great Change"

In 1934 the goals of the Second Five-Year Plan were scaled down as regards industrial investment and production, and at the same time shifted somewhat in favor of industrial production and the consumer. This was the direct consequence of growing high-level opposition to the hardships wrought by the economic tempos Stalin had sought, and it was clearly one of the factors that triggered the launching of the Great Purge (see below). Good harvests later in the 1930s helped to restore economic balance, though at the same time the rise of Nazi Germany and the other fascist powers prompted great increases in Soviet military outlays.

Repairing the incredible devastation wrought by the German invasion in World War II (1941–45) did not mean a greater relative emphasis on agriculture and on consumers' goods. With Russia still far behind the United States in both heavy industry and armaments, Stalin was determined to set his nation back on a course which in the not too distant future would close this gap. The related goal of maximum economic self-sufficiency was pursued just as relentlessly after 1945 as it had been before the war. This meant, for example, producing goods domestically which could have been purchased more cheaply abroad, and it called for more belt tightening by Soviet consumers. As in the 1930s, few concessions were made to the collective farmers, those who bore the brunt of the national investment priorities. Many collective farms had broken up as a result of the war, and in some places the farmers hoped that the land they had possessed in the 1920s would be restored. This was not to be: the prewar collective farm policies were now restored in full force. Heavy industry retained its top priority, and the single-minded pursuit of economic autarky once more held sway, reinforced by the Soviet Union's ability to exploit the economies of the East European nations which had fallen under its domination in the wake of the war. National security through economic might, whether it was pursued in the name of Holy Mother Russia or to defend the world proletarian movement, added up to a difficult, costly economic strategy.

POLITICAL CONSEQUENCES

Industrialization and the Great Purge

The hardships of the industrialization drive, and the outright brutalities which were inflicted on parts of the peasantry, had political consequences which obliged Stalin to agree to moderate the pace of growth. Discontent in high circles had increased rapidly in the last years of the First Five-Year Plan, to the extent that Stalin at the end of 1932 actually tendered his resignation to the Politburo (it was waved aside by his colleagues without discussion). The original indices of the Second Five-Year Plan (1933–37) continued the harsh priorities of the First Plan. At the 17th Party Congress, however, which met early in 1934, industrial growth indices were reduced significantly. Soon afterwards, concessions were made to the consumer (abolition of bread rationing) and especially to the peasantry; the Model Collective Farm Charter of 1935, and the 1936 Constitution, guaranteed continuation of the collective farmer's all-important individual plot.

Economic concessions were accompanied by political concessions at this same 17th Congress. The leaders of the former "Right," Bukharin, Rykov, and Tomsky, having been reduced to minor posts since 1929, now regained a tentative foothold in the power structure by promotion to candidate membership in the Central Committee. Pyatakov, a former Menshevik and leading spokesman for the "Left" in the Great Debate, was now made a full member. These and certain other indications pointed to the growing influence of a Politburo group that sought a period of relaxation. This group probably sought to damp down the regime's war against the peasants, to moderate a further purge which Stalin was probably urging after the Ryutin affair of 1932, a plot to remove him which was nipped in the bud. Doubtless the group also sought to reduce the sacrifices being made for industrialization. Analysts of this period have also speculated that the figure whose support was sought by the "moderates" was Sergei Kirov, head of the Leningrad Party organization after Zinoviev's political demise. Kirov was no "moderate," but on the contrary a thoroughgoing Stalinist. But policy stances change to suit political needs, and the support of the moderates may have been sought by Kirov for strategic reasons. Youthful, handsome, and a forceful speaker, Kirov received as much of the limelight and the applause at the 17th Congress as did Stalin himself. For Stalin the most ominous political concession was the omission of a single word in his title: Instead of being reelected to the Party Secretariat as General Secretary, the title he had borne since the post was created for him in 1922, he was now designated merely as one of four Party Secretaries (Kaganovich, Kirov, and Zhdanov were the others). In view of the great importance of symbolic relationships in Soviet politics, the omission could hardly have been a printer's error.

Partial economic reverses, therefore, were now threatening not only Stalin's economic priorities, but his power as well. Though in 1934 harmony prevailed on the surface, the rehabilitated oppositionists having renounced their old views and given full public support to Stalin, the Party Congress had given political leverage to influential people who might now wish to remove Stalin. It was two years before the great public trials and mass arrests began, but Stalin began laying the groundwork of the Purge within months after the 1934 Congress. That same summer, a superagency for policy and security matters was created in the form of the Commissariat for Internal Affairs, the NKVD. In December 1934, ten months after the "Congress of Victors," Kirov fell victim to an assassin's bullet. Khrushchev in his 1956 de-Stalinization speech accused Stalin of having ordered the murder, and the circumstances surrounding it certainly invited suspicion. However that may be, for Stalin the act which eliminated his most formidable political rival was also the pretext for launching the campaign of repression which eventually grew into the Great Purge of 1936–38.

Did the Growth Tempo Require Political Repression?

Among the documents captured by the invading Germans in World War II, and which later passed into Allied hands, was the Economic Plan for 1941. While overall plan figures were generally made public, this was the only detailed document for official use which became available in the West. One of its most interesting items was the allocation to the security police, the NKVD, of 1.2 percent of total industrial pro-

duction, including extractive operations, logging, and fishing. Separate
information confirmed the fact that during most of the Stalin period
the NKVD and its successor the MVD controlled a large complex of
gold-mining operations in northeastern Siberia. Certain published decrees
from the 1930s and later showed that the NKVD was engaged in running
still other operations, including some state farms, plus furniture and clothing production.[17]

The forced-labor system was also important as a supplier of labor
to regular civilian undertakings. Both labor camp inmates and others
who were exiled to given localities without being placed in camps found
themselves working side by side with free labor in some situations. This
was a continuation of the Tsarist practice of selling prison labor by
contract to private businesses, often foreign firms, as for example in the
building of the Trans-Siberian Railroad at the turn of the century.

Estimates of the forced labor population for the late 1930s and the
latter Stalin period have run as high as 12.5 million and not lower than
3.5 million.[18] The use of forced labor on this scale raises the question
of its economic importance. One sometimes hears the argument that it
represents labor waste, since part of the labor camp population was
skilled; therefore Moscow's primary motive could not have been the
full use of economic resources, but was largely political. To begin with,
the Soviet regime did succeed in using skills within the context of forced
labor, a circumstance which at last received wide publicity outside the
Soviet Union with the publication of Alexander Solzhenitsyn's *The First
Circle*. This novel is about a *sharashka*, a prison facility for scientists,
who would be rewarded for achievement with early release, or punished
for malingering by being sent to an ordinary labor camp. Also, the "prisoner specialist" was a familiar institution in the 1930s, a person living
under surveillance at a given place of exile, whose location was determined by the need for his skill.[19]

Another use of prison labor was in labor-intensive operations in remote
parts of the country, where hiring free labor would have been very
costly. Where some of the most infamous camps once functioned in
northern Siberia, for example, Soviet workers and specialists are now
lured to perform three-year work contracts with wages which are several
times the wage for the same work elsewhere, plus two months of vacation
per year and other generous benefits. Though skills among the forced
labor population were put to work in some situations, the lack of modern

---

[17] Robert Conquest (ed.), *The Soviet Police System* (New York: Praeger, 1968),
pp. 84–87.

[18] S. Swaniewicz, *Forced Labour and Economic Development: An Enquiry Into
the Experience of Soviet Industrialization* (London: Oxford University Press, 1965),
ch. 3.

[19] See the description of one such specialist in John Scott, *Behind the Urals*
(Boston: Houghton Mifflin, 1942), pp. 22–23.

equipment meant that massive inputs of unskilled labor were used to perform the same jobs in the absence of equipment. In a sense, the labor camps were making up for the stringent limitations on the Soviet Union's ability to obtain modern technology from abroad. Also, prison-run logging and mining operations provided valuable exports to help finance the early five-year plans.

On the other hand, one may argue that the massive security apparatus necessary to keep the camp system functioning reduced its economic benefit. There is evidence, in fact, that the cost of maintaining one labor camp inmate was not significantly below the cost of maintaining an ordinary worker. If the NKVD required little from the state budget because of its self-contained economy, it also returned little to the general economy.[20]

In brief, it is very difficult to establish any hierarchy of motives in explaining the forced labor system. The steps by which the forced labor system was established, from the 1920s to the end of the 1930s, can be seen as the result of successive decisions, some of them stressing security goals, others stressing economic needs. For the incredible wave of arrests in 1937, which sent the labor camp population soaring to what could have been 10 million or more, there seems to be no good political *or* economic explanation.

As regards control of the rest of the labor force, it is not difficult to show that in Stalin's time a degree of repression was necessary if the extreme economic goals were to be met. Strikes were prohibited, labor unions were turned to the goal of increased output and labor discipline, labor mobility was controlled through an internal passport system, and collectivization required a system of political commissars to preserve order in the countryside (see chapter 2). One may argue that the means chosen by Moscow were more drastic than the circumstances required, especially because it was also possible in these same years to stimulate high performance through morale and enthusiasm. But, in Soviet circumstances, controls and repression were a particularly tempting means for solving labor problems. If they went far beyond the means used to curb labor unrest in Western nations at comparable stages of the industrial revolution, then one may only observe that Russian political culture and Soviet ideology offered few inhibitions to the use of drastic solutions.

Consequences for Administration and Government

The 1930s saw the transformation of centralized economic direction into the system of ministries which exists today. The Supreme Economic Council had become a sprawling collection of departments whose conflict-

---

[20] These and related arguments are discussed in Swaniewicz, *Forced Labour and Economic Development*, ch. 14.

ing needs were not easily reconciled. During the First Five-Year Plan it was divided into three commissariats: heavy industry, light industry, and forestry. From that point on, the commissariats continued to divide and multiply until there were more than 50 in the last years of the Stalin era; in 1946 they were redesignated "ministries." From the point of view of planning and control, the ministerial system had the great advantage of fixing responsibility for meeting production targets. Because Moscow's primary economic objective in these years was quite simply volume of output, success or failure could now be laid at the door of a specific ministry directed by a minister, who governed a large number of plants and factories throughout the country. If the ministry was among those designated as "Union-Republic" rather than "All-Union," responsibility was shared between the minister in Moscow and his counterparts in the Union Republics (11 at the time the 1936 Constitution was adopted, 15 today), who directed their own branch ministries within the framework of the republic governments. However, the difference in Stalin's time was not great. All the ministers came under the jurisdiction of the Council of Ministers, of which they were all members. By the end of the Stalin period the Council of Ministers or cabinet had grown to unwieldy proportions, about 70 members in all, of whom somewhat over half were in charge of economic ministries. During the latter years of Stalin's rule the Council rarely met as a whole; its ministers reported to specialized subcabinets coordinated by various deputy ministers without portfolio.

The one central economic institution from the 1920s which remained was Gosplan, the State Planning Commission. Then, as later, its function was to plan rather than to manage. In spite of the purge of many capable economists in the 1930s, its staff had become a large and well-experienced one by the end of the Stalin era. Its task was an unenviable one, considering the huge number of individual items it undertook to plan. It was not surprising that Soviet plans were in some respects unreal, and that crash programs promoted by top economic officials often upset its calculations. But Stalin had made Gosplan a key agency, and the two officials who headed it by turns during Stalin's last dozen years were among the politically powerful.[21]

The ministerial system had serious drawbacks. Each ministry attempted to hoard resources of all kinds at the expense of other ministries. Each tried to build up subsidiary enterprises which were important to it—for example, the many coal mines operated by the Ministry of Ferrous Metallurgy, which wanted a reserve coal supply for its blast furnaces which would free it from total dependence on the Ministry of the Coal Mining Industry. The nation's railways were under strain from the eco-

---

[21] Nikolai Voznesensky was executed in the 1949–50 purge; Mikhail Saburov opposed Khrushchev in the mid-1950s and was dismissed from all his posts in 1957.

nomically nonsensical crosshauling of supplies from one part of a ministry's far-flung "fiefdom" to another.

All this had a most serious result for the nation's governmental structure. The middle and lower levels of government, from the Union Republics on down to cities and districts, exercised scant control over the
many industrial hierarchies which had operations in their territory.
Among the resources which ministries and their enterprises hoarded were
housing, transport, retail trade networks, local utilities, and everything
else that they needed to provide for their workers. There were cities
where one factory ran the public transportation network, another controlled the water supply, and all the factories combined controlled three
quarters of the housing supply. Within the economic priorities of the
Stalin era, there were little enough resources at best for providing these
things. The budgets of provinces and municipalities were a fraction of
what they needed to meet the demands of their populace. Local government became very much a junior partner in the Soviet system, and the
republic governments did not fare much better. The local soviets, which
in Lenin's time were regarded as the true "grass roots" of the Soviet
system, fell into disuse. Ministries of the Union Republics, and administrative departments in the lower levels of government, became nothing but
branch offices of various ministries in Moscow. By the end of the Stalin
period, the structure of government below the national level bore little
resemblance to the elegant pyramid set forth in the USSR Constitution.
The country's main business was industrial production, and all else had
to give way before it.

ECONOMIC AND POLITICAL MOTIVES

It is much easier to find political calculation in Stalin's economic radicalism than it is to make sense out of it in conventional economic terms.
And to the extent that it may have represented a coherent economic
choice, it is easier to describe the main component of the choice as a
psychological tactic. On the surface, Stalin was arguing that breakthroughs in a few critical investment and production sectors would enable
production in many sectors to leap to a much higher plane within a
few years. Stalin shared with Witte the conviction that the advance
sectors of the economy would pull all else in their wake. The Witte
system did not last long enough either to prove or disprove this, and
Soviet planning confused the issue by attempting to plan virtually everything instead of a few sectors only.

Politically, Stalin's manner of launching both industrialization and collectivization was a strategy designed to prove *all* the participants in the
Great Debate to be wrong. One might think that, from 1929, Stalin
would willingly have courted the support of the Leftists whom he had

defeated politically in 1923–26; not Trotsky, probably, but at least Zinoviev and Kamenev. Though their Left position after 1925 was by no means as radical as what Stalin was now promoting, in a sense they could claim justification. Quite the contrary, the Left received much the same treatment as the Right. Readmitted to the Party at the end of 1928, Kamenev and Zinoviev received humble posts, were arrested briefly in 1932, then readmitted to the Party. The leaders of the Right, Bukharin, Rykov, and Tomsky, were permitted to confess their errors at several Party gatherings in 1930. At the 17th Party Congress, in 1934, with the first Five-Year Plan declared a success and the second plan under way, both Left and Right were permitted to speak, this time without the accompanying chorus of catcalls. All confessed their former "errors" and the atmosphere was one of reconciliation. This congress was intended by Stalin to place the ultimate seal on his victory over both the "deviations" and their leaders.

There is hardly a political leader in history who could have wished himself a more complete triumph over his rivals: defeat in open discussion, demotion, humiliation, readmission to the fold of the believers, detailed public confessions of old errors, and acceptance of humble assignments thereafter. Not without reason were some foreign observers calling Stalin's system a pseudoreligion, a religion with strong medieval overtones. Yet all this turned out to be not sufficient for Stalin and certain figures around him. Within less than four years all the major figures of both Left and Right had been branded heretics, placed beyond the pale of the Party and Marxism, and executed.

So Stalin's manner of attack in launching the Five-Year Plan can be explained readily in political terms. But it is not difficult to reverse the terms by explaining political attack as a means of promoting an economic policy, in order to save the industrialization drive from the attacks of its foes. Witte had been obliged to fight a running battle with his enemies during the dozen years of his program. Stalin defeated his enemies, actual and potential, *before* embarking on his radical course. And because even defeated enemies could reappear on the political scene if the Five-Year Plan ran into serious difficulty, political danger had to be warded off by striking blow after blow at them. Economic radicalism as Stalin pursued it meant dealing with high political tensions; managing these tensions meant building a formidably powerful security apparatus and using it to keep his political and economic leaders off balance.

Stalin's decisions of 1929 display a logic of their own in that they were mutually supportive. Economically, they formed a strategy for assuring the attainment of what was possible by demanding the apparently impossible. Politically, they were a vehicle which could be used to undercut opponents and supporters alike. By evoking still further opposition, quite apart from the opposition that had been defeated in the 1920s, they provided justification for perfecting totalitarian rule. This in turn assured absolute control of the nation's resources: sabotage of industry on a large scale was now unthinkable, and there would be no repetition of farmers' withholding grain from the cities. Witte's dilemma was resolved at last by radical demands backed by force.

FOR FURTHER READING

A reliable history of the Russian economy up to the Soviet period is that of James Mavor, *An Economic History of Russia* (2 vols.; New York: Dutton, 1914). It is interesting to compare this with the standard Soviet account, P. I. Lyashchenko, *History of the National Economy of Russia* (New York: Macmillan, 1949). Hugh Seton-Watson, *The Decline of Imperial Russia* (New York: Praeger, 1952) integrates economic developments with both internal politics and foreign policy. Theodore H. Von Laue, *Sergei Witte and the Industrialization of Russia* (New York: Columbia University Press, 1963) deals with Witte's career as Finance Minister; though weak in analyzing economic policies, it presents a vivid picture of the controversies which Witte's policies generated. See also Von Laue's interpretation of the whole period from 1890 to 1930, *Why Lenin? Why Stalin?* (Philadelphia: Lippincott, 1964).

William L. Blackwell, *The Industrialization of Russia* (New York: Crowell, 1970) offers an introductory survey from the mid-19th century to the present. The best single account of Soviet economic history is Alec Nove, *An Economic History of the U.S.S.R.* (Baltimore: Penguin, 1969). See also his *Was Stalin Really Necessary?* (London: Allen and Unwin, 1964) for brief analyses of some of the crucial economic choices. A defense of the Soviet choices is offered by Maurice Dobb, *Soviet Economic Development Since 1917* (3rd ed.; London: Routledge, 1966). The "Great Debate" is analyzed in Alexander Erlich, *The Soviet Industrialization Debate, 1924–1928* (Cambridge, Mass.: Harvard University Press, 1960), and in Nicolas Spulber, *Soviet Strategy for Economic Growth* (Bloomington, Ind.: University of Indiana Press, 1964). The most important statements of the Great Debate can be found in a volume edited by Nicolas Spulber, *Foundations of Soviet Strategy for Economic Growth* (Bloomington, Ind.: Indiana University Press, 1964).

The human side of the Soviet industrialization drive is described at first hand by an American who worked as an engineer in Magnitogorsk in the 1930s: John Scott, *Behind the Urals* (Boston: Houghton Mifflin, 1942). Compare this with the most famous of the Soviet "industrialization novels" of the same period, Valentin Katayev's *Time, Forward!*

2

COLLECTIVIZATION

A visit to the villages of Russia and the Ukraine is in some ways a journey back into the 19th century. The farm people, in their dress, their habits, and their manner of speaking, are a world apart from the population of the fast-growing cities. Water is carried from wells or outdoor spigots into two-room log houses, or, in the south, into picturesque stuccoed and thatched dwellings. Here a bewhiskered grandfather tends the family cow by the roadside, there a cheerful barefoot lad rounds up the geese. Young people in their 20s and 30s are in a small minority; farms seem to be run largely by the elderly. The roads are unpaved and deeply rutted, and horse-drawn vehicles are a common sight. Though any given village is probably part of a collective or state farm which may embrace dozens of villages, an air of isolation and remoteness hangs over each and every one. While electric wires now lead to the village dwellings, and television antennae sprout from a good many, one need only squint a bit, imagining the scene without them, in order to behold the countryside described by Tolstoy, Gogol, and other writers of the past.

There can be no mistaking the changes of the last half-century. Those of the dreamy old villages which became farm centers now boast communal dairies, tractor parks, agronomists' offices, and cultural centers. Some have new housing which can be called modern by comparison with the traditional dwellings. If some collective farms have been slow to acquire these things, others have prospered enough to give their members a secure living. In some of the non-Slavic areas of the south, especially in Transcaucasia and Central Asia, farms have a cheerful and prosperous look about them.

But almost anywhere one travels in the Soviet countryside, one cannot avoid seeing in rural conditions the long-term consequences of Stalin's relentless collectivization drive of 1929–34. In judging these results, the

64

fact of collectivization itself is not necessarily the most important cause. Even in other political circumstances, some kind of collectivization might have been a vehicle for bringing Russian agriculture abreast of European agriculture generally. More important for our purposes is a look at the process: the way in which the collectivization drive emerged; the type and pace of collectivization employed; the way in which the decision was enforced; the political warfare against the rural population which accompanied it; and the economic priorities which for long decades were to keep the farmers in poverty in order to feed the cities and build industries.

THE GRAIN CRISIS

In 1913, the last full year of peace before the World War, Russia had exported 12 million tons of grain; in that same year, grain constituted about 40 percent of the nation's total exports. Under the Bolsheviks, as under the Tsars, industrialization at this stage depended heavily on exports of agricultural products and other raw materials. Foreign loans could hasten matters, but these too must be paid for with exports. Anyway, the large loans of the Witte era were no longer to be had, as we saw in the last chapter. With the introduction of NEP, the Soviet leaders had to abandon whatever hope they had of reaching the prewar level of grain exports in any short space of time. The harvest of 1925 was a poor one, and yielded but 2 million tons for export. The next year's exports were just slightly better, but this was followed by disaster in 1927, when a bare 3 million tons were exported. Russia, the "breadbasket of Europe," was faced with the dismal prospect of having to import grain instead of export it.

Who Was to Blame?

Bad weather could not be held to blame, but rather the fact that grain and other agricultural products were simply not being marketed as they had been in the past. In the last decades of the Empire, half the total grain production had come from the large estates and the farms of kulaks, the relatively well-to-do farmers. More important, the large landowners and kulaks had produced more than 70 percent of the grain brought to market. Now most of the large estates had been divided, in spite of Lenin's wish to keep part of these lands intact as state-run farms.

The kulaks of the 1920s were by no means as prosperous as the kulaks of prerevolutionary times. Large kulak holdings had shared the fate of the estates, often being cut into small plots and divided strip holdings by the poorer peasants themselves, who had no notion of waiting for the new Soviet government to reorganize the land. Many former "bat-raks," the landless agricultural laborers, had at last gained a bit of land for themselves. On the eve of the World War there had been 16 million farm households in possession of land. By the end of the NEP period, in 1928, there were 10 million additional households. To say "farms" could be misleading, since a large proportion of these households had received their land from the swiftly reconstituted peasant communes, which assigned it in scattered strips. This, actually, was part of the marketing problem: the communes were still the least efficient agricultural producers in terms of the proportion of their output which was brought to market.

All the nation's farms, large or small, consolidated or in communal strips, were inefficient producers by the European standards of that time. Chemical fertilizers were virtually nonexistent, and organic fertilizers were limited in quantity because of the nation's low supply of livestock, which had been depleted during the war years. Agricultural extension services were only in their beginnings.

Low productivity was only a small part of the immediate problem. The real problem was that farmers in every category, from kulaks to the poorest communes, were increasingly withholding their grain from the market. Prices on manufactured goods remained high, and farmers were motivated to consume their own output, to use it on their farms, and to hoard it in anticipation of higher prices. Even the basic agricultural equipment which was readily available for purchase—steel ploughs, for example, to replace the traditional wooden plough—went begging for buyers because of the prevailing price levels.

The government was itself to blame for most of this. Procurement prices followed an erratic course: when the government tried to hold grain prices at a low level, peasants switched to better-priced industrial crops; to increase grain procurements, the government would then reverse the price relationships, the changes sometimes occurring in the middle of the growing season. While private middlemen in grain marketing had to pursue their business illegally, the government was increasingly forced to buy part of its grain from them in order to keep the cities fed and provide for exports. By the end of the NEP, nearly one fourth of government purchases were being made in the agricultural "grey market." Even this measure did not halt the decline in grain procurements during the latter 1920s. Purchases of food grains were dropping alarmingly, from 8.3 million tons in 1926–27 to 6.2 million in 1928–29.[1]

---

[1] See the data in M. Lewin, *Russian Peasants and Soviet Power* (Evanston, Ill.: Northwestern University Press, 1968), pp. 175–92, and Alex Nove, *An Economic History of the U.S.S.R.* (London: Allen Lane The Penguin Press, 1969), pp. 105–113.

The Kulak Question

The great irony of the Soviet grain dilemma in these crucial years was that the state depended on grain marketings by the category of farmers whom it attacked as politically suspect: the kulaks. Soviet leaders during these years took the loose system of labels which in former years had distinguished the various classes of peasantry, and substituted their own inconsistent distinctions. After the kulaks came the "serednyaks," or middle farmers, the "bednyaks," or poor farmers, and the "batraks," or agricultural laborers.

Who was a kulak? Farm acreage was unsatisfactory as a criterion, and income data were not available. Some official surveys of rural classes used the hiring of labor or the renting out of farm implements as criteria. In fact, a lot of attention was paid to nonfarming business activities as defining the kulaks, including moneylending. Whoever has seen Chekhov's play *The Cherry Orchard* (1904) may recall that Lopákhin, a literary prototype of the Russian kulak, bought the cherry orchard in order to replace the trees with vacation cottages. In general, Soviet economic officials saw kulaks first of all as farmers who used hired hands and had succeeded in branching out into small capitalist undertakings.

During 1927–28, the last two years of NEP, official estimates on the proportion of kulaks in the agricultural population ranged between 2 and 8 percent, which is between a half million and four million households.[2] Understandably, estimates of the economic power of the kulaks varied, too; the most commonly cited statistic is that they controlled 20 percent of the marketable grain, but this cannot be verified. From the point of view of the Soviet leaders, the kulaks' social and political role may have been more important than whatever economic weight they possessed. Wrote one student of this question:

> Despite what was often alleged in propaganda statements, the kulak, under Soviet conditions, was not a man who was hated by the peasants. Their anger might be aroused by certain extreme cases, in particular those kulaks who engaged mainly in speculation and moneylending, and did not themselves work, but these were not typical. The typical kulak was primarily a worker, and for this reason he was looked on by the villagers as a peasant like the rest of them. He was prosperous, and envied, but respected too.[3]

If the kulak often prospered at the expense of his fellow peasants, he was their helper in time of need as well. The symbiotic economic relationship, far from generating class conflict in the villages, was making the kulaks increasingly the political leaders of the rest.

---

[2] Lewin, *Russian Peasants and Soviet Power,* pp. 43–49 and 71–78.

[3] Ibid., p. 76.

ALTERNATIVES FOR SOCIALIZING AGRICULTURE

Marxism and Farmers

Marx's prophecies about the future society rested on his prediction that most of capitalist society would be "proletarianized." As large-scale capitalism grew and consolidated its hold, all classes would be swept into its clutches, until all society was divided into a small minority of capitalists and a huge majority of proletarians. Nowhere did Marx deal at length with what he believed would happen to farmers. But we can gather from Marx's passing comments that farmers, too, would find themselves the victims of "agri-business," which would sooner or later invade the countryside, gobbling up both small holders and traditional-type estates.

On the other hand, Marx saw no important political role for the peasantry in the overthrow of capitalism. Farmers were too scattered for this, and their level of political awareness was low. Above all, they had not been through the harsh "school" of class cooperation which the capitalists were unwittingly teaching to the urban workers by organizing them into great social groups. Marx, after watching the behavior of the French farmers during and after the upheaval of 1848, saw in the small proprietors a conservative, antirevolutionary social stratum. He proposed that the proletariat, in seizing power, keep the large estates intact in order to convert them to some kind of socialist management. Yielding to the inevitable demand for distributing this land to households would only promote more capitalism in the countryside.

Lenin sought to forge an "alliance" between the Russian proletariat and part of the peasantry, an alliance which existed mainly as a propaganda phrase. The Bolsheviks, in the confusion of the Civil War years (1918–21), were powerless to stop land seizures by the farmers. The NEP program of 1921 placed Moscow's blessing, with limits and reservations, on small family farms. From the experience that followed, the Bolsheviks learned to mistrust the farmers even more than before.

It is important to note that the Bolshevik coup of 1917 represented the triumph of an urban-oriented movement over a rural-oriented movement, the Social Revolutionaries. To the Bolsheviks, the farmers were at best only junior partners in the new regime, and only part of them qualified even for this humble role. Bolshevik slogans spoke of "workers, peasants, and soldiers" as the true revolutionary groups. But the Party's recruiting efforts in the villages produced only marginal results, and local organs of government set up in the countryside were often dominated by farmers opposed to Bolshevik rule. The villages, in the eyes of the new leaders, were still the captives of hidebound tradition, superstition, dissipation, and covert resistance to authority. Marx, many Bolsheviks concluded, had been right in speaking of peasant conservatism. Only long years of proletarian-generated discipline could overcome this.

Can Farmers Be Allies of the Proletariat?

In its political relations with the more affluent farmers, the Soviet regime was working under a severe handicap of its own making. Any attempt to secure grain through means other than the market would immediately conjure up the specter of the *prodrazvyórstka* of 1918–21, the confiscation of grain by armed detachments of workers, Moscow at that time had sought cooperation only from the poor farmers and landless laborers. For a few months in 1918 they were formed into "committees of the poor" to help ferret out the kulaks' grain supplies and livestock. These were the same farmers who in the early months of revolution had attacked the great estates and begun to divide the land among themselves. Now they were called on to be actors in a rural class struggle for which Lenin claimed a Marxist justification.

The great irony of this tactic was that the Revolution had opened up to the poor farmers the prospect of getting more land, and to the batraks the prospect of having their own small farms at last. Those whom Lenin called the rural allies of the proletariat wanted nothing more than to become small capitalists of the type they were supposed to be combating. By 1919 Lenin had quite abandoned the tactic of setting the poor farmers off against the rest. But the grain confiscations continued, for the Civil War had to be fought and the cities fed.

With the beginning of NEP in 1921, the confiscations were stopped. In their place a tax in kind fixed the amount of produce which the peasant owed the state without recompense; this amount was eventually set at 10 percent of output. The farmers were free to market the remainder. Labor could now be hired legally, and land leased, although the sale and purchase of land were forbidden. Farmers were free to choose their form of land tenure, particularly as between individual plots and membership in a peasant commune. The concessions were those of the Soviet regime, and the gains were those of the farmers. But in retrospect, there was little to show that an "alliance" had been forged in the sense of political support from the middle peasants. For one thing, the kulaks were benefiting from NEP even more than they. For another thing, the farmers were more apt to regard the concessions as the real goal of the Revolution, not as the way station to collectivization.

Early in the 1920s, the farmers saw one thing that could happen to their newly won economic security. The "scissors crisis" of 1923–24, so called because of the scissors-like appearance of the indices on a graph, saw the price of manufactured goods rise steeply as the prices paid for foodstuffs fell. Unlike the first years after the Revolution, the farmers could now withhold most of their output from the market legally. They did so, and this helped bring the price relationships back into line. There was a lesson in this for the farmers: resistance pays. In fact, their whole experience since 1918 had taught them this. Moscow's options in finding a system that would get more grain from the countryside had now been narrowed.

Which Way to Socialist Agriculture?

Various forms of cooperative agriculture existed in Russia already, and had existed even before the Revolution, quite aside from the traditional repartitional villages. About a third of all farm households, in fact, took part in some kind of cooperative relationships under a national organization called *Selskosoyúz*. Three types of cooperative farming arrangements had emerged spontaneously. These were *toz*, which pooled implements but not land; the *artél*, which pooled most of its land but left small household plots intact; and the *kommúna*, whose production was totally collectivized. But collective farming in all three variants was miniscule in scope. *Selskosoyúz*, for its part, was in fact helping individual farms to bolster their position as capitalists.

Left to its own devices, Soviet agriculture appeared very unlikely to move in a socialist direction. Attempts by Moscow to prod it toward socialism by stages would be very likely to meet with the same kind of resistance which the peasants had used against earlier policies. Unless the Soviets were willing to set up some kind of stern control over peasant sowings and marketings, all their choices appeared unsatisfactory. How long must the state and the industrial sector continue to pay tribute to the peasants, in the form of high agricultural prices and diversion of industrial output to peasant needs? Or was there a clear alternative to the drastic "primitive socialist accumulation" at the peasants' expense, as proposed by the Left?

AGRICULTURE IN THE "GREAT DEBATE"

Bukharin and the "Right"

Nikolai Bukharin's search for a gradualist solution which would avoid compulsion produced an alternative of sorts. The weak point of the Bukharin thesis was its solution to the *political* problem of peasant resistance. To guarantee grain procurements in the present, Bukharin proposed that the NEP be made more favorable for agricultural marketing. The problem with the NEP, he said, was not that guided peasant capitalism had failed to supply the towns and the export trade, but that a true NEP solution had not even been given a fair trial. In order to do this, the laws prohibiting the use of hired labor must be modified, and other penalties and discrimination against the well-to-do peasants must be lifted.

What of collectivization? It must be voluntary, insisted Bukharin, it must proceed by stages, and at each stage it must demonstrate its value so as to attract increasing numbers of peasants. Bukharin would start by promoting cooperative ventures that did not involve merging land: this meant cooperative marketing, purchases, and credit arrangements. The poor and middle peasants would improve their farming income; they would be freed by degrees from their dependence on the kulaks; further forms of cooperation would naturally emerge which would pool land and lead to large-scale agriculture. The kulaks' role and status would dwindle in importance, and joining the cooperatives would become increasingly attractive to them. But in the immediate future, Bukharin believed, cooperatives would be a means of bolstering the private farm. By one means or another, by both stimulating cooperation and fostering private gain, the peasantry at all levels could soon be brought to marketing enough produce to assure the basis for industrial growth. In 1925 he summed up the immediate goal in a much-quoted statement which he was soon forced to retract, even if he did not renounce the idea behind it: "We have to tell the whole peasantry, all its strata: get rich, accumulate, develop your economy."[4]

What of industrialization? Some spokesmen for the Right advocated a slow progression of investment towards the goal of high investment in heavy industry. Agriculture should come first, then agricultural industries capable of exporting, then light industries supplying Soviet consumers, and finally heavy industries. Bukharin, on the contrary, believed that industrialization could proceed simultaneously with the kind of agricultural development he proposed. Part of the savings created in the agricultural sector could be drawn off to pay for new industries. The whole secret lay in finding an optimal level of savings used thus. Bukharin rejected the Left's charges that industry was lagging behind agriculture, or that it would continue to do so under his agricultural proposals. He charged, in return, that high industrial prices and the recurrent "goods famine" which was obstructing trade between town and country could be dealt with by attacking inefficiency and monopolistic abuses in the state-run industries.[5]

Bukharin's failure to deal with the Left's political doubts about growing peasant capitalism may be ascribed to his great optimism about the benefits of peasant cooperation. Why should cooperatives organized for

[4] Quoted in Alexander Erlich, *The Soviet Industrialization Debate, 1924–1928* (Cambridge, Mass.: Harvard University Press, 1960), p. 16.
[5] Nicolas Spulber, *Soviet Strategy for Economic Growth* (Bloomington, Ind.: Indiana University Press, 1964), pp. 63–66.

marketing and purchasing, much less credit cooperatives, lead peasants to the further step of pooling their lands and their profits? In the United States and many other countries outside the communist world, such co-ops are basically an aid to private farming. If cooperation of this kind could build the peasant prosperity that Bukharin predicted, would it not also build an ever larger class of well-to-do peasants unwilling to risk their gains for the very uncertain benefits of collectivization? And if the future of industrialization depended on offering ever more consumer goods to a prosperous peasantry, how much would be left for basic heavy industries?

Under the impact of these and other arguments, and perhaps disheartened by the low procurements of 1927–28, Bukharin shifted his case somewhat. He now approved heavier taxes on the kulaks. Together with Rykov, he devoted careful attention to a balanced investment program as between investment-goods and consumer-goods industries. The views of these two men dominated, in fact, the tone of the 15th Party Congress at the end of 1927. Party statements stressed the danger of tying up too much capital in projects which would not even begin to pay off for several years. The Right, let it be said, was reckoning in economic realities just as much as the Left.

Bukharin's final defense of his position on agriculture came in a *Pravda* article in the fall of 1928, at a time when he already sensed the direction Stalin was about to take. He repeated his arguments for gradual socialization of the countryside, but at the same time argued that individual farms needed help as well if the procurement crisis was to be solved. He dismissed as a myth the Party's charges that the well-to-do peasants were hoarding grain. The problem of procurements, said Bukharin, was quite simply a matter of low production. For this the Party, with its vacillating policies toward individual farming, had to bear much or most of the blame.[6]

How much of an alternative did Bukharin present? He agreed with collectivization as a goal, and saw no other mode of agricultural organization compatible with Marxist ideology and practical political requirements. He supported fully the decision of the 15th Party Congress (1927) to aim for collectivization of 20 percent of the nation's farms by 1933, the end of the first Five-Year Plan. He did not challenge the assumption that the poor and middle peasantry could be made productive only by collectivization in some form. He did not even weigh the Stolypin alternative, the breaking up of the peasant commune, as a means of making the peasantry as a whole capable of delivering surpluses. His call for aid to private farming was in a sense undermined by his belief that only collectivized agriculture could be highly productive in Soviet cir-

---

[6] *Pravda*, Sept. 30, 1928.

cumstances. In brief, for all of Bukharin's sound practical insights, he too was a prisoner of the Bolsheviks' ideological commitment to collectivization and of their equally strong ideological opposition to the well-to-do peasantry.[7]

"Primitive Socialist Accumulation"

Yevgeny Preobrazhensky had served briefly as one of the original Party Secretaries in 1920–21. An economist, he became the most articulate spokesman of the Left in the early 1920s. In spite of the fact that Stalin in 1929 not only adopted Preobrazhensky's recommendations, but applied them with extreme measures that Preobrazhensky had cautioned against, the latter suffered the same fate as other leaders of the Left. His confession at the 1934 Party Congress placed him in the role of one who would enslave the peasants, as against Stalin's supposedly triumphant appeal for peasant support:

> You know that my chief error consisted in . . . elaborating the law of primitive socialist accumulation. . . . I thought that by exploiting the peasants, by concentrating resources of the peasant economy in the hands of the state, one could build a socialist industry and develop industrialization. This was a crude analogy with the epoch of primitive capitalist accumulation. . . . Events totally disproved my ideas, and those prognoses triumphed which Lenin made and which the party made reality under the leadership of Comrade Stalin. Collectivization, that was the point! Did I anticipate collectivization? I did not . . . Collectivization of the peasants is the greatest of our conquests. . . .[8]

Consider that Stalin's collectivization had meant shipping masses of well-to-do peasants off to the labor camps and the death by starvation of perhaps 10 million Ukrainians—this by Stalin's own later admission. Now, via this extorted confession, the old Left was being accused of pressing for a policy of "exploiting the peasants" and "concentrating agricultural resources in the hands of the state." There were episodes in Stalin's long reign in which the boundless self-assurance with which the General Secretary stood facts on their heads could hardly be described adequately by any English word.

"Primitive socialist accumulation" had a fearsome ring. As a watchword for the Left it was almost as unfortunate as Bukharin's "enrich yourselves" was for the Right. In one context, it referred to the Soviet system's need to accomplish what capitalism had had not time to do: to squeeze savings from the agricultural sector in order to pay for building

[7] See Herbert J. Ellison's telling critique of Burkharin's position in "The Decision of Collectivize Agriculture," *The American Slavic and East European Review* 20 (April 1961): 198–201.

[8] Nove, *An Economic History of the U.S.S.R.*, p. 220.

new industries. In another context, it suggested the grain raids of the War Communism period.

Preobrazhensky was against forcible grain collections. He even opposed taxation as a principal means of laying hold of the surplus. Instead, there would be a period of high prices on manufactured goods and low prices on agricultural output. The "scissors crisis" must return, in other words, as a long-term policy. The Soviet state, through its control of socialized industries, is a monopoly producer of many important things and can control their prices. The peasants, because they are many in number, cannot respond by manipulating grain prices. In both manufacturing and trade, wrote Preobrazhensky, there would be a necessarily unequal contest "between the united fist of the state economy and the unorganized sea of simple commodity production."[9]

Was a Compromise Possible?

At first glance, it appears that Preobrazhensky and the Left were quite simply willing to overlook the forms of resistance of which the peasantry was capable. The state could indeed manipulate prices—no one doubted this—but would the peasants willingly grow and market a reliably large surplus year after year with prices tilted heavily against them? If the winter of 1923–24 had not been a sufficient lesson for the Left, the winter of 1927–28 offered a similar lesson, one even harder to overlook.

The seeming unreality of the Left's argument on how to obtain grain is one oft repeated justification for Stalin's collectivization program. For, aside from the whole question of whether collectivization would raise the whole level of agricultural output, there is no disputing the point that collective farms were a solution to Moscow's problem of deciding what and how much should be sown and how much should be delivered to the state. How this was done is explained below.

Actually, a close look at Preobrazhensky's proposals shows that he was indeed aware of the political peril in his program. As an economist, he had set forth the economic necessity of "squeezing the peasants" in its blunt form. But his approach to policy, which he never got around to describing in detail, took peasant resistance into account. In fact, it may be said that Preobrazhensky and Bukharin, as the intellectual leaders of Right and Left in economic matters, were not at all far apart in their views on dealing with the peasantry. Neither of them regarded collectivization as a solution to agriculture's short-range problems; both agreed on its desirability as a long-term goal. They agreed further that the peasantry must be shortchanged in the marketplace (though Bukharin

---

[9] Quoted in George R. Feiwel, *The Soviet Quest for Economic Efficiency* (New York: Praeger, 1967), p. 28.

conceded this only at the end). Both urged that careful tactics be employed with the peasants so as to keep their cooperation.[10]

In other circumstances, these two persuastive debaters and writers,
Preobrazhensky and Bukharin, might have forged a common program
for the countryside. But the ideological bitterness of the Left-Right debate, the intense feelings that led to rigid positions, drove both them
and their supporters to the extremes. For example, it is true that the
Left was inclined more and more to massive collectivization in the latter
1920s. The secretly drafted "Platform of the Left," which came out
in the fall of 1927, urged a major effort toward collectivization, repeating
the Left's familiar argument that major agricultural progress must depend
on industrial progress.

Two years later, Stalin began using some of the Left's ideas and arguments. But in another sense, the drastic collectivization drive which he
launched in 1929 was not at all a resolution of the Great Debate. Just
as Stalin's industrialization targets threw conventional economic thinking
to the winds, so the collectivization which occurred was born of motives
many of which did not figure in public discussions. One sees Stalin as
we saw him described in the last chapter, sitting apart from the brilliant
give-and-take of policy discussions in which he felt so ill at ease. His
talents were of a different sort.

COLLECTIVIZATION

Stalin's Decisions and Assumptions

Stalin's collectivization drive of 1929–36, which ended with the abolition of 90 percent of private farming, looks like a single decision, a
decision at once resolute and cruel, one which cut at last the Gordian
knot of agricultural crisis which the economists of both Right and Left
had failed to untie. In fact it consisted of several important decisions
taken together. Each of them left a lasting impact on Soviet agriculture,
including a number of other Gordian knots with which Soviet agricultural
administrators have been wrestling for decades. The decisions were these:
(1) Collectivization was *forced* nearly everywhere, while only the bare
facade of a voluntary process was maintained. (2) It was a *swift and
overwhelming process*, leaving no period of time in which private agriculture could compete for productivity with the new collective farms.
(3) *No transitional forms* of agricultural cooperation were tried as an
intermediate step, such as China was to employ in the 1950s. (Actually,
the collective farm itself has always been regarded by Soviet policy-
makers as a transitional form, the final form being huge state farms,

---

[10] Lewin, *Russian Peasants and Soviet Power*, pp. 154–55.

or some kind of very large agricultural association run like a factory.) The form of the agricultural cooperative involved *immediate and drastic changes in the farmer's work habits*, skills required, and psychology; of private farming, only the farmer's small private plot was left, embracing a couple of acres at most, and often less than a single acre. (4) The legal position of the new farms, their status as cooperatives rather than state enterprises, meant that *the state bore no responsibility* for maintaining minimum wages, fringe benefits, pensions, and the like. (5) *The political drive against the kulaks* ended with the deportation of over a million peasant households.

These decisions were not as tightly interrelated as they appear. Compulsion could have been used to produce gradual and partial collectivization; a transitional form of cooperative could have been used at first, the *toz* or something similar; different investment and consumption policies could have offered a minimal living standard for the countryside; and kulak opposition could have been dealt with in different ways, as the Chinese were to demonstrate two decades later. What unifies this group of decisions is not any theory of agricultural economics, but Stalin's own convictions about how the farmers should be dealt with politically. His political purpose was to deprive them of the control they exercised over the supply of agricultural output to the cities.

Stalin's political purpose was also his main economic purpose: whether or not collectivization increased the nation's agricultural output, the state would now be guaranteed its share, which it could collect at advantageous prices. Whatever else might evolve from the collective farm system, it made possible a system of control which eliminated the peasants' capacity to bargain with the state. The keystone of this control was the system of Machine-Tractor Stations or MTS, which in addition to controlling the use of major agricultural equipment embraced a whole network of officials whose main duty was surveillance and political control.

It is likely that Stalin believed that collectivization would lead directly to increased production. Given a plentiful supply of equipment, fertilizers, and expertise, this assumption is certainly reasonable. The problem was that in spite of the economy's efforts to provide all these inputs, they remained in very short supply on most of the collective farms. If Stalin had believed that there was any magic in collective farm organization alone, he was soon proven wrong. It is also possible that Stalin believed he could rally the poor and middle peasants to the cause of building agriculture, initially by mobilizing them against the kulaks during the process of collectivization. While the evidence on this question includes—understandably—no public opinion polls, but only data on specific situations (see the Smolensk data below), what we know indicates that opposition to collectivization could come as easily from poor peasants as from the well-to-do. In some areas, however, it does appear that collectivization was accepted by the poor peasants as a form of security. But as a consequence of expelling the kulaks from their land and driving them out of the collective farms altogether, the Soviet system lost the services of the last traditional class of people who were capable farmers, having already driven out the stewards and estate managers of Tsarist times. That Stalin and those who pushed the collectivization drive did not at least consider how they might retain the services of the kulaks is evidence that the motive of political control prevailed over the motive of economic gain.

From the point of view of political strategy, Stalin used an approach that he would later repeat in other spheres: solving a political problem by breaking resistance at the outset in drastic fashion, rather than giving it time to build up. From an historical point of view, Stalin was reenacting the aggression of Russian Tsars against the people they ruled. Just as Peter the Great and others had bound diverse elements of Russian society to the service of the state, so Stalin was restoring the peasant servitude that Emancipation and Revolution had dissolved. From a Soviet Marxist point of view, the idea of "primitive socialist accumulation" was to be realized with a vengeance. The farmers were to pay the price for building a proletarian industrial state in a land whose industrial revolution was still incomplete.

The Human Consequences

From a purely human point of view, the collectivization process meant suffering and disaster for the majority of the farmers. Some eloquent testimony came to light after World War II in the form of a large secret archive of documents taken by the German invaders from a rural province of western Russia. Among the documents are letters written by farmers to a local newspaper. Following is a letter from 1930:

> We have bad land and little of it in the village of Muzhyno, and we had grain and potato requisitions, and they took them from us by force, both from the poor peasants and from the middle peasants. Simply speaking, it was robbery. . . . We ourselves do not know what to do. Every day they send us lecturers asking us to sign up for such-and-such a kolkhoz for eternal slavery, but we don't want to leave our good homes. It may be a poor little hut, but it's mine, a poor horse, but it's mine.

Another farmer wrote:

> Comrades, you write that all the middle peasants and poor peasants join the kolkhoz voluntarily, but it is not true. For example, in our village of Podbuzhye, all do not enter the kolkhoz willingly. When the register made the rounds, only 25% signed it, while 75% did not. They collected seeds by frightening [the peasants] with protocols and

arrests. If any one spoke against it, he was threatened with arrest and forced labor.

In spite of the threats, many farmers resisted collectivization to the point of attacking officials and harrassing their fellow farmers who had joined. A police report records that in a certain village

> . . . a mob of 200 people made an open attack on the kolkhozniks who were going out to work the fields. This attack consisted of the dispersal of the kolkhozniks from the field, the destruction of their equipment, clothes, etc. . . They chased after the leaders of the kolkhoz, but the latter succeeded in saving themselves by fleeing. The majority of the attackers were women, who were armed with staves, pitchforks, spades, axes, etc. . . On the night of September 3 a threshing floor with all the harvest, belonging to a member of the kolkhoz, was destroyed by fire.[11]

The countryside was overrun with army and police detachments, who performed the double function of deporting all those unlucky enough to be classified as kulaks, and of shattering peasant resistance for the benefit of the civilian organizers sent out from the cities to head the new farms. Of the deportees, an eyewitness account relates:

> Trainloads of deported peasants left for the icy North, the forests, the steppes, the deserts. These were whole populations, denuded of everything; the old folk starved to death in mid-journey, new born babies were buried on the banks of the roadside, and each wilderness had its crop of little crosses of boughs or white wood. Other populations, dragging all their mean possessions on wagons, rushed towards the frontiers of Poland, Rumania, and China, and crossed them—by no means intact, to be sure—in spite of the machine guns.[12]

In the 1950s Nikita Khrushchev was to disclose that the nation's supply of livestock was still smaller than it had been before the outbreak of World War I. While war and civil war had taken their toll of livestock, the most serious blow had been struck by the farmers themselves during the collectivization drive. Rather than see their cows, geese, and all the rest confiscated by the military or seized for the collective farms, they slaughtered recklessly and gorged themselves. Mikhail Sholokhov, author of *The Quiet Don* and today regarded as politically conservative, wrote a less well known novel about collectivization in his native Don Cossack territory which describes this:

> . . . [L]ivestock began to be slaughtered every night in Gremyachy. Hardly had darkness fallen when the brief and stifled bleating of a

---

[11] Merle Fainsod, *Smolensk Under Soviet Rule* (Cambridge, Mass: Harvard University Press, 1958), pp. 252–53.

[12] From an account by Victor Serge, cited in M. Lewin, *Russian Peasants and Soviet Power*, p. 506.

sheep, the mortal scream of a pig, or the bellowing of a calf would be heard piercing the silence. Not only those who had joined the collective farm, but individual farmers also slaughtered. They killed oxen, sheep, pigs, even cows; they slaughtered animals kept for breeding. In two nights the horned cattle of Gremyachy were reduced to half their number. The dogs began to drag entrails and guts about the village, the cellars and granaries were filled with meat. . . . "Kill, it's not ours now!" "Kill; they'll take it for the meat collection tax if you don't." "Kill, for you won't taste meat on the collective farm." The insidious rumors crept around. And they killed. . . ."[13]

Managing the Crisis

It may have been this disastrous slaughter of livestock that persuaded Stalin to allow the countryside a temporary respite in the spring of 1930. Like many a Russian Tsar, he blamed the failures of collective agriculture on overzealous officials. Stalin's newspaper article of March 1930 went down in the annals of Soviet history as his condemnation of "dizziness with success," and he conceded that force had been used against the farmers in some places. Collectivization, he protested, must be a voluntary process. At this point 55 percent of all peasant households had been collectivized; but by summer the proportion had fallen to less than one fourth. Yet the retreat was only a tactical one. A year later the proportion had risen over the 50 percent mark once more, and by 1936, seven years after the onset of the campaign, 90 percent of the households were enrolled.

The use of force went on, Stalin's pious statement about a voluntary process notwithstanding. Where collectivization was already a fact, force had to be used to collect foodstuffs for the cities and the growing armed forces. The collective farms were assigned delivery quotas to the state at low prices, and it often happened that these deliveries ate into the food supply the peasants needed simply to keep their own households fed. The peasants concealed grain, pilfered it, sold what they could at high market prices, and used every means to resist the procurement agencies. Moscow responded in 1932 with a law threatening grain pilferers with death. In some areas the vendetta against the kulaks was resumed, and the net of arrests and deportations caught a good many ordinary peasants and Party officials as well. When in 1933 the writer Sholokhov, whose novel on collectivization was quoted above, protested to Stalin about the excesses in his area, Stalin replied that his officials were dealing with nothing less than mass sabotage, a "silent" war against the Soviet regime.[14] Little wonder that in a wartime conversation with

---

[13] Mikhail Sholokhov, *Seeds of Tomorrow* (New York: Alfred A. Knopf, 1959), p. 131.

[14] Nove, *An Economic History of the U.S.S.R.*, pp. 176–77.

Churchill ten years later, Stalin described his struggle against the peasants as more terrible than his struggle against the German invaders.

As if these man-made disasters were not enough, yet another disaster descended in the form of the 1933 famine. The weather was not to blame, either. Russian agriculture has ever been at the mercy of the weather; a severe winter or a dry summer have an immediate impact on what the Soviet consumer will find or not find in the food stores. But the harvest was somewhat better in 1933 than in 1932. Moscow, after relenting somewhat in its procurement targets in 1932, had raised the quotas again in 1933. It was the policy of taking grain out of the countryside at all costs, and the singling out of the Ukraine and the North Caucasus for drastic measures, that contributed to a famine in which millions died.

SOCIALIZED AGRICULTURE

Organizing the Collective Farms

The kolkhoz or collective farm itself was a half-dozen years in taking shape, but its organization was finally standardized by the Model Kolkhoz Charter of 1935. This remained the basis of the nation's kolkhozes for the next 30 years. Juridically the kolkhoz was a voluntary cooperative, its affairs managed through self-government. The members met to elect a chairman and a management committee, whom they could also recall and replace. The kolkhoz was linked to the Soviet state through the procurements system, which in turn required that the kolkhoz plant whatever the state needed to purchase. In practice this led to minute regulation of the kolkhozes' affairs by the district government and Party offices, as well as by the Machine-Tractor Stations (MTS). Kolkhoz chairman were in effect appointed and dismissed by the district Party chairmen.

The MTS, established by a decree of 1929, began as a state-run tractor service, but quickly assumed a supervisory role over kolkhoz operations. It was a logical step, initially, to set up agencies for allocating the services of power-driven agricultural equipment. This equipment was in very short supply, and individual kolkhozes lacked trained personnel to operate and service it; so the MTS provided both equipment and operators to the farms in return for a percentage of the harvest. In 1933, on the heels of the second political offensive against the farmers, political departments were set up in all the MTS. These were supervised directly from the central Party bureaucracy in Moscow, and hence could not be controlled by the otherwise powerful district Party leaders. Besides providing Moscow with an additional check over farm operations, the political departments were charged with purging the "subversive elements" whom Stalin accused of sabotaging agricultural output. They remained a key feature of agricultural management until Khrushchev abolished the entire MTS system in 1958.

Kolkhozes of the 1930s averaged some 75 households and two square miles of land, though there were great regional variations in size. Often there were several villages in a single farm, one of them serving as farm headquarters and the site of new service structures. One must not imagine that collectivization entailed herding farmers and their families into barracks. Moscow had even discouraged a few early experiments in changing the peasant style of domestic life. Besides, to rehouse 100 million people at this point, in any fashion, was quite out of the question. What did change for the peasant household was the land allotted for its own private use, which was now reduced to not more than 1.2 acres, and sometimes half that, depending on the locality. The household could market its output from this tiny plot at market prices, and in addition raise a cow (with calves), a sow (with piglets), four sheep, and poultry and rabbits in any quantity. Private livestock could be pastured on kolkhoz land. Though these plots seem an insignificant concession, they have been intensively cultivated right up to the present, and their output supplies a significant proportion of some kinds of foodstuffs.

Labor for the kolkhoz itself was measured in a workday unit called the *trudodén*. Kolkhoz members were rewarded in cash and produce for the number of workdays they put in. An earnings differential was introduced by assigning more workday units per unit of time to skilled types of work. Moreover, the value of the workday unit itself fluctuated with the output and income of the kolkhoz. During the whole Stalin era, the farmer's income for workdays performed was extremely small, and the proportion of income paid in cash often negligible. Because of this, income from the private plots was of vital importance to the peasant household, which accordingly worked its tiny plot intensively and neglected working for the kolkhoz to the extent it could. Consequently compulsion had to be used to get farmers to devote time to the kolkhoz, and a statute formalized this in 1939. But the farmers, because they were not state employees, had no claim to any kind of minimum wage, pensions, workmen's compensation, or other fringe benefits enjoyed by industrial labor.

In addition to the quarter-million kolkhozes, about 4,000 state farms, or sovkhozes, were in existence in the 1930s. These "grain factories," as they were dubbed at the time, were intended as a start toward the agricultural wave of the future, a scientific agriculture on an enormous scale, manned by specialists operating the most modern equipment. The early state farms were enormous in territory and unprofitable in operation, so that a number of the early farms were broken up and their land assigned to the kolkhozes. Their turn had to wait until after World War II.

Controlling the Rural Population

For more than three centuries, a major agricultural problem of Russia's rulers had been to find an effective way of binding rural labor to the land. A related problem had been to assure a supply of rural manpower for nonagricultural purposes, whenever that was necessary. The emancipation of the serfs in the 1860s had unlocked a potentially very large supply of manpower for the industries and cities, even though most of it was unskilled. But legal restrictions on rural population movements and peasant continued almost unchanged up to the Revolution.

Under serfdom, these restrictions rested on the feudal-type dues exacted from the peasantry. With the sanction of landlords and officials, a peasant could work part of the year at a nonfarm job in order to get money for these dues. This often meant permission for the peasant to spend a time in a distant city. The Emancipation replaced these dues with redemption payments, and the peasant commune in many places stepped into the landlord's former role as collector. Only with the commune's permission could one of its members leave to earn his redemption payments elsewhere; and only a local court could approve this arrangement. It was not the purpose of the Emancipation to release masses of rural labor for industrial purposes; only the former household serfs, who received no land allotments, were free to choose their employment. State programs encouraged the migration of surplus population to start farms in sparsely settled areas of the Russian Empire. After the early revolutionary years, the NEP agricultural policies encouraged farmers to stay on the land by distributing available land to households which had previously been without land of their own.

Stalin and the Soviet leaders could not have failed to forsee that tens of millions of peasants would attempt to flee to the cities at the first blows of the collectivization drive. Part of this manpower was needed for the nation's rapidly growing industries and construction projects. Industries signed contracts with collective farms which obliged the latter to supply a specified number of workers. In the early years, this was accomplished largely by compulsion, although the exfarmers, once employed in industry, were then able to change jobs. But most of the farmers had to remain to work the collective farms. Besides, the cities could not be permitted to fill with unemployed exfarmers, who would be both a burden on the urban economy and possibly a political danger to the regime. The internal passport system introduced in 1932 provided a legal and administrative framework for barring unauthorized migration from the villages to the cities. Collective farmers in most areas were denied passports under this system. At the same time they were forbidden to take up permanent residence in areas where carrying passports is required, namely in cities, industrial regions, and border areas.

Migration from the villages to the towns and cities has taken place on a massive scale during the whole period of Soviet rule, and it was not Moscow's intention to stop this. For rural young people, today just as in the 1930s, there are a number of ways of gaining urban residence and nonfarm occupations. Soviet newspaper articles ask whether it is not possible to keep more young people on the farms, and in the 1960s Soviet sociologists began to gather data on the reasons for the youth exodus from the countryside. Regional differences in employment patterns are very pronounced: areas such as the western periphery of the Ukraine and Byelorussia have a surplus of labor not only in farming, but in nonfarm occupations as well, so that an exodus of young people from the farms is a normal state of affairs, promoted by labor recruitment policies.

It has always been common for kolkhoz men to hold nonfarm jobs outside the kolkhoz, jobs to which they sometimes commute long distances. So common is this phenomenon that even the more prosperous kolkhozes which are shown to foreign visitors often have a labor force consisting predominantly of middle-aged to elderly women. From the early years of collectivization efforts were made to regulate these outside jobs also, important as they were in assuring a cash income where the kolkhoz itself could assure little or none. Soviet authorities became concerned about those households whose links with the farms had become tenuous, but which hung on to their membership because of their private plots and the opportunity of pilfering foodstuffs at harvest time. In the early 1930s and through the peak of the Great Purge, kolkhozes had expelled their own members right and left; included in the expulsions were households where the father had found an industrial job. Once again there was official concern about an uncontrolled flow of people from the farms to the cities, since a 1938 decree forbade expulsion from the kolkhozes of any but the worst malingerers.

Soviet efforts to regulate, promote, and block population movements in various contexts have usually been only partly successful. There is generally a good deal of "slippage" in the process of enforcing such regulations, and immediate economic needs usually take precedence over long-range measures for population distribution. But even so, Soviet collective farmers today are not free to leave the farms simply at will.

Controlling the Rural Living Standard

There is little doubt that the Soviet farmers bore the main burden of paying for Stalin's industrialization drive. No matter whether the new kolkhozes fared well or badly, or whether the country's unpredictable weather smiled on the harvest or not, the cities, the industrial labor force,

and the growing military establishment had first claim on what the farmers produced. What the farms received from the new industries in
equipment was far from what they needed to meet their delivery quotas.
It was to be another quarter-century before the Soviet economy began
to turn out the kind of technology, fertilizers, and all the rest that would
raise the farms' productivity to the level it might have reached in Stalin's
time.

As for the farmers themselves, their rewards were kept deliberately
meager, the responsibility of the state for their welfare was minimal,
and often the individual plots were their only real security. The passport
system reimposed a serfdom of sorts, and in this and other respects the
farmers were made third-class citizens. The Soviet regime thus took on
itself an enormous economic and social debt to the farmers.

It was not until the 1960s that Moscow began to make major changes
in the condition of the Soviet collective farmer as consumer and citizen.
Until that time, the farmers had no claim to pensions, sickness and accident benefits, or paid holidays, as did the urban population. They had
to content themselves with whatever their collectives could provide as
substitutes, which was often meager. State investments in housing, medical
services, schools, and urban-type amenities for the villages constituted
only a small fraction of what the cities received. Distribution of consumers' goods was carried on through a woefully inadequate system of
village co-ops. A familiar sight in Soviet cities was the farmers who
travelled long distances to shop in the cities, their dress setting them
apart sharply from urban shoppers. They carried great sacks in which
they hauled many months' worth of shopping—often including foodstuffs—back to the railroad stations for the return trip.

It was hard to persuade university graduates to go out to the small
towns and villages to teach, staff the hospitals, and provide technical
services for the farms. Very few of them, even those who had come
from the villages and had earned their diplomas in agricultural specialties,
wanted to return to the 19th-century Russia were more than half the
Soviet population still lived. Even those who joined the "rural intelligentsia," the Soviet name for all professionals in the countryside, usually
enjoyed urban-type salaries and benefits which set them apart in status
from the rest of the farm population.

To be sure, it was not the farmers alone who paid for Stalin's industrialization drive with their deprivations. Urban wages remained low
by European standards, housing became fearfully crowded, and urban
services were greatly overburdened. But the difference between urban
and rural living standards was great. Where choices had to be made
between city and country, it was the countryside that suffered. During
the 1933 famine, the cities were fed while the villages quite literally
starved, particularly in the Ukraine.

POLITICAL CONSEQUENCES

The political consequences of Stalin-style collectivization were of two kinds: 1. The disaster which descended on the countryside became a focal point for actual and potential opposition to Stalin's rule, and could have served to topple him from power in 1932 or 1933. 2. The experience of the Soviet leaders in overcoming peasant resistance and high-level criticism hardened their negative opinion about collective farmers' willingness to make the new system a success. After 1932, no basic alteration in the collective farm system occurred until after Stalin's death.

Political Crisis, 1932–33

Stalin's decisions about collectivization resulted, three years after the drive had begun, in a political crisis for the Georgian dictator to which he responded with yet another series of fateful decisions. Recall his famous speech of 1931 about slowing down the tempo, quoted in chapter 1. The criticisms at which Stalin struck in his speech were not only about the headlong tempo of industrial investment itself. There were also voices among the upper Party hierarchy which protested the rape of the countryside. Probably some of the critics feared first of all that repression in the villages might plunge the country into political chaos, with disastrous results for the Party's rule. Others doubtless feared for the harvests and foresaw the ruin of agriculture. And finally, there were those who saw first of all the human misery inflicted by the brutal collectivization drive, and believed this contrary to socialist ideals.

Stalin's position in the years 1930–32 bore one interesting resemblance to that of Witte in 1900–1903: the high tempo of industrialization was under heavy attack from a variety of foes, and the leader of the industrialization drive must either strike back or yield. A massive party purge was visited on the Ukraine in 1933, the area which had suffered most of all from collectivization; a highly respected veteran Bolshevik, Mikola Skrypnik, committed suicide in protest against the political, economic, and cultural oppression of the Ukraine. As during Witte's last years in the Ministry of Finance, some of the protest came from politically powerful figures who believed that the industrialization program would be ruined by haste, and some of it from circles that foresaw the ruin of the peasantry and were horrified at the suffering inflicted on the villages.

As we saw in the last chapter, the rest of the story is quite different from what happened in the Witte period. By 1932, the crescendo of behind-the-scenes criticism had shaken Stalin's confidence in the Five-Year Plan and in himself as leader. His second wife, Nadya Alliluyeva, became a channel for much of the criticism, and was despondent over the human suffering wrought by the regime's harsh policies. In November 1932, in the presence of some of his close political associates, Stalin in a fit of temper heaped vulgar abuse on her. She left the gathering and took her own life the same night. Not long after this, Stalin tendered his resignation as General Secretary to a session of the Politburo. While this is a familiar and usually safe tactic of dictators for bolstering their position, in Stalin's case it also reflected genuine self-doubt. But Stalin's most important high-level foes had been purged by this time. Of the more or less loyal Party leaders who remained, none would risk his position by suggesting that the resignation be accepted. After an embarrassed silence, according to one report, Molotov said: "Stop it, stop it. You have got the Party's confidence." The matter ended there, and by stages Stalin regained his old confidence.[15]

At the beginning of 1933, Stalin broke his long public silence to address the Party Central Committee in a confident tone. A year later, at the 17th Party Congress of 1934, the so-called Congress of Victors, he admitted many weak spots in the nation's agriculture. But he declared flatly that collectivization had the firm support of the farmers: "Our Soviet peasantry has departed from the shores of capitalism for once and for all, and has gone ahead to socialism in alliance with the working class." Assertions to the contrary, he said, the rumors that farmers would like to return to individual farming, were vicious calumny spread by old Trotskyites, Mensheviks, and other defeated groups.[16]

Political Rigidity, 1935–53

While the political crisis of collectivization passed, and some of the subsequent harvests were good by Russian standards, a long-term political consequence remained: political suspicion of the peasantry on the part of the leaders, an aversion to listening to the now muted protests from officials concerned about the farmers' lot, and a refusal to make even a few obvious concessions to the collective farms. Proposals for setting up a nationwide organization of collective farms were nipped in the bud; instead, the farms were placed under the political supervision of the Machine-Tractor Stations, already described. The Model Collective Farm Charter issued in 1935 appears to call for democracy and a degree of autonomy in farm management, but in practice the collective farm chairmen were Party appointees.

In the mid-1940s, in the wake of World War II and the destruction of vast farming areas, farmers and many junior officials acted on the

---

[15] Victor Serge, *Portrait de Staline* (Paris, 1940), pp. 94–95, as quoted in Isaac Deutscher, *Stalin: A Political Biography* (New York and London: Oxford University Press, 1949), pp. 333–34.

[16] I. Stalin, *Voprosy Leninizma* 11th ed. (Moscow: Gospolitizdat, 1953), p. 487.

assumption that the rigorous collective farm system would now be modified somewhat for the farmers' benefit. Farmers had even begun adding land—illegally—to their private plots, in hopes that the tight acreage restrictions on these plots would be relaxed, or their extension at least tolerated. These hopes were crushed when a decree of September 1946 reaffirmed tight central control over collective farm affairs. It flayed farm officials for relaxing discipline and called for a return to strict observance of the prewar collective farm regulations. A high-level Council on Collective Farm Affairs was set up to supervise the enforcement of discipline.

Stalin, to all appearances, resisted efforts to make any kind of important changes in the collective farm system he had established 15 years before. The two important programs that were undertaken did not affect the nature of the collective farm system itself. In 1949 a grandiose program for changing the climate of the south was undertaken, involving large-scale afforestation and irrigation. In the same year, the policy of amalgamating the collective farms into larger units was pressed; the 240,000 farms that existed in 1949 were merged in just a few years' time so as to reduce the number of units by two thirds. On the occasion of the Nineteenth Party Congress (1952), Stalin did state that collective farms should be converted gradually into state farms, one result of which would be control by the state over the nation's entire agricultural output. But reform proposals which would have had a direct, immediate effect on the life and work situation of collective farmers were rejected: Andrei A. Andreyev's proposal for replacing the brigade with the much smaller "link" (which had been used as a wartime emergency measure) as the collective farm's basic work unit; and Nikita S. Khrushchev's plan for building "agro-cities" which would both concentrate the farm population and offer it urban-type amenities. In 1950 Andreyev was publicly censured (though not dismissed or purged), and Khrushchev had to amend his *Pravda* article by stating that he had written it "for discussion purposes only." Whatever may have been the advantages of the "link," it was small enough to coincide with a large farm household and used an incentive system which could be interpreted as a step back in the direction of private farming. The "agro-city" would have meant an enormous diversion of resources to improve rural living standards, which Stalin firmly opposed regardless of possible long-term benefits for agricultural output.

Finally, the multitude of initiatives and reforms in agriculture which were launched within months of Stalin's death suggests strongly that Stalin in his last years had at least postponed them long beyond the point where his knowledgeable lieutenants considered the time ripe for them: the Virgin Lands campaign (see chapter 3), relaxation of restrictions on private plots, a drive to produce more agricultural equipment, price reforms, and much else, culminating in 1958 with abolition of the Machine-Tractor Stations. In short, one may say that Stalin entertained only such proposals as would have increased control over the agricultural system as he had established it in the 1930s; whatever might have made control more difficult was shunted aside.

OPTIONS AND CHOICES

During the 1920s, there was no debate about the desirability of large-scale socialized agriculture as a goal. It was in keeping with Karl Marx's assumptions about socialism (admittedly Marx gave no specific plans for a socialist economy) and it followed the trend toward large, mechanized farms in some countries of the capitalist West, whose production technology the Bolshevik leaders so admired. There was nothing foreordained about the specific form of cooperative farming, the *artél*, which Moscow imposed as a universal pattern for collective farms. The *toz* could have been used as an intermediate stage. On the other hand, there was no practical possibility of going beyond the collective farm system by transforming the whole countryside into state farms and the peasants into state-paid workers, particularly in view of the great managerial problems the existing state farms were having. But above all, the development of farm output as such certainly did not require abrupt collectivization of the entire countryside. It would have been far better to collectivize first those areas which could profit by it most, and to concentrate farm machinery and other inputs there.

Stalin's choices, as should be clear from this chapter, can be explained only in terms of his decision to force an immediate solution to the problem of grain supply. This in turn required that the farmers most likely to resist this measure, the kulaks, be removed from the land by force. The decision to use force impelled Stalin to apply it in the way he considered most effective. The attack on the kulaks must be sudden and complete; resistance must not be given time to build up. Secondary advantages could be derived from a "short victorious war" against the kulaks: it could be used to win the loyalty of the rest of the peasantry and to elicit their cooperation in building a new Soviet agriculture. If loyalty did not result, the antikulak drive offered an occasion for reestablishing the kind of political controls over the peasantry that Tsarist Russia had long maintained. The campaign to organize collective farms was Stalin's chosen vehicle for crystallizing this hoped-for loyalty and imposing political controls; consequently it was not desirable to stretch the collectivization process over many years. Whether sudden collectivization led to any immediate increase in farm output, as Stalin claimed it would, may not have been of central importance.

Small wonder, then, that Stalin specifically attacked the economists who called for a balanced development of agriculture. Whatever other reasons he may have had for throwing even eminently sensible economic advice to the winds, the very idea of measured agricultural progress stood in the way of Stalin's solution to a crisis that endangered his rule. On the other hand, Stalin's apparent decision after World War II not to undertake agricultural reforms in the immediate future is harder to explain in terms of political realism. The state of Soviet agriculture was in fact a growing political liability which Stalin, cut off as he was from the lives of ordinary people during his last years, simply failed to recognize. Instead of looking within the collective farm system itself for possible changes, he relied on stern administrative control for the present and grandiose future plans external to the system. His successors, consequently, inherited a whole mountain of pressing agricultural problems.

FOR FURTHER READING

On agriculture under the Tsars, a widely respected standard work is Geroid T. Robinson, *Rural Russia Under the Old Regime* (New York: Longmans, Green and Co., 1949). D. M. Wallace, *Russia on the Eve of War and Revolution* (New York: Vintage Books, 1961) contains some fascinating first-hand accounts of the life of both peasants and gentry. Detailed accounts of the condition of agriculture and the peasantry in the 1920s may be found in M. Lewin, *Russian Peasants and Soviet Power* (Evanston, Ill.: Northwestern University Press, 1968), and D. J. Male, *Russian Peasant Organisation Before Collectivisation* (Cambridge: At the University Press, 1971).

Mikhail Sholokhov, author of *The Quiet Don*, wrote a surprisingly frank novel about the process of collectivization on the lower Don, *Seeds of Tomorrow* (New York: Knopf, 1959), which was published earlier under the title *Virgin Soil Upturned*. A grim picture of collectivization in a predominantly rural province emerges from Soviet documents captured in World War II, and analyzed in Merle Fainsod, *Smolensk Under Soviet Rule* (New York: Vintage Books, 1963); see especially Chapter 12. Other chapters provide an excellent inside view of agricultural administration in the 1930s. See also Fedor Belov, *The History of a Soviet Collective Farm* (New York: Praeger, 1955). An economist's view of the agricultural system under Stalin is that of Naum Jasny, *The Socialized Agriculture of the USSR* (Stanford, Calif.: Stanford University Press, 1949). An introductory overview and interpretation of collectivization and its results is given in Roy D. Laird and Betty A. Laird, *Soviet Communism and Agrarian Revolution* (Baltimore: Penguin Books, 1970).

3

THE POLITICS OF A MATURE
ECONOMY

$\mathbf{B}_\text{Y THE TIME}$ of Stalin's death in 1953, his economic priorities of the 1930s had been transformed into a rigid dogma. These included the priority of investment over consumption; the priority of heavy industrial investment over investment in light industry, consumers' goods, and agriculture; a high defense budget in peacetime; and priority for consumption by the nonfarm population over consumption by the farmers. The first two of these were stated explicitly, and the remainder assumed. Arguments over actual priorities never quite stopped during the Stalin era. Clearly the matter of priorities had been a bone of contention in 1934, and it was to crop up again after World War II, but none of Stalin's lieutenants questioned the dogmas themselves.

In chapters 1 and 2 we saw that Soviet leaders from Lenin's time on were agreed on the importance of investment, and of heavy industrial investment specifically. Their disagreements sprang from different views about the pace at which it could be carried out, and the degree of sacrifice that could be imposed on the population. The specific policies which Stalin imposed in 1929, more extreme in pace and sacrifice than anything considered up to then, sprang from his strategy for dealing with immediate economic and political problems. But the priorities became enshrined in dogmas, again because in this form they were useful in meeting further crises, notably postwar reconstruction needs and the disarray of collective farming in 1945–46.

Small wonder, then, that any proposal for reordering economic priorities raised basic political questions. It is no less surprising that economic policies became the natural weapons of the leaders who contended for power in the years 1953–57, the period which ended with Khrushchev's supremacy. There were episodes during this period which make one wonder whether the Soviet leaders regard economic policies as nothing but handy political weapons, and trade one for another as political circumstances dictate. Malenkov started in 1953 as an outspoken advocate of more consumer-oriented investment, then switched back to a Stalinist position when he needed allies; Khrushchev in 1954 upheld the old priorities as against Malenkov, but by 1957 had reversed himself in the process of building a successful combination of leaders. There were analogous switches in the Great Debate of the 1920s, as we saw in chapter 1.

In the Soviet experience, not only were economic policies politicized right from the time of the Revolution, but after Trotsky's defeat they were the main political issue. In a political system whose very justification is derived from its relation to economic systems and economic change, it could hardly be otherwise. But this is not the same as saying that economic issues were derived from power struggles. The strength of the Soviet system, indeed its very legitimacy, is closely tied to its success in solving the double problem of building its strength against foreign rivals and making at least a modicum of progress toward realizing the ideological promise of full prosperity for its citizens. The power struggles of the 1920s and 1950s were both fueled by the fear of each faction that the opposing faction would make the Soviet Union vulnerable on one or both counts. It was such fears that quickly reignited the debate over economic priorities within months after Stalin's death.

CONSUMER WELFARE AS A POLITICAL WEAPON

This debate, in fact, was threatening to get out of hand in 1954. Those who studied the nuances of speeches and editorials in the tightly controlled Soviet press were treated to the unseemly spectacle of *Izvestiya* disagreeing flatly with *Pravda* on economic priorities. *Izvestiya*, the government newspaper, was calling for a shift of priorities to consumers' goods; *Pravda*, the top Party daily, defended the traditional policies. Foreign analysts quickly spotted *Izvestiya's* line as that of Premier Malenkov, the formal head of government. By the end of 1954, *Izvestiya* had shifted its position back to the old line.

Something had happened to Malenkov's authority—would he now submit to his opponents? On February 8, 1955, he sat impassively before a session of the Supreme Soviet as a deputy read his statement of resignation from the premiership. The first chapter of the bitter post-Stalin political struggles was over.

The Rise of Malenkov

Georgi M. Malenkov's career was hardly the stuff of which biographies and novels are made. His rise to power, even more than Stalin's, had been accomplished entirely within the Party bureaucracy. Very much a behind-the-scenes figure during Stalin's long rule, he was in charge of the all-important Cadres Directorate. It was this office that decided on appointments and promotions both inside and outside the ranks of the Party. This included, among others, a great many offices which on paper were supposed to be elective. Stalin himself had gained vast power through his appointments function as General Secretary, and from the 1930s on Malenkov was right-hand man in these matters. During the Great Purge of 1936–38, while the top security and law-enforcement officials were in the center of political attention—Yagoda, Yezhov, and Vyshinsky—it was Malenkov's office that was making many of the key decisions. Though later on he gained some experience managing industry and transport, basically he remained a top-level manipulator of internal Party affairs. A thickly built man with a round fleshy face ("a face like a woman's," wrote the poet Yevtushenko some years later), he was suited even less than Stalin for persuasive oratory, or for cutting a vigorous figure in public.

Several months before Stalin's death, it was Malenkov and not Stalin who delivered the Report of the Central Committee at the 19th Party Congress, the first such congress in 13 years. Hence it was no surprise that Malenkov, two days after Stalin died, gained the premiership. This office, together with the Party Secretaryship he had occupied since 1939 plus a dozen years' service on the Politburo, placed him very nearly in Stalin's shoes as head of both Party and state hierarchies. During Malenkov's first days of power, the Soviet press gave him a buildup resembling the countless glorifications of Stalin which were produced on command to suit all occasions. Perhaps Stalin's charisma could be transferred to another person after all, who knows? A surprising reverse ended these brief days of glory: On March 21st, *Pravda* announced that Malenkov had given up his all-important Secretaryship at his own request. Though he remained premier and a member of the Politburo, and though Stalin's old office of General Secretary had apparently been dropped, Malenkov's political power was placed under a severe restriction. He had to strike out on a new political course or else succumb to his rivals, actual and potential.

The last months of Stalin's reign had seen some very complex political maneuvering involving the power of the Soviet security machinery. While Stalin's death cut short what probably would have been another wave of purges, these unsettled questions occupied the political stage until the summer of 1953. With the arrest and eventual execution of Lavrenti Beria, the top security official and a formidable contender for power, Malenkov was free to launch a program that might rebuild his diminished strength.

A Bid for Popularity

The program he announced in August 1953 was a bold stroke aimed at identifying the Malenkov regime with the needs of the long-neglected Soviet consumer. Said Malenkov to the Supreme Soviet:

> The Government and the Central Committee of the Party consider it necessary to increase significantly the investments in the development of the light, food and fishing industries, and in agriculture, and to improve greatly the production of articles of popular consumption . . .

> Our immediate task is within the course of two or three years to raise sharply the supply to the population of foodstuffs and manufactured goods—meat and meat products, fish and fish products, butter, sugar, confectionary, fabrics, clothing, footwear, utensils, furniture and other articles of cultural and household goods, to raise considerably the supply to the population of all consumer goods. . . .[1]

Malenkov did concede two points: his program could not be carried out without some basic improvements in agriculture, and heavy industry must remain strong. These concessions summarized the two grave risks of his program. First, basic agricultural improvement might be impossible to bring about within a few years, even in the best of circumstances. Secondly, failure to deliver the consumers' goods which he promised, many of which depended so heavily on agriculture, would give his rivals the chance to accuse him of having betrayed the principle that heavy industry must come first.

What Malenkov actually did was more froth than substance. A series of retail price reductions had already been splashed over the front page of the newspapers, the first of them less than a month after Stalin's death. Yet the reductions made no sense in the case of goods in short supply; it only increased the length of the queues for them. Stalin had tried the same thing back in 1949. Getting rid of compulsory purchases of state bonds by workers accentuated the shortages by increasing purchasing power before the supply of goods could be improved. The sharp increases in consumer goods production which Malenkov ordered were in some cases impossible, and a disappointing harvest in 1953 did not help matters. The whole campaign was symbolized by setting up a large department store right across Red Square from the Kremlin. Government offices were moved out of an arcaded prerevolutionary structure, and GUM—the initials stand for "State Department Store"—became a crowded mecca for shoppers from near and far.

---

[1] Speech to the Supreme Soviet of Aug. 8, 1953, quoted in Robert Conquest, *Power and Policy in the U.S.S.R.* (London: Macmillan, 1962), p. 249.

Khrushchev and the Farms

The new regime made some immediate changes in the collective farm system as well. These changes were the work of the man who was soon to emerge as victor over Malenkov, Nikita S. Khrushchev. Khrushchev had been named a Party Secretary in 1949 after a decade of ruling his native Ukraine, where he acquired an encyclopaedic knowledge of agriculture. He not only stayed on in the Secretariat when Malenkov was removed, but six months later emerged as First Secretary (a title not capitalized for several years, let it be noted). The title of "First Secretary" at this pinnacle of the Party bureaucracy was something new, a concession to anti-Stalin feelings, and possibly an indication that, as of 1953, Khrushchev was meant to be only "first among equals." Not until 1966 did the Party restore Stalin's old title of General Secretary.

While these first agricultural reforms did not deal with the basic ills of the system, they did lead to some real improvements within a few years, both in agricultural output and in the lot of the farmers. Prices paid to the collective farms by state purchasing agencies were increased, transport and marketing costs were reduced, and the volume of compulsory sales to the state was in some cases reduced. Taxes on the use of private plots were reduced, farmers were encouraged to raise private livestock, and their freedom to market their private output was extended. The collective farms were promised more farm machinery, fertilizers, electrical supplies, and building materials. However, the hold of the MTS over the collective farms was strengthened, and farm directors were given new disciplinary authority over the farmers.

Khrushchev had staked his reputation on getting quick results in agriculture, and by the end of 1953 he was already in difficulty. Having revealed that the nation's livestock supply was still below that of prerevolutionary times, he promised an increase within two or three years. Yet the output of fodder, and especially of fodder grain, was low and not likely to increase rapidly. So, rather than stake his campaign on increased productivity per acre, Khrushchev instead won approval for his campaign to plough the virgin lands of a vast dry area: northern Kazakhstan, parts of southern Siberia, and the southeastern part of European Russia, beyond the Volga. Early in 1954 an army of young people migrated to these areas, some of them voluntarily, others under pressure. At the risk of turning the area into a vast dust bowl, the virgin lands were sown almost exclusively with grain crops. The first harvest year, 1954, saw good results on the first huge farms, 1955 turned out to be a drought year, but 1956 again saw a good harvest. Khrushchev's immediate gamble had paid off.

Why Appeal to the Soviet Consumer?

Why should Malenkov, or any other Soviet leader, consider it important to woo the Soviet population with promises of more and better goods? The votes which Soviet citizens cast under their constitution had no effect on the selection of leaders. Their complaints about low earnings and empty stores did not find their way into the press, except where the authorities found it expedient to print some critical letters. Stalin had actually reduced living standards in some respects in order to build the kind of heavy industry he wanted; but, save for his initial faltering in 1932, which we saw in the last chapter, public unhappiness about living conditions seemed not to threaten his power in any way. And finally, two years after Stalin's death, a majority of his former associates in the Politburo—including at this point Khrushchev—were persuaded that the old economic priorities could be restored. Why, then, Malenkov's promises to the consumer?

To begin with, in 1953 Malenkov's new course on consumers appeared to have the assent of his Party associates; at least there is little to suggest controversy over it at that time. On the other hand, Khrushchev's agricultural program seems to have been under attack from the beginning, particularly his Virgin Lands campaign. But a large part of the controversy over agriculture was over specific methods for increasing output and not over the need for some kind of new emphasis on agriculture. The collective farm reforms already described did not figure in the controversy. For a number of months after Stalin's death, it appeared that Soviet leaders were agreed on some kind of new deal for the Soviet citizen as consumer.

One can speculate on what united the Party leaders in this opinion. First of all, they more than anyone else were aware that the Soviet system had been operating under high tension for a quarter-century; with Stalin gone, this tension might lead to disturbances. Opening a safety valve was therefore a wise course. Secondly, leaders newly arrived in power generally try to reinforce their image at once by putting a distinctive stamp on their administration. Malenkov with his superficial gestures to consumer welfare was only doing what others—save perhaps Molotov—would have done in his place. Finally, Marxism proclaims that socialism will bring abundance to the people who live under it. Realizing this promise in some small degree was the next logical step for any leader who wishes to give evidence of forward movement. Stalin in the 1930s had built the Moscow subway at great cost for this very reason.

How, then, did support for Malenkov's program become transformed into opposition? Where a leader is only first among equals, and especially in a situation where the magnitude of his authority is in doubt, any attempt to build his public image will be regarded with mistrust. New programs may constitute an act of aggression against those political leaders who are strongly identified with the old programs. Moreover, the new program may be used as justification for removing them from power. Both Malenkov and Khrushchev were engaged in building their power by overtrumping rivals with economic breakthroughs. Khrushchev, the more adept of the two, rescued his position in 1954–55 by siding with Malenkov's enemies, the ones who were using part of the press to criticize the new consumer line. Just a few years later, Khrushchev too would switch again to championing the consumer. A wise politician tries to fight only one major battle at a time.

KHRUSHCHEV'S CRUSADE

The Man and His Several Images

In his own way, Khrushchev was just as much a phenomenon as Stalin had been. It is true that he did not wield Stalin's formidable power over his associates. Nor, once in power, did he recklessly inflict death and suffering on the population. And, while he encouraged a "cult of the personality" which saw his picture displayed icon-fashion on important occasions, this was only a pale imitation of the artificial sainthood which Stalin had bestowed on himself. He shared Stalin's political cunning without being as ruthless in political triumph.

But Khrushchev was much more than just a humanized version of his awesome predecessor. He possessed a restless urge to reform and experiment, and this in a system now managed by a vast antireform bureaucracy. He was an indefatigable student of reports and statistics; his retentive mind enabled him to talk circles around both his Soviet rivals and foreign interviewers. Though not a brilliant orator, he had a ready tongue and a persuasive manner. Unlike Stalin, but very much in the Lenin tradition, he enjoyed mingling with crowds in a way that would horrify the U.S. Secret Service were an American President to do the same. In political dealings, too, he took risks that others in his place would have shunned. He capitalized ably on his successes, and never abandoned the effort to recoup his defeats. Finally, during his early years of power, he possessed a gift for striking a responsive note among his fellow countrymen. To the Soviet public of the latter 1950s, he offered a refreshing antidote to Stalin's ways, a cause for genuine hope.

Two other images of Khrushchev must not be permitted to obscure these basic qualities. One is the image conveyed by some of the Western press, which pictured him first of all as arrogant, ruthless, and overbearing. One recalls the Khrushchev of 1960, angrily denouncing the Eisenhower administration over the U-2 spy plane incident; the Khrushchev who lashed out at Soviet intellectuals and "parasites," who gloated over the 100-megaton nuclear tests with which Moscow ended an unofficial testing moratorium, who sometimes treated foreign correspondents like ignorant schoolchildren. Along with this image goes Khrushchev the vulgarian, his boorish antics in Belgrade when the old feud with Yugoslavia was patched up in 1955, and his shoe-pounding episode in the United Nations. Reinforcing this image was the famous potato sack figure, the piggish features, the country mannerisms of speech, and the vulgar expressions with which he sometimes emphasized a point.

The other image is one composed in retrospect by foreign scholars and journalists after Khrushchev's overthrow in 1964. This image stresses the First Secretary's political failures after 1960, his attempts to regain the positions he thought he had won during 1957–59. Even when he appeared to be at the height of his power, he paid a price for every reform he put into operation. His political triumphs over his rivals were partial triumphs at best. While the original rivals of the mid-1950s never returned to challenge him—Molotov, Malenkov, and Kaganovich—others who shared their mentality did score telling points against the Khrushchev reforms. One may point to Khrushchev's increasing arbitrariness, his growing impatience with criticism, and the ever more frequent tactic of catching his colleagues unawares in announcing policy changes. Finally, this image underscores what some observers saw as Khrushchev's decline in popularity with the Soviet man in the street. His ouster in October 1964 produced hardly a ripple in Soviet society, while Stalin's death had evoked a numbing shock.

Economic Choices and Limits

The economic reports which flooded Khrushchev's desk in the Central Committee building during 1955–56 contained a lot of hopeful news. The nation's economic recovery from the devestation of World War II had been swift. The industrialization drive which Stalin had begun, for all the failures to meet targets set in the early Five-Year Plans, was now bearing real fruit. Agricultural output, thought still at the mercy of the weather, had responded to Khrushchev's reforms enough to justify further steps along the same line. Khrushchev certainly must have compared the actual possibilities for a new era of consumer welfare with Malenkov's political ineptness and economic naïveté in trying to realize it.

We noted in chapter 1 that Soviet economic data must be treated with caution. Vague percentage increases must somehow be translated into real terms, and this is not always possible; ruble figures must be converted not just into dollars, but into a set of price relationships meaningful to non-Soviet economists; and even raw data on economic output—tons of steel, centners of wheat, square meters of housing space—must be qualified by examining Soviet data-collection methods. Khrushchev, as he pored over this mountain of data, doubtless made some mental adjustment for overoptimistic statistical results. Certainly he had a lot of additional data that were not made public, which probably offered a more sober picture. Even assuming that Khrushchev used all the skeptical caution of Western specialists in making sense of Soviet data, he saw strengths in the Soviet economy which could now be turned to good account. First a look at some raw production data for industry (Table 3-1). In agriculture the results appear good at first, but the statis-

TABLE 3–1
Industry-Related Output
(in selected years)

	1928	1940	1956
Steel (millions of tons)	4.3	18.3	48.7
Electrical generating capacity (millions of kilowatts)	1.9	11.2	43.
Truck and automobile production (thousands of units)	0.8	145.	465.
Coal (millions of tons)	35.5	165.9	420.2
Oil (millions of tons)	11.6	31.1	83.8

Source: *Dostizheniya Sovetskoi vlasti za sorok let v tsifrakh* (Moscow, 1957), pp. 53, 64, 70, 87.

tics were systematically inflated, and one must take into account the territorial and population acquisitions of the World War II period (see Table 3-2). Downright alarming was the livestock situation. To the livestock slaughter caused by collectivization had been added wartime livestock losses, so that at Stalin's death there were less cattle than before the Revolution, with smaller livestock not much better off (Table 3-3).

TABLE 3–2
Agricultural Output in Selected Years
(million tons)

	1926	1940	1953	1956
Grain	10.3	38.3	35.8	61.2
Raw cotton	0.53	2.24	3.85	4.35
Potatoes	3.0	12.9	12.1	15.7
Fruit	1.9	6.1	5.1	6.9
Meat and fat	2.4	4.2	5.4	6.3
Milk and milk products	4.3	10.8	13.7	20.4

Source: *Dostizheniya Sovetskoi vlasti za sorok let v tsifrakh* (Moscow, 1957), p. 154.

TABLE 3–3
Livestock on Hand in Selected Years
(million head)

	1928	1941	1953	1956
Cattle.	66.8	54.5	56.6	70.4
Pigs .	27.7	27.5	28.5	56.5
Sheep and goats	114.6	91.6	109.9	145.7

Source: *Dostizheniya Sovetskoi vlasti za sorok let v tsifrakh* (Moscow, 1957), p. 180.

It was these statistics on livestock with which Khrushchev had shocked both Party and public in his September 1953 speech to the Central Committee. The abrupt rise in all agricultural indicators between 1953 and 1956, a statistically exaggerated but still genuine development, was trumpeted in the press as evidence of Khrushchev's quick success with agriculture.

That all this had resulted in some long-term gains for the consumer is evident both from Soviet statistics and from their interpretation by Western economists. Evidence of this may be seen in the following computation of the gross national product (GNP) by use categories. Here a leading American specialist on the Soviet economy used 1937 Soviet ruble prices as the basis of value (Table 3–4). More refined calculations

TABLE 3–4
Gross National Product by Use Categories
(billions of rubles)

	1928	1940	1950	1955
Gross national product .	181.9	331.8	410.8	609.8
Household consumption outlays .	151.7	194.1	226.6	356.7
Health services, education, and related services .	6.6	30.2	36.3	44.6

Source: Abram Bergson, *The Real National Income of Soviet Russia Since 1928* (Cambridge, Mass.: Harvard University Press, 1961), p. 48.

support the overall message of the figures in this table, which is that the GNP, and with it the volume of consumption, nearly tripled from the beginning of the First Five-Year Plan to the mid-1950s, a span of less than 30 years which included an incredibly destructive war fought on Soviet soil. During the same period the Soviet population had increased by a third, roughly from 150 to 200 million; territorial annexations, which accounted for a third of the increase, compensated statistically for the many millions who died in World War II.

The lot of the consumer in the mid-1950s was still a difficult one. Housing space was fearfully crowded: per capita urban housing space at the end of the Stalin period (1950) was a meager seven square meters, scarcely above what it had been in 1913; this was due partly to the ravages of two world wars.[2] Shopping queues were long, meat was scarce and very expensive, and clothing was likewise a difficult item in the Soviet family budget. While a beginning had been made in dealing with some of these problems, the backlog even of essential consumer needs was large.

While the figures Khrushchev examined showed encouraging increases on the face of things, in some ways they were deceptive. Farm production had been raised during 1953–55 by a series of adjustments in collective farm management and incentives; this source of gain would soon have reached its limit. Private farming had been promoted, and its growth accounted for much of the increase in food consumption. Increases in housing space owed much to a 1948 decree encouraging the building of private homes. If, however, the trend of consumption were to continue upward, there would have to be a decisive shift in investment priorities, and it would be several years at least before the impact of this shift would be felt by the consumer. The one major step in this direction had been the launching of the Virgin Lands campaign in 1954, a program vigorously promoted by Khrushchev, designed to expand the nation's supply of arable land by putting the plough to the Kazakh steppe.

Malenkov's brief consumer campaign had made little real impact on priorities. The Korean War of 1950–53 had alarmed Moscow into increasing its military outlays and its investments in defense-related industries. The period of international calm which began in 1954 could serve as the basis for reducing direct military outlays somewhat. But changing basic investment priorities involves a great deal more than retooling some factories. If one wants an upswing in agriculture and consumer goods output, one must begin by acquiring producers' goods of a different kind: more machine tools for turning out agricultural equipment, more chemical processing devices for producing fertilizer, more casting machinery for making prefabricated housing components, and so on. From concentrating on more producers' goods of the kind which equip yet more basic heavy industries, one turns to producers' goods which result in diverting raw materials to consumption. Moreover, the *immediate* effect of such a choice may be to slow the growth of present consumption levels for a few years. The Malenkov, Khrushchev, and Brezhnev-Kosygin administrations were all to discover that reordering economic priorities was not analogous to turning off one faucet and turning on another.

Khrushchev's solution was, in fact, to risk present consumption by

---

[2] Ellen Mickiewicz (ed.), *Handbook of Soviet Social Science Data* (New York: The Free Press, 1973), p. 122.

increasing overall investment. During the latter 1950s this was done by cutting back defense expenditures, as the proportions given in Table 3–5 show. Khrushchev was able to take advantage of the fact that any

TABLE 3–5
Expenditure Composition of the Soviet GNP
(percent)

	1952	1955	1958	1960
Consumption	60.1	59.6	58.9	58.1
Investment.	21.4	24.3	28.1	29.9
Defense	14.7	13.2	10.4	9.6
Administration	4.1	2.9	2.6	2.4

Source: Stanley H. Cohn, "The Economic Burden of Soviet Defense Outlays," in U.S. Congress, Joint Economic Committee, *Economic Performance and the Military Burden in the Soviet Union* (Washington, D.C.: U.S. Government Printing Office, 1970), p. 169.

maturing industrial system is able, in the proper circumstances, to devote a larger proportion of its resources to investment without any drastic curtailment of consumption. But given the Soviet Union's difficulties in raising agricultural output, and the need for creating whole new branches of industry (e.g., chemical fertilizer plants) to provide a basis for more consumption, a real risk was involved. For several important years, Khrushchev's strategy was able to surmount the risk.

Questions of Strategy

On the vital matter of economic priorities, Khrushchev did not repeat Malenkov's mistake of moving ahead too soon. Malenkov had misread a general feeling among the leaders that something should be done for the consumer as political support for his splashy initiatives in that direction. What he actually did, as we saw earlier, was to expose himself to political attack by moving too soon. His consumer campaign thus became a political liability.

Khrushchev for the time being had aligned himself with Malenkov's enemies, with those who believed that Stalin's strong priority for building heavy industry should be continued. His power as First Secretary of the Party had been greatly enhanced by Malenkov's removal from the premiership. Malenkov had been replaced by Nikolai A. Bulganin, who despite his prestige as former head of the military establishment was not a major contender for power. This in itself represented a compromise among the politically powerful, and a victory of sorts for Khrushchev. But the ebullient First Secretary had not been able to get Malenkov removed from the Politburo, where two other rivals likewise kept their places, Molotov and Kaganovich.

Until the end of 1956, Khrushchev waged his political battles in fields other than the Soviet economy. The year 1955 saw a series of startling foreign policy initiatives: the rapprochement with Yugoslavia, the Austrian peace treaty, the Geneva summit conference with Eisenhower and other Western leaders, the beginning of support for Nasser's Egypt with arms and help for the Aswan Dam project, and the beginning of a massive foreign aid program in Asia. Among other things, these initiatives served as a vehicle for attacking and (in June 1956) demoting Molotov, who resigned as Foreign Minister but stayed on the Politburo. He had opposed some of Khrushchev's most important foreign moves. Kaganovich, another powerful rival, was handed a similar political setback at the same time.

The year 1956 had begun with Khrushchev's famous "secret speech" (in reality not so secret) at the 20th Party Congress. This was a dramatic condemnation of Stalin's ruthless treatment of the Party, which will be discussed in chapter 5. It ended with the Soviet Union's reaping the harvest Khrushchev had sown, in the form of the Hungarian uprising and the Polish disturbances which ultimately returned Gomulka to power. Khrushchev, whose condemnation of some of Stalin's crimes had won him a lot of support in the Party elite, now faced his colleagues' suspicion that he had opened a Pandora's box of unrest in the communist world by the way he had handled de-Stalinization.

Meanwhile the Sixth Five-Year Plan was in trouble, a plan adopted less than a year previously, at the beginning of 1956. While it contained few surprises and retained the traditional priority for basic industrial investment, some of its major goals were now clearly unrealizable. Khrushchev bore a major responsibility for the plan's difficulties. This was not only because he was head of the Party's vast bureaucracy, but because he had involved the Party officialdom more and more in economic planning and management.

On the surface of things, this seemed an unlikely time for Khrushchev to come forward with major proposals for economic reform—would he not thus expose himself and share Malenkov's fate? Canny merchant of power that he was, he saw his only sure rescue in a blunt counterattack. The goal of this counterattack must be twofold: It must isolate his top rivals politically, and it must place his own stamp on future economic programs in a manner that would garner him long-term support among top Party administrators and economic executives.

1957: Economic Reform and Political Crisis

The vehicle which Khrushchev chose for this risky strategy was a massive overhaul of the nation's economic administration. Already Molotov and Kaganovich had proceeded to the attack in this area. Both had regained some of the power they had lost earlier, and in December 1956 they put their weight behind a plan which, when it came into full operation, would cut down Khrushchev's influence over economic policy. An existing body, the State Economic Commission, was given vast authority over the economy; the Party, whose bureaucracy was full of experts deeply involved in economic matters, was assigned a subordinate position.

During the 1930s, after some years of experimenting with different forms of socialized planning and management, Stalin's economic lieutenants had settled on a system of several dozen central ministries, each responsible for a specialized industrial empire (e.g., coal, ferrous metallurgy, nonferrous metallurgy, heavy machine building, electric power stations). Each ministry maintained tight central control over its operations; each competed with others for scarce resources, which were sometimes obtained and hoarded at great expense to other branches of the economy. By and large, the success of the ministries was judged by the physical output of their plants. Many received large annual subsidies from the budget because they could not break even under the country's Alice-in-Wonderland price system, much less show a profit. Hidden costs, unreported losses, and systematic waste abounded. The ministries had long ago adjusted to all this, and were only too willing to live with waste and inefficiency as long as their output was rewarded by Moscow.

In theory, economic operations were coordinated in the Council of Ministers, on which each minister had a seat, together with a number of deputy ministers plus the chairman (or premier), who was now Bulganin. This was a body of unwieldy size, which was hardly in a position to coordinate economic management even if it had met regularly. A variety of top-level planning and management systems had been tried, of which the newly invigorated State Economic Commission was only the latest. Each change in the system of economic management had roots in the Kremlin's political contests, though the economic matters at stake were also very real. (We saw in chapter 1 how Stalin played the Supreme Economic Council off against the State Planning Committee during the "Great Debate" of the 1920s.)

The men who occupied the important ministerial chairs, those for basic industries, were the Soviet "captains of industry." They saw their several empires threatened from two directions: from a possible shift to priority for consumer goods production, and from increased interference by high Party officials. Under Stalin, as we shall see in chapter 4, the Party itself had been downgraded in the Soviet system as a whole. Many of Stalin's most important lieutenants held high posts in economic management rather than high Party posts. Together, the men who ran these industries could act as a giant "lobby" whenever their favored position was threatened. Kaganovich, with his long experience in economic matters, was the most prominent spokesman for these men. Molotov was in political alliance with him, and they were eventually joined by Malenkov, the one who had begun his brief term as leader by threatening the old heavy industrial priority.

If it makes these men appear cynical that they were capable of reversing their positions on issues at a moment's notice, one should remember that they were following a common practice of politics: in the face of a common threat, differences should be buried and policy positions reconciled. A corollary to this practice is that the one who threatens may be able to break his opponents' unity by his own policy shifts. Stalin and his rivals operated by these rules in the 1920s; now Khrushchev and his rivals were doing the same.

Before his opponents' economic reforms could be put into operation Khrushchev struck back in February 1957 with an economic reform proposal of his own. What he proposed was nothing less than the abolition of most of the central ministries, together with abolition of the State Economic Commission. In their place would be over 100 regional economic councils (*sovnarkhozy*). The most important of their tasks would be the direct supervision of industries within their respective territories, particularly from the point of view of allocating resources and making rational use of transport. They would be coordinated at the level of the 15 Soviet Republics, and would be responsible ultimately to the Council of Ministers in Moscow. The State Planning Commission was retained, though it was given no operating responsibilities.

Khrushchev's reform was enacted by the Supreme Soviet in May 1957, in the midst of a major leadership struggle of which it had become the focal point. For the reform carried a triple political edge: 1. It cancelled the December reform, which had been supported by Khrushchev's rivals, by substituting apparent decentralization for the extreme centralization favored by Kaganovich and Molotov. 2. It would be used to send many of the "captains of industry" away from Moscow and out to the provinces, where they would be physically dispersed and assigned to humbler posts. The political power of the great industrial ministries would be gone. 3. It had the potential for placing day-to-day supervision of economic matters under the provincial Party chiefs. As the delineation of the regional economic councils worked out in practice, the bulk of the councils coincided in territory with the provinces (*oblasts*). Each province in fact was ruled over by a powerful Part first secretary, and a good many of these secretaries had seats on the Party Central Committee. Foreign observers have since argued over the question whether the Party stood to gain influence in this manner, and whether this was Khrushchev's intention in the first place. For Khrushchev's opponents, however, this danger must have appeared real.

Khrushchev was very soon to need the support of the provincial party secretaries, since in June he was outvoted in the Politburo and hastily assembled the Central Committee to reverse the vote and support his reform. The immediate result was that Khrushchev succeeded in ousting six Politburo members, including his three major rivals, whom he now labeled the "anti-Party group." In reality Khrushchev's victory was only a partial one, although foreign observers generally did not interpret the evidence this way at the time. To all appearances, the way now seemed open for Khrushchev to choose the nation's economic priorities, whatever his inclinations might be. Early in 1958, as if to seal his dominance of the political scene, he had Bulganin removed from the premiership and then rapidly demoted from his other posts under a political cloud. Khrushchev himself then became premier, hence head of both Party and state, as Stalin had been in the last dozen years of his life.

The Khrushchev Program

Khrushchev lost no time in putting his stamp on the economy. After a brief attempt to redraft the Sixth Five-Year Plan, it was scrapped as unworkable, and planning efforts were focused on drafting a Seven-Year Plan to cover the years 1959–65. For all of Khrushchev's talk about increasing consumption, the new plan did not in fact stress consumer needs to the detriment of the existing rate of industrial growth. In spite of this, the First Secretary insisted on setting his consumer goals high. Already in the spring of 1957 he had promised to overtake the United States in per capita production of meat and milk products, a promise that even today remains unfulfilled. A decree on housing construction set the goal of an apartment for every family by the 1960s. Though the construction goals were not reached on schedule, the decree signalled the beginning of mass production housing which moved many millions of Soviet families into apartments of their own.

But Khrushchev's two major economic campaigns during these years were not of the kind that could be measured in terms of producers' versus consumers' goods. Both of them trod on dogmas of the Stalin period. First, Khrushchev proposed abolition of the Machine-Tractor Stations (MTS) and the acquisition by collective farms of their own agricultural machinery and automotive equipment. Secondly, he attacked the traditional priority for steel production as the lynchpin of heavy industry, proposing instead a new stress on chemicals.

Under Stalin, the MTS had been a vital political watchdog over the collective farms, and the most immediate regulator of their deliveries to the state. Now, a quarter-century after collectivization, there was scarcely any danger that abolishing the MTS would pave the way for political opposition of some kind; many other means of control were at hand for any such eventuality. But the MTS during all these years had symbolized the firm hand of both state and Party in the countryside. Should agriculture now falter, the blame could also too easily be traced to Khrushchev's reform.

Khrushchev was vulnerable on this score, for during his remaining six years in office, until 1964, agriculture remained the Achilles' heel of the Soviet economy. The Seven-Year Plan aimed at raising agricultural output by 70 percent; in fact, the increase was less than 15 percent. The MTS reform was partly to blame, too. Collective farms had to cut back other vital investments in order to pay for their machinery; and once they had it, maintenance and repair became a serious problem. The Repair-Technical Stations, which were supposed to cope with this latter problem, were ineffective for some years.

Other ills resulted from Khrushchev's compulsive urge to experiment and reorganize. He toured the countryside repeatedly to advertise his various campaigns: his campaign for growing maize, his attack on the grassland rotation system, his insistence on wheat as the sole crop for the Virgin Lands. His many administrative reforms were unclear as to motivation and baffling in execution. Khrushchev began imposing restrictions on private plots at a time when their increased output could have been most useful economically and politically. Yet, for all these mistakes, Khrushchev's strong personal rule over agriculture offered some hope that the nation's age-old dependence on weather might be overcome.

The campaign to build the Soviet chemical industry contained particularly interesting political strategy. For all his advocacy of consumer welfare, Khrushchev in drawing up the Seven-Year Plan did not attempt to alter the old principle of primacy for producers' goods. In promoting more chemical plants, however, he could support heavy industrial investment of a kind which could soon benefit the consumer. It would provide the basis for a plastics industry and at the same time radically improve the supply of chemical fertilizers for agriculture. The "lobby" of the basic industries immediately saw in this proposal a threat to the position of the steel and metalworking industries. Khrushchev had his way when the Plan figures were set up, but already by 1959 one could note that the chemical buildup was lagging badly, while steel and other industries were meeting their targets. This was the result of not very subtle sabotage by the old industrial establishment, which apparently was alive and well in spite of the 1957 reorganization.

In other ways Khrushchev did a great deal for the lot of the Soviet citizen. In all too many cases, and in ways frequently unnoticed by foreign observers, he had to settle for half a loaf. But much was done just the same. A 41-hour work week was introduced by stages, wage differentials were narrowed, wages themselves were improved, pensions and benefits were raised, and benefit coverage extended. A much publicized school and university reform of 1958 sought to equalize the opportunities for gaining admission to higher education, and also to reintegrate curricula in secondary education with actual employment needs. Housing, as we have noted, entered a boom era. Medical services likewise expanded dramatically. The qualitative results of these campaigns often left much to be desired. But the gains of Soviet citizens as consumers, employees, and students were very real during these years.

Guns versus Growth versus Butter

One thing that Khrushchev's program seemed to require was an era of international relaxation. He made this point repeatedly in public. Having watched the consequences of the Korean war for the Soviet budget during Stalin's last years, he had learned at first hand the lesson which Sergei Witte and his several predecessors in the Finance Ministry had learned by bitter experience: international emergencies will upset the best-laid programs of economic progress.

If Khrushchev indeed sought a relaxation of tensions—the phrase was on his lips in ever so many speeches—then how can we account for the seeming belligerency of some of his international moves? From one point of view, he was a perpetrator of crises, whose ambitions thrived on keeping international tension high. His 1958 ultimatum on Berlin touched off several years of anxious East-West maneuvering, including the building of the Berlin Wall in 1961. What of the angry denunciations which broke up the Paris summit conference of 1960? What of the way in which Moscow, by its 100-megaton test series of 1961 and subsequently, ended the informal nuclear testing moratorium begun in 1958? What of the Cuban missile crisis of 1962, the result of a Soviet attempt to plant nuclear missile sites 90 miles from American soil? What of Soviet arms shipments to parts of Asia and Africa, the Soviet role in the Congo crisis of 1960–61, the massive Soviet buildup of the Indonesian armed forces?

These steps, which so alarmed the Western capitals at the time, had a variety of causes, and one can study them from different angles. Here we are interested in their relationship to Khrushchev's economic goals. The Khrushchev era had begun with the Geneva summit conference of 1955, massive Soviet emphasis on the need for peaceful coexistence, the beginning of negotiations on arms limitation, and the settlement of some lesser European problems. All this was not a complete departure from Soviet policies before 1955. Malenkov had paved the way for some of this (the first arms talks were actually in 1954), and there is evidence that even Stalin, had he lived longer, might have moved in this direction. Khrushchev, though, staked much of his career on reaping gains from the peaceful coexistence line.

One explanation is that Khrushchev was making a supreme effort to reduce arms expenditures in order to divert more resources to both industrial investment and consumers' goods. We saw in chapter 1 that expenditures on armaments as such is a type of "consumption" which returns nothing to the economy. High output of arms diverts resources from other economic tasks, including the task of expanding the basic industries (e.g., steel, oil, chemicals), which are themselves the economic foundation of military might. Maintaining large armies has the same effect in a less direct way. The choice is not necessarily guns versus butter; it can also be guns versus basic economic growth. To say that massive arms production spurs basic economic growth is to obscure the actual choice it represents. Certainly it is true that the goal of a high output of arms requires high investment levels in many basic industries; Stalin's relentless drive for metallurgical investment in the 1930s was motivated first of all by his fear of Soviet weakness in an eventual war. But the route to industrial strength would have been far easier had the resources diverted to an arms buildup during the 1930s been ploughed back into industrial growth.

Economic data support the conclusion that, until 1960, Khrushchev was bent on cutting back the cost of military outlays. This is shown both in Soviet statistics and in interpretations of these figures by foreign specialists. The interpreted data of one of the tables above show that the proportion of defense expenditures in the Soviet GNP declined from almost 15 percent in Stalin's last full year (1952) to less than 10 percent in 1960. Ruble outlays, likewise interpreted, show that military expenditures remained virtually constant at about 11 billion rubles during 1952–60, while the GNP rose from 79 to 133 billion. Military personnel during this same period declined from 6.4 million to 3.6 million. It is true that technological innovation was making it possible for all the great powers to cut back their military manpower needs; the Soviet figure has stayed at just above 3 million during the 1960s and early 1970s, unaffected by periods of international tension.[3] But Soviet cutback is still significant in view of the nation's historical vulnerability to land invasion. Khrushchev made a great point of these manpower reductions, and for a time in the latter 1950s the Soviet press carried many items on career military people who had shifted to civilian occupations. Also, it was not uncommon for army units to be set to work on civilian projects, such as housing construction—and this to the displeasure of Defense Ministry officials, who saw this as an infringement on military professionalism.

From the point of view of Soviet economic needs, a persuasive interpre-

---

[3] Stanley H. Cohn, "The Economic Burden of Soviet Defense Outlays," in U.S. Congress, Joint Economic Committee, *Economic Performance and the Military Burden in the Soviet Union* (Washington, D.C.: U.S. Government Printing Office, 1970), pp. 168, 183–85.

tation of the Berlin ultimatum of November 1958 is that it was Khrushchev's means of pressuring the Western powers into a settlement of
European questions. This might enable the Soviet Union to make its position in East Germany more secure, to bolster its grip on other Eastern
European countries, and perhaps even to reduce the American military
presence in Central Europe. Successes of this kind would not require great
additional investment in arms. They would also bolster Khrushchev's
contention that the Soviet Union was now secure from outside threats,
that Stalin's doctrine of a "capitalist encirclement" was no longer valid.
But far from disrupting relations with the West because of the Berlin
crisis, Khrushchev then used it as a lever for arranging a trip to the
United States, which culminated in the Camp David meeting with President Eisenhower in September 1959. He postponed the Berlin ultimatum
further in order to meet with Western leaders at the Paris summit conference in 1960, and to invite Eisenhower for a reciprocal visit on Soviet
soil. Alas for both Khrushchev and his détente with the West, the U-2
spy plane incident disrupted the summit and cancelled the visit.

Amid this program of restraint on military spending, Khrushchev did
not cut back the Soviet drive for a nuclear capacity to match that of
the United States. Moscow had come from well behind in this race,
but was closing the gap rapidly during the 1950s. The first atomic device
had been exploded in 1949, and the first hydrogen bomb in 1953, a
bit ahead of the first U.S. hydrogen test. The development of a Soviet
missile force had suffered badly from Stalin's military traditionalism, his
unwillingness to weigh the value of surprise attack in future wars. Soviet
military docrine changed rapidly after Stalin's death, and the missile
forces were placed in a branch of the armed services all their own,
so as to prevent their being hampered by the outlook of the older services.

The Soviet missile drive meant more to Khrushchev than just catching
up with the United States in striking power. Comparatively speaking,
emphasis on missile defense, coupled with de-emphasis of the other services, meant cheap defense. This, perhaps, was the real motive behind
much of Khrushchev's missile rattling: He was by no means threatening
war against the West, certainly not with the Soviet Union still seriously
behind in both warheads and delivery vehicles; rather, he was persuading
Soviet military leaders and their allies in the Party that the Soviet defense
posture could be reoriented without jeopardizing the nation's defenses.
The same reasoning probably lay behind his decision to set up missile
sites on Cuba in the fall of 1962. It would have been a cheap, quick
way of redressing the nuclear imbalance, and thereby a way for Khrushchev to recoup his political defeats at the hands of his Kremlin rivals.
Military leaders, meanwhile, argued not against catching up with U.S.
missile strength, but for retaining the other services at a high level of
strength. Defense minister Malinovsky, himself a Khrushchev appointee

of 1957, promoted his doctrine of "combined arms," which asserted that future wars would require strength in all types of military force.

The Crusade Is Undermined

At first sight it seems improbable that the shooting down of an American U-2 spy plane on May Day of 1960 could serve as a weapon for reversing Khrushchevs economic program. The incident itself was a triumph rather than a defeat: An air-to-air missile downed the plane, then crossing Soviet territory at a very high altitude. It was the latest in a series of flights, which Moscow had known about but had also kept silent about; there would have been no gain in admitting Soviet impotence against this spy work by railing publicly at it. Now the feat had been accomplished and the United States had halted the overflights for the time being.

Immediately after the U-2 incident, the debate over economic priorities came out into the open. From that time until his removal from office in the fall of 1964, Khrushchev waged campaign after campaign against those who were returning the Soviet economy to its pre-Khrushchev priorities. His criticisms sounded like denunciations at times, as in his campaign against the "metal eaters" at the 22nd Party Congress in 1961, the officials who successfully defended the old priority for steel production. His campaigns used wearisome saturation propaganda, for example his drive in 1963 for massive investment in the chemical industry. His administrative reorganizations were more frequent and apparently less well thought out than before; they became thinly veiled pretexts for shifting officials about in a way that would reduce opposition to this or that program.

For Khrushchev, there could be no compromise on the issues of priorities in the long run. He had suffered enough partial setbacks even before the U-2 affair at the hands of top leaders and other officials who were in a position to undermine his program, as in the first campaign on behalf of the chemical industry. He now stated flatly that the old doctrine of consumption was outmoded, the principle that the growth of production will lag behind the growth of consumer demand, as least until socialism gives way to the ultimate stage of communism. Instead, argued Khrushchev at a Central Committee plenum in January 1961, consumer production should always be greater than demand. The Soviet Union, he continued, could not win the economic contest with the West until it had overtaken the United States in consumption.[4]

Khrushchev now reinforced his stand on this and other issues through the use of ideology and symbols. At the 22nd Party Congress, the Party

[4] See the account in Carl A. Linden, *Khrushchev and the Soviet Leadership, 1957–1964* (Baltimore: Johns Hopkins Press, 1966), pp. 105–108.

adopted a new Party Program which, though it lacked many of the utopian-sounding prophecies which Khrushchev had indulged in earlier, promised an era of complete abundance in 20 years, the end of all shortages. Then, in order to place a seal of finality on the changes he had either wrought or attempted during his half-dozen years of power, Khrushchev attacked Stalin and Stalinism once again. The dictator's remains were thereupon removed from the Lenin Mausoleum on Red Square to a more modest resting-place under the Kremlin walls. The "anti-Party group" of 1957 was villified again likewise, and warnings rang out against a return to the evils of the past.

Molotov, Malenkov, and Kaganovich were in retirement and unlikely to return to power. Among those whom foreign observers believed to be leaders of the opposition to Khrushchev's priorities, the names of Mikhail Suslov and Frol Kozlov figured most prominently, both Politburo members. Specialists who have studied the politics of the Khrushchev era have not identified any clear-cut opposition "faction"; there were various degrees and areas of opposition. However one may characterize the opposition at this point, what united its adherents was the desire to raise the defense budget and the rate of investment in heavy industry. Khrushchev had tried to link these old priorities with the name of Stalin, and by condemning once again the evils of that era in order to condemn the former economic policies as well. Now he was obliged to make some concessions in resource allocation, but without retreating from his pro-consumption principle, and without letting slip any opportunity to out-maneuver his opponents. In three years, 1961–63, the annual defense outlays jumped 50 percent, and it was consumption that suffered most from this. Khrushchev, undeterred, launched a further public campaign against the "metal eaters" early in 1964. His proposal at this time to abandon the old distinction between "group A" (capital goods) and "group B" (consumer goods) would have shattered a long-standing economic dogma. But the "metal eaters" were able to strike back in a *Pravda* editorial calling for increased metallurgical capacity.[5] That fall, a month before Khrushchev was removed, a Presidium (Politburo) meeting on economic planning produced evidence of another serious clash over economic priorities. Khrushchev's position on this all-important issue was still a strong one; whenever he accepted compromises, he returned to the attack later with his original priorities. It was an embattled leader who was removed by his colleagues, but not a weakened or already defeated one.

The Soviet economy during these same years was having other problems which were not necessarily traceable to increased defense requirements. The annual rate of increase in investment had decreased from 16 percent in 1958 to 5 percent in 1963. Part of the blame for this

---

[5] See the account in Michel Tatu, *Power in the Kremlin From Khrushchev to Kosygin* (New York: Viking Press, 1970), pp. 369–70.

could be assigned to Khrushchev's frequent administrative reorganizations and his arbitrary shifting of economic targets. While his goals were not unreasonable ones, the abruptness with which he changed economic strategies caused a number of serious shortages and disproportions. Because he wanted prefabricated concrete substituted for bricks in construction, there were serious shortages of bricks. His campaigning for the chemical industry threatened shortages of steel and coal. State-constructed housing was cut back, while at the same time Khrushchev's campaign against private housing construction—still legal in itself, but now facing increasing handicaps—nearly halved the output of this important supplement to state housing.

Economic planning and management were, if not quite in chaos, at least in turbulence. A number of the old central ministries had been resurrected in shadowy form as "state committees," a partial victory for opponents of the 1957 reorganization. The regional economic councils were merged so as to halve their number; the State Planning Committee was split into two bodies, one for long-range planning, the other for coordinating operations; a Supreme Economic Council was created to bring some order to the economic scene, its title harking back to Lenin's economic system. The reform which sat least well with Khrushchev's rivals, amid all this organizational tinkering, was the splitting of the provincial and local Party organizations into halves, one half for industry, the other for agriculture. Khrushchev had been complaining that Party officials in the provinces were neglecting agriculture; now he not only could fix the responsibility, but with the stroke of a pen had doubled the number of first secretaries he could appoint. When Khrushchev was removed in 1964, this reform was immediately rescinded and Party officials moved back to their old posts.

We noted earlier the woes of agriculture during Khrushchev's last four years. The wretched harvest of 1963 complicated the agricultural scene still further. As in the fateful year 1928, the Soviet Union was compelled to buy grain abroad, this time from the United States and Canada. One may well ask whether any leader in Khrushchev's shoes could have wrought a basic improvement in Soviet agriculture within the span of six or eight years. Most of the basic ills of the collective farm system dated back to the early period of collectivization, and had been compounded by a quarter-century of neglect.

It is all too easy to portray Khrushchev the economic leader as the sum of his many blunders. But even considering the way in which he was removed from office, and the economic ills which contributed heavily to his ultimate defeat, his performance was a remarkable one. His willingness to undertake massive experiments was a badly needed antidote to the methods of the Stalin era; his concern for the consumer was genuine and deeply felt, quite aside from the way in which he played politics with consumer priorities. His ability to counterattack under pressure, his use of the peaceful coexistence theme to undercut his opponents on economic questions, his ceaseless tours of collective farms—all these distinguished his style from that of the Brezhnev-Kosygin administration.

BREZHNEV AND KOSYGIN: THE SEARCH FOR ECONOMIC BALANCE

The economy that Khrushchev's successors inherited at the end of 1964 had been mismanaged in some important ways, but it was not by any means a disaster area. It was a system operating well below its potential, in need of reforms in areas which Khrushchev's experimentation had passed over. Indeed, the "new men" of the 1960s had been responsible for a good deal of the mismanagement themselves. These were none other than some of Khrushchev's former colleagues in the Politburo, Party Secretariat, and Council of Ministers; foreign observers marvelled at how few new faces showed up in leadership roles, and how high the average age was. The most important of the post-Khrushchev leaders, beginning with Party General Secretary Leonid I. Brezhnev and Prime Minister Alexei N. Kosygin, had come to political prominence not under Khrushchev, but in the latter Stalin era. Also important is the fact that the most important single post-Khrushchev economic reform, the enterprise incentive legislation of 1965, had been drafted under Khrushchev and was strongly advocated by him.

While the new leadership washed its hands of Khrushchev the leader by condemning his "harebrained scheming," there was no sharp break in either personnel or economic policies. The intensity of political struggle during 1960–64 conveys to some observers the impression that the struggle over economic policy was clear-cut. Actually, policy differences offer a blurred and shifting picture at best. Khrushchev had not been, in fact, a thoroughgoing opponent of the priority for industrial investment; his successors were not, in turn, against making a major effort on behalf of the consumer. For one thing, much of Kosygin's career had been connected with light industry and consumers' goods, and after 1964 he continued to speak out on behalf of this part of the economy.

Economic Priorities: Gains for Consumption

The dismissal of Khrushchev was not followed by any clear shifts in investment priorities. In spite of all the heat this issue had generated during Khrushchev's administration, it does not appear to have played a role in his political downfall. During the first three years of the new leadership, 1964 to 1967, Brezhnev and Kosygin more than once gave indications of differing emphases in their statements, Kosygin favoring more emphasis on consumption. Though foreign "Kremlin watchers" scrutinized all such evidence in search of a budding struggle for power like that of 1953–55, with investment priorities as the key weapon on both sides, nothing of that magnitude developed. The Brezhnev era still displayed much evidence of debates and struggles, such as over the 1965 economic reforms, and later over agricultural priorities. But there appeared to be no sharp polarization of factions and no direct struggles for power which would have promoted polarization. Furthermore, the areas of agreement were larger than they had been in the 1950s, so that there was now less to be gained for any leader or group by further politicizing the resource allocation issue.

Only after 1967 did the outlines of a new resource allocation policy start to emerge, a policy of moderate shifts in favor of consumption. The Eighth Five-Year Plan (1966–70) saw several "firsts" in the use of resources: for the first time, the consumption goals of a five-year plan were actually fulfilled; consumption increased at a somewhat greater rate than the Gross National Product; during 1966–68 consumer-oriented investment increased at a more rapid rate than producer-oriented investment; and as a result of this, the growth rate of output for industry-produced consumers' goods in 1968–70 exceeded the growth rate for producer goods, which in past decades would have been ideological heresy (see Table 3–6). For the first time, also, substantial amounts were being

TABLE 3–6
Planned Annual Output Increases for
Heavy and Light Industry—
Group A and Group B
(percent increase)

Plan Year	Group A	Group B
1966	6.9	6.0
1967	7.5	6.6
1968	7.9	8.6
1969	7.2	7.5
1970	6.1	6.8
1971	7.9	8.3
1972	6.8	7.1
1973	6.3	4.5

Sources: *Izvestiya*, Dec. 8, 1965; Dec. 16, 1966; Oct. 11, 1967; Dec. 10, 1968; Dec. 17, 1969; Dec. 9, 1970; Nov. 25, 1971; Dec. 20, 1972.

spent from the Soviet Union's precious supply of foreign currency—the ruble not being an international currency—to purchase manufactured consumers' goods abroad. (Foodstuffs were purchased abroad in years of bad harvests, notably in 1963 and 1972.)

The Ninth Five-Year Plan (1971–75) confirmed the policies of the latter 1960s, while moderating the drive for increased consumer output in many areas as a consequence of a slower growth rate for the GNP. The publicity which accompanied the launching of this latest plan—particularly at the 24th Party Congress in 1971—laid great stress on its provision for a more rapid growth rate for manufactured consumers' goods than for producer goods. It was the first time that this policy received such a clear seal of official approval, an important step because it cancelled an old dogma, a key point of Stalin's application of Marxist economics.[6]

Actually a lower rate of growth in production of most manufactured consumers' goods was planned for the period 1971–75 than the rate achieved during the preceding plan period. The one striking exception to this pattern is the planned output of passenger automobiles, which in spite of their high cost to the consumer will meet some of the pent-up consumer demand represented by growing private savings. By 1975, annual output is scheduled to reach 800,000 automobiles, at which point there will be 3.7 million private cars, better than triple the figure for 1970.

Plans for agricultural output and investment, far from moderating Khrushchev's efforts in this area, show the present regime's determination to eliminate Soviet agriculture's decades-old lag. The rate of increase for the output of meat, fish, and vegetables is scheduled to grow, while the rate for milk and eggs was cut back somewhat. But certain of the increases planned for 1971–75 look impressive when compared with a probable 6 percent population growth for this period: 16 percent for grain production, 23 percent for meat, and 15 percent for dairy products. Such gains are becoming increasingly expensive, however: 43 billion rubles were invested in agriculture during 1961–65, 71 billion was planned for 1966–70 (actual investments probably fell short of this), and 128 billion is the figure set for 1971–75. According to one calculation, Soviet agriculture now receives what amounts to a massive subsidy from the state budget. If so, the present state of affairs stands in sharp contrast to the early decades of the Soviet industrialization drive, when enormous subsidies went to key industrial and mining operations, and collective farmers paid much of the actual price for this.[7]

Meanwhile consumption itself has continued to grow, the most signifi-

---

[6] Those economists and officials who objected to the "violation" of Lenin's law of preferential development of means of production were mollified by the fact that the relationship between the two rates of growth can be calculated in more than one way. In 1970–71 Soviet leaders preferred to leave the new priorities somewhat fuzzy in respect to the traditional Soviet economic law. See the discussion in Werner G. Hahn, *The Politics of Soviet Agriculture* (Baltimore: Johns Hopkins Press, 1972), pp. 246–51.

[7] See Roy D. Laird, "Prospects for Soviet Agriculture," *Problems of Communism* 20 (September-October 1971), pp. 31–40.

TABLE 3–7
Average Earnings of Soviet Workers and
Employees, and the Minimum Wage
(in post-1960 rubles)°

Year	Average Monthly Earnings per Worker	Legal Minimum Wage†
1940	33.0	–
1950	63.9	22
1955	71.5	22
1960	80.1	27 to 35
1965	95.6	40 to 70
1968	112.5	60 to 70
1972	128.5	60 to 70

*One post-1960 ruble is equivalent to $1.40 at the official Soviet-determined exchange rate. The "workers and employees" category excludes collective farmers, but includes workers on state farms.
†There are different minimum wage levels for different categories of workers and employees.
Source: *Narodnoye khozyaistvo SSSR, 1965* (Moscow, 1966), p. 567; *Pravda*, Jan. 25, 1968, and Jan. 26, 1969; *Ekonomicheskaya gazeta* No. 31 (July) 1972, p. 1.

cant indicators being average earnings (see Table 3–7) and the skyrocketing increases in savings deposits, which quadrupled in the 1960s. The latter are often used to buy cooperative apartments, automobiles, and summer homes, though only a small minority of the population will attain the latter two for some time to come. The post-Khrushchev regime has shown a sensible self-restraint on the matter of private property, by contrast with Khrushchev's efforts to curtail private houses and cars, together with his highly unpopular effort to phase out the garden plots assigned to many city-dwellers, which after 1965 received official blessing once again.

Farmers as consumers have scored some gains since 1964, although it will take more years to show just what these improvements amount to in their overall standard of living. The latter 1960s saw a guaranteed minimum wage for collective farmers, and their inclusion in the state pension system. According to Soviet figures, in 1970 average rural incomes were only 15 percent behind urban wages.[8] This ratio must be seen against the background of earlier disparities shown in Table 3–8. Note that these figures do not include income from private plots, which according to one calculation constituted more than two thirds of all collective farmers' income in 1953, and about half in 1967.[9] It is important to note that in spite of all the ominous statements made during Khrushchev's last years of power about the need for restricting private plots, and ultimately abolishing them, the private plot gained a new lease on life in 1965, shortly after Khrushchev was dismissed. The same was done

---

[8] Laird, "Prospects for Soviet Agriculture," p. 34.

[9] See Bronson and Krueger, "The Revolution in Soviet Household Farm Income, 1953–1967," p. 241. Cited in Table 3–3.

TABLE 3–8
Average Annual Wages for 1953–1967
(in post-1960 rubles)

Year	Industry	State Farms and Subsidiary State Agricultural Enterprises	Collective Farms
1953	917	494	164
1960	1,096	647	276
1965	1,240	894	525
1967	1,344	1,007	647

Source: David W. Bronson and Constance B. Krueger, "The Revolution in Soviet Farm Household Income, 1953–1967," in James R. Millar (ed.), *The Soviet Rural Community* (Urbana, Ill.: University of Illinois Press, 1971), p. 247.

for plots worked by city dwellers, which are numerous. This was in part a response to the bad harvest of 1963, which was a warning sign that no reliable means of adding to the nation's agricultural output should be overlooked. The private plot has received official encouragement, in fact, in the form of promises of fertilizer and equipment adapted to small-scale farming.

The Growth Rate Puzzle

Both Soviet statistics and foreign interpretations of Soviet data showed that the rate of economic growth had slowed markedly in the early 1960s. During the 1950s, the GNP had grown at an annual rate of around 7 percent; during 1960–64 this had decreased to 5 percent and perhaps less. The rate of increase in investment had declined sharply, from 16 percent in 1958 to 5 percent in the early 1960s. Industrial growth rates, according to official statistics, had fallen below 8 percent in 1963–64, something that had not happened in peacetime since the early 1930s. We have already noted the sorry state of agricultural output during this period, capped by the very poor harvest of 1963. The 1964 harvest was good, but that of 1965 was once again less than bountiful. Despite all of man's efforts to guarantee the Soviet food supply during the preceding three decades, King Weather was still in charge of the harvests.

Actually the Brezhnev administration did not have to be alarmed unduly by the falling growth rate. Between 1928 and 1955, not counting the war years, the growth rate of the Soviet GNP had averaged about 5 percent.[10] A growth rate of this order had been typical of other industrial nations during their respective periods of massive industrialization,

[10] Abram Bergson, *The Real National Income of Soviet Russia Since 1928* (Cambridge, Mass.: Harvard University Press, 1961) p. 261.

among them the United States in the half-century preceding World War
I. Reconstruction after wartime destruction has produced similar growth
rates in the industrial world: Germany, Italy, and Japan have averaged
well over 5 percent for much of the period following World War II.
Japan during 1958–64 achieved a phenomenal rate of 12 percent, and
a variety of other countries have displayed rates almost as high, including
Israel, Yugoslavia, and Mexico. Aside from these unusual periods of
growth, however, the growth rate of mature industrial systems tends
to settle somewhere below the 5 percent level, sometimes well below,
without placing their prosperity in jeopardy. Such appeared to be the
case with the Soviet Union in the 1960s.

The reasons for this became clear to the Soviet leaders only gradually.
They would have done well to set their economists to work studying
the economic history of industrial growth under capitalism, in order
to find out whether there is a sequence of tasks or problems which must
be overcome in any industrializing economy. But, alas, Soviet Marxist
doctrine since Lenin had proclaimed that socialist industrialization would
be a radically different process. Soviet Marxism laid great stress on Marx's
suggestions that socialism would open limitless economic possibilities to
mankind. Capitalism, in Marx's vision, was a giant in fetters; its technology was capable of almost any feat, but its private property system
of measuring goals kept its performance well below its capacities. Friedrich Engels gave philosophical expression to this notion: A much quoted
statement of his holds that with advent of socialism there will be a leap
from the realm of necessity into the realm of freedom. Only Stalin,
in his last major statement on matters of doctrine, in 1952, rebuked those
who believed that socialism could abolish all existing laws of economics
and create new laws at will.[11]

One major shortcoming of Soviet economic thought in the 1950s and
1960s was its failure to distinguish types of growth. Modern economic
thought in the West distinguishes between quantitative and qualitative
growth. By "qualitative" is meant changes in technology, methods, and
manpower skills; in economic terms, it embraces money spent for research
and development together with outlays for improving skills at every
level. In earlier stages of economic growth, and particularly in nations
with the vast unexploited natural resources, rapid increases in manpower
will produce rapid increases in output. The rate of increase will then
sink as these possibilities have been exploited, and as more refined methods
are necessary to produce the same things. In Soviet agriculture, for example, Khrushchev's campaign for cultivating the Virgin Lands can be
seen as a last-ditch effort to spur the growth of farm output by the
old means.

---

[11] J. Stalin, *Economic Problems of Socialism in the U.S.S.R.* (Moscow: Foreign
Languages Publishing House, 1952), pp. 5–13.

Economists today are able to distinguish that part of economic growth that occurs because of qualitative improvements in all the things that go into production—manpower, methods, and technology. In Stalin's time, and up to 1958, qualitative improvements accounted for less than a third of growth, the same relationship that prevailed in the U.S. economy at the turn of the century. At present over two thirds of the U.S. increases come from these qualitative changes.[12] For all the stress that Moscow has placed on using up-to-date technology and raising levels of training in the labor force, it has had to struggle to get some branches of the economy to use the latest machines and methods.

Cautious Changes in the Economic Structure

Economic management under Stalin left a troublesome legacy for future administrations that would have to cope with the whole problem of quality. The entire economy, after Stalin's death, was geared to producing quick results and to measuring these results first of all in quantitative terms. The tales and anecdotes which sprang from this priority are countless: the company that produced gigantic chandeliers because its output was judged by weight; or the railroad branch that ran water in its tank cars in order to overfulfill its hauling quota, then saw a trainful of tank cars stand idle for months because the water had frozen in them.

The 1965 reforms in economic management, promoted by Khrushchev but enacted by his successors, were greeted by some newspapers in the West as the Kremlin's admission that capitalist-type incentives are really best after all. This was hardly the case. At no point in the history of the Soviet economy had profits been abandoned as a measure of performance, and at no point had labor or managerial rewards been divorced from performance. With the end of the last private enterprises in 1929–30, all enterprises saw their operations directed in detail by the state plan. In order to realize its part in the plan, an enterprise had to carry out a number of subplans, covering such matters as: production cost, power requirements, raw materials, utilization of plant equipment, organizational and technical measures, labor force size and composition, payroll, investment, use of new processes, and, finally, the financial results to be achieved. And there were other items in the list. Financial results were important. Most enterprises used what was called economic accountability, or *khozraschót*, as a vital measure of performance. This meant that an enterprise, besides carrying out its whole list of subplans, had to strive for maximum profitability. Ordinarily a certain profit was specified in the financial plan; beyond this, "profits above plan" were encouraged.

---

[12] Joseph S. Berliner, "Economic Reform in the USSR," in John W. Strong (ed.), *The Soviet Union Under Brezhnev and Kosygin* (New York: Van Nostrand Reinhold, 1971), pp. 53–54.

Management and workers were rewarded for these profits, in the form of bonuses and fringe benefits, whose distribution was likewise regulated closely from above.

Many things went awry with planning under Stalin and Khrushchev, but what concerns us here is what was actually expected of enterprises. To begin with, they were given far too many different kinds of targets, and reaching them all was usually an impossibility even before the plan year had begun. These planning disproportions, together with the arbitrary price levels that were set from Moscow, meant that many enterprises had to operate in the red. Far from penalizing their management and workers for doing so, higher authorities would arrange for annual subsidies. The more important an industry, the more protection it enjoyed in this respect, and the less compulsion its management felt to fulfill the subplans. The Soviet coal industry, for example, operated in the red through most of the Stalin era, and this was openly acknowledged.

One subplan was vastly more important than all the rest: physical output. Tons of steel, coal, and oil, numbers of railroad carloadings (as in the anecdote), kilowatt hours of electricity—these were watched intently by the Kremlin, which willingly forgave all kinds of managerial sins as long as the physical targets were met. Hence the deeply ingrained antiquality bias in Soviet economic management. Quality suffered in two respects: products were below standard, and qualitative inputs in production were spurned if they would not guarantee quick results. Khrushchev, while he talked much about both types of quality, shared Stalin's reflexes in his drive to get quick results. His successors were left to cope with a problem whose solution was already 10 or 15 years overdue.

The 1965 reforms, far from being a step in the direction of capitalism, were a sensible approach to making socialism efficient. The many subplans which enterprise managers had had to deal with were now reduced to eight only. Enterprises were given much-needed "elbow room" in a number of matters: they can now alter the size of their labor force, exercise a certain freedom in deciding what to produce, and have a freer hand in disposing of profits. As an effort to control quality, physical output targets are not considered reached until the products are actually sold and their quality approved by the enterprise or agency which has contracted to buy them. Profits were definitely made the prime criterion of enterprise success. Together with these and other reforms at the enterprise level, there were changes of broader scope. Khrushchev's regional economic councils were abandoned, the Supreme Economic Council likewise, and the administrative system of Stalin's day restored, at least in its major features. The price system was revised, and steps were taken to control the quality of consumers' goods.

By the early 1970s, with all enterprises at last converted to the new management system, it was evident that the reform had mainly streamlined an existing system rather than laid the foundation for something different. In output, the results were very modest: industrial output in 1966–70 grew at a rate slightly less than the rate of 1961–65. The annual increase in labor productivity grew by one percentage point and Soviet figures claimed a large increase in the return on capital.[13] The enterprises themselves, far from taking a step in the direction of Yugoslav-type "market socialism," found their choices regulated from above in far greater detail than the original 1965 reform documents suggest they should be.

A structural reform was decreed in the spring of 1973 in order to provide the kind of autonomy and flexibility in economic management that the 1965 reforms had hardly begun to provide. Soviet enterprises have been grouped into several thousand "production associations," each of which is meant to exercise much greater autonomy than was intended earlier for the individual enterprises. Direct controls by the central economic ministries in Moscow are now reduced, research and development functions come under the association's aegis, and in some import-export decisions have been taken over also, the latter a remarkable step in view of the hitherto rigid channelling of foreign dealings through Moscow. The individual enterprises had to cede some of their powers of decision to the association, including decisions on fringe benefits and housing. Foreign observers have compared the new structure to that of large American corporations, whose operations have been the object of many studies by Soviet researchers in the past decade.[14]

Reforms in the structure and operating principles of the collective farms have been more cautious than those in industry. The principle has been the same, however: the Soviet leadership will make structural changes to promote both efficiency and public welfare, but will not change the basic features of the system as they were fixed in Stalin's time. In agriculture, even the idea of a nationwide organization of collective farms, a move which Stalin had so flatly rejected and Khrushchev had then advocated, proved to be too radical a step for the Brezhnev administration. Moscow's fear, apparently, was that even the modest degree of autonomy which such an organization might embody could reduce the state's all-pervasive control of collective farm output. A similar fear, however irrational, made the Brezhnev administration very cautious about the idea of using small work teams or "links" instead of the usual brigades on the collective farms. The idea received a new impetus in 1969, however, when a new Model Collective Farm Charter was under discussion, the first such since 1935. The Brezhnev administration avoided

---

[13] Gertrude E. Schroeder, "Soviet Economic Reform at an Impasse," *Problems of Communism* 20 (July-August 1971), p. 44.

[14] The text of the reform is translated in *Current Digest of the Soviet Press* 25 (May 2, 1973), pp. 1–4.

making any direct judgment for or against the link, but the ambiguous wording of the Charter's final draft left the door open for more experiments in this direction. The idea had remained alive, there has been some favorable publicity in the Soviet press, and links of a half-dozen persons each have actually been functioning in some areas, each tilling a segment of collective farm land comparable in size to traditional family farms in the United States.

THE CHANGING CHARACTER OF DECISIONS

It was not only that the content of economic decisions in the Khrushchev and Brezhnev eras differed from that of the Stalin era; rather, the economic options themselves had changed, and the manner of making decisions had changed too. The mechanism and political setting of decision-making is dealt with in future chapters. Here the purpose is to note what influence the content of economic decisions might have had on the basic character of the political process. The opposite causation—economic policies as the weapons of political struggles—is dealt with in later chapters.

As regards the content of major economic decisions since 1953, probably the most important single circumstance is that none of the options required aggression against this or that part of society, or increased consumer austerity. With the defeat of Malenkov, Molotov, and Kaganovich in 1957, no group of leaders was left that would argue even for a continuation of Stalin-era consumer austerity as it existed in the early 1950s. At issue was only the tempo at which consumer welfare could rise, and the degree to which this tempo must be moderated in the interest of major investment and defense needs.

Next, the regime's information about economic options was vastly better in the latter 1950s and 1960s than it had been earlier. The most important type of information lay in the record of earlier experiences to increase output through massive public campaigns, overt or hidden subsidies, and simplistic ideas of economic growth. While the very complexity of the economy was increasing the number of decisions that had to be made, the options that were taken seriously by the leadership fell within a narrower range than those of the 1920s. Hence disagreements about the options were unlikely to breed factions sharply divided on basic matters.

Finally, the specific links that Stalin had sought to create between Marxism and Soviet economic development had been set aside wherever they impeded a rational discussion of options. In some cases, for example Stalin's assertions about the Soviet-model collective farm as the one true bridge to socialism in the countryside, his successors found it wise to let the ideological assertion stand untouched. The same applies to the

Soviet brand of central planning and control, derived from some comments by Karl Marx via Lenin's elaboration of them. But the whole field of resource allocation, which had been more explosive politically than the issue of centralization or the idea of collectivization as a goal, was now cut loose from any kind of narrow ideological constraints. Khrushchev in the latter 1950s tried to enshrine his own economic priorities in new ideological constraints, notably in the field of consumption and how it ought to be organized in the communist future. But the Brezhnev administration treated these innovations with silence, restoring some of the options (e.g., indefinite continuation of private plots) which otherwise would have been in conflict with ideology.

The changes in the content of economic decisions have helped shape certain political circumstances of decision-making. All the developments just described have given more weight to economic and managerial expertise. It is not a case of "experts" influencing "politicians," but rather of political leaders in possession of expertise, who must justify their proposals to other leaders who are similarly expert because of their professional backgrounds. A headstrong leader would be less likely than in past decades to gain the support of his colleagues for an extreme economic measure if its flaws would create great problems for the latter. All this has not prevented the Brezhnev regime from attempting to place Party officials more firmly in charge of economic operations and of the state bureaucracy that supervises them (see chapter 9).

The leaders of the Brezhnev period have carried on their debates within a fairly narrow range of economic options. No doubt their success in reducing the areas of disagreement owes something to memories of Stalin's arbitrary decisions and to Khrushchev's sometimes erratic campaigns and panaceas. However that may be, it appears that the present leaders have sought a more orderly type of procedure for compromise than the noisy advances and retreats which Khrushchev used. In economic organization and management, restoration of the ministerial system so soon after Khrushchev's removal served to win the cooperation of officials who might otherwise have engaged in the sabotage of the new regime's priorities, as they had done under Khrushchev.

The stability of the top leadership in the Brezhnev period is one indication of the success of a compromise course. Among the small number of top personnel changes that have occurred, the only demotions that can be traced to economic issues have been those associated with agricultural failures and the sometimes sharp disagreements over agricultural priorities: Gennadi I. Voronov was dropped from the Politburo and from his post as head of government in the Russian Republic, and Vladimir V. Matskevitch was dismissed as Minister of Agriculture, both in 1973, in the wake of the very poor 1972 harvest.

Thus a number of circumstances have led to the way big economic decisions are now handled and the place they occupy in the Soviet political system: the maturing of the industrial economy itself, the growing weight of expert judgment, removal of important ideological constraints, and a style of compromise which has discouraged the hardening of factional lines. The one development which could upset this style of compromise would be a massive failure of some part of the economy, such as several bad harvests in a row. Barring such disasters, the present approach to managing economic decisions has the advantage of offering political security to the top leadership, both as a group and individually. The successors to the present aging leaders will probably find it a desirable approach for that reason.

FOR FURTHER READING

For readers unfamiliar with the study of economics, a useful introduction is Marshall I. Goldman, *The Soviet Economy: Myth and Reality* (Englewood Cliffs, N.J.: Prentice-Hall, 1968). Likewise quite readable for the layman are parts of the collection by Harry Shaffer (ed.), *The Soviet Economy: A Collection of Western and Soviet Views* (New York: Appleton-Century-Crofts, 1963). More technical introductory works include Robert W. Campbell, *Soviet Economic Power* (Cambridge, Mass.: Houghton Mifflin, 1960), Alec Nove, *The Soviet Economy* (rev. ed.; London: Allen and Unwin, 1968), and Nicolas Spulber, *The Soviet Economy: Structures, Principles, Problems* (rev. ed.; New York: Norton, 1969).

On the level of consumption and related problems, two recent works are Philip Hanson, *The Consumer in the Soviet Economy* (London: Macmillan, 1968), and Margaret Miller, *The Rise of the Russian Consumer* (London: Institute of Economic Affairs, 1965). See also Gertrude E. Schroeder, "Consumer Problems and Prospects," *Problems of Communism* 22 (March-April 1973), pp. 10–24. On economic planning see Eugene Zaleski, *Planning Reforms in the Soviet Union, 1962–1966* (Chapel Hill, N.C.: University of North Carolina Press, 1969), Abram Bergson, *The Economics of Soviet Planning* (New Haven, Conn.: Yale University Press, 1964), and a recent article by Bergson, "Toward a New Growth Model," *Problems of Communism* 22 (March-April 1973), pp. 1–9.

On the relation between agricultural issues and Soviet politics, detailed studies include Sidney I. Ploss, *Conflict and Decision-Making in Soviet Russia: A Case Study of Agricultural Policy* (Princeton, N.J.: Princeton University Press, 1965); Werner G. Hahn, *The Politics of Soviet Agriculture, 1960–1970* (Baltimore: Johns Hopkins Press, 1972); and Abraham Katz, *The Politics of Economic Reform in the Soviet Union* (New York: Praeger, 1972).

An interesting array of views on the relation between economic development and political change in industrial societies may be found in the following: Raymond Aron, *The Industrial Society* (New York: Praeger, 1967); A. F. K. Organski, *The Stages of Political Development* (New York: Knopf, 1965); and W. W. Rostow, *Politics and the Stages of Growth* (Cambridge: At the University Press, 1971).

Part II
CONTROL OF THE POLITICAL PROCESS

4

PARTY UNITY AND THE
MONOPOLY OF POWER

In the practical struggle against factionalism, every organization of the party must take strict measures to prevent any factional actions whatsoever. Criticism of the party's shortcomings . . . must be conducted in such a way that every practical proposal shall be submitted immediately, without any delay, in the most precise form possible, for consideration and decision to the leading local and central bodies of the party. Moreover, everyone who criticizes must see to it that the form of his criticism takes into account the position of the party, surrounded as it is by a ring of enemies, and that the content of his criticism is such that, by directly participating in Soviet and party work, he can test the rectification of the errors of the party or of individual party members in practice. Every analysis of the general line of the party, estimate of the practical experience, verification of the fulfillment of decisions, study of methods of rectifying error, etc., must under no circumstances be submitted for preliminary discussion to groups formed on the basis of 'platforms,' etc., but must be exclusively submitted for discussion directly to all members of the party. . . .
— From the "Resolution on Unity" adopted by the 10th Congress of the Russian Communist Party of Bolsheviks, March 1921.[1]

---

[1] Robert H. McNeal, ed., *Lenin, Stalin, Khrushchev: Voices of Bolshevism,* © 1960, p. 60. By permission of Prentice-Hall, Inc., Englewood Cliffs, N.J.

THIS 1921 RESOLUTION, Lenin's own work, is in a way the culmination of his 25 years of striving for the perfectly united political organization. Seen in the perspective of Stalin's rise to power in the 1920s, it is an ironical epitaph to the fate of democracy within the Party. By decreeing an end to group politics, it undercut later efforts to rally Party members and officials against Stalin. By requiring that criticism be communicated at once to the entire Party membership, it exposed and isolated the critics who might have pressed for rules that could have been used to stop Stalin's rise to power. Once firmly in power in the early 1930s, Stalin carried the doctrine of unity a step further by ascribing a mystical will to the Party, which made it possible to demand the treatment of critics as heretics. While Stalin's style of vengeance against his opponents is a thing of the past, the doctrine of a unified Party as the custodian of a unified ideology, the prohibition of factions, and the absolute monopoly of political power within the larger political system are all explicit features of the Soviet political system today. Even Stalin's device of charging opponents within the Party with heresy may not be entirely abandoned, since Khrushchev used it vigorously in labelling his vanquished opponents of 1957 the "anti-Party group."

Three of Lenin's decisions shaped the doctrine of Party unity: (1) his struggle at the Second Party Congress in 1903 to secure a tightly disciplined Party and a unified ideology; (2) his decision in 1917–18 first to seize power in the name of a small, disciplined minority, then to use his Party as the sole ruling party, excluding any possibility of coalitions; (3) his decision in 1920–21 to eliminate organized dissent in the Party (though not all discussion and debate). Each of these decisions was the response to a crisis; yet all of them flowed from interpretations of Marxism that Lenin had developed before 1903. Each of the crises, in turn, was the product of specifically Russian circumstances, which Marx and Engels could not have foreseen: (1) the suppression of liberties and the existence of police-state rule required a small, professional, conspiratorial party, according to Lenin, instead of the large parties and movements that had arisen in the West; (2) the circumstances of the Russo-Japanese War (1904–05) and World War I gave the Russian proletariat a chance to hasten a European revolution by seizing power, though in Marx's thought Russian circumstances were far from ripe for this; (3) the failure of a European revolution to develop led to Lenin's decision to retain proletarian power anyway, which required tight discipline in view of the Party's minority position. In each case, Lenin's brand of Marxism combined with the need for mastering a crisis to produce doctrines which shaped the entire Soviet political system, and are considered valid by Soviet leaders today.

THE ORIGINS OF PARTY DISCIPLINE

Lenin's concepts of Party discipline were born amid the early factional struggles of Russian Marxists, both in Russia and among Russian political emigrés in Europe. The major effort in 1903 to build an all-Russian party succeeded, but at the same time produced a sharp and permanent cleavage within the new party's ranks over the issue of discipline and organizational questions related to it. Almost immediately, the capacity of the new party to act in unity was tested by two decisions: how to respond to Russia's revolutionary crisis of 1905, and how to exploit the possibilities offered by participation in the Duma, Russia's new parliament. The type of maneuvers which Lenin advocated in response to these circumstances—notably the pursuit of "permanent revolution"—required great tactical flexibility on the part of the leaders, and hence absolute cooperation among the rank and file. To this end, Lenin forged his doctrine of "democratic centralism." Finally, in the bleak years of Tsarist repression between 1905 and World War I, Lenin demonstrated the lengths to which he was prepared to go to keep the Party's legitimacy and resources under tight Bolshevik control. Let us look at these problems in sequence.

Lenin and the Early Marxist Groups

There was factionalism among Russian social democrats even before there was a Party, and the most enduring factional differences occurred over questions of Party organization. In 1895 the 25-year-old Lenin went to Switzerland to see Georgi Plekhanov, the acknowledged dean of Russian Marxists though long an exile. Plekhanov and his small circle had been arguing for cooperation between the proletariat and liberal democratic circles; Lenin, his political philosophy still only in its beginnings, was firmly against this. To the end of his life, Lenin's insistence on a tightly organized, centrally led proletarian organization as the sole valid instrument of revolution remained one of the great overriding constants of his thinking.

Lenin soon tried to put his views into practice. Together with Julius Martov, a Jewish labor activist, he organized a circle of 18 persons in St. Petersburg under the name "Petersburg Union of Struggle for the Liberation of the Working Class." Lenin concentrated on converting this group to his specific views on organization; here as throughout his life, a small organization boasting tight discipline and unity on theory was worth far more to him than a mass organization. The group became involved in a wave of strikes in December 1895, its members were promptly arrested, and Lenin was sent off for three years of exile in a Siberian village. It was there, living under surveillance but free to study, write, and correspond, that Lenin began his polemics against "economism," the tactic of stressing workers' immediate economic demands rather than the broad political struggle. On this subject Lenin found himself generally in agreement with Plekhanov and the emigré group around him. Activist groups set up in Russia itself, including several underground newspapers, tended to be "economist" in spite of the formal links they tried to maintain with Plekhanov's groups.

By the time Lenin was released from exile and was able to return to Europe, the main lines of controversy had already emerged on two issues: strategy and organization. For the time being these issues caused no basic split among Russian social democrats, since there was no one all-embracing social democratic organization. What the Communist Party of the Soviet Union (CPSU) today numbers as its First Party Congress, a small gathering in Minsk in 1898, was one abortive effort among several to forge an all-Russian organization; most of its delegates were arrested soon afterwards, and its press discovered and seized.

Early Organizational Questions

Lenin, after following these early struggles from afar during his three years of exile, came to Switzerland in 1900 with a program of organization firmly in mind. The struggle over doctrine and strategy must be resolved, he maintained, *before* a unified organization could be founded. The best means for waging this initial struggle would be a newspaper for all Russian social democrats. It would admit various points of view to its columns at first, but for the purpose of combating them, and would be a vehicle for putting down heresy. The newspaper, published in Western Europe, would be a party in embryo, with its own agents in Russia. By this means, the lines of battle among Russian social democrats could be sharply drawn, and only then should a national party be founded. Wrote Lenin: "Before uniting, and for the purpose of uniting, we must first decisively and definitely mark ourselves off from those who are not with us."[2] *Iskrá*, "The Spark," published its first issue at the end of 1900. The paper was soon attacking its two most important competitor papers and the small circles that sponsored them, branding their views as "economism" even where this epithet was undeserved.

Lenin meanwhile busied himself with building the skeleton of a party, first of all by directing a network of a dozen agents at work in Russia. In 1902 he came out with his plan for a party organization, in a lengthy pamphlet later to become famous as his basic statement on organization: *What Is To Be Done?* More important than the strategy of organization

---

[2] Quoted in Leonard Schapiro, *The Communist Party of the Soviet Union* (New York: Random House, 1960), pp. 36–37.

as such was Lenin's blunt conclusion about the relationship of the new party to the proletariat, its role within this fast-growing social class. The justification for this role rested, in turn, on a highly elitist perception of the proletariat as a class. The proletariat could neither unite nor take meaningful action, wrote Lenin, until it possessed a specific knowledge of its own potential and its historical mission. Lenin labeled this knowledge "political class consciousness." The problem was that the proletariat, left to its own devices, would not develop this type of consciousness. Workers, unless they have received special indoctrination, are politically short-sighted. They see the advantage of organizing for immediate gains, such as improving working conditions by means of strikes and trade union work. But their activity suffers from "spontaneity": it is uncoordinated and not aimed at definite political goals. The belief that pursuing economic gains would lead the workers naturally into political action, wrote Lenin, had already been proven false. Therefore political class consciousness can be brought to the proletariat "only from without, that is, only from outside of the economic struggle, from outside of the sphere of relations between workers and employees."[3]

A great problem in interpreting Lenin's thinking about organization is that it is so hard to separate his basic philosophy of organizations from what he believed Russian circumstances dictated. One finds Lenin arguing that conspiracy and discipline are essential for building any kind of organization under the noses of the Tsarist police, which sounds logical enough. In other passages of *What Is To Be Done?* the highly disciplined "core party" is called necessary in order to build the right class consciousness. Discipline and conspiracy were closely interwoven in Lenin's mentality. There was yet another reason for party discipline: Socialist ideology, said Marx, had been produced by members of the bourgeois intelligentsia, beginning with Marx and Engels themselves; workers' movements had not produced it. What the bourgeois-turned-revolutionary intelligentsia brought to workers' movements was of extreme importance. The danger of "infection" from false socialisms was ever present. Therefore the Party's first major battle would have to be against its own immediate competitors among the intelligentsia, and to win this battle discipline was essential. This also meant that the Party could carry on its work among any section of the population receptive to socialist doctrines, and not just among the proletariat. Here Lenin ran the danger of defining proletarians according to their receptivity to a given ideology, a far cry from Marx's attempts to find a sociological definition. His sociological use of the term "proletariat" was becoming broader at this point, and included some categories of both peasants and intellectuals (who could be said to sell their labor to capital). It is even possible to argue that

---

[3] V. I. Lenin, *What Is To Be Done?* (Moscow: Foreign Languages Publishing House, 1952), p. 133.

Lenin did not ascribe consciousness to the proletariat at all, but only to the professional revolutionaries (mainly intellectuals, actually) whose mission was to lead it.[4] If so, then the split between Bolsheviks and Mensheviks was fundamental since the Mensheviks identified consciousness with the working-class movement.

From these conclusions sprang some of the constant features of Lenin's conception of the Party, which he considered valid even after the Party had come to power. Most important was the concept of a *revolutionary organization* as distinct from a proletarian party or movement. Its custodianship of doctrine, the absence of any democratic control over it by proletarian organizations, its manipulation of mass organizations, all became explicit features of the system Lenin established after 1917. The Party, as Lenin saw it in the 1900s, should consist of professional revolutionaries in order to serve as an instrument for leading and directing the working-class movement. The revolution should not wait for class consciousness to penetrate the entire proletariat; there might even be some danger in this. When the time was ripe, "spontaneity" among the working classes would be harnessed by the professionals in order to move the working classes in the direction ordained by history. Though Lenin did not say so flatly, one can only conclude that the relation between Party and proletariat in such circumstances can only be a manipulative one.

Did Lenin Violate Marx?

Here we should note—if only to "set the record straight"—the things Lenin shared and did not share with Marx concerning the business of organizing the proletariat. Both men insisted on doctrinal correctness. Both devoted much energy to defeating socialist trends of thought which contradicted their doctrines. Both believed that intellectuals of bourgeois origin could join and even lead the proletariat because of their intellectual capacities. Both believed that it was better to work with a small, dedicated, doctrinally united movement than with a large one which needed to paper over important differences in order not to fall apart. Both believed that the rule of the oppressing classes could be shattered only by massive political blows, not by reforms.

There were important differences. Marx assumed that industrial workers, the true proletarians, would become politically conscious because of their very position in bourgeois society. He believed that economic victories, strikes, and trade union activity all helped build political consciousness. He was against the idea of an *elite party* within the proletariat, or within the revolutionary movement as a whole. The *Communist Mani-*

---

[4] This is argued very convincingly in Alfred G. Meyer, *Leninism* (New York: Praeger, 1962), chapter 1.

festo said flatly: "The Communists do not form a separate party opposed to other working-class parties. They have no interests separate and apart from those of the proletariat as a whole. They do not set up any sectarian principles of their own, by which to shape and mold the proletariat movement." Marx's short-lived Workingmen's International was composed of a great variety of European socialist organizations. Marx did believe that Communists are a vanguard among the proletarians, since they understand the course of history. Far from forming a sect of their own, however, Communists should be "the most advanced and resolute section of the working-class parties of every country, that section which pushes forward all the others." If Marx's concept of their role makes them something more than simply the leaven in the loaf, it stops well short of Lenin's concept of a separate revolutionary organization.

The Second Party Congress, 1903

The debates over organization, strategy, and a number of related issues all came to a head at the Second Party Congress, held in Brussels and London. This was yet another effort to put together a single Marxist party for Russia. While the Russian Social Democratic Labor Party did emerge from the sessions, it was a Party bitterly and permanently divided into Bolshevik and Menshevik wings.

A rising tide of strikes, demonstrations, and other forms of unrest had been sweeping Russia during 1900–1903. In these same years the *Iskra* group had outmaneuvered its rival groups in Russia, and its members dominated the Congress. But neither *Iskra* nor any other group was in command of the protest movement in Russia; there "spontaneity" won out over the maneuvers of Marxist professionals. Furthermore, the *Iskra* group itself was divided as to how to exploit the unrest. Lenin's "hard" position saw the coming overthrow of Russian autocracy as the prelude to a socialist revolution which would not be long in coming; he therefore stressed the "maximum" part of the draft Party Program which charted strategy for this ultimate event. Plekhanov was the most prominent of those who foresaw a longer road to the socialist revolution. His "soft" position stressed cooperation between the proletariat and the bourgeoisie in overthrowing the autocracy, a strategy to which Marx long ago had given his blessing in the case of Germany. In the "maximum" program, Plekhanov foresaw peasant participation in the "dictatorship of the proletariat," Marx's phrase describing the initial stage of proletarian rule; Lenin would have none of this. At the Congress, Lenin's draft won the day.

On organizational questions, so close to Lenin's heart, he appeared headed for defeat. Here Lenin's former collaborator Martov switched sides, to join a growing "soft" opposition which included some advocates of "economism" and the Jewish *Bund*, a radical ethnic organization dating from 1897 which insisted on its autonomy within the framework of the Party. Lenin was defeated in his bid to set up strict Party discipline, and Martov carried his majority on a number of other points as well. But when the *Bund* members walked out of the Congress over a challenge to their status, Martov's majority evaporated, and Lenin now commanded 24 votes against 20. Even with this majority, it cost him a bitter struggle to gain command of the two Party bodies that were most important: the new *Iskra* editorial board, which would provide ideological guidance from abroad, and a Central Committee of three, which would operate inside Russia. It was these final votes that earned Lenin's supporters the title of Bolsheviks (*bolsheviki*), the "men of the majority," and Martov's group the damaging epithet Mensheviks (*mensheviki*), those seemingly doomed to be a permanent minority.

1905: Factional Victory Before All Else

One would think that Russia's political crisis of 1905—usually misnamed a revolution—would have served to draw Bolsheviks and Mensheviks together. Here, barely two years after the Second Congress, was at least the beginning of the bourgeois revolution which the "minimum" program had foreseen, brought on by Russia's humiliating defeat at the hands of Japan. In fact, neither Bolsheviks nor Mensheviks had much influence on the behavior of the proletariat in that year. If either, it was the Mensheviks who played a role. The St. Petersburg Menshevik group had a part in forming the Petersburg Soviet (Council) of Workers' Deputies, a mixture of strike committee and embryo government. But the Soviet itself was neither Bolshevik nor Menshevik. In the last days before the authorities closed it down, it was presided over by Trotsky, who had broken with Lenin in 1903 and then had left the Mensheviks in 1904. The one action that Bolsheviks and Mensheviks agreed to sponsor jointly with a quixotic barricade episode in Moscow in December 1905, a symbolic act of defiance which was doomed from the beginning.

For Lenin, 1905 offered not a year of glorious revolutionary activity, but only the first of a dozen years of political infighting which ended with the Bolsheviks in firm control of the vital organs of the Russian Social Democratic Labor Party (RSDLP). This was an activity at which Lenin proved himself very adept; he was able to demonstrate his principle that a dozen loyal men are to be preferred to a mass organization whose loyalty is only conditional. There was little danger, in fact, that the RSDLP would turn into a mass organization, however much the Mensheviks may have desired this. Lenin's main accomplishment in 1905 was not anything he or his Bolshevik agents did in Russia, but the holding of the Third Party Congress in London, a Congress which Lenin later admitted was not legal according to the Party Statutes. It was a thoroughly Bolshevik conclave, and it enacted some of the organizational measures Lenin had urged unsuccessfully two years before. This included most especially Lenin's definition of Party membership, with its stress on discipline and professionalism. Lenin did offer reconciliation with the Mensheviks, and a year later the Fourth Congress, meeting in Stockholm, actually saw the Mensheviks in a slight majority. But the two major factions showed little sign of reconciling their important differences—indeed, Lenin encouraged hard factional lines. From then on, factionalism degenerated into organizational guerilla warfare as the fortunes of the whole Russia Marxist movement went into decline.

Democratic Centralism

Lenin managed to return to Russia in the fall of 1905, after an absence of five years. Except for brief trips to western Europe for Party meetings, he spent the next two years in Russia, keeping carefully out of the hands of the police. The way he spent his time during this period was characteristic: instead of propagandizing and seeking recruits among ordinary workers, he was building a disciplined Bolshevik organization, starting with the mere skeleton of an organization which he found on his arrival. The enemies against whom Lenin directed his attacks were neither Tsarism nor the Russian bourgeoisie, but rival socialist parties. To maintain an organization against its close rivals in the same field, doctrine, discipline, and commitment were essential. Looking beyond the kind of discipline that was imposed on the Bolsheviks by their semi-underground existence in Russia, Lenin foresaw his organization's working during another revolutionary upsurge such as that of 1905, fighting a life-or-death struggle with other socialist groups over leadership of the revolution.

In this situation, discipline and correct doctrine were not by themselves enough. Participation, commitment, and enthusiasm of the followers were just as essential. But how to reconcile the opposites? Looking around him in the aftermath of 1905, Lenin could see that both the Social Revolutionaries and the Mensheviks, his chief rivals, had decided against discipline. In riding a wave of revolutionary feeling they gave the appearance of a formidable force, but in a protracted struggle for leadership of the revolutionary movement their internal divisions would come to the fore and place them at a disadvantage. Internal democracy could be a strength in some circumstances and a handicap in others. Could democracy and discipline be built into the same organization?

Lenin's solution to this problem was capsuled in four principles which today any Soviet schoolchild can recite from memory: (1) election of all leading Party bodies, from the lowest to the highest; (2) periodic reports of Party bodies both to the organizations that elected them and to higher bodies; (3) strict Party discipline, and subordination of the minority to the majority; (4) the obligatory character of decisions by higher Party bodies for lower bodies. The key provisions are the last two, which leave certain matters unclear. Is there to be majority rule, and if so, how can this be reconciled with obligatory orders from above? If the minority is to be subordinated to the majority, may it continue to work for its point of view in hopes of becoming a majority?

Neither of these questions was to be resolved in practice until the 1920s. Lenin's own answers to these and other questions left much to be desired by way of clarity. Consider his attempt to make a sharp distinction between policy making and the execution of policies: Until a policy issue has been resolved, there shall be open debate; once the issue is resolved and the policy put into operation, discussion must cease, and every Party member must bend his will to carrying it out. Here Lenin overlooked the circumstances that policy problems are often matters of constant concern. Many political situations require constant "tending," an ongoing adjustment of policies to situations. What Lenin meant by "policy" was a statement of policy at a given point in time. As long as the statement stands, there can be no criticism of it. If the issue is to be opened upon for Party discussion, the initiative to do so must come from the top Party organs, and not from below.

It is also fair to ask what the purpose of elections is, in view of the subordination of elected Party officials at each level to officials at the next higher level. In Lenin's view, elections should have no policy content; that is to say, a Party committee member or Party bureau officer at any given level is chosen not because he represents a certain set of policies, but presumably for his personal qualities and his ability to carry out decisions handed down from above.

Undergirding Lenin's thinking on democracy in the Party was his insistence on doctrinal correctness in Party decisions. If the Party's policies are to be developed by applying Marxism to concrete circumstances, why ask the Party's members what these policies should be? A rank-and-file Bolshevik, by his act of entering the Party, subordinated himself to leadership based on specialized knowledge, not to leadership based on an understanding of the members' opinions and aspirations. Democratic devices were built into the Party for the purpose of gaining the commitment of the members. Commitment is to be gained through discussions and elections, but it must also be based on a conviction that the leadership possesses knowledge that is not open to question. This is not to say, of course, that Marxism left no questions open. Questions of strategy, as we have already seen, could not necessarily be resolved by referring to Marx, and questions of organization were scarcely dealt with by Marx. The early history of the Bolsheviks saw much discussion on both topics, for they were the Party's central concern. Yet for Lenin, discussions and elections had no purpose other than serving as a medium for persuading the rank-and-file of the correctness of the leadership's decisions. Democratic processes, within these very narrow confines, were intended to make the difference between blind obedience and obedience based on enthusiastic conviction.

STRATEGY INFLUENCES ORGANIZATION

Permanent Revolution

The notion of "permanent revolution" was Marx's invention, not Lenin's. It followed from Marx's advice of 1849 to German revolutionaries, whom he urged to assist the bourgeois revolution against feudalism as a first step. Marx had written that the still small German proletariat would serve as the foot troops of the bourgeoisie in this task. He advised them that when the revolution was accomplished, the proletariat could hasten the day of its own revolution against the bourgeoisie by keeping its weapons, by staying organized, by pressing the bourgeoisie to put its own ideals into practice, and by keeping the bourgeoisie constantly off balance in a growing political struggle. Trotsky, in evaluating the events of 1905, saw the proletarian revolution following immediately on the heels of the bourgeois triumph: the two revolutions could be "telescoped" into one. Lenin's position was closer to that of Marx: the proletariat must bring pressure on the bourgeoisie to establish the "democratic republic," a last phase of bourgeois rule in which the bourgeoisie has been forced to concede the most important goals of democracy: representative government and individual freedom, both manipulated by the ruling class. Within this system, the proletariat will at least have some "elbow room" in which to press for the coming revolution.

Both versions of permanent revolution called for a high degree of discipline in the ranks of Russian social democrats. When a radical organization makes common cause with a less radical organization or movement, there is often a danger that the moderate leaders will try to "take it into camp" by offering rewards to the radical leaders: cabinet posts, economic concessions, and political and legal protection are the most common lures. Lenin's fears on this score were realized in part in 1917, when leading Mensheviks cooperated with the Provisional Government, and were duly rewarded. Lenin's version of permanent revolution, because it foresaw a period of time between the bourgeois and proletarian revolutions, foresaw also a greater danger from the lures of coalition politics than did Trotsky's version. The kind of discipline necessary to reject the fruits of temporary cooperation with the bourgeoisie was a specialty of Lenin's, and an important factor in the differences between the conduct of Bolsheviks and Mensheviks in 1917 (see below).

Revolutionaries in a Bourgeois Parliament

The Russian Government's Manifesto of October 1905, its most important concession in the face of serious unrest, established a State Duma
chosen (in the beginning) by an indirect but surprisingly representative
electoral system. Unfortunately for Russia's nascent democracy, the Tsar
and his top officials regarded the Duma as an advisory body only, and
even in this role as a necessary evil. The Constitutional Democratic Party
("Kadets") and others saw it as a British-style parliament in the making.
Plekhanov followed a Marxian prescription in urging that the Social
Democrats help the bourgeoisie—in this case the Kadets—in completing
their own revolution. The Mensheviks, 18 of whom were elected to the
524-member Duma, were little disposed to accept this strategy. Instead,
they devoted their energy to rather empty revolutionary rhetoric in
which they attacked the Kadets and tried to appeal to the nation. Lenin
had instructed the Bolsheviks to boycott the elections. He saw the Duma
as a trick to undermine the revolutionary movement, and he saw the
Kadets in particular as betrayers of the proletariat who would soon make
a deal with the Tsar's government.

The Kadets soon found themselves at loggerheads with the Tsar's
ministers, the Duma was dissolved, and elections to a new Duma were
set in motion. Lenin now reversed his position, and Bolsheviks and Mensheviks cooperated to elect 65 deputies, while the once-powerful Kadets
lost much ground. It was not only that Lenin saw the Duma's potential
as a means of communicating to the nation; he doubtless feared that
the Mensheviks might gain immeasurably in influence if they commanded
the parliamentary forum. As it was, 36 of the 65 social democratic
deputies were Mensheviks, 18 were Bolsheviks, and the rest neither. (A
number of Social Democrats were content to stay away from both frac-
tions.) The Social Democrats' role in the Duma continued to be one
of propaganda. They did, in 1914, use the chance of opposing Russia's
entry into World War I by voting against war credits. This was something few of the social democratic deputies in other European parlia-
ments had the courage and doctrinal consistency to do. By this time
electoral rigging and political repression had reduced their number to
a mere dozen; then the five who were Bolsheviks were arrested in 1914,
while the remaining Mensheviks continued to oppose the war effort as
best they could.

In sum, both Bolshevik and Menshevik deputies followed Lenin's prescription that they take a radical stance and not be drawn into any
kind of coalition with the moderate parties. In the circumstances, however, there was little temptation to join coalitions after the first two
Dumas had been dissolved, since the Kadets and other moderates had
no rewards to offer them. The fact that Lenin was prepared to

see a Bolshevik grouping enter the Duma speaks both for his sureness about Bolshevik discipline and also for his concern that a Menshevik sellout to other parties might damage the Social Democratic cause generally.

Revolutionary Legitimacy

The 1905 disturbances were followed by a period of successful official repression in Russia, together with discouragement and a great slackening of activity among radical organizations. Only in 1912 were there again strikes and demonstrations, until an outburst of public patriotism that attended the beginning of World War I gave the Tsar's government a respite from these as well. The socialist emigrés in Europe, and their few remaining agents within Russian borders, fought intense struggles over the control of miniscule organizations, plotted the strategy of nonexistent socialist "troops," and quarrelled over their slim sources of funds. As a fruit of years of complicated maneuvering, Lenin's faction gained recognition for its own Central Committee and thereby at least nominal control of the RSDLP.

That Lenin and the Bolsheviks did not quit the Party altogether, as other groups might have done in a similar situation, is a tribute to Lenin's appreciation of political legitimacy. This was not legitimacy as political philosophers generally use the term, but legitimacy as the true embodiment of Marxist doctrine. The Party's "firm name" was important. To the same extent that Lenin was bent on cutting off all groups within the Party that disagreed wih Bolshevik strategy, so he was bent on keeping up the Bolshevik claim to the name of the Party that had once enjoyed the support of Russia's most important Marxists. This tactic did not prevent Lenin from maintaining a separate Bolshevik Center within the Party. He gained control of the Party's funds, but was less successful in dominating its newspapers.

These tactics were not always successful by any means. In fact, by the time World War I broke out, the Mensheviks had regained some of their leverage in the RSDLP by appealing to the Second Socialist International (not Marx's International, which had dissolved, but the one founded in 1889). The year 1914 found the Bolshevik Center close to dissolution. Yet the role Lenin had found for his Bolshevik faction within the Party had not been entirely unsuccessful; the adroit interplay of "splitting tactics" with the tactic of maintaining the Party formally intact was to be used later with stunnng success.

Consequence for the Party's Role

It is easy to look cynically on Lenin's rapid shifting of positions, his facile use of slogans, and his concealment of ultimate intentions. His

Bolshevik Center was very small, and very small groupings can afford to be opportunistic, adroitly and diabolically so. This is especially the case where one figure clearly dominates the grouping. Mass organizations are much harder to lead in such maneuvers, unless their following is sufficiently docile or mesmerized to accept its strategy from the dictates of a small leadership circle. The Social Revolutionaries, the peasant-oriented competitors of the Social Democrats, suffered all the inconvenience of striving for a truly mass following amid a continuing debate over both goals and strategy. Their leadership, for example, tried to proclaim public seizure of the land while being somewhat coy about what would happen with the land after that, and this ideological maneuver cost them a good deal politically.

Lenin's concept of a small party of professional revolutionaries offered distinct advantages in manipulating mass movements. It is well adapted to carrying out a program whose long-range consistency required highly flexible current strategies. Cynical and opportunistic this might be: "The end justifies the means" is a judgment of reproach in today's world. But the problem lies deeper: Do the means also shape the end? The type of organization which Lenin built did, in spite of its vast increase in size and functions, carry some of its important "underground traits" into its postrevolutionary rule. The Party leadership, once in power, was not likely to abandon organization and strategies which had succeeded before 1917. Reinforcing this continuity was the circumstance that the Party after 1917 ruled over a society still in need of basic transformation, quite the opposite of what Marx had foreseen for a revolution in Western Europe. If the Party had succeeded in maintaining itself before 1917 as a small minority movement in a hostile environment, it was well prepared to maintain itself later in a largely hostile society.

The organizational measures which Lenin found most effective were the following: He maintained a core of associates totally in agreement with his views, who acted as a bloc even though their views were usually those of the minority among the social democrats. He drew others into sharp polemics in order to refute their views publicly and shatter the tendencies they represented. His "splitting tactics" aimed at reducing both the leadership and Party in size, while he retained control of the Party's name, traditions, and aura of "Marxist legitimacy." He strove to bring factions and factionalism out in the open with the ultimate end of ending all factionalism. "Democratic centralism," a slogan Lenin first used in 1906, envisaged the replacement of factionalism by voluntary unanimity. A question once resolved remains resolved until the leadership chooses to reopen it. Unanimity was essential to the Party's success. Lenin held, therefore, that Party members must feel a strong constraint to support this unanimity at all costs.

Lenin saw the Central Committee as the guarantor of unanimity; hence his relentless efforts to keep it under the control of a Bolshevik majority. Until circumstances permitted, Lenin believed, the Central Committee must co-opt its members. This central command organ, whose members shared a special capacity for charting the Party's strategy, was a guarantee of correct decisions.

The idea of the Party as an organization of professional revolutionaries, for all Lenin's insistence on this in 1903, was not realizable in any strict sense. The broader definition which Lenin actually settled for was a constantly active membership penetrated and guided by professionals. There is some justice in saying that Lenin "bureaucratized" the Party from the very beginning: decisions were made by an elite group not subject to democratic control, and they were executed through a command structure responsible only to the leadership.[5]

On questions of strategy, Lenin believed that the role of the Party must be to change the whole fabric of political and social relations in a planned manner. He did not agree with Marx on this point. Marx saw the future society as being created by capitalism; the day of revolution would find the proletariat a well-functioning social organism, fully conscious of its destiny, well able to unite against its capitalist foes. Thereafter, Marx believed, a brief period of practical training in the ways of socialism would enable the proletarians to enter the ultimate stage of communism.

Lenin was a manipulator of social change. Part of his manipulative urge stemmed from his impatience with history, his great urge to compensate for Russia's wide historical lag by devising shortcuts. This much is clear from his writings. But in studying Lenin's discussions of strategy, one senses a parallel conviction that social change does not take place *except* through manipulative leadership. The term "manipulative" is used here in a definite sense. As we saw in the case of his appeals on land seizures, he revealed his program only by stages. He advertised only those goals which would command the kind of support he needed, omitting the succeeding goals if revealing these would erode support. The distinction between theory, propaganda, and agitation rested not just on how to present a Marxist program to ever wider audiences. It depended even more on what parts of the program should be urged to whom and when, and what else should be kept within Party circles.

THE DECISIONS OF 1917

The choices that Lenin made during the eight months that followed the Tsar's overthrow not only led to the opportunity to seize power, but also shaped further the Bolsheviks' view of their relation to other

---

[5] See the excellent discussion of these organizational principles in Meyer, *Leninism*, chapters 2–5.

parties and to the system of soviets which sprang into existence in March. These same eight months also saw Lenin search for an opportunity for his minority Party to wield power in the name of an entire people. Questions of Party structure and discipline remained in the background during this year. Party membership grew rapidly during these months, so that the strict discipline of previous years had to be loosened. Also, the counsels of Party leaders were divided on many things, including Lenin's proposal to seize power. In order to hold the Party together, Lenin sought to separate its role sharply from that of other parties and the soviets, not to mention the Mensheviks. Here was the practical political foundation of the Party's elitism, which Lenin hitherto had argued from the point of view of Marxist thought. For the present, unity would be created through agreement on revolutionary action itself; later, when the Party consolidated its rule, democratic centralism would be adapted to its much enlarged membership.

Political Instability and Political Opportunity

The tangled events of 1917 were to offer the Bolsheviks a unique change for seizing power at little immediate cost. Lenin exploited a number of circumstances which happened to coincide in time: the nation's war-weariness after three long years of trying to stem the German invasion; the atmosphere of freedom which resulted from the overthrow of the Tsar; the divided counsels of the Provisional Government, which ruled from March to November; mass desertions from the armed forces together with political agitation in many military units; and the slowness of efforts to create a regular constitutional order for Russia. As we saw at the very beginning of this book, the actual seizure of power was simple. The real Bolshevik feat was retaining power for the next three years during a prolonged civil war coupled with military intervention by four of the Great Powers, including the United States. But here, too, Lenin profited from the mistakes, handicaps, and divided counsel of his foes.

No party or network of agents planned the demonstrations of March 8–15. Neither Bolsheviks, nor Mensheviks, nor Social Revolutionaries could claim they persuaded units of the Petrograd garrison to side with the demonstrators. The crowds which took possession of unused rooms in the Taurida Palace, the same building in which the Duma met, carried no directives from radical political leaders when it proceeded to form the Petrograd Soviet of Workers' Deputies.

By March 13 many of the Tsar's ministers were under arrest. The Tsar himself, who at this time had taken over command of the Russian armies and lived in a railroad car at the front, had unthinkingly prorogued the Duma. The Duma met anyway, and soon dispatched two of its leaders to ask for the Tsar's abdication. Nicholas agreed reluctantly, handing the throne to his brother, Grand Duke Michael; but the latter wisely refused to accept his office unless it be at the hands of a constitutional assembly of some kind.

To the Kadets and many Duma conservatives, a new era of constitutional monarchy was at hand. To the Marxist factions, the hitherto weak-kneed Russian bourgeoisie had completed its revolution according to Marx's old prescription for Germany—that is, with massive aid from proletarian "troops." To the Social Revolutionaries, majority rule would mean a peasant-based government, which in turn would open the door to some form of agrarian socialism. To the man in the street, the air of freedom was exhilarating; the cancelled promises of 1905 were to be granted after all. Peaceful demonstrations filled the streets day after day, as parties and organizations of every stripe made their views known.

The Duma soon elected a Provisional Government as custodian of rule until a Russian constitution could be adopted. It was headed for several months by Prince Lvov, a Kadet, and the Kadet leader Paul Miliukov became Foreign Minister. From the revolutionary parties there was only one representative, Alexander Kerensky, who had been leader of the *Trudoviki* in the Duma. He was a Social Revolutionary of sorts, but maintained relationships with the several parties of the Left without attaching his political fortunes to any one of them.

The Provisional Government soon had its hands full with matters other than drafting a constitution. Much of the Left urged a prompt end to the war; troops at the front were swept up in political debates; army desertions multiplied, and in Petrograd demonstrations both for and against the war surged through the streets. Kerensky, who became War Minister in May (he had been Minister of Justice), vigorously supported the war in what seemed a nonstop speechmaking campaign.

The Petrograd Soviet offered a classic example of what today is called a "parallel government." Its first act, which went down in history as Order Number 1, directed that elective committees be set up in every military unit and declared that the Provisional Government's orders should be obeyed only if they were in keeping with the Soviet's orders. While the Soviet could not thereafter enforce the authority which it asserted, and indeed seemed reluctant to expand its authority further, it had aroused much public support because it claimed a share of legitimacy. If the Provisional Government's legitimacy was derived from the Duma and its formal inheritance of the old Imperial rule, the Soviet's leaders maintained that its legitimacy came from the people themselves, who alone could validate the Government's acts. The Petrograd Soviet came to be Menshevik-dominated, and for the time being it equivocated on the war issue while pressing the Provisional Government for democratic reforms and a prompt convening of the Constituent Assembly.

Spontaneous militant activity spread to some of the farthest corners of the old Russian Empire, and to different strata of society. Trade union membership grew rapidly, strikes and lockouts became frequent. Where there were Bolsheviks groups in the factories, they organized Factory Committees in order to undercut the more cautious trade unions, which were often under Menshevik or Social Revolutionary influence. Soviets of Workers' and Soldiers' Deputies sprang up about the country. The revolutionary novelties of the capital were quickly initiated in the provinces, as had happened in the French Revolution. There were Soviets of Peasants' Deputies as well, dominated by the Social Revolutionaries, who organized a national conference in May. The next month saw the First All-Russian Congress of Soviets; there too the Social Revolutionaries were strong, the Mensheviks likewise, while the Bolsheviks were in a small minority.

The Tsar's abdication found most of the Bolshevik leaders scattered and caught them unawares. Lenin was in Switzerland, Trotsky was in New York, and a good many others, including Stalin, were in Siberian exile. In April the German Government assisted Lenin's return to Russia via Germany and Scandinavia, well knowing that he would use the opportunity to foment opposition to the Provisional Government and the war. Trotsky returned in May after some delays and difficulties, and the Provisional Government's policy of amnesty for political prisoners served to release all the important Bolsheviks.

Lenin's Shifting Strategy

Before his return to Russia from Switzerland, Lenin had understood the soviets as the main vehicle of a working-class revolution, which embraced the aspirations of both workers and peasants, as against the urban bourgeois forces which were the mainstay of the Provisional Government. But seizure of power by the soviets would be only the next step in the revolution, with a proletarian assumption of power still to come. In 1905, impressed with the scope of unrest among the Russian peasantry, Lenin had come forth with the demand for a "revolutionary democratic workers' and peasants' dictatorship." Now he revived this slogan, emphasizing that attainment of this goal meant only the final smashing of bourgeois power and provisional rule by the masses; it was not yet a proletarian order, and a long way still from the establishment of socialism. The proletariat would lead the other classes. Only after contradictions had arisen in this new state would the proletariat establish its own dictatorship and thereby open the socialist era.

Lenin's theories about the transfer of power were actually somewhat unsettled. Though it may be pardonable if in the excitement of those months he paid little attention to niceties of theory, still it is surprising that his accustomed rigor of definitions and formulae was missing when it was most needed. Be that as it may, Lenin was baffled on the eve of his return to Russia to learn that the soviets had made accommodations with the Provisional Government which amounted to abandonment, for the present, of any moves toward overthrowing it. He ascribed this partly to the fact that no peasant revolution had occurred, and none seemed in the offing.

Consequently Lenin brought to Russia a new formula for action. His arrival on April 16 at Petrograd's Finland Station is enshrined in Soviet historiography as the starting point of his unswerving drive toward a Bolshevik seizure of power. The "revolutionary democratic dictatorship" had failed; it had occurred simultaneously with the bourgeois revolution, but had surrendered to the latter. The proletariat remained, for the time being, the only truly revolutionary class. While Lenin continued to support the slogan "All Power to the Soviets," it now meant that the left-wing parties which dominated the soviets must first break off their agreement with the bourgeois-dominated government. Meanwhile the Bolsheviks must do everything to win the rest of the left wing to the overthrow of the government, and themselves prepare to lead the way to a dictatorship of the proletariat.

Up to that point, the Bolsheviks in Petrograd had been largely in accord with the Mensheviks and the other left-wing parties. Lenin's call for revolution met with considerable skepticism among his own followers, and incredulity among Mensheviks and Social Revolutionaries. With the Bolshevik Party in a ferment of growth and activity, Lenin no longer possessed the mechanism of Party discipline that he had built up during his years of organizing a small network of professionals. At this point persuasion was his main weapon, and events his main helper.

Events first gave support to his call for a Bolshevik-led dictatorship of the proletariat, then supplied the weapons for a coup, and finally provided the political disorganization which made an easy coup possible. The Provisional Government, by the summer of 1917, was promising more war instead of peace, and had made no progress toward land reform, an all-important issue in a country still largely peasant, whose armies were now filled with peasant soldiers. In order to demonstrate to the Western allies its intent to continue fighting, the Provisional Government mounted an offensive in Galicia which turned into a rout. Armed Bolshevik demonstrations, which neither Lenin nor the other Bolshevik leaders had ordered, and which Lenin was obliged to pacify, surged through the streets of Petrograd. A cabinet crisis brought both Social Revolutionaries and Mensheviks into the government of Alexander Kerensky, now the Prime Minister, himself a socialist of sorts. In this way the Bolsheviks' chief rivals compromised themselves on the war issue, for the war continued in spite of defeats at the front. The Bolsheviks were driven underground, and Lenin went into hiding outside of Petrograd.

At this point Lenin dropped all support of the soviets, which were still dominated by his left-wing rivals, now thoroughly discredited in his eyes as a revolutionary force, not least of all because they had joined the Provisional Government in trying to suppress the Bolsheviks. His view of how power would be transferred, and to whom, now changed sharply. Power could no longer be assumed more or less peacefully by the soviets, but must be seized by the Bolsheviks with the use of force. In his Finnish hideout, Lenin wrote a lengthy tract which later became a classic of Soviet Marxism, *State and Revolution.* In it he assembled numerous passages from the writings of Marx in an effort to show that a truly proletarian revolution is necessarily violent because its task is to smash the bourgeois state altogether. Although not all of his associates were convinced, for Lenin there no longer remained any doubt that a Bolshevik seizure of power should be carried out as soon as circumstances permitted.

Alone among the contending parties, the Bolsheviks had organized their own military units, the Red Guard. Kerensky had not disbanded these after the "July Days," as logically he should have done. In September, the Provisional Government was threatened from the Right in the form of an imminent attack on Petrograd by troops from the front mustered by General Kornilov, who suspected treason in the capital. Now the Provisional Government called on the Red Guard to help defend Petrograd, which the Bolsheviks agreed to do. The attack was fended off without a fight, and the Bolsheviks rode a sudden wave of popularity. Besides this, the public mood was growing more sullen; impatience with the war was rising sharply; desertions were reducing the front to a shambles; and in the countryside peasants were seizing what land they could.

Lenin now reversed again his view of the soviets' potential. Elections to the soviets were returning Bolshevik majorities in many areas. The Second Congress of Soviets was scheduled to meet early in November, and Lenin now saw his chance to capture this as his needed organ of revolutionary legitimacy. And, in fact, more than half of the 650 delegates were Bolshevik or pro-Bolshevik. There was an important reservation: The revolution would be a Bolshevik act, and the results would be approved by the Congress while the Bolsheviks maintained sole command of the armed detachments they had created. The Central Committee was anything but unanimous in its support of Lenin (Kamenev and Zinoviev were firmly against him in this adventure), but he finally won the majority vote he needed. Trotsky, whose advocacy of "permanent revolution" now appeared fully justified, was in command of the operation, whose culmination we saw in the Introduction. Potentially troublesome troops were neutralized, vital communications points were seized, the Winter Palace was infiltrated with little real trouble, and the Provisional Government's cabinet was arrested (minus Kerensky, who was away trying to round up some loyal troops). Lenin then hastened to announce to the Congress of Soviets that the deed was done, and the era of socialism at hand.

Lenin, by some accounts, was not as convinced as other Bolsheviks about the need for legitimizing the Bolshevik coup through the soviets, but in the end he too embraced this. Though he would have preferred to devote all his time to the Party and let others manage the formal machinery of rule, his colleagues persuaded him to accept the post that corresponds to Prime Minister in parliamentary democracies. The Congress of Soviets was in the process of electing a cabinet to be styled the "Council of People's Commissars," and Lenin now became its Chairman.

The Impact on the Party

Lenin's shifting strategy of 1917 displayed one very important constant: the Party, lacking though it was in the tight organization that Lenin stressed, had been kept well apart from other left-wing parties and organizations by Lenin's insistence on a hard, radical doctrine. At the time Lenin returned to Russia in April, this had not been so—Bolsheviks and Mensheviks in Petrograd had been cooperating in their support of the soviets. Lenin was undiscouraged by the skepticism about his hard line in Bolshevik ranks, convinced as he was that events would prove him right. It was his persuasiveness that drew a hard line between Bolshevik objectives and those of other left-wing organizations. This characteristic was carried over into the new system of rule, where a tightly disciplined Party worked within the soviets and bureaucracy, maintaining its own clear identity and policy objectives.

Next, the Party's distinct radical line had made it possible for Bolsheviks to wage a political battle in the soviets with enough success to enable Lenin to use the soviets as his legitimizing institution. If the lines of division between Bolsheviks and the rest had been unclear, very likely the struggle over the question of revolution versus cooperation could have gone on and on without result. Instead, the Bolsheviks had succeeded well enough in the choice of delegates to the Second Congress of Soviets that Lenin was certain of approval, hence legitimacy, for his seizure of power. His followers, therefore, were furnished with the immediate reward of power in return for their adherence to a radical line.

This same strategy of seeking legitimacy by capturing control of the soviets also set the pattern for the Party's role within the government, which will be treated in detail in later chapters. Party members were now asked to form part of a "hard core" within a system of assemblies which embraced a variety of left-wing tendencies, many of them hostile to the Bolsheviks at this point. After the Revolution, even more than before, it was important for the Party's leaders to maintain an obedience and dedication strong enough not to be eroded by the larger political environment in which they worked.

Finally, the Bolsheviks had seized power as a small minority in the country, with between 200,000 and 300,000 members,[6] claiming leadership of an industrial proletariat of about 2.5 million workers, which constituted less than 2 percent of the population.[7] While Bolshevik propaganda claimed the support of the vast majority of the peasants and the lower classes generally, the events of the next few years showed how narrow was the regime's actual base of support. The most immediate evidence is the elections to the Constituent Assembly in December, where the Social Revolutionaries won a decisive majority. Further evidence is Lenin's policy of formenting class warfare among the peasantry from the summer of 1918 on, done partly in the hope of bringing the poor peasants over to support of the Bolsheviks. Lenin had led his Party into a situation where enthusiasm would serve for a time to hold the ranks together, but where in the long run a strong internal mechanism of control would be needed. By 1921, Lenin had reestablished the principal mechanisms of control he had used in the prewar years. To these were added, as we shall see, devices for shattering factions within the Party and for placing discussion itself under the firm control of the leadership.

THE BANNING OF OPPOSITION

In the short space of three and one-half years, November 1917 to March 1921, the Bolsheviks succeeded in prohibiting every form of opposition. This was done in stages, from the banning of the bourgeois parties immediately after the seizure of power to the 1921 Resolution on Unity, which attempted—though without immediate success—to end the practice of allowing formal factions within the Party. Most of this period was occupied by the Russian Civil War, and for a time in 1918 and 1919 the very existence of Bolshevik rule was endangered. Ordinarily, a regime that is fighting for its life will seek broad support from many groups. Lenin's reaction in this situation followed from his choices in 1917: strong Party unity is essential, and this unity can be forged most readily by emphasizing differences and attacking those who differ. Only one episode in this series of attacks produced doubts in Lenin's mind:

---

[6] The exact membership figure at the time of the Bolshevik seizure of power is not known. The figure given in August 1917 was Sverdlov's estimate of 200,000. Schapiro, *The Communist Party of the Soviet Union*, p 171.

[7] See the figures in David Lane, *Politics and Society in the USSR* (New York: Random House, 1971), p. 29.

the vendetta against the Georgian Mensheviks, described below. But while Lenin was disturbed by the kind of brutality which Stalin and Ordzhonikidze used to enforce Lenin's policy, he did not question the principle of subordinating national (non-Russian) communist parties within a strictly unitary Party. As virtually the last act of his career he tried to remove Stalin from his position of power, then lay ill and died without having realized that his own principles of unity and subordination had opened the door to misuse by Stalin and others. We shall look at the stages of banning opposition in sequence.

Coalition versus Sole Rule

According to the commonsense rules of Western politics, Lenin after his coup should have assembled a revolutionary coalition, including a sizable representation for the Social Revolutionaries. The SR's, as they were called, were loosely organized and embraced a variety of political tendencies. But they had real political appeal, as they promptly demonstrated. The Bolsheviks had promised after seizing power to go ahead with the planned elections to the Constituent Assembly, which would then meet early in 1918 to draft a new Russian constitution. Lenin had hoped that the Bolshevik political victory would sweep all else before it at the polls. It is true that Bolshevik electoral strength was impressive in the major cities. Professional agitators and publicity spread by pro-Bolshevik armed forces had a strong effect. But of 707 seats in the Constituent Assembly, the Social Revolutionaries won 370, a clear majority. The left-wing Social Revolutionaries, who were likely to side with the Bolsheviks on important matters, held another 40. The Bolsheviks themselves garnered 175 seats, less than half the SR figure. Of nearly 40 million votes cast, the Bolsheviks received just under one fourth, while the Social Revolutionaries received about 45 percent. The Kadets made an impressive showing in the cities, with one fourth of the vote in Petrograd and one third in Moscow, but gained only 17 seats overall. The Mensheviks had 16 seats.

Lenin, undaunted, interpreted the results as a mandate from history because of the huge Bolshevik majority among urban workers and among the largely peasant armies. In any case, arithmetical majorities had little to do with the proletariat's mandate from history, as Lenin interpreted this from Marx's dialectical progression of history. Besides, Lenin considered his true majority to include the proletariat of Europe, which was expected to carry out its own revolution very shortly. By temperament and political philosophy, as we have seen, he was little disposed to accept any but the most temporary alliances; a true coalition was out of the question. During the first two weeks of Bolshevik power, the coalition issue split the Bolshevik leaders, some of whom were even inclined to consider a compromise with the Mensheviks that would exclude Lenin from the government. Lenin expelled some of the waverers from their posts, but ultimately brought all but a few to join his tough stance.

There was an equal reluctance on the part of the other parties and factions of the left to enter even a temporary alliance. Few of their leaders expected the Bolsheviks to retain power, so they did not want to attach their political fortunes to such a risky venture. The left SR's, who by this time were a separate party, were offered a token representation on the new Council of People's Commissars, but refused. They together with the other Social Revolutionaries, Mensheviks, and others had walked out of the All-Russian Congress of Soviets in protest against the Bolshevik coup. There were those who later regretted this step; they might have learned something from Lenin's belief that fighting for control of a legitimizing institution, even against improbable odds, is far preferable to forming a splinter group apart from it.

The Bolshevik offer of cabinet posts to the left SR's had been calculated to present the image of a broadly based government without incurring any of the real dangers of a coalition. This branch of the Social Revolutionaries was very young, divided, and inexperienced. Three weeks after the coup, the Bolsheviks meanwhile having scored their first military victories, several left SR's did in fact accept cabinet posts. They resigned three months later in protest against the conclusion of peace with Germany. From that day on, the Bolsheviks ruled their system alone, an embattled minority using drastic expedients in order to stay in power. By 1921, when the NEP brought about a truce in the countryside and some kind of coalition might have been possible, Bolshevik repression and the Civil War had shattered the SR organization.

The Bolsheviks had also sought the presence of Social Revolutionaries and others in the new soviet organs, primarily in the interest of legitimacy. As the Second All-Russian Congress of Soviets, the same body that had approved Lenin's Council of People's Commissars, was dispersing in haste, it elected a Central Executive Committee of 116 members, only 67 of them Bolsheviks, plus 29 left-wing Social Revolutionaries, and the remainder a miscellany of left-wing figures. Though countless decrees were issued in its name, the Central Executive Commitee's one real function was to serve as a legitimizing body for the Bolsheviks in the interval before the next Congress of Soviets. As such, it symbolized the idea of a broad revolutionary front, in which the Bolsheviks could claim sole leadership while accepting certain other political groupings as junior partners. Lenin lost no time in embodying the same organs and their symbolism in regular constitutional form: the first Soviet constitution, that of the Russian Republic (RSFSR), went into effect only eight months after the November coup. It organized the soviets into a pyramidal system, from the local soviets at the base to the All-Russian Congress of

Soviets at the top; each of these elected an executive body which presided over the appropriate organs of state administration.

An End to Party Politics

The Bolsheviks' elimination of competing parties and movements proceeded just as swiftly as circumstances allowed. A minority party which is beset with enemies and refuses all genuine coalitions must eliminate its competitors or go under. The Constituent Assembly posed a serious threat, as it possessed a stamp of legitimacy more potent than that of the Congress of Soviets. Its sessions had hardly begun when it was closed down under a flimsy pretext by armed Bolshevik detachments. After that, the parties which had held seats in the Constituent Assembly were dealt with one by one. The nonsocialist parties were the first victims, above all the Kadets. Opposition newspapers, including those supporting the Kadets, had been shut down soon after the Bolshevik seizure of power, and a number of Kadet leaders remained under arrest. Both wings of the Social Revolutionaries were attacked in the summer of 1918, a political assassination serving as the pretext for repression. At this point the Central Executive Committee was cleansed not only of all its Social Revolutionary members, but of Mensheviks as well.

After this, the only legal opposition groups were factions of Bolsheviks, and these played a vigorous political role during the entire Civil War period (1918–20). With the end of the war emergency and the beginning of NEP, one might imagine that Lenin would at least be content to allow free rein to these factions in discussions within the Party. Quite the contrary, his need for a tightly knit political instrument was even greater, now that concessions to capitalism were necessary. At the 10th Party Congress, in March 1921, the "Resolution on Unity" (quoted at the beginning of this chapter) proclaimed an end to all factional activity. No longer could groups of Party members, regardless under what banner, offer their proposals and platforms at Party gatherings. The possibility of initiative was taken away from the Party rank and file. Initiative thereby became a prerogative of the Party leadership and of the swiftly growing bureaucracy which it now commanded. The philosophy of organization which Lenin had employed during the years in exile, when the Party had numbered a few thousand, was now applied to the half-million members of the Party in power.

Lenin and Stalin both learned that opposition and division are not ended by the stroke of a pen. Parties could be proscribed, but party loyalties remained and provided a basis for action when the opportunity came up. Factional activity could be prohibited, as was done in 1921, but factions persisted to the end of the 1920s, and in fact have never been entirely absent from Soviet politics. Stalin could order the Politburo to take its decisions unanimously, as he did in 1929, but this did not put an end to sharp divisions among Politburo members.

Both Mensheviks and Social Revolutionaries survived the Civil War as movements, if not as organized parties. Adherents of both played a role in the mutiny of March 1921 on the island of Kronstadt, a key naval base in the Gulf of Finland not many miles from Petrograd. Bolshevik troops were storming this island across the ice at the same time the 10th Party Congress was debating the Resoluton on Unity. Lenin, in advocating this ominous resolution, was occupied not just with divisions "within the family," among loyal Bolsheviks; he was thinking also what might happen if the Mensheviks and Social Revolutionaries, in the more permissive atmosphere of the 1920s, were to exploit these divisions. Such a thing had already happened, in fact: Only a few months after the Bolsheviks assumed power, Lenin had seen the left-wing Social Revolutionaries make common cause with Nikolai Bukharin and a group that was to be known as the "Left Communists." These opposed Lenin's proposed peace with Germany on the ground that it meant betrayal of the coming international revolution.

Party Factions Are Undermined

In reviewing the demands that were being put forth by dissident Bolshevik groups in 1920–21, one is struck by the extent to which these groups accepted the kind of tactics which were creating a Party autocracy. The "Workers' Opposition," headed by A. G. Shlyapnikov, consisted not primarily of workers but of Bolshevik trade union officials. Many of them had attained their positions by electoral fraud and pressure tactics, which had served to oust Mensheviks and other non-Bolsheviks from union leadership. Their demands centered around a larger role and more autonomy for the unions. They objected, for example, to continued Party meddling in union elections, even though it was by such methods they were kept in their posts. They regarded the employment of noncommunist experts in industry as class betrayal. Finally, and most importantly, they maintained that control over industry should be effected by a central trade union organization. This was something of a concession to syndicalist sentiment, which called for direct worker control in each industry separately. But it also met the Marxist requirement that the proletariat exercise central control over the economy.

The "Democratic Centralists," who had once included Bukharin, objected to Lenin's increasingly authoritarian management of the Party. They objected likewise to the Party's high-handed management of the local soviets. At the same time, they made no protest over the way in which Party majorities were secured in the local soviets. The Democratic Centralists, like the Workers' Opposition, stopped short of demanding that democracy be thoroughgoing. Each accepted the degree of authoritarian control by which it had attained its privileged position.

As the time for the 10th Party Congress approached, serious dissent outside the Party was on the upswing too. The emergencies of the Civil War had passed, Lenin had made some enormous economic concessions in introducing the NEP, and the Party appeared very much on the defensive. The political groups that had been formally suppressed, though still in existence, had let slip whatever chances they may have had to resist and overthrow the Bolsheviks. This was partly because they feared playing into the hands of the White forces in the Civil War. In their weakened state, they now attempted a reckoning. Mensheviks and Social Revolutionaries were being elected in large numbers to the local soviets. There were serious disturbances in the countryside, and in February 1921 Petrograd saw an alarming series of strikes and workers' demonstrations. Then, just a week before the Party Congress was to open, the Kronstadt rebels (see above) set forth a truly radical list of demands: political freedoms for all working-class parties, an end to the Communist Party's privileged position, an end to Party domination over the soviets, peasant proprietorship of the land, liberation of political prisoners, and other demands of this kind.

The Kronstadt uprising was short-lived: Within two weeks it was suppressed by a Red Army invasion of the island, and it had sparked no similar rebellions in the rest of the country. Nevertheless the Bolshevik leaders were shaken by this episode, and it doubtless hastened the tightening of discipline within the Party. In preparation for the 10th Congress, Lenin and the leading Bolsheviks had encouraged the presentation of alternative platforms, including those of the Workers' Opposition and the Democratic Centralists. Indeed, Lenin himself sponsored a "Platform of Ten" as a counterweight to these; on paper, at least, it embodied a good many concessions to the two dissident groups. But by the end of the Congress, this form of Party debate had been banned; the Central Committee had been given enormous powers over the Party's membership; and the distinctions among opposition within the Party, working-class opposition outside the Party, and counterrevolutionary activity had been blurred in a fashion that could be used to equate opposition with treason.

While the Resolution on Unity did not succeed in putting an immediate end to factionalism as such, it did greatly accelerate the process of narrowing the scope of policy discussions at Party gatherings. It benefited the Party bureaucracy at all levels by removing the basis for attacking whatever policies the bureaucracy put forth. Without the swift growth of a centrally directed bureaucracy, however, factionalism might have gone on indefinitely. At first, during the Civil War period, it was not mainly the great national policy issues that created local factions,

since these issues were only taking shape. Local factionalism was such
more a product of local issues, personality clashes, and microcosmic struggles for leadership. But these were pervasive phenomena, and if factionalism was not to become a way of life for the Party, which would expose
the Party to the incursions of its political foes, a permanent antidote
must be found. From 1920 on, an antidote was swiftly concocted in
the form of a centralized bureaucratic apparatus capable of serving as
the real backbone of a partially democratic policy-making structure.
Chapter 6 explains this in detail.

Non-Russian Bolsheviks

During these same early years of Soviet rule, one more kind of dissident
Party organization was brought to heel in Lenin's drive for discipline:
the non-Russian national parties. Lenin's policy of self-determination for
the non-Russian peoples of the Empire, formulated some years before
the Revolution, was affirmed by a decree of the new Bolshevik regime
immediately after the coup. The idea of self-determination was soon modified to mean self-determination for the working people of a given nationality; separatist movements of non-working-class parties were to be
resisted. There was never any doubt that the Bolshevik leaders were
working toward two objectives: revolutions in the non-Russian areas carried out by Bolshevik parties, and federal union with these areas. The
Russian Republic Constitution of 1918 established a federal structure.
A larger federal union, embracing all or most of the nations within the
former Russian Empire, was declared by the 1919 Party Program to
be a transitional form to complete unity.

All this was obvious from Lenin's statements on the subject, and from
many Party pronouncements. What was now added—though one might
have deduced this already from Lenin's views on Party unity—was the
Russian Party's claim to jurisdiction over the non-Russian parties. In
the eyes of the Bolshevik leaders, the Ukrainian, Georgian, Armenian,
and other parties were branch organizations subject to the Central Committee just as were the Russian provincial organizations. Enforcing this
view was a task left to none other than Stalin, who from 1917 on headed
the People's Commissariat for Nationality Affairs. Non-Russian though
he himself was, he was responsible for staffing the local communist parties
with a high proportion of Russians. Part of this was understandable in
view of the fact that the non-Russian areas were little industrialized,
had no proletariat to speak of, and, except in Georgia, had produced
few social democrats. Yet Stalin and others were sufficiently heavy-
handed in imposing Russian leadership that they kindled resentment
among the non-Russian communists.

Georgian Mensheviks and "Great-Russian Chauvinism"

During the Civil War, some of the non-Russian areas had been in effect conquered by the Red Army, and Russian-dominated Party organizations had been set up on the heels of the conquest. The case of Georgia was different. There the social democratic movement had established itself firmly long before the Revolution, and it was Mensheviks who dominated the movement. In 1919 the Mensheviks had won four fifths of the seats in the Georgian National Assembly. The Menshevik-led Georgian Republic had been recognized not only by major foreign powers, but by Moscow itself, in a treaty of May 1920. Unfortunately, a secret clause of this same treaty had legalized the miniscule group of Georgian Bolsheviks, and they now helped prepare for Russian reconquest. Stalin together with Sergo Ordzhonikidze organized a brief, successful invasion early in 1921. Lenin had opposed this plan at first, then changed his mind. However, he was increasingly disturbed at the vengeance which Stalin and Ordzhonikidze had brought on the heads of Georgian Mensheviks and Bolsheviks alike. Ordzhonikidze, in particular, was ruling Georgia like a viceroy as head of the Party's North Caucasian Bureau.

For a year and a half, Lenin publicly supported Stalin and Ordzhonikidze on the Georgian matter, whatever private doubts he may have harbored. He was much occupied with the question of nationalities and federation, since 1922 saw the approval of a draft constitution which would bring four nominally separate socialist republics into the Union of Soviet Socialist Republics. In May 1922 he suffered a stroke which removed him from active leadership, though he still continued to dictate orders and correspondence. In the fall of 1922 he suddenly changed his mind about the Georgian problem; in three sharply worded memoranda, he attacked "Great-Russian chauvinism," blamed Stalin and Ordzhonikidze directly for the troubles of the Georgian communists, and expressed his fear that Moscow's administrative domination over the Georgian party was only imperialism in Soviet disguise.

There is an aura of tragedy about the last year of Lenin's life. Because Lenin's insight into the root of his problems with Stalin and others remained partial at best, his life could not but end in half-grasped tragedy. He saw the Party's mistakes in Georgia as the fault of wrongheaded leadership, which he now ascribed to Stalin's power hunger and inability to deal tactfully with those who crossed him. In his "Testament" of December 1922, a memorandum known to other Party leaders but half-suppressed at the time, he found fault with all his potential successors. But Lenin's judgment of his associates was faulty too. He had entrusted none other than Trotsky with the job of bringing his memoranda on "Great-Russian chauvinism" and other matters before the 11th Party

Congress. Trotsky, for reasons of his own, made no use of the memoranda. He thereby let pass a magnificent opportunity to undercut Stalin, and he was in some embarrassment when the existence of the memoranda was discovered on the eve of the Congress. Meanwhile Lenin's relations with Stalin had become quite embittered. In a codicil to the "Testament" dictated in time to be used at the Congress, Lenin criticized Stalin both for his rudeness and for his dangerous accumulation of power. He proposed that Stalin be removed as General Secretary, the post created for him just eight months previously. Both the Testament and its codicil were read to the 13th Party Congress in 1924, just after Lenin's death, but not circulated in printed form. Stalin offered his resignation to the Central Commitee, but the latter unanimously—including Trotsky—urged him to stay in his post, and the whole matter was dropped. The Testament was not to raise its head again in the Soviet Union until Khrushchev pulled it out in 1956.

PARTY UNITY BECOMES A MYSTIQUE

In tracing the principle of Party discipline and the end of such democracy as had existed within the Party, it is possible to end the main narrative with 1921 or 1923, and call the rest epilogue. Such is the interpretation in this book. It is all too easy to come under the impression that the fate of democracy within the Party was resolved by the final triumph of Stalin over his colleagues. But how would his rivals have ruled, had the triumph been theirs? Zinoviev ruled his important Leningrad fiefdom with an iron hand; an impassioned orator and demagogue, he also managed the affairs of the Communist International (Comintern) in a way that gave no suggestion of democratic leanings. Kamenev, the very prototype of the future Party *apparatchik*, ruled the Moscow organization similarly. Both men gave Stalin emphatic support at a Party conference early in 1924, where they condemned Trotsky's plea for a revival of Party democracy. Stalin at this point published the hitherto secret seventh clause of the Resolution on Unity, which empowered the Central Commitee to expel any member from the Party, including Central Commitee members, for factional activity.

As for Trotsky, his *Pravda* article "The New Course" (of December 1923) was indeed a plea for Party democracy and an attack on the power of the Party bureaucracy. He had argued against Lenin on this score at the 10th Congress and subsequently. But his leadership of the Red Army in the Civil War, and later his management of the Central Transport Commission (*Tsektran*), show an autocratic disposition not unlike that of his rivals. As head of *Tsektran* he sought to bring the labor unions under strict government control and pressed for a kind of labor discipline that resembled military organization. Even while fulminating against violations of Party democracy by the apparatus (bureaucracy), he was urging a Party dictatorship over the nation which even Lenin found extreme. He disdained Party infighting, a trait which certainly hastened his defeat; he had attempted to stand above factions, joining neither Bolsheviks nor Mensheviks until after the Revolution; he was not averse to building up a personal following with which to bolster his position among the leaders. All in all, the fears of Trotsky's rivals that he could become the Napoleon Bonaparte of the Russian Revolution were not unfounded.[8]

What bound the Bolshevik leaders together in spite of all their disagreements on policy was the belief that the Party, exercising its dictatorship over the nation, must itself be tightly disciplined. The real argument between Trotsky and the rest on this score was not over discipline, but how to achieve it. Since Trotsky had no entering wedge in the Party apparatus whereby he could maintain his grip on the making of policies, he could safely argue against the growing bureaucratization of the policy process. Had Trotsky succeeded in clearing the way for open factionalism, his conduct leaves little doubt that he would have used the weight of the Party bureaucracy in order to smash opposing factions, much as Stalin did. After the death of Lenin in January 1924, not even Trotsky was willing to risk an open confrontation. At the 14th Party Congress in 1925 he refused to make use of Lenin's "Testament," to the extent of denying its existence, just as he had refused to use Lenin's memoranda on "Great-Russian chauvinism" two years earlier. Thus even the leader most likely to profit by splitting the Party leadership and capitalizing on dissent balked at this step. It remained for Stalin to employ this tactic, but only at such a time as he was certain that the split would outflank his rivals and make their surrender inevitable. Trotsky, unwittingly, had already set the terms of his surrender in a statement to the 13th Congress, acknowledging a resolution that condemned his article on "The New Course": "My party—right or wrong. . . . I know one cannot be right against the party . . . for history has not created other ways for the realization of what is right."[9]

The Politics of the "Great Debate"

We saw in chapters 1 and 2 the positions of the "Right" and "Left" during the 1920s on economic issues, and the political use of these positions. An oft-told story full of policy switches and zigzags, it began with Stalin, Kamenev, and Zinoviev united against what appeared to be a threat from Trotsky in 1923–24. Trotsky counterattacked from a

---

[8] See Isaac Deutscher, *The Prophet Armed: Trotsky: 1897–1921* (New York: Vintage Books, 1965), chapter 14.

[9] Schapiro, *The Communist Party of the Soviet Union*, p. 284.

rather shaky platform of militancy in pressing for an international proletarian revolution. In 1925 Stalin, more for reasons of power than because of policy disagreements, undercut Zinoviev's Party fiefdom in Leningrad (as Petrograd had been renamed) and removed Kamenev from both his top national economic post and his leadership of the Moscow municipal government. Bukharin at this point rendered full support to Stalin, defending him against the charge that the NEP's land policy was a backward step toward capitalism. In 1926, Trotsky, Zinoviev, and Kamenev patched up their own feuds in an effort to form a united front against Stalin. The Resolution on Unity notwithstanding, they presented a platform of their own on economic policy to the Central Committee, which resulted in Zinoviev's expulsion from the Politburo. When Trotsky and Zinoviev attempted a counterattack at the Party's "grass roots," in a number of important Party cells, Stalin succeeded in frightening them into a public statement admitting their violation of Party discipline. Zinoviev, already removed as head of the Leningrad party organization, now lost his position in the Communist International. Stalin, who for the moment was restrained by the "Right" wing of the Politburo, had the Central Committee expel Trotsky and Zinoviev, then accepted a compromise which restored their seats.

At the 15th Congress, in the summer of 1927, the opposition once again tried to present its own platform, which aimed at nothing less than a removal of Stalin and other leaders. Balked in this attempt, they took to the streets in a series of demonstrations on the tenth anniversary of the Bolshevik seizure of power. This ultimate, futile gesture resulted in immediate expulsion from the Party for Trotsky, Zinoviev, and nearly 100 key members of the opposition. Trotsky was deported to Alma-Ata, thousands of miles to the east, then in 1929 expelled from the Soviet Union itself. Zinoviev and Kamenev were readmitted to the Party in 1928, suffered a year of penal exile in 1933, and reappeared at the 17th "Congress of Victors" in 1934 to confess their errors once again. Early in 1935 they and others were tried in secret and imprisoned, only to be called as star performers in the great purge trial of 1936, which charged them with leading a Trotskyite "terrorist center."

Party Unity and a Bolshevik Conscience

In chapter 2 we saw the defeat of Bukharin, Rykov, and the "Right" on the agricultural question. These two plus Tomsky, the trade union leader, were removed from their leading posts during the first fall and winter of collectivization (1929–30). They occupied lesser bureaucratic posts thereafter, and were reelected to the Central Committee as candidate (probationary) members in 1934 after making their recantations once again before the 17th Congress. Tomsky committed suicide in 1936, when he fell under the shadow of one of Vyshinsky's investigations. Bukharin and Rykov were the principal defendants of the show trial of March 1938, which labeled them as leaders of the "Anti-Soviet Bloc of the Rightists and Trotskyites."

Bukharin's conduct at this trial illuminates in almost agonizing fashion the hold of the Party's mystique over men's lives. Where others under similar pressure had confessed to all the absurd charges of treason and subversion in order to spare themselves further torture, and also in the conviction that they could thus serve the Party as their dying act, Bukharin turned out to be a somewhat unsatisfactory defendant. True, he did follow the example of his co-defendants in confessing to the crime of "counterrevolution," meaning that he had endangered Party unity by his opposition. However, Bukharin had, in fact, approached the defeated Left in 1928 after Trotsky's banishment, in hopes of forming a united front against Stalin. Already there were rumors that Stalin was about to take up the Left's policies and perhaps reinstate its leaders. Nothing came of the effort—Trotsky himself thought the gulf between Right and Left still very wide—but this desperate gambit doubtless weighed heavily on his conscience after his arrest. Bukharin denied having taken part in a plot on Lenin's life, and he denied likewise having conspired with foreign governments. Throughout his defense he gave the impression of one who, while desiring to cooperate with the Party to which he had devoted his life, sought to preserve his integrity in so doing. After echoing Trotsky's admission of a dozen years earlier that no one could be right against the Party, he then reconciled personal integrity with abject surrender to the needs of the Party:

> When you ask yourself: 'If you must die, what are you dying for?'—an absolute black vacuity suddenly rises before you with startling vividness. There was nothing to die for, if one wanted to die unrepentant. And, on the contrary, everything positive that glistens in the Soviet Union acquires new dimensions in a man's mind. This in the end disarmed me completely and led me to bend my knees before the party and the country. And when you ask yourself: 'Very well, suppose you do not die; suppose by some miracle you remain alive— again what for? Isolated from everybody, an enemy of the people, in an inhuman position, completely isolated from everything that constitutes the essence of life.' . . . The result is the complete internal moral victory of the USSR over its kneeling opponents.[10]

While the spectacular trials and confessions of the 1930s were never repeated, the whole concept of Party orthodoxy and heresy which attended them has remained to this day. It has been both an advantage and a liability, depending on the circumstances. In times of stress, such

[10] Robert Vincent Daniels, *The Conscience of the Revolution* (New York: Clarion Books, 1969), pp. 389–90.

as the period following Khrushchev's denunciation of Stalin's misdeeds in 1956, it has served to hold the ranks together. But it has also served to inhibit discussion and initiative in the Party's middle and lower levels. In situations where more ideas might have been advantageous, for example in the debate over economic reforms in the 1960s, discussions reported by the Party press indicate that it was only the narrow range of alternatives generated by the Secretariat and Party leadership that was under consideration. It is but a few steps from unity to rigidity, and since Stalin's time the Party has been in constant danger of succumbing to the latter.

FOR FURTHER READING

The best history of the Communist Party, from its earliest origins, is that of Leonard Schapiro, *The Communist Party of the Soviet Union* (New York: Vintage Books, 1964). Somewhat less satisfactory is the account of John S. Reshetar, Jr., *A Concise History of the Communist Party of the Soviet Union* (New York: Praeger, 1960).

Concerning the origins and early struggles of the Party, one of the most interesting and readable accounts is a triple biography of the careers of Lenin, Stalin, and Trotsky up to 1917, Bertram D. Wolfe, *Three Who Made a Revolution: A Biographical History* (New York: Dial Press, 1948). See also Leopold H. Haimson, *The Russian Marxists and the Origins of Bolshevism* (Cambridge, Mass.: Harvard University Press, 1955); J. L. H. Keep, *The Rise of Social Democracy in Russia* (Oxford: The Clarendon Press, 1963); and Donald W. Treadgold, *Lenin and His Rivals: The Struggle for Russia's Future, 1898–1906* (New York: Praeger, 1955).

No biography of Lenin is completely satisfactory, but a good introductory account is David Shub, *Lenin* (New York: Mentor Books, 1950). Louis Fischer, *The Life of Lenin* (New York: Harper Colophon Books, 1964) devotes its main attention to Lenin's few years in power, and is a detailed and highly competent account. A complete English translation of the 4th Soviet edition of Lenin's *Collected Works* is available in 45 volumes (Moscow: Foreign Languages Publishing House, 1960–1970). Of the many collections of Lenin's main writings, a very useful one, embracing a great many writings in chronological order, is James E. Connor (ed.), *Lenin on Politics and Revolution* (New York: Pegasus, 1968). Trotsky's major writings are easily available. *The Permanent Revolution* is placed in a single volume with *Results and Prospects* (New York: Pioneer Publishers, 1965). Others are *The Real Situation in Russia* (New York: Harcourt, Brace, 1928) and *The Revolution Betrayed* (New York: Pioneer Publishers, 1945).

One way of approaching the enormous volume of literature on the Russian Revolution is to compare the accounts of its major actors. After sampling Lenin's writings of 1917 and afterwards, one may read the following: N. N. Sukhanov, *The Russian Revolution 1917: Eyewitness Account* (2 vols.; New York: Harper Torchbooks, 1962), a Menshevik view; V. M. Chernov, *The Great Russian Revolution* (New Haven, Conn.: Yale University Press,

1936), the account of the Social Revolutionary leader and chairman of the Constituent Assembly of 1918; and Trotsky's *The History of the Russian Revolution* (3 vols.; New York: Simon and Schuster, 1932). John Reed's *Ten Days That Shook the World* (New York: Vintage Books, 1960) is a gripping first-hand account by an American socialist sympathetic to the Bolsheviks.

Two excellent volumes detail the manner in which the Party consolidated its monopoly of power after the Revolution: Robert V. Daniels, *The Conscience of the Revolution: Communist Opposition in Soviet Russia* (Cambridge, Mass.: Harvard University Press, 1960), and Leonard Schapiro, *The Origin of the Communist Autocracy* (Cambridge, Mass.: Harvard University Press, 1955). Trotsky's role in this period is dealt with in the middle volume of Isaac Deutscher's excellent three-volume history, *The Prophet Unarmed; Trotsky: 1921–1929* (New York: Vintage Books, 1965).

The only English edition of Stalin's writings is incomplete (as is the Russian edition too, incidentally), ending in 1934: J. Stalin, *Works* (13 vols.; Moscow: Foreign Languages Publishing House, 1954). A "must" for those approaching his writings for the first time is his 1925 essay *Foundations of Leninism* (New York: International Publishers, 1939). Two rather different accounts of his career are Isaac Deutscher, *Stalin: A Political Biography* (New York: Oxford University Press, 1949), and H. Montgomery Hyde, *Stalin: The History of A Dictator* (New York: Farrar, Straus and Giroux, 1972). New light was shed on Stalin the man, and to a limited extent on his political milieu, in the accounts of his daughter, Svetlana Alliluyeva, *Twenty Letters to a Friend* (New York: Harper and Row, 1967), and *Only One Year* (New York: Harper and Row, 1969).

Schapiro's history of the Party, cited the outset, covers the politics of the Stalin period admirably, also the structural evolution of the Party. Penetrating and well-informed essays are offered by Boris I. Nicolaevsky, *Power and the Soviet Elite* (New York: Praeger, 1965). Robert Conquest, *The Great Terror* (New York: Macmillan, 1968) is an authoritative and highly detailed account of the Great Purge. A "Kremlinological" account of Stalin's rule from 1934, and carried into the early Khrushchev period, is John Armstrong, *The Politics of Totalitarianism* (New York: Random House, 1961).

5

PARTY LEADERSHIP AFTER STALIN

STALIN'S DAUGHTER, Svetlana Alliluyeva, was a witness to the first scene of the power struggle that followed upon Stalin's death, one which began even as Stalin lay dying in the presence of his Politburo associates on March 5, 1953:

> There was only one person who was behaving in a way that was nearly obscene. That was Beria. He was extremely agitated. His face, repulsive enough at the best of times, now was twisted by his passions— by ambition, cruelty, cunning and a lust for power and more power still. He was trying so hard at this moment of crisis to strike exactly the right balance, to be cunning, yet not too cunning. It was written all over him. He went up to the bed and spent a long time gazing into the dying man's face. From time to time my father opened his eyes but was apparently unconscious or in a state of semiconsciousness. Beria stared fixedly at those clouded eyes, anxious even now to convince my father that he was the most loyal and devoted of them all, as he had always tried with every ounce of his strength to appear to be. . . .
>
> During the final minutes, as the end was approaching, Beria suddenly caught sight of me and ordered: "Take Svetlana away!" Those who were standing nearby stared but no one moved. Afterward he darted into the hallway ahead of anybody else. The silence of the room where everyone was gathered around the deathbed was shattered by the sound of his loud voice, the ring of triumph unconcealed, as he shouted, "Khrustalyov! My car!" [Khrustalyov was the head of Stalin's personal bodyguard.][1]

---

[1] Svetlana Alliluyeva, *Twenty Letters to a Friend* (New York: Harper & Row, 1967), pp. 7–8.

Beria's maneuvers at this point were not, in fact, the beginning of a power struggle, but a renewal of struggles that had never entirely stopped during Stalin's quarter-century of rule. Stalin himself had been wary of the amount of power Beria had concentrated in his hands. Beria had become general overseer of the nation's internal security at the close of the Great Purge. While Stalin clearly valued his services in this role, he was careful not to give Beria absolute control over the nation's several police forces, the security police (today the KGB) having been separated from the Ministry of the Interior, which controlled the regular police. Furthermore, in 1951–52, a number of Beria's close political associates in his native Georgia were arrested (the "Mingrelian conspiracy") and V. S. Abakumov, a longtime supporter of Beria, was removed from his post as head of the security police. Less than two months before Stalin's death, a group of Jewish doctors was accused of having caused the death of Zhdanov in 1948 and of complicity in a major plot against other Soviet leaders. Hence Stalin's death cut short what would very likely have turned into a major purge, in which Beria would doubtless have been prominent among the victims. Stalin's ruthless personal dictatorship, far from having crushed factional intrigue and struggles for power, served rather to intensify them.

Beria, after his boorish exit from the dead dictator's house in a Moscow suburb, moved swiftly. The very next day, at the same time Malenkov was made head of government, Beria took all the nation's police forces under his control as Minister of the Interior. It was his troops and armored units, not those of the Soviet Army, which stood about the capital in readiness for any eventuality. He, along with Malenkov and Molotov, delivered the major eulogies at Stalin's funeral. It is not clear why he then hesitated for several months in using his vast police power to seize political control from his associates. Possibly he needed to strengthen his hold in several ways before taking the risky final step. Late in June he was placed under arrest, charged with attempting to seize power, spying for foreign governments, and attempting to overthrow the whole Soviet system. In December he and six other defendants were tried *in camera* and shot at once. As this was happening, it was the Soviet Army's tanks that stood in readiness around Moscow, not those of the Interior Ministry. In a sense, Beria was the last victim of Stalin's several purges, though Stalin was now dead. While leading political figures since 1953 have been removed from their posts against their will, to face retirement, demotion, and sometimes demotion to obscurity, none has been executed or charged with fantastic crimes.[2]

---

[2] See the account of these events in John A. Armstrong, *The Politics of Totalitarianism* (New York: Random House, 1961), ch. 18.

INTERPRETING SOVIET LEADERSHIP

Beria's bid for power led some observers to believe that the Soviet system required an all-powerful dictator, whose death or overthrow could only result in a life-and-death struggle among his erstwhile lieutenants (as in the 1920s) until another absolute dictator gained power. Events after 1953, however, suggest that while strong individual leadership appears necessary, the manner of leadership is too complex to be understood through any such simple formula. The most interesting question is whether the nature of leadership is undergoing any kind of long-term change. Is the Soviet political system becoming pluralistic, with the leader's assuming more and more the role of mediator and persuader, and abandoning that of dictator?

Here we are concerned with the manner of leadership at the very top. However, much of the evidence we possess concerning this leadership can be found in the ways in which the top figures deal with the relations of "groups," however defined. More evidence may be gained from the policies and statements of leaders concerning Soviet society. One example is the way in which Malenkov, Khrushchev, and Brezhnev each in turn, at a time he believed auspicious, made a major appeal to the Soviet consumer; this suggests that each believed that such an appeal would build his leadership role. Unfortunately for the purpose of studying Soviet leadership, most of the overt evidence consists in the public initiatives taken by the top leader. All else must be deduced from fragmentary data, such as perfunctory rather than enthusiastic support of a policy on the part of a Politburo member. More concrete evidence may wait for years before coming to light: counterarguments presented by other leaders, the slow sabotage of policies by various administrative hierarchies, temporary alliances for the purpose of reducing a leader's influence, and much else.[3]

The core of the Soviet political process, the way in which important political decisions are made, involves several kinds of relationships. One is the relationship among the top leaders, the nature of their discussions and other interactions, and the way in which their work produces political choices. At a minimum, this group includes the 25 men who are either Politburo members or Party Secretaries (seven of them are both); students of Soviet politics often include a much larger circle. Another relationship is that between the top leaders and the various institutions which comprise the Soviet system. Do the top leaders speak for "groups," and are they able to use these "groups" in order to make their weight felt in top decisions? Groups may be highly specific structures, such as the

---

[3] Those who may be skeptical about the kind of evidence used by "Kremlinologists" will profit by reading chapters 4 and 5 in Sidney I. Ploss (ed.), *The Soviet Political Process: Aims, Techniques and Examples of Analysis* (Waltham, Mass.: Ginn, 1971).

Ministry of Defense; they may be presumed combinations of structures, such as the heavy industrial ministries, or a Soviet version of the "military-industrial complex"; they may be categories of people which cut across structures, such as agricultural officialdom (some speak of an "agricultural lobby"), the directors of the mass media, or agencies dealing with housing questions.

A third relationship is that between the central decision-making process and the entire society. This relationship is most commonly seen as determining the interactions of leaders and groups in certain important ways. Beria's bid for power, for example, was made possible by his control of an enormous, all-pervasive security police, which in turn had grown out of Lenin's and Stalin's determination to maintain thoroughgoing control over social processes. Or, one may see the expanded top-level consultation and discussion processes of the post-Stalin era not only as the source of loosened social control, but eventually as its result as well.

Theories of leadership are important here insofar as they help explain whether the Soviet Union—or any system similarly organized—can expect stable and effective leadership in the long run. One of the most familiar (and today most criticized) theories, that of Friedrich and Brzezinski, finds that a Soviet-type system requires a strong, charismatic figure as a guarantee of stability. Unlike many despots and monarchs of earlier systems, the totalitarian leader operates through a mystique or charisma adapted to the society of the present century, which unites him with the mass of his followers. He uses mass propaganda and terror to bolster his rule. He operates through an oligarchy of powerful lieutenants, but takes care that none aspires to his position. And in consequence of these methods, according to the totalitarianism theory, the modern totalitarian ruler is more powerful than the absolute rulers of the past.[4]

Other observers believe quite the contrary, that developments in the Soviet system after the death of Stalin have changed the nature and tasks of the leadership. The application of interest-group concepts to the Soviet system has produced the suggestion that the Soviet Union is producing some features of interest-group politics as they are known in the West, even if this process is unlikely to lead to a Western-type democratic system:

> In the post-Stalin era, with the circle of decision-making widening and public discussion less restricted, the party chiefs must more and more give attention to forming a consensus among competing policy groups, specialist elites, differing viewpoints within the party, professional and other associations, and broader amorphous social groupings.[5]

---

[4] Carl J. Friedrich and Zbigniew K. Brzezinski, *Totalitarian Dictatorship and Autocracy*, 2d ed. rev. (New York: Praeger, 1965), chapter 3.

[5] H. Gordon Skilling, "Interest Groups and Communist Politics," in Ploss, *The Soviet Political Process*, p. 32.

However, it has yet to be shown that the role of groups in the Soviet Union might one day be able to transcend the limits imposed by one-party rule. Brezezinski, in a study which departed in some respects from the notion of totalitarian rule, compared American and Soviet decision-making processes in terms of the stages of initiation, persuasion, decision, and execution. The four stages, he found, are closely linked in the Soviet Union through the Party bureaucracy; in the United States they are performed through different, specialized institutions. Thus in the Soviet Union the impact of interest groups is contained in a manner that permits policy making to be dominated by a small circle of leaders, whatever the differences may be among the latter. Therefore the growth of the interest-group phenomenon in Soviet politics is unlikely to lead to any "convergence" of Soviet-type and Western-type political systems.[6]

Another dimension of Soviet leadership is that of conflict versus stability in relationships among the top leaders, quite apart from the institutions, groups, and policy issues which give rise to their debates. Conflict and instability may be endemic to the top leadership without being reflected in the system as a whole. "Kremlinology," which stresses leadership conflicts, is often criticized for underestimating the importance of substantive issues and developments in the political system as a whole. In some ways the "Kremlinological" writings offer a static picture of Soviet leadership, in that they stress recurring patterns of conflict which assert themselves in spite of changes in the larger system.[7] Great importance is attached to the lack of an effective legitimizing organ of power—a point disputed by other observers—and to the Soviet system's apparent failure to develop an orderly manner of succession to the top leadership post, the General Secretaryship. While to all appearances the Brezhnev administration has been the most stable one so far in its ability to cope with differences and tensions, one knowledgeable observer found "a continuing struggle by Brezhnev's rivals to curb his assumption of greater authority and to preserve a balance of power between party and state."[8] In defense of this approach, it must be said that certain problems of power relationships, particularly those having to do with succession, seem endemic to nondemocratic systems generally, including the monarchies and empires of past centuries. We shall note these problems and the way in which they have cropped up in the Soviet setting. The larger question, however, is whether the way in which they have occurred

---

[6] Zbigniew Brzezinski and Samuel P. Huntington, *Political Power USA/USSR* (New York: Viking Press, 1965), chapter 4 and Conclusion.

[7] See for example R. Conquest, *Power and Policy in the U.S.S.R.* (London: Macmillan, 1962), chapters 1–3; and John A. Armstrong, *The Politics of Totalitarianism* (New York: Random House, 1961), especially chapter 25.

[8] Sidney I. Ploss, "The Rise of Brezhnev," in Ploss, *The Soviet Political Process*, p. 293.

tells us anything about the tendencies of the Soviet decision-making process as a whole, and its possible future paths of evolution.

THE DILEMMA OF THE SUCCESSION TO STALIN

The aftermath of Stalin's death showed one of the grave flaws of absolute rule: The absolute ruler needs lieutenants to enforce his rule; they must be entrusted with power in their own right, but their hold on power must be sufficiently ambiguous to prevent them from entrenching themselves too well in their separate empires. They are a danger to the ruler, and they become more of a danger as the ruler grows older. None of them can be appointed crown prince, for such a step promptly turns the crown prince into the object of high-powered intrigue. Even genuine hereditary princes had this problem in Russia: Peter the Great imprisoned his own son for this reason; after Alexis died in prison, Peter issued a decree enabling him to appoint his own successor, then (perhaps wisely) made no use of it.

There is an analogous danger in the ruler's building a powerful instrument of control and reprisal to break up centers of opposition. Those who wield the instrument can turn it against the ruler, and police instruments have a way of running amok once they are in action. Beria during 1950–53 was an obvious case of the first danger; Yezhov, his predecessor, not only had developed a psychopathic urge to shoot and imprison during 1937, but may not have been able to control the terror apparatus which was then filling the labor camps and the execution cellars. Thus, also, Ivan the Terrible's *oprichniki*, the elite caste he created to fight the hereditary nobility, ran amok for seven years until Ivan was forced to disband it in 1572. Like the Soviet secret police, it had become a threat to the very foundation of government.

Restrictions on the Successor

Another problem of succession is that when a powerful ruler departs from the scene, for whatever reason, the nation's other powerful men may try to combine to avoid permitting such power to be concentrated in the hands of one person again. Thus, after Ivan the Terrible's death in 1584, the boyars (leading nobility) were lucky that Ivan's son was a weak and manipulable figure; a boyar-controlled rule was much to their liking. There are two dangers in such a development, however: the state may be weakened and become a prey to foreign powers, and the instability of what is in effect committee rule may provide a would-be absolute ruler with the chance he needs. Resurgent boyar power after Ivan's ime led to factional struggles which invited Polish intervention as well as internal rebellion in the "Time of Troubles." We have already seen how Stalin's political chances were enhanced when an unstable and noninstitutionalized triumvirate (Stalin, Zinoviev, and Kamenev) succeeded Lenin, who had found no one of his associates able to step into his shoes. The aftermath of Stalin's death produced a similarly unstable triumvirate of Malenkov, Molotov, and Beria.

The triumvirate did not fully emerge until Malenkov had briefly occupied Stalin's dual position as head of both Party and state. The day after Stalin died, a joint meeting of the Central Committee, Council of Ministers, and Supreme Soviet Presidium—at least the conclave was announced in these terms—made the first major changes: Malenkov was to be Chairman of the Council of Ministers, assisted by Beria, Molotov, Bulganin, and Kaganovich as his deputies, named in that order. The recently inflated Politburo ("Presidium" now) was restored to roughly its old size and composition; Beria was placed in charge of a unified police system; and some of the 50-odd ministries were consolidated. For a week, Malenkov was both head of government and the senior Party Secretary among seven Secretaries. These included Khrushchev, who had already been a Secretary for several years, but who now saw his control of the important Moscow Party organization snatched from under him. And during this same week, March 7–14, the Soviet press wrote Malenkov's name larger than the rest, so to speak, as the leader most worthy to succeed Stalin.

Stalin's Office Vanishes

One kind of political alternative probably did not occur to the boyars who descended like vultures on the remnants of Ivan the Terrible's rule after his death: smashing the throne and abolishing the office of Tsar. Nor would there have been any point in this: better to continue this useful institution while gutting its power by keeping a pliable ruler on the throne; to do otherwise would create the impression that Muscovite rule was in dissolution. Stalin's office of General Secretary, though it was recognized as quite important in the beginning, was not originally intended to be the supreme throne of the Soviet system. Lenin had ruled as Chairman of the Council of People's Commissars, also as a member of the Politburo, which had no formal head. Stalin, aside from membership on the Politburo and Orgburo, ruled *only* as General Secretary until 1940, when the international crisis impelled him to take over from Molotov as head of government.

Now, after Stalin's death, the General Secretaryship no longer existed. It was unclear, after the original announcement concerning appointments, what Malenkov's position among the Secretaries would be. Just a week later, this question was resolved in dramatic fashion when it was announced that Malenkov had given up his post as Secretary altogether.

Clearly there had been differences over this, for otherwise it would have been made public with the first round of appointments. Then the new leaders delayed yet another week before making known the Central Committee's action in a brief item in *Pravda*, another sign that it was a hotly disputed issue.

No one man was in command at this point; committee-style rule was in operation, the composition of the "committee" and the strength of its members varying with circumstances. Was another Stalin waiting in the wings, after Beria's arrest removed the one obvious claimant to this role? Few foreign commentators at this point mentioned Khrushchev as a successor. But Kremlinologists in the West were interested first of all in the fact that the same announcement which removed Malenkov as Secretary listed the five remaining Secretaries in nonalphabetical order, with Khrushchev first (the Russian letter X with which the name begins would otherwise have placed him fourth). Khrushchev spent the spring and summer of 1953 cutting a wide swath for himself among the Soviet leaders with his revelations about agriculture and his proposals for reform, as we saw in chapter 3. Early in September the Central Committee met again for the first time since it had expelled Beria, devoted itself entirely to Khrushchev's agricultural proposals, and then announced that he was elected *first* secretary. This title was not capitalized in print until 1955, a significant nuance. Leadership of the Party bureaucracy was thus restored, while the name of the office that had been occupied thus far only by Stalin was changed so as to connote a new style.

The Use of Symbols

To some this may seem an unimportant detail. Actually, if it had been unimportant, there would not have been six months of indecision about what to do with Stalin's trappings of office. The symbols of office can be of crucial importance in a situation where many men are trying to widen their grip on power. The order in which leaders are listed in official announcements, the sequence in which they stand in the tribune atop Lenin's mausoleum in Red Square to review parades, the presence or absence of certain leaders on official occasions—all these are means by which those in a position to manipulate the symbols communicate about their power, both to their influential associates and to Party members and the public. Though symbols are an indispensable tool of political leadership everywhere, there are two reasons why they loom so large in studying Soviet politics: 1. Information about the inner workings of policy making is particularly scarce in the case of the Soviet Union, so that symbols form a large part of the total information at our disposal. 2. Where advancement to leading positions occurs only within the framework of a single party-state hierarchy, rather than in substantive public discussions among candidates and groups, the use of symbols is likely to be more important as a vehicle for political contests.

Dropping the General Secretaryship for the time being was not quite the equivalent of smashing the Tsar's throne, since the principal organs of Soviet rule remained: the Party Central Committee, its long-neglected symbolic status somewhat restored by the 1952 Party Congress; the Council of Ministers; and the Presidium of the Supreme Soviet, whose functions were mainly symbolic and always had been. Since 1946, when Russian nationalism was toned down somewhat and the system's ideological basis given new emphasis, the symbolic stress on the Party's legitimizing role compensated for the reduction of the Party's status in the Great Purge. What was at stake in abolishing Stalin's office was leadership. The change sprang from the search for an acceptable formula for collective leadership in which both responsibilities and the symbols of power would be distributed somewhat, and not concentrated in the hands of one person. The Party press had begun stressing the slogan of "collective leadership" not long after Stalin's death. The term had been used not only in Lenin's time, but in the Stalin era as well, Stalin's own autocratic style notwithstanding. The use of the slogan in this context served to justify the division of leading posts and the absence of one all-powerful leader. It may also have been an admonition—from whom and to whom one may only speculate—about the danger that another Stalin might arise and seek to eradicate his opposition. By way of additional reassurance, Party statements now stressed that the Central Commitee and the Party's other leading organs were functioning regularly once more after years of neglect.

Collective Leadership

"Collective leadership" had been championed by Soviet leaders ever since Lenin, even by Stalin in his years of despotic power. The slogan has not meant, and probably was never intended to mean, rule by the Central Committee, Politburo, and Council of Ministers as groups of political equals, with no one figure having ultimate responsibility for policy. A realistic explanation of the phrase in its post-Stalin meaning would have to include: (1) decision of important policy matters in and through the legitimate leading bodies, especially the Central Committee; (2) full consultation between the political leader and the leading bodies in advance of decision; (3) abstention from extreme political reprisals as a means of ending opposition to the leader's policies within the leading bodies; and (4) the leader's agreement to remain "first among equals" and to refrain from attempting to use the symbols of Stalin-like dominance. Official commentary on these points has been something less than explicit, save for the first. The Central Committee, perhaps because it now numbered over 200 and included representatives of most of the nation's importance power structures, became the prime example of assertions that legitimacy had been restored through the device of collective leadership. Take for example a statement at the 20th Party Congress (1956) by Mikhail Suslov, the leading expert on theory in the Politburo then and now:

> One may say without the slightest doubt that the principle of collective leadership has been fully established in the Central Committee. Resolution of all the most important questions has passed into the hands of the Central Committee plenum meeting in regular sessions, a broad Party organ which functions on the basis of collegiality, and which is very closely linked to the most decisive parts of the structure of communist society.[9]

Accommodation between the necessity for a strong executive and the requirements of collective leadership is a never-ending problem. The extremes of political instability on the one hand and arbitrary leadership on the other have been recurrent dangers in Soviet political history. The two periods—the mid-1920s and 1953–55—in which the Soviet Union was without a powerful executive, one recognized by his associates as such, were also periods of leadership instability in the sense of strong factional strife, each factor reinforcing the other. Khrushchev, who publicly laid such stress on collective leadership and was also a strong executive, was removed in 1964 partly for his increasingly arbitrary personal leadership. Brezhnev and the men around him have clearly learned something from the past in this respect, even though there has been recent evidence of Brezhnev's attempts to heighten his leadership role, against a certain amount of opposition within the Politburo.

Legitimacy of the Central Committee

The term "legitimacy" has a number of possible meanings, only some of which are useful for understanding the workings of the Soviet Union's top political institutions.[10] What is important here is the recognition by Party members, particularly by those in important positions, that key decisions and the most significant personnel choices are made only through certain institutions and procedures. Whatever private political negotiations may transpire in order that these procedures be complied with, the important thing is that the institutions and procedures not be sub-

---

[9] *XX S'yezd KPSS*, vol. 1 (Moscow: Gospolitizdat, 1956), p. 278.

[10] For example, a definition of legitimacy which presupposes contests among candidates or parties for political leadership in a popular vote is clearly inapplicable here. To call the Soviet Union's leading political institutions "illegitimate" on the basis of such a definition hardly advances our knowledge of how their authority is actually derived.

verted or replaced. Stalin's decimation of the Central Committee in the Great Purge, for example, certainly qualifies as subversion, as does his failure to call Central Committee meetings at all during the last years of his rule. Yet the Central Committee's structure and symbolic value remained, so that after 1953 it was possible for Stalin's successors to restore its legitimacy as the nation's primary decision-making body.

Was it actually the Central Committee that made the decisions on leadership and succession in the post-Stalin period? The four plenums of 1953 were all concerned with personnel changes, but it is impossible to say whether it met only to ratify decisions already made by an inner circle. Clearly Beria's arrest could not have been decided in the full Central Committee, which met several days later. Khrushchev's elevation to First Secretary may or may not have been decided at the September 1953 plenum, the occasion on which he spoke so frankly about the ills of Soviet agriculture.

More interesting is the Central Committee plenum which met in the last week of January 1955, for it was here that Malenkov's removal from his post as head of government may have been discussed. He was not formally removed until February 8, when a note in which he asked to resign was sent to a session of the Supreme Soviet, a procedure which was in keeping with the formalities of state. At the plenum it was Khrushchev who led the attack on Malenkov's consumers' goods program along the lines we saw in chapter 3, linking this program with Bukharin, Rykov, and the "Right deviation" of the 1920s. This was strong language, and according to some accounts it was reinforced by implicating Malenkov in some of the misdeeds of Stalin's last years.[11] In perspective, this plenum was the culmination of indirect attacks on Malenkov which used the consumer program as his vulnerable point. All four plenums of the Malenkov period which discussed economic problems were reported as dealing only with agriculture, while the consumer program was apparently ignored. In the Central Committee plenums of the Union Republics, the silence on consumers' goods was equally deafening. Khrushchev was making full use of his top position in the Party apparatus, while Malenkov now sorely missed the leverage in the Party he had once enjoyed as Secretary.

The conclusion suggested by the evidence is that when the Central Committee met in January 1955, a demotion of Malenkov was virtually a certainty. If so, the plenum served several purposes: it enabled Khrushchev and his supporters to make their majority as firm as possible before any kind of vote was taken—if in fact a vote was necessary; it set the Party's highest body on record as having condemned Malenkov; and, possibly, the manner and extent of Malenkov's demotion was resolved during the proceedings. If Khrushchev wanted to dismiss Malenkov from

---

[11] Armstrong, *The Politics of Totalitarianism*, p. 263.

the Politburo as well, which he probably did, the plenum served as a final indicator of just how severe an action would be supported by its members. In this case, leaving Malenkov's Presidium (Politburo) seat intact was an important concession, one which could have been decided at the plenum.

Actually, it would make little difference from an institutional point of view whether Khrushchev had lined up his support among the Central Committee members before the plenum or during it (and beyond doubt it was before the plenum). The point is that a majority of the Central Committee's members had to be persuaded to give the opposition to Malenkov their votes. An institution is nothing but a collection of people interacting according to certain norms. Here one may say that the institution functioned as such even though its important work could be done before its members took their seats in the same hall. This is hardly different from the actual working of deliberative bodies elsewhere in the world. Rarely, in the world's democracies, does the outcome of an important vote in a legislature depend on what is said "on the floor" while the legislature is in session. Either parties determine in advance how their members shall vote, or, in the absence of strict party discipline, votes are lined up in private discussions, via persuasion, pressure, and deals.

Therefore, we may say that the Central Committee, in the period after Stalin's death, was legitimate not only in its symbolism as the Party's highest authority, but also in the sense that no one dictated its decisions from above or outside. Within its ranks, differences were discussed, pressure and persuasion were applied to gain votes, and the outcome of a vote was regarded as authoritative by its members. Beria in 1953 obviously threatened this second kind of legitimacy, just as Stalin had undermined its legitimacy in both senses, without completely destroying it. The Central Committee's first act as a separate body after Stalin's death, its session of March 14, had sought a guarantee of this legitimacy with the removal of Malenkov as Secretary, assuring itself—at least for the time being—that no one leader could again undermine it as Stalin had done.

Rebuilding the Party's Legitimacy

The evolution of the Party's decision-making role during the 1950s can best be seen in the pledges of various leaders, implicit and explicit, concerning which practices would be shunned and which ones upheld. All these pledges had to do with legitimacy in the functioning of the Party mechanism. The regular functioning of Party organs from top to bottom was one; the limited mandate of the top political leader was another; the separation of Party leadership from leadership of the state was a third. Khrushchev violated this second implicit pledge in 1958 when he dismissed Bulganin from the Premiership and took the post himself; it was restored after Khrushchev's removal in 1964, when Brezhnev and Kosygin occupied the top Party and state posts respectively, with Brezhnev—as it turned out—serving as political leader.

A third pledge was that there would be no drastic reprisals against leading Party members, no forced confessions, no executions or prison sentences, save in the most extreme cases where actual treason had been shown. This was by no means a dead issue after Beria's execution, since the trials of Beria's former associates went on until the spring of 1956, with more than a dozen of them receiving the death sentence. These trials, like all the other steps taken to right the wrongs of the Stalin era, had a sharp political cutting edge in the post-Stalin contest for leadership. If the lesser figures who had served as Beria's henchmen in the Stalin-era repressions could be put on trial and executed, what about the top Party figures still in power who had either ordered or supported these acts? Most of the Presidium members of the 1950s had profited from either the Great Purge of the 1930s or the lesser purges of 1949 and subsequently, even though not all had participated in doing the purging. Would the trials of those implicated in Beria's misdeeds eventually develop into trials of the top leadership? Would righting past wrongs lead to another Great Purge, this time with confessions of the truth wrung from the defendants, instead of confessions fabricated for them to sign after months of isolation and torture?

Less than two months before Malenkov's resignation in February 1955, the trial of former State Security Minister Abakumov and five associates raised the ghosts of the "Leningrad case" of 1949. After the death in 1948 of Andrei Zhdanov, the Leningrad Party chief and Malenkov's rival for the role of Stalin's chief lieutenant, the whole Leningrad organization was purged, together with a Politburo member, a Party Secretary and others who had been Zhdanov's close associates. Malenkov, whatever his role may have been, was the immediate beneficiary of the purge. Khrushchev was to accuse him in 1957 of having plotted the whole thing, and other Party leaders joined the chorus then and later. The Abakumov trial was plainly timed in order to undercut whatever support Malenkov still retained in the Central Committee and elsewhere. At the time, this was probably the single most effective way of influencing votes in the Central Committee. But it was a highly dangerous weapon, one which could be turned against its users. Had not Khrushchev been the main beneficiary of Yezhov's slaughter of the Ukrainian Party leadership, when Stalin sent him to the Ukraine at the end of the 1930s to restore order as head of the Ukrainian party?

DE-STALINIZATION

The story of Khrushchev's success in outmaneuvering a majority of the Presidium members in the years 1955–57 is one of the most fascinating episodes of Soviet politics, and one of the most revealing in what it says about problems of succession and legitimacy. In chapter 3 we saw how Khrushchev used economic policy as his main ideological weapon, and how both he and his opponents used economic reorganization as a weapon for undercutting the key organizational positions held by the other side. Now we must look at this in political perspective.

There were two big political issues. The first was the problem of whether Stalinism would be permitted to survive Stalin, whether the Party would now proclaim an end to repression against both its own members and the Soviet population generally. The second was the question of whether the Presidium and Central Committee should embody a balance of economic and political views, or whether the losers of a political struggle should be excluded from the main arena of decision making.

Khrushchev's "de-Stalinization speech" at the 20th Party Congress was a bold effort to turn the unresolved questions of Stalinism to his own political advantage. Certain steps had been taken to eliminate some of the worst features of the system as Stalin had shaped it, but the most agonizing questions still remained. Amnesties in 1953 and 1955 had released many of the millions of labor camp inmates; the "special tribunals" of the Interior Ministry had been eliminated, the ones set up to imprison and execute without trial; political interference with the machinery of justice was reduced; the secret police, now called the Committee of State Security or KGB, was once again separated from the Interior Ministry; and the USSR Supreme Court, acting for the most part in privacy, started to "rehabilitate" some of the victims of the Great Purge, even if in many cases posthumously.

The 20th Congress: A Time to Speak Out

But if the new leaders were to make a convincing pledge to Party and people that Stalin's abuses would not be repeated, must Stalin be condemned publicly for them? If so, who else besides Beria should be blamed as having supported Stalin in these abuses? Should Stalin's management of collectivization be condemned too? Did his attacks against the non-Russian nations deserve an apology and restoration of certain national rights? If his stifling of frank discussion in Party ranks was to be condemned, did this mean a return to the relatively open Party congresses of the early 1920s? Were Trotsky, Bukharin, Kamenev, and the leaders of the opposition to Stalin to be rehabilitated? Should Stalin be blamed for his pact with Hitler, and the non-Russian western territories which he reaped from this pact returned to the East European nations they were taken from? Should he be held responsible for the military disasters of 1941—his refusal to listen to warnings from Western

capitals of an impending German invasion, and the incredible unprepared-
ness of the Soviet armed forces?

For nearly three years after Stalin's death no Party congress had been
held, nor did the Party Rules require that a congress be held before
the fall of 1956. All the top Party figures were probably relieved at
this. Holding a congress would mean dealing with Stalin's legacy in some
depth; to have a congress and ignore the Stalin issue would reduce the
credibility and position of the entire Party. An investigation of the
Stalin-period executions and other injustices had been under way since
1953 or 1954, and this was known to the upper ranks of the Party.
Now a report was due. Besides, even if the Presidium as a whole decided
to paper over the whole issue, would this not hand a golden opportunity
to the Party's younger, second-echelon leaders, themselves somewhat less
to blame for Stalin's crimes, and only too eager to use the issue for
their own advancement?

Khrushchev gave himself a year in which to prepare for the 20th
Congress. It was a year full of startling international initiatives from
Moscow, with Khrushchev prominent as Soviet spokesman: the reconciliation with Yugoslavia, the Austrian peace treaty, the Geneva summit
conference, and a new program of aid and friendship in Asia. Molotov
clearly opposed these initiatives, but was outmaneuvered. At the time
the 20th Congress opened in February 1956, Khrushchev and Bulganin
had recently completed a whirlwind tour of South Asia, and the First
Secretary's prestige was being regarded with some awe in foreign capitals.

In view of Khrushchev's capacity to build his position, it is surprising
to note that, as the 20th Congress opened, he had been unable to secure
agreement as to what should be said about Stalinism. Khrushchev's long
opening report contained no attack on Stalin, though it did make indirect
jabs at Malenkov and Molotov. It was Mikoyan who opened the debate
on Stalin by criticizing the "cult of the individual" (the official euphem-
ism for Stalinism) and urging corrective action in ideological and historical matters. Kaganovich argued lamely that the leaders other than Stalin
had raised the "cult" question, albeit in indirect form, at the 19th Congress, before Stalin's death; he made this a veiled argument for moderation
in dealing with the Stalin legacy. The battle lines were being drawn.
The Congress was ten days old and approaching an end when a special
evening meeting was announced without warning. There, behind closed
doors, Khrushchev roundly condemned Stalin's excesses in a long statement that has never been published in the Soviet Union.

Which Crimes? Which Victims?

Khrushchev minced no words and spiced his account with anecdotes
that illustrated Stalin's growing paranoia and his personal callousness to

injustice. But it covered only a limited part of the dead dictator's misdeeds, which were mainly abuse of the *Party*—his undermining of the Party as an institution, and even more his reprisals against individual Party members. Even within the area of Party politics, Khrushchev had been obliged to do a good deal of picking and choosing. He compared Stalin's brutal liquidation of Party leaders unfavorably with Lenin's generous treatment of Kamenev, Zinoviev, and Trotsky over his differences with them; yet he referred to "the completed political liquidation of the Trotskyistes, Zinovievites and Bukharinites" as one would speak of an inevitable and necessary development. He made much of the fabrication of evidence against loyal Party workers, including accusations of "Trotskyism," while making no reference to the equally fantastic evidence brought against Zinoviev, Kamenev, Bukharin, and the other oppositionists of the 1920s. Perhaps more important than any other single point, Khrushchev left the impression that Stalin's crimes had begun only in 1934, with his arranging the murder of Sergei Kirov. This left out the entire period of collectivization, the trials of Mensheviks and others in the late 1920s and early 1930s, and Stalin's manipulation of the Party in the 1920s. Only Lenin's "Testament," now after 33 years made available in printed form, suggested that Stalin had strayed from the true Bolshevik path before 1934.

All of Khrushchev's important colleagues in the current Presidium (Politburo) figured somewhere in the speech. Mikoyan came off better than the rest; he was depicted criticizing Stalin to his face, while Bulganin was recorded as complaining about him in private. Twice Malenkov was portrayed as Stalin's spokesman in refusing justified requests; Molotov and Kaganovich were described receiving Stalin's instructions to step up the purges. Ordzhonikidze's suicide in 1937 was imputed indirectly to Malenkov's threats. On the whole, it was an unlovely picture of Stalin's old associates.[12]

THE 1957 CRISIS

With his secret speech, Khrushchev sowed a whirlwind that he was forced to reap in Eastern Europe before the year 1956 was out. The speech had been passed to leaders of foreign communist parties, including some outside the orbit of communist nations, with the intention that its message become generally known, even to the Soviet population. The "little Stalins" who still ruled in Eastern Europe were thrown into a quandary. According to one report, the death of Poland's party boss Boleslaw Bierut in Moscow two weeks after the secret speech was a suicide. Hungary's Mátyás Rákosi had to be removed four months later

---

[12] See the account in Conquest, *Power and Policy in the U.S.S.R.*, p. 282 ff.

at Moscow's order. Unrest in both countries led to the restoration of
Poland's Wladyslaw Gomulka to power in October, and to revolution
in Hungary in the same month. A top-level Soviet delegation, including
Khrushchev, rushed to Warsaw at the last moment in a futile attempt
to stop Gomulka. For the Hungarian uprising the Soviet leaders found
no solution but to send Soviet tanks.

A Majority Coalition against Khrushchev

Khrushchev's enemies in the Presidium were now forced into a make-
shift coalition in spite of their many disagreements of the past: Malenkov,
Molotov, and Kaganovich. The latter two had suffered demotions in their
government jobs several months after the speech. Now the threatening
volcano in Eastern Europe delivered power into their hands once more,
bringing some wavering members of the 17-member Presidium over to
their side. Molotov and Kaganovich accompanied Khrushchev on the
Warsaw trip, and Molotov received a state post (Minister of State Control) that enabled him to investigate the affairs of the entire government
structure.

In December 1956 the gauntlet was thrown down: a Central Committee plenum transferred central economic management to the State Economic Commission, a body that was endowed with power such that
only the Presidium could override its decisions. Khrushchev's problem
was not just that he had been promoting the idea of partial decentralization of the economy; it was that his chief opponents were entrenched
in the vast central bureaucracy of economic management. At the next
plenum, in February 1957, this decision was reversed in principle before
it had been put into effect, and it appeared that a majority of the Central
Committee now supported Khrushchev. Khrushchev now staked his political reputation on the decentralization program; he went on speechmaking tours and marshalled the Party press in his support. At the Supreme
Soviet session in May he got his law passed; but the complete silence
of his opponents at this session was ominous.

Now even Bulganin, the head of government and a Presidium member,
joined the opposition, making a total of 11 Presidium members opposed
to the reorganization and only three besides Khrushchev in favor. Khrushchev returned from a brief foreign trip to find his Presidium colleagues
seeking his overthrow. A debate raged in the Presidium for three days.
Though our information on who took sides on what specific issues in
circumstantial, Khrushchev after losing the policy question won two tactical advantages: the Presidium would not publish its decision immediately, and a Central Committee plenum would be called. Actually the
second point remained in doubt, for Bulganin had posted guards about
the Kremlin in order to keep out some Central Committee members

who wanted to know what was going on and were demanding a plenum. Since the 1952 Congress the Presidium was endowed with the power to act on the Central Committee's behalf between sessions of the latter. Had its decision now been announced, in advance of the next plenum, it could well have undermined Khrushchev's presumed majority in the Central Committee. As it was, Khrushchev had to act in haste before his shaky position became common knowledge. Marshal Zhukov, the World War II hero, whom Khrushchev had made Minister of the Defense recently and appointed as candidate member of the Presidium, rendered powerful assistance by bringing Central Committee members from the far corners of the Soviet Union on military planes.

The June Plenum

The plenum opened on June 22, deliberated for a record eight days, and handed Khrushchev the policy victory he sought on both the economic reorganization issue and the dismissal from the Presidium of Khrushchev's chief opponents. We do not know whether votes were taken which divided the ayes and nays, or whether there were only unanimous votes, which had become the practice in Stalin's time. In any case Khrushchev prevailed over his opponents after a struggle, had them ousted from the Politburo (but not from the Party), and saw his economic reorganization plan affirmed, with a few modifications.

Had Khrushchev been packing the Central Committee with his supporters as blatantly as Stalin did in the 1920s, the legitimacy of this body might have been placed in jeopardy by what appeared to be a lopsided Khrushchev victory. But the membership of the Central Committee elected at the 20th Party Congress (1956) was not sharply different from the preceding Central Committee that had been elected in 1952. Ninety of the 133 full (voting) members elected in 1956 had been carried over from 1952. It is true that Khrushchev had had ample opportunity to promote some people to Central Committee membership, and that he had made use of it. As a Party Secretary and head of the Moscow Party organization from the end of 1949 until Stalin's death, he was especially concerned with appointments of Party first secretaries to the agriculturally important provinces. As First Secretary from 1953 on, his control over appointments was enormous, as had been Malenkov's as Party organization specialist under Stalin. The purge of Beria's associates in 1953–54 had provided a certain number of key places for him to fill. During his dozen years as Party chief of the Ukraine (from 1938 to 1949), interrupted though his duties were by the German occupation, Khrushchev had had plenty of opportunity to promote his own appointees to leadership of those grain-rich provinces.

In view of this, the enormous place occupied by provincial Party secretaries in the Central Committee is significant: if one adds a few provincial government leaders to the figure, they constituted 68 out of the 133 full members, just over half.[13] Representation from the central apparatus of rule was small by comparison: eight from the Secretariat, and 15 from the industrial ministries. The latter were most certainly hostile to Khrushchev's plan for industrial reorganization. The numbers of the industrial officials had been cut back sharply in 1956, since in the previous Central Committee (that of 1952) there had been some three dozen of them. Such was the kind of arithmetic the First Secretary used in appealing the Politburo's adverse vote.

Certainly Khrushchev had no automatic control of a majority. Even the people who owed their promotions to him at one time did not necessarily owe him their support in 1957. Had Khrushchev lost his gamble, their careers might be in jeopardy too for having supported their former patron. But it helped Khrushchev's case with the provincial officialdom that the economic reform he proposed would increase their responsibility and prestige at the expense of the various central bureaucracies. In any case, Khrushchev had "counted noses" early in 1957 and found enough support to warrant an appeal to the Central Committee on this issue, an issue which was central because his opponents had selected it as the field of battle in their bid to unseat him.

Two Succession Crises Compared

The parallels between the succession to Stalin in the 1950s and the succession to Lenin in the 1920s are many. Both had begun with a triumvirate which quickly fell apart: Malenkov-Molotov-Beria and Stalin-Kamenev-Zinoviev. Both ended with the ascendancy of a single strong figure, who promptly set about to put his individual stamp on policies, even where he had argued for different policies not long before. Stalin and Khrushchev were both in charge of the Party bureaucracy, wielded enormous control over appointments both in and outside of the Party, and used the power of appointment to improve their position in the Central Committee and other Party bodies. Both men fought their political battles in terms of the most important issues of the time: in the 1950s, investment priorities, Stalin's political legacy, and to a lesser extent national security; in the 1920s, the tempo of industrialization, the manner of socializing agriculture, and the program for world revolution. The issues of both successions can be summed up as the problem of "getting the country moving again" after a period of economic lag and political demoralization. Stalin and Khrushchev both sought to win their victories

---

[13] Armstrong, *The Politics of Totalitarianism*, p. 272. The provincial government leaders, far from being a category apart from Party officials, were often Party men assigned to governmental posts as a steppingstone in Party-oriented careers.

in the Central Committee, the Politburo, and Party congresses (Khrushchev had only the 1956 Congress). Both used ideology as a major weapon, and sought to innovate in ways that suited their purposes. Finally, both men emerged from the power struggle without having defeated their opponents as completely as they had wanted to do.

The differences lie mainly in what happened after the succession problem had been resolved—that is, after 1927 and 1957, respectively. Stalin humbled his ex-foes far more completely than did Khrushchev, but, fearing that they might yet be the nucleus of a new opposition, solved his immediate problem through judicial murders. Khrushchev's mandate for power included a renunciation of terror, so that making arrests would have been doubly risky; consequently he was also balked in his efforts to humble the "anti-Party group" after 1957. Other than this, the main differences are those having to do with individual approaches to power, and the specific issues of the time. The most important similarity is that the succession crisis in each case was "contained" by the Party's proper institutions. It is true that institutional changes outside the Party between the 1920s and 1950s created major issues that were important in the succession: the size and importance of the security police and armed forces, and the influence of the state economic hierarchy. The 1920s produced no Beria or Zhukov episodes. Whether by luck or because of skillful political management, these threats were dealt with swiftly, and they throw into relief the apparent agreement among the political leadership, from the 1920s to the present, that major disputes can be resolved only through the instrumentality of the Party.

KHRUSHCHEV ON THE OFFENSIVE

Over a period of four years from the time of Stalin's death, therefore, the Central Committee had apparently regained the status within the system that it had occupied under Lenin. While it did not manufacture policy at its sessions, and was never intended to supervise the day-to-day guidance of policy, it was a legitimate forum of appeal when the Presidium (Politburo) found itself divided. Its composition had been fairly stable, by its own standards, from 1939 on. This was an important factor in its legitimacy, since any repetition of the mass ouster (not to mention slaughter) of its members such as occurred in the Great Purge would have reduced it to a mouthpiece of higher authority. It was still unlikely that any Central Committee would resist the policy initiatives of a united Presidium, even were a majority of its members privately opposed. Presidium members were also Central Committee members, elected from its midst, and in ordinary circumstances their presence and their statements set the framework for whatever the Central Committee might decide. But it seemed equally unlikely that Khrushchev or any future leader would embark on a radical policy initiative without first having taken soundings among a good many Central Committee members.

Khrushchev's Policies for the Nation

Khrushchev's initiatives on domestic issues in the latter 1950s were as impressive as his 1955 foreign policy initiatives had been, both in their boldness and in the rapidity with which they were launched. We reviewed some of these in chapter 3. He scrapped the unworkable Sixth Five-Year Plan and replaced it with a Seven-Year Plan (for 1959–65) containing altered indices. He abolished the Machine-Tractor Stations, a major change for the farms. He placed a realistic new emphasis on consumers' goods and services, first of all on housing. He called for massive investment in the investment-starved chemical industry, partly with the intent of building fertilizer production. He reduced expenditures on conventional military forces, and reduced the size of Soviet ground forces somewhat as well, in favor of emphasizing what he believed would be cheaper defense via reliance on missiles.

Khrushchev's political measures were no less important than his economic drives on behalf of the consumer. The release and rehabilitation of persons falsely accused during the Stalin era had begun before the de-Stalinization speech, as had reform of the Public Prosecutor's Office, whose sweeping competence is so important for enforcing adherence to the laws. The law codes of the 1920s, which had been undermined and bypassed for over two decades in the course of political repression campaigns, were now redrafted completely. The special tribunals and arbitrary procedures spawned in the 1930s were either abolished or reduced greatly in jurisdiction; the Vyshinsky doctrine of placing the burden of proof on the accused in political cases was repudiated; crimes were defined more precisely, particularly the old category of "counterrevolutionary crimes"; and in many other ways, there was a restoration of procedural due process of law.[14]

The structure of soviets, parts of which had been allowed to decay in the Stalin era, was infused with new life. A campaign was begun to make sessions of the soviets meaningful, to enlist the cooperation of more people in the work of local government and to encourage the growth of local civic bodies operating under the aegis of local government and Party organizations. Both the soviets and civic groups were encouraged to perform the function of watchdog over state administration and economic management. The "standing commissions" of local soviets were revived in an effort to maintain specialized watchdog groups. "Popular justice," devices for bringing the influence of ordinary people to bear

---

[14] See the excellent account of these reforms in Harold J. Berman, *Justice in the U.S.S.R.*, rev. ed. (New York: Vintage Books, 1963), chapter 2.

on some aspects of law enforcement, was promoted vigorously in the form of comrades' courts, voluntary patrols to assist the police, and popular legal education. An effort was made to deal with the perennial problem of inattention to the complaints of citizens against (mainly local) authorities, though not to the extent of opening new subjects for lawsuits.

As to the Party itself, reforms in the functioning of the top Party organs were applied to the lower levels as well. Party committees at all levels, from the Central Committee down, resumed regular meetings and were attended by much publicity, beginning with the practice of publishing the stenographic records (incomplete and heavily edited, to be sure) of Central Committee plenums. Party secretaries, who had ruled as "little Stalins" in their jurisdictions, now had to pay more attention to opinion in their committees. The identity and specific role of the Party in the Soviet political system was bolstered by a massive "recodification" of Soviet Marxism. Ideology as a whole had been long neglected by Stalin, save for the arbitrary pronouncements with which he sought to reinforce certain political stands. The 21st Party Congress in 1959 was accompanied by a mass of pronouncements about the transition from a socialist order to full-blown communism, and about the Party's leading role in this process.

The Khrushchev era reforms dealing with social relations are noted in later chapters—the drive for equal educational opportunities and a more equitable reward system, attempts to improve communication between Party and people, changes in policy regarding nationalities, and other areas of social policy. To all appearances, Khrushchev's administration was busy converting a political system with many rigidities and blocks to performance into a usable instrument of change, capable of enlisting mass support for its efforts. Though some reforms failed, others were blocked, and though Khrushchev himself was later obliged to set limits to change, this was a serious and partly successful effort to make one-party rule dynamic, adaptable to change, and genuinely popular.

Belated Revenge on the "Anti-Party Group"

Through most of these developments, Khrushchev created the impression of being thoroughly in command of the Party and the entire policy-making process. Only in 1960–61, particularly when he launched his 1961 campaign against the "metal eaters" (those who favored the heavy industrial priority), did it become evident to the outside world that he was having difficulties. On the surface, it was economic priorities that were being discussed; ever since the U-2 incident in May 1960 Khrushchev's economic program had been under some kind of attack. Actually, the evidence shows that his difficulties began right at the time of his apparent triumph over the "anti-Party group" in 1957. Furthermore, the central issue may not have been economic priorities, but Khrushchev's alarming inroads into the Party's structure and procedures.

The Central Committee resolution which expelled Malenkov, Molotov, and Kaganovich from the Presidium labelled them the "anti-Party group" and alleged that they had violated Lenin's Resolution on Unity of 1921 (see chapter 4). It claimed that they had attempted to bypass the Central Committee altogether, and that they had tried to sabotage some major policies, including the reconciliation with Yugoslavia and the whole de-Stalinization campaign. The resolution did not, however, expel them from the Party. But a very different line was taken, immediately after this resolution was issued, in public statements by Khrushchev, Zhukov, Frol Kozlov, and several others who had supported the ouster. Accusing the trio of complicity in some of Stalin's worst crimes, they strongly suggested that it was time to bring the culprits to trial. Khrushchev returned to this demand again and again, notably at the party congresses of 1959 and 1961.

KHRUSHCHEV THREATENS THE PARTY

Khrushchev offered a deeper and more serious threat than his wish to bring vengeance on the heads of his fellow ex-Stalinists. Whether he fully realized it or not, he repeatedly threatened the institutional legitimacy he had built up and used in the mid-1950s. His motives in doing this will still be disputed when the whole Khrushchev era lies many decades in the past. Probably his largest single motive was that he faced considerable opposition from within the Party when he tried to reorder the nation's priorities, internally and in foreign policy. A thoroughgoing Stalinist now turned pragmatist in the post-Stalin era, his aim was to make the Soviet system more flexible in handling problems and more responsive to public needs, all without sacrificing the leadership's monopoly of power within the system, or its capacity for absolute control of important situations. The Party was Khrushchev's chosen instrument for doing this. But the Party's central bureaucracy was skeptical and in part hostile; the provincial leaders whom Khrushchev had promoted began to have doubts about the leader's increasing his personal grip on the Party and becoming a new Stalin. Ultimately, a majority in the Central Committee proved willing to go along with a majority of the Presidium, men whom Khrushchev had alienated. Khrushchev's removal from all his posts in the fall of 1964 came about when a majority of the Presidium resolved that it was time to act before the unpredictable leader brought disaster on all their heads.

Opinions differ as to how the Presidium saw impending disaster. Some believe, for example, that it would have been some kind of risky initiative against China. There was certainly some objection to Khrushchev's negotiations with West Germany. But a more likely reason was that Khrushchev, frustrated in his initiatives by the very Party which he had restored to its pre-Stalin role, was on the point of yet another Party reorganization. This could have meant not only shattering the various oppositions which were now coalescing into one opposition, but destroying the legitimacy which the Party had exercised within the system during the preceding ten years. What Stalin had done after his frustration at the 1934 Congress by murdering the opposition, Khrushchev would do by reorganizing the opposition out of his path and reducing the Party once again from a legitimate controller of policy to an instrument of personal rule.

Khrushchev in his de-Stalinization speech had placed great emphasis on the need for adhering to the Party Rules, for Stalin's careless violations of them had opened the way for the latter's emasculation of the Party. Between 1957 and 1964, Khrushchev exposed himself in five ways to the accusation of trying to violate the Party's role in the Soviet system: (1) he was promoting his own "cult of the personality"; (2) he was reducing the role of the lower Party organs to that of economic overseers, one hierarchy among many for managing the nation's economy; (3) he was trying to eliminate the deliberative and decision-making functions of the Central Committee, replacing these with a planned script; (4) he was trying to eliminate the deliberative and decision-making functions by coming out with highly publicized proposals with no advance warning; and (5) he sought to cut down his critics in the Party by creating otherwise needless opportunities to shift them about.

A New Cult

If one can speak of a "cult of Khrushchev," it was certainly not on the same scale as the Stalin cult had been. But it would be no exaggeration to call Khrushchev's image-building a blatant campaign to set him far above his colleagues in authority. While much of the symbolism of collective leadership was maintained, the media were full of symbols of Khrushchev's primacy as well, both subtle and gross. Part of the decor for great celebrations in Moscow, such as May Day or the October Revolution festivities on November 7th, consisted of equal-sized portraits of the 12 full members of the Politburo, arranged in a line atop various buildings, with a larger portrait of Lenin exactly in the middle. Khrushchev, invariably, occupied the space immediately to Lenin's right.

More blatant was the way Khrushchev personally took the lead in promoting every policy initiative, and the frequency with which his long speeches (plus the inevitable portrait) occupied the first several pages of many newspapers. His scolding and chiding interventions at Party conclaves, and the way he sometimes treated his close associates like ignorant schoolchildren, even in the presence of foreign delegations, was disquietingly remindful of Stalin. He lost little time in gaining Stalin's old position as head of both Party and state by ousting Bulganin. That was in March 1958, nine months after the fall of the "anti-Party group," and by the end of 1958 Bulganin was off the Presidium as well and had confessed publicly that he too had been "anti-Party" in 1957. Khrushchev at this point renewed his demand for further action on his vanquished foes, which among other things was a ploy to keep himself at the head of the whole anti-Stalin campaign.

The Party as Economic Manager

The second issue, that of debasing the Party's status by using it as an economic manager, certainly did not originate with Khrushchev. The extent to which Party committees should intervene in day-to-day matters of economic management and planning had been an issue back in the 1920s and ever since. After the 1957 economic management reform, the whole Party bureaucracy, and especially the provincial Party organizations, became a vital channel of economic guidance in the absence of most of the central ministries. The Party bureaucracy by this time included far more economic expertise than the bureaucracy of the 1930s. Increasing numbers of Party secretaries in the province and city organizations, particularly, had advanced degrees in technology and years of industrial experience. Some observers believed that one major goal of the 1957 reform was to place the Party first secretaries at the provincial level in direct control of economic management, because in most areas of the Russian Republic the territory of each Regional Economic Council coincided with the boundaries of a province. One of the Party's most important roles at the middle and local levels has been, and remains today, that of mediator among industries, also between industries and local governments, particularly because the lines of responsibility for most industries (except small local enterprises) go above the level of the city or province. Now, it seemed, the first secretary of a provincial Party organization would have the directing agencies for most industries (there were important exceptions) entirely within his jurisdiction.

On the other hand, it may be argued that this arrangement actually reduced the role of the Party as an authoritative organization which could instill dynamism into both economy and government. Heightened concentration on economic tasks could reduce the Party's attention to its role in important noneconomic functions—propaganda, recruitment, education, and the management of nongovernmental organizations. Even within the sphere of economic management, a multitude of articles in the Party press during the Khrushchev era conveyed the message that Party officials were often losing their capacity as enforcers of policy by getting too involved in the details of management. In some ways it appears that it may even have been Khrushchev's intention to reduce the Party's overall political capacities by tying its functions so closely to those of economic management. In any case, given the still highly centralized character of Soviet economic planning, even after the 1957 reforms, it is clear that some kind of directing mechanism had to replace the many central ministries that had been abolished; whatever may have been Khrushchev's further intention, it was now Party officials who had to assume much of this function of direction.

After Khrushchev's political reverses of 1960–61, the top industrial administrators began resurrecting their old pre-1957 empire, at first in somewhat shadowy form as "state committees" for various economic branches. While Khrushchev had left the State Planning Committee (Gosplan) in place as the supreme economic coordinator, his foes on this issue now outflanked Gosplan by creating another central body for economic coordination.

At the end of 1962 Khrushchev abruptly counterattacked with a reform of both Party and local government which was certainly intended to put the Party bureaucracy in direct charge of many parts of the economy. At the province level and below, both Party and government were split amoeba-fashion into two completely separate components, one for industry, the other for agriculture. Among other things, this reform doubled the number of provincial Party secretaryships, thus exposing Khrushchev to the final charge in our list. That the bifurcation of Party and government had provoked strong opposition was evident in the haste with which the Brezhnev-Kosygin regime restored the old system after it assumed power.

Diluting the Central Committee

As concerns the Central Committee, Khrushchev had begun by fulfilling his original promise of 1956 that Party bodies would meet regularly, according to the Party Rules, and would debate and resolve real issues. The next step was to turn Central Committee plenums into major events, attended by publicity for general consumption (including the display of Lenin and the 12 apostles described above). Red-bound stenographic reports of their proceedings began to be published; these, although necessarily incomplete and well edited, gave interested Soviet citizens some idea of the content of debates. The last step, taken when Khrushchev's position in the Central Committee had definitely weakened after 1960, was to turn the plenums into conventions. Outside specialists were brought in by the dozens, and the Central Committee sessions were broken down part of the time into working parties in which the members were lectured on a variety of problems. There was a danger that Khrushchev was using this device not to elicit better-informed decisions from the Central Committee, but to reduce its political role by turning the plenums into glorified briefing sessions. Khrushchev's successors roundly criticized this practice and put a swift end to it.

One-Man Decisions

Immediately after Khrushchev's fall, an editorial in *Pravda*, though it did not mention Khrushchev by name, attacked "subjectivism," "empty phrases," "harebrained schemes," and "rash decisions."[15] An editorial in a Party magazine was more explicit:

> We cannot permit even the most authoritative person to get away from the control of the leading collective or party organization and to get the idea that he knows everything and can do everything and that the knowledge and experience of his comrades is of no use to him.[16]

Khrushchev's increasing reluctance to engage in real policy consultations with his colleagues, plus his habit of overwhelming them with well-publicized pronouncements on policies that had not yet been resolved, were not just signs of megalomania. They were also the tactics of a man who knew that he could only lose in an orderly process of discussion. His first known use of the surprise attack had been the de-Stalinization speech in 1956. While this and later initiatives were probably discussed with his colleagues in advance, what galled them was Khrushchev's rushing ahead with his cannon-shot statements, whereby he attempted to commit the Party willy-nilly to a given course of action.

A Fight for Survival

Khrushchev had indeed been a master of the counterattack. Though the main ends he sought in using it were never reached, without this skill he might have fallen sooner than he did. His performance at the 22nd Party Congress in 1961 was as grotesque as it was shrewd. Here Khrushchev and his supporters launched a shrill attack against Molotov, Malenkov, and Kaganovich, suggesting that they had been implicated in even more crimes than Khrushchev had already indicated. The real surprise came when delegates began demanding that Stalin's remains be taken out of Lenin's mausoleum on Red Square and buried elsewhere. An elderly woman delegate, an Old Bolshevik who had known Lenin and served time in Stalin's labor camps, reported how Lenin had appeared

---

[15] *Pravda*, Oct. 17, 1964,

[16] Editorial in *Partiinaya Zhizn*, October 1964 (signed to press Oct. 17).

to her in a dream and protested having to share the mausoleum with Stalin, who had done so much damage to the Party. Hardly had these demands rung out than the mausoleum was boarded up and Stalin's embalmed body transferred unceremoniously to a nearby grave beneath the Kremlin walls, all while the Congress was still in session.

Even this was a Pyrrhic victory for Khrushchev, since his demand to try Stalin's accomplices went unheeded. Mikoyan, Kosygin, Suslov, and others, while condemning Stalinism, asserted that the "ideological defeat" of the leading Stalinists had already accomplished its purpose. Khrushchev's attack on the "metal eaters" at this same Congress was linked to his anti-Stalin outbursts, since steel output had been the sacred cow of Stalin's economy. The Stalin issue was also a blow aimed at the Chinese leadership, but, even more, it was a bid to rally the Party in support of measures for using the world communist movement to condemn Peking formally. On none of these issues did Khrushchev win the day, although the vigor of his onslaught gained him enough time and support to return to the attack later, as in his bid for building the chemical industry (at the expense of steel, among others) in 1963–64. Defeat and stalemate only goaded him to further efforts. By 1964 his colleagues doubtless viewed him as irascible, unpredictable, and a danger to the stability of the Party itself.

Khrushchev's Sudden Fall

Khrushchev's removal was a swift "surgical operation," accomplished in three days (October 12–14, 1964). It showed both that his colleagues had learned the lessons of 1957, and that they had a good grasp of the legitimacy issue. The Presidium held its decisive meeting on October 12, minus Khrushchev, who was vacationing in the south, and Mikoyan, who was with him and probably had knowledge of the plot. It is not certain how Khrushchev was persuaded to return to Moscow, and perhaps he needed no persuasion when he understood what threatened him. He arrived on the afternoon of October 13 to face the Presidium, and the indications are that this body was already united in its decision to remove Khrushchev from all his posts. In 1957, Khrushchev had argued with the Presidium for three days over whether the Central Committee should be convened, and this gave him time to rally support. The plotters of 1964 had already summoned the Central Committee to meet tht next day, October 14, and unlike 1957 the Presidium this time could offer a united front. At the Central Committee plenum, early on October 14, Gennadi Suslov presented the Presidium's indictment. There was probably little discussion, and Khrushchev submitted his resignation as First Secretary and Presidium member without a fight. On the following day, the Supreme Soviet Presidium went through the formality of removing him also from the premiership (i.e., from chairmanship of the Council of Ministers).[17]

The whole incident created few immediate ripples in the political system, and almost none in public life. Khrushchev's widely disliked bifurcation of the Party into industrial and agricultural hierarchies was promptly cancelled, and the officials who had been shuffled in the process returned to the posts they had held in 1962. A small number of officials whose careers were intimately bound to Khrushchev's support departed the scene (e.g., Alexei Adzhubei, Khrushchev's son-in-law, editor of *Izvestiya* and a Central Committee member), with the mass media singled out for special attention. But there was no major Party shakeup. No army units appeared in the Moscow vicinity, as they had in 1957 at Zhukov's direction; Khrushchev's portraits disappeared swiftly from their accustomed places; ordinary citizens had little to say and showed no emotion one way or another. Aside from the indirect but obvious criticism in a few editorials immediately after Khrushchev was removed, he was not subjected to any campaign or vilification. No one demanded his trial, and no other officials were accused of "Khrushchevism." He simply became an "unperson," living out his days in comfortable, isolated retirement outside of Moscow. The memoirs he is alleged to have dictated could have been an attempt at self-justification, but they could also have been the hoax of an intelligence service.

KHRUSHCHEV'S HEIRS

No Soviet leader thus far has, on assuming the highest office, brought a fresh new set of faces with him into the Politburo (or Presidium) the Secretariat, and the leading posts in the Council of Ministers. Stalin and Khrushchev each waged a long battle to get rid of some of the chief lieutenants inherited from the previous regime. Each time, the new leader and his associates were implicated with the policies of the previous regime. Stalin came to power in the 1920s supporting NEP and a moderate line toward the peasantry. Malenkov and Khrushchev assumed office deeply implicated in Stalin's crimes and committed to his economic priorities. Brezhnev had loyally served the Khrushchev regime, and had lent his voice to the "Khrushchev cult" along with many others.

Leonid Brezhnev had come up through the Ukrainian Party apparatus with Khrushchev's assistance and had been the first director of Khrushchev's controversial Virgin Lands campaign. When Khrushchev's power was shaken in the early 1960s, Brezhnev's position was threatened too—he spent 1960–63 away from the Secretariat as titular head of state, then regained his former powerful post in the Party bureaucracy.

---

[17] I have followed closely the account in Michel Tatu, *Power in the Kremlin: From Khrushchev to Kosygin* (New York: Viking Press, 1970), pp. 408–18.

New Commitments

Like Khrushchev, Brezhnev assumed power in need of placing his own stamp on Soviet policies. If the leadership selection is such that the new leader must be chosen from among the old leader's close associates, there is little chance that the new leader will come in with a reputation for having a distinctive set of policies. Khrushchev was a partial exception to this rule, since even in Stalin's last years he had made a name for himself with some bold proposals on agriculture, which at the time he had been prevented from realizing. Malenkov, Khrushchev, and Brezhnev all came to power with the problem of creating distinctive policies, in a system which afforded them little chance of presenting the alternatives openly so as to test their support in the upper echelons of Party and government. Moreover, all three came to power with the immediate, pressing problem of deciding just which of their predecessors' policies they were going to repudiate.

Some important decisions had to be made before the Central Committee confronted Khrushchev as to what parts of Khrushchev's policies and methods were to be repudiated. One day the indictment which Suslov read on October 14 will come to light, just as Khrushchev's 1956 de-Stalinization speech found its way to the West. Until then, we can guess the contents of this statement only from later statements and policies in the Brezhnev period. In drawing up this indictment, the safest course in what could have been a risky undertaking would have been to concentrate on the issues most likely to unite the Central Committee against Khrushchev. These would not be the then controversial substantive issues—economic priorities, the approach to West Germany, or a possible political offensive against China—for each of these would have exacerbated existing divisions of opinion. Instead, Khrushchev's style of managing the Party could be made a common target. Though opinions probably differed widely over what should now be done about Party management, hardly any major category of officials was without serious grievances at this point.

The subsequent conduct of Party affairs by the Brezhnev-era leaders suggests the following: The notion of collective leadership was amended; the leader will not commit the Presidium (Politburo) or the Central Committee without thorough discussion and advance consultation. Next, he will not threaten, even indirectly, the drastic purging of his opponents on policy—that is, purging in the sense of sweeping demotions, expulsions from the Party, accusations of fractionalism, and the like. He will not undertake demotion-style purges in the guise of reorganizations. Accusations of "Stalinism" will no longer be used as a weapon in policy disagreements. There will be no attempt to undercut the functions of Party bodies by the means Khrushchev employed: packing Central Committee plenums with outside specialists, or debasing the policy-making functions of Party committees at various levels by turning them into part of the mechanism for controlling the economy. And, finally, Khrushchev's own pledges concerning the regularity of Party work, the faithful observance of the Party Rules, will continue to be upheld.

A Divided Leadership?

Hardly had Alexei Kosygin been chosen as head of government than foreign observers began to speculate what kind of struggle for power might be brewing. Was this duumvirate fated to go the way of the Malenkov-Khrushchev arrangement of 1953, and the Khrushchev-Bulganin team of 1955? Could two powerful men share rulership over a system that seemed fated to produce only strong-minded dictators tempermentally incapable of dividing their power? Brezhnev's career had been concentrated in the Party hierarchy, while Kosygin had served exclusively in the state's economic hierarchy; Brezhnev tended to favor emphasis on heavy industry, while Kosygin had shown signs of partisanship for more consumers' goods. Was this not, then, a patched-up alliance of two Presidium factions which was bound to come apart?

These speculations overlooked a long-term development that offered a chance of stability to any post-Khrushchev regime, and for which the Brezhnev-Kosygin regime had none other than Khrushchev himself to thank. The top organs of the Party, had, during Khrushchev's nine years of power, been restored as the locus of decision-making. The office of First Secretary (or General Secretary in Stalin's time) had been established by Khrushchev as the system's primary executive post, and was no longer regarded simply as the formal title of a dictator who had discovered he no longer needed to rule through the Party. It is true that the choice of Kosygin as head of government was meant to appeal to elements that might have been less enthusiastic had Brezhnev filled this post with another Party *apparatchik* like himself. Kosygin, who had shown his lack of enthusiasm for the way Khrushchev had dismantled the ministerial system of economic management, stood for economic rationality within the pre-Khrushchev system. His favoring of a balance between producers' and consumers' goods made his appointment a sort of pledge to all who valued Khrushchev's pursuit of consumer welfare. Very much a specialist, not a flamboyant speaker or a seeker of the limelight, and not given to pronouncements on matters of ideology, he offered scant political threat either to Brezhnev or to the newly restored primacy of the Party within the system. From one point of view, he had been chosen much the way an American presidential candidate picks his vice-presidential candidate. Kosygin's duties, however, were just as specific as the vice-president's duties are indefinite, and he soon had his hands full with the first crisis of the new administration.

The Politics of Economic Management

This was the economic management reform, described in chapter 3. Briefly, it was a move to give enterprise managers a broader framework within which to make their management decisions, and a more rational set of incentives which offered both meaningful success criteria and a more promising rewards for success. It was definitely not a step in the direction of capitalism, but an effort at rational reordering of the Soviet Union's particular style of central economic management. Khrushchev had encouraged debate of this measure starting in 1962. By the time Khrushchev was deposed, the Soviet press and economic journals were full of discussions on the proposed reforms. Something had to be done with the proposals, the more so because the choice of incentives and success indicators had to be embodied somehow in the new five-year planning period that would begin in 1966.

Brezhnev was remarkably silent about the whole reform idea, Suslov likewise. On the whole, those of the Presidium members whose careers lay in the Party apparatus showed themselves skeptical.[18] The evidence suggests that the Presidium was deeply divided as to whether to go ahead with the reforms at all. The doubts of the Party apparatus were well founded, in fact, for the reforms threatened what had become one of the Party's central functions, and confronted the Party with an identity crisis. Under Stalin's system of management, in which enterprises were guided by a mass of direct instructions from the ministries (usually via an intermediate layer of offices), the role of Party organizations was necessarily large. They were the intermediaries, the interpreters, and the "fixers" when things went awry. Enterprise managers had come to rely heavily on Party directives to get them out of difficulties which the myriad instructions from above made inevitable. When Khrushchev abolished most of the central ministries and put the Regional Economic Councils in their place, the Party's role as arbiter and fixer increased. Now came Kosygin, in the spring of 1965, with his talk of economic rationality: a rational planning process meant a degree of autonomy both for Gosplan and for the enterprises. Old economic laws must give way to new laws, the application of which will foster rational decision-making at all levels of the economic structure. Kosygin's position had once suffered a sharp setback on this issue in the fall of 1962, when he argued for the proposals of Professor Yevsei Liberman, whose articles had served

---

[18] Nikolai Podgorny, soon to be appointed titular head of state, was an exception. He returned from a trip to Czechoslovakia in May 1965 praising the Czech reforms, which had already gone further than what was being proposed in the Soviet Union.

to open the debate on reform.[19] Now the whole issue was out in the open again, and articles for and against—the attacks by each side on the other only thinly veiled, that is—were appearing in the press. The issue of material versus moral incentives as spurs to production entered into the debate as well. Meanwhile, a parallel discussion had been going on with regard to the management of agriculture.

A Presidium session in May 1965, which may have been a stormy one, resolved the main issues. Then a Central Committee plenum in September placed its approval on the detailed legislation, which was quickly approved by the Supreme Soviet and has been in force ever since. It was the political compromise, far more than the specific terms of the economic reform—whose practical benefits are debatable—that laid another one of the foundation stones of the Brezhnev regime. Briefly, the compromise consisted in the following: (1) greater autonomy for enterprise management was granted, though less than had been proposed; (2) Stalin's old system of central ministries was resurrected, the Regional Economic Councils were abolished, and a large number of central economic officials were restored to the posts they had held before 1957; (3) at the same time as the reforms threatened to deprive the Party apparatus of many of its customary tools for intervening in economic and management decisions, this loss was compensated both by transfers of certain top Party *apparatchiki* to state economic offices, and by the authority conferred on Party organizations within enterprises; (4) the Party was given back its most important functions in the management of cultural life, functions which during the Khrushchev period and even earlier had been transferred to the Ministry of Culture and a variety of state committees. The last change represented a change of emphasis among the Party's several roles: if its authority over and within the nation's economy was to be cut back, its authority over culture, education, and propaganda must be increased.

Later, in the fall of 1965, this fairly pragmatic agreement received an interesting codicil. In 1962, at the same time he divided the Party into industrial and agricultural hierarchies, Khrushchev had merged the Party Control Committee (see chapter 6) and State Control Committee into one powerful body, the Commission of Party and State Control. (This was a repetition of the merger of 1924, which had been done at Lenin's earlier insistence, then undone by Stalin in 1934.) The Commission was entrusted to one of the rising younger leaders, Alexander N. Shelepin, whom Khrushchev had made head of the KGB four years earlier, and who now became a Party Secretary also. Shortly after Khru-

---

[19] Tatu, *Power in the Kremlin*, pp. 285–86. His setback was only temporary, and did not result in his being demoted from his post of first deputy premier. The impact of the Cuban missile crisis in October 1962 may have given his opponents the upper hand on a number of issues, including this.

shchev's fall, Shelepin had vaulted to full membership in the Presidium without having first served as a candidate member. As one of several deputy premiers, he also had a foothold in the state apparatus. In December 1965 the Commission was broken up into its state and Party components, and Shelepin was removed from his government post. Already a serious threat to the integrity of Kosygin's newly resurrected state economic structure, he may have become a threat to Brezhnev as well. In 1967 he was removed as Secretary, while remaining on the Presidium. In any case, removing Shelepin from his key investigative position, which would have enabled him to intervene in the most minute concerns of economic administration, was the Party's pledge to Kosygin that its relation to the economy would at least exclude arbitrary interference by an ambitious young Party leader.

The tendency of the Brezhnev regime has been to strengthen the Party's hold over the state apparatus—indeed, over all components of the Soviet system—in an undramatic but persistent fashion. The 24th Party Congress in 1971 decreed that Party organizations functioning within ministries and other state bodies, which hitherto had been authorized only to pass their criticisms to higher Party authorities, were now told to make sure "that directives of the Party and government and observance of the law are carried out."[20] This restored to the Party some of the power of direct interference which it lost when Shelepin's agency was abolished. Concerned also with the loyalty of professional people, the Party at this same Congress extended the right of "control" (i.e., supervision plus responsibility for policy and its implementation) to educational, research, design, and medical establishments.

Stalin Sanitized

Another foundation stone of the Brezhnev regime has been a compromise on the issue of Stalinism, which by the end of the 1960s had restored the Georgian dictator to a position of respectability without condoning his regime's excesses of violence. Just as with Khrushchev's anti-Stalin campaign, Brezhnev's cautious but firm "re-Stalinization" has been a weapon for dealing with current problems. As with so much else that the Brezhnev regime altered, this change must be understood first of all as an antidote to the negative consequences of what had gone before, as the new leaders perceived these consequences. Judging by the way they handled the issue, the post-Khrushchev leaders saw both the Party apparatus and the military leaders alienated by the lengths to which Khrushchev had gone in his anti-Stalin campaign. Those responsible for security saw de-Stalinization as symbolizing an era of dan-

---

[20] Leonard Schapiro, "Keynote—Compromise, *Problems of Communism* 20 (July-August 1971), p. 5.

gerous permissiveness in culture, thought, and ideology. And probably most of the leadership feared that, in the vituperative extremes to which he carried de-Stalinization, Khrushchev was preparing the groundwork for a ruthless Party purge of his own (though not likely one to be accompanied by executions). All these fears must be stilled—the anti-Stalin campaign could not be permitted to take its own course, any more than Malenkov and Khrushchev could have escaped dealing with the whole Stalin issue in the 1950s. Besides, for Brezhnev there was definite political gain in presenting himself as "the man who set the record straight."

"Re-Stalinization" did not mean returning Stalin to his old Olympian pedestal. It began in 1965 with an effort by military leaders to set the record straight concerning Stalin's record as leader in World War II, which Khrushchev had gone to great lengths to belittle. After that, newspaper articles and Party magazines began balancing Stalin's merits against his defects, stressing the positive social and economic developments of the Stalin era without taking Khrushchev's line that these had taken place in spite of Stalin. The tenth anniversary of the 20th Party Congress (which had been February 1956) went unnoted by the mass media. The executions and injustices of the purge period were now played down. Also, the anti-Stalin literature of the Khrushchev period was singled out for condemnation, with indications that the leadership now regarded this as a particularly dangerous tendency.

The 23rd Party Congress (of April 1966), Brezhnev's first congress as leader, might have been a forum for publicizing the new line on Stalin. To the surprise of foreign observers, the whole issue was passed over in silence, which suggested that there were still differences. Then, paradoxically, Brezhnev's title of First Secretary reverted to its Stalin-era designation of General Secretary, while the Presidium now became the Politburo once again. The General Secretary title must be interpreted more as a symbolic repudiation of Khrushchev's style of leadership than as an indication of Stalin-type ambitions on the part of Brezhnev. Restoration of the Politburo's original name, which Stalin himself, and not Khrushchev, had changed in 1952, was a gesture to tradition and to the people who still found the Stalin era basically good.

Surprising as it may seem, not only a proportion of Soviet officialdom of the older generation, but also ordinary Soviet citizens of middle age and older hold Stalin in some awe even today. They readily admit his faults, but maintain that his system was debased in many ways by Khrushchev, on whom they blame the nation's increasing problems with discipline and intellectual dissent. Returning to the symbolism of the Stalin era had something of the appeal to "law and order" sentiments in America. It was also Brezhnev's way of undergirding the Party's legitimacy as well as the legitimacy of his own rule, by stressing the continuity of Soviet rule. Khrushchev, too, had tried this when he tried to present himself as the restorer of Lenin's style of rule. Since the 1966 Party Congress, the Brezhnev regime has promoted a balanced view of Stalin, though it has been defensive about Stalin's record as leader in World War II. The issue remains a delicate one; consequently the regime has reserved the Stalin issue for its own attention, instead of following Khrushchev's tactic of turning an army of writers, film makers and commentators loose to improvise their own versions of de-Stalinization.

The Brezhnev Style of Leadership

Kremlin watchers abroad were intrigued to notice that Brezhnev, in delivering his concluding address to the 23rd Party Congress (1966), listed the new composition of the Politburo and Secretariat in order of political importance rather than in alphabetical order. This had been the practice in Lenin's time, it was done during the Great Purge, and, having been resumed at the 1952 Party Congress, it was then dropped two years later, a little over a year after Stalin had died. Hierarchical listing, therefore, had accompanied some but not all periods of leadership struggle. Was a new struggle now brewing? Brezhnev's speech had been broadcast, so there was no mistake about his list, but the "complete version" of his speech given subsequently by TASS (the Soviet press agency) gave an alphabetical listing. This was even stranger—had Brezhnev's colleagues objected to his list? In the years that followed, the Politburo was listed alphabetically. Then at the 24th Party Congress in 1971, the mystery was solved: exactly the same procedure was followed, Brezhnev giving the hierarchical listing orally, the newspapers and all subsequent printed accounts giving the alphabetical listing. Brezhnev himself had little to worry about—his name came first on the alphabetical list too (see Diagram 5–1).

More important than the eternal question of "Who will be next?" or "Who is struggling with whom?" is the question of the style of leadership, and its meaning for the Party as an institution of rule within a larger political system. The delicate insertion of a hierarchical list of the Politburo at both Party congresses could only have been Brezhnev's own work (no one else would dare organize the hierarchy for him), and it illustrates his style. He had never been a vociferous supporter of the collective leadership idea, least of all after Khrushchev's removal. By the end of the 1966 Party Congress he had established himself as the executive both of the Party and of the entire political system. Important functions could be shared, including representation of the Soviet Union in international negotiations (e.g., Kosygin's "Glassboro Summit" with President Johnson in 1967). Ultimate responsibility for policy, however, could not be shared. The hierarchical list served at both Party

DIAGRAM 5–1
Interlocking Membership of the Top Party and State Bodies as of 1973

Name	Politburo (with date of appointment)*	Secretariat and Other Party Posts	Government and Other Non-Party Posts
L. I. Brezhnev	Member 1957 (1956)†	General Secretary	
N. V. Podgorny	Member 1960 (1958)		Chairman of the Supreme Soviet Presidium
A. N. Kosygin	Member 1960 (1957)‡		Chairman of the Council of Ministers
M. A. Suslov	Member 1955	Secretary	
A. P. Kirilenko	Member 1962 (1957)	Secretary	
A. Ya. Pelše	Member 1966	Chairman of the Party Control Committee	
K. T. Mazurov	Member 1965 (1957)		First Deputy Chairman of the Council of Ministers
D. S. Polyansky	Member 1960 (1958)		First Deputy Chairman of the Council of Ministers
A. N. Shelepin	Member 1964		Chairman of the All-Union Council of Trade Unions
V. V. Grishin	Member 1971 (1961)	First Secretary of the Moscow Party Committee	
D. A. Kunayev.	Member 1971 (1966)	First Secretary of the Kazakh Party	
V. V. Shcherbitsky§	Member 1971 (1965)	First Secretary of the Ukrainian Party	
F. D. Kulakov	Member 1971	Secretary	
Yu. V. Andropov	Member 1973 (1967)		Chairman of the State Security Committee (KGB)
A. A. Grechko.	Member 1973		Minister of Defense
A. A. Gromyko	Member 1973		Minister of Foreign Affairs

DIAGRAM 5-1 (continued)

Name	Politburo (with date of appointment)*	Secretariat and Other Party Posts	Government and Other Non-Party Posts
P. N. Demichev	Alternate 1964	Secretary	
Sh. R. Rashidov	Alternate 1961	First Secretary of the Uzbek Party	
D. F. Ustinov	Alternate 1965	Secretary	
P. M. Masherov	Alternate 1966	First Secretary of the Byelorussian Party	
B. N. Ponomaryov	Alternate 1972	Secretary	
M. S. Solomentsev	Alternate 1972		Chairman of the Russian Republic Council of Ministers
G. V. Romanov	Alternate 1973	First Secretary of the Leningrad Party Committee	
I. V. Kapitonov		Secretary	
K. T. Katushev		Secretary	

*The dates in parentheses designate the earlier appointment as alternates of those who are now full members. Names of the Politburo members and alternates are given in the nonalphabetical order announced by Brezhnev at the close of the 24th Party Congress in April 1971. Those appointed since that date are added at the end of the lists of members and alternates respectively.

†Brezhnev was also an alternate in Stalin's enlarged Presidium (as the Politburo was renamed at that point) from October 1952 to March 1953.

‡Kosygin was also an alternate in 1946–48, a full member in 1948–52, an alternate once more in the enlarged body of 1952–53, after which he was dropped entirely until his appointment as an alternate in 1957.

§Shcherbitsky was an alternate in 1961–63 as well.

congresses as a symbol of the kind of executive responsibility that necessitates control over the position of the executive's top associates.

What caught the attention of Kremlin watchers in the 1971 list was that Kosygin had dropped to third place, behind Nikolai Podgorny. Podgorny had been an ardent supporter of a consumers' goods priority during the Khrushchev period, and he was equally outspoken after Khrushchev's fall. An attack on some of his close associates in the Kharkov Party organization, and his elevation to the dubious honor of serving as chief of state, at the end of 1966, would ordinarily have meant that his political star was in decline. The head of state, formally the Chairman of the

Supreme Soviet Presidium, had ordinarily not ranked with the most powerful leaders. But Brezhnev's appointment to this post in 1960 had removed him as Party Secretary in the midst of personnel changes which Khrushchev had been obliged to make in the wake of the U-2 crisis; here was a different use for this largely ceremonial office. In 1965 the same thing apparently happened to Podgorny, in circumstances which left no doubt that he was being chastised for his strong advocacy of an increase in consumer-oriented investment. Still, he occupied the third place (after Brezhnev and Kosygin) in Brezhnev's political ranking at the 23rd Party Congress in 1966. In 1967, when Brezhnev gave his support to a new emphasis on consumers' goods (the sudden escalation of the Vietnam conflict in 1965–66 had delayed this) Podgorny's liability on this score vanished. He began performing important functions in contacts with foreign governments, and in other ways displayed ability and initiative without, apparently, being disposed to use his talents to build a political following. Alexander Shelepin, who showed every sign of seeking support in both Party and state organs, was deprived of his key posts in the manner already described. Now he found himself at the tail end of the incumbent Politburo members on the 1971 list, ahead only of the new appointees.

Coping with Stresses

While on the surface the Brezhnev administration appears not to have experienced the intense top-level struggles that characterized much of the Khrushchev period, there has been ample evidence of conflict from 1965 on. Observers who stress the stability of the Brezhnev period can point to the absence of mass expulsions from high office, the compromise character of the major decisions, and the fact that decisions once taken have been long-lasting, and have not been subverted in the process of execution. On the other hand, those who stress Soviet politics as a process of unending conflict can also point to some evidence. Adoption of the 1965 economic management reform showed a strong cleavage between the leading state officials on the Politburo and spokesmen for the Party bureaucracy, and there are indications that the reform was salvaged by Brezhnev with some difficulty.[21] Podgorny's removal from the Secretariat at the end of 1965 can be seen as a consequence of his having supported the proponents of a thoroughgoing consumer-oriented reform. The unending debate over resource allocation, and the accompanying debate over the Party's economic role, have played a part in most top-level personnel changes. It is possible to argue that the absence of sweeping changes in the Politburo and Secretariat does not by itself indicate har-

---

[21] Tatu, *Power in the Kremlin*, pp. 429–60.

mony. Brezhnev has dealt with his policy opponents in cautious fashion, one by one, and may have been blocked in his efforts to oust or demote them more rapidly than he did.[22] The increasing amount of publicity sought by Brezhnev himself may indicate his growing conviction that strong personal leadership is necessary for a stable decision-making process. While the Brezhnev-oriented publicity is not aimed at building a Stalin-like charisma, it represents a significant change from the restrained image of the mid-1960s, the effort to publicize the two-man team of Brezhnev and Kosygin and to stress the "collective" in collective leadership.

The first major Politburo reshuffling came in April 1973, when two full members and an alternate were replaced. However, this change did not come in the form of a sudden attack on a group of opponents; it was quite unlike Khrushchev's expulsion of his foes in 1957. Each man had already suffered demotion in his assignment outside the Politburo, and the probable reasons for the demotions were various. Pyotr Shelest had been removed as Party chief of the Ukraine a year before, and was moved into the relatively unimportant assignment of deputy prime minister in Moscow. His uncompromising hard-line stance against the reformist Czech leaders in 1968 had now become an obstacle to better relations in Eastern Europe, and his failure to stem manifestations of Ukrainian nationalism probably played a role too. Gennadi Voronov had been removed as head of government in the Russian Republic in 1971, probably because of his opposition to a 1970 decision on improving agricultural output.[23] He too had been assigned to a comparatively minor ministerial post in the central government. Vassili Mzhavanadze, an alternate Politburo member and for 20 years the Party chief of Georgia, was clearly marked for removal when he was retired from his Georgian post in the fall of 1972 without further assignment. Besides his age (he was 70 at the time), he had presided over an increasingly scandal-plagued republic, which was also displaying some unsettling (to Moscow) signs of national consciousness.

The way in which the three vacancies were filled represented a striking new departure in the composition of the Politburo. Yuri Andropov became the first internal security chief to sit on the Politburo since Beria; Andrei Grechko was the first Defense Minister on the Politburo since Zhukov's brief term in 1956–57; and Andrei Gromyko, Foreign Minister since 1957, was the first person in his post since Molotov to attain the top policy level.[24] The appointments meant several things: they rewarded men

---

[22] See the interpretation in Werner G. Hahn, *The Politics of Soviet Agriculture, 1960–1970* (Baltimore: Johns Hopkins Press, 1972), pp. 261–68.

[23] Ibid., chapter 11 and Postscript.

[24] At the time Trotsky was Commissar for Foreign Affairs, November 1917 to March 1918, the Politburo had not yet been established in permanent form.

who had supported Brezhnev in important policy initiatives, a standard practice in making appointments; they gave weight to "groups" (well-defined agencies in this case) whose influence was historically suspect in Soviet politics; and they added weight to Brezhnev's policy of seeking accommodation with Europe and the West, which in turn has become an important buttress of his increasingly strong personal leadership.

CONTINUITY AND CHANGE

Neither the differences and tensions among Soviet leaders, nor the removal of some because of the policy positions they have taken, nor the General Secretary's strong personal leadership at present, distinguish the Soviet system from many other political systems, including the democracies. These characteristics could very well persist even while other features of the Soviet political process change.

The outward features of the policy-making process have remained fairly constant during the Khrushchev and Brezhnev periods. Both leaders have described to foreign correspondents how the Politburo meets once a week to discuss major issues. Unanimity is sought through discussion, but when differences still remain, they may be settled by a simple majority vote (according to Khrushchev) or by appointing a committee to work out the differences (according to Brezhnev).[25] While we do not know what issues, if any, are actually decided in the course of Central Committee discussions and votes, this semiannual gathering of (currently) 396 members and alternates is primarily a forum in which the top leaders seek advice, information, and support. The Central Committee members (apart from the top leaders, who are also members) are closer to the day-to-day problems of their specialities than are the Politburo members and Party Secretaries. They can exert an important influence on decisions because of their expertise. Party congresses, while far too large (4,963 at the 1971 Congress) to do more than ratify decisions, are an important sounding board for both the top leaders and the Central Committee members, including those who wish to register dissent from prevailing politics, albeit in guarded and usually technical language.

Another kind of constant has been the Party's continued monopoly of the decision-making processes. Even those officials who have challenged certain policies by using non-Party agencies for support (e.g., opposition to Khrushchev's 1958 educational reforms from within various education ministries) have had to carry their case to Party authorities. The Party

---

[25] Khrushchev's statement is cited in Jerome M. Gilison, *British and Soviet Politics: Legitimacy and Convergence* (Baltimore: Johns Hopkins Press, 1972), pp. 147–48. Brezhnev, shortly before his June 1973 trip to the United States, described Politburo meetings to a group of foreign correspondents who met with him in the same room used by the Politburo.

Secretariat, through its all-pervasive power of appointment, is able to reshuffle high-level personnel both inside and outside the Party so as to prevent any agency or group of agencies from imposing its own will on the decision-making process. The Secretariat and the whole Party bureaucracy is sufficiently equipped with its own expertise to deal with the claim of any agency or "group" to ultimate wisdom on a given policy issue.

Finally, the close interdependence of the top leaders has not changed, in spite of Khrushchev's efforts (and, possibly, Brezhnev's in the 1970s) to lessen it. If the General Secretary does not command a majority for his policies in the Politburo and among the Party Secretaries, it is risky to push ahead in spite of their opposition. Khrushchev took an enormous risk—though it was probably the only course left open to him—in 1957 when he appealed to the Central Committee; and his removal in 1964 came about in part—and perhaps mainly—because he persisted in seeking ways to circumvent objections. An American president can appeal to the public over the heads of a recalcitrant Congress; he can also fire Cabinet officials with relative impunity. A British prime minister can renew his party's mandate by calling for elections, and thereby hold opposition among his fellow leaders at bay; he can also fire cabinet members with (apparently) greater ease than the General Secretary can dismiss his Politburo colleagues.[26]

A corollary of this interdependence is that the problem of succession remains a touchy and potentially explosive matter. There is only one precedent for the removal of a Party leader (Khrushchev in 1964), and no precedent for dealing with a resignation.[27] Unlike the prime minister of a parliamentary democracy, the General Secretary cannot warn his colleagues that all of them will be out of office at the next elections if their policies fail. The other Politburo members, for the most part, cannot warn the General Secretary that electoral disaster—or failure of a bill in parliament—will serve to force his resignation as leader of the Party. Discussions among Politburo members about the desirability of removing the General Secretary could bring about their demotions. One can only imagine the extreme care with which Suslov—for we presume it was he—served as intermediary for the discussions that led to Khrushchev's removal in 1964. Those observers who stress that Party institutions are, in spite of all these difficulties, the legitimate institutions through which to replace the leader, can of course point to the fact

---

[26] Gilison points out that the greatest purge of the 1960s in a major power was that carried out in 1962 by British Prime Minister Macmillan, not the changes effected by Khrushchev or Brezhnev. Gilison, *British and Soviet Politics*, p. 149.

[27] When Malenkov was obliged to give up his post as Party Secretary shortly after Stalin's death, he was not the General Secretary, and had had very little time to consolidate his position as de facto Party leader.

that Party protocol was indeed observed when Khrushchev was dismissed. But it is hard to defend the legitimacy of a *process* which has been used only once, and which demonstrated the necessity of working through those institutions by means of a highly secret, swiftly executed plot.

Changes in the policy-making process since 1953 stand out far less clearly than the constant features. The one truly significant change lies in the degree and type of consultation on policy matters which have been promoted by the top Party leaders. The details of many domestic issues have been opened up for discussion in the press and at public meetings: economic reforms, social welfare, education, and legal matters have figured prominently. The increasingly complex problems of a mature industrial society have heightened the role both of specialists not directly involved in policy-making, and of administrators who are necessarily involved because of their positions. A study of Khrushchev's 1958 educational reforms found top political leaders to be increasingly dependent on expert judgment and "policy groups" whose influence in politics is increasingly felt.[28]

A major study of the Khrushchev period concluded that the influence of various groupings has been promoted by the fact that autocratic one-man rule has ended, leaving an oligarchy to settle its policies by debate:

> Inevitably, conflicts among the leaders also reflect the rivalries among the various apparatuses and bureaucracies in both the party and state structure. A leader must win and hold the support of a combination of such organizational groupings adequate to secure his position. His actual or potential rivals can look for aid from those bureaucratic elements discontented with the leader's policy. With the loss of an absolute political will such as Stalin's and the waning of the system of terror, conflict and controversy both within and among the bureaucratic, professional and intellectual groupings staffing the modern Soviet state increasingly resonate in the politics of leadership.[29]

Probably the most interesting single question in the present-day study of Soviet politics is whether or not this development has become stabilized in the sense that the Party is able to contain policy-making within its own framework, or at least within a framework which is entirely determined by the Party leadership. Far from being a threat to the Party's dominance of the policy process, the involvement of many outside groups and points of view may actually be an advantage: it brings out different points of view, it gives many middle-level officials and specialists a sense

---

[28] Joel J. Schwartz and William R. Keech, "Group Influence and the Policy Process in the Soviet Union," *American Political Science Review* 62 (September 1968), pp. 840–51.

[29] Carl J. Linden, *Khrushchev and the Soviet Leadership, 1957–1964* (Baltimore: Johns Hopkins Press, 1966), p. 20.

of involvement in policy-making, it can be used to elicit wider cooperation in carrying out decisions, and it casts the Party somewhat more
in the role of wise mediator and somewhat less in the role of collective
autocrat. In the Brezhnev period, however, there is so far little evidence
that group involvement of this kind is the harbinger of any basic changes
in the core of the policy-making process, the oligarchy presided over
by a strong if not all-powerful leader.

FOR FURTHER READING

Biographical accounts of the first two successors to Stalin include Martin
Ebon, *Malenkov: Stalin's Successor* (New York: McGraw Hill, 1953); Ed-
ward Crankshaw, *Khrushchev: A Career* (New York: Viking Press, 1966);
Konrad Kellen, *Khrushchev: A Political Portrait* (New York: Praeger, 1961);
and Lazar Pistrak, *The Grand Tactician: Khrushchev's Rise to Power* (New
York: Praeger, 1961).

On the issue of succession, see Howard R. Swearer, *The Politics of Succession in the U.S.S.R.* (Boston: Little, Brown, 1964), a largely documentary
survey; also Myron Rush, *Political Succession in the USSR* (New York:
Columbia University Press, 1965). The de-Stalinization speech of 1956 is
translated, with other documents of the period, in *The Anti-Stalin Campaign
and International Communism* (New York: Columbia University Press, 1956).
See also the analysis of this speech in Bertram D. Wolfe, *Khrushchev and
Stalin's Ghost* (New York: Praeger, 1957).

Wolfgang Leonhard, *The Kremlin Since Stalin* (New York: Praeger, 1962)
is a good introductory overview of the early post-Stalin period. An excellent
analysis of Khrushchev's leadership strategy is Carl Linden, *Khrushchev and
the Soviet Leadership, 1957–1964* (Baltimore: Johns Hopkins Press, 1965).
The 1957 crisis is analyzed in Roger Pethybridge, *A Key to Soviet Politics:
The Crisis of the Anti-Party Group* (New York: Praeger, 1962). The last
events of the Khrushchev period are covered in William Hyland and Richard
Wallace Shyrock, *The Fall of Khrushchev* (New York: Funk and Wagnalls,
1968).

As to documentation, a handy source of Khrushchev's statements is
*Khrushchev Speaks; Selected Speeches, Articles and Press Conferences,
1949–1961* (Ann Arbor, Mich.: University of Michigan Press, 1963). Abbrevi-
ated stenographic records of the Party congresses have been prepared by
the *Current Digest of the Soviet Press* (itself the best single primary source,
presently published weekly in Columbus, Ohio); these appear under the general heading *Current Soviet Policies*, beginning with the 19th Party Congress
(1952) as vol. I, and including all successive congress, the latest being the
24th Congress, vol. VI. A handy source of the text of the 1961 Party Program
is Arthur P. Mendel (ed.), *Essential Works of Marxism* (New York: Bantam,
1961).

So far no truly definitive works on the Brezhnev-Kosygin era have appeared. Michel Tatu's *Power in the Kremlin* (New York: Viking Press,
1969), a very detailed "Kremlinological" study, covers the period 1960–66.

Collections of studies include Alexander Dallin and Thomas B. Larson (eds.), *Soviet Politics Since Khrushchev* (Englewood Cliffs, N.J.: Prentice-Hall, 1968), and John W. Strong (ed.), *The Soviet Union Under Brezhnev and Kosygin* (New York: Van Nostrand Reinhold, 1971). The relation of politics to economic issues is covered in two detailed works, Werner G. Hahn, *The Politics of Soviet Agriculture, 1960–1970* (Baltimore: Johns Hopkins Press, 1972), and Abraham Katz, *The Politics of Economic Reform in the Soviet Union* (New York: Praeger, 1972).

Pioneering studies which attempt to relate Soviet and Western democratic political processes are: Zbigniew Brzezinski and Samuel P. Huntington, *Political Power: USA/USSR* (New York: Viking Press, 1963); and Jerome M. Gilison, *British and Soviet Politics: Legitimacy and Convergence* (Baltimore: Johns Hopkins Press, 1972). A valuable collection comparing facets of the Soviet leadership with leadership in other communist countries is Carl Beck et al., *Comparative Communist Political Leadership* (New York: McKay, 1973). Collections of analytical studies restricted to the Soviet scene are Sidney I. Ploss (ed.), *The Soviet Political Process: Aims, Techniques and Examples of Analysis* (Waltham, Mass.: Ginn, 1971), and H. Gordon Skilling and Franklyn J. C. Griffiths (eds.), *Interest Groups in Soviet Politics* (Princeton, N.J.: Princeton University Press, 1971).

Periodicals which frequently publish analyses of recent political developments in the Soviet Union include *Problems of Communism, Soviet Survey, Studies in Comparative Communism,* and *Survey.*

6

PARTY ORGANIZATION
AND MEMBERSHIP

The Communist Party, which began as a small, conspiratorial organization designed to undermine established regimes, became after the Revolution a government within a government. In addition, it built a following large enough to penetrate and control the vital processes of tens of thousands of factories, collective farms, schools, government offices, trade unions, and much else; but its membership was held to a size which was intended to maintain an elite morale based on political consciousness rather than on privilege. Today, having recovered from Stalin's attacks on some aspects of its role and on much of its membership, the Party has grown to be an intricate mechanism for coordinating the affairs of a centralized socialist economy and a centrally guided social order. Its organization is highly bureaucratized, which enables it to perform many functions which in other systems are performed by governmental agencies. Its membership from top to bottom displays an ever increasing stress on specialists to oversee the many functions of government, and of economic and social management. It has so entrenched itself in the very heart of the whole Soviet system that were the Party for some reason to be abolished, substitute agencies would have to be devised to take over its more important functions. Yet many foreign observers see the present-day Party as undergoing an identity crisis, its officials fearing that their tasks are useful but no longer essential.

The basic decisions on the Party's role in the Soviet system had been made by the middle of the 1920s, when Stalin was presiding as General Secretary over a process of bureaucratization which formed the Party apparatus much as we see it today. Decisions on membership policy have continued up to the present day, though the membership concepts of

208 The Evolution of Soviet Politics

Lenin's time and the 1920s have not changed in their essentials. A detailed survey of the evolution of both organization and membership will place in perspective the whole question of the Party's present roles within the Soviet system. As regards organization and bureaucratization, the present chapter will focus on their origins in the early years of Soviet rule, while the next three chapters will cover Party organization as it relates to the government and the economy. Membership policies will be surveyed from their beginnings right up to the present day.

Bureaucratization in the sense it is used here means two things: (1) dominance over the Party's policy-making process by its full-time staff, the "apparatus," and (2) the Party's assumption of managerial functions in the government and the economy. In the first meaning, the Party's most important business was preempted by the apparatus to the extent that by the end of the Stalin period its inner politics could be understood only as taking place within the apparatus. The "collegial" or deliberative organs of the Party from top to bottom—all the Party committees, conferences, congresses, and even the Central Committee and Politburo themselves—had been stripped of the decision-making functions they once had. Between 1939 and 1952 no Party congresses were called; Stalin had given up summoning the Central Committee, and the Politburo (at least according to Khrushchev's de-Stalinization speech of 1956) was treated by Stalin as a group of ad hoc committees. The situation in the Party's middle and lower levels was similar.

Bureaucratization in the second sense meant that Party officials intervened in the work of the state in a thoroughgoing way; no detail was too unimportant for them. While the Party's structure remained separate from that of the state, the two were merging into a single pyramid whose tendency was to reduce the Party's importance as a separate entity. Symbolic of this new relationship was the Politburo in Stalin's last year, which had come to consist predominantly of the nation's top economic managers, whose full-time posts were in the Council of Ministers and not in the Party.

We shall consider the process of bureaucratization as it developed under Lenin and Stalin in three major areas: the top command, the Party structure as a whole, and membership policies.

THE TOP COMMAND

Two Party institutions have a history that is continuous from 1903: the Central Committee and the Party Congress. One might also add the centralized Party press, so important to Lenin from the very beginning; but the very mixed fortunes of social democratic newspapers make a discontinuous history. Both the Central Committee and the congresses have evolved into very different bodies from what they were in the beginning. Today they are not only vastly larger in size and meet far less frequently than they once did, but their functions within the Party structure have changed as well. Today's Politburo appears closer to the Central Committee of 1917 in its role than to the original Politburo. Today's Central Committee resembles the old Party congresses more than today's convention-like congresses do.

The Central Committee of prerevolutionary years derived its formal mandate from the Party Congress, which elected it anew at each session. In one sense, the Central Committee of those years was more directly accountable to its constituency than it is today. Initially it was a small body, numbering three at the outset, and 22 on the eve of the Bolshevik seizure of power. It reported to the Party far more frequently than it does under the present norm of once every five years.

Between 1903 and the end of 1917 there were five congresses and seven Party conferences. Until conferences were dispensed with in the 1940s, the Rules provided that a conference be held once during each interval between congresses. Conferences met very much in the manner of congresses, except that they were not empowered to elect a new Central Committee. But, just like congresses, they did give a large number of leading Party members the opportunity to hear the top leadership render an accounting of its work.

The diminishing frequency of both congresses and conferences was an indicator of the way in which the numerically growing Central Committee was replacing them: during 1921–25 there were ten, during 1926–30 there were four, during 1931–35 a mere two, and but one in 1936–40. The last conference met in 1941, and after that the final dozen years of Stalin's rule saw only the 19th Congress in 1952, a few years before his death. While it is understandable that no congresses met during the war years, after 1945 the omission was in flagrant disregard of the Rules; the 1939 Rules, in particular, called for a congress not less than once every three years, and for an annual conference.

The Central Committee declined in importance, too. In the 1930s, the frequency of its plenums never even approached what was specified in the Rules (until 1934, bimonthly, thereafter three times a year). But it met at least once every year, and usually twice. After World War II there were only two meetings, perfunctory ones at that, in 1946 and 1947. Thereafter, we know of no meetings at all except one which convened the 19th Congress in 1952. Stalin's political system still needed the mystique of the Party to sustain its legitimacy, and yet Stalin in his last years found the Party dispensable as an instrument of rule.

The Central Committee

With the exception of the World War II period and Stalin's last years, it is the Central Committee that has served as a sort of legislative body for the Party. It grew in membership from its original "cabinet proportions" in 1917 to a size more characteristic of a legislature. By the 1930s it had passed the 100-member mark, both full members and alternates included, and in 1952, at Stalin's last Party Congress, the total jumped to 236.

There was logic in the growth of this and other organs of rule. Part of the reason lay in Stalin's artful packing of the Central Committee during the 1920s, one vital tactic which enabled him to outvote his rivals during the succession struggle. Another reason was the convenience of using Central Committee seats as rewards for service to the Party, particularly service by the top administrators of the Party apparatus. Like Privy Council rank in the history of English government, Central Committee rank endowed its holders—and the institutions in which they worked—with a sense of participation at the highest level. Finally, because the active working out of policy questions had passed to the Secretariat during the 1920s, the Central Committee came to serve more and more as a "chamber of reflection," an assembly which gave draft policy statements a final check before issuing them. This function is one which can be adapted to assemblages numbering in the hundreds; and if this is the main function, size is not of great concern. That Central Committee plenums (as its meetings are called) could also be the scene of vital, meaningful policy discussion is supported by a good deal of evidence. The usefulness of a Central Committee vote as a means of appealing questions from the Politburo was shown by Stalin a number of times in the 1920s. Thereafter it declined in importance together with the other leading Party institutions. At the time of Stalin's death, when these institutions had been neglected for years in favor of Stalin's highly personal channels of rule, there was a real question whether they could be resurrected to serve an active role once more.

One interesting thing about the decline of the Central Committee under Stalin—and the same applies in different ways to the Party congresses and the Politburo—is that his neglect of these Party institutions reflected a genuine fear of them. One would imagine that, after the Great Purge, nothing more was to be feared from any Central Committee Stalin might pick. However, political assemblies have a way of gaining a certain leverage as against the holder of executive power if they can meet certain requirements: (1) they must be endowed with a formal legitimacy, a formal capacity to make binding decisions, as the Central Committee certainly was; (2) their membership must have some continuity, and include a certain proportion of men who are powerful in their own right because they stand in authority over some segment of the political or economic system; (3) they must meet with some regularity, and their leading members must remain in communication with one another; and (4) there must be a precedent whereby the executive, at least in the past, has had to appeal to the assembly for support. All these circumstances assisted the English Parliament, for example, in defending its privileges against the incursions of many monarchs. There were many times in English history when Parliament appeared to have no more chance of survival than did the Central Committee under Stalin. Perhaps this is a risky parallel, because none of Europe's royal houses possessed the enormous bureaucratic apparatus that Stalin put to such effective use in undercutting the leading Party organs. Still, it is impossible to avoid the conclusion that Stalin's drastic cutting down of the Party—its leading members, its procedures, its status within the overall political system—was born of a fear that opponents might find in the Central Committee or Politburo an entering wedge against his arbitrary command. The alternative is to work in and through the legitimate decision-making organs, as did the more sensible English kings and queens of past centuries.

The Party Congress

Of the evolution of the Party congresses during the Stalin period, it can only be said that their death knell as an active institution in the policy process had sounded in 1921, before Stalin's rise to power, with the Resolution on Unity. It was not just that they occurred less and less often. More important was the way in which they ceased being an accessible forum for presenting differing views on key questions. In size and manner of proceeding, they could more aptly be called conventions than deliberative bodies. The number of delegates had reached 1,000 by the 1921 Congress, and it continued to increase through the 1920s. The sessions grew longer and more wordy, and the published stenographic records filled ever thicker tomes bound in the standard red; the congresses of 1927, 1930, and 1934 ran over two weeks each. The 1934 "Congress of Victors" saw some 2,000 delegates meeting in the hall of the Kremlin Grand Palace. They listened to a fixed agenda of speeches which on the surface of things consisted mainly of praises for the triumphs of the five-year plans and eulogies for Stalin's leadership.

Leafing through the stenographic records of these early conferences, one is struck by the vast difference in tone between the three congresses of the 1930s and those of the 1920s. The latter, at least, had seen a type of vigorous debate which the Resolution on Unity had failed to stifle. Clearly there were still factions and alliances among the Party leaders, and clearly there was an appeal by these factions to the congress delegates, whose support was decidedly worth something. By the 1930s, the intent of the congresses was to promote policies already decided upon, and to turn the searchlight of criticism on those who were laggard in carrying them out, or who had made the mistake of opposing them in the past.

While Stalin's last four congresses, spread out unevenly over more than two decades, looked like staged celebrations of the regime's triumphs, they also harbored their share of the struggles over policy that continued right up to the dictator's death. What had changed, as concerns the congresses, was not the fact of differences within the Party elite, but rather the way in which these differences found expression in Party procedures. The 1934 "Congress of Victors" is particularly instructive on this point (see chapter 1).

The type of evidence we must use to discover what policy differences were dealt with at the 1934 Congress is characteristic of the evidence that has been available from later congresses, including those of the Khrushchev and Brezhnev periods. One must look for differences between policy statements produced by a congress and what the Party leaders had been saying earlier on the same subjects; differences between draft resolutions submitted to a congress and the final resolutions which it approves; differences between draft economic targets and approved targets; the order of speaking at the congress; the use of watchwords and slogans by different speakers; and the amount of time and emphasis the speakers devote to different points of the main report delivered by the Party's leader.

At each congress a new Central Committee must be elected, plus a Central Auditing Commission. The newly elected Central Committee, while the congress is still in session, then elects the Politburo, the Orgburo (until 1952, when it was abolished), and the Secretariat. The Party Control Committee (to use the current terminology—it went through several designations and reorganizations) is elected also, originally by the Congress itself, then after 1939 by the Central Committee. True, the Party Congress is not necessarily an occasion to make dramatic changes in the Politburo or any other body—this can be done between congresses just as easily. However, changes of personnel are a means by which both the leader and those who may differ with him underscore their positions and attempt to gain a better foothold in policy decisions.

All such pieces of evidence can crop up at any time, not just at Party congresses. But this evidence also tells us something about the Party Congress as an institution. It is an occasion when many decisions must be made public at once, and an occasion when all the powerful figures in the Party have a chance to state their positions. The manipulation of symbols is of great importance; even the slogans which deck the thousands of red banners that festoon Moscow as a congress meets are drawn from a carefully prepared list of slogans. While each Party Congress, from the 1930s on, has had the surface appearance of a carefully managed spectacle, each one has also brought many deep-seated disputes to a head. The congress is a test for everyone whose voice carries weight in the Party; any politically important figure who fails to score some points at the congress is in danger of seeing his position eroded as a result. In this sense, the congress remained in Stalin's time and afterwards a politically alive institution, a place where politically important things were happening, and a setting that caused a good many of them to happen. After Stalin's experience with the 1934 Congress, described in chapter 1, one can understand this reluctance to summon congresses as frequently as Lenin had done.

Politburo and Orgburo

The original Politburo was a council of seven set up for the purpose of directing the Bolshevik seizure of power; it was abolished soon afterwards. The 8th Party Congress in 1919 set up the Politburo and Orgburo ("Organizational Bureau") on a permanent basis. The Politburo hardly added anything new to established practice, since in fact Party policy was being made by an inner circle of the Central Committee, which by this time numbered over 25. There is evidence that Lenin and the top leaders were hesitant to make this group formal, and indeed the proposal ran into opposition at this Congress. An effort was made to allay suspicions by allowing Central Committee members to attend Politburo meetings, and by guaranteeing a Central Committee meeting at least once every two weeks. The impression was given that the Politburo would deal with urgent matters only, and report to the Central Committee on all its deliberations. It was accorded no formal powers— these remained with the Central Committee. Its first members were Lenin, Kamenev, Trotsky, Stalin, and Krestinsky, plus Zinoviev and Bukharin as alternates.

The Orgburo was set up for the purpose of making personnel assignments, both in and out of the Party. As we shall see a bit later, this became a key function of the Party, and one which continued to be important under Stalin when most of the Party's other functions had been greatly reduced. Stalin, the only leader who was a member of both Politburo and Orgburo, immediately began to build his influence over Party personnel matters by making full use of the Orgburo. This, indeed, was the key weapon in his rise to power. With the creation of the Secretariat in 1920, and Stalin's appointment to it as General Secretary two years later, the activities of Secretariat and Orgburo became virtually indistinguishable. It remained in existence until 1952, when it was abolished by the 19th Party Congress.

While the Central Committee grew and grew, reducing its capacity as a deliberative body, the Politburo stayed a manageable size almost until Stalin's death. In 1952 it numbered only a dozen, and had never been more than a handful above that figure. The comings and goings of its members reflected the power struggles of the 1920s and Stalin's rise to power. Rykov and Tomsky, the future "right deviationists," were added early in the NEP period. Molotov and Kalinin in 1921 became the first of a number of Stalin's appointees, followed by other "Stalinists," who included Kuibyshev, Voroshilov, Kaganovich, Kirov, and Mikoyan.

Elevation to the Politburo as Stalin's protégé was no guarantee of political security. The higher a person is raised by his political protector, the more he becomes a potential threat to the protector's power. Certainly this was the case with Kirov, whose murder in 1934 was probably arranged by Stalin. During the Great Purge the Politburo was hardly a safe place to be. Of the 15 members elected at the "Congress of Victors" in 1934, no less than seven became purge victims during the next five years, and to this number one may add Kirov himself plus one more who was appointed after 1934. Bear in mind that the 1934 Politburo no longer included the leaders of the Right and Left from the 1920s; without exception, the nine victims owed their careers to Stalin and had professed the utmost loyalty to him.

At the 19th Party Congress in 1952, Stalin's last, the Politburo and Orgburo were abruptly "merged" into a new and much larger body with 25 full members and 10 candidate members. While the Politburo had been, in form, a subcommittee of the Central Committee, the Presidium was formally authorized to carry on the Central Committee's business during the intervals between the latter's sessions. It appeared that the Politburo would now, officially, go the way of the Central Committee by suffering enlargement and transmutation into a formal decision-making body. Khrushchev in his 1956 speech stated that Stalin had plans to finish off the old Politburo, and a good deal of evidence suggests that a top-level purge of some kind was in the making. Stalin had been dead only two days when his successors, even before they had resolved other key issues, cut the Presidium's size back to 14 while retaining the new name. One interesting tidbit that came to light afterward was the existence of a Bureau as the directing body of Stalin's enlarged Presidium. We do not know its membership, or the reason for its creation, but it was in the same tradition as the early Politburo itself: a new "inner circle" made into a formal institution.

MANAGING THE ORGANIZATION

Lenin's vision of the Party was that of a dedicated corps of trained members who would be employed in all branches of the nation's work: in factories, on state and collective farms, in schools and universities, in the professions, and above all in government offices. They would be present at assemblies and conferences of every kind, beginning with the Congress of Soviets itself, to assure that their votes would go in the way the Party desired. They would serve as the main channel of Party propaganda; they would serve as examples to their fellow citizens; and they would assist their employers and organizations in achieving their goals. Like a gigantic nerve system, this great body of loyal Bolsheviks would transmit commands from the center to the many branches, and also transmit information, opinion, and even protests from the branches to the center.

The Party Rules embodied Lenin's wish for "control from within" of the nation's economic and governmental life. The Rules of 1919, particularly, devoted much attention to setting up what were then called "Party factions," today "Party groups." These were to be formed in any situation, including temporary situations such as conferences of different organizations, where more than three Party members were present. The Rules, while giving these groups autonomy in their day-to-day activity, placed them in strict subordination to the local Party committee at their particular level. Their main function was to see to it that Party directives were carried out by the non-Party bodies in which they functioned. In the early 1920s, this device was aimed particularly at the local soviets.

The 1919 Rules set forth for the first time the functions of the "Party cell" as well. Unlike Party factions, cells were permanent bodies formed at places of employment wherever at least three Party members were present. The cell was intended to be "an organization which links the masses of workers and peasants with the leading organ of the Party in a given locality." To do this, it propagated Party slogans and decisions among the masses, recruited new members, cooperated with the local Party committee in carrying on agitation and organizational work, and took "an active part, as a Party organ, in the economic and political life of the nation."[1]

The Growing Party Bureaucracy

When Lenin attacked "bureaucratism," as he did with increasing frequency toward the end of his life, he meant the state bureaucracy. The Party bureaucracy had just begun the process of expansion, which, by the end of Stalin's time, made it a rival of the state bureaucracy in its all-pervasiveness, if not in size. When Lenin in his "Testament" criticized Stalin's accumulation of power, he was referring to the man and not to the structures which had been entrusted to Stalin's command. Yet by 1921 or 1922, there were plenty of signs that the Party, too, was on the road to becoming a bureaucratic organism in its own right. The full-time officials of the Party were beginning to direct the Party's work as a network of authority within the Party, which was not the

---

[1] *KPSS v rezolyutsiyakh*, vol. 1 (Moscow: Gospolitizdat, 1954), pp. 466–67.

intent of the 1919 Party Rules. Just as the Party was meant to be the nerve system of the entire Soviet political system, so the Party bureaucracy was now becoming the Party's own nerve system. Out in the provinces, the provincial Party secretaries had become, by the end of the Civil War, the actual executives. Their local organizations were also operating with great independence of Moscow in some cases, which is not surprising in view of the confusion of those times and the haste with which the Party structure had been expanded. The same was true of Party organizations which had been improvised to keep watch over the Army, the all-important railway network, and other vital activities. It was the need to bring these organizations under the Central Committee's control that launched the Party bureaucracy.

Until his death in 1919, Yakov Sverdlov as secretary to the Central Committee had managed the Party's internal structure with the assistance of a very small staff. Since he was also the titular head of state (as Chairman of the Central Executive Committee of the Congress of Soviets) he used the hierarchy of soviets for carrying out Party directives, rather than local Party organizations. It was Krestinsky, his successor, who freed these local organizations from dependence on the soviet bodies, and consequently created the need for a central Party hierarchy to direct their affairs. He began by establishing a regular system of reports and communications between his office and the provincial organizations. At about this time, the provincial Party secretaryships became paid full-time positions; thereafter the growth of the Central Committee's bureaucracy ran parallel to the growth of a provincial bureaucracy. The "apparatus," the Party bureaucracy, was quickly taking shape.

Krestinsky's second contribution was to organize the Central Committee's apparatus into specialized departments, as had been directed by the 8th Party Congress in 1919. Of a projected nine departments, the four most important were the following: (1) *Orgotdel*, the Organization and Instruction Department, which supervised the growth and functioning of the Party's structure; (2) *Uchraspred*, the Records and Assignment Department, which set up personnel records which then served as a basis for making appointments to Party posts (and, ultimately, to important non-Party posts as well); (3) *Informotdel*, the Information and Statistics Department, which assembled data on the functioning of Party organs; and (4) *Agitprop*, the Department of Agitation and Propaganda, which first took over the propaganda functions of other Party agencies, and then by stages added supervision of the nation's press and publishing. There were also a Rural Department and a Department for Work Among Women.[2]

---

[2] For a detailed account of the setting up of the departments, see Leonard Schapiro, *The Communist Party of the Soviet Union* (New York: Random House, 1960), chapter 13.

The departments were to undergo many reorganizations, transformations and changes of name, but the functions performed by these four
important ones remained. By 1923, *Orgotdel*, now headed by Lazar
Kaganovich, had absorbed both *Informotdel* and *Uchraspred*, and was
now called *Orgraspred*—how the Bolsheviks loved to spawn acronyms!
Later in the 1920s *Informotdel* was given its original status, responsibility
for the press was separated out from *Agitprop*, and departments for
statistics and accounting were added. *Orgraspred*, because it handled assignments, was the key department. By the end of the 1920s it made
about 5,000 assignments annually, and was so swamped with work that
it was divided into sections, most of them handling specific branches
of the economy. Stalin's 1934 "Congress of Victors" saw the creation
of separate departments for industry, agriculture, transportation, and certain other economic activities, but five years later this division was replaced by the old functional approach of the 1920s. After World War
II the economic branch system of 1934 was tried once again, on a broader
scale, and this system has prevailed up to the present. The focus on
spheres of economic activity reflects the Party's increasing emphasis, since
the 1930s, on expertise in the Central Committee bureaucracy as the
best instrument for watching over the performance of the economy.

Together, these departments of the Central Committee constitute the
Secretariat. Lenin had appointed one secretary to watch over a very
small office; by the end of Stalin's rule there were five secretaries, each
entrusted with supervision of several departments; and by the end of
Khrushchev's period of power there were ten. Under Khrushchev, and
perhaps because of his great stress on Party expertise in production, the
number of departments reached about 30; his successors have reduced
this to around two dozen. (The exact number of departments is always
somewhat in doubt because the Party does not make public any kind
of official table of organization for its Secretariat. Diagram 6–1 shows
the present state of our information.) The size of the central apparatus,
which had begun with a bit more than a dozen workers under Sverdlov,
had risen to 600 by 1921, and one estimate from the 1960s puts the
figure at between 1,300 and 1,500.[3] Considering that the Party's membership had risen to nearly 15 million by the early 1970s, roughly a 30-fold
increase over 1921, the increase in the Secretariat is a very modest one.
Of more interest is the size of the overall Party apparatus, that is, how
many paid staff pesons are employed by the Party. While no figures
of this kind have been published, one careful estimate for the latter 1950s
put the number at 240,000, which means that roughly one out of every
40 members at that time was in the apparatus.[4]

[3] Abdurakhman Avtorkhanov, *The Communist Party Apparatus* (Cleveland:
World Publishing Co., 1968), p. 209.
[4] Schapiro, *The Communist Party of the Soviet Union*, pp. 572–73.

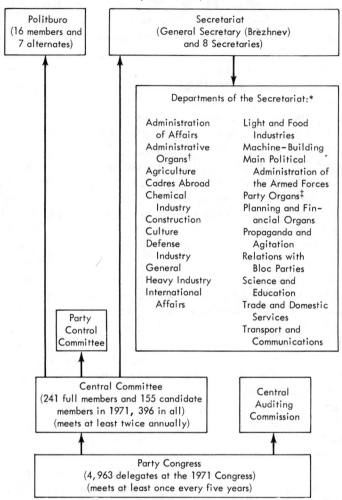

DIAGRAM 6-1
Central Organs of the Communist Party
(as of 1971)

*Official lists of these departments are not published. The only basis
for our knowledge about them is occasional identification in Soviet publications; hence the possibility that this list may be incomplete.
†Oversees law-enforcement agencies.
‡In charge of the most important appointments to both Party and
governmental posts.

The Uses of the Apparatus

More important than just the size or structure of the Party apparatus
were—and are—the uses made of it. The term "bureaucratization" as
we are using it here means the making of decisions by paid staffs which
are supposed to be made instead by elective bodies. The important decisions are of three kinds: appointments and elections to Party posts, ques-

tions of Party organization, and Party policies for the nation. From 1920, there is no doubt that the first two kinds of decisions were heavily influenced by the Records and Assignments Department (*Uchraspred*) and the Organization and Instruction Department (*Orgotdel*). As to personnel decisions, Party directives from the early 1920s provide a chronicle of the assignment by *Uchraspred* of over 50,000 Party cadres to various posts during the 1920s and early 1930s. The term "cadres" means Party members with the training and qualifications for leading positions, primarily positions outside the Party itself, in government, the economy, and the armed forces. But the same personnel files which were used to fill non-Party posts also enabled the Secretariat to select Party secretaries, other apparatus workers and Party committee members at different levels. During a 12-month period in 1922–23, for example, some 42 provincial Party secretaries were approved by the Secretariat, a rank that for many Party members was to be a stepping-stone to membership on the Central Committee and the Politburo.

The Secretariat's power to transfer Party officials from one post to another became one of its principal weapons for bringing faction-ridden local organizations in line. Individuals in such cases were assigned to other jobs in other areas, without reduction in rank. Initially this was used simply for the purpose of achieving harmony. Later on, from 1921, it was used for political purposes as well, local supporters of the Workers' Opposition being among the first victims of the system of "honorable exile." In this way, a device that began as a politically neutral way of disciplining a squabbling Party organization turned into a way of breaking up dissident groups.[5]

The growing influence of the Secretariat over matters of organization, exercised largely through *Orgotdel*, may be traced in the numerous regulations it issued concerning procedure. Provincial Party secretaries, for example, were required not only to report in person to the Central Committee in Moscow every month (meaning, in practice, to the staff of the Secretariat) but to submit secret reports on local political matters as well. The Secretariat also issued detailed regulations on the status and pay of local Party staffs.[6]

Stalin in Charge of the Bureaucracy

Stalin's appointment as General Secretary in 1922 was his greatest single coup in climbing the ladder of Party organization. It must also

[5] See the case history of the Samara organization described in Robert V. Daniels, "The Secretariat and the Local Organizations in the Russian Communist Party, 1921–1923," *The American Slavic and East European Review*, 16 (February 1957), pp. 32–49.

[6] Schapiro, *The Communist Party of the Soviet Union*, pp. 253–54.

be set down as one of Lenin's greatest mistakes. Only nine months after the appointment had been made, Lenin dictated the "Testament," in which he warned that Stalin had "concentrated enormous power in his hands" and was not always cautious in using it; this was followed by a postscript ten days later in which Lenin proposed that a way be found for removing Stalin from his new post. One can only surmise that Lenin's doubts about Stalin were mingled with an enormous confidence in him as an administrator. Lenin may have been disturbed more by Stalin's abrasive personal manner than by his bureaucratic manipulations: the postscript to the Testament was occasioned by Stalin's rudeness toward Lenin's wife as Lenin lay ill. Until 1922, there is every indication that Lenin had a high regard for Stalin.

In any case, Stalin had arrived at his high posts with the full support of the Party's "inner circle"; he was a member of the temporary Politburo of 1917, of the full Politburo of seven that was created in 1919, and of the Orgburo, likewise created in 1919. We noted earlier that Stalin was the only Politburo member who also sat on the Orgburo. Until the Secretariat was able to handle the large volume of work involved, the Orgburo itself was directly responsible for making appointments and supervising the growth of the whole Party structure. As the Politburo's specialist in matters of Party administration, therefore, Stalin was the logical person to coordinate the whole apparatus. In the growing Soviet state structure, Stalin in 1919 was put in charge of a superagency that also happened to be one of Lenin's pet ideas: The Commissariat of Workers' and Peasants' Inspection (*Rabkrin*). This was meant to be an all-pervasive intelligence service for overseeing the work of the civil service, much of which the Bolsheviks had inherited from Tsarism. As such, it was to be an incorruptible guardian, free of the bureaucratic evils it was supposed to ferret out. While *Rabkrin* itself succumbed to the same evils even before Lenin's death, Stalin's appointment to this post had been a signal expression of Lenin's confidence. True, Trotsky's autobiography reports that Lenin was having doubts even at the time (April 1922) Stalin was made Secretary General ("This cook can serve only peppery dishes");[7] but the appointment was made with Lenin's full knowledge and support.

Lenin and Stalin

It is not likely, either, that Lenin and other Party leaders thought of the new General Secretary's post as a routine job of administrative coordination. Stalin, already the Orgburo's one link with the Politburo, would now be given formal administrative control over functions that

---

[7] Isaac Deutscher, *Stalin: A Political Biography* (New York: Oxford University Press, 1949), p. 232.

he had already been supervising. While running the Secretariat involved a huge burden of administrative detail which the other leading Bolsheviks were temperamentally loathe to handle, its large and growing power over personnel matters was actually promoted by Lenin. Lenin's concern for the Party during the period of demoralization that followed the Civil War led him to weld it together into a unified, efficient, maneuverable political instrument. The centralized bureaucracy, the apparatus, was to be the key link for day-to-day operations.

It was characteristic of Lenin during his brief years of power that he came to regard the structures he set up as Frankenstein monsters. The solution he sought to "bureaucratic distortions" was to install more bureaucratic structures and control mechanisms; we have already noted *Rabkrin*. Central direction, central coordination, highly centralized policy-making—these were very much in the blood of the man whom later critics were to call a "revolutionary with a bureaucratic mind." So the power that Lenin placed in Stalin's hands was no accident at all. That Stalin would then use this power to pack Party congresses, the Central Committee and lower Party bodies with his supporters should not have surprised Lenin either, had he lived to see this. He, Lenin, had let no opportunity slip to do the same during his years of exile; if his behind-the-scenes maneuvering to this end was less flagrant than Stalin's later became, it was because he had a persuasive tongue and was able, if necessary, to meet opposition head-on in public.

In retrospect we wonder why Stalin's rise to power should have surprised anyone. The position he started with at the time of Lenin's illness was not an obscure administrative job which he somehow parlayed into great power; the job of General Secretary was politically important when it was established. Nor was it having this job that gave him his grip on Party appointments and organization; he had exercised great influence in this area before 1922, and would have continued to do so without the new job. There had been no opposition to Stalin's various high-level appointments from the leading Bolsheviks who were soon to become his political foes, not even from Trotsky, though the latter had already squabbled with Stalin over other matters.

The surprise and anguish at Stalin's rise to power came rather from the assumptions which the leading Bolsheviks had derived from Lenin's hopes, while playing down Lenin's fears. Because Lenin had led the Party as its persuader-in-chief, his lieutenants assumed that his successor must lead in the same style: everyone's eyes were fixed on Trotsky. Lenin had assumed that Party democracy in the top organs must prevail in the end, that a solid majority would form around suitable leadership in the Central Committee and the Party congresses. He had assumed, further, that a close watch over Party procedures, especially that exercised through the Control Commission established in 1921 (see below), would suffice to curb abuses of power. On all three counts, it would be easier to pardon Lenin's optimism were it not he who had undermined the last two, one through the Resolution on Unity, the other through according the apparatus an arbitrary power that no watchdog device within the Party structure could curb.

A Watchdog for the Party

The origin of the Central Control Commission (today called the Party Control Committee) furnishes another example of the politicization of Party bodies. Here too, a mechanism set up to promote smooth functioning of the organization became a weapon used in factional struggles. With the Party's enormous growth after 1917, some means became necessary for dealing with Party members who used their membership for private ends, who violated the Party Rules for advancing their political fortunes, or whose private misconduct became a liability to their Party work. During the Civil War period the Central Committee had set up a group for dealing with these cases, which meant assembling the facts and deciding on the appropriate action: a reprimand, demotion to candidate membership, withdrawal of Party membership, and so forth. At the 10th Congress, in 1921, it was decided to entrust this function to a whole separate hierarchy of commissions headed by a new Central Control Commission. This was the same Congress that passed Lenin's Resolution on Unity, and there was a fine irony in the fact that a body which was to play a major role in purging the opposition started as a concession to demands by the "Democratic Centralists," an opposition group.

A genuine effort was made to maintain the independence of these commissions, but it was not enough. They were to be elected by Party conferences and congresses, in the same manner as the Central Committee and the local Party committees, and no dual membership was permitted; that is, no member of a Party committee, or holder of a Party office, could sit on a control commission. Immediately the problem arose of conflicts between a control commission and the Party committee whose affairs it watched over. Members of the control commission were entitled to participate in Party committee sessions and have access to all their records. On the other hand, the control commissions were dependent on the regular Party structure for carrying out their decisions, for they had no staff of their own. Jurisdictional disputes arose between committee and commission, which could be settled only by a joint meeting of the two, or by appeal to the next higher Party committee. It might have been possible to set up some kind of formal judicial structure, with the "judges" carefully removed from the day-to-day disputes in which the control commissions were embroiled. That, however, was not in the

Bolshevik mentality; furthermore, the authority conferred upon the growing Party apparatus was by now such that Party secretaries were not likely to put up with any diminution of their authority.

The solution to this dilemma, again a typical one for the Bolsheviks, was to turn the control commissions into a tightly centralized hierarchy in their own right, equipped with their own staff. In 1922 Stalin reorganized the seven-member Commission in order to fill it with his own supporters; it was headed by Kuibyshev, whose career thus far owed everything to Stalin's help. One should say, in fact, that Stalin packed the Commission with a vengeance: it rose from seven to 50 members in its first two years and numbered around 200 by the end of the 1920s. Stalin's idea of holding joint meetings of the Commission and the Central Committee proved an effective way of packing the latter in deciding important disciplinary cases. The Commission now became a weapon for disciplining—and in some cases dismissing—local Party leaders. The concept of violations of the Party Rules was broad enough to permit politically motivated dismissals. Earlier, before 1922, the control commissions had assumed authority over government officials as well as Party officials; now this authority was used to discipline local government bodies which attempted to assert their independence. In 1924 the Central Control Commission's political purpose was stated openly in a new set of regulations. These referred to its role in struggling against groupings, tendencies, and factions, its surveillance of unhealthy ideological phenomena, and its duty to purge "ideologically alien, harmful and demoralizing elements."[8]

Ultimately, Stalin was to use the state security organs, not the Commission, as his principal weapon for dealing with Party dissidents. For the time being, the Commission served the purpose of keeping the OGPU (then the top state security agency) out of Party business. Yet Kuibyshev stated to the 1925 Party Congress that the Commission maintained close relations with the OGPU, and that the latter was a supplier of information on Party members. Stalin obviously knew the value of keeping independent hierarchies, while at the same time he did not hesitate to fuse Party and government bodies in the same task where it suited his purposes. In the case of the Commission, it was Lenin's idea—the last one he ever contributed, in 1923, to the system he had built—to fuse the Commission with the ailing *Rabkrin*, the Workers' and Peasants' Inspectorate. Like so many of Lenin's other organizational cures, this temporary Party-state experiment served only to amalgamate administrative problems rather than solve them.

What began as a mechanism for resolving lower-level political disputes within the Party in an impartial fashion attained its real day of glory

---

[8] Schapiro, *The Communist Party of the Soviet Union*, p. 319; see also pp. 255–58.

by being brought right into the mainstream of high-level Party politics. The 1934 Congress had voted to elect the Commission henceforth in the entire Congress, rather than let the Central Committee elect it as in the past. This was in order to give it authority to discipline Central Committee members themselves, a clear indication of Stalin's intentions. As if the message were not clear enough already, Stalin placed his purge expert Nikolai Yezhov in charge of the Commission in 1935. At the end of the Great Purge, in which Yezhov himself had become a victim, the Commission was relegated to a lesser role, and was once again selected by the Central Committee.

Control over the Provinces

From what we have seen of the Party's central supervisory mechanisms it is not hard to deduce the realities of the Party's lower structures. From the early Party Rules of 1919 and 1922 on, these structures display some constant features: 1. The various levels of Party organizations correspond to the levels of government, and the territory covered by each Party organization coincides with a governmental jurisdiction. 2. The same principle was applied to the federal level after 1924; national parties have retained their identity and organization, but as components of the Communist Party of the Soviet Union (CPSU). Only the Russian Communist Party was abolished as such, in consideration of the fears of the non-Russian parties; the provincial Party organizations in Russia are accountable directly to the CPSU's central organs. 3. Party organizations at the lowest level are usually functional rather than territorial: these are the Party cells and party factions.[9] They work under the supervision of one or another territorial Party organization. 4. In form, each territorial organization consists of (a) Party members, who select delegates to (b) a conference, which meets at stated intervals and elects (c) a Party committee, which makes decisions for the whole Party organization, but entrusts ongoing supervision to (d) a bureau, a small body which ordinarily consists of the top officials of Party and state, plus one or two important economic administrators, the top trade union officials, the Komsomol leader, or other local "notables." 5. Each Party organization is called to exercise detailed supervision over the organizations immediately below it, including the power of vetoing appointments and policy decisions.

Appendix 2 gives the Party Rules as they stand at present, embodying all these principles just as their predecessors did from Lenin's time on.

---

[9] Until World War II, there were many rural primary Party organizations based on groups of villages, and today the Party Rules permit territorially based primary organizations both in villages and in urban districts corresponding to the jurisdiction of housing administrations.

The last point needs some elaboration, since the one important feature about which the Rules have little to say is the extent and interrelations of the Party bureaucracy or apparatus. First of all, democratic centralism is upheld explicitly in the Rules. Next, each Party organization must be "confirmed" or "ratified" by the organization immediately above it in the pyramid. This means in practice that the personnel of each Party committee and its bureau not only must be selected from within their own jurisdiction, but must pass muster at the next higher level as well. Next, a point mentioned only obliquely in the Rules but referred to in other Party documents, officials of the lower Party organs are assigned to their posts by the Secretariat in Moscow; their presence is then legalized through local election. And finally, the early 1920s saw the provincial Party secretaries called to Moscow periodically to report to the Secretariat on their work, a type of communications which bypassed the reporting functions set forth in the Rules.

The provincial secretaries, who were made full-time officials in the 1919 Rules, soon became key persons in the Party's actual structure of power. The relationship of the provinces to the center was not that of provincial Party committees reporting to the Central Committee and receiving instructions from it, but of full-time Party secretaries communicating with officials in various offices of the growing Secretariat staff in Moscow. The bureaucratization of the Party meant very precisely the assumption of its members' functions by its paid staff, the selection of personnel and the making of policy by way of communication among its full-time workers. This was not something which grew up with time—it was there from the beginning, the Party Rules left plenty of room for it even if not elevating it to a principle, and the haste and fears of the top Party leadership promoted it.

PARTY MEMBERSHIP:
FROM ACTIVISTS TO SPECIALISTS

At the beginning of 1917, the Party probably numbered less than 25,000; at the time of the Bolshevik coup, though exact figures are lacking, it had already passed the 200,000 mark. Recruitment had been open; membership was offered to anyone willing to join, and consequently Party ranks now included many thousands who had joined the bandwagon mainly for their own advancement or protection. The new Party Rules adopted at the April 1917 Congress attempted to tighten discipline by requiring subordination to all Party directives, and made detailed provisions for expelling members. It was not until early 1919 that the Bolshevik leaders took serious steps to sift out the "careerists," as they were called. While something like 100,000 members were expelled as a result, this was only the prelude to a new wave of recruiting. This was the most critical period of the Civil War, when Party membership carried personal risk. By the spring of 1920 the figure was above 600,000, and at the crucial 10th Party Congress a year later there were nearly 750,000. The beginning of NEP, the new regime's "breathing spell," offered a chance to carry out a second purge. This together with voluntary resignations—the consequence of apathy following war and crisis— brought membership rolls back to a half million by 1922 (see Table 6–1).

TABLE 6–1
Party Membership, 1917–1972
(in thousands)

Year	Full Members	Candidates	Total
1917	24		24
1921	732		732
1924	350	122	472
1929	1,090	445	1,535
1933	2,204	1,351	3,555
1938	1,406	514	1,920
1941	2,490	1,382	3,872
1945	3,956	1,795	5,751
1949	5,335	1,018	6,352
1953	6,067	830	6,897
1957	7,001	493	7,494
1960	8,017	691	8,708
1964	10,183	839	11,022
1968	12,485	695	13,180
1972	14,109	522	14,631

Sources: T. H. Rigby, *Communist Party Membership in the U.S.S.R., 1917-1967* (Princeton, N.J.: Princeton University Press, 1968), pp. 52–53 (data for 1917 through 1964 printed by permission of Princeton University Press); *Partiinoye stroitelstvo—uchebnoye posobiye* (Moscow: Politizdat, 1970), p. 54; *Kommunist*, no. 3 (February) 1972, p. 85.

Proletarians and Others

The Party's social composition in these years is not easy to determine. According to official statistics the proportion of workers in its ranks fell from 57 percent in 1918 to 41 percent in 1921, at the beginning of the NEP. But here, as in later years, "proletarian" or "worker" as definitions could refer to a member's origins but have no reference to his occupation at the time of the tally. In 1919, at the height of the Civil War, only 11 percent were actually employed as manual workers, while over 60 percent were officials of the government, the trade unions, and the Party itself. Joining the Party offered a chance to get a job in one of several bureaucracies. The same circumstances held true for those listed as "peasants," who numbered about one fourth in the early 1920s. Judging from the large number of expulsions carried out against

Party members who were charged with concealing their bourgeois origins, these must have been a sizeable element.[10]

Even allowing much benefit of the doubt for the Party's own statistics, two conclusions emerge: 1. The Party's rank and file, far from being the "leaven in the loaf" in the factories and farms, consisted very heavily of officials. 2. The Party was proletarian more in the sense of political loyalty than it was in the sense of class background. By the early 1920s, less than half of its members were described in official statistics as proletarians, while nearly 30 percent were from a white-collar background.

By the end of the 1920s, the proportion of members engaged in nonmanual work was nearly half. Moreover, scattered data suggest that among Party cadres and officials the proportion was much higher. With the beginning of the five-year plans, a determined effort was made to increase recruiting from among industrial workers. A directive of 1929 specified that 90 percent of all recruits from industrial areas must be workers in production. By the next year, the proportion of members engaged in industrial production was closer to 50 percent than to 40 percent, where it had been a few years before.

Such rapid change was possible because the Party was in the midst of massive recruiting at this point. Membership had passed the 1 million mark in 1926; by 1930 there were 1.5 million; and just two years later the last figure had more than doubled, to 3.2 million. Inevitably there was a weeding-out process, which occurred on a scale just as massive and abrupt as the recruiting. During 1933–34 no less than 1.2 million, a third of the membership, had been expelled, so that on the eve of the Great Purge the Party was down to 2.3 million. This massive reduction was not itself related to the Purge; the bulk of those who departed at this point were the fresh recruits who had not been equal to their assignments. Recruitment was stopped early in 1933, and not resumed until the end of 1936. At that point the "Yezhov purges" were approaching their height. According to one careful estimate, the Party once again shed a third of its members; this time those dropped from the rolls included a substantial proportion of Party members of older vintage than the early 1930s. In 1939 the membership, including candidates or probationary members, had risen again to 2.5 million, over a third of them candidate members. Of the full members, something like 70 percent had joined during the previous ten years, i.e., since the beginning of the five-year plans. What had happened to the upper Party echelons, the Central Committee, and the delegates to the 1934 Party Congress had happened to the membership as a whole.[11]

The Great Purge not only changed the Party's personnel from top

---

[10] Schapiro, *The Communist Party of the Soviet Union*, pp. 233–36, analyzes such figures as are available.

[11] Ibid., pp. 435–37.

to bottom, and eliminated Stalin's former and possible future rivals. It also had the effect, whether or not Stalin intended this, of completing a process of bureaucratization that had begun under Lenin, who certainly had not intended that it go so far. The Chinese Cultural Revolution of 1966–69 was among other things a deliberate attack on the Chinese Communist Party's growing bureaucratization and the Party officials who promoted it. Stalin's Great Purge, by contrast, had no similar goal; quite the contrary, it was the continuation of the Party's old style of organization and management that made possible its swift rebuilding in 1939. To be sure, the Party's role as an entity distinct from the state and the hierarchy of economic management was a somewhat diminished one during the remainder of Stalin's rule. But its style of operation was then, and remains today, one of the overriding constants of the Soviet political system. The decisions that set the Party on this course began in Lenin's time.

After the Purge

The men Stalin brought into the Party from 1938 on, after the Great Purge had subsided, were of a different stripe than those who had been purged. They had made their early careers during the industrialization drive of the 1920s, and not in the revolutionary underground or in the Civil War; these careers were mostly technical; the men were better educated than their predecessors; and, finally, it appears that almost half of all newly admitted Party members came from a "middle class" background, i.e., their parents were employed in nonmanual occupations. The Party's admissions records of 1938–39, the protocols of the 18th Party Congress (1939), and the changes which this Congress made in the Party Rules all point to a massive effort to recruit the best from among the new generation of technicians, with little reference to class background.

Education was now stressed at the expense of working-class social origin. Having relied largely on noncommunists as technicians, engineers, and in some cases industrial managers, the economic system now had a rising generation of Soviet-educated specialists at its disposal. Soviet higher education, having stressed working-class origins in its admissions policies until the early 1930s, was now drawing increasingly on the sons and daughters of the middle classes. By 1938, over half of the students in higher education were in this category, and their proportion was increasing. As they were promoted to responsible positions in industry, they became a prime object of Party recruitment. All this did not represent a sudden shift of policy on the part of Stalin and the leadership. Stalin, in the same 1931 speech in which he talked of the need for maintaining the industrialization tempo, laid great stress on the place of the intelligentsia:

. . . [O]ur country has entered a phase of its development where the working class must create its own industrial and technical intelligentsia, capable of defending the working class's interests in the sphere of production, as the interests of the ruling class.

No ruling class has been able to do without its own intelligentsia. There is no reason to doubt that the ruling class of the USSR could not get along without its own industrial and technical intelligentsia either.[12]

The Party itself, of course, was not the immediate consumer of technical expertise, though its bureaucracy did increasingly need specialists to oversee the nation's growing economy. What the Party needed even more was political responsiveness on the part of those who served the economy with their expertise. There had been a time when loyal Bolsheviks had been sent out to manage industries, having little managerial experience and no technical knowledge to speak of. The younger generation of managers had received its professional education first. With the planned decline in the use of foreign specialists during the 1930s, these men were now a potential force that needed watching. That they never did develop into any kind of autonomous force in the Soviet system probably confirms the wisdom of recruiting them.

This change in recruitment policies was evidence of another and more fundamental kind of change. Many of the Party's functions had withered. No longer was it the bloodstream of the entire system, the mechanism which made and carried out the system's major policies. Of the functions that remained, personnel work was probably the chief one. Recruitment into the Party itself was only part of the personnel function. Even more important was keeping watch over the qualifications, performance, and advancement of specialists and managers in every branch of the nation's work. Here was a task that could be performed by a bureaucratic structure with little reference to democratic procedures. That this function survived the Great Purge is itself evidence of bureaucratization. Where an organization depends on the activity of all its members, on group activity in carrrying out decisions, a purge can destroy this activity because it requires group experience and group morale at many levels. A bureaucratic structure carrying out specific functions can be purged and rebuilt in a much shorter space of time. One of the basic concepts of modern bureaucracy is that the people in it *are* replaceable parts. The way in which the Party survived the Purge indicates the extent to which its full-time officials dominated its work even before 1934.

Campaign-Style Recruiting

If there was one central reason for the ups and downs of Party membership, it was the manner in which recruiting was carried out. When

---

[12] I. Stalin, *Voprosy Leninizma*, 11th ed. (Moscow: Gospolitizdat, 1953), p. 374.

in the 1920s there was at last a chance to recruit at a measured pace, the mass campaign was used instead. The "Lenin Enrollment" of 1924, its designation a tribute to the late leader, was first of all a maneuver by Stalin and the Secretariat to undercut the Left: the new recruits, though only candidate (probationary) members at that point, had voted for delegates to the 13th Party Congress that year in violation of the Rules. Another reason for campaign-type recruiting was that there was yet no reliable system of processing applicants' credentials. The one basis of evaluation was observation of young recruits after admission. The campaigns were also massive efforts to increase the proportion of industrial workers in Party ranks, which, as we have seen, began to show results in the late 1920s. After the 1920s, each new crisis brought in its wake the need for masses of recruits: replenishing Party ranks after the purges; getting a share of the specialists trained during the 1930s; building morale among the troops and war production workers in World War II by conferring Party status; and replacing wartime losses.

Several motives linked all of the recruiting campaigns. We have already noted the political motive, the use of new members as a counterweight to the existing membership. The ability to hand out new jobs, responsibility, and honors in a boon to any political organization, these being the best means of keeping and enlarging a loyal following. As the membership multiplied, positions in the Party apparatus multiplied as well, and assignment to these places became an important political weapon in Stalin's hands. From an ideological point of view, Soviet leaders after Lenin appeared unanimous in their desire to see the Party a large and expanding organism, which as things turned out meant expanding as a proportion of the population. At the time of Lenin's death, Party membership constituted less than a third of 1 percent of the population; at the time of Stalin's death, 28 years later, it was about 3.5 percent; by the early 1970s it was about 6 percent, which means close to 9 percent of the population over 18, the age of eligibility for Party membership. The drive for mass membership, as opposed to the training of a small vanguard, has seemingly been an end in itself as well as the end result of countless individual drives to gain more recruits in specific categories at various times: first more industrial workers, later more peasants, more women, more non-Russians, and so on.

After World War II, during Stalin's last seven years of rule, campaign-style recruitment was no longer employed. The great swelling of Party ranks during World War II, by almost two million, had produced a membership consisting about half of recent recruits, many of whom had to be weeded out in the latter 1940s. During the last seven years of Stalin's rule, the emphasis was on quality rather than quantity. As in the early 1930s, an effort was made to increase the proportion of workers and peasants. However, analyses of Party statistics show that white-collar occupations now predominated in the membership. In particular, a large proportion of those officially listed as workers and peasants in fact occupied positions of authority in the factories and on the farms.

It is understandable that Party members were recruited increasingly from among people already holding responsible jobs. This followed from one of the basic ideas of recruitment, which was to find Soviet citizens who combined good performance in their regular jobs with a high level of political awareness. These were exactly the people who were most needed in positions of responsibility; furthermore, joining the Party was a step up the ladder of promotion for those anxious to make a successful career in their chosen specialties. The political leadership, for its part, was just as anxious to get reliable communists into administrative posts. From there, it was only a step to situations in which Party membership became virtually a requisite for holding certain posts.

Lenin's wish to build a truly working-class Party membership was genuine. As for Stalin, whatever his intentions may have been in his various Party recruitment drives, he at least made a serious effort in the early 1930s and again in the latter 1940s to increase the proportion of workers. But recruitment policies had to be adapted to the kind of role the Party assumed in relation to the state and the economy. Its close interaction with both, its growing tradition of direct intervention in administration, and the watch it kept over the performance of managers and specialists, all demanded a membership with more than just the experience of lathe operators or tractor drivers. The Great Purge, however one may describe its causes, served the purpose of clearing out the Party's upper echelons to make way for a loyal young generation of technocrats. Whether they worked in the Party's apparatus or in executive positions in the economy, they became part of a specialized mechanism of management and control without which the nation's new industries and farms would have been vastly more difficult to manage in the context of a centralized economy. If bureaucratization of the Party's several functions had made it possible to purge its membership without destroying the functions, the purge in turn made it possible to complete the process of adapting the Party bureaucracy to the new tasks of economic management that followed the crash programs of the early five-year plans.

HOW REPRESENTATIVE A PARTY?

The Problem of Numbers

At the time of Stalin's death, the Party numbered 6.9 million (see Table 6-1). During the five preceding years, the membership had increased by only a half million, a slow rate of growth compared with other periods. The emphasis during this period had been on the "best people," which meant a stress on recruiting officials, and the intelligentsia generally, at the expense of ordinary workers and farmers. Khrushchev, concerned particularly about broadening the Party's representation in agriculture, pushed the annual rate of membership increase up to an annual 5 and 6 percent. In 1964, membership had passed 11 million and was increasing by well over a half million annually. Under Brezhnev, the rate of increase was cut back to an annual 3 percent, so that in 1972 the Party had 15 million members, or 9 percent of the nation's adult population. Even so, this growth rate is higher than the growth rate of the population. If both rates continue at their present level for a decade, into the early 1980's, the Party will number over 20 million.[13] As of 1972, 45.8 percent of the Party's membership had entered within the previous ten years. At the 1971 Party Congress, Brezhnev placed great stress on quality in Party recruitment, and praised the increased rate of expulsions which had been urged at the last congress five years earlier. But there is great pressure for continued expansion from within the Party bureaucracy, and apparently Brezhnev's management of the Party has only partly succeeded in slowing the pace of its growth. It is the 374,000 primary Party organizations which admit members and candidates, and these must be approved by the Party committee under whose jurisdiction they stand (usually a city or district committee). Enrollments are one of the chief indicators by which the lowest-level Party functionaries measure their success, in spite of admonitions to refrain from "chasing after numbers." City, district and provincial Party officials often play the same "numbers game."[14] One can also appreciate the motives of the leaders of the non-Russian parties in wanting to bring their memberships within the overall Party membership up to their nationalities' population ratios in the total population. In the 1960s, only the Georgian and Armenian parties had more than their "fair share" of Party members; at the same time, the three Baltic nations, the Moldavians, and some of the Central Asians had achieved only half their share or less.[15] Party committees have been known to impose admissions quotas on primary organizations, and they in turn receive membership guidelines from above. But such is the nature of the Communist Party that the top officials have refrained from imposing absolute limits on the rate of growth, at least in recent years.

A long-expected Party purge was announced at the 24th Party Congress in April 1971. A later *Pravda* editorial called for weeding out those "who are not real political fighters, who are passive." No longer are class enemies the problem, said the editorial, but rather those who joined

---

[13] Darrell P. Hammer, "The Dilemma of Party Growth," *Problems of Communism* 20 (July-August 1971), p. 21. *Kommunist*, no. 3 (February), 1972, p. 89.

[14] T. H. Rigby, *Communist Party Membership in the U.S.S.R., 1917–1967* (Princeton, N.J.: Princeton University Press, 1968), pp. 314–23.

[15] Ibid., p. 378.

the Party for its benefits were then in order to work for its goals. In 1973 and 1974, all Party cards will be replaced, and in the process the records of members will be reviewed.[16] The term "purge" was avoided, and in any case the membership review is unlikely to produce any sensations. What it does mean is that the Party's leaders have been taking a cautious view of their membership policies, which may threaten the effectiveness of the Party as the instrument which directs the entire Soviet system's affairs. A well-controlled, undramatic weeding out of members may be a way of avoiding more sweeping measures later on. The example of Czechoslovakia in the latter 1960s may have made Soviet leaders wary on this score, for, in proportion to population, the Czechoslovak Communist Party before 1968 was the largest in the world; from the Soviet point of view, its inability to maintain discipline through proper training contributed to the dangerous trends of the Dubček era. Khrushchev's recruitment policies had been leading the Soviet Communist Party in that direction, and a retrenchment has been long overdue.

Social and Occupational Composition

Khrushchev's recruitment drive was a sharp reversal of the policy that prevailed at the time of Stalin's death. Not only did he seek to restore the pace of growth, but he made a determined effort to raise the proportion of workers and farmers in Party ranks. During the years 1956–61, 41 percent of all recruits were workers at the time they joined the Party, and 23 percent were collective farmers, both a great increase over the partial figures available for 1945–55.[17] The figures on the "social position" of Party members, unsatisfactory as they are in the vagueness of their definitions, show in percentages the modest but perceptible results of Khrushchev's recruitment policy (see Table 6–2). The figures in Table

TABLE 6–2
"Social Position" of Party Members

	1924	1932	1956	1964	1972
Workers	44.0	65.2	32.0	37.3	40.5
Collective farmers	28.8	26.9	17.1	16.5	14.8
White-collar workers and others	27.2	7.9	50.9	46.2	44.7

Sources: *Pravda*, June 24, p. 325; *Kommunist*, No. 3 (February) 1972, p. 85.

6–2 probably err in the direction of understating the proportion of white-collar workers and intelligentsia, since they are based on basic occupation

[16] *Pravda*, June 24, 1972.

[17] Ibid., p. 306.

at the time of admission to the Party. The decrease in the proportion
of farmers reflects the fact that state farm employees are classified as
"workers," and their numbers have been on the increase as the state
farms take over an ever larger portion of agricultural production (see
chapter 12). It should be kept in mind that, of these who are listed
as "collective farmers" in Party statistics, specialists and equipment operators are overrepresented.[18] Khrushchev's success in recruiting collective
farmers was actually considerable, though one would not guess this from
the broad statistical result. Part of the increase was due to the disbanding
of the Machine-Tractor Stations (MTS) in 1958 and the consequent
shifting of their specialists and equipment operators to the collective
farms. One clear result, evident in comparing the final two columns
of Table 6–2, is that the Brezhnev regime has thus far continued Khrushchev's effort to build up the Party's non-intelligentsia, non-white-collar
membership.

Additional evidence of this effort can be seen in figures on the present
employment of Party members. Within the Party organizations of collective farms, the proportion of members directly engaged in production
(as opposed to administrative personnel, and others not in production
roles) rose from two thirds to over four fifths during the Khrushchev
period.[19] There was a similar but less decisive trend in industrial Party
organizations during 1956–61. In the latter Stalin period, the available
evidence indicates that at least half the Party members in industry and
construction were managerial, specialist, and other white-collar personnel.
During 1956–61 the proportion of workers increased 7 percent in industry
and 10 percent in construction. In the 1960s, however, there was little
further change. The proportion of members in Party and state administration has decreased since Stalin's time from roughly 15 percent to about
half that in 1972.[20] No separate figures are available on the proportion
of this category employed in the Party bureaucracy, but the widely
accepted estimate of 200,000 to 250,000 represents less than 2 percent
of the membership. Those employed in science, health, education, and
culture number about 14 percent, which means that since Stalin's time
their proportion has increased by about 50 percent; the emphasis of both
the Khrushchev and Brezhnev administrations has been to increase representation of scientists and specialists and to reduce that of bureaucrats.
The proportion of members in the armed forces (including the KGB's
border guards) has likewise been reduced; it stood at 7 percent in 1967.[21]

---

[18] See the figures in David Lane, *Politics and Society in the USSR* (New York:
Random House, 1971), p. 137.

[19] Rigby, *Communist Party Membership in the U.S.S.R., 1917–1967*, p. 336. The
time span involved is 1956–1965.

[20] *Kommunist*, no. 3 (February), 1972, p. 89.

[21] Rigby, *Communist Party Membership in the U.S.S.R., 1917–1967*, pp. 326–48.

In sum, the whole post-Stalin period has seen an effort to make the Party's membership somewhat more representative of the nation's occupational pattern. From the end of the Great Purge on, the Party had threatened to become the preserve of those occupational categories whose prestige was so emphasized in Stalin's time: the Party and state bureaucracy, economic administration, and national security. Today the Party is hardly less well represented in these three categories than it was under Stalin, if one reckons in terms of numbers or of the proportion of persons in these categories who are Party members. The difference today is that Party membership policies have returned at least partly to Lenin's concept of a working people's party, a concept that was failing in practice even in his day, and has not been fully realized since.

The Party Leadership

Two important facts stand out in any analysis of Party executives and the leading Party bodies: (1) the Party has been able to recruit its top leaders largely from among members of working-class origins, but increasingly from those who have completed higher education; and (2) the composition of leading Party bodies is intended to represent the Party bureaucracy, and to a lesser extent the state and other bureaucracies, much more than the social composition of the Party or the nation.

A study of those who occupied the Party's 230 top executive posts during the Khrushchev period, from Party secretaries down to the first secretaries of provincial Party organizations, showed that those of professional and white-collar origins were in a small minority. They constituted only 8 percent of the group, whereas 57 percent were of peasant origin and 35 percent from the families of workers. While Party executives in the Stalin era typically had no higher education, or had acquired it when they were well beyond student age, the trend today is toward executives who have joined the intelligentsia early in their careers by finishing a higher degree. Of the sample from the Khrushchev era, only 12 percent had had no education beyond secondary school, while 26 percent had been to the Party's school system, usually after beginning their ascent up the Party hierarchy. For those under 50 years of age, the proportion without a higher education dropped sharply, so that it is likely that in the future all top Party executives will have higher degrees, a small proportion of them from Party schools only.[22] Somewhat lower down the Party ladder, the same trend is evident. Studies of city and district Party secretaries showed that while in 1939 only 40 percent had completed even secondary education, those holding the same posts

---

[22] George Fischer, *The Soviet System and Modern Society* (New York: Atherton Press, 1968), pp. 68, 96, 100, et passim.

between 1950 and 1966 include 40 percent who had completed higher education.[23]

The top Party leadership is occupied by a greater proportion of persons who came from families of manual workers than is the Party membership as a whole. Of the full Politburo members elected in 1971, 12 out of 15 (or 80 percent) were in this category.[24] At the Republic and provincial levels, 80 percent of all Party Secretaries were in the same category as of 1972, and 70 percent of the USSR Council of Ministers likewise.[25]

The Party Central Committee's membership is selected not primarily for the individual qualifications and background of its members, but because they have attained certain high positions in the Party apparatus, or in state administration, the trade unions, and certain other important organizations. All the Party Secretaries who rule the Secretariat in Moscow are members of the Central Committee, and usually over half of the heads of departments whom they supervise. The First Secretaries of the Republic Party organizations are members, and the bulk of the provincial first secretaries (though a far smaller proportion, interestingly, from the provinces of the non-Russian republics). Most of the USSR Council of Ministers are members, and the heads of the republic governments. Top Defense Ministry personnel are included, together with a few military district commanders. Even the KGB has a few seats: three after the 1971 Party Congress. An analysis of the known occupations of the full Central Committee members elected in 1966 (184 out of 195 were known) showed Party officials far in the lead with 55 percent of the seats, and top echelon government officials second with 25 percent. In the 1971 Central Committee 107 out of 241 full members were Party officials, or 44 percent. In 1966 there were 14 military officers (7.6 percent) and six trade union officials (3.3 percent); the rest were a scattering of scientists, writers, journalists, and so forth.[26]

This manner of selection reflects both the origins of the Central Committee as a council of the Party's most powerful members, and the need to confer the elevated status of Central Committee rank on a rapidly growing number of executives inside and outside the Party. Thus, the Central Committee's membership is not intended to reflect the Party membership as a whole. It is a parliament of the powerful, today numbering 241 full members and 155 candidates, whose influence on the policy process varies with circumstances, but which on occasion can take decisive action.

---

[23] Lane, *Politics and Society in the USSR*, p. 141.

[24] T. H. Rigby, "The Soviet Politburo: A Comparative Profile 1951–1971," *Soviet Studies* 24 (July 1972), p. 9.

[25] *Kommunist* no. 6 (April) 1972, p. 83.

[26] Michael P. Gehlen, *The Communist Party of the Soviet Union: A Functional Analysis* (Bloomington, Ind.: Indiana University Press, 1969), p. 45; *New York Times*, April 11, 1971, p. 23.

The composition of the Politburo reflects that of the Central Committee, and for much the same reasons. Foreign observers follow carefully the numerical shifting of its membership as between top Party executives and state officials. During the post-Stalin succession struggle of 1953–57, government executives predominated (including Malenkov, who until 1953 had pursued his career entirely within the Party bureaucracy); Khrushchev in 1957–60 tipped the balance in favor of the Party apparatus, and after 1960 equilibrium was restored, usually with the Party at a slight advantage. The military establishment was unrepresented between the time of Marshal Zhukov's sudden dismissal in 1957 and the appointment of Defense Minister Andrei Grechko as a full member in 1973. Similarly the security establishment was unrepresented between the time of Beria's arrest in 1953 and the appointment of Yuri Andropov in 1967. Andropov had been a Party Secretary in charge of relations with foreign communist parties, so that in a sense his simultaneous appointment as KGB head and candidate member of the Politburo represented a "civilian" (i.e., Party) control over the security forces. In 1973 Andropov became a full member. Foreign relations had been even less represented on the Politburo than was the case with the military and security establishments. Of the Soviet Union's Ministers of Foreign Affairs, only Molotov was a Politburo member (although one may count Trotsky too, even though the permanent Politburo had not yet been established during his few months as Commissar of Foreign Affairs). In 1973 Andrei Gromyko, Foreign Minister since 1957 and hitherto regarded abroad as a "diplomatic executive" rather than a weighty political figure, was suddenly elevated to full Politburo membership. The appointment of all three of these officials reflects the priority the Brezhnev administration has given to foreign affairs; the inclusion of the defense and internal security chiefs is also a recognition of the weight these two branches have carried in policy-making for many years.

AN EVALUATION

The qualities of the Party can be judged only in terms of the tasks it is expected to perform. To measure it against external standards of bureaucratization or representativeness is to miss the point that it had to be adapted to the needs of the larger political system of which it formed the core. The first of these needs, when the country had emerged from the Civil War, was to unify the Party itself in order to save it from the apathy, bickering, and lack of discipline which were reducing its effectiveness. The same forms of control which accomplished this task then proved well adapted to controlling vital sectors of the economy, in particular the great crash projects of the early five-year plans.

In Khrushchev's time, the Party's function as the maker and supervisor of economic policy was reinforced, and in some cases carried to lengths that displeased some of the top leadership. As concerns its personnel function, the Party's intricate system of *nomenklatura* requires much staff work and record keeping, plus a degree of central coordination which facilitates the promotion of able people to important national posts. In its function as educator and propagandist also, the Party's tight co-ordination was deemed necessary by the top leaders in order to be sure that the same messages were being transmitted to Party members and the entire population, swiftly and in step with economic and social policy. Therefore there is little point in saying that bureaucratization grew like a cancer in the Party's structure. On the contrary, its growth was functional to the tasks the Party had assumed.

Similar reasoning applies to the Party's recruitment and membership policies. Whether or not the Party's membership reflects the composition of the Soviet population may be regarded as secondary. If the Party has been overweighted with managers, professional people, and specialists, it is precisely these people whose responsiveness to Party directives is essential for carrying out national policies. The campaigns which sought to increase the proportion of worker and peasant members have had an important psychological value. But they have also been used to broaden the search for talent, to take ordinary people and transform the best of them into specialists and managers.

It may be that certain of the Party's traditional functions have become less relevant than they once were to realizing overall policy goals. There is certainly plenty of evidence that, from the Party Secretaries on down, the Party bureaucracy has considered its role threatened by economic reforms which give enterprises and ministries greater autonomy; if this increasing autonomy is the long-term trend, Party officials may find their old role of brokers among enterprises, ministries, and other agencies much less needed. Party membership itself may become less important in a society which has accepted the values of the Party leaders and has become responsive to their wishes. And what of the future—will the Party be necessary at all when full communism has arrived? Khrushchev argued emphatically that it would; his successors have let his views stand without much added comment. The changes at the 24th Party Congress in 1971 which heightened the functions of Party organizations in the economy and research establishments have been the Brezhnev regime's practical response to the question.

FOR FURTHER READING

Leonard Schapiro, *The Communist Party of the Soviet Union* (New York: Random House, 1960) traces the growth of both the Party bureaucracy and the Party's membership; see chapters 13, 14, 17, 24, and 28. Abdurakhman

Avtorkhanov, *The Communist Party Apparatus* (Cleveland: Meridian Books, 1966) offers extensive factual coverage of most aspects of the Party bureaucracy and membership. T. H. Rigby, *Communist Party Membership in the U.S.S.R., 1917–1967* (Princeton, N.J.: Princeton University Press, 1968) is very thorough, the only major study devoted exclusively to this question. For recent developments in Party membership see Darrell P. Hammer, "The Dilemma of Party Growth," *Problems of Communism* 20 (July-August 1971), pp. 16–23. An interesting analysis of Party recruitment policies is in Michael P. Gehlen, *The Communist Party of the Soviet Union: A Functional Analysis* (Bloomington, Ind.: Indiana University Press, 1969).

Case studies of the organization of the Party bureaucracy at the provincial level are in Merle Fainsod, *Smolensk Under Soviet Rule* (New York: Vintage Books, 1963), chapter 2, and Philip D. Stewart, *Political Power in the Soviet Union* (Indianapolis: Bobbs-Merrill, 1968), a study of the Party organization in Stalingrad (today Volgograd) Province. Another specialized study relevant to this chapter is George Fischer, *The Soviet System and Modern Society* (New York: Atherton Press, 1968), which examines the careers and background of 230 top Party officials, from the Party Secretariat in Moscow down to the level of Party leaders in provinces and major cities.

7

THE ONE-PARTY STATE I:
EVOLUTION OF THEORY
AND STRUCTURES

At what point did Lenin and his fellow Bolsheviks decide that the Communist Party would continue to function after a proletarian revolution? Looking over the protocols of the early Party congresses, Lenin's writings in 1917, and other Party documents, one finds little evidence that the question was even discussed. At what point, then, did the Bolshevik leaders decide that their Party would exercise some of the central functions of governance, in a manner that interlocked with the functions of a formal governmental structure? Had they always assumed that proletarian rule would include a formal constitutional order? Did they assume that their Party would form one component of a permanent hierarchy of interlocking Party and state systems? Was the Party's specific role in this hierarchy already set in Lenin's thinking at the time the Bolsheviks assumed power, or did it have to be worked out in later decisions?

THE EVOLUTION OF THEORY

Marx on the State

Karl Marx devoted his major studies and most of his career to analyzing the trends in capitalism that must, he contended, inevitably lead to the new society. For the purposes of his theory, it was enough for him to point out the basic characteristics of this society: It would be composed of a single class; this class, by the time of the revolution, would have learned to function as a single organism, and to direct its energies to common goals. The absence of competing classes after the revolution, plus the potential for producing material abundance for the entire population (thanks to modern technology developed by capitalism) meant that no group of people would have to be oppressed in order to maintain a system of production. Consequently there would be no mechanism for repression, and no need for compulsion in order to keep masses of people in a deprived status.

It was this mechanism of repression that Marx termed the state. He made a very particular use of the word, tying it to a more down-to-earth definition that what political philosophy and jurisprudence had produced thus far. The state, said Marx, is an instrument of class rule, to be understood not in any abstract philosophical or legal sense, but as a means of dominance. Wrote Marx in the *Communist Manifesto:* "The executive of the modern state is but a committee for managing the common affairs of the whole bourgeoise." Elsewhere in the *Manifesto* one encounters the term "political power," defined as "the organized power of one class for oppressing another."

After watching the birth and death of the Second French Republic (1848–51), Marx came to some further conclusions about the nature of the bourgeois state. He noted that power in French politics had passed from the parliament to the executive during the Republic's brief life. As to control of the executive, the bewildering interrelationships of various categories of the bourgeoisie led Marx to drop his earlier notion of the executive as "a committee for managing the affairs of the whole bourgeoisie." Instead, he focused his attention on the modern bourgeois state as an *instrument,* regardless which faction of the bourgeoisie controlled it at a given time:

> This executive power with its enormous bureaucratic and military organization, with its ingenious state machinery, embracing wide strata, with a host of officials numbering half a million, besides an army of another half million, this appalling parasitic body, which enmeshes the body of French society like a net and chockes all its pores, sprang up in the days of the absolute monarchy, with the decay of the feudal system, which it helped to hasten.[1]

This formidable instrument, continued Marx, had survived the transition from the feudal economic order to the bourgeois, capitalist economic order; in the bourgeois era it had passed from one part of the bourgeoisie to another at certain points, growing in repressive force the whole time. The bureaucracy served the purpose of bolstering and regulating the capitalist economy, for the benefit of the capitalists; the standing army

---

[1] K. Marx, *The Eighteenth Brumaire of Louis Bonaparte* (Moscow: Foreign Languages Publishing House, n.d.), p. 121.

served the same purpose in a different way, by acting as policeman to quell lower-class unrest, break up strikes, and stop proletarian movements from forming.

As to how the proletariat would organize itself politically after it seized power, Marx's thinking must be culled from a few key passages that are not elaborated, and from his analysis of the Paris Commune of 1871. All his comments are clear on the point that the proletariat, too, must organize itself as a class in order to repress and crush the last remnants of the classes which had formerly oppressed it. The proletariat's second task, equally important, would be to seize all means of production and organize them into an integrated system of production. In the *Communist Manifesto*, Marx spoke of the postrevolutionary order as "the proletariat organized as the working class." Nearly three decades later he defined this as the "dictatorship of the proletariat."

Marx's reason for avoiding the term "workers' state" or "proletarian state" should be noted. Instead, the "dictatorship of the proletariat" excluded any idea that proletarians could simply take over the existing machinery of state and wield it for their own purposes. The term occurred in a memorandum which in 1875 Marx sent to some of the leading German social democrats, whose recent platform included the formula that "the German workers' party strives by all legal means for the free state." This, according to Marx, opened the door for a campaign merely for reforms in the political structure which would not change its capitalist class nature. It would negate the whole idea that the proletariat must assume power over all of society. Hence proletarian rule must be defined so as to leave no ambiguity about the idea of class rule:

> Between capitalist and communist society lies the period of the revolutionary transformation of the one into the other. There corresponds to this also a political transition period in which the state can be nothing but *the revolutionary dictatorship of the proletariat.*[2]

The *Communist Manifesto* contains some suggestions about the initial policies the proletarian dictatorship should follow: (1) transitional measures for equalizing wealth, such as a graduated income tax, abolition of inheritance rights, and nationalization of land; (2) centralization of all production and financial operations in the hands of the state (Marx had not yet abandoned the use of the term in connection with proletarian rule); and (3) universal labor duty, central mobilization of all manpower. Two decades later, in his tract *The Civil War in France*, Marx placed his stamp of approval on certain aspects of the Paris Commune of 1871, a radical government that ruled Paris for two months in the confusion that followed the Franco-Prussian War. The features of the Commune

---

[2] K. Marx, *Critique of the Gotha Programme* (Moscow: Foreign Languages Publishing House, 1954), p. 41.

which Marx lauded were those of its political organization rather than its economic and social policies. (Actually the Commune was more the work of old-style Jacobin Republicans than of socialists, and in any case hardly had an opportunity to begin transforming French society.) However, Marx hailed its proletarian character, the universal suffrage by which it elected its officials, the fact that the officials received only workingmen's wages and were subject to recall by the electorate, and abolition of the distinction between executive and legislative functions—lawmakers had to administer their own laws. (Actually the Commune used a committee-style administration which greatly hampered its ability to function.)

Marx offered no advice on the situation of a proletarian minority ruling over a peasant majority, nor did he dwell on what kind of repression would be necessary. The "dictatorship of the proletariat" phrase left many questions open: how long it would last, how the proletariat would be organized to exercise the dictatorship (Marx said nothing about party rule), or what should be done about divided opinions among the revolution's supporters. A few years after the Russian Revolution, Lenin and Trotsky found themselves engaged in bitter polemics with the German socialist leader Karl Kautsky over whether Marx had meant a specific form of the state or only a general political phase.

Marx gave no indication that he thought a party necessary to the unity and political action of the proletariat. While he found proletarian organizations useful, and attempted to bring them under a common political "roof" when he founded the Communist International in the 1860s, he opposed both the notion of an elite party and the notion that one party alone should lead the proletariat. In the *Communist Manifesto* he wrote that communists "do not form a separate party opposed to other working-class parties," that they "have no interests separate and apart from those of the proletariat as a whole," and "do not set up any sectarian principles of their own." Nowhere in Marx's writing about the Paris Commune, which itself embodied a great mixture of parties and tendencies, is there any comment that a single leading party would have given the proletariat better leadership. Marx assumed, rather, a proletariat already unified by the common experience of all its members in capitalist society.

Lenin on Proletarian Dictatorship

While he was in hiding in Finland during the summer of 1917, Lenin was at work on a lengthy theoretical statement entitled *State and Revolution*, which today ranks with *What Is To Be Done?* and *Imperialism* as one of Lenin's most fundamental works. Here he explained in detail how he conceived of the dictatorship of the proletariat. Curiously, *State and Revolution* scarcely mentioned the place of a proletarian party, and there are two possible explanations for this: either Lenin believed at this point that the Party would no longer be essential after the coming revolution, or he assumed that the term "proletariat" meant a Bolshevik-organized and Bolshevik-led proletariat. Only the latter explanation is consistent with the course of action he then took in calling for Bolshevik majorities in the soviets as a condition for the seizure of power. Considering the battle still to be fought against those parties of the left which were still cooperating with the Provisional Government, dissolution of the Bolshevik political organization on the morrow of the revolution would only play into the hands of the Bolsheviks' rivals.

But two other factors were more basic than the immediate political battle: (1) the Party, in Lenin's thought, embodied the consciousness of the proletarian masses—it was the "brain" without which there could be no correct strategy and organization; (2) the dictatorship of the proletariat, as Lenin conceived it, simply would not function as it should without the Party's tutelage.

The guiding principles of proletarian dictatorship, as Lenin elaborated them in *State and Revolution*, embodied what appeared to be a great confidence on Lenin's part in the high proletarian consciousness and self-discipline of the masses. But if one looks closely at just what he expected the proletarian masses to do on behalf of the new political order, the need for a guiding political organization becomes very apparent, unstated though it was. These expectations included the following: 1. A true proletarian revolution must completely smash the old bourgeois state; neither armed forces nor administrative agencies can be taken over by the proletariat. 2. While the proletarian dictatorship would use force to suppress the last remnants of bourgeois resistance, it will need "no special machinery for repression." Instead, the armed people themselves will deal with their own security, because the formerly exploited masses are the vast majority of society, as against a small minority of former oppressors. 3. The administration of the new proletarian state (or "half-state," as Lenin called it) will be carried out not by highly paid administrators possessed of special knowledge, but by ordinary citizens receiving workers' wages. "We will reduce the role of the state officials," wrote Lenin, "to that of simply carrying out our instructions as responsible, revocable, modestly paid 'foremen and bookkeepers.' "[3] No special corps of civil servants will be permitted; on the contrary, with time the functions of administration will be performed in rotation by workers released from their jobs for this purpose. Referring in numerous passages to Marx's view of the Paris Commune, Lenin even advocated a system whereby the whole distinction between legislative and executive functions will

[3] V. I. Lenin, *The State and Revolution* (Moscow: Foreign Languages Publishing House, n.d.), p. 79.

be erased. Those who legislate will also supervise the carrying out of their measures. 4. The proletarian dictatorship will be highly centralized, for two reasons: it must smash the last remnants of a bourgeois regime that has centralized its own power in self-defense; and it must operate a vast integrated economic mechanism which the bourgeoisie has built up. According to Marx, the building of the capitalist productive mechanism is a historically positive accomplishment, which will be used by the future classless society to guarantee the abundance for all which capitalism as an economic system was unable to provide. Because this economy is complex and highly integrated, under socialism and communism it must be centrally directed.

Lenin's assumption that a tightly disciplined Party must preside over all these operations can be found mainly in the way he actually used the Party after the Revolution. Doubtless he himself did not guess the extent to which the Party would be involved in day-to-day management of the new political system, though it was he who set this process in motion; for it was the growth of the Party's bureaucracy that made possible the Party's growing practice of direct involvement in state administration and economic management. Lenin's assumptions of 1917 created the foundation for all this, particularly the assumption that the Party is both the architect and builder of the proletarian dictatorship.

Stalin and the Socialist State

Morale in the Communist Party had reached a low point early in the 1920s, just at the point when Lenin was incapacitated by strokes and the short-lived Stalin-Kamenev-Zinoviev triumvirate took charge. The end of the various Civil War emergencies and the reintroduction of limited capitalism under the NEP program had contributed to the decline in morale. Furthermore, after completion of the governmental structure in the form of the USSR Constitution of 1923, it was not at all certain in the eyes of Party members how important the Party would be from then on. Party officials had rushed to occupy governmental positions, in the belief that the governmental structure would now be more important than the Party. At the same time, foreign socialists had accused Soviet leaders of arrogating to themselves, in the form of Party dictatorship, the power that should be shared by an entire class. Stalin replied in his *Problems of Leninism* (1925) by justifying the Party's leading role in language suggestive of a mediaeval theological polemic:

> . . . Lenin does not by any means identify the leading role of the Party with the dictatorship of the proletariat. He simply says that "only the conscious minority (i.e., the party—J.S.) can guide the broad masses of the workers and lead them," that it is *precisely in this sense* that "by the dictatorship of the proletariat we mean *in essence* (my

italics—J.S.), the dictatorship of its organized and conscious minority."
    When we say "in essence" we do not mean "wholly." . . . . Although the Party carries out the dictatorship of the proletariat, and in this sense the dictatorship of the proletariat is, *in essence,* the "dictatorship" of its Party this does not mean that the "dictatorship of the Party" (its leading role) is *identical* with the dictatorship of the proletariat, that the former is *equal* in scope to the latter. There is no need to prove that the dictatorship of the proletariat is wider in scope and richer in content than the leading role of the Party. The Party carries out the dictatorship of the proletariat, but it carries out the dictatorship *of the proletariat,* and not any other kind of dictatorship. Whoever identifies the leading role of the Party with the dictatorship of the proletariat substitutes "dictatorship" of the Party for dictatorship of the proletariat.[4]

Stalin at this point was striving to fill Lenin's role as the Party's leading interpreter of Marxist theory, and also to be the leading exponent of Lenin's ideas. At the same time, he combined Lenin's pronouncements on the Party in ways that underscored his view—at that time—that the Party must be the active director of the entire Soviet system. Stalin's political characterization of the Party became a dogma of Soviet Marxism: "the advanced detachment of the working class," "the organized detachment of the working class," "the highest form of proletarian class organization," and "the instrument of the dictatorship of the proletariat."
    In a formal sense, said Stalin, the organs of state exercised the dictatorship of the proletariat. At the same time, the state was nothing but the Party's instrument; whenever the Party acted to carry out its decisions, it did so through this instrument, and in some matters through the trade unions, cooperatives, and other technically nongovernmental organizations. He called these the Party's "transmission belts" and "levers," the "mass organizations without whose aid the dictatorship cannot be realized."[5] At the very top level, Party organs and governmental organs merged, not formally as structures, but in their overlapping personnel and their day-to-day deliberations. Here Stalin employed quotations from Lenin which used the word "merge"; there was little difference between the two on this score, for neither had ideological qualms about mixing the affairs of Party and state this way. It was Lenin who proposed fusing the Party Control Committee with the Workers' and Peasants' Inspectorate, which was the arrangement during 1924–34; Khrushchev thus had a precedent for doing the same thing in 1962 (although this was quickly undone by his successors). The practice of issuing joint Party-state decrees dates back to the very beginning of the Bolshevik regime. Article 126 of the 1936 Constitution finally wrote the Party's role into

---

[4] I. Stalin, *Voprosy Leninizma,* 11th ed. (Moscow: Gospolitizdat, 1953), p. 127.
    [5] Ibid., p. 123.

the foundations of the state, by citing one of Stalin's four characterizations of the Party: "the leading core of all organizations, both public and state."

Until the 1930s, the existence of a Soviet state could be justified as the instrument of the dictatorship of the proletariat, which would continue until the attainment of socialism, the first or lower stage of the new classless order. The attainment of socialism was understood in Marx's sense as reorganization of the economy so as to eliminate all exploitation, a new type of socialized productive mechanism which would pave the way for a new type of distribution ("to each according to his need") in the future communist order. Stalin, understandably interested in preserving the Soviet state as an instrument of force and control, now came forth with some blunt theoretical innovations. Summarizing the results of the First Five-Year Plan, he added a new twist to Engels' idea that the state (understood by Lenin to mean the proletarian "half-state") would wither away:

> The withering-away of the state will not come about through weakening the state's power, but rather through its maximum strengthening, which is necessary in order to deal the final blow to the remnants of the dying classes and to defend ourselves against the capitalist encirclement, which has by no means been annihilated and which will not soon be annihilated.[6]

The stronger state was necessary, continued Stalin, because the dying bourgeoisie and the defeated opposition groups were still capable of striking serious blows at the new order, and were becoming even more dangerous as the might of the socialist state grew. This statement, made almost two years before Kirov's murder and the beginning of the Great Purge, is very revealing of Stalin's political intentions.

Socialism was officially proclaimed with the adoption of the USSR Constitution of 1936. But Stalin, in explaining the meaning of this important threshhold of the nation's development, made it plain that the main features of the dictatorship of the proletariat were to remain for the indefinite future:

> I must confess that the draft of the new Constitution leaves the system of working class dictatorship in force, just as it preserves unchanged the present leading position of the Communist Party of the USSR. If our respected critics consider this a defect of the draft Constitution, that is only to be regretted. We Bolsheviks, however, consider it a merit of the draft Constitution.[7]

---

[6] Ibid., p. 429.
[7] Ibid., pp. 561–62.

However, Stalin also depicted the new Constitution as marketing the end of the bourgeoisie and as a milestone in the progressive obliteration of distinctions among three remaining groups: the working class, the peasant class, and the "laboring intelligentsia." At the 18th Party Congress three years later (1939), Stalin once again rebutted critics—real or hypothetical—who suggested that it was high time for the state to begin withering away. The theme of the "capitalist encirclement" was used as the primary justification for keeping the state's role as an instrument of force, though its force would henceforth be directed against foreign enemies. Even under communism, said Stalin, the state would remain as long as the capitalist encirclement had not been overcome. Meanwhile, the state's constructive or nonrepressive functions had been growing: its function as organizer of the socialist economy, and its function as educator and promoter of culture. Here Stalin (and his successors too) departed altogether from Marx's use of the term "state," which had meant an instrument of repression and control of class over class. As for the Party's function, Stalin from this point on no longer felt it necessary to rebuff challenges, real or imagined, to the Party's central role as maker, transmitter, and controller of policy within the now enormous state mechanism.

This same 1939 Party Congress, the first held after the attainment of socialism and the first following the Great Purge, crystallized a pattern of Party-state relations that has been followed ever since. The Party's efforts were now concentrated heavily on practical questions of economic policy and management. True, the 1939 Congress listened to Stalin's report on the international situation and to his discourse on the state and social classes. But the idea of the Party as a fighter for the correct political line now gave way completely to the idea of the Party as the driving force of the nation's economic program. The need for trained managers, well-educated specialists and a new Soviet intelligentsia was a leading theme in 1939. The "right of supervision" (*kontrol*) which changes in the Party Rules now granted to Party cells in factories and on farms appears at first glance as a move to heighten the Party's authority in production. But more important, it was recognition of the fact that the bulk of managerial personnel and specialists were now loyal Party members, people whose middle-class backgrounds would have kept them in a suspect category only a few years before.

Stalin died without having provided any more major statements concerning the Party's role in the Soviet system. No Party Program had been issued since 1919, although the 1952 Party Congress approved the idea of drawing up a new one. Stalin's major pronouncement at this Congress had to do with economic theory, not with political tasks or the Party's role. The succession struggle of four years which followed Stalin's death likewise produced no major statements on the Party's relation to the Soviet system; more urgent matters were at stake.

Khrushchev: The Party as Guide to Utopia

Just as Stalin had burst into print with major theoretical statements less than a year after Lenin's death, so Khrushchev sought to bolster his leadership with a massive "recodification of theory," so to speak. Soon after his triumph over the "anti-Party group," a commission set to work on a massive restatement and updating of Soviet Marxism, which appeared in 1959 as a tome of nearly 900 pages.[8] This plus a number of Khrushchev's own statements, especially those at the 21st Party Congress (1959), made foreign observers wonder whether the new leadership was actually bringing Soviet policies back to Marx. At any rate Khrushchev, whose capacity for abstract thought was not much greater than Stalin's had been, was engaged in placing his stamp indelibly on the Soviet system by creating some specific Marxist goals for the future.

Not only did Stalin's neglect of the Party's role require a lot of updating of theory concerning the Party's role, but some of his views about the state had to be repudiated. An important example was his statement of the early 1930s that the withering away of the state would be achieved via building the most powerful state in history; this was his blunt theoretical justification for the vast power given the NKVD, the security police. Khrushchev was a match for Stalin in the political use of theoretical concepts, and he had the advantage of a straightforward and occasionally earthy style. In brief, he said, the state would certainly wither away, and in fact was starting to wither in the present. The Party, on the other hand, would keep society and the economy together, centrally directed as always, until at last it would merge with the remnants of the former state structure and a number of nongovernmental organizations into some kind of all-embracing public organization. The state was temporary and bound to phases of history. It had now entered the stage of being the "state of all the people," no longer a repressive force except to a few incorrigibles at home and potential enemies abroad, but an expression of voluntary social coordination. The Party was virtually immortal, on the other hand. Like the third member of the Trinity, it dwelt in men's hearts:

> The Party has stronger foundations than the state organs. It arose and exists not as a result of the duties of a lawmaker. Its development was evoked by circumstances stemming from the political concepts of the people, . . . from principles of a moral nature. And mankind will always need moral factors.[9]

---

[8] The English translation was published as *Fundamentals of Marxism-Leninism* (Moscow: Foreign Languages Publishing House, n.d.).

[9] Khrushchev interview with A. I. MacDonald of the *London Times*, as reported in *Pravda*, Feb. 16, 1958.

The Party, as Khrushchev saw it, would enter into the various roles from which the state withdrew, performing them by persuasion and coordination rather than by orders and compulsion:

> A certain loosening of the administrative ties among districts, provinces and Republics is now taking place here. At the same time the *ideological* ties among regions and Republics and the unity of the Soviet nations are being strengthened. The Communist Party plays an important role in this process, and this role will grow stronger. . . .[10]

Just as in Stalin's old formula about the Party's operating through the "levers" and "transmission belts" of other organizations, the Party of the future will direct the transition to communism by using nongovernmental organizations:

> As the state gradually transfers many of its functions to public organizations, the Party increasingly comes to the foreground as the leader of all of society and the guiding force among all public organizations. The Party directs both the process of the withering away of the state and the activities of the trade unions and other public organizations, helping them to assume the new place which they are called upon to take with the approach to communism.[11]

Since the economy would remain centrally directed and planned (as Marx also had said it would) Khrushchev maintained that technical and economic expertise would be increasingly necessary in Party ranks. In short, not Stalin's state but Khrushchev's Party was now destined to grow stronger right up to the threshold of the communist era, which Khrushchev rather optimistically scheduled for the 1980s.

Back to Earth Again

It was probably a good thing that Khrushchev got his vision on the record before 1960, when he began coping with a series of political obstacles to the more far-reaching features of his program. The Party Program of 1961, the first issued in 42 years, represented a cooling of enthusiasm for certain of Khrushchev's long-range proposals. It did contain some of Khrushchev's pet slogans: "the state of all the people," "public self-government" as the wave of the future, guided by "the Party of all the people." But its rather brief tribute to utopia consisted in paraphrasing the standard utopian prophecies of Marx and Engels. It had virtually nothing to say about the gradual substitution of social influence for compulsion in dealing with deviant behavior, another of Khrushchev's favorite topics. Above all, the whole burden of the docu-

---

[10] Ibid.

[11] *Fundamentals of Marxism-Leninism*, p. 843.

ment is a down-to-earth assessment of current tasks, chiefly economic. The Party got no more than its due in customary slogans, and there was not even a hint that the Party might one day step into roles vacated by a withering state.

Politicians' visions of the future, if they are publicized, are usually intended to serve present-day political needs. In view of Khrushchev's great battle of the 1950s to put the Party in charge of the nation's economy at the expense of the state bureaucracy, it is not surprising that this wish should turn up as a Marxist utopia too. The Yugoslavs had unwittingly given Khrushchev some assistance in this campaign, with their 1958 program and its prediction that the Party would now begin to wither away. Even Khrushchev's worst enemies among the captains of industry—the ones he had exiled to the provinces in 1957—must have agreed with him that the Yugoslav position was dangerous, and that a weakening of the Soviet Communist Party now might possibly start its long-term decline.

Be that as it may, Khrushchev's successors had to give some features of Khrushchev's Party-managed utopia a quiet burial. These features included the statements calling for unsettling social experiments and those relegating various state functions to the familiar Marxist "scrap heap of history." The "state of all the people" was therefore set aside by the explanation that the state had already become such, and hence that the phrase, while true, added nothing. The phrase last appeared among the official slogans for the 1965 celebration of the October Revolution anniversary, although Politburo theorist Suslov resurrected it in 1971. From 1966 on, the annual batches of slogans did not even mention the 1961 Party Program. The slogans issued for May Day 1973, for example, made four references to the decisions of the 24th Party Congress, and none to the Program.

In the mid-1960s, it appeared that the main reason for official silence about Khrushchev's version of Party-state relations was the resurrection of a strong state apparatus under Kosygin's auspices. The 1971 Congress, on the other hand, furnished strong evidence of a major campaign to build the Party's control over and within the mechanism of state, primarily the great pyramid of economic administration. Doubtless one of the reasons for delaying—perhaps indefinitely—the writing of a new USSR Constitution (see below) is that any major reordering of the state structure necessarily raises the difficult question of the future of Party-state relations.

CONSTITUTIONAL FORM AND PROLETARIAN CONTENT

No institution, according to Marx, is neutral; all institutions are established to serve a given interest, or, if already long established, may have been taken over by other groups with their own interests. Therefore governments, laws, and constitutions cannot possibly serve the interests of an entire society, even though modern bourgeois governments claim that this is the case. After the proletarian revolution, while remnants of the bourgeoisie still exist, the new political order is still a class instrument, this time in the hands of the proletariat, which has no need to conceal the fact. Lenin gave great emphasis to this idea:

> The crux of the matter is that the bourgeois state, embodying the dictatorship of the bourgeoisie through the means of the democratic republic, can not admit before the people that it is serving the bourgeoisie, cannot tell the truth, and is forced to be hypocritical.
>
> But a state of the commune type, a soviet state, openly and directly tells the people the *truth* by declaring that it is the dictatorship of the proletariat and the poorest peasantry, and by this very truth it attracts tens and tens of millions of new citizens who are oppressed in any one of the democratic republics, but whom the soviets draw into political life, into democracy, into the governing of the state.[12]

Bourgeois and Proletarian Democracy

For both Marx and Lenin, democracy was a stage of development in both capitalist and proletarian politics. Marx, who in his lifetime watched the birth struggles of democratic institutions in Western Europe, concluded that this signalled the beginning of the end of capitalism. The "democratic republic," as he termed it, was both a concession to proletarian demands and a deception to make the lower classes believe they had a voice in the government. It embraced universal suffrage, representative government, and the political liberties proclaimed in 1789, but not economic and social rights. Actual power remained with the ruling circles of the bourgeoisie, which knew how to manipulate these institutions to their own advantage, and whose hold on the economy continued undiminished. Nevertheless, the democratic republic offered a definite advantage to the proletariat in its struggle to overthrow the capitalist order: though it could not come to power by the route of elections, the proletariat could use these bourgeois institutions to organize and propagandize in preparation for the eventual seizure of power.

At first sight it appears inconsistent for Lenin to have urged a constitutional democracy as the form of the dictatorship of the proletariat. Formal liberties, according to both Marx and Lenin, are claims *against* an authority or *against* interference by society. The victorious proletariat would scarcely need these to perform its first and only genuine political task, the crushing of the last remnants of bourgeois rule. The society

---

[12] V. I. Lenin, "The Proletarian Revolution and the Renegade Kautsky," quoted in Alfred G. Meyer, *Leninism* (New York: Praeger, 1962), p. 191.

it would then set to work to build would be a great organism of people for whom cooperation was second nature, who would need no formal protection against authorities, or against incursions from their fellow citizens. Human nature would come back into its own, and society would discover its own means of setting problems without any necessity for formal liberties and intricate procedures for safeguarding them. Whatever legislative bodies remained would not rest on highly formal procedures either. Bourgeois legislatures had been designed to contain the strife of factions, which would no longer occur in the communist future. "Politics" in the old sense would now have disappeared. So why the need for a formal constitution such as the document adopted by the Russian Republic in 1918, only eight months after the seizure of power?

Lenin's answer was twofold: proletarian democracy was a framework for organizing proletarian cooperation in the cause of building a future society, hence was not an institution fixed for all time; furthermore, it was democracy with a difference, a new type of political organization which stressed the interaction of all men as equals rather than the claims of men against society. Governing would cease to be a special art; everyone would be drawn into the task of governing society by rotation; and within government itself, the separation of executive and legislative functions would be replaced by a fusion of these functions. More was needed than just a constitutional structure in order to realize these aims. A vigorous campaign must be waged in order to get the masses involved. The 1919 Party Program sets forth the Party's duty "to encourage the working masses to enjoy democratic rights and liberties and to offer them every opportunity for doing so."[13] Lenin's idea of democracy, therefore, embraced not only the idea of training all working people in performing the functions of government, but also the idea of the Party as the initiator of this process. The Program also contains the germ of the idea of Party-supervised control over the workings of government:

> The aim of the Party consists in endeavoring to bring the Government apparatus into still closer contact with the masses, for the purpose of realizing democracy more fully and strictly in practice, by making Government officials responsible to, and placing them under the control of, the masses.[14]

The new Party Rules, adopted at the same time as the Program, instructed the Party committees at each level to guide the work of the executive organs of the soviets, by means of the Party's "factions" or groups of members working in each institution. Thus, while it was uncertain in

---

[13] This Program is translated in Jan F. Triska (ed.), *Soviet Communism: Programs and Rules* (San Francisco: Chandler, 1962), pp. 130–53.

[14] Ibid., p. 137.

how great detail the Party would manage the structure of soviets, its authority to do so was made explicit at the very outset.

The Concept of the Soviets

Lenin's manner of dealing with the soviets was central to his later decisions on a constitutional order for two reasons: they were the Bolsheviks' first legitimizing organ, the first political structure outside the Party which had to be captured and infused with a "Bolshevik content"; and they were intended to be the very basis of the new government. They were incorporated into the Russian Republic's Constitution of 1918, and into all subsequent constitutions.

In 1917, the soviets at the local level were a combination of strike committees, talking shops, and improvised action groups with shifting membership. The Congress of Soviets met three times during 1917. It was an enormous, disorderly body, capable of acting only by acclamation, and its Central Executive Committee (see below) was far too large to be any kind of real executive. The soviets were a symbol, a loose movement, a collection of political forums, but they were not a government until the Bolsheviks transformed them into a government after 1917.

In fact, what Lenin had captured for use in his new regime was, initially, mainly the name of the soviets. (As he had learned from his Party maneuvering in the years of exile, possessing the "firm name" can be quite important.) The soviets' link to the growing bureaucracy of the new government was tenuous at best during the Civil War and the early 1920s. With the beginning of the NEP period in 1921, it turned out that Social Revolutionaries and Mensheviks were still in control of a large number of soviets. The opposition slogan "Soviets Without the Party" cropped up in the Kronstadt uprising of 1921 and elsewhere. Yet the Bolsheviks, having captured the name of the soviets, promptly fixed their place in the new regime through the constitutions of 1918 and 1923. The actual political conquest of the soviets had to be delayed until later in the 1920s.

Lenin, skeptical though he was of loosely knit mass organizations, saw in the mass character of the soviets an educational experience for ordinary workers and peasants. During the eight months' interval between the two revolutions of 1917, the soviets had been effective vehicles of political communication. This was not only because their deputies listened to speeches and passed resolutions, but because many of the soviets regarded themselves as governments in embryo, alternate power centers responsible for the fate of ordinary people. Now, after the Revolution, Lenin wanted to press for growing practical activity on the part of the soviet deputies. They are not, he insisted, "parliamentarians," whose functions are limited to debate, voting, and engaging in parliamentary politics.

Just as every person must have the experience of serving as deputy, so every deputy must have the experience of administering the measures he votes on. In this way the evils of bureaucratism will die out of their own accord. The same process will deal with another evil, the "heritage of the masses" supreme hatred and suspicion of everything that is connected with the state."[15]

Fusing the soviets to the Bolshevik monopoly of political power was to be the backbone of the new political system, a guarantee that the Bolsheviks' ideals of rule would be supported actively by the masses:

> . . . For Soviet power is nothing but an organizational form of the dictatorship of the proletariat, the dictatorship of the advanced class, which raises to a new democracy and to independent participation in the administration of the state tens upon tens of millions of toiling and exploited people—who by their own experience learn to regard the disciplined and class-conscious vanguard of the proletariat as their most reliable leader.[16]

Here we see once again Lenin's root belief that the "vanguard" of the new political order, far from drawing guidance from the mass of the population, must instead teach and lead the masses. The new form of government, therefore, was not primarily a mechanism by which ordinary people were to focus their needs and take action on them, but a school for training them to follow the proletarian vanguard.

Is it fair to regard Lenin's concept of the soviets as elitism masked by deception? Lenin fully intended to "capture" institutions which were intended to channel the political desires of ordinary people, and whose original concept was therefore a democratic one. He then decreed that the main channel of communication be reversed: henceforth the soviets would transmit the teachings and policies of the vanguard to the masses, who would then assist in carrying out the policies. This did not negate the soviets' role in communication from people to vanguard. This was still a vital function, for the Party had to check on popular moods and respond to needs. The soviets also had a large role to play, in Lenin's conception, in exposing the kinds of bureaucratic malpractices which were his despair during his brief period of rule. But the idea of the soviets as democratic bodies, an idea supported by many Mensheviks and Social Revolutionaries, was now excluded.

It can hardly be said that Lenin was attempting to deceive the adherents of the soviets as to what they might expect from "proletarian democracy," as he now termed it. The soviets, said Lenin in 1918, formed

---

[15] V. I. Lenin, *The Immediate Tasks of the Soviet Government* (Moscow: Foreign Languages Publishing House, 1951), p. 31.

[16] Ibid., p. 50.

the "best mass organization of the vanguard of the toilers," which enables
the vanguard "to lead the vast masses of the exploited, to draw them
into independent political life, to educate them politically by their own
experience."[17] The result of political education would be not any kind
of parliamentary skill, but rather a knowledge of the art of administration.

From Lenin's concept of the vanguard and the soviets, it is but a
step to Stalin's blunt exegesis of this point, in the political writings he
hurried to complete very soon after Lenin's death. Here the soviets are
relegated to the role not just of an instrument of the Party, but one
of a number of instruments—others include trade unions, cooperatives,
youth organizations, and other nongovernmental associations. The only
important feature which distinguishes the soviets from the rest is the
fact that they are all-embracing; they represent entire populations.[18] It
cannot be said that either Lenin or Stalin evaded stating their actual
belief about the primacy of the Party over the soviets, or about the
narrowly restricted character of democracy within the soviets.

Both Lenin and Stalin made it clear that there would be no return
to what they termed "parliamentarism." By this they meant two things:
the interplay of parties and factions in elected assemblies, and the role
of elected representatives as specialists in parliamentary business. Just
as Lenin's utopianism about the state bureaucracy ruled out specialization
(in the future, anyway), so the soviets, the main links between the people
and the proletarian state, were forbidden to develop any special life of
their own which might well cut them off from public understanding.

EVOLUTION AND NATURE OF CONSTITUTIONS

The outward features of the Soviet constitutional system are not, for
the most part, startlingly different from those of constitutions outside
the communist world. Executive, legislative, and judicial functions are
separated. The council of ministers (cabinet) and its chairman (prime
minister) are elected by the bicameral Supreme Soviet (parliament),
which can also vote them out of office. A federal structure unites 15
republics, and local governments are organized in a conventional system
of "layers"—provinces, districts, and localities. From the present (1936)
Soviet Constitution (appendix 1), one can deduce readily that it under-
girds a socialized and centrally run economy, and imposes tight limits
on channels of individual gain outside of regular wage employment or
membership in a collective farm. A bill of rights sets forth political, social,
and economic rights all at once. The Communist Party is mentioned
in only one of the 146 paragraphs (see below), and here there is only

---

[17] Ibid., p. 62.

[18] Joseph Stalin, *Foundations of Leninism* (New York: International Publishers,
1939), pp. 57–60, 115–17.

a suggestion of what is in fact the Party's thoroughgoing dominance of the constitutional structure.

However, it is a mistake to see the Soviet Constitution and the formal structure of government as a massive exercise in deception. Quite the contrary, they are adapted to one-party rule and to a highly centralized decision-making process. Social and economic purposes are set forth clearly enough to make it plain that the Constitution is not meant to appear as a neutral framework for ordering public powers, but as the instrument of building a particular kind of social order. Rights and liberties are qualified so as to make sure they cannot be used to obstruct the goal of building this social order. The line between what is governmental and what is nongovernmental is deliberately kept vague. The competence of various units of government is hedged sufficiently to rule out the possibility of obstructionism. Far from being a mask with which to conceal the reality of Party rule, the Soviet constitutional system was designed to complement the Party's role as policy maker by offering well-ordered channels for eliciting public support and putting policies into effect.

The Evolution of Constitutions

The structure of the new government grew from the top down. The first organ of government was the Council of People's Commissars, with Lenin at its head, which derived its legitimacy from the Congress of Soviets which elected it. The Central Executive Committee was chosen at the same time in order to carry on the legislative functions of the Congress between sessions of the latter. Yakov Sverdlov, its chairman, was in effect the first president of the new state, a president with residual powers and ceremonial duties; he died shortly after the Revolution and was succeeded by Mikhail Kalinin, who remained in the post until his death in 1946. The provincial and local soviets were assigned their functions in January 1918, in a pair of brief decrees. Finally, the entire structure was put together in the constitution of June 1918, which formally established the Russian Socialist Federated Soviet Republic (RSFSR). This included only European Russia and Siberia, and not the Ukraine, Byelorussia, and the non-Slavic national areas of the south, which at the time were in the hands of anti-Bolshevik forces. The final constitutional step came in 1923, with the federal constitution that formally inaugurated the Union of Soviet Socialist Republics. The Ukraine, Byelorussia, and the three Transcaucasian nations were placed under a common government together with the Russian Republic.

In the mid-1930s, a whole new set of constitutions was approved, which embodied some interesting changes of detail but no very great changes in the overall framework of government. The USSR Constitution of 1936 served as yet another symbol of Stalin's ascendancy (it was designated the "Stalin Constitution"). It was the first federal constitution to embody a statement of rights and liberties, which were now extended beyond the former class lines to all persons—ironically, just at a time when warfare against alleged "class enemies" was gaining momentum in the Great Purge. The new constitutions of what were then 11 Union Republics followed shortly, all of them virtual copies of the parts of the USSR Constitution that related to their competence, though with small variations of structure. These constitutions all remain in force today. They have been amended many times, but nearly always for the purpose of bringing them into conformity with successive administrative reorganizations.

Khrushchev from 1959 on argued for a rewriting of the Constitution in order to reflect his newly proclaimed guidelines for the eventual "withering away" of the state. In 1962 he appointed a Constitutional Commission, with himself as chairman; his intent was probably to crown his administration by replacing Stalin's constitution with a new document not later than 1967, the 50th anniversary of the Bolshevik Revolution. After Khrushchev was ousted, Brezhnev in 1966 revived the project by appointing a new Constitutional Commission to ready a draft for the following year. But the revision was then quietly buried, possibly because it might have encouraged demands for reform of a type that was already causing official concern, and this in a period of increasingly tight legal controls. Amendments aside, the essential story of Soviet constitution writings ends in the mid-1930s.[19]

Basic Characteristics

Soviet constitutions were never intended to be the object of searching judicial interpretation, or an exact set of legal norms, or a fixed political structure for the ages. It is well to recall that Russia's one experience with a written constitution, the October Manifesto of 1905 and its enabling legislation, had shown Russians of all political persuasions the instability of a basic document in the face of political pressures. Not only were the 1905 provisions interpreted quite differently by different political groups, but they proved highly manipulable. The RSFSR Constitution of 1918, similarly, was meant to be no more than a political instrument to suit the needs of the new regime during a given period. Though nowhere in its provisions was there any mention of the Party, Bolshevik statements made it plain that the Constitution was a form or framework, whose true political content was to be found in the fact of proletarian rule, guided by the Party. The Party Rules of 1919 stated clearly that

---

[19] See the detailed account in Jerome M. Gilison, "Khrushchev, Brezhnev, and Constitutional Reform," *Problems of Communism* 21 (Sept.-Oct. 1972), pp. 69–78.

the work of the soviets and the state administration were subject to the Party's political direction. Party congresses and conferences passed well-publicized resolutions concerning the work of the government which were nothing less than directives, and soon became law. The whole relation between Party and government was openly proclaimed, and the Party's dominance openly exercised. To say that the Party's manipulation "violated the constitution" is to misunderstand the declared meaning of these constitutions.

All the Soviet constitutions contain the following basic elements: (1) broad statements of principles, and sometimes of programs as well; (2) specific objectives stated as principles, sometimes including a justification, and occasionally embellished with detail; (3) structural and procedural matters, including detailed provisions for the central organs of power, rather general provisions for lower units of government, and electoral provisions. The specific objectives are mostly declaratory; that is, only legislation renders them valid, and only on the basis of specific laws (and not constitutions) can a Soviet citizen claim his rights or be required to perform duties. These objectives were expanded into an impressive list of economic and social rights in the 1936 Constitution, all of which are likewise declaratory. The structural and procedural provisions are about as specific as they are in constitutions outside the communist world. Acting as judge of the correctness of these procedures is the Presidium, a sort of collective president and legislative appeals body of presently 32 members, chosen from among the Supreme Soviet deputies in both houses. Its chairman is the equivalent of the president of the Soviet Union, the head of state, whose duties as such are largely ceremonial.[20]

Statements of Principle

The RSFSR Constitution of 1918 began with a propagandistic statement of current foreign policy and a justification of the way the Bolsheviks had dispersed the Constituent Assembly. This was the "Declaration of the Rights of the Toiling and Exploited People," which had been promulgated as a separate document five months before the RSFSR Constitution was adopted as a whole. It summarized the major economic measures taken thus far, including nationalization of land, workers' control of industrial enterprises, seizure of the banks, and universal labor service.

---

[20] Under the 1918 Constitution, the Central Executive Committee filled the role of Presidium. In the federal Constitution of 1923, the new Central Executive Committee of the entire Soviet Union was made into a two-chamber legislature in its own right, while its Presidium took over the functions of interim legislation and appeals. Since 1936 it has been designated the Presidium of the Supreme Soviet. Nikolai Podgorny, Chairman of the Presidium since December 1965, is indeed politically powerful (second after Brezhnev in the 1971 political listing), but this is by virtue of his Politburo membership rather than because of his leadership of the Presidium.

Neither the 1923 nor the 1936 Constitution has anything similar, save perhaps for Article 2 of the 1936 Constitution, according to which the soviets "grew and became strong as a result of the overthrow of the power of the landowners and capitalists and the victory of the dictatorship of the proletariat."

The 1918 Constitution defined itself as a transitional order, set up to enable the urban proletariat, rural (landless) workers and the poor peasantry to finish their work of suppressing the bourgeoisie. This was a constitution for the working classes only, and it barred other classes from voting and standing for public office: those who employed the labor of others, those who lived from capital and large landholdings, businessmen of all kinds, all clergy, and former officials of the Tsarist police and secret service. These restrictions were dropped in the 1936 Constitution, the reason being the advent of socialism, the end of the bourgeoisie as a class, and therefore the end of class antagonisms. Article 4 noted that a socialist economy had been built, private ownership of the means of production abolished, and the exploitation of man by man finally ended. All Soviet citizens were therefore entitled to vote and to hold office.

Specific Objectives

While the 1918 and 1923 constitutions have little to say about the economic order—economic programs were set forth in the Party Program of 1919—the 1936 Constitution devotes most of its first section to the specific objectives of socialism. These dozen articles begin by specifying socialist ownership of the means of production, which includes both state ownership and ownership by cooperatives, chiefly collective farms. The state is assigned ownership of natural resources, productive enterprises, means of transportation and communication, state farms (as distinct from collective farms), and most urban housing. Collective farms are assured ownership of their livestock, implements, and common buildings; the land they use belongs to the state but is assigned to them rent-free in perpetuity. Very important is the paragraph which guarantees collective farmers their own small plots of land and miniature farm operations. Here too the plot belongs to the state and is assigned to households; livestock and equipment are the farm household's property. Another paragraph creates a small niche for individual farmers and artisans, who may carry on their occupations on condition that they use no hired labor. Article 10 guarantees the personal property of individuals: incomes, savings, houses, and even "subsidiary home enterprises," which are usually agricultural plots. Inheritance is protected as well, a provision which sometimes surprises foreigners. The planning system merits its own special paragraph (Article 11), which states that the economy shall be planned for the purpose of increasing national wealth and public well-being. Finally, the provision (Article 12) which sets forth the citizen's obligation to work quotes Marx's first principle of socialism, "From each according to his ability, to each according to his work."

Rights and Duties

Political rights are substantially the same in both constitutions. They are defined in the simplest possible phrases: "freedom of opinion," "freedom of assembly," "freedom of association," and in the 1936 Constitution "freedom of speech" and "freedom of street processions and demonstrations." The provisions are often criticized as the sheerest hypocrisy. But it takes only a brief look at the documents themselves to see how these familiar norms are adapted to proletarian dictatorship. The state itself guarantees the material support needed for publishing newspapers, holding meetings, arranging street demonstrations, and building organizations. Take for example the 1918 provision on freedom of the press:

> *Article 14.* To ensure effective liberty of opinion for working people, the Russian Socialist Federated Soviet Republic puts an end to the dependence of the press upon capital; it transfers to the working class and to the peasants all the technical and material resources necessary for publishing newspapers, pamphlets, books, and other printed matter; and it guarantees their unobstructed circulation throughout the country.

Here it is stated flatly that the state will subsidize newspapers. As for freedom of assembly, the constitution "recognizes the right of its citizens freely to organize meetings, processions, and so on," and guarantees that they shall have meeting places at state expense, complete with lighting, heating, and furniture (Article 15). Freedom of association is similarly supported in that the state "lends to the workers and peasants all its material and moral assistance to help them unite and to organize themselves" (Article 16). Here and elsewhere, there is little regard for the Anglo-American insistence on separating the public from the private, the governmental from the nongovernmental; the new order of things is a total interacting society where such distinctions, where they are used, are matters of organizational convenience and not of principle. Under the 1918 constitution, the bourgeoisie and the former ruling classes were clearly set outside this new system. But what of maverick groups that might want to avail themselves of state support? Article 23 leaves this to political judgment:

> In the general interest of the working class, the Russian Socialist Federated Soviet Republic deprives individuals and sections of the community of any privileges which may be used by them to the detriment of the socialist revolution.

Far from being hypocritical, the 1918 Constitution said fairly plainly that the new regime was taking a partisan political stance, and was not to be hindered in doing so by legal niceties. The 1936 Constitution altered little in its approach to political rights except to abbreviate the language. In guaranteeing the "right to unite in public organizations," it made specific mention of the Party, the first time this had cropped up in any constitution. The CPSU was set above other nongovernmental organizations in that it embraced "the most active and politically conscious citizens," formed the "vanguard of the working people" and—most important—constituted "the leading core of all organizations of the working people, both governmental and nongovernmental" (Article 126). Here was Stalin's idea of nongovernmental organizations and the soviets as "transmission belts" for the Party's policies, embodied in rather loose legal form.

It can hardly be overemphasized that the thinking of Lenin and his successors did not separate the structure of government from that of the Party, trade unions, and various other organizations which performed vital tasks on behalf of the system. Stalin's contribution was to effect what in German is called a *Gleichschaltung:* the nongovernmental organizations were grouped and amalgamated according to the needs of the system. Henceforth there would be one writers' organization, one massive trade union structure, and so forth, all of them assigned their policies and tasks by the Party.

Other specific objectives included equality, social and economic rights, certain conventional legal rights, rights for national minorities, and duties to the state. The 1918 document specified equality for all races and nationalities, and the 1936 Constitution added a paragraph on equality for women. The one social right singled out in 1918 was equal access to education, while the 1936 Constitution added some important ones: the right to work, the right to rest and leisure, the right to old-age and disability pensions, and the right to a free education through seventh grade. Conventional rights included inviolability of the home, freedom from arbitrary arrest, and the right of asylum for foreigners of the right political persuasion. Duties in both constitutions are the duty to work ("He that does not work shall not eat") and the duty to bear arms; in 1936 the duty to safeguard socialist property was added, with an ominous warning: "Persons committing offenses against public, socialist property are enemies of the people" (Article 131).

Let it be said once more that these provisions are declaratory. In order to understand how they are defined, or whether they have any reality at all, one must sift through masses of legislation and legal codes. Even where legislation is specific on this or that guarantee, one must ask what remedies or avenues of appeal are offered. Legislators and not judges have been the formal interpreters of Soviet constitutions, and those who legislate are bound by the wishes of the leadership.

STRUCTURAL AND PROCEDURAL FEATURES

The procedures of the Soviet constitutions appear loose and inexact to anyone schooled in reading the constitutional documents of Western Europe and the English-speaking world. Even where the procedures are elaborate, their very "fussiness" leaves one with an impression of inexactness. Wherever the Russian genius may lie, it is not found in the way Russians have coped with the problem of legal relationships, either before or after the Revolution. It was not, of course, the Bolshevik leaders' intention to stress the exactness of norms and procedures. In drawing up constitutions, they were interested first of all in a broad framework for exercising power, the reality of which lay elsewhere than in constitutional dealings. The framework was to be dominated by a ready-made majority, and consequently its norms were not made so tight as to encourage political minorities to use them as openings for gaining a foothold in the system.

The constitutional relationships which strike outsiders as being deliberately loose are these: (1) the provisions for substituting the decisions of a smaller body for those of a large body, and for encouraging overlapping functions; (2) lack of clearness in delimiting functions among different levels of government; (3) lack of clear-cut authority for the soviets in their relations with the executive organs they elect. There are others, but these are the most important.

Powers Are Fused, Not Separated

The practice of "constitutional substitution," as it might be called, arose at once after the Bolshevik seizure of power. The Council of People's Commissars, of which Lenin was the first chairman, derived its mandate from the Second All-Russian Congress of Soviets, the same turbulent body described in the Introduction, which met for just two days and passed the Bolsheviks' first decrees by acclamation. Its last act, as the delegates were rapidly leaving the hall, was to vote in a new Central Executive Committee (CEC) of about 100 to carry on its business (see Diagram 7-1). The Congress, like its successor Congresses, was not iteslf a lawmaking body—it had no machinery or procedures to process legislation—but a legitimizing body. During the long intervals (up to six months) between its sessions, the CEC made laws in place of the Congress, laws which were routinely approved by each succeeding Congress. This arrangement was written into the 1918 Constitution, which, among other things, increased the CEC's number to 200. While according

DIAGRAM 7-1
Central Organs of Government Under Three
Soviet Constitutions

1. RSFSR Constitution of 1918

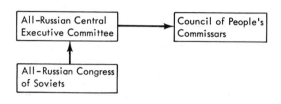

2. USSR Constitution of 1923

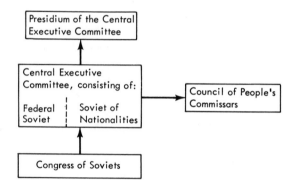

3. USSR Constitution of 1936

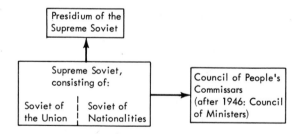

to the Constitution the CEC was "responsible in all matters" to the Congress, when the Congress was not in session it was the "supreme authority of the Republic." It was required to report to each session of the Congress, but nothing required approval from the Congress for the CEC's actions.

Relations between the CEC and the Council of People's Commissars, the system's formal cabinet, were downright contradictory in the Constitution. While the CEC was set up as "the supreme legislative, administrative and controlling body," the cabinet had "general direction of the affairs of the Republic." True, the CEC held the authority to annul any of the cabinet's decisions "of general political importance." Both bodies, and not only the cabinet, were intended to be involved deeply in matters of day-to-day administration; there was no intention of separating the CEC's lawmaking functions from its overall responsibility for government operations. As if this were not enough, the CEC's 200 members were *required* by the Constitution to work in the bureaucracy. Here, with a vengeance, was embodied Lenin's idea that lawmakers should administer their own laws; in a proletarian democracy they were not to have the time or opportunity to play parliamentary politics.

The 1923 Constitution, which founded a federal system in the form of the Union of Soviet Socialist Republics (USSR), incorporated the pattern of Congress-CEC-cabinet, but inserted yet another body between the CEC and the cabinet. This was the Presidium, a body of 21 (later 27) elected by the all-Union CEC and functioning as the "supreme organ of power" between sessions of the CEC. The Congress of Soviets, the other "supreme organ of power" according to the Constitution, was now relegated to a thoroughly ceremonial status, and summoned to meet only once a year. The CEC, a bicameral body of 371 members, performed mainly legislative functions, unlike its counterparts in the Russian Republic and the other Union Republics. The Presidium was not assigned the same kind of administrative involvement which the CEC had theoretically practiced under the 1918 Constitution; all that remained of this was the phraseology describing it as the "supreme organ of legislative, executive and administrative power." The Presidium, possessing these same powers expressed in the same words, was given the job of checking on the decisions and orders not only of the federal cabinet (Council of People's Commissars), but of the Republic governments as well. This included the power to abrogate these decisions, on any grounds whatever; and this power was shared by the CEC.

The 1936 Constitution retained all these basic features while simplifying the structure of the top organs. Henceforth there would be only the Supreme Soviet, its 32-member Presidium, and the Council of People's Commissars (today called the Council of Ministers). The Presidium was now removed completely from supervision over administration. Furthermore, its power to annul decisions of the federal and Republic cabinets was limited to cases in which these did not conform with law. It may still issue decrees on its own initiative, often on important matters, which are then ratified at the subsequent session of the Supreme Soviet by turning them into ordinary laws. The Presdium is also the interpreter of laws, and not the Supreme Court. Otherwise, its functions are rather like these of a narrowly limited constitutional monarch. Its power to dissolve the legislature, to declare war, to appoint and fire ministers, to ratify treaties, to send and receive ambassadors, are all very much the ceremonial expression of decisions that are made elsewhere.

All of these arrangements would have given rise to serious problems had it not been for the type of one-party management that undergirded them. Where the actual decision-making structure is tightly organized, a loosely designed constitution is an advantage. It permits the formal organs of rule to be large, too large for most types of real decision-making. It permits several different constitutional bodies to regard their power as "supreme." It brings a large number of people into the formalities of "checking out" decisions and ratifying them, often introducing minor but needed changes. The practice of maintaining a large turnover of deputies at each new election multiplies the number of people who have this experience. Finally, since a major purpose of these constitutional arrangements is to instruct those who are assigned a part in them, one of the lessons they bring home from these many types of sessions is that procedures and precise relationships are unimportant. The important thing is the involvement of ordinary people in discussing, supporting, ratifying, and regulating the application of policies set by the Party and its high command. Lenin and his successors intended Soviet constitutions to provide a setting for all these goals. While Bolshevik oratory sometimes overflowed with phrases about placing all power in the hands of the people via the system of soviets, the Party's actual relationship to this system was publicized also, and in no uncertain terms.

Levels of Government

Fundamental to the state structure is the absence of any clear delimitation of functions and powers as among the various levels of government. At first it appears that the relationship between the USSR and the Union Republics is one of enumerated powers at both levels. A look at the powers listed shows a great deal of intentional overlapping, or perhaps a better expression is "integration" of the exercise of power. For example, the Union Republics are given authority over their own budgets, taxation, and economic plans; but all of these must be integrated with the national budget, national tax legislation and national economic plan. Another kind of relationship is the capacity of Moscow to legislate the "principles" of various law codes, while the actual codes are drawn up by the Republics. What happens in practice is that the most critical laws are passed by the USSR Supreme Soviet under the heading of "principles," which are then adopted word for word in the 15 Republics.

The system of ministries established by the 1923 Constitution made the Union Republics the custodian of a good many ministries within their own cabinets which must answer to their opposite numbers in Moscow. Besides the many all-Union ministries, 28 at present, which are directed from Moscow independently of all lower levels of government, there are the Union Republic ministries, presently 30, which operate both in Moscow and in the 15 Republic capitals (see Diagram 7–2). Their number and type have varied over the years. The same is true of the Republic ministries, which have no counterparts in Moscow, and perform largely local functions: utilities, water supply systems, local industry, local fuel supplies, elementary and secondary education, and social security were the categories that remained for Union-Republic administration by the end of the Stalin era. During the same period, the early 1950s, there were 22 Union-Republic ministries as compared with 29 all-Union ministries; at the founding of the federal system in 1923 there had been five all-Union ministries, four Union-Republic ministries, and six more exclusively under Union-Republic jurisdiction. The Union-Republic ministries of 1953 included all those dealing with agriculture and light industry, plus some dealing with social welfare and education, which left only a handful of functions to the exclusive competence of the Republics.

The high degree of centralization within the federal framework was intentional. Before concluding that the Bolsheviks simply had a mania for central control of everything important, one must consider that the bulk of the all-Union and Union-Republic ministries controlled operations that noncommunist industrial nations usually leave to private enterprise. If for some reason the United States Government were to nationalize General Motors, DuPont, General Electric, and U.S. Steel, it is doubtful that the job of running them would be shared with the 50 states in any significant way.

Aside from this obvious point, what is most significant about Moscow's tight economic control was the way in which this type of centralization "spilled over" into other governmental operations which need not have been run from Moscow. This effect might have been moderated if Lenin's original conception of industrial management had been followed, which was a completely separate pyramid of industrial operations connected to the state structure only at the top, through the Supreme Economic Council. It was the idea of running vertical lines of economic management from Moscow to the republics, sometimes through the republic level to the local level, that made the difference. This was then reinforced by financial and planning systems which coordinated local budgets, taxation, and economic plans with national plans in great detail. Inevitably, Republic and local governments became collections of branch offices, each separate office concerned with implementing the directives that came from the corresponding office at the next higher level.

Among the world's governments, the implementation of central directives by local governments is common enough. This is true even of some federal systems, such as that of the German Federal Republic, whose

DIAGRAM 7–2
Composition of the USSR Council of Ministers
(July 1973)

A. Leading personnel:
   Chairman (A. N. Kosygin)
   First Deputy Chairmen (K. T. Mazurov and D. S. Polyansky)
   Deputy Chairman (10)*
B. Chairmen of the Councils of Ministers of the Union Republics

Armenian	Kazakh	Russian (RSFSR)
Azerbaidzhanian	Kirghiz	Tadzhik
Byelorussian	Latvian	Turkmenian
Estonian	Lithuanian	Ukrainian
Georgian	Moldavian	Uzbek

C. Ministers of all-Union Ministries:

Aircraft Industry	Machine-Building for Heavy Industry,
Automotive Industry	Power and Transport
Cellulose and Paper Industry	Machine-Building for the Light and
Chemical Industry	Food Industries and Household
Civil Aviation	Appliances
Defense Industry	Machine-Building for the Oil and Gas
Electrical Engineering	Industry
Electronics Industry	Machine-Building for Tractors and
Foreign Trade	Agricultural Equipment
Gas Industry	Medical Industry
General Machine-Building	Medium Machine-Building†
Instrument Manufacture, Automation	Merchant Marine
and Control Systems	Oil Extracting Industry
Machine-Building	Radio Industry
Machine-Building for the Chemical and	Shipbuilding
Oil Industry	Tool-Making Industry
Machine-Building for Construction,	Transport
Roads and Municipal Services	Transport Construction

D. Ministers of Union-Republic Ministries

Agricultural Deliveries	Higher and Specialized Secondary
Agriculture	Education
Building Materials Industry	Industrial Construction
Coal Industry	Installation and Special Construction
Communications	Internal Affairs
Construction	Justice
Culture	Light Industry
Defense	Meat and Dairy Industry
Electric Power and Electrification	Nonferrous Metallurgy
Ferrous Metallurgy	Oil Refining and Petrochemical
Finance	Industry
Fisheries	Public Education
Food Industry	Public Health
Geology	Rural Construction
Heavy Industrial Construction	Soil and Water Conservation
	Timber and Woodworking Industry
	Trade

E. Chairmen of State Committees

Cinematography	Prices
Construction	Science and Technology
Labor and Wages	Security (KGB)
Material and Technical Supply	Standards
Planning (Gosplan)	Television and Radio Broadcasting
Publishing Houses, Printing and Book	Vocational Training
Trade	

Diagram 7–2 (*continued*)

F. Heads of other agencies:
Administrative Board of the State Bank   Central Statistical Administration
All-Union Board for the Supply of   People's Control Committee
Farm Machinery, Fuel and Fertilizers

*Four of the Deputy Chairmen are also chairmen of State Committees.
†This is the Ministry in charge of nuclear energy.

Länder, or states, bear heavy responsibility for enforcing federal laws. What characterized Soviet centralism was the direct, vertical penetration of separate ministerial hierarchies right down to the local roots of the state bureaucracy. Local executive committee chairmen, the equivalent of mayors and governors, faced an insuperable problem in trying to co-ordinate local operations. At meetings of their executive committees (the local cabinets) they would confront financial administrators whose first responsibility was to the Finance Ministry in Moscow, educational admin-istrators who were bound by directives from the Republic's capital, public health officials who answered both to the Republic's ministry for public health and the corresponding ministry in Moscow, and so forth. Little wonder that it took the efforts of powerful Party secretaries to enforce at least a minimum of coordination through their own channels of influence.

Soviets and Bureaucracy

Moscow's particular style of centralization was not only the result of economic centralization. Since, among other things, we are trying to trace the interaction of economic and political development, this point deserves attention. Centralization was also the result of Lenin's early efforts to bind the new soviets and the old bureaucracy together into a single instrument of government. This problem became acute at the time when Lenin was trying to weld together the Party's competing local factions. The same kind of emergency solutions which were used with the Party, and became permanent solutions, were used with the state apparatus and soviets too—and needless to say became permanent likewise. The first solution was the tutelage of higher bodies over lower bodies: initiative, training and direction must come from the top down. The 1918 Constitution made this explicit in Article 62 by giving soviets and their administrative organs the right of supervising all the soviets in the lower levels of government within their jurisdiction. This included the right to cancel decisions of lower units.

The second solution, and by far the more effective one, was to establish direct administrative links from top to bottom (see Diagram 7–3). The practice of "dual accountability" is one of those notions which foreigners

DIAGRAM 7–3
Dual Accountability in the Structure of Government

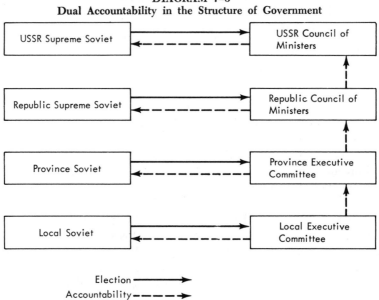

Election ————————▶
Accountability ———————▶

accustomed to Western constitutions find puzzling. It existed from the very beginning of Soviet rule, even before the 1918 Constitution, and was made formal by the 1936 Constitution:

> *Article 101.* The executive organs of Soviets of Working People's Deputies are directly accountable both to the Soviet of Working People's Deputies which elected them and to the executive organ of the superior Soviet of Working People's Deputies.

In other words, the administration of a province, city, district, or other local government unit serves two masters: the local soviet which elected it, and the administration of the next higher level of government. Given a conflict of policies as between the two, it is not hard to imagine that local administrators would be more responsive to bureaucratic authority from above than to the local soviet. While this accountability was meant to be collective, a lower executive committee answering to the next higher executive committee, it naturally left the door open for splintering into separate functional hierarchies.

Earlier we reviewed Lenin's hopes of erasing the centuries-old barrier between people and state by bringing ordinary people into administrative work on a rotating basis. While he never abandoned this notion as a goal, he turned instead to emphasizing channels of control through popular assemblies: workers' control for industry, and the soviets for the state bureaucracy. When this too failed, he set up a separate hierarchy of control, which was *Rabkrin*. In 1923, near the end of his life, Lenin condemned *Rabkrin* roundly, saying that it neither wielded the slightest authority nor, in its present state, deserved to have any.

Stalin, *Rabkrin*'s first head, never returned to the idea of popularizing administration or stressing public control, and the 1936 Constitution reflects this. The authority which was given to the soviets, from the USSR Supreme Soviet down to the localities, is of a formal legislative kind. The vital, active connection between the work of soviet deputies and state administrators which Lenin envisaged was nowhere spelled out adequately. Local government statutes attempted to fill this gap; for example, a 1925 regulation on city soviets divided the deputies into "sections," each attached to a branch of municipal administration, and each forming its own mini-bureaucracy in the form of a bureau for day-to-day business.[21] What happened in fact was that, during Stalin's time, the soviets were summoned only at irregular intervals for the purpose of rubber-stamping actions taken by their executive committees. The officials who comprised the executive committees, far from being answerable to the soviets, were appointed by the Party bureaucracy and served at the Party's pleasure.[22] It remained for Khrushchev to try to breathe some life into the soviets. While Party supervision of the soviets and their executive committees remains firm today, especially control over elections and appointments, the soviets themselves have at least been meeting regularly. The old sections are now called standing commissions, whose areas of competence include most administrative functions at any given level (see Diagram 7–4). The old ideological goal of erasing the distinction between representation and administration remains unrealized, but in many localities the soviets and their standing commissions have performed a significant function as watchdog, though in fact they are only one watchdog among many. At the national and Union-Republic levels, the various Supreme Soviets and their standing commissions act as a final "chamber of reflection" which irons out the details of legislation before its final enactment. On a number of politically nonvolatile issues, including social welfare, housing, public services, and some aspects of education, they have been the scene of policy debates which have affected the final drafts of legislation.

TRENDS AND EVOLUTION

Both the concepts and structures of the Soviet constitutional order have remained surprisingly static since the 1930s. In the Western political

---

[21] James H. Meisel and Edward S. Kozera (eds.), *Materials for the Study of the Soviet System* (Ann Arbor, Mich.: George Wahr, 1953), pp. 170–71.

[22] See the evidence from Smolensk Province in Merle Fainsod, *Smolensk Under Soviet Rule* (Cambridge, Mass.: Harvard University Press, 1958), pp. 93–94.

DIAGRAM 7–4
Structure of Government of a Province (*Oblast*)

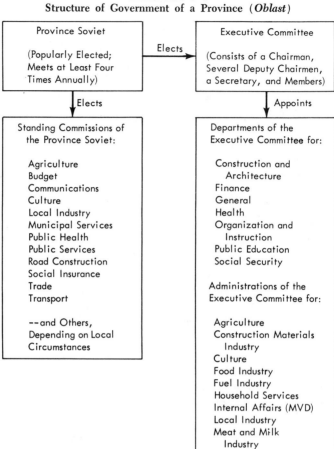

Province Soviet (Popularly Elected; Meets at Least Four Times Annually)	Elects →	Executive Committee (Consists of a Chairman, Several Deputy Chairmen, a Secretary, and Members)
↓ Elects		↓ Appoints
Standing Commissions of the Province Soviet: Agriculture Budget Communications Culture Local Industry Municipal Services Public Health Public Services Road Construction Social Insurance Trade Transport --and Others, Depending on Local Circumstances		Departments of the Executive Committee for: Construction and Architecture Finance General Health Organization and Instruction Public Education Social Security Administrations of the Executive Committee for: Agriculture Construction Materials Industry Culture Food Industry Fuel Industry Household Services Internal Affairs (MVD) Local Industry Meat and Milk Industry Municipal Services Trade

tradition a stable constitution and structure of government are usually regarded as a sign of political health. But Soviet Marxism calls for a process of evolution that will end with the demise of the organs of force and repression. Formal administrative authority will give way to the cooperative efforts of nongovernmental bodies, whose activity is based on mass public involvement. While central economic planning will remain, self-government in other spheres of activity will grow. In view of this, one would expect numerous constitutional changes reflecting experiments in citizen involvement and self-government, a process resembling that of Yugoslavia in the 1950s and 1960s, though not necessarily leading to the same goals.

Instead of this, significant constitutional changes have been few and cautious. To be sure, there have been countless amendments in the field of economic organization. Most of these have simply rearranged the administrative and planning mechanism without affecting its basic principles; the only really significant reform, the Regional Economic Councils set up in 1957, was abolished in 1965 and the old system of ministries was restored. The Union Republics have gained somewhat in authority since Stalin's time, but one cannot speak of any dramatic change in this area either. A number of decrees and campaigns have sought to activate the local soviets and to increase the functions and authority of deputies to the soviets at all levels. The USSR Supreme Soviet and its counterparts in the Union Republics have experienced some gains in the form of open debate in certain policy areas. They now enjoy more direct involvement in legislation through their standing commissions, which have grown in number over the years. As to legal reforms, if one considers that many of the significant changes of the post-Stalin era have merely served to erase the barbaric practices which had grown up under Stalin, changes since the first law codes of the 1920s have been interesting in some fields, but on the whole less than dramatic (see chapter 11). Khrushchev's campaign of the latter 1950s to press the development of "popular justice" was largely reversed by his successors, so that here too the net change has not been great.

Thus, in the midst of truly dramatic economic and social transformations of the past half-century, the framework of government has been managed with great conservatism. The basic structural principles had been decided on by the early 1920s, and the 1936 Constitution added symmetry to the whole. All the same, it is worthwhile to note some of the more noticeable trends of recent years in order to assess the further changes that they might lead to.

The Supreme Soviet: Standing Commissions and Debates

Until the mid-1960s, each house of the Supreme Soviet had four standing commissions, numbering from 21 to 39 members each: a Credentials Commission, a Commission on Legislation, a Budgetary Commission, and a Commission on Foreign Affairs; the Soviet of Nationalities also had an Economic Commission. In a legislature of over 1,500 deputies (divided about equally between its two chambers, to be sure) which meets only twice a year for not more than 10 days, and often less, and whose votes are invariably unanimous, it is not inconceivable that some kind of real legislative procedures take place in the commissions. Under Stalin, however, this definitely was not that case. Khrushchev in 1955 began the practice of calling commission hearings well before the Supreme Soviet sessions, and in other ways promoted consultation with specialists in different areas who sat on the commissions, as legislative proposals were being put into final shape. In 1966 the number of commissions was increased to 10 in each chamber, and the following year a decree expanded their functions. Most significant were the rights given to the commissions to summon government officials to answer questions, and to demand official documents.

By 1970 the list of commissions had expanded to add precisely those topics on which there has been relatively open discussion in the Soviet press. The total list then embraced the following:

Credentials	Agriculture
Planning and Budget	Public Health and Social Welfare
Legislative Proposals	Education, Science and Culture
Foreign Affairs	Trade, Everyday Services and Local
Transport and Communications	Economy
Construction and Construction	Youth Affairs
Materials Industry	Conservation

Note that no commissions are concerned with the nation's armed forces, police, and judicial system. A number of law codes, however, have received close scrutiny in one or another commission: the codes for marriage and divorce, aspects of conservation, social security rights, health services, and others. The commissions' membership includes a number of deputies who hold responsible positions in their fields and who are in some cases Party Central Committee members as well. This is not surprising, since the Supreme Soviet's membership invariably includes most of the top Party and state officials, plus a number of middle-level officials, as well as a proportion of ordinary Soviet citizens. Separation of powers is not a Soviet concept, and the separation of functions is provided for only partially in the USSR Constitution, so that the phenomenon of committee members investigating the doings of agencies which they serve is not out of order.[23]

The topics dealt with by the last six of the list of commissions given above are also the topics on which there has been a degree of genuine debate on the floor of both chambers of the Supreme Soviet. Reform of the pension and social welfare system in the mid-1950s was the first major occasion for debate; housing, education, public services, and conservation have occasioned debates also from time to time. While the Soviet constitutional system does not pit the "politicians" against the "administration," and was expressly designed to eradicate this distinction, the Supreme Soviet does show signs of growing into a useful forum for the more rational consideration of proposals and drafts which, as a rule, originate within the Party's upper bureaucracy. At present, however, the process by itself does not seem destined to work any substantial

---

[23] See the description in Jerome M. Gilison, *British and Soviet Politics: Legitimacy and Convergence* (Baltimore: Johns Hopkins Press, 1972), pp. 106–17.

alteration in the top decision-making process, but on the contrary is proving to be a useful support for the existing process.

The Local Soviets

During most of the Stalin period, Soviet local government had all but ceased to exist: the immediate contact between government and people which Lenin had seen as the main reason for the soviets had fallen by the wayside. Part of the reason was that local governments as such were the creatures—and victims—not just of one higher agency, but of many, including the economic enterprises operating on their territory. In 1957 Khrushchev mounted a campaign to breathe life into the local soviets, which with varying emphases and results has continued up to the present. Up to that time, sessions of the soviets were called only infrequently, and when called were perfunctory, and dominated by local government administrators. The role of their deputies, who were supposed to form a direct and active link between the population and the organs of local government, had fallen by the wayside altogether.

The first job was to get the machinery of the soviets functioning again, which was accomplished in a fairly short time. The next task, among other things the subject of a press campaign extending over most of the Khrushchev period, was to involve the deputies in the solution of concrete local problems. At election time, once every two years in the case of local soviets, voters are encouraged to give their needs and requests to the local soviet in the form of "mandates" to their deputies. Deputies, in turn, are obliged to take action, whether by raising the question at a soviet session, or dealing with local government authorities, or enlisting the aid of local committees and citizens' groups to solve a problem. Standing commissions, in which all deputies are now obliged to take part, became a major channel for dealing with mandates. In order to deal with other requests, deputies were obligated to keep weekly reception hours. The role of the ideal deputy became that of a social service worker, neighborhood activist, and intermediary between the citizen and local authorities.

The press from the 1950s on carried many examples and anecdotes about the soviets and their deputies, including both praise and criticism: the deputy who had a bus line extended to serve an outlying community; the standing commission that mobilized the residents of a new housing district to lay a water main; the citizens' group that persuaded the soviet to investigate housing space allocations, which resulted in removal of the town's top housing official; the group of deputies who successfully protested the illegal felling of trees by a local factory.

Khrushchev had something further in mind, beyond reactivating the soviets and building citizen confidence in local government. The soviets, their standing commissions, and a whole host of civic groups operating in close conjunction with them represented the means by which the state would "wither away." Voluntary public action would replace bureaucratic agencies in one area after another. By this route, part of the future communist order could be realized in the present. This was one of the developments that Khrushchev used to substantiate both his claim to be a Marxist theoretician, and his assertion that the transition from socialism to communism was under way, heralded among other things by transformation of the socialist state into the "state of all the people."

Just as this last-mentioned slogan was quietly set aside a year after Khrushchev's removal, the whole idea of volunteers replacing paid workers, and standing commissions taking over the tasks of government agencies, was shelved as well. The emphasis of the Brezhnev period has been on the efficiency and responsiveness of government agencies, not on any notion of replacing them or transforming them into something different. Interestingly, the "state of all the people" concept came back into limited use after 1971 in theoretical writings following an address to Party ideologists and social scientists by Suslov, the Politburo's leading theoretician. However, the utopian associations of this doctrine were now omitted, and Suslov stressed instead the need for more economic progress and ideological maturity among the people before changes could be made in the political superstructure.[24] A later theoretical writing published in the Party's own journal *Kommunist* warned that

. . . it is incorrect to assume that the socialist state of the entire people is on the point of withering away and of handing over its functions to public organizations. It is incorrect to think this, because mature socialism is not a way station on the road of social development but a prolonged period in society's forward movement. . . . In today's conditions, the matter at hand should not be the weakening but the strengthening of the socialist state of the entire people, which in our country is taking place on the basis of the comprehensive development of socialist democracy.

While advocating mass public participation in both the soviets and nongovernmental organizations, the article warned that even the "communist self-government" of the future does not arise outside of governmental agencies, but springs primarily from them. "Thus," it concludes, "the development of socialist democracy and the strengthening of the Soviet state are inextricably connected tasks."[25]

The role of deputies and standing commissions is by no means ne-

[24] *Pravda*, Sept. 30, 1971.

[25] A. Yegorov, "On the C.P.S.U.'s Theoretical Generalization of the Experience of Communist Construction," *Kommunist*, no. 2, January 1973, pp. 36–55. Translated in *Current Digest of the Soviet Press* 25 (April 25, 1973), p. 11.

glected today, and actually there have been some improvements in the laws and regulations undergirding their authority. A law of 1971 greatly improved the definition of city soviets' rights; and a law of 1972 considerably broadened the competence of deputies at all levels, particularly their right to gather information and to be actively involved in the work of administrative agencies.[26] But official criticism that accompanied the first law made it clear that the role of the local soviets remained weak in many ways, although this was primarily the fault of both local government administrators and the corresponding Party organizations.

But from the early 1960s on, Soviet commentary has placed increasing emphasis on the smooth functioning of administrative agencies, as well as on management of the soviets and voluntary organizations from above, through the "organization and instruction departments" of local government.[27] Khrushchev's vision, whether it was practical or not, has gone the way of history. His successors appear far more concerned with governmental stability than with any dialectical transformation of the nature of government.

FOR FURTHER READING

A very useful collection of constitutions and basic laws in force today is Harold J. Berman and John B. Quigley, Jr. (eds.), *Basic Laws on the Structure of the Soviet State* (Cambridge, Mass.: Harvard University Press, 1969). For the early constitutions and laws, consult James H. Meisel and Edward S. Kozera (eds.), *Materials for the Study of the Soviet System* (Ann Arbor, Mich.: George Wahr, 1953). Major speeches and portions of debates at sessions of the USSR Supreme Soviet are regularly published in *Current Digest of the Soviet Press*. See also the periodical *Soviet Law and Government*, which specializes in translations of current major legislation.

A comprehensive reference work on Soviet political institutions is Karel Hulicka and Irene M. Hulicka, *Soviet Institution, the Individual and Society* (Boston: Christopher, 1967). Other texts include: Frederick C. Barghoorn, *Politics in the USSR* (2nd ed.; Boston: Little, Brown, 1972); David Lane, *Politics and Society in the USSR* (New York: Random House, 1971); Derek J. R. Scott, *Russian Political Institutions* (4th ed.; London: Allen and Unwin, 1969); John N. Hazard, *The Soviet System of Government* (4th ed.; Chicago: University of Chicago Press, 1968); and Lloyd G. Churchward, *Contemporary Soviet Government* (London: Routledge and Kegan Paul, 1968).

Soviet descriptions and commentaries on the state system are ordinarily of a formal kind, and generally do not go into the specifics of relations between Party and state organs. Published mainly by Progress Publishers

[26] These are translated in *Current Digest of the Soviet Press* 23 (April 27, 1971) pp. 27–30, 38, and 24 (Oct. 25, 1972), pp. 9–13.
[27] One student of the question contends that this trend began as early as 1962. George A. Brinkley, "Khrushchev Remembered: On the Theory of Soviet Statehood," *Soviet Studies* 24 (January 1973), p. 398.

278 The Evolution of Soviet Politics

and the Foreign Languages Publishing House, recent titles include: L. Grigoryan and Y. Dolgopolov, *Fundamentals of Soviet Constitutional Law;* V. M. Chkhikvadze (ed.), *The Soviet Form of Popular Government;* V. M. Chkhikvadze, *The State, Democracy and Legality in the USSR;* B. Bayanov et al., *Soviet Socialist Democracy;* and M. Saifulin (ed.), *The Soviet Parliament.*

Western studies of Soviet local government, which understandably stress Party rather than state structures and processes, include: David T. Cattell, *Leningrad: A Case Study of Soviet Urban Government* (New York: Praeger, 1968); Philip D. Stewart, *Political Power in the Soviet Union: A Study of Decision-Making in Stalingrad* (Indianapolis: Bobbs-Merrill, 1968); and William Taubman, *Governing Soviet Cities: Bureaucratic Politics and Urban Development in the USSR* (New York: Praeger, 1973). See also B. Michael Frolic, "Decision Making in Soviet Cities," *American Political Science Review* 66 (June 1972), pp. 38–52, L. G. Churchward, "Soviet Local Government Today," *Soviet Studies* 17 (April 1966), pp. 431–52, and Jerry F. Hough, "The Soviet Concept of the Relationship Between the Lower Party Organs and the State Administration," *Slavic Review* 24 (June 1965), pp. 215–40.

8

THE ONE-PARTY STATE II: CONTROL OF ADMINISTRATION AND THE INSTRUMENTS OF FORCE

Wᴇ ꜱᴀᴡ ɪɴ ᴛʜᴇ ʟᴀꜱᴛ chapter Marx's characterization of the bourgeois state as the standing army and the bureaucracy. The dictatorship of the proletariat, according to Lenin, would perform these same functions during its brief period of existence, since it too would be a form of state power. But Lenin's *State and Revolution* (1917) called this new system a "semi-state," because the two functions of repression and control would no longer be the province of specialized segments of the population. Rather, the proletariat would perform the most essential functions on a volunteer basis, and most of the population would be involved in this in some way. The proletariat's class solidarity, said Lenin, would guarantee that this work was done effectively. Repression of the remaining bourgeoisie would be carried out in a short time by a proletarian militia; the functions of control and accounting, to regulate the new socialist economy, would be performed by volunteers working in rotation.

Hardly had Lenin announced the Bolshevik seizure of power to the Congress of Soviets than he began retreating from his extreme stands. Far from dismantling the entire apparatus of state, he sought to keep large chunks of it intact. Officials were ordered to stay at their posts. When civil servants went on strike, he ordered their return. Thereafter he made little progress in eliminating the distinction between volunteer and professional, elected delegate and paid administrator. He did continue

279

to talk about a volunteer civil service whose tasks could be performed by ordinary people. What he saw happening, and was in fact powerless to stop, was the mushrooming of bureaucratic structures, an improvised command system bypassing democratic procedures, which was probably necessary in order to prevent all government from disintegrating during the Civil War years.

On the matter of compensation for the new civil servants, Lenin made some temporary concessions that turned into more or less permanent concessions, and then were made official policy under Stalin. Several months after the Bolshevik coup Lenin defended the high salaries paid to administrators and specialists who were carried over from the old regime. This, he said, was the only way to keep their services until such time as proletarians could take over their functions. More important than the matter of pay differentials was the fact that the new civil service was in fact a paid bureaucracy, in which experience and expertise were recognized just as they are in other governments.[1]

As for dispensing with any special machinery of repression, one must give Lenin credit for attempting to create voluntary bodies for maintaining public order, in place of the old police and army. He started a worker's militia, designed to supplement the Red Guard forces that had overthrown the Provisional Government. But the Bolsheviks had been in power less than two months when the *Cheka* was organized, the "Extraordinary Commission to Fight Counter-Revolution." This quickly grew into a large apparatus possessing armed forces of its own. Its title and manner of organization have changed a number of times—*Vecheka*, GPU, OGPU, NKVD, and today the KGB—but its status as a highly professionalized, highly specialized force has not changed. The Red Army, likewise, was formed as a professional force within months after the Bolsheviks were in power. By the spring of 1918 Trotsky was defending the employment of former Tsarist generals who had agreed to serve the new regime.

In the circumstances, one certainly cannot criticize Lenin for sidetracking his utopian prescriptions. There had been no successful proletarian revolutions elsewhere which might have aided the Bolsheviks in their struggle for survival, and the governmental and economic chaos left in the wake of World War I and the Civil War could not possibly have been dealt with by volunteers, however dedicated. But if proletarian élan could not by itself cope with these problems, a substitute had to be found. This was the origin of all-pervasive Party control of the bureaucracy and the instruments of force. It is a long and complex history, in the course of which the Party itself became bureaucratized, as we saw in chapter 6.

[1] V. I. Lenin, *The Immediate Tasks of the Soviet Government* (Moscow: Foreign Languages Publishing House, 1951), pp. 22–27.

THE PARTY AND THE STATE BUREAUCRACY

Within months after taking office as Chairman of the Council of People's Commissars, Lenin found himself coping with some of the same evils that had long beset the Tsarist bureaucracy. The Tsarist structure, in its time, had been a byword for cumbersome central controls, floods of paperwork regulating the most minute acts, governors ruling as despots over their provinces, all-pervasive surveillance of the comings and going of ordinary people, and, permeating the whole system, routinized evasion and corruption. In spite of all its flaws it proved effective—if not efficient—as a vehicle of administration right up to the Revolution.

But the old bureaucracy's shortcomings were deeply rooted in Russian political culture; it was unlikely that any successor regime would escape them. It was Lenin's battle against these shortcomings, which had reached a head just at the time he was incapacitated in 1922, which cast the Communist Party in the role of guarantor of efficiency. Up to that point, the Party's main role in the state bureaucracy had been to assure its loyal subordination to Party rule and to campaign for the speedy implementation of Party decisions. Now it confronted the further task of assuring that the bureaucracy not only functioned loyally, but functioned well.

Two important pieces of evidence confirm the impression that the new Soviet civil service inherited some of the worst vices of the old one. The first is that the state apparatus continued to be dominated, numerically, by officials from prerevolutionary times; this was so until the end of the 1920s.[2] The second is Lenin's own testimony in a memorandum written in 1923, less than a year before his death—the last thing he ever wrote, as it turned out:

> Our state apparatus is so deplorable, not to say disgusting, that we must first think very carefully how to combat its defects, bearing in mind that these defects are rooted in the past, which, although it has been overthrown, has not yet been overcome, has not yet reached the stage of a culture that has receded into the distant past. I say culture deliberately, because in these matters we can only regard as achieved what has become part and parcel of our culture, of our social life, our habits.[3]

It is interesting that Lenin explicitly recognized the notion of political culture, so important today in political science outside the communist world, and that he applied it mercilessly to the system he had created.

---

[2] Alf Edeen, "The Civil Service: Its Composition and Status," in C. E. Black (ed.), *The Transformation of Russian Society* (Cambridge, Mass.: Harvard University Press, 1967), pp. 284–85 et passim.

[3] V. I. Lenin, "Luchshe menshe, da luchshe," ("Better Fewer, But Better"), in *Polnoye sobraniye sochinenii*, 5th ed., vol. 45 (Moscow: Politizdat, 1964), p. 390.

He added that a cure must be discovered by way of developing the social sciences, for "the good in our social system has not been properly studied, understood, and taken to heart."

It would have been better for Lenin had he devised a program for transforming the Tsarist bureaucracy by stages. The only theory he had to work with was his central conclusion in *State and Revolution*, that the old regime would be "smashed" and a radically different one set in its place immediately. Even had it been possible for the Bolsheviks to fire every last official and filing clerk who had served the old regime, it would have been more realistic for Lenin to assume that bureaucratic functions could be deprofessionalized and despecialized by stages. This process would be accompanied by a rising level of public involvement in the affairs of government, with more and more volunteers and non-governmental organizations taking over a number of functions. There was even a Marxist basis for some kind of transition like this, for Marx stressed that the first or socialist phase of the future society would be one of training an entire society to become involved in self-government. Lenin, instead, stressed the dialectical side of the social transformation, which led him to envisage the replacement of the old bureaucracy as a veritable cataclysm of public involvement. Here was an ideological disaster which, among other things, delayed the serious analytical study of public administration (as distinct from its formal and legal aspects) until the 1960s.

Rebuilding and controlling the machinery of state was one of Lenin's major justifications for retaining the Party after the Bolshevik seizure of power. From a political point of view alone, the many civil servants carried over from the Tsarist regime needed strict watching. Even more important for the Party's rule was the need for injecting some efficiency into this vast, creaking machinery to enable it to handle the nation's urgent economic tasks. The soviets as bodies for mobilizing public support left much to be desired, too. Many were dominated by Social Revolutionaries, Mensheviks, and other suspect political categories. At the close of the Civil War, many of the soviets had simply ceased to function.

Little wonder, therefore, that each territorial Party organization was given the job of supervising the corresponding unit of government. This was done openly and explicitly, both at the top level and in the provinces. Party congresses and conferences passed resolutions directing the organs of state on a wide variety of questions. Since the top posts in the national government were headed by loyal Bolsheviks, there was initially no problem of enforcing the Party's will at that level. In the middle and lower levels of government, the 1919 Party Rules instructed the Party committees at each level to "guide" the work of the government at that level. It was this direct involvement in the day-to-day affairs of government which provided a major impetus for the Party's own bureaucratization.

The Party's ultimate sanction for assuring both the loyalty and efficiency of state officials was the power of *nomenklatura*, perhaps best translated as "patronage," which is now a permanent feature of the Soviet system. All major appointments within any given jurisdiction must be approved by the top Party official in that jurisdiction, no matter whether the positions to be filled belong to the Party itself, the government, or nongovernmental organizations, including for example the leading trade union posts and collective farm chairmanships. The *nomenklatura* list applies even to posts which are formally elective, for example the chairman and executive committee of a city soviet, who are nominally elected by the soviet at its first session following public elections. During the 1920s there was a great shortage of qualified administrative personnel for posts in the government bureaucracy; the Party itself and the organs of economic management quickly absorbed what talent there was. The Party members who found themselves in state administrative posts initially resisted efforts by the Party committees in whose jurisdiction they found themselves to issue orders to them. Later the friction spread to the central government, as the Party officials assigned to the commissariats began to chafe at the amount of supervision attempted by the growing Party Secretariat. Chapter 9 provides details on how the Secretariat was reorganized in 1934 so as to place all the commissariats under the direct supervision of one or another department of the Secretariat. Abandoned in 1939, this production-branch organization of the Secretariat was reinstituted in 1948, as part of Stalin's campaign for improving his central command system.

Khrushchev-era criticism of Stalin's administrative practices suggests that, in Stalin's last years, the Party's role in the machinery of government suffered from a lack of distinctness. So commingled were the lines of authority that the Party was no longer usable to initiate changes and inject dynamism into the vast government structure. Stalin, neglecting more and more the concept of the Party as the "leading core" of all agencies, used whatever lines of authority suited an immediate purpose. His political lieutenants were assigned increasingly to state rather than Party posts. It remained for Khrushchev to breathe new life into the notion of the Party's primacy in the system.

The evolution of Party-state relations during the Khrushchev and Brezhnev periods shows a basic continuity in spite of many differences on specific questions. For example, while Khrushchev's 1957 decentralization of economic management was dropped less than a year after he was removed from office, the provincial Party secretaries' increase in functions which the reform encouraged has remained. Khrushchev's 1962 bifurcation of the provincial and local Party structure into industrial and agricultural subsystems was abolished very soon after his removal from office in favor of the old system. However, statements at the 24th

Party Congress (1971) encourage the very type of immediate Party supervision which Khrushchev had sought in his reorganization. Even Khrushchev tempered his view on the need for direct Party involvement in administration, particularly in economic administration. Not long after the 1962 reorganization he cautioned that Party committees are first of all "organs of political and organizational leadership" which must not seek to preempt the functions of economic management bodies.[4]

This same continuity can be seen in basic developments that have bolstered the Party's capacity to cope with the central problems of state administration, economic management, and public involvement in the political system. One such development concerns the background and skills of Party officials. The educational qualifications and professional expertise of Party officials have risen steadily, a long-term trend that reaches back into the Stalin era. One important study of Party officials' backgrounds stresses the importance of "dual leadership skills," the combination of political and technical training.[5] Career patterns have become increasingly stabilized, and tenure in Party administrative positions has been growing longer. There is less crossing over between posts in the Party and those in the state administration.[6] Since Stalin's time, large-scale reshufflings of Party officials have been infrequent, and most have been confined to specific situations, for example the Georgian Republic in 1972–73, or the replacement of Party and state officials in the mass media and propaganda shortly after Khrushchev's removal from office. Skills plus stabilization of Party careers have enabled Party officials to gain expert knowledge of the territories and functions they supervise.

Another development is that, in the post-Stalin era, Party officials at every level have emerged more and more in the role of mediators in an endless process of consultation with state administrators, economic managers, trade union officials, and others in important posts. Stalin's autocratic style of administration had made "little Stalins" out of the top Party officials at each level. Consequently, when he began to bypass the Party's chain of command, the Party officialdom was unable to adapt to a different role. Khrushchev stressed the Party's role as mediator, and by so doing provided one of the elements of what is today a process of group politics within a rather narrow political framework.[7] To be sure, Party officials are far more than mediators, for they hold the

---

[4] Carl A. Linden, *Khrushchev and the Soviet Leadership, 1957–1964* (Baltimore: Johns Hopkins Press, 1966), p. 170.

[5] George Fischer, *The Soviet System and Modern Society* (New York: Atherton, 1968).

[6] B. Michael Frolic, "Decision Making in Soviet Cities," *American Political Science Review* 66 (June 1972), p. 51.

[7] See the interpretations of this process in Philip D. Stewart, *Political Power in the Soviet Union: A Study of Decision-Making in Stalingrad* (Indianapolis: Bobbs-Merrill, 1968), chapter 9; and Jerry F. Hough, *The Soviet Prefects: The Local Party Organs in Industrial Decision-Making* (Cambridge, Mass.: Harvard University Press, 1969), chapter 13.

actual power to impose policies and to remove from their posts the officials who obstruct them. But, increasingly, it is the mediating and coordinating role that is proving crucial in getting the nation's business done; consequently the careers of Party officials have come to depend more and more upon this skill.

A third development, made formal at the 24th Party Congress in 1971, is the increasing degree of involvement of primary Party organizations (formerly the Party "cells") in the running of ministries and administrative agencies. This is a newer and less certain trend than the ones just discussed, and will be dealt with in chapter 9.

THE DUAL PYRAMID: DOES IT WORK?

Local government officials in the Soviet Union, who in the writer's own experience talk willingly about their normal procedures and problems, are quite reticent about the role the Party plays in their work. One encounters some general phrases—"the Party assists us in all phases of our work," "the Party determines the main lines of policy," and so forth. Literature on local government, which is usually formal to the point of dullness, is especially formal and unrevealing when it comes to the matter of Party-state relations. Thanks to anecdotal materials in the Party press and assiduous work by Western researchers, a fairly consistent picture of present-day local administration has emerged.

The Party's structure below the level of the Union Republics appears at first glance to be redundant on a massive scale (see Diagrams 8–1 and 8–2). Only the primary Party organizations are not duplicated in the state hierarchy, and yet each of them operates within the framework of an agency, organization, or economic enterprise of some kind. At the provincial and local levels, the Party bureaucracy appears to duplicate the state bureaucracy (see Diagram 8–2). The Party's staff, to be sure, is smaller than its counterpart staff in the government, and its administrative subdivisions are far fewer in number. But the intent of the Party's organization is clear: each government office must come under the supervision of a Party office. The correspondence is by no means exact, but this is partly because the provincial Party organization is responsible for much more than the concerns of the provincial government. Its industrial department, for example, will be involved in the affairs of large industries over which the province government has no jurisdiction at all. But allowing for some variation in local structures, the officials who head the departments in the left-hand column of Diagram 8–2 are in constant communication with the offices in the right-hand column.

Party Command and Party Priorities

Who communicates what, and to whom? We know the broad outlines of this communication from press reports and other accounts of the meet-

DIAGRAM 8–1
Levels of Administration for Party and State

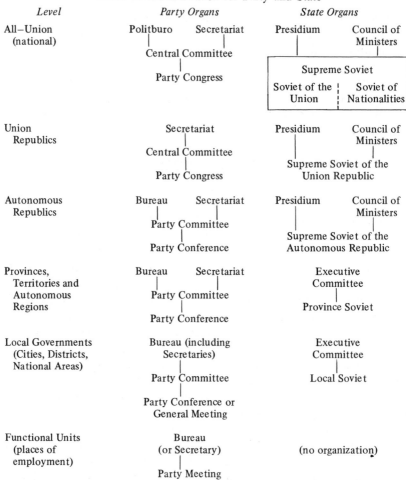

Level	*Party Organs*	*State Organs*
All–Union (national)	Politburo Secretariat | | Central Committee | Party Congress	Presidium Council of | Ministers | | Supreme Soviet Soviet of the | Soviet of Union | Nationalities
Union Republics	Secretariat | Central Committee | Party Congress	Presidium Council of | Ministers | | Supreme Soviet of the Union Republic
Autonomous Republics	Bureau Secretariat | | Party Committee | Party Conference	Presidium Council of | Ministers | | Supreme Soviet of the Autonomous Republic
Provinces, Territories and Autonomous Regions	Bureau Secretariat | | Party Committee | Party Conference	Executive Committee | Province Soviet
Local Governments (Cities, Districts, National Areas)	Bureau (including Secretaries) | Party Committee | Party Conference or General Meeting	Executive Committee | Local Soviet
Functional Units (places of employment)	Bureau (or Secretary) | Party Meeting	(no organization)

ings of local Party committees and their bureaus. The bureau is usually nothing more or less than a collection of the top administrative "notables" from several different hierarchies. Besides all or most of the Party secretaries (typically five in number), the bureau will typically include the chairman of the executive committee (that is, the head of government), the head of the trade union council, the head of the Komsomol, and sometimes the director of an important enterprise.[8] They meet every two weeks or so, perhaps more frequently, to discuss and make decisions on almost any problem that falls within their common territorial jurisdic-

---

[8] See the example of the Stalingrad *obkom* bureau in Stewart, *Political Power in the Soviet Union*, pp. 89–99.

DIAGRAM 8–2
Correspondence of Party and State Administrative Departments
at the Provincial (*Oblast*) Level

		State Structure	Party Structure
A.	Executive level	Chairman of the soviet executive committee Several deputy chairmen	First secretary Second secretary Three other secretaries
B.	Departments and administrations	1. Local Industry Fuel Industry Utilities Road Construction and Repair Food Industry Meat and Milk Industry	Industry and Transport
		2. Construction and Architecture Building Materials Industry	Construction
		3. Trade Everyday Services Social Security Planning Commission	Administration, Trade and Finance
		4. Agriculture	Agriculture State Farms
		5. Public Education Culture	Science and Schools
		6. Cadres Sector Organization and Instruction	Party Organs
		7. General Internal Affairs	Special Section Administrative Organs
		8. (none)	Propaganda and Agitation

Sources: Constitution of the RSFSR, Articles 81 and 92; Philip D. Stewart, *Political Power in the Soviet Union* (Indianapolis: Bobbs-Merrill), p. 182.

tion, be it a province, city, or district. The Party committee, a much larger body that meets typically between three and six times annually, includes a much larger circle of "notables." The lower levels of Party and state, therefore, are nearly as interlocked as the top policy-making organs. State officials, in many cases, are persons whose careers lie basically within the Party bureaucracy, but who are "on loan" to the state apparatus. A provincial government chief, for example, may later become Party chief of the same province when the first secretary is transferred or retires. Communication between Party and state offices, both formal and informal, is part of the system's life blood.

The topics discussed at both bureau and committee sessions are concentrated very heavily on problems of production. What kind of production problems are discussed depends on the type of governmental unit. Provincial Party organizations must divide their time between industry and agriculture, depending on their relative importance in the province's total output. City Party organizations concentrate on the industries falling within their jurisdiction, and district organizations usually have agriculture as first priority. Next after production topics comes the topic of personnel, and occasionally sessions are devoted to matters of ideology.

Therefore, the things that are treated as the ordinary functions of government in much of the noncommunist world—public services, law enforcement, education, urban problems, and the like—must share the agenda with much other pressing business. This is understandable when one reflects that the careers of Party officials are usually bound to production indices in the areas of their jurisdiction. Whether a city's streets are kept adequately repaired and a district public health system is operating efficiently are not matters that show as clearly as production indices on the record of Party officials. Where local governments operate factories of their own, the attention of Party executives tends to focus on these to the exclusion of other local government concerns. A Central Committee resolution of 1971 pointed out that cities and districts, the lowest units of government, get lopsided treatment from their corresponding Party organizations:

> In the practice . . . of city Party committees there are still a good many instances of petty tutelage over the soviets or of the usurpation of their functions, as well as the adoption of Party decisions on questions that fall wholly within the jurisdiction of the soviets. Some Party committees give instructions to economic executives while bypassing the soviets and soviet agencies to which these economic managers are subordinate.[9]

The same resolution criticized Party organizations in the cities for not giving enough attention to the quality of personnel in local government.

The Party as Supercoordinator

Are Party organizations supposed to issue orders to local governments, then? Sometimes they do, obviously, and occasionally they are chastised for doing it in particular situations. But considering that local government, trade union, and economic officials are part of the Party bureaus and committees that pass judgment on these orders, the process is a more complicated one than it seems on the surface. Party and state officials at the local level must both work within the framework of economic plans, budgets, laws, and policy directives which are put together in Moscow. Their problem is finding ways of using local resources to carry out all these commands. The Party is the one agency which is in a position to coordinate resources and operations. Furthermore, its officials

---

[9] *Pravda*, March 14, 1971.

suffer the consequences when their region falls short; laying the blame on government officials is of little use, since all the important ones fall within the Party committee's *nomenklatura*.

Thus, in spite of the collective procedure of decision-making in local Party organizations, it is invariably the full-time Party officials—the first secretary and the handful of other secretaries who are his immediate subordinates—who take the initiative and put through their decisions and resolutions. They are the real executives of the unit of government within whose jurisdiction they function, notwithstanding the many Party instructions from above which chide them from usurping the decisions of local governments.

The powerful executive role of the Party first secretaries and their organizations is not by any means the product of malevolence or suspicion in Moscow. The principle that we saw in the case of economic management applies to local governments as well; many things simply would not function, or would function with very low efficiency, were it not for constant Party supervision, intervention, and in some cases direct orders. Intertwined as it is with the organs of government and economic administration, the Party bureaucracy is nevertheless a reliable, self-contained chain of command. At meetings of Party bureaus and Party committees, it is the voices of the first secretaries and the other secretaries —the top Party staff officers, that is—that predominate. They are indispensable as coordinators of all the authorities within their jurisdiction, for there is no state agency that plays this role. Theoretically it would be possible to set up a superagency of the state to do this; but as long as the Party already exists for this purpose, there is hardly any reason to do so. Party officials wield an influence that would be hard to bestow on any state agency, especially considering the number of specialized superagencies of the state that have been tried already. Also, the avalanche of orders that arrives on the desks of government officials has the unintended effect of increasing their options. They must pick and choose among the countless demands that are made of them, deciding which ones are important, which can be treated perfunctorily, and which can be evaded or ignored. Here the backing of Party officials is invaluable, for they have the ultimate responsibility for what is done (and the government officials they advise are, after all, their own appointees).[10]

THE PARTY AND THE MILITARY ESTABLISHMENT

It is one thing for the Communist Party to act as coordinator of policy and operations in the vast state structure, with its overlapping jurisdictions,

---

[10] These arguments are ably defended in Jerry F. Hough, "The Soviet Concept of the Relationship Between the Lower Party Organs and the State Administration," *Slavic Review* 24 (June 1965), pp. 235–40.

multiple chains of command, and overwhelming burden of petty regulations and combersome procedures. It is quite another thing for the Party to act as a separate chain of command in a structure which, like the military, depends so heavily on a strong and unified system of command. On the other hand, the Party leadership from the very founding of the Red Army in 1918 could not permit the military establishment to remain insulated from Party control, in spite of the leaders' ability to appoint and dismiss the defense chiefs and the General Staff. Initially, strict watch had to be kept over the former Tsarist generals and officers who were employed; later on, Stalin had to find some means of assuring that the military would not step in to play a political role during times of pressure and crisis, such as 1931–32, or at the height of the Great Purge in 1937. As with so many other Soviet institutions, the instruments that were so useful in dealing with early crises became fixtures in the Soviet system, often in modified form. But control through the Main Political Administration has justified itself in the eyes of Soviet leaders, in that it has encouraged military professionalism and discouraged politicization.

The rise and fall of Marshal Georgi K. Zhukov during the 1950s stands out as an "exception which proves the rule." It was the one episode in Soviet history where a career military leader not only gained entrance to the top Party leadership, but sought an active leadership role which could have endangered his colleagues' positions. Since Zhukov's swift dismissal in October 1957 as Minister of Defense and full member of the Presidium (Politburo), the politically subordinate role of the whole military establishment has been reaffirmed countless times. Though politically subordinate, the military has successfully defended its professional status. It has also taken sides—with the Party leaders' assent—in those political decisions which affect its status and its views on defense priorities. The Party leadership has achieved this state of affairs in three ways: (1) by strong political assertion of control over military policies, (2) by granting the military a well-defined professional status, and (3) by a compromise on the status of Party organizations in the military structure.

For a political system that has devoted so much of its efforts and resources to building military power, it seems remarkable that the threat of military coups seems hardly to have arisen in the Soviet Union. The self-congratulatory statements made by Zhukov in the fall of 1957, which immediately preceded his ouster, may or may not have been the prelude to some kind of military takeover. More likely, Zhukov was trying to expand the political influence he already had, counting on support from Party leaders which never materialized. It looked like the blunder of a military man who had been thrust into high Party office as a political amateur.

Charges of a military coup in the making furnished the pretext for the decimation of the top officer ranks of the Soviet Army in 1937, beginning with the sudden trial and shooting of Marshal Tukhachevsky, the Chief of Staff. He and many others were accused of treason and of espionage on behalf of foreign governments. Many of the higher officers had been Tsarist officers before 1917, including Tukhachevsky himself. They played a prominent role in stressing military professionalism, had won a privileged status for themselves socially, and were in the process of reintroducing the old ranks from 1935 on. Of all the groups hit by the Great Purge, this was the one that might have taken swift action to defend itself. But if the nation's top military men had been preparing to overthrow Stalin, or had conspired with the German High Command to commit treason (as they were charged with doing), no credible evidence has come to light.[11]

Officers and Commissars

The development of Party organization in the armed forces at first parallelled the events by which the central Party bureaucracy gained control over the provincial Party organizations. Until 1919 Party cells in the Red Army and the fleet functioned with great autonomy, and also asserted their authority over the officers at all levels, a large proportion of whom were holdovers from Tsarist times. Political departments were then set up in most military units, with responsibility for supervising all political activity. These in turn were subordinated to the Main Political Administration, which initially operated under Trotsky's Revolutionary War Council, but very soon developed close ties to the growing Secretariat of the Central Committee. Many Party cells objected to Party control from outside the military establishment, but they were swiftly disciplined by transfers and mass recruiting, the same methods that were working so well in the provincial Party organizations. Special detachments responsible for security within the armed forces were placed under political commissars.

At the end of the Civil War, there were two kinds of opposition to central control: demands from the ranks that local committees regain their autonomy, and demands from higher officers that the Main Political Administration be subordinated entirely to the military command structure. Trotsky, who had advocated strict military discipline from the beginning, opposed the first demand while supporting the second. His

---

[11] Quite the contrary, the key evidence that was used had been forged by German security officials and passed to the NKVD, which almost certainly knew that this was a hoax. See Robert Conquest, *The Great Terror* (New York: Collier Books, 1963), chapter 7.

political defeat in 1925 was accompanied by Stalin's placing the Main Political Administration directly under the Central Committee's control. From that time to this, Party control has been exercised through complete separation of the military Party structure from nonmilitary Party organizations, except at the very top level, since the Main Political Administration is directly accountable to the Party's Central Committee.

The struggle over the authority of the political commissars was equally hardfought. In the Civil War, these commissars had kept watch over the former Tsarist officers by holding a sort of veto power over their decisions, which could be made effective by appealing decisions to the next higher Party instance. With Trotsky's departure, there was the appearance of a compromise on this issue, but gradually the principle of undivided command was established. Henceforth, military decisions could be overruled by Party officials only at the top; that is, the struggle for military professionalism was being won. Besides, with over half the officers Party members in the latter 1920s, and with the increasing practice of regular officers' taking over Party leadership duties, the old gulf between Party organization and officer corps was fast disappearing. Only in the topmost ranks did there remain friction between the relatively well-educated political officers and the old-line generals who had won the Civil War.

Just at the time of the arrest of Tukhachevsky and the first group of high officers, in May 1937, the old dual command system was reintroduced. Far from being a move in favor of the existing political commissars, it was a security measure to restore this vital supplementary control within the armed forces. The Great Purge fell as heavily on the ranks of the political commissars as it did on the military commanders. Jan Garmarnik, who had headed the Main Political Administration since 1929, committed suicide when he was faced with arrest. For the next two years, great stress was placed on the role of the political commissars, whose signatures were required on the orders of the corresponding commanding officers at each level. After this awkward command system had contributed to the Soviet Army's very poor showing in the "Winter War" of 1939–40 against Finland, it was dropped, only to be revived in desperation after the German attack in 1941, then dropped once again a year later, on the eve of the Battle of Stalingrad.

The Main Political Administration's network of officers pervades the entire defense establishment, from the General Staff down to the regimental level. Its members have military ranks corresponding to the levels at which they work. Both Khrushchev and Bulganin were political commissars during World War II, attached to military districts and with the rank of general. Party organizations at many levels repeat in somewhat simplified form the organizations of the civilian Party hierarchy. Far from being a competing hierarchy of command, the *zampolits*—deputy commanders for political affairs—and their organizations perform specialized functions which are complementary to regular military activities. Political education and propaganda are major functions; reporting on the performance of military personnel is another; recruiting Party members goes on as it does in civilian Party organizations; and much time goes to assisting commanders in training programs and other tasks while acting as a semi-independent channel of advice and criticism. As with the civilian Party organizations, if the Main Political Administration were not there to perform these functions, other channels would have to be devised. On balance, the goals sought by the Party leadership through a modernized version of the old political commissars are probably better achieved with the present system than they would be if entrusted solely to the military profession as such.

The Soviet military establishment, considering its drastic importance in the history of national priorities, enjoys no more than its share of representation in the leading political organs, measured in terms of the number of Party members who serve in the military establishment. This is important mainly in symbolic terms, for in reality the Ministry of Defense gets far more attention from the leadership than most other ministries, and its influence is correspondingly greater. The appointment in 1973 of Defense Minister Grechko to full Politburo membership came as a surprise to foreign observers, since truly professional military figures have been a rarity in the Party's top policy level. Zhukov, Defense Minister from 1955 until his abrupt dismissal by Khrushchev in 1957, was briefly a Politburo alternate in 1956–57, then even more briefly a full member. Of the other Defense Ministers who achieved political prominence as well, only Voroshilov served on the Politburo, during his 15-year service as head of the military (1925–40), and until the end of the Stalin period. However, it does not appear that he was an important figure in the political struggles of that period, outside of his concern with military affairs. Bulganin, unlike Voroshilov, was not a career military man, and in any case he was not a weighty figure in the Politburo. Grechko's appointment may be seen as two things at least: as recognition of the great importance of military requirements at a time when the Soviet leaders have been seeking political accommodation and arms limitation, and as confidence on the part of the top leadership that the influence of military leaders does not threaten Party control over the military establishment.

Military representation on the Central Committee has not risen over 10 percent in the postwar period. The proportion was much lower in Stalin's last years. It rose to 9.7 percent at the 1961 Party Congress, then decreased by stages to 7.5 percent at the 1971 Congress. These percentages correspond very roughly to the percent of all Party members who serve in the armed forces.

The Zhukov Case

The basic relationship of the military establishment with Party and state has thus been a fairly secure one for the party leaders. How, then, can the Zhukov phenomenon be explained? Zhukov, hero of the defense of both Moscow and Leningrad, conqueror of Berlin, and a flamboyant figure in celebrations at the close of World War II, was soon demoted by Stalin to a regional command and removed from the Central Committee. His name turned up on the Central Committee list in 1952 as an alternate member, but it was clearly Khrushchev who made possible his meteoric rise after Stalin's death. Zhukov became Defense Minister at the same time Malenkov was removed from the premiership (early 1955); he became a candidate Presidium member at the 20th Congress in 1956, then a full member of Khrushchev's enlarged Presidium in the wake of the 1957 crisis, where he had rendered such powerful assistance. In return for this service, Khrushchev exempted the two most important defense-related industrial ministries from his economic reorganization. Zhukov's fall came only three months after the defeat of the "anti-Party group," and the two ministries were soon decentralized as well.

The aftermath of Zhukov's fall showed that the blame for his clash with Khrushchev rested with both men. Zhukov, besides the politically questionable figure he cut in public, showed signs of wanting to reduce the Party's grip on the military. He had discovered that he might gain support from the top military figures who now opposed certain of Khrushchev's policies. Khrushchev had offered the military several favors: he had opposed Malenkov's emphasis on consumers' goods; he had encouraged the military to develop modern strategic doctrines to replace the legacy of Stalin's now dangerously antiquated concepts; and he had modified Malenkov's version of peaceful coexistence, which had banished the thought of any major clash with the United States because both countries would be destroyed. By 1957 Khrushchev's stance had changed. He had now switched to a consumers' goods emphasis, he had destroyed most of the central ministries that had been a mainstay of the military, he was placing great stress on peaceful coexistence with the West, and he was moving to cut the strength of Soviet ground forces. There is still no clear picture of whether Zhukov really had the support of his top colleagues in the military establishment; but certainly Zhukov believed he was on his way to gaining this support, which meant overcoming a number of old feuds among the commanders who had fought World War II.

In the speeches he made in 1957, Zhukov did not attack the peaceful coexistence doctrine or pose any direct challenge to Khrushchev's new economic priorities. He did indicate more than once his displeasure with the degree of Party control over the defense establishment. But more important was the vehemence of his attacks on the "anti-Party" group which he had helped defeat, in which he indicated plainly that much more remained to be disclosed. In all likelihood, the immediate reason for his dismissal was the threat to use against Khrushchev the same de-Staliniza- tion tactic that Khrushchev had used against Malenkov and the rest.[12] After Zhukov's dismissal, the appointment of another career military man to the post (Malinovsky) and a slight loosening of Party involvement in military affairs produced a temporary truce in the long struggle over the proper degree of Party control.

Professionalism Attacked and Restored

After Zhukov's departure, some of Khrushchev's foreign policy initia- tives threatened further the prerogatives of the military leaders. Any political leader is bound to have his own conceptions of security policy, and basically the Soviet military leaders were prepared to accept this in the 1950s and 1960s. What did arouse opposition was the precipitous way in which Khrushchev took sides and launched policies. To take one example, Khrushchev's great emphasis on missile defense raised some hackles in the air force, for the nation's missile defense is a completely separate branch of service. But the idea of placing missiles on Cuba in 1962 did not necessarily please the missile commanders, whose professional outlook may have regarded this as reckless exposure of their most ad- vanced military hardware. The removal of Marshal Zakharov as Chief of Staff early in 1963 certainly indicated military objections to the Cuban missile venture and its aftermath. He was promptly reappointed to the post after Khrushchev's fall.

On the surface, the decades-old debate over Party-military relations appears to have quieted down in the Brezhnev period, suggesting a suc- cessful accommodation of some kind. Marshal Zhukov reappeared in pub- lic, restored to a position of honor once again, and his supporters revived some old debates about World War II strategy which had pitted a Khru- shchev faction against a Zhukov faction. But Kolkowicz's detailed study suggested that the military leaders had found public debates and struggles unprofitable, because of the way in which they tied the influence of the military establishment to the political fortunes of Party leaders:

The chief lesson the military leaders owe to the cumulative effect of political changes followed by periods of military assertiveness is that it is safer and more profitable for the military professionals to

---

[12] See the account in Otto Preston Chaney, Jr., *Zhukov* (Norman, Okla.: Univer- sity of Oklahoma Press, 1971), chapters 14–16. The issue of military professionalism versus Party influence, as it relates to Zhukov's dismissal, is dealt with in Roman Kolkowicz, *The Soviet Military and the Communist Party* (Princeton, N.J.: Prince- ton University Press, 1967), pp. 113–35.

remain politically aloof, with primary loyalty to their own institution, than to serve the ephemeral ideals of the Party.[13]

A closer look at Party-military relations in the Brezhnev period, however, shows that debate over the basic issues has indeed continued: defense allocations and military professionalism. Military leaders promptly used the fall of Khrushchev as the occasion for reasserting their priorities. Marshal Zakharov, resinstated as Chief of Staff, used the Party's charge about Khrushchev's "subjectivism" to claim that Party interference could be damaging to military doctrine and strategy. He and others became quite outspoken in urging continuation of the post-1960 policy of high military expenditures, together with continued primacy for the heavy industries which formed the backbone of military production. Brezhnev supported this view, and the mid-1960s saw increased expenditures for defense.

The debate over military versus civilian priorities has been as central to the politics of the Brezhnev era as it was to those of the Khrushchev era. Brezhnev himself has on occasion supported the military point of view, in spite of the shift of emphasis toward consumer priorities that began in 1967. At the meeting of world communist parties in the summer of 1969, where Soviet spokesmen defended the invasion of Czechoslovakia the year before, Brezhnev emphasized his support for continued high military allocations even if this reduced overall economic growth. A *Pravda* editorial reiterated this the next year, on the anniversary of the founding of the Soviet armed forces.[14] At the 24th Party Congress (April 1971), however, Brezhnev's picture of the world situation was one which, though still troubled by pretensions of some of the capitalist powers, did not threaten Soviet secruity to the extent the Soviet Union would be distracted from its primary task of building the economy in all spheres. But Defense Minister Grechko, a career military figure, who had succeeded Malinovsky after the latter's death in 1967, stressed those international developments which he maintained did not permit any relaxation of vigilance and preparedness.

Two more recent examples will show this difference in emphasis, which is particularly evident in any assesssment of the intentions and capabilities of the Western ("imperialist") powers. Politburo member Kirill Mazurov, in his major address on Revolution Day in 1972, first conceded something to the "hard line" view by accusing the "reactionary circles of the West" (he did not specify entire governments or leaders) of "obstructing the process of detente in every way and instigating a

---

[13] Kolkowicz, *The Soviet Military and the Communist Party*, p. 219 (copyright [C] 1967 by the Rand Corporation; reprinted by permission of Princeton University Press).

[14] *Pravda*, Feb. 23, 1970.

further acceleration of the arms race." But later on, he added that the West now had no choice but to abandon its military pretensions and content itself with peaceful competition:

> Under the mighty pressure of today's revolutionary forces, capitalism is being compelled to maneuver, to adapt itself to new conditions. As imperialism's possibilities for maneuvering in the military and political spheres of the class struggle are reduced, the battle between capitalism and socialism on the ideological front assumes an ever broader scale. . . .[15]

Three months later Grechko, while noting the Peace Program adopted at the 24th Congress, made clear his stress on external dangers and Soviet military vigilance:

> Even now there are persons abroad and in Europe itself who are still placing obstacles on the path to a lasting peace on the earth. The most militantly disposed reactionary circles in the West would like not only to preserve the existing hotbeds of aggression but also to fan new conflicts and push the world back to the time of the "cold war." The 24th C.P.S.U. Congress, which adopted the Peace Program, pointed out at the same time that increasing the country's defense capability in every way possible and instilling in the Soviet people a spirit of high vigilance and constant readiness to defend the great gains of socialism should continue to be one of the most important tasks of the Party and the people.[16]

While these statements have a certain ritual character, and indeed the institutionalized groupings of the Soviet system are expected to press the causes for which their institutions exist, still the vigor and sequence of these public expressions cannot be seen as other than evidence of a genuine difference of opinion.

While one would expect the Defense Ministry and the top Soviet military figures to have grave doubts about Brezhnev's agreements with West Germany, the United States, and other major noncommunist nations in the early 1970s, this is not necessarily the case. Grechko's appointment to the Politburo in the spring of 1973 may be seen as a concession to the military leaders' views, but it may also be the fruit of agreement on certain policies. Far from taking a belligerent stance on international problems involving Soviet interests, professional military men are likely to be more concerned that belligerent international stances of the Party leadership do not require more military strength than the Defense Minis-

---

[15] *Pravda*, Nov. 7, 1972. Translated in *Current Digest of the Soviet Press* 24 (Dec. 6, 1972), p. 6.

[16] Translated copyright 1974 by *The Current Digest of the Soviet Press*, published weekly at the Ohio State University by the American Association for the Advancement of Slavic Studies; reprinted by permission of the Digest.

try can provide. Khrushchev's decision to emplace Soviet missiles in Cuba (1962) was opposed by three top military figures, who were all dismissed as a result: Chief of Staff Marshal Zakharov, missile force chief Marshal Moskalenko, and Marshal Golikov, head of the Main Political Administration. Zakharov, reinstated in 1965, has consistently opposed preventive military action against China. There are indications of military opposition to the rearmament of Egypt after its crushing defeat in the war of 1967.[17]

To the extent that the Kremlin's campaign of the 1970s for international agreements has reduced the prospect of major clashes which military leaders consider risky, as in the Middle East, the Ministry of Defense is likely to support the agreements. Soviet proposals for some kind of all-European security arrangement, which Moscow has pressed since 1966, are designed among other things to bring about an eventual reduction of direct American military involvement in Europe, and a limit to West German military development. Unless the Brezhnev administration uses the climate of negotiations as justification for reducing military appropriations, Grechko and his colleagues are likely to acquiesce in this policy.

Differences over military professionalism, military appropriations, and "adventurist" foreign commitments by civilian leaders appear to be just as much part of civil-military relations in the Soviet Union as they are in other countries. The Party's grip over the military establishment and military policy has been a secure one during most of Soviet history, but has not served either to abolish the "built-in" differences or to find magic solutions for them.

CONTROLLING THE POLICE

Felix Dzerzhinsky, a Pole, was the first chief of the security police. He died in 1926, and remains as one of the few Old Bolsheviks whose names were consistently held in honor from Lenin's time until the present. Today his statue stands near the center of Moscow in the center of a square that bears his name. On one side of this square stands the Lubyanka, long the headquarters of the security police, and also the place to which most of the country's illustrious opposition figures were first taken for interrogation after their arrest. Dzerzhinsky's successors fared much less well. Vyacheslav Menzhinsky, who effectively took over in 1924 and ruled the security apparatus for a decade, was removed not long before Kirov's assassination and was probably killed the next year. Later Stalin charged him indirectly with having delayed the prosecution of those who subseqently became the major Purge victims. Genrikh (Henry) Yagoda, who succeeded him, was accused in this same statement of being "incapable of unmasking the Trotskyite-Zinovievite

---

[17] See John R. Thomas, "Soviet Foreign Policy and the Military," *Survey* 17 (Summer 1971), pp. 129–56.

bloc," which made him a "right deviationsist" and landed him in the same prisoners' dock with Bukharin and Rykov at the 1938 trial. Nikolai Yezhov, who presided over the climax of the Great Purge's insanity in 1937–38, was removed suddenly at the end of 1938 and simply vanished. Lavrenti Beria replaced him; in chapter 5, we saw the end of his 15–year rule of the security establishment. Of Dzerzhinsky's four successors, only Menzhinsky still occupied a position of honor in the post-Stalin era.

Beria's bid for power after Stalin's death had begun with unification of the security police with the Ministry of the Interior. The two organs had been merged and separated several times from 1917 on; during the Great Purge the Ministry (then the NKVD) had controlled the security police, the regular police, the border forces, and several other security-related functions. During World War II the security police was separated from the rest, a measure which can be ascribed partly to Stalin's caution in dealing with Beria. A year after Stalin's death the security police was once again made a separate organ, now call the Committee of State Security or KGB; this arrangement has remained up to the present.

This separation of police functions represents both administrative common sense and political caution. Its also makes the Party's control functions easier, since the official in whose hands the various threads of police control come together is a Party official, the director of the Department for Administrative Organs in the Central Committee Secretariat.[18] One has only to consider the grip that the security police alone have on the entire Soviet system. KGB representatives, responsible only to their own hierarchy, sit on local government bodies, Party committees, and Party bureaus, and are present in the more important enterprises. It is true that the Party itself has a more pervasive "omnipresence" simply because of numbers. The Public Prosecutor's Office, like the KGB, has a formally independent hierarchy of local prosecutors who check for legal violations, can order arrests, interrogate, and indict. The KGB, besides reserving many types of more serious crimes for its own jurisdiction, combines the functions of police, intelligence, and—to the extent that it conducts preliminary investigations—prosecution. The Party has its own organizations within KGB units, and local KGB operations formally come under the supervision of the Party's territorial committees at every level, which is quite unlike the arrangement in the armed forces.

---

[18] Nikolai Mironov, who had headed this department since 1959, was killed in an air crash outside of Belgrade just a few days after Khrushchev's ouster in October 1964. The circumstances of the crash were accompanied by a bit of mystery—for one thing, Yugoslav authorities were not allowed to inspect the wreckage—and foreign observers voiced the suspicion that Mironov had not given his cooperation to the succession move. Lack of cooperation by the security police at such a vital juncture could have been damaging, and in the case of Beria, quite dangerous.

Precious little is known about the Party's exact area of competence in the work of KGB units. It is chiefly the concern of the top Soviet leadership with the authority of the security police that leads one to suppose that Party controls within the KGB are not considered sufficient by themselves to maintain "civilian" control.

One type of control has been the trend toward appointing Party functionaries to head both the KGB and the MVD (Ministry of the Interior). Since Yezhov and Beria had both come up in the Party apparatus rather than in security work, this could have been an unsettling development. The young Alexander Shelepin became head of the KGB in 1958 after serving as leader of the Komsomol. When in 1962 he moved from that post into the chairmanship of the Party-State Control Commission, a body given additional powers just at that time, it appeared that he could be another Beria in the making, holding various posts but always responsible for security matters.[19] He gained full membership in the Politburo in 1965, but his authority was cut back not long afterward.

None of the recent heads of the security police has been a professional security official. Some observers would qualify this by pointing out that Shelepin and his successor Vladimir Semichastny had made their recent careers as Komsomol officials, and that the Komsomol is assumed by many people in the Soviet Union to serve as an intelligence arm of the regular police and KGB, in addition to its public role as the organizer of voluntary militia units. Semichastny, in any case, had not been politically prominent otherwise, played no conspicuous public role, and certainly did not rank with the top leadership stratum. Yuri Andropov, who succeeded Semichastny in 1967, had served as Party Secretary in charge of relations with ruling foreign communist parties, and as such was reckoned as a leading political figure. His appointment to the KGB in 1967 was regarded among other things as yet another assertion of the Party's "civilian" control over what in the not-too-distant past had been a dangerous organization. Also, Brezhnev may have made this appointment as part of the new regime's campaign to toughen its treatment of dissidents, in the wake of the trials of Daniel and Sinyavsky (1966) and the demonstrations and further prosecutions they had led to. Andropov did, however, give up his possibly more prestigious Secretaryship.

Andropov's sudden elevation in 1973 to full Politburo membership, exactly two decades after Beria's unsuccessful bid for power, was no more expected than the similar appointments of Grechko and Gromyko. Like the Grechko appointment, Andropov's presence on the Politburo reflects the Brezhnev administration's preoccupation with foreign affairs

---

[19] Khrushchev in 1962 merged the Party Control Committee and the Committee of State Control into a single body, as had been done in the 1920s. The reform was cancelled soon after his ouster.

in the 1970s. Besides its foreign intelligence–gathering function, the KGB commands a frontier army of some 250,000, whose conduct in incidents on the Chinese border has been of some importance. The Andropov appointment also brings the Politburo's composition more into line with the actual influence of hierarchies and agencies in the Soviet system. It is a gesture to neo-Stalinist opinion among Soviet leaders, which among other things considers that Khrushchev had denigrated the prestige of the security police more than was necessary. Most significantly, it places the KGB directly in the midst of top-level politics, where it had been in Beria's time. This is one method for assuring the complete responsiveness of the security apparatus to Party demands, which may forestall any further incidents such as that in 1964, when the KGB was suspected of having created incidents for the purpose of disrupting Khrushchev's negotiations with West Germany. But the Andropov appointment also opens a door which could conceivably be used by a future Beria.

The division of responsibility between the KGB and the MVD is of some interest. The KGB, besides its regular security police, has charge of foreign intelligence, the border troops, and most probably several different kinds of security forces which are organized and equipped more like an army than a police force.[20] The MVD went into decline after Stalin's death. Its labor camps went to the Ministry of Justice, and its economic enterprises to the appropriate economic ministries. In 1960 the all-Union MVD was abolished, while its 15 counterparts in the Union Republics were renamed "Ministries for the Protection of Public Order," a gesture to remove the Stalinist associations of the MVD. These ministries retained control, chiefly, over the ordinary police and the nation's complex internal passport system, and they regained jurisdiction over the much-reduced system of labor camps and other penal institutions. Like so many other Khrushchev-era reforms, this too was undone when a central Ministry for the Protection of Public Order (MOOP) was set up in 1966 and placed under a Party official close to Brezhnev, Nikolai Shcholokov. In 1970 it again became the MVD, yet another step in removing stigmas from the memory of the Stalin era.

However, there are no signs that the Brezhnev administration has wished to unify the regular police and security police in the manner of the Great Purge era. It is not that these two hierarchies are political rivals, for according to a great deal of legal and journalistic literature they cooperate closely in many spheres. Instead, their separation represents one kind of safeguard which the Party leadership retains in order to help forestall the rise of future Berias or Yezhovs.

---

[20] One defector who served until 1953 in the MGB, the KBG's predecessor, gave the total strength of these troops as one million. There are no reliable estimates for more recent years. Robert Conquest (ed.), *The Soviet Police System* (New York: Praeger, 1968), p. 26.

FOR FURTHER READING

The studies by Cattell, Frolic, Stewart, and Taubman cited in the readings at the end of chapter 7 are applicable here too. Abdurakhman Avtorkhanov *The Communist Party Apparatus* (Cleveland: Meridian Books, 1968) provides separate chapters on the role of the Party in government, the economy, the armed forces, and the security police. Merle Fainsod, *Smolensk Under Soviet Rule* (New York: Vintage Books, 1963), already cited in other connections, provides an invaluable inside picture of relationships in all these fields at the provincial and local level during the 1930s; see especially chapters 3, 8, and 17.

The most comprehensive and detailed study of the Party's role in the armed forces is Roman Kolkowicz, *The Soviet Military and the Communist Party* (Princeton, N.J.: Princeton University Press, 1967). See also Littleton B. Atkinson, *Dual Command in the Red Army* (Maxwell Air Force Base, Alabama, 1950), Zbigniew Brzezinski (ed.), *Political Controls in the Soviet Army* (New York: Research Program on the USSR), and B. H. Liddell-Hart (ed.), *The Red Army* (New York: Harcourt, Brace, 1956). Studies of specific episodes and periods of Party-military relations include Victor Alexandrov, *The Tukhachevsky Affair* (Englewood Cliffs, N.J.: Prentice-Hall, 1964), John Erickson, *The Soviet High Command, 1918–1941* (New York: St. Martin's Press, 1962), and Raymond L. Garthoff, "The Marshals and the Party: Soviet Civil-Military Relations in the Postwar Period," in Harry Coles (ed.), *Total War and Cold War: Problems in Civilian Control of the Military* (Columbus, Ohio: Ohio State University Press, 1962). On the Zhukov affair of 1957, see the biography by Otto Preston Chaney, Jr., *Zhukov* (Norman, Okla.: University of Oklahoma Press, 1971), chapters 14–16, and Zbigniew Brzezinski and Samuel P. Huntington, *Political Power: USA/USSR* (New York: Viking Press, 1963), ch. 8.

Information on Party controls over and within the security police is sparse, outside of the broad political events surrounding the coming and going of the various top security chiefs. A good factual summary is Robert Conquest (ed.), *The Soviet Police System* (New York: Praeger, 1968); somewhat dated but still useful is Sheldon Wolin and Robert M. Slusser (eds.), *The Soviet Secret Police* (New York: Praeger, 1957).

9

THE PARTY AND THE
ECONOMY

A VISITOR TO ANY Soviet factory or plant, if he keeps his eyes open
as he is being escorted to an interview with the director, will notice that
other organizations are present besides the factory management itself.
Near the director's office is a door bearing the inscription "Party Bureau,"
and just down the hall is another door that says "Factory Shop Committee," which is the trade union local. The question-and-answer sessions
that the director organizes for his visitors may include a trade union
representative, a member of the Party committee, and the head of the
factory's Komsomol, or Young Communist League.

The trade union representative recites a long list of functions his organization performs, beginning with the fact that every single person
employed by the factory is a member. While the union does not bargain
over wages (which are rigidly controlled by Moscow) or go on strike,
it organizes a union-management grievance committee, consults with management on a large variety of production problems, administers most
of the fringe benefits (which can be very important), handles social
insurance on behalf of the state, and has a large voice in determining
working conditions, investigating safety standards, and so forth. The
union can be quite important in the life of the individual factory worker,
especially in the realm of grievance procedures and housing assignments.
The Komsomol's representative likewise offers a long list of functions,
though these are not usually central to the lives of young workers as
workers.

The Party representative, if one is present, is apt to be very reticent
about the Party's specific functions in the factory, and to speak only
in the most general terms. Everyone present is likely to be a Party mem-

ber, but the others offer little enlightenment either. The Party "assists the management and the trade union in all phases of their work," or it "concerns itself with matters of policy," or it "speaks for Party interests in the overall operation of the factory." Some Party bureaus will admit to having a concern for political education in the factory, or to devoting special attention to personnel questions. But it is generally useless to inquire what, precisely, the primary Party organization discusses at its meetings or even what a typical agenda might look like. Since it is quite hard to get separate interviews with Party officials of any type and at any level, one must be content with these generalities and seek information on the Party's work in published sources.

There are Party officials outside the factory who might have something to say on the subject, were it possible to interview them. The city Party committee has its own separate building, a structure in the center of town, often resembling a large American post office of the New Deal era. This houses the staff of the city Party organization's secretariat, and among its full-time officials is the chief of the Department for Industry and Transport. One might also wish to spend a day eavesdropping on the life of the corresponding Party official at the province level, whose Party organization may even be in the same building, if the city is a provincial capital. But while we can form only an approximate idea of how any of these officials spends his time—the Party's city and province industrial specialists, or the Party chairman at the factory—we do know a good deal about the kinds of tasks they are given and the situations they confront.

For one studying the Soviet system for the first time, the role of the Party in industry and on the farms probably appears more confusing than the Party's relationship with governmental bodies. It is one thing for a political agency to direct the workings of government bodies whose tasks are diverse, and which are not intended to build their efforts around a few all-important production norms, or to show a planned profit on their operations. It is another thing for a Party secretary to issue to a plant director directives which, if followed, might upset a delicately balanced input plan or production schedule. To the Western mind, the usual functions of government are compatible with policy coordination by a political organization; business and production need a unity of command which can only be disturbed by subjecting them to a constant flow of political demands. Lenin, an admirer of American efficiency in business and production, was not unmindful of the risk of reducing efficiency through too detailed political control, particularly after the experience of the War Communism period. But as a Marxist, he necessarily shared the conviction that factories and farms could not be politically neutral; somehow they too had to be infused with a politically determined direction for their efforts.

HAS THE PARTY'S ROLE CHANGED?

The proper role of Party organizations in industry and agriculture is a perenniel issue in the Soviet press, and always has been. The larger issue is not just how a primary Party organization (formerly the "cell") should function within an enterprise, but what kinds of functions are in the domain of the entire Party structure. May the first secretary of an important industrial province tell the plant directors there to revise their production schedules, or to divert more of their profits to build housing for their workers?

Even a casual review of Party directives on this subject, from Lenin's time to the present, shows that whatever the reality of the Party's role may have been, Soviet leaders have seen this role in different ways at different times. At the beginning of the First Five-Year Plan, for example, Stalin's emphasis on the enterprise director's responsibility ("one-man management," Lenin's slogan also) apparently sought to reduce the Party's role in managerial decisions. To take a much later example, Khrushchev's bifurcation of the whole provincial and local Party structure into industrial and agricultural hierarchies may be seen as a move to increase the role of the Party apparatus and the primary Party organizations. Some analysts dispute this conclusion (see below), but in any case it was a politically divisive issue among Soviet leaders.

It is not surprising that the issue of the Party's role in running the economy has produced debate and division. The Soviet Union was the world's first country to set up a socialized economy; Lenin and his associates could hardly have predicted what kind of lines of control would be needed to guarantee the effectiveness of central planning and direction. While they agreed that basic economic goals were the domain of the top Party organs, it did not necessarily follow that the Party should be able to interfere in the workings of the economy at every level.

Two Views of the Party's Role

Studies of the Party's economic role are not in agreement about the ways it has changed with the passage of time. Jeremy Azrael's history of the Soviet managerial elite found that the Party's role in management was high during the 1930s but was cut back greatly during Stalin's last dozen years; then the Party's importance grew during what Azrael terms Khrushchev's struggle with a "united managerial opposition" in 1955–57, only to be cut back drastically after Khrushchev had dealt with this problem[1] Jerry Hough's study of the role of local Party organs in industrial decision-making came to quite the opposite conclusion: ". . . [T]he

---

[1] Jeremy R. Azrael, *Managerial Power and Soviet Politics* (Cambridge, Mass.: Harvard University Press, 1966), chapters 5 and 6.

most basic functions of the local Party organs have remained fundamentally the same during the last forty years."[2] Even the short-term campaigns to increase or reduce the role of Party bodies have not made as much change as the publicity which accompanied them suggests. On the other hand, Hough found some variations in the Party's authority as between one economic management situation and the next, and between planning and management processes. Long-term changes which he identified include more orderly and professionalized career patterns for officials in both the Party and economic hierarchies, and growing technical and professional skills among Party officials.

Therefore the possibility of differing interpretations of the Party's authority within the economic structure must be kept in mind in any study of how the Soviet economic system is related to the political system. Also, one must be wary of assuming that directives from Moscow ordering the Party to change its role in industry and agriculture have had anything like the intended effect; administrative inertia may have enabled the Party's officials to keep the functions and authority they had built up from the 1920s on and to resist the imposition of new responsibilities, regardless of Moscow's efforts to increase or diminish them.

The Party's Continuing Functions

One circumstance which argues for the continuity of a strong Party role in the economy is that the broad functions devised for Party bodies in the 1920s, when the Party's authority was high, are all performed today. While all these functions may have experienced periods of emphasis and deemphasis, there have been no serious moves either to drop them, or to replace them with something radically different:

1. Guidance (*napravleniye*) and leadership (*rukovodstvo*) have long been the key terms describing the Party's overall authority. In writings on the role of Party organizations, the use of these terms is commonly coupled with the injunction that the Party must not usurp the functions of economic administrators. Instead, the authority of the local Party bureaucracy and the primary Party organizations is derived from the authority and policies of the Party as a whole. Guidance and leadership mean that each Party organization must assure that the Party's overall policies are carried out; and this entails constant communication with executives in industry and agriculture, including trade union leaders. Just how and in what circumstances a Party secretary may impose his interpretation of policy on an enterprise director is a difficult question. The principle of "one-man management," advocated by Lenin and estab-

---

[2] Jerry F. Hough, *The Soviet Prefects: The Local Party Organs in Industrial Decision-Making* (Cambridge, Mass.: Harvard University Press, 1969), p. 272.

lished virtually as a matter of doctrine in the First Five-Year Plan, may not be infringed.

2. Supervision (*kontrol*) is much less a matter of dispute: it embraces the Party's function as inspector and generator of criticism and recommendations in all phases of an enterprise's activity, and its purpose is to make sure that both state and Party directives are being carried out. By contrast with the mandates of a variety of other agencies (mainly governmental) which have supervision functions, the Party's mandate is an all-embracing one, intended to bring to light situations that need correction from the point of view of the *intent* of national policies.

3. Expediting, mediating, and "fixing" together constitute a crucial role, because Party officials are in a position to make sure that things are done when the normal channels of economic administration are too cumbersome. A provincial or city Party secretary must know how to negotiate to keep his industries supplied, to settle disputes both among them and with enterprises outside his jurisdiction, to act as an intermediary between enterprises and their ministries, and to resolve conflicts between enterprises and local governments, which are frequent.

4. Personnel selection and policies are central to the Party's role. Through his *nomenklatura*, a Party secretary has a voice in the selection of leading economic personnel, just as he plays a role in the selection of local government officials within his jurisdiction. While the most important personnel decisions must be approved by higher Party agencies, and not infrequently by the Party Secretariat in Moscow, the local Party secretary's role is extremely important here. The supervision function is among other things a process of checking constantly on the performance of economic administrators.

5. Education, propaganda, and morale-building constitute a function very specific to the Party, but one that is clearly less important today than it was in the 1930s. Today there are many alternate channels of political socialization, including those addressing themselves to work situations, that were not fully developed four or five decades ago. Also, enthusiasm is a far less important ingredient of labor morale today than it was in the early industrialization drive.

These, then, were and are the ingredients of policy debates concerning the proper role of the Party in industry. These same functions all existed in the 1920s, so that in a sense all that has transpired since that time has been by way of variations on the same set of themes. Meanwhile, as Soviet managers acquired skills and experience, the Party's role may have been subjected increasingly to the threat of being rendered superfluous in one area after another. If there is a long-term trend underlying the short-term fluctuations of policy concerning the Party's role, this is surely it.

INDUSTRIAL ADMINISTRATION

The Party Controls the "Red Directors"

The early failure of Workers' Control, the chaotically swift national-ization of industries, the ambiguity of the trade unions' position in the nationalized industries, and the need to employ managers and specialists from the capitalist era all contributed to a serious problem of control over enterprise operations. Party cells, linked to the central Party ap-paratus through Stalin's growing hierarchy of Party secretaries, offered the safest solution. While Soviet sources sometimes referred to factory management by a "triangle" of management, Party and trade unions, Lenin early insisted on the principle of "one-man management" as the only rational principle. There was much opposition to this at the 9th Party Congress (1919), where Lenin was accused of wanting bureaucratic authoritarianism and of opening the door to a restoration of capitalism by giving such authority to prerevolutionary managers and specialists. In fact, the Party's interference in managerial questions was considerable during the 1920s. This was just as true in those enterprises which were run by loyal Bolsheviks who had acquired their managerial skills by being thrust suddenly into responsible industrial jobs—these were called the "red directors."[3]

While Stalin too came out repeatedly in favor of "one-man manage-ment," urging a supportive role for the Party and an end to petty inter-ference, he may actually have encouraged this interference because of his political mistrust of the "red directors." A decree of 1929 bolstered the managers' position, and Stalin promised to curtail the role of the "production conferences" which had hitherto served as a device for bring-ing all kinds of criticism and pressure to bear against management. To-ward the end of the First Five-Year Plan, however, Party organizations were being urged to become more involved in matters of production, rather than confining their activities to propaganda and personnel. Mean-while the spokesmen for the "red directors" protested the degree of interference to which they were still being subjected in spite of Stalin's decree. It was a struggle between the old way and the new, between the urge for collective enterprise management that stemmed from the Revolution, and Stalin's need for managerial authority in order to achieve production goals. A secret Central Committee decree of June 1931 for-bade Party organizations to "change, correct, or delay the operative orders of the directors of the factories." It also ordered secret police

---

[3] This category is taken to include many officials who held posts above the level of enterprise management, in the commissariats and the planning mechanism. For a description of the "red directors" see Azrael, *Managerial Power and Soviet Politics,* chapter 4.

representatives out of the factories, and forbade other law-enforcement agencies to interfere without management permission.[4]

While all evidence indicates that one-man management in the 1930s was an operating principle rather than only a slogan, the same leaders who supported this principle also sustained a strong role for Party organizations. If strong managerial authority offered practical advantages, so did strong Party authority. Actually, one-man management within the enterprise was found to be compatible with active supervision by Party officials from the outside, particularly supervision by local and provincial Party secretaries. John Scott's firsthand account of Magnitogorsk in the 1930s, a major new steel center, described the city's Party organization as the real driving force of the economy. By comparison, the soviets, trade unions, and Young Communist League were ineffective: they held no meetings for months at a time, while "the leaders sat in their offices, almost completely out of touch with the memberships and passed resolutions." A dynamic city Party secretary by the name of Lominadze ruled the economy directly. The lines of the Party's authority, wrote Scott, ran to every factory, mine, office, shop, and school. The men who ran the industries were usually Party members, and the Party's authority among the workers was strong. The Party was "the source of initiative and energy" which made the economy move. While the Party made mistakes, particularly in its efforts to ferret out ideological heretics, Scott concluded that Magnitogorsk would not have been built as swiftly or efficiently without it.[5]

A large proportion of the "red directors" vanished in the purges, including Lominadze: summoned to the district NKVD office just two weeks after Kirov's assassination, he shot himself en route. Among the primary victims were those who had supported the move at the 1934 Party Congress to reduce the rate of industrial investment. It was they who had been placed under formidable pressure to meet production goals and get massive new industries into operation. Ordzhonikidze, whom we saw earlier (chapter 4) in the role of crusher of the Georgian Menshevik government, was the chief spokesman for this group. He attempted to protect the "red directors" from the purges, only to commit suicide in 1937 when he too came under threat. Shortly before this, a show trial had sentenced the other leading "red directors" to death. The most notable of these was Grigori Pyatakov, who was vulnerable as an exsupporter of Trotsky, though after Trotsky's departure he had become deputy commissar for heavy industry and one of the First Five-Year Plan's chief planners.

[4] Merle Fainsod, *Smolensk Under Soviet Rule* (Cambridge, Mass.: Harvard University Press, 1958), p. 319.
[5] John Scott, *Behind the Urals* (Boston: Houghton Mifflin, 1942), pp. 83–84.

Do Loyal Specialists Need Party Supervision?

The men who were brought in, starting in the late 1930s, to replace the purge victims have been called the "red specialists," the ones who had received their technical education under Soviet auspices. Some were already active Party members and officials before they received their training; others were young graduates of technological institutes who not only were encouraged to join the Party, but found that active Party membership was essential to their advancement. All of them, from plant managers up to commissars and planning officials, were beneficiaries of the Great Purge in two ways: they owed their rapid advancement to the purges, and once in their posts they found—at any rate after 1939— that the policy was to reduce the Party's functions in industry. No matter whether they had served in the Party apparatus before joining the ranks of the new technocrats, their interests and security now lay with the highly centralized "command economy," which for all its glaring faults and inner divisions of interest was a system they had adapted to.[6]

The Party as Supervisor of Management

The urge of Party officials at all levels to be directly involved in decisions concerning economic management remained a perenniel issue, for in the eyes of at least some of the top leaders it diverted their attention from propaganda, personnel problems, and other nonproduction concerns. At the 18th Party Congress in 1939, the Party Secretariat was reorganized once again, this time to stress specific Party functions rather than the supervision of industrial branches. In 1934, four of the nine departments of the Secretariat had been organized on the production-branch principle; in 1939, only the Agriculture Department was left in this category, while the remainder were organized once again according to the Party's own functions (see Diagram 9–1). The departments themselves, according to spokesmen at the 1939 Congress, had been too involved in management questions and too little concerned with political work. Consequently Party officials at the lower levels, including the secretaries of primary Party organizations in the enterprises, could hardly be blamed for applying the same imbalanced emphasis in their work.

The same sequence of events was repeated in the postwar period. In 1948, the Party Secretariat reverted to its 1934 pattern of production-branch departments, including this time the separation of heavy and light industry. The change was occasioned both by the death of Zhdanov

---

[6] The foregoing historical sketch follows generally the account in Azrael, *Managerial Power and Soviet Politics*, chapters 3, 4, and 5. In dealing with this account, one must bear in mind that the Party's actual authority and functions in industry may not have changed as much from one period to the next as Soviet policy documents suggest.

DIAGRAM 9-1
Departments of the Party Secretariat

1930	1934	1939	1948
Organization and Instruction	Agriculture	Cadres Directorate	Party, Trade Union and *Komsomol* Organs
	Industry		
Agitation and Mass Campaigns	Transport	Propaganda and Agitation	Propaganda and Agitation
Secret	Planning, Finance, and Trade	Organization and Instruction	Heavy Industry
Culture and Propaganda	Political and Administrative	Agriculture	Light Industry
			Agriculture
Administration of Affairs	Leading Party Organs	Schools	Transport
Assignment (subdivided by economic and other branches)	Culture and Propaganda	Special Section	Planning, Finance, and Trade
		Administration of Affairs	Administrative (security organs)
	Special Section		
	Administration of Affairs		Foreign Affairs
			Special Section
			Main Political Administration

Source: Merle Fainsod, *How Russia Is Ruled* (Cambridge, Mass.: Harvard University Press, 1963), pp. 192, 194, 197, 199. Some designations have been altered for the sake of clarity.

and Malenkov's consequent assumption of control over the Secretariat, and by the need to bend all the Party's efforts to rebuilding the nation's war-ravaged economy. (This, actually, has remained the Secretariat's prevailing pattern of organization: At the time of the 1971 Party Congress, 10 of 22 departments were production-branch units.) But after the 19th Party Congress in 1952, the Party press once again began flaying local Party officials for what one article called "a one-sided interest in current economic questions and hardly any interest at all in ideological problems." Some officials had virtually taken command of enterprises and were running them in defiance of Party discipline.[7] The problem now was not only that local Party organizations were neglecting political tasks, but that even as supermanagers of enterprises they had become too strongly identified with the economic establishment as it existed, and hence too little able to act as a force for change.

[7] Ernst Kux, "Technicians of Power Versus Managers of Technique," in Sidney I. Ploss (ed.), *The Soviet Political Process* (Waltham, Mass.: Ginn, 1971), p. 163.

The Khrushchev Reforms

We have reviewed in several different contexts Khrushchev's attack on the mighty industrial establishment, which was directed at the part of the hierarchy above the enterprise level. His 1957 reform, the vehicle he used to topple the "anti-Party group," had quite a number of motives, both political and economic. Strengthening the role of the Party within the industrial establishment was only one motive. The immediate beneficiary of the reform was the provincial (*oblast*) Party organization. A mass of evidence indicates that the provincial first secretaries and their staffs dominated the Regional Economic Councils, which had now taken the place of most of the central ministries. Party officials in effect appointed the councils' staffs; the most important questions of economic priorities and management were settled at joint meetings of the councils and their respective Party committees; communications between the councils and the central planning organs duplicated communications between the provincial first secretaries and the Party secretariat in Moscow; and provincial Party directives interpreting central economic requirements were issued to the councils.[8]

Party organizations in the enterprises, therefore, continued to be immediately and deeply involved in management questions. Above all, they carried the mandate from the provincial Party offices to enforce Party directives concerning production. A flood of newspaper articles admonished the organizations at the enterprise level not to substitute their authority for that of the management, and at the same time warned them to deal resolutely with major questions instead of losing themselves in detail work. The Scylla and Charybdis of Party organizations in enterprises were ever present, and the Party seemed to be forever running into one or the other. Either it dissipated its independent authority by serving as management's handmaiden in handling details, or it arrogated too much authority to itself and started issuing orders to the director.

In 1962 Khrushchev opted for Charybdis. The bifurcation of the provincial and local Party structure into industrial and agricultural subhierarchies, like the 1957 industrial form, had a variety of political and economic ends. In one sense it reduced the importance of the Party hierarchy, by enabling Khrushchev to flood the lower Party organizations with new first secretaries (since every province would now have two such officials instead of one). It divided the authority of the formerly all-powerful provincial Party secretaries. Khrushchev was now doing directly what he had done indirectly in the 1957 reforms: in 1957 he had caused most of the new economic jurisdictions (the Regional Economic Councils) to coincide with provincial Party jurisdictions; now,

---

[8] Philip D. Stewart, *Political Power in the Soviet Union: A Study of Decision-Making in Stalingrad* (Indianapolis, Ind.: Bobbs-Merrill, 1968), pp. 107–19.

in 1962, he reorganized Party jurisdictions to coincide with the two basic economic activities in each province, industry and agriculture. In the latter reorganization, Khrushchev's intention to bind the Party's main energies to the immediate supervision of the economy was made plain. The Central Committee's resolution stated:

> Setting up Party organs along production lines will make it possible to secure a more immediate and better planned direction of industry, construction and agriculture, to concentrate the Party's main attention on questions of production. Such a reorganization will help activate all facets of the Party's activity, and will bind its organizational and ideological work still more closely to the tasks of creating the material and technical base for communism and forming the new type of human being.[9]

Just as with the 1957 measure, one may ask whether the actual effect was to tighten the grip of the Party apparatus over economic management or to dilute its authority by causing it to be so closely involved with day-to-day management questions. If Khrushchev's intention was the former, then his further intention was probably to rescue the system of Regional Economic Councils from its growing difficulties. He may also have sought to check the growth (since 1960) of "state committees" for various branches of the economy, which were reasserting some of the features of the ministerial system that Khrushchev had largely abolished in 1957. But a major study of Soviet economic management argues that, after assuming the office of Prime Minister in 1958, Khrushchev took the lead in recentralizing the economic mechanism he had partly decentralized the preceding year. From this assumption, it follows that the 1962 reform was designed to reduce the position of the Party apparatus at the province level by turning it into "a corps of glorified low-level economic controllers."[10] If this was the case, however, then it is surprising that Khrushchev failed to restore the pre-1957 system of central ministries, since his successors did this promptly after he was removed from office.

The Brezhnev Restoration

The Brezhnev administration's resurrection of the ministerial system in 1965 apparently caused Party officials to fear that their role in industrial management was about to be cut back. The Party press waged a campaign to persuade primary Party organizations in enterprises to focus their attention on the broader functions which they were accused of having neglected for so long:

[9] *Spravochnik partiinogo rabotnika; vypusk chetvyortyi* (Moscow: Gospolitizdat, 1963), p. 193.

[10] Azrael, *Managerial Power and Soviet Politics*, pp. 145–46.

Without substituting themselves for the directors of economic enterprises, Party organizations must focus their main attention on organizational work, on the selection, assignment and education of cadres, on
supervising the execution of Party and state directives, and on strengthening the communist education of the workers.[11]

The press was full of articles by and about enterprise directors, asserting
the need for full authority over their factories.

What the 1965 economic reform had done was to open up new fields
for potential conflict among management, Party, and unions. Directors
now had authority to make more decisions. No longer were Moscow's
planning agencies and ministries meant to specify a factory's output in
great detail, or dictate the exact number of workers to be hired, or
set precise norms for labor productivity. The means by which a factory
could increase its profits were now greater than before. The old guaranteed profits that depended on volume of production were gone, for profits
would henceforth spring from goods *sold* under contract to other enterprises or trade agencies, and accepted by the latter as meeting the quality
specified in contracts. Management's discretion in using profits was expanded: within certain norms, profits could be used for increasing production, improving technology, offering added incentives to the labor
force, and providing more fringe benefits for the workers, including
housing. Little wonder that managers were arguing at this point that
added authority must accompany added responsibility. Without this authority, others would step in to influence these decisions, including not
only Party and union organizations, but a whole long list of other agencies
that have a hand in enterprise decisions: the State Bank, the Ministry
of Finance, local governments, police agencies, and above all the ministries
themselves.

Party organizations have continued their deep involvement in day-to-
day production matters during the first years of the Brezhnev period,
all exhortations to the contrary notwithstanding. This is partly because
the reputations of Party organizations—at provincial and city levels and
in enterprises—are judged in Moscow largely by how well the enterprises
in their jurisdictions are meeting production goals. The same goes for
agricultural production, needless to say. A recent study of the political
advancement and demotion of provincial Party leaders in the Russian
Republic tested the political importance of economic performance. The
224 cases studied, covering a 13-year period, tested political patronage
against economic performance as motives for changes in assignment. It
found a tendency for performance to increase as the more important
criterion, as against patronage. The results were so equivocal as to leave
the impression that performance and patronage are both of great impor-

---

[11] *Pravda*, editorial, Nov. 18, 1965.

tance, but that their relative importance varies from situation to situation in ways that cannot be fully explained.[12]

By all accounts a major role of Party officials is that of production "fixers" who are needed as such by enterprise directors. Soviet industries are forever battling bottlenecks of different kinds which delay obtaining the resources they need in order to meet their quotas: raw materials, parts, and availability of transport are the most critical items. The *tolkach* or "fixer" is a hallowed if still unofficial institution in Soviet industry. The lower Party organizations have long played the role of institutionalized "fixers," even while they are enjoined not to get bogged down in this activity. One local Party official wrote frankly about this kind of work:

> Many deficiencies arise in planning, in the day-to-day management of the economy, bottlenecks crop up in raw material supply, and lo and behold, the [city Party organization's] industrial department starts acting as dispatcher: it communicates with various authorities; it decides questions of supply; it "knocks heads together" among factory directors; its instructors [a type of Party official] "hang on the telephone," and naturally they keep writing a quantity of memoranda and reports. . . .
>
> The question arises: Under such circumstances, how is it possible to avoid interference by Party officials in the decision-making functions of enterprise management? A charmed circle is formed: on the one hand, we direct them not to act in place of management, but on the other hand we require them to investigate matters and create order. Such an approach makes duplication of the economic administrators' work unavoidable.[13]

A New Drive for Party Authority

With the introduction of the 1965 economic management reforms and restoration of the old ministerial system, the details of the Party's role in industry were unclear. Khrushchev's bifurcation of the provincial and local Party structure into industry-oriented and agriculture-oriented components had been abolished. Some observers presumed that all this represented a victory for those who advocated managerial independence and freedom of enterprises from Party interference in decisions concerning production. At the time, this may well have been so. The greater "elbow room" enjoyed by enterprise managers, their freedom from the more petty kinds of control exercised by the ministries and the intermediate *glavki*, made them also less dependent on the services of Party

---

[12] Philip D. Stewart et al., "Political Mobility and the Soviet Political Process: A Partial Test of Two Models," *American Political Science Review* 66 (December 1972), pp. 1269–90.

[13] *Partiinaya zhizn*, No. 22 (November), 1965, p. 41.

officials as intermediaries between level and level, and between one ministerial hierarchy and another.

The 1965 reforms turned out to be more problematic in execution than any of their supporters had probably imagined. Ministries, plus the *glavki* which served as intermediate links between ministries and enterprises, devised numerous ways of restricting the initiative of enterprise directors. A survey of the latter showed that over half of the respondents believed that they had gained no significant amount of managerial independence after 1965.[14] Consequently the role of Party officials as intermediaries and "fixers" appeared to be just as necessary after the reform as before. It is possible to argue that even had enterprise managers gained a significantly greater degree of independence, this in itself might have prompted them to rely on Party officials to buttress their positions as against the ministries. However that may be, there is plenty of evidence that Party officials saw their authority threatened by the reforms, and therefore encouraged their partial sabotage. Also, it should be noted that the 1965 reforms were not accompanied by any corresponding changes in the Party's structure which might suggest a reduction of the Party's role in economic management. As long as a structure remains that is geared to involvement in the affairs of industries—not just the primary Party organizations, but all the industrial departments in local Party bureaucracies—Party officials will be drawn into managerial questions like iron filings to a magnet.

It is not certain how the 1973 reforms in the structure of management (see chapter 3) will affect Party involvement in industry. The grouping of enterprises into "production associations" will not by itself increase the autonomy of the now enlarged basic units as against either the Party structure or the industrial ministries. While it has the potential for doing so, the old practices of detailed regulation by the ministries, and detailed involvement by Party agencies, are too deeply imbedded in managerial procedures to be altered in any short space of time, or by any single reform. A change in the Party Rules at the 1971 Party Congress paved the way for creation of primary Party organizations covering entire production associations, rather than their individual enterprises alone.

Meanwhile, in the wake of the 1971 Congress, the Party press has carried on a campaign urging the most direct kind of Party involvement in managerial decisions. The immediate occasion for this was another amendment to the Party Rules, which expanded significantly the function of supervision (*kontrol*). Supervision in this context denotes an ongoing process of inspection and verification, to make sure that economic plans, ministerial directives, and, above all, Party resolutions are put into effect. It means a formal Party presence at all meetings where decisions are

---

[14] Gertrude E. Schroeder, "Soviet Economic Reform at an Impasse," *Problems of Communism* 20 (July-August 1970), p. 43.

made, the right to check documents of every kind, and observation of work on the spot. Supervision was now extended to two spheres which had hitherto been exempt: (1) central ministries and other central government agencies, plus local government offices and economic management agencies; and (2) research institutes, design bureaus, and educational and cultural establishments, together with a miscellany of organizations such as those for local trade and services. Never before had the Party's mandate been so sweeping, although in the second category Party organizations had in many cases long exercised the supervision that was now made formal.

Those "Kremlinologists" who have stressed rivalries between the Party bureaucracy and state economic bureaucracy as basic to Soviet politics have watched with interest the Party's campaign in the early 1970s to assert its presence in industry and elsewhere. For example, the director of a farm machinery plant in Novosibirsk wrote a tribute to Party supervision which was published by *Pravda* as an example and rebuke to other enterprise directors who have resisted the Party's recently growing role. Given the task of speeding up the production of seed drills, he turned to his Party committee for help and guidance:

> After consulting with the Party committee, we turned first to the Communists. Party meetings were held in all of the shops involved in this difficult job. Related Party meetings were then held for the collectives involved in the technological process. Measures were mapped out to improve the organization of production, and concrete assignments were spelled out for every collective. All this work was summarized in a decision by the Party committee and an order from the plant director. . . .
>
> Today, in looking back at those months of intensive effort, I can see what a great role consistent, determined Party supervision by the Party committee and shop organizations played in this success—in surmounting all the difficulties. To tell the truth, I am surprised to read from time to time that the directors of certain enterprises and organizations are oversensitive about the Party committee's right to oversee their work and consider that such supervision virtually undermines management's authority. This is a mistaken viewpoint![15]

The Party committee, continued the director, operates not only through its shop organizations, but through six specialized commissions whose main function is supervision: technical progress, economic questions, output quality, safety, production of consumer goods, and construction of cultural and social projects. These commissions prepare items for the agenda of the Party committee as a result of their investigations, then supervise the fulfillment of the committee's decisions. In short, the direc-

---

[15] F. Kotov, "The Director's Position," *Pravda*, Aug. 12, 1972, p. 2. Translation from *Current Digest of the Soviet Press* 24 (Sept. 6, 1972), p. 14.

tor's account gives the impression of a ramified policy-making and pol-
icy-executing structure, whose only limitation is that it is enjoined not
to get bogged down in petty details.

Another *Pravda* item, also from Novosibirsk, provided an illustration
of how the Party committee at a research institute which studies the
processing of minerals was exercising its newly granted function of
supervision:

> The Communists at the Institute are making vigorous use of the
> right to supervise management activity, a right granted by the 24th
> Party Congress. They constantly keep the main scientific and production
> questions in their field of vision. The plan for the experimental-industrial
> testing and introduction of completed projects in 1969–1971, a plan
> drawn up on the initiative of and with the active participation of the
> Party bureau, was successfully fulfilled. The implementation of a similar
> plan to cover the period to the end of the five-year plan has begun.
> The recent Party meeting on the state of discipline and the organization
> of labor in the institute and on the introduction of the results of scien-
> tific research in the national economy was very important in the life
> of the collective. . . .[16]

The Party bureau, continued the article, hears reports from the 13 labora-
tory chiefs at its sessions. It recently investigated the poor management
of one of the laboratories, and made recommendations which were
adopted by the Institute's managing board. The Party also distributed
a questionnaire to the Institute's younger professional workers, which
turned up job dissatisfactions and low output and became the subject
of more recommendations.

Finally, there is the enhanced status of Party committees in the USSR
and Union-Republic ministries, particularly in those which manage
branches of the economy. Here too, press accounts in the form of "testi-
monials" offer a picture of what Party committees are now supposed
to be doing, no matter what changes may be taking place in practice.
In the ministries, the Party's role as management consultant and efficiency
expert stands out quite strongly.

To take one example, the Party committee of the USSR Ministry
of Machine Building for the Oil and Chemical Industry decided in 1971
to concentrate on speeding up technological change in this industry. A
general Party meeting within the Ministry was called to consider proposals
that had been solicited through Party members from the Ministry's research and design organizations. As a result, the Party established its own
procedures for checking on the introduction of new processes throughout
the industry, plus a special Party commission for handling this. One specific objective was to achieve the delivery to other industrial branches of

---

[16] *Pravda*, July 31, 1972, p. 2. Translation from *Current Digest of the Soviet
Press* 24 (Sept. 6, 1972), p. 14.

complete sets of equipment for producing mineral fertilizers, and to shorten delivery time on all equipment. This in turn gave rise to meetings of the Ministry's Party committee with Party committees in other ministries which are purchasers of this equipment, for example with the Party committee in the Ministry of Cellulose and Paper Industry. Another project was the Party's introduction of a system for checking on the preparation and handling of documents, and yet another was the analysis of the responsibilities of the Ministry's officials, and their fulfillment.[17]

If such is the reality of the Party's role within a ministry, it stops well short of the Party's issuing direct orders to the minister (who typically is an important member of the Party committee himself). Rather, the Party has now been given additional encouragement to perform actively and efficiently the same roles which it had been lax in performing previously. In any case, the Party's role as a voluntary team for devising ways of promoting efficiency is central, as it has been in the past. If anything is new in the Party committee's present situation, it is perhaps a better-established right of access to documents and information.

One must balance reports such as the three summarized above against other reports, very common in the past, which charge Party secretaries with forming "family circles" together with the directors of enterprises. Mutual support is advantageous when it makes production records and other success indicators look better than they actually are, since the careers of both directors and their Party secretaries depend heavily on practical results. But the 1971 changes in the Party Rules, together with the ensuing campaign for heightening the impact of Party decisions on state enterprises and organizations, show that Brezhnev and the Party Secretaries do not intend to permit the erosion of the enormous instrument which enforces their priorities within the cumbersome machinery of economic administration.

ON THE AGRICULTURAL FRONT

Party organization in the villages started very nearly from "ground zero" at the time collectivization began, in 1929. Figures from the preceding year show that, of a total Party membership of 1.3 million, 200,000 lived in the villages. But of the latter number, less than half were actually of peasant background; and of those who were of peasant stock, roughly one fourth had been recruited to work in the Party apparatus, away from their villages. Over 80 percent of the rural Party cell secretaries were of worker origin. Party members who worked and lived as farmers,

---

[17] P. Kalitin, Secretary of the Party Committee of the Ministry of Machine Building for the Oil and Chemical Industry, "When Responsibility Has Grown," *Pravda*, Nov. 29, 1972. Translation from *Current Digest of the Soviet Press* 23 (Dec. 28, 1971), pp. 8, 20.

therefore, were in very short supply. A massive recruitment drive in the countryside accompanied collectivization, and raised rural Party membership to 800,000 by 1934. But just at this point, a large scale Party purge was under way in the countryside which fell heavily on the new recruits, so that, by the end of the 1930s, actual Party membership on the collective farms was still low. In 1939, there were only 153,000 Party members for some 243,000 collective farms, and only one farm out of 20 had a Party organization at all.[18]

Commissars in Tractor Parks

If agriculture, therefore, was to be brought under Party control, urban communists would have to do the job. During the early 1930s, around 50,000 experienced organizers—many of them "Old Bolsheviks" whose membership antedated the Revolution—were sent out to build Party control in the villages. The leadership avoided attempting to start with a regular Party structure—i.e., with organizing cells on the collective and state farms and strengthening the district (*rayon*) Party committees. Cells, particularly, were openly recognized as politically unreliable, often siding with the opponents of collectivization, who were still numerous. Instead, an extreme type of centralization was adopted in an effort to bridge the vast gulf between Party and farmers, in the form of political departments attached to the Machine-Tractor Stations (MTS). The 25,000 department heads were appointed by the central Party bureaucracy in Moscow, and reported directly to the Central Committee. Their authority was vast, and they were encouraged to foment political warfare in the collective farms to weed out hostile elements. A representative of the OGPU, the name at that time of the security police, was attached to each. Their immediate lieutenants were the collective farm chairmen, who theoretically were elected by the entire collective farm membership, but in reality were Party appointees.

The political departments were modified after less than two years, partly because they had earned such a bad reputation in the countryside, and partly because the leaders had decided to build up the weak district organizations. The MTS continued to have deputy directors for political matters, and these headed regular Party organizations. Their power over the farms continued to be great because of the power of the MTS themselves. Because they controlled the equipment that made collective farm operations possible, they also controlled the farms' major decisions and enforced the directives of the Ministry of Agriculture concerning crop selection and harvest delivery schedules. The MTS tractor brigade leaders and chief agronomists easily overruled any farm director's decisions they

---

[18] Leonard Schapiro, *The Communist Party of the Soviet Union* (New York: Random House, 1960), pp. 454–56.

thought incorrect. A team of Party inspectors served as the main channel for orders from the MTS, and each one was responsible for the success of certain farms. Meanwhile the district Party organizations were being equipped with agricultural departments, which in the course of time acquired their own specialists. From 1934 on, there was an Agricultural Department in the Party's central bureaucracy to give it the necessary support, and analogous departments were formed at the Republic and province levels as well.

If it appears that the Party mechanism was in direct charge of the nation's agriculture—which in the 1930s was not far from the truth—it must be borne in mind that the collective farms were not state agencies and possessed no central organization of their own. So as to preserve the appearance of voluntary nongovernmental organization, the MTS themselves had been organized in 1929 as joint stock companies in which the collective farms were to own shares. Later on the MTS became state agencies. The collective farms' formal tie to the state has been through the procurement agencies that collect crop deliveries, and through the hierarchy of the Ministry (then People's Commissariat) of Agriculture. From the beginning, the Ministry had been working through departments in the various levels of government, down to the district level. The state farms, few in number though they were in the beginning, were creatures of the Ministry; their workers received state wages while at the same time they had the use of private plots, just like collective farmers. But the state farms, too, fell under the Party's direct control, first of all because each one possessed an active and usually reliable Party organization.

The Party Sows and Harvests

The following summary of bureau meetings of a *raikom* (district Party committee), from the captured Smolensk archives of the 1930s, gives some idea of the Party's directing role in agriculture. Because the Party secretary was held directly responsible for agricultural output within his district

> . . . the protocols of raikom bureau meetings . . . read like an agricultural calendar. Each season had its own characteristic preoccupations, with the raikom prodding and threatening, persuading and agitating to get the work done. During the late winter and early spring there were the tools and machinery to be repaired, the seeds to be sorted and delivered. With the spring came plowing and sowing; as the summer approached there was weeding and care of the fields. In late summer the raikom moved toward preparation for the harvest, the struggle to bring it in, and finally the deliveries to the state. Each part of the process found almost frantic reflection in the bureau protocols,

though the urgency of the party directives was not necessarily accompanied by a similar sense of urgency in the fields.[19]

The same was true of the provincial Party organization. Since Smolensk Province was an important agricultural area, the first secretary of its Party organization was under tremendous pressure to meet crop delivery quotas, and his career quite literally depended on his ability to do this. Agricultural departments of the local governments did much of the "leg work" for the Party organizations, attending to the execution of Party orders. But even so, Party representatives were constantly on the move, visiting collective farms and MTS, ordering, prodding, and arranging.[20] On the whole, this description of Party management in agriculture during the 1930s is applicable today as well. The main differences are the absence of the MTS and the fact that the collective farms are much better able to enforce their own output quotas. They are much larger and better staffed than farms of the 1930s, and each is now equipped with a primary Party organization that serves as the district Party's agent on the spot.

After World War II, the Party had to go through the whole process of imposing its authority once again. Many collective farms had been broken up in the Ukraine, Byelorussia, and western Russia; individual plots had been enlarged illegally; and local officials profited from the chaos by pilfering farm property and bartering land. Stalin set up a superagency to deal with all this, the Council on Collective Farms, which worked largely through the Party structure and within a few years had restored the old collective farm structure.

The Khrushchev Reforms

It was at this point that Khrushchev began coming forward with his proposals for building agricultural strength by enlarging and strengthening the collective farms themselves. This occurred during Stalin's last years, and the boldness with which Khrushchev made his proposals was remarkable for that politically oppressive period. He proposed first of all that the collective farms be greatly enlarged through amalgamation. He proposed further that the farmers be rehoused in "agro-cities," where they would live in apartments, have most of the amenities of urban life, and work private plots located on the outskirts of the new towns. Khrushchev may also have inspired a proposal by some economists to permit collective farms to buy some of the equipment hitherto managed by the MTS. The first proposal, that of amalgamation, was readily accepted by Stalin and the leadership, and would probably have occurred even without Khrushchev's support. Part of its popularity with the leadership

[19] Fainsod, *Smolensk Under Soviet Rule,* p. 115.
[20] Ibid., pp. 70–72.

lay in the fact that it was bound to have the effect of enabling each collective farm to have its own Party organization in the immediate future. Between 1949 and 1952, the number of collective farms was reduced from 250,000 to 95,000, while at the same time the number of farms having their own Party organizations increased from about one third to four fifths.

The abolition of the MTS in 1958 appeared to have been one of Khrushchev's fundamental goals in agriculture, so that it is not unlikely that he was the one who actually raised the issue back in 1950. A most delicate issue it was, too—for a quarter-century the MTS had been the Party's guarantee of security in the countryside; to abolish them now might relax some the Party's control over the collective farms in a dangerous way. Khrushchev's arguments stressed economic and managerial advantages rather than the issue of Party control. As it turned out, the enlargement of the farms in the early 1950s, and the higher concentration of specialists which it made possible on each farm, made control through the farms' own cadres vastly easier than it had been in the 1930s. Agronomists, equipment operators, and other specialists had long enjoyed a status apart from that of ordinary collective farmers anyway. Shifting the MTS personnel to the farms along with their equipment simply multiplied the personnel who identified themselves with the agricultural bureaucracy, or the Party, or both. These specialists, therefore, together with the collective farm chairman, now offered the district Party organizations a responsive core of supporters which simply had not existed on the smaller and ill-equipped farms of the 1930s and 1940s.

After Khrushchev

The important changes in agriculture during the Brezhnev period have been almost exclusively in the field of investment priorities and work incentives. The Eighth Five-Year Plan (1966–70) saw a dramatic increase in farm investments by the state, and the following plan (for 1971–75) continued the upswing at a more modest rate. For the collective farmers, there were guaranteed wages and a full range of social security benefits for the first time. However, the new administration's efforts in the direction of restructuring the farms were instances of the mountain's laboring to bring forth a mouse. At the first post-Khrushchev Central Committee Plenum devoted to agriculture, in March 1965, Brezhnev called for a new Model Collective Farm Charter (the last one, also the first, had been that of 1935) and suggested that some of the farms had become too large for efficient management. Amalgamation of the collective farms continued, however, so that by the end of the 1960s there were just under 35,000, as compared with 45,000 in 1960.

The Evolution of Soviet Politics

As for the Charter, endless pages of newsprint were devoted to proposals of different kinds, but the result was largely a codification of arrangements that already existed. The issue of the "link" was left unresolved by making provision for it in certain cases, but without prescribing its widespread adoption. In view of the fears of many Soviet officials that a work unit as small as a half-dozen people, cultivating its assigned portion of collective farm lands, would lead to inefficiency at best and capitalism at worst, the compromise came as no surprise. It had been strongly opposed by Agriculture Minister Matskevich, while its chief advocate, Gennadi Voronov, suffered demotion later and was finally removed from the Politburo in 1973. Had it been adopted on a mass scale (it has long been used in some areas) it might have provided the Party with a major new task, that of keeping the links from pursuing narrow material gain at the expense of collective farm interests.

The idea of a nationwide organization of collective farms, long opposed by Stalin, was discussed during debate over the Charter. This too would have increased the scope of the Party's tasks in agriculture, by providing an all-embracing organization for which the Party would be directly responsible, in view of the fact that Party agencies could not directly interfere (until 1971, at any rate) in the workings of the Ministry of Agriculture. But the idea of an agricultural union was dropped in favor of a system of collective farm councils, whose mandate is very limited and whose main function to date has been assuring that delivery schedules to state agencies are met.

Otherwise both collective and state farms are operating within much the same framework of state and Party agencies that prevailed at the beginning of the Khrushchev era, before the agriculture-minded First Secretary began his series of increasingly confusing reforms. The MTS are gone, and Party organizations in the individual farms are today far more important than they were when the collective farms were smaller and more numerous. The provincial and district Party secretaries continue to play their important role in exerting pressure and mediating among agencies: the Ministry of Agricultural Deliveries gathers the annual output due to it, the Association for Agricultural Equipment and Supplies acts as agent for what the farms are able to purchase, and a host of other agencies make their demands on the farms as well.

The campaign to increase the Party's involvement in management decisions, begun at the 1971 Party Congress, has been pressed in agriculture as well as industry. However, given the relative weakness of Party organizations in agriculture, both numerical and qualitative, use of the Party as a supervisor of management occupies a smaller place on the farms than it does in the factories. But the ritual exhortations to Party organizations place this supervision at the head of the list of duties. A 1972 Central Committee resolution read in part:

The Party organization should exercise fuller control over the activity of the collective farm board and focus its activity on fundamental questions of developing the economy, increasing the production and sale to the state of agricultural output and improving cultural and everyday services for the collective farmers. The unswerving maintenance of the interests of the state and the heightening of the responsibility of cadres for the unconditional fulfillment of plans and assignments for the sale to the state of all types of products of farming and animal husbandry is to be regarded as the main task of the Party organization and the collective farm board. . . .[21]

However, two other Party tasks have received almost equal emphasis in recent years: persuading more collective farmers to take part in the governance of farm affairs, and getting and keeping qualified personnel for the specialist positions. On the whole, the issue of Party interference in the management decisions of both collective and state farms has not generated the same amount of discussion and differences as has the Party's role in industry.

THE NATURE OF THE DECISIONS

The history of decisions concerning structures and roles in economic management resembles the history of government institutions described in chapters 6 and 7; since the 1930s, truly fundamental changes have been few. Khrushchev's Regional Economic Councils represented a dramatic change, but the old system was restored by his successors; the 1962 reorganization of the Party might possibly have produced some basic changes in the Party's role in the economy, but it too was cancelled; abolition of the MTS in 1958 was a striking change, but the functions of the MTS are being performed today through other channels. Seemingly, the "seed time" of economic organization was in the 1920s and early 1930s; all else appears to be little more than piecemeal adaptation of the components and relationships that were created under Lenin and Stalin.

The strategy of the Brezhnev period reinforces this impression. After returning to structures and procedures that had been well tested under Stalin, the Brezhnev administration used a policy of gradual and experimental change. The 1965 management reforms, in themselves only a partial solution of earlier management problems, were introduced on a gradual basis. The link system in agriculture was left as an experiment for the time being, and the transition from collective to state farming, including the amalgamation of collective farms as a preparatory step, was carried on at a moderate pace. In many respects, this approach seems

---

[21] *Pravda*, Oct. 6, 1972. Translation from *Current Digest of the Soviet Press* 24 (Nov. 1, 1972), p. 8.

far sounder than Khrushchev's penchant for pushing through reorganization plans immediately and totally. (Khrushchev, for his part, was well aware that gradual reform would give his opponents time to organize against the reforms.)

The study of recent decisions, therefore, must be primarily the study of incremental policy changes, whether they are planned that way or simply happen to follow an incremental pattern. Whatever their internal differences, the Soviet leaders of the past decade have sought security in working within the array of economic institutions and control procedures inherited from the Stalin era, adapting them by stages to new problems and circumstances. The major question confronting them today is whether this style of change will be adequate to meet the pressing economic goals which must also be part of their political security.

FOR FURTHER READING

The most comprehensive study of the Party's role in economic administration is Jerry F. Hough, *The Soviet Prefects: The Local Party Organs in Industrial Decision-making* (Cambridge, Mass.: Harvard University Press, 1969). See also Grey Hodnett, "The Obkom First Secretaries," *Slavic Review* 24 (December 1965), pp. 636–52, and Philip D. Stewart, *Political Power in the Soviet Union: A Study of Decision-Making in Stalingrad* (Indianapolis: Bobbs-Merrill, 1968). For an evaluation of Khrushchev's 1962 effort to bring the Party structure closer to production matters see Jerry F. Hough, "A Harebrained Scheme in Retrospect," *Problems of Communism* 14 (July-August 1965), pp. 26–32. A good overview of recent problems is in Michael P. Gehlen, *The Communist Party of the Soviet Union: A Functional Analysis* (Bloomington, Ind.: Indiana University Press, 1969), chapters 4 and 5.

Much has been written on the relations between Party and industrial management which focuses on the situation of management. A basic study of the historical evolution of this relationship is Jeremy R. Azrael, *Managerial Power and Soviet Politics* (Cambridge, Mass.: Harvard University Press, 1966). See also David Granick, *The Red Executive: A Study of the Organization Man in Russian Industry* (Garden City, N.Y.: Doubleday, 1960); J. S. Berliner, *Factory and Manager in the USSR* (Cambridge, Mass.: Harvard University Press, 1957); and B. M. Richman, *Soviet Management* (Englewood Cliffs, N.J.: Prentice-Hall, 1965).

Studies specifically devoted to the Party's management of agriculture are not as plentiful. See first of all the works by Belov, Jasny, and Laird in the bibliography at the end of chapter 2. Laird has written and edited a number of surveys of recent problems, whose titles include: Roy D. Laird (ed.), *Soviet Agricultural and Peasant Affairs* (Lawrence, Kans.: University of Kansas Press, 1963); Roy D. Laird and Edward J. Crawley (eds.), *Soviet Agriculture: The Permanent Crisis* (New York: Praeger, 1964); and Roy D. Laird, *Collective Farming in Russia* (Lawrence, Kans.: University of Kansas Press, 1958). For a basic work on control through the MTS, see Roy

D. Laird, Darwin E. Sharp, and Ruth Sturtevant, *The Rise and Fall of the MTS as an Instrument of Soviet Rule* (Lawrence, Kans.: University of Kansas Press, 1960).

On Party control of agriculture in the Stalin era, an excellent source is once again Merle Fainsod, *Smolensk Under Soviet Rule* (New York: Vintage Books, 1963), chapters 5–7 and 12–15. See also Gregory Bienstock, Solomon M. Schwarz, and Aaron Yugow, *Management in Russian Industry and Agriculture* (New York: Oxford University Press, 1944), and Harry Schwartz, *Russia's Soviet Economy* (2nd ed.; Englewood Cliffs, N.J.: Prentice-Hall, 1954), chapter 8.

Part III
THE RESHAPING OF SOCIETY

10

SHAPING A NEW TYPE OF MAN

THE SOCIETY which the Bolsheviks set out to reshape when peace returned at last to Russian soil offered little promise of becoming an orderly, industrious citizenry, let alone a utopian fraternity of all men. Industrial workers, whatever their feelings about the new regime, were inefficient performers in the factories, hard to discipline, and heedless of authority now that the Tsar was gone and the trade unions had grown strong. The farmers had returned to their old village ways of prerevolutionary times, many returning to the repartitional commune system, and shunning modern implements even where some might have afforded them. Mistrustful of the cities and city people, fearful that the Bolshevik grain-raiding parties might descend on them again, the poor households clung to their small holdings, while the more well-to-do sought to expand theirs. Millions of homeless youths roamed over the land, and all the social evils that one can expect on the heels of a long-drawn-out war descended on the population in full force. The non-Russian nationalities, though not unmindful of Bolshevik promises of national equality, could see with their own eyes that most of the commissars who came to organize their lands were Russians, so that old national attitudes hardened after a brief period of hope.

Russians and non-Russians alike shared the centuries-old conviction that the state held sway over them somewhat in the manner of a foreign conqueror. "Submit and evade" was the watchword now as in the past. The Party members and sympathizers who believed that the state was now something vastly different were a small minority of the population; and, in any case, even Lenin's doctrines declared that nonproletarians would continue to be ruled over as subordinate classes. The Cheka, Felix Dzerzhinsky's security police, had become a symbol of this class rule and a household word. For the time being, the NEP and all that went with it had greatly relaxed the demands of the state on the population; a true breath of freedom swept across the land, and this was associated with Lenin's name even after his death. But the old attitudes toward the state's authority remained and would spring to life as soon as new demands were made on the population.

The Bolshevik leaders faced a formidable task in reorganizing this society, a task made far more difficult by the kinds of prophecies they brought with them to power. They were pledged to carry on a phase of industrialization which in the experience of other countries had brought labor strife and more general social unrest. They promised to persuade the farmers to abandon both centuries-old ways of work and the security which the NEP system of land tenure offered them. Material abundance and social freedom were to be the reward of these changes, but both these goals clearly had to be deferred.

SOVIET CONCEPTS OF SOCIAL CHANGE

The conceptual tools which the Bolsheviks possessed had been improvised from Marxian concepts and modified in the light of the Bolsheviks' experience in the Revolution and Civil War. Adaptation was necessary because Marx had assumed that the proletarian society would be built under the hammerblows of capitalism. What would emerge on the morrow of the revolution would be a society embodying a Rousseauian type of solidarity in its inner relationships, particularly in its capacity for self-discipline and coordination. A training period would be necessary before the full-blown communist order could emerge. According to the Marxian dialectic, the future order of things is always formed in the midst of the present order, but having freed itself from the restraints of the outmoded present, it bears for a time the scars of its origins. After the full conquest of political power, therefore—carried out by the dictatorship of the proletariat—there will follow a socialist period, in which each member of society will internalize the new way of life. "To each according to his work," the principle of socialism, is a temporary concession to the mentality carried over from the capitalist past, when one worked in order to gain an existence. Work in communist society will be performed because it has again become part of man's true nature, his most fundamental link to his material environment. Given the kind of abundance which Marx foresaw, the whole need for petty arithmetic measurement of rewards would fall by the wayside; hence "to each according to his needs."

Materialism and Consciousness

The Marxian doctrine most important for Bolshevik adaptation was the idea of materialism. Much more than the simple notion of the primacy of matter, this meant the primacy, as a social force, of man's adaptation to matter by his use of the material world to sustain himself. What men produce beyond the means for their existence—culture, social relations, and political organization—is necessarily a product of the way they are able to organize to stay alive. In this sense, according to Marx, men's ideas are derived from matter. More precisely, Marx believed ideas to be the product of men's *active* relationship to nature:

> The production of ideas, of conceptions, of consciousness, is at first directly interwoven with the material activity and the material intercourse of men, the language of real life. Conceiving, thinking, the mental intercourse of men, appear at this stage as the direct efflux of their material behavior. The same applies to mental production as expressed in the language of the politics, laws, morality, religion, metaphysics of a people. Men are the producers of their conceptions, ideas, etc.—real, active men, as they are conditioned by a definite development of their productive forces and of the intercourse corresponding to these, up to its furthest forms. Consciousness can never be anything else than conscious existence, and the existence of men is their actual life-process. . . .[1]

The Soviet system, from Lenin's time to the present, has never maintained the policy that the nation's economic transformation was by itself sufficient to transform the consciousness of the population. Quite the contrary, it was the Soviet leaders who first made propaganda, education, and control of mass communications into a modern art that has been followed by other governments in the present century. The fact that socialism was declared attained in 1936, and the "full-scale building of communism" begun at the end of the 1950s, did not lead to any reduction in the use of all these means of shaping human consciousness.

The notion that consciousness might in some cases develop *ahead* of the material environment had its beginnings in Marx's own thought, when he wrote that

> . . . consciousness can sometimes appear further advanced than the contemporary empirical relationships, so that in the struggles of a later epoch one can refer to earlier theoreticians as authorities.[2]

Lenin began with the Marxian idea that oppressed classes in each stage of history must, in order to be capable of overthrowing the ruling class,

---

[1] Karl Marx and Friedrich Engels, *The German Ideology* (New York: International Publishers, 1947), pp. 13–14.

[2] Ibid., p. 72.

develop a common consciousness of their own based on a common perception of their material situation. Marx had advocated propaganda and uniting the efforts of proletarian organizations as a means of hastening the spread of proletarian consciousness. Lenin argued for the role of a united proletarian party as the bearer and embodiment of this consciousness. From this view, it was only a step to the further conclusion that consciousness was the same as submission to the leadership of this party.[3]

After the Revolution, and particularly in view of the economic policy compromises of the NEP, direct means of instilling proletarian consciousness into ever widening circles of the population were again necessary. Until the structure of socialism was complete, the new regime would remain without broad support unless most of society were deliberately reeducated. The same techniques of propaganda that had assisted the success of a premature proletarian revolution, well ahead of the material circumstances that Marx considered necessary for it, would now serve to promote a socialist consciousness before the full economic base for it existed.

Freedom in a Highly Organized Society

Another Marxian premise had to do with the place of the individual in society. Marx and Engels spoke repeatedly of the free fulfillment of human potential under communism. While Marx foresaw a centrally regulated economy, he did not foresee the need for outside regulation of social conduct in the manner later parodied in the famous anti-utopian tracts (e.g., Orwell's *1984* and Zamyatin's *We*). The human being, for Marx and Engels, is a creature of infinite potential, who needs freedom in order to develop. This freedom is to be found in true community, which means a society without class divisions, without domination of man's productive relationship to his environment by one part of society. Once this division is abolished, the personal freedom which hitherto was enjoyed by members of the ruling class will pass to all men: "Only in community with others has each individual the means of cultivating his gifts in all directions; only in the community, therefore, is personal freedom possible."[4] The *Communist Manifesto* speaks of "an association in which the free development of each is the condition for the free development of all." Freedom in this definition is linked to material abundance:

> The possibility of securing for every member of society, by means of socialized production, an existence not only fully sufficient materially,

---

[3] This conclusion is argued persuasively in Alfred G. Meyer, *Leninism* (New York: Praeger, 1962), chapters 1 and 2.

[4] Marx and Engels, *The German Ideology*, p. 74.

and becoming day by day more full, but an existence guaranteeing
to all the free development and exercise of their physical and mental
faculties—this possibility is now for the first time here, but *it is here.*[5]

That freedom means freedom within a community is a truism. That
it depends partly on the absence of political domination by a minority,
and partly on the material resources which men have at their disposal,
few will dispute. Marx and Engels rather wisely left their definition
simple, refraining from any predictions about how men would organize
their free existence once they had emerged from the confines of class
rule. On one point, however, Marx was quite specific: this ultimate freedom cannot be defined by establishing economic rights. "To each according to his work" is a principle that embodies a bourgeois right. Since
men are unequal in their abilities, and have different needs, one man's
assertion of his right to an equal wage means another's proportionate
loss.[6] As to political rights, Marx nowhere described them in detail.
Rights, he maintained, are claimed *against* a person or an authority. To
assert a right is to demand a remedy for an imperfection that is built
into one's society, including a state that dominates this society. Under
communism, one may assume that rights too would be consigned to
Engels' "museum of antiquities" along with the state itself.

Lenin accepted Marx's reasoning thus far. He was explicit in talking
about rights generally, and not only about the right to the fruits of
one's labor. Democracy itself is a necessary holdover from the bourgeois
era, the framework of "formal equality" as opposed to "actual equality."
Equality for Lenin consisted in "the equal right of everyone to determine
the structure of the state and to administer it."[7] This excluded the bourgeoisie and other former ruling classes, whose power would be crushed
by this new state. As for the laboring classes, democracy consists in
universal participation: "*All* citizens are transformed here into hired employees of the state . . . *All* citizens become employees and workers
of a *single* nationwide state 'syndicate.' "[8] The main task of the state,
after it has crushed the old oppressors, will be accounting and control.
Keeping account of who produces what and who gets what will enter
into the nation's bloodstream, to the extent that escape from this control
will become an impossibility. Finally, the necessity of observing the rules
of social conduct becomes internalized. At this point the whole formal

---

[5] F. Engels, *Socialism: Utopian and Scientific* (Moscow: Foreign Languages Publishing House, 1954), p. 113.

[6] K. Marx, *Critique of the Gotha Programme* (Moscow: Foreign Languages
Publishing House, 1954), pp. 25–26.

[7] V. I. Lenin, *The State and Revolution* (Moscow: Foreign Languages Publishing
House, n.d.), p. 159.

[8] Ibid., p. 161.

framework of democracy can be dropped, for the era of communism is at hand.

This prophecy came from Lenin in the role of utopian, as he penned *State and Revolution* in the summer of 1917. Control and accounting were to be his despair during his brief years in power, but Lenin's specific vision of mass participation was never repudiated, and it remained to plague future writers on ideology. *State and Revolution* did not stop Lenin and his successors from maintaining a professional bureaucracy to do the controlling, nor did it keep them from putting a bill of rights in two of the three key constitutions (those of 1918 and 1936), or from setting up a full-blown system of law codes and courts for guaranteeing individual rights in the traditional way. It did, however, give future leaders a mandate to de-emphasize the claims of the individual against the state's authority, specifically to forbid the use of rights where this gave an advantage to hostile political tendencies.

Democracy and Authority

It was characteristic of Lenin's thought about society that he was forever trying to combine things that common sense says are not reconcilable. His vision of universal administration attempted to combine the concepts of "community" and "society," which early sociologists at that time were taking such pains to separate. In a revolution, the turbulent upsurge of the masses must be combined with absolute discipline. Factory labor must do the same:

> We must learn to combine the "public meeting" democracy of the toiling masses—turbulent, surging, overflowing its banks like a spring flood—with *iron* discipline while at work, with *unquestioning obedience* to the will of a single person, the Soviet leader, while at work.[9]

That is to say, between spontaneous mass action and dictatorship there is no firm middle ground, for the essence of Lenin's democracy was linking one extreme to the other.

While this notion is repugnant to democratic thought in the West, it is one of the ways in which Lenin's Marxism complements Russian culture. First, the Russian urge toward group unity is a strong one, a trait which some scholars ascribe to the doctrines and rituals of the Orthodox Church. Next, the boundary between self-discipline and anarchy in group behavior is traditionally a thin one, and it can be crossed in both directions: as the Bolsheviks were infiltrating the Winter Palace in search of Kerensky's cabinet, spontaneous discipline stopped the looting that had begun. Finally, Russians in the past have displayed erratic work

---

[9] V. I. Lenin, *The Immediate Tasks of the Soviet Government* (Moscow: Foreign Languages Publishing House, 1951), p. 61.

habits, in which idleness alternates with frenzied drives to meet targets. Many a Russian will say even today that back in the 1920s and 1930s the country needed Stalin, for without massive discipline the nation might have relapsed into its old ways in the midst of the early five-year plans. Russians, consequently, may chafe at discipline while recognizing its necessity; they may think of democracy as the setting for an outpouring of opinions and feelings, but a setting which still leaves room for decisive leadership which can put an end to discussions in favor of united action. In the course of modern Russian history, Western concepts of democracy and rights were known, but mainly to a small intellectual and political minority. While Russia had produced able parliamentarians who had held sway in the first two Dumas, and courageous lawyers who battled to extend the rights granted in the 1860s, they were working with ideas which had little opportunity to take root in the public consciousness.

Lenin was an able practitioner of group relationships, even if not always a successful one. He saw groups locked in combat, groups infiltrating other groups, groups absorbing groups. The individual found his identity only as a member of this or that group. He might think himself free, but his conduct in the end would always hang on group membership, consequently also on class membership. The notion of the individual as a constant unit of society was rejected by Lenin as a relic of idealist philosophy. Marx's idea of the human being as an unfolding potential was quite compatible with his outlook. Marx, too, denied constant human characteristics, save for man's drive to sustain himself in cooperation with his fellow men, and to improve his lot where possible. Furthermore, it was easy enough for Lenin to assert with Marx that realizing the human potential must wait until after the new society had developed out of the various social elements that survived the Revolution. A number of early Russian Marxist philosophers were very explicit on this point. Some of them went further than either Marx or Lenin in their assertions that future man could be truly human only in close harmony with his society, and not in asserting his individuality against society.[10]

Man and Possessions

The human urge to acquire, own, and multiply possessions is not, in Marx's thought, a universal trait, but one which arose in history, and which will come to an end with the arrival of communism. Private property, though its origin was ancient, became the dominating principle of economic relationships as feudal relations and the old absolutist regimes came to an end. The use of property as capital, as a means for multiplying

---

[10] See George L. Kline, "Changing Attitudes Toward the Individual," in Cyril E. Black (ed.), *The Transformation of Russian Society* (Cambridge, Mass.: Harvard University Press, 1967), pp. 618–24.

itself, was neither an expression of human nature nor the result of perverse human passions unleashed. Rather, it was a system of relationships which many men found advantageous in seeking their survival and well-being. These relationships came to dominate the economy of Europe and North America, but in so doing they produced their opposite. Initially they had offered a tolerable means of existence to a large part of society, including hired workers who had no capital; now they turned into the means for existence of only a very few who now dominated the capitalist system, and a threat to the very existence of the many whose wages were pushed down to the level of bare subsistence.

The use of possessions as capital had led to this state of affairs through its own internal laws of development. All goods that were produced had now become commodities, whose production and distribution was determined by their exchange value in commerce, not by their use to society and individuals. Early capitalism could not be restored; the way back was closed. Property itself had to be transformed to solve the dilemma. The new form of property, *personal* property, must be so regulated that it is henceforth used or consumed by individuals, but cannot be used to multiply wealth. The great capitalist accumulation of property will be preserved and even multiplied further, but by society as a whole and for the ultimate benefit of its members. Such was Marx's solution to the property question.

Marx's formula for possession and consumption in the future society scarcely required communal barracks and common soup pots. It certainly did not presume austerity. "Man, at last the master of his own form of social organization, becomes at the same time the lord over nature, his own master—free," wrote Engels.[11] Marx had waged a long ideological battle against proposals for sharing the wealth in utopian communes. The future society, far from returning to a simple mode of existence, would have as its disposal the vast productive mechanism bequeathed to it by the capitalists. Expanding and improving this mechanism would at last free man from economic necessity. The future society would then solve the problem of distribution in its own way: "Communism deprives no man of the power to appropriate the products of society," said the *Communist Manifesto*, but only "of the power to subjugate the labor of others by means of such appropriation."

Marx left little indication of how he envisaged the distribution of goods under communism. His rigorous mode of thinking was focused entirely on the broad premises of the future. We know only that he foresaw a society of abundance, a society based on a complex and highly integrated productive mechanism, and a society capable of shaping its own social relationships in the interest of all its members.

------

[11] Engels, *Socialism: Utopian and Scientific*, p. 118.

ENTHUSIASM AND MATERIAL INCENTIVES

What is the cause of excessive labor turnover? It lies in the incorrect organization of wages, in incorrect pay scales, and in a "leftish" levelling of wages. A number of enterprises have set up their pay scales in such a manner that the difference has almost vanished between skilled and unskilled labor, and between difficult and easy work. Wage levelling creates a situation in which the unskilled worker has no interest in moving up into the ranks of skilled labor, and thus is deprived of the chance of getting ahead. . . .[12]

Stalin was addressing a conclave of economic administrators in 1931, not the same gathering that had heard his speech about refusing to slacken the economic tempo, but another one just four months later. If 1929 was the year of the "Great Change" for Soviet agriculture, 1931 was a year of similarly great changes for industrial policy. It was a return to conventional industrial administration after a decade of experimentation. One-man management now definitely triumphed over the "triangle" of the 1920s, the trade unions had been purged and disciplined so as to support management, and now wage levelling was declared anathema. Marx's principle of socialism, "To each according to his work," was now put into effect with a vengeance.

Wage Levelling in the Early Years

Soviet wage policies had begun with a brief and unsuccessful attempt in 1917–18 to reduce all administrative and managerial salaries to the level of earnings of the average worker.[13] Even before the beginning of the NEP, practical necessity had led to increases in pay differentials, both within pay scales and among different branches of industry. In the mid-1920s Tomsky, head of the trade unions, pushed to restore the Left's policy of greatly reduced differentials (which did not stop him from joining the Right toward the end of the economic debates). A few groups of workers had turned into real enthusiasts for levelling, to the extent of pooling their wages and dividing the sum evenly among themselves.

Had the Soviet economy been able to depend on enthusiasm as the main motive of its labor force, or had Moscow assumed the power to assign workers to their jobs and professions, wage levelling might have been possible. Moscow commanded both enthusiasm and the power of assignment; there were the young people who endured every sacrifice

---

[12] I. Stalin, *Voprosy Leninizma* (11th ed.; Moscow: Gospolitizdat, 1953), p. 367.

[13] This account is a condensed version of the summary of Soviet wage policies in the author's *Soviet Social Policies* (Homewood, Ill.: Dorsey Press, 1970), pp. 165–79.

to build the town of Komsomolsk in the Far East, and the growing army of labor camp inmates who toiled in the Siberian mines and forests; there were specialists who volunteered for the most difficult posts, and growing numbers of university graduates who were assigned for three years to jobs not of their own choosing. But these methods alone would have been awkward to use on the entire labor force. Money incentives provided an easier way of distributing the bulk of the industrial workers.

Stalin Introduces High Differentials

From 1931 on, workers in mining and metallurgy enjoyed pay scales substantially higher than those of other industries, and the scales themselves showed the greatest differential from bottom to top. John Scott's account of the Magnitogorsk metallurgical industry in the 1930s reported that in 1933 unskilled workers were earning 100 rubles, skilled workers 300, experienced engineers 600 to 800, and top managerial personnel from 800 to 3,000.[14] Bonuses also were proportionately larger in the favored industries. A majority of the labor force was shifted to some form of piecework, in many cases a combination of time-rate scales with piecework, plus a wage bonus system that itself was a further form of piece rate. The bonus system of the 1930s provided enormous incentives in the critical industries. The pay scales of a Magnitogorsk steel-rolling operation give some idea of this: for underfulfillment of the plan, 75 percent of the regular wage scale was paid; for up to 20 percent overfulfillment, there was an added 30 percent in wages; for 20 to 30 percent overfulfillment, the wage bonus went up to 70 percent; above 50 percent overfulfillment yielded three times the base wage rate. This was at a time when many of the new industries were operating at a fraction of their potential, and powerful incentives were proving quite effective.[15] Later in the decade the bonus incentives were cut back, and in the post-Stalin era the proportion of wages paid on a piecework basis had been greatly reduced. However, both are still used in many branches of the economy.

The 1931 policy offered substantial rewards to specialists and managerial personnel. Engineers and technical specialists received salaries that, for all of Soviet industry, were typically 2½ times the average wage in any given enterprise. While no systematic data exist on the salaries of directors and top administrators during the Stalin era, fragmentary data suggest that they were rewarded generously if not exactly in princely fashion. Many of them received, in addition to a comfortable

---

[14] John Scott, *Behind the Urals* (Boston: Houghton Mifflin, 1942), p. 49. Ruble-dollar comparisons, complicated enough even today, are even harder to state for the 1930s, since the Soviet economy then was going through a severe inflation.

[15] Ibid., pp. 148–50.

executive salary, a "Party envelope" with supplementary pay. Social insurance, pensions and fringe benefits were for the most part proportional to wages for all workers: that is, they tended to reinforce differences instead of mitigating them.

Khrushchev Reduces the Differentials

At the 20th Party Congress in 1956, Khrushchev launched a campaign for reducing but not eliminating all these differentials. In doing so he did not argue that this was a step in the direction of wage levelling, or that enthusiasm could now be substituted for money incentives. He stressed that the economy must "make full use of the powerful lever of material interest" for the purpose of increasing labor productivity. Mikoyan pointed out that the gap between low-paid and high-paid workers had been necessary back in the 1930s because of the crying need for skilled workers. It was the rise in levels of training and skill throughout the labor force that now made it possible to close the gap somewhat.[16]

By the early 1960s, there had been good if not spectacular progress toward fulfilling these promises. While wage differentials themselves were not reduced, minimum wage legislation raised the monthly wage "floor" to 60 and 70 rubles, and differentials among industries were lessened. Whereas the differential between the lowest-paid and highest-paid workers in a given industry in Stalin's time was often over 1 to 3, now it was reduced to 1 to 2 in many branches of heavy industry, and 1 to 1.8 in the light and food industries. Engineering and technical personnel were assigned salary scales overlapping the pay levels for skilled workers. A 1958 decree limiting executive salaries to 350 rubles monthly remained a dead letter, however.[17] The one area in which incentive differentials were increased was in the pay scales for industries in the remote and climatically harsh areas of Siberia. In areas where formerly the bulk of the labor force was provided by the NKVD's prison camps, workers were now offered three to five times the pay that they would receive in the same kind of employment elsewhere in the country. It was not until after Khrushchev's removal that serious steps were taken to bring the income of collective farmers up to the level of industrial wages. In the latter 1960s a guaranteed farm wage was enacted, the farmers were brought into the social security system, and income for a large proportion of the rural population at last moved "to within hailing distance" of urban incomes.

---

[16] *XX Syezd KPSS*, vol. 1 (Moscow: Gospolitizdat, 1956), pp. 74–75, 307.

[17] While this was only $385 at the official exchange rate, Soviet prices, the tax system, and the free provision of things for which Americans must pay (e.g., medical services) all combine to make this a comfortable salary.

Moral Stimuli and Industrial Psychology

Soviet leaders, philosophers, and social scientists have been concerned about the great emphasis on adjusting material rewards. Where are the work motivations that will operate in the future communist society? Can the enthusiasm of the early five-year plans be created anew? "Combining material and moral stimuli" is a much used phrase, but whether this principle has been successfully applied is a matter of debate. From the very beginning of Soviet rule, psychological rewards for good job performance have been handed out by the bushel. Competition among and within industries has produced a variety of such rewards. There are "Certificates of Merit," "Red Banners," "Rolls of Honor," and the like. The Stakhanov movement of the 1930s combined these publicity devices with high money rewards; the "Brigades of Communist Labor" which the Khrushchev regime initiated in 1958 attempted to stress moral satisfaction sweetened somewhat by bonuses. The way "moral stimuli" are interpreted publicly suggests the motivation of creating material abundance for future years by dedication to one's work in the present. All in all, Soviet leaders and economic administrators have had a hard time making use of Marx's interpretation of work under communism, which is that work will be a part of man's nature, an everyday necessity, freely performed without any connection to specific rewards.

The 1960s saw the beginning of Soviet sociology, a field that had been pre-empted hitherto by the dogmas of Soviet Marxism. Much of the effort of sociologists has been directed toward work and work motivations. For the first time, the Soviet policy makers are equipping themselves with tools which will tell them what has been happening to the motives of the ordinary working man. Karl Marx had prophesied the end of the worker's alienation from his own work, from the system in which he worked, and from the very products he turned out. Had the Soviet regime ended this state of affairs in its own factories? Industrial psychologists in America have been discovering that, beyond a certain point, neither increased material rewards nor honorific recognition will improve labor performance. Instead, labor performance is a correlate of creative participation in the work process. A team of sociologists at Leningrad University conducted surveys of workers very much like those that are being done in the West. While agreeing with the thesis of creative participation, they found that "social circumstances" are a still more important determinant of work performance. These include social and political awareness, participation in service activities outside of work, and voluntary participation in improving the work process itself.[18]

This conclusion leaves open the Marxian question of whether labor

---

[18] A. G. Zdravomyslov, V. P. Rozhin, and V. A. Yadov, *Man and His Work: A Sociological Study* (New York: International Arts and Sciences Press, 1969).

will become one of man's prime needs under communism. A socially aware, civic-minded worker may be motivated to work well even at a dull factory job, if the Leningrad group's findings are correct. On the other hand, this does not make labor itself part of man's being. Sociologists in the communist countries of Eastern Europe have recognized that alienation from one's work can and does occur under a socialist economic system, first of all because of the monotony of the work itself. Soviet Marxism denies that this is alienation in any more than a superficial sense. Soviet philosophers and social scientists have sought an answer to this problem with prognoses of what labor will become in the future: all labor will be skilled, the work week will be 20 or 25 hours, occupational choices and changes can be made at will, and labor will continue to occupy high respect in society.[19] Such, at any rate, was the optimism promoted by Khrushchev. While this view is still accepted, the optimism which accompanied it has given way to sober efforts in social science research. Meanwhile, manipulation of material rewards is still the first concern of economic administrators. The results of social science research will be used if they serve to raise productivity and to solve other practical problems. The question of *intrinsic* work satisfactions, posed by Marx's prophecy, has only begun to be dealt with seriously.

INFORMATION, PROPAGANDA, AND ATTITUDES

Visitors to the Soviet Union generally leave with a very mixed set of impressions about the system's efforts to shape public opinion. It begins with an innocent request for foreign newspapers at the newsstand in the hotel lobby, and the discovery that only communist party newspapers are available—*L'Humanité* from France, *Unità* from Italy, an assortment of others, and occasionally an offbeat Marxist newspaper from the United States. A tour of the main city streets may turn up some large red banners with yellow or white letters, offering a variety of slogans: "Hail to the great and indestructible unity of Party and people!" "Working people of the Soviet Union: Participate actively in the election campaign!" "May the fraternal friendship of the peoples of the U.S.S.R. eternally live and flourish." "The Party is our glory, our honor, and our conscience!" If a Party congress, a Central Committee plenum, a Komsomol congress or something similar is in progress, the banners are especially thick. Lenin's profile is prominent in many situations—a bookstore display, the portico of a meeting hall, the bronze commemorative plaque on an historic building.

A closer look at the kind of everyday political communication the

---

[19] *Fundamentals of Marxism-Leninism* (Moscow: Foreign Languages Publishing House, n.d.), p. 861.

citizen gets from the system reveals a multiplicity of channels carrying
the same messages. Government announcements, Party statements, and
editorials on ideological questions are carried in identical form by a large
variety of newspapers; radio broadcasts repeat the same messages. When
a public campaign of some kind is on, the media are full of similar exhortations—for physical fitness, for some new and growing industry,
for public support of law enforcement, for honoring Soviet writers, and
so forth. Bookstores offer a large variety of books on political questions,
nearly all of them published in the Soviet Union, from the works of
Lenin and the protocols of Party congresses to handbooks for propagandists and popular pamphlets on Soviet foreign policy. One sees notices
of public lectures on a variety of topics, some of them political. Often the
sponsoring agency is listed as the *Znaniye* (Knowledge) Society, which
is also the publisher of a great many books on political and social themes,
popularized for mass distribution. A look at the theater and film adver-
tisements shows that some of these have a direct political message: typical
are plays about the Revolution in which actors portray Lenin, Dzerzhinsky, and the few Old Bolsheviks who were not later anathematized;
a number of films deal with the Soviet Army in World War II; many
films and plays are devoted to the life of factories and farms.

   A visit to a factory turns up another setting for political communication. Posters abound, touching on every kind of theme, from the importance of safety goggles to the danger of imbibing imperialist ideology.
The factory has an auditorium, and a glance at the notices of events
shows a wide variety of items, including amateur evenings and folk con-
certs on the one hand, and political lectures and films on the other.
A "red corner" offers a library of Party and Komsomol publications,
a small meeting room, and a director who is in charge of a staff of
volunteer propagandists and agitators from among the factory's employees. The honors awarded to leading workers and work teams stress their
role in fulfilling the nation's economic plan, which in turn is linked to
quotations from the most recent Party congress, thus placing production
goals in a political setting.

   In short, the channels of everyday political communication both per-
vade the system and enjoy a near monopoly. Foreign films that are shown,
and foreign books that are translated (which are quite numerous, actually), are selected for their conformity to the official interpretation of
the countries and societies they represent. Foreign visitors, in whatever
capacity they arrive, must "go through channels" in all their travels
and contacts with institutions. While no one prohibits foreigners from
mixing informally with ordinary Soviet citizens, and many do, the authorities can discourage this by warning (or creating trouble for) those
Soviet citizens whose contacts with foreigners seem too frequent or too

intimate. The one major breach in the communications monopoly consists in foreign radio broadcasts, which today are sometimes jammed and sometimes not.

What Manner of Communication?

Foreigners usually find the repetitive slogans crude, the newspapers' political coverage dull, and the whole idea of communications saturation repugnant. One has the feeling that the Party's ideological chiefs are using the communications techniques of the past, which must have been tremendously effective when the Revolution was still young and when most of the population was not yet aware of what the Bolsheviks stood for. One also gets the impression that the ordinary citizen pays little attention to these forms of political communication: people go about their business unmindful of banners and posters; bookstore shoppers cluster around the novels and poetry instead of the Party publications; and in a society of avid readers, who keep their noses in books on park benches and in subway cars, literature rather than newspapers is the choice of most.

The conspicuous forms of communication are only one facet of a total process of shaping the attitudes and feelings of citizens. The banners and the profiles of Lenin are ritualistic symbols, addressed to a people whose cultural heritage includes the repetitive ritual expressions of the Russian Orthodox Church, monotonous to outsiders but a balm to the faithful. The outpouring of political literature may be regarded as mere commentary on familiar and unchanging scriptures; once the basic teachings are taken to heart, it is not of great importance if the mass of the faithful find little interest in the commentaries.

Here the parallel ends. The Communist Party has communications functions which the Orthodox Church did not: It must interpret changing events and changing demands on the populace, and it must summon people to specific acts. It must be persuasive with a populace whose level of education has been rising steadily and whose patterns of association are no longer restricted to traditional village ties. Forms of communication which were once effective must give way to new and sophisticated forms. The things that are communicated must engage the thought processes of ordinary people in a way that persuades them of the continuing validity of Soviet Marxism.

Information about the effectiveness of communications from Party to people is fragmentary, but thanks to a growing official interest in sociology and questionnaires there are some interesting recent data. *Izvestiya*, published as the central organ of the Soviet government, conducted a reader survey in 1967 which turned up both strengths and limitations in the newspaper's job of transmitting political information and propaganda. Though intended as a mass-circulation newspaper for the general reader, its readership had an average level of education far above the national average: 44 percent of *Izvestiya's* readers had had a higher education, as opposed to 9 percent nationally; 21 percent had not completed secondary education, as opposed to 49 percent nationally. Articles published under the following rubrics were read regularly by the following percentages of readers:[20]

1. On moral themes 75
2. Surprising stories 71
3. International surveys 69
4. Family circle 66
5. Feuilletons (anecdotal material, generally on moral and political themes) 64
6. Events in countries of Asia, Africa, Latin America 55
7. Man, the collective, and society 52
8. Science 49
9. Sports 47
10. Meetings with interesting people 47
11. Events in socialist countries 45
12. World of the intelligent man 44
13. Juridical problems 40
14. Pedagogy 38
15. Literature and art 37
16. Lead article 30
17. Economics 23
18. Propaganda articles 18
19. Work of the soviets 17

Other surveys indicate a high preference for international news, family life, and accidents and crime (the last two only scantily represented in the press), and a relatively low preference for domestic economic and political news. The number of newspapers printed each day is now over half the nation's population figure, and they are a key source of news for the bulk of the population, no matter whether their highly selective content is understood skeptically or taken at face value. But apparently a saturation point has been reached on the kinds of topics most central to the Party's concerns.

Agitation: An Outmoded Type of Communication?

The role of the agitator is an interesting example both of adaptation and reluctance to alter traditional patterns of communication. Even before

---

[20] Gayle Durham Hollander, *Soviet Political Indoctrination: Developments in Mass Media and Propaganda Since Stalin* (New York: Praeger 1972), pp. 63–65.

the Revolution, the Bolsheviks had been real pioneers in the art of mass oral communication. The agitator, a "soapbox orator" who conveyed simple messages by linking them to popular discontent, was particularly effective in the ranks of the Tsarist armies in 1917. Propaganda, as distinct from agitation, meant communicating many ideas to relatively few people, instead of the other way around. After the Bolsheviks were in power, agitators typically operated in teams under the supervision of Party activists. They spoke to captive (though not necessarily unwilling) audiences at factories, on farms, and during campaigns for elections to the soviets. For many ordinary people, this face-to-face contact was more effective than the Party-controlled press in getting across basic messages. The agitator represented the Party, even though many were not Party members, and the response to his talks provided the Party with a barometer of public feeling. Leaflets and "wall newspapers" were used by agitators to supplement their oral communications.

With time, agitators came to focus more and more on the practical economic tasks of the people they addressed. Their ideological and political messages were so widely duplicated in other media that they were not often of prime importance. But the agitators had a strong institutionalized "lobby" in the form of the Central Committee's Department of Agitation and Propaganda (Agitprop). Operating through its own network of departments right down to the base of the Party hierarchy, Agitprop keeps a close check on the activity of its more than two million volunteers. Its publications, several magazines plus handy pocket manuals that set agitation themes and offer background information, stress a variety of political, social, and ideological themes. The Khrushchev regime made a determined effort in 1962 to upgrade the work of agitators in a reorganization which concentrated this work under a new Ideological Commission, headed by the then-powerful Leonid Ilyichov. There was a renewed emphasis on combating the infiltration of "bourgeois ideology," attacking religion at its roots through conversations with believers, and reaching people in many settings other than their places of work.

After Khrushchev's fall, Ilyichov was demoted and the Ideological Commission scrapped in favor of the old Agitprop arrangement. In 1966, as a result of a debate within the Party over the value of agitation, a new type of Party publicist was recruited, the propagandist-commentator or Politinformator. The Politinformator was drawn from the ranks of the intelligentsia, and received training for propaganda discussions in one of four special areas: domestic policy, foreign affairs, economic questions, and cultural life. In other words, the old distinction between agitation and propaganda could now be finally erased after a half-century, and well-educated propagandists could now achieve a better result than simple but forceful orators from among the working people. It is likely that this reform was too much for tradition-minded officials in Agitprop, for after a three-year tussle the old concept of agitation was restored to its former status, without, however, removal of the Politinformators.[21]

Coordinating Propaganda

Since every form of public expression is of potential propaganda value, central coordination of propaganda has been very important to the Soviet leaders. One must not get the impression that propaganda means simply the ritualized repetition of doctrines; if it did, the management of political communication would not be such a delicate matter. Propaganda involves applying complex doctrines to what is happening in the present and what is planned for the future. After the fall of Khrushchev, the only area in which there was a large-scale shifting of personnel was in propaganda and mass communications. Not only was Ilyichov dismissed and his Ideological Commission dropped, but within a year after Khrushchev's ouster the chief editors of *Pravda* and *Izvestiya* were replaced not once but twice, and the heads of both the State Committee for the Press and the State Committee for Radio Broadcasting and Television were replaced likewise.

The daily press and much of the periodical press that is nontechnical is under the Party's direct supervision in fact, if not always in form. A number of central agencies and organizations have their own newspapers, including the Central Committee (*Pravda*), the Supreme Soviet Presidium (*Izvestiya*), the All-Union Central Council of Trade Unions (*Trud*), the Komsomol (*Komsomolskaya Pravda*), and the Union of Soviet Writers (*Literaturnaya Gazeta*, now a weekly newspaper). Each of the Union Republics has a newspaper published jointly by Party and government, both in Russian and in the predominant local language. Their content is determined by a combination of Party directives, cautious self-censorship, and occasional direct intervention by the Central Committee. The Party maintains a similarly direct watch over the two central news agencies: TASS, which is governmental, and Novosti, which is technically a nongovernmental organization. The Ministry of Communications assures thorough distribution of the press through the All-Union News Agency. The Agency also has the function of determining which foreign periodicals are to be distributed in the Soviet Union, in what quantity and where.

Other areas of mass communication follow the pattern of central coordination through governmental and nongovernmental agencies, coupled with Party responsibility for coordination at the local level. Besides the

---

[21] Aryeh L. Unger, "Politinformator or Agitator: A Decision Blocked," *Problems of Communism* 19 (September-October 1970), pp. 30–43. See also the background information in Frederick C. Barghoorn, *Politics in the USSR* (2nd ed.; Boston: Little, Brown and Co., 1966), chapters 5 and 6.

two State Committees mentioned above, there is a State Committee for Cinematography. The Ministry of Culture has jurisdiction over theaters, libraries, and cultural institutions. The *Znaniye* (Knowledge) Society, a much-refined reincarnation of the League of the Militant Godless of the 1930s, specializes in public lectures and informational pamphlets on a wide variety of topics, political, social, and scientific. Certain controls over output are exercised by the Union of Soviet Writers, the Union of Soviet Composers, and the Union of Soviet Journalists.

While the Writers' Union promotes the politically favored literary trends and condemns those which are not approved, actual censorship is performed by Glavlit, the Main Administration for Literary Affairs and Publishing. In a nation where no individual may possess printing and reproducing equipment, or use it without specific authorization, it is Glavlit that issues the authorizations. Like the Public Prosecutor's Office, it was a Tsarist agency resurrected in 1922 for Soviet use. Its function of both prepublication and postpublication censorship was stated explicitly in the decree which established it, as well as the subsequent extension of its jurisdiction to art, films, and stage presentations of all kinds. Likewise, its connection with the security police was made explicit: the original 1922 decree reserved one of its two posts of deputy director for the security police.[22]

The entire mechanism for coordinating mass communications and public expression was already well established by the early 1930s. It was crowned by the abolition of a variety of literary organizations and the founding, in their place, of the Union of Soviet Writers in 1932. Since that time, while policy regarding the content of mass communications has fluctuated, the Party's tight grip on propaganda content in the mass media, the arts, and all organized public expression has remained strikingly constant.

Informing and Persuading the Soviet Citizen

Lenin, Stalin, and Khrushchev each left a particular stamp on Soviet propaganda. Lenin was a master persuader; logic was a formidable weapon in his hands, as was his capacity to demolish opposing arguments from all angles, driving home his conclusions with vivid language. If his premises were often open to attack, his ability to divert attention from their weaknesses carried the day. To the end of his life, he was adapting his Marxist convictions to new circumstances and presenting his conclusions in propagandistic form.

Stalin all but destroyed propaganda, if we understand the term in

---

[22] An interesting account of the evolution of Glavlit is that of Maurice Friedberg, "Keeping up With the Censor," *Problems of Communism* 13 (November-December 1964), pp. 22–31.

Lenin's sense as the presentation of facts and ideas with the partisan intent to persuade. His last major contribution to Soviet Marxism had been in his *Problems of Leninism* of 1925. From that point on, the ritualization of propaganda robbed it of both the capacity to persuade with ideas and the ability to explain changing phenomena. In the last years of his life, Stalin displayed a frustration with propaganda's lack of effectiveness which caused him to want to change its very nature.

Andrei Zhdanov in the last two years of his life (1946–48) took command of Stalin's campaign to end wartime permissiveness by harnessing literature, the arts, and all the mass media to specific Party goals. As a campaign of censorship and cultural intimidation, it succeeded; as a campaign to arouse enthusiasm and willing cooperation to rebuild society along the lines sought by Stalin, it was a failure. Exhortations and political education were not inducing workers and farmers to work harder, nor were the strict controls over literature and the arts completely successful in wiping out skepticism. Something else was needed to bolster the effectiveness of propaganda, which was no longer true propaganda in Lenin's sense. This partly explains the odd way in which Stalin, silent for so long on basic questions of Marxist theory, wrote his 1950 essay on the seemingly irrelevant subject of linguistics, and then proceeded to demand a new psychology. What he was seeking was a direct connection between words and human responses. Taking a Pavlovian concept which actually was incidental to Pavlov's psychology, the "second signal system," Soviet psychologists at the Party's direct order began to treat words as verbal stimuli rather than as the bearers of concepts which evoke thought. Robert C. Tucker, who first identified this part of Stalin's social psychology, described its political intent as follows:

> The practical importance discerned in the neo-Pavlovian movement, its electrifying educational implications to the Stalinist mind, depended entirely upon reducing language to its signal-function exclusively, upon regarding words as "proxy for their objects." The whole movement would have collapsed instantly had its initiator forced himself to consider the possibility that words can be employed purely symbolically as neutral vehicles for the conception of objects. The goal was to treat language as an instrument of social control.[23]

Bear in mind that little had been added to Soviet Marxist ideas since the 1920s. Ideology had simply stopped growing as a vehicle for explanation. A growing body of ideas not only would have suggested lack of consistency, but even more, would have reduced the ritual value and the desired emotional impact of what was already familiar. Such, at any rate, was the fear of Stalin and of many men around him, a fear that

---

[23] Robert C. Tucker, *The Soviet Political Mind* (New York: Praeger, 1963), p. 113.

continues to be shared by part of the Soviet leadership today. Khrushchev and some of the men around him considered Stalin's approach to propaganda counterproductive and destructive of propaganda's educational function. Additions to Soviet Marxist theory went hand in hand with changes in the approach to propaganda: (1) major restatements of theory were undertaken; (2) theory was coupled with fairly specific prognoses about future changes in the Soviet system; (3) adult education in Marxism received a strong injection of education in practical applications of theory; (4) whereas political education in Stalin's time had concentrated on the educated and on people in positions of responsibility, mass political education was now the goal, with strong emphasis on drawing in nonparty members. In sum, propaganda was once again to appeal to the reasoning powers of a population whose overall level of education was vastly higher than it had been in Lenin's time, and would be rising steadily for several decades to come.[24]

To bring about mass political education, the Party improved and expanded a variety of existing devices, including the "political schools" and the "Universities of Marxism-Leninism." Both of these institutions offer two-year courses in Marxism and its applications. The political school (*politshkola*) is the first rung of political education. It is an evening institution, offering a basic survey curriculum in courses conducted by the group discussion method. Included in its program are a survey of Marxist theory, the history of the Communist Party, basic economics, and some contemporary applications of theory. After completing the Party school, one may go on to study specialized topics in a variety of seminars and study groups. Those who have done all this are qualified to enter the ranks of agitators or to perform propaganda functions in conjunction with their regular jobs. The Universities of Marxism-Leninism offer the same topics at a higher level of sophistication. Although they too are evening institutions, they require a heavier workload and use more formal methods of instruction than the *politshkola*. Formerly their programs were directed at specialists, managers, and the intelligentsia generally, but in Khrushchev's time they were reorganized to accommodate future propagandists from every walk of life. The core of the Party's educational system consists of the Higher Party Schools, full-time institutions offering two-year and four-year programs, aimed at mid-career training of Party officials, managers, and specialists—a select student body. A certain proportion of graduates then become the directors of the Party's adult education programs.

The Khrushchev reforms were retained under Brezhnev, for the most part. While there is far less emphasis on training ordinary citizens to take over tasks heretofore performed by the bureaucracy—which had

---

[24] The differences between the Stalin and Khrushchev approaches to political education are described in detail in Barghoorn, *Politics in the USSR*, chapter 4.

been a major public justification of Khrushchev's mass education program—the whole mechanism of adult education is considered useful in
reinforcing the effects of early political training in the schools and youth
organizations.

EDUCATION FOR SOCIALISM

The Soviet experience with political education for the young is a
vast and complex topic. It is of greater interest than propaganda for
adults, first because it operates for the most part in controlled group
situations, and next because its effectiveness appears to be high. Foreign
accounts of Soviet youth, particularly in the United States, tend to focus
on problems: unorthodox attitudes, apathy toward political questions,
and antisocial behavior. It is true that the Soviet press and frequent statements by Soviet officials take a serious view of these problems, sometimes
admitting that they are growing more serious with time. But the writer's
experiences in conversing with Soviet young people, and the experiences
of many others who have had similar opportunities, show that political
education has created acceptance of the basic features of the Soviet
system.

Such a statement must be qualified by many "ifs," "ands," and "buts."
Supportive attitudes range everywhere from 100 percent patriotism to
pragmatic acceptance of some features but not others. One not infrequently meets young people who take pride in their socialist economic
order but deplore specific phenomena such as censorship, the lack of
opportunity to travel abroad, and the high-and-mighty attitudes of officialdom. Nor is it uncommon to find well-informed students who consider
their system a stagnant bureaucracy but will defend Soviet foreign policy
to the hilt. There are, too, the totally disaffected, and the foreign visitor
is likely to encounter more than a representative proportion of them,
since they know that foreigners from the noncommunist world will lend
a sympathetic ear and provide uncensored information about the outside
world. There are distinct differences between the Russians and non-Russians: the latter show a certain detachment in their support for the system,
are less inclined to argue about ideologies and systems, and are only
rarely "gut patriots." Patriotism and Marxist beliefs are not necessarily
linked. Acceptance of Marx's dialectical materialism may be accompanied
by criticism of Soviet policies for having ignored Marx. Said one physics
student to the writer: "Our leaders and bureaucrats have forgotten their
Marxism. They don't know that one day the dialectic will sweep them,
too, onto the scrap heap of history."

The Soviet Union was the first modern country to experiment with
shaping the attitudes of youth on a nationwide scale. This has been
done through both schools and the mass youth organizations, chiefly the

Young Pioneers (for ages 10 to 14) and the Komosomol (for ages 15 to 27). In differing ways, the schools and youth organizations have sought to shape the consciousness of young people according to definite goals in three areas: (1) attitudes toward work, careers, and education; (2) attitudes concerning social relations, their place in society; and (3) political attitudes.

Shaping Attitudes toward Work, Careers, and Education

The evolution of the Soviet school system is an oft-told and very instructive tale. Each generation of Soviet leaders has demanded that the schools serve the nation in different ways; each has had to solve anew the question of how much emphasis to put on skills, how much on liberal arts subjects (with their large propaganda value), and how much on relating the school experience to the world of work so as to prepare a smooth transition from one to the other. Lenin was inclined to stress skills, but his first Commissar for Education laid overwhelming emphasis on the world of work, to the great detriment of skills. Anatoli Lunacharsky was a romantic "left communist," one of the visionaries who believed that the communist future must begin in the present. Partly under the influence of the American educator John Dewey, Lunacharsky did away with the traditional classroom, traditional subjects, and even examinations. Learning by doing, learning by observing the outside world, were now the watchwords. Political education was stressed likewise. Foreign educators flocked to the Soviet Union to see this educational revolution in action, and many returned impressed. Actually, the results were fairly chaotic, and it is doubtful that more than a part of the school system actually did adopt the new methods.

The need for Soviet-trained engineers, scientists, and technicians, already a problem in the 1920s, became critical with the beginning of the five-year plans. The school system and higher education had been dealing admirably with the restlessness of youth, but they had done precious little to train the large corps of specialists the country needed. Stalin reversed educational policy abruptly after 1929. From a utopian experiment, education did not merely revert to traditional practices and objectives, but became both elitist and authoritarian in the process. The regular secondary schools became university preparatory institutions; students not able to meet the academic requirements were weeded out early and shunted to trade schools and other training programs. Examinations were reintroduced, and teacher qualifications were upgraded. Class origins were now relegated to the background as a criterion for university admissions, and both secondary schools and higher education were filled with the sons and daughters of the upper occupational strata.

After Stalin's death, there appears to have been some feeling among both political leaders and education specialists that schools and universities should have functions other than just training an elite of specialists. In a system which had long sought to elevate the status of ordinary labor, the educational system was reinforcing the prestige of professions to which only higher education gave access. The upper stratum of Soviet society was reproducing itself by means of its easier access to higher education; potentially damaging resentments were building up; and students were being sent out to their specialties with no direct knowledge of the world of work.

Among the many ideas under discussion, it was not Khrushchev's own radical version of reform that was enacted, though certain of his ideas were realized. Khrushchev attempted to re-inject something of Lunacharsky's ideals into the system. The reform sought to transform the secondary schools so as to incorporate production experience into their curricula. Khrushchev wanted to require university students to study for their first two or three years on a part-time basis, a proposal which was rejected; and he wanted secondary school graduates to have worked for two years before going on to higher education, which was accepted with considerable modifications. The original proposal had an admirable sweep, but parts of it would have been damaging to the specialist-training function had they been put into effect fully. Besides, teachers and educational administrators were skeptical and in some cases hostile, and it proved easy to undermine the reforms by reinterpretation and administrative delays. Parts of the reform had been quietly dropped even during Khrushchev's years in office, and less than a year after his removal the work-experience criterion for university admission was formally cancelled. What remained of the reform was a pledge on the part of the public education system to imbue Soviet schoolchildren with some kind of appreciation of the world of work.

In the early 1970s, there are signs that the worm has turned once again. Talk of the schools being "divorced from the real world" is remindful of Khrushchev's rhetoric of the 1950s on this subject. Vocational schools and technical schools, whose low prestige had only served to reinforce the low prestige of manual labor among students, were reorganized so as to remove their "dead-end" stigma and enable their students to complete a regular secondary-school education while learning a trade. Another important trend is that a balanced system of vocational guidance is at last coming into its own. The time has passed when education officials worked on the assumption that aptitude is measured by grades alone, and the transition to the world of work effected mainly by the assignment system.

Lunacharsky's experiment, and Khrushchev's unsuccessful proposals to relate schools and vocations through direct contact, were crude, one-sided, and difficult to administer. Today, in the 1970s, educational authorities, officials concerned with labor supply, psychologists, sociologists, and other professions have been coming to grips with the complexity of the relationship. One labor resources official outlined the process of career entry in the following stages:

> Labor upbringing; the study of personality, including medical study; forecasting the cadre requirements of the national economy; work with children; propagandizing of vocations, enterprises, and educational institutions; professional counseling and selection; placement; adaptation of young people to production.[25]

Apparently the days of ideologically based panaceas are over in this field, and the day of social science analysis and painstaking administrative coordination has begun. Indirectly, the Brezhnev administration has conceded that Khrushchev was right in his desire to change the attitudes of schoolchildren and students toward the world of work.

Shaping Attitudes toward Social Relations

The Young Pioneers function in symbiosis with the school system in shaping social attitudes at an important stage in child development. The majority of schoolchildren of Pioneer age (10 to 14) belong to the organization, 10 percent of them attend Pioneer camps in the summer, and "Pioneer Palaces" in the cities offer a wide variety of activities throughout the year. Much of their activity is like that of the Boy Scouts. The scale, however, is much larger, the school system is an active supporter, and the emphasis on patriotism and social values is greater. The social values, moreover, are in a class by themselves.

Pioneer organizations, whether functioning within schools or elsewhere, provide the setting for a system of collective responsibility and discipline. Under adult supervision, Pioneer units form the first of a number of "collectives" which every Soviet citizen experiences in different versions during his life. The idea of the collective is based on the self-discipline of a group of coworkers, schoolmates, or others whose common tasks bring them in daily or at least frequent contact. Not only are decisions and problems shared, but the individual is pledged to subordinate himself to the wishes of the majority. And actually, majorities and minorities within collectives have little meaning, since the idea is to secure unity of will and effort following discussion—here we have Lenin's concept of unity as a vital root of social relations. Equally important is the responsibility of the entire collective for each and every member. For the misbehavior or poor performance of one of its members, the entire group shares the blame. Everyone is responsible for disciplining

---

[25] A. Solovyov, "A Place in the Workers' Ranks," *Izvestiya*, Feb. 3, 1970, as translated in *Current Digest of the Soviet Press*, vol. 22, p. 21.

and educating those who do not live up to the collective's standards; expulsion of a member from the collective is an extreme measure, an admission of failure by the rest. Necessarily, members of the collective must not protect the misbehavior of their co-workers or fellow students, for otherwise they share his guilt. At a court of honor, a meeting to judge the conduct of wayward members, appropriate punishment and educational measures are determined, accompanied by a process of shaming.

From one point of view, the collective appears to be the Party's "ultimate weapon" of social control, totalitarianism at the grass roots. On the other hand, it has produced a self-discipline and a feeling of responsibility for one's fellow man. Foreigners are repelled by the way in which even Soviet schoolchildren are encouraged to report on the activities of their classmates, and to denounce them before a group, if necessary. (One still sees memorials to Pavlik Morozov, the schoolchild of the 1930s who denounced his own father to the authorities as a traitor.) But more positive sides of the Soviet experience with collectives commend themselves to the attention of other societies.

The American psychologist Urie Bronfenbrenner reported witnessing the disciplining of a group of fifth-graders by their classmates, the misbehavior in this case being that eight boys had gone swimming without permission. A Pioneer council of 13, representing all classes from the fifth upwards, judged the case in a somewhat formal procedure, then discussed possible penalties in the presence of the offenders. It was finally decided that the boys be required to shave their heads and perform two additional work assignments connected with school maintenance. But in reviewing the overall work of this Pioneer unit, Bronfenbrenner concluded that the carrot is much more in evidence than the stick.[26] His conclusions on collective-oriented discipline, coupled as it is with firm authority exercised through the school system, are quite positive:

> What impressed this observer, like others before him, about Soviet youngsters, especially those attending schools of the new type, was their "good behavior." In their external actions, they are well-mannered, attentive, and industrious. In informal conversations, they reveal a strong motivation to learn, a readiness to serve their society, and—in general— ironically enough for a culture committed to a materialistic philosophy, what can only be described as an idealistic attitude toward life. In keeping with this general orientation, relationships with parents, teachers and upbringers are those of respectful but affectionate friendship. The discipline of the collective is accepted and regarded as justified, even when severe as judged by Western standards. On the basis not only of personal observations and reports from Soviet educators, but also

---
[26] Excerpted from *Two Worlds of Childhood: U.S. and U.S.S.R.*, by Urie Bronfenbrenner, © 1970 by Russell Sage Foundation, New York.

from entries in the minutes of Pioneer and Komsomol meetings which I had an opportunity to examine, it is apparent that instances of aggressiveness, violation of rules, or other anti-social behavior are genuinely rare.[27]

The collective's autonomy, in the school setting and in Pioneer and Komsomol units, is limited by the authority structure within which it operates. But it was not historically the creature of authority, nor does the collective depend on authority for its existence. Both Lunacharsky's experiments and Russian culture contributed their share. Since the 1920s, the collective has been one of the most durable features of Soviet social management. From conversations with Soviet citizens who remember the Stalin period, the writer gained the impression that political pressures and the extreme authoritarian practices of the 1930s and 1940s diminished the collective's importance: people grew warier, more fearful of exposing themselves, and less willing to assume responsibility for the actions of others. It also remains to be seen what several generations of urban life will do to the collective. It is not hard to find young people who feel stifled by the demands of collectives, who try to organize their work and lives so as to avoid pressure from this source. Though much in Soviet culture continues to sustain the collective, any prognoses on its long-range future are hazardous.

Political Education

The methods used in the political education of youth have less that is distinctive about them. In secondary education, the amount of specifically political education is surprisingly small. Before Khrushchev's time, there was only a course on the Soviet Constitution, which dealt not just with the document but with the whole Marxist theory of governments and its modern applications. Early in the 1960s a course called "Fundamentals of Political Knowledge" was added, and another called "Social Studies," both of them emphasizing Marxist theory, Lenin's writings, and interpretation of current political events. Each grade has its own history course, and the approach of these courses naturally follows Marx's interpretation of history. After the 1964 curricular reforms, history in the two upper grades of secondary school occupied 9 percent of instructional time, and social studies less than 3 percent.[28]

In higher education, the workload in Marxism and the social sciences constitutes about 10 percent of the five-year program. This proportion is more significant than the ratio suggests, since Soviet universities and

---

[27] Ibid. But see also the strong reservations about making a general conclusion from this in Barghoorn, *Politics in the USSR*, pp. 98–102.

[28] See the table in Robert Lane, *Politics and Society in the USSR* (New York: Random House, 1971), p. 495.

institutes follow the European pattern of specialization from the first year on, as opposed to the American liberal arts curriculum. The courses required include Dialectical and Historical Materialism, the History of the Communist Party of the Soviet Union, and Political Economy. From many conversations with Soviet students, the writer gained the impression that these courses could be counterproductive from the point of view of political socialization. Their curricula are rigidly controlled by a branch of the Ministry of Higher Education, with the result that the manner of presentation is dull at best, and the instructors often third-rate. On the whole, they are regarded as a nuisance to be endured. While it is not likely that the poor quality of these courses changes the students' attitudes toward Marxism one way or another, it certainly does reduce interest in Marxist theory. The courses create the impression that Marxism is a set of dogmas rather than the vital (if flawed) tool of inquiry that it was in the hands of Marx and Engels.

The Komsomol plays a large role in the life of university students, who have already been exposed to its influence in the last two years of secondary school, where many of them become members. Over 90 percent of the students in higher education are members. Unlike the Young Pioneers, its role is well separated from the process of instruction. It has its own office and staff on the premises of the university or institute, and it stands under the immediate supervision of the university's Party committee. Its extracurricular activities are many: sports events, lectures, films, outings, workdays, and some disciplinary functions. The Komsomol has been a prime organizer of the "people's detachments" (voluntary police) initiated by Khrushchev. Its "light cavalry raids" are spot checks of how well or badly the public is being served in stores and local offices. It was the main recruiting agency for the many thousands of students who were sent out to Kazakhstan each summer from 1954 on to help with harvests in the Virgin Lands campaign. It also serves as the recruiting ground for Party membership, although most of those who ultimately join do not do so until one or several years after graduation. The Komsomol apparatus—the full-time staff—serves as an early testing ground for some who then move up the Party's own apparatus. The Komsomol's role in factories and on farms is similar, although it is necessarily a smaller role because only a certain proportion of any work force is within the required age limits.

The impact of the Komsomol on its members is harder to assess than that of the Pioneers and the schools. Its political education program at the universities, which includes study circles on Marxist topics, lectures, local newspaper editing, radio broadcasts, and the like, shares the strengths and flaws of the Party's adult education programs. As an agency for building morals and discipline, it has the same means at its disposal as the Pioneers. But it must work with less impressionable age groups than the Pioneers, and satisfy interests which go beyond what its formal program has to offer. In the writer's experience during a year of residence among Moscow University students, the Komsomol was effective in organizing mainly nonpolitical extracurricular activities, effective in taking disciplinary measures only with the active backing of University authorities, and ineffective in arousing interest in the study of political topics. Komsomol leaders are frequently well past the upper age limit of 27, they identify strongly with the Party bureaucracy, and for both these reasons are apt to be somewhat out of touch with the feelings and thoughts of young people.

LENIN'S VISION OF SOCIETY REVISITED

Clearly Soviet management of society has wrought enormous changes in relationships and attitudes. It is equally clear that progress toward Lenin's vision of "disciplined enthusiasm" has been hampered in a number of ways. The means by which negative or destructive traits were curbed have become all too permanent features of social management; the route to a future society of close harmony and little outward control is too fraught with risks.

Experimentation with labor rewards may be entering a fluid stage because of the findings of industrial psychologists. Stalin's extreme use of material rewards created expectations which it was disadvantageous to alter later on. Khrushchev's campaign to narrow the gap between low and high pay was made possible only because the "floor" of the lowest wage brackets (and pensions) could be raised without creating inflationary pressures, not because there was any agreement on a new principle of equalization. Here, too, the Party leaders have long recognized the stabilizing effect of high reward differentials, while seeking to curb the worst anomalies. Major changes in the reward system are now unlikely.

The direct political education of the adult population has yielded very mixed results. From World War II on, it has been plagued with the continued preference for outmoded techniques, although the worst features of Stalin-era propaganda have been done away with or adapted to the present. Here, too, it is difficult to see that major changes are in the offing under the present leadership. The political education of youth has been effective in the younger age groups, but markedly less so among those in their late teens and early twenties. Maintenance of the collective as a basic social relationship, plus an ability to use authority relationships to good effect, have been notable achievements of the primary and secondary schools.

The Brezhnev regime's reactions to Khrushchev's effort to create some forward motion toward the "new man" and the self-regulating society indicate that we must wait at least until the leaders now in their 60's have departed the political scene. Their concern with present problems apparently had induced them to regard future-oriented measures as unjustified risks. Meanwhile some of the initiative has passed to social scientists and educators, and the Soviet press today is filled with debates on a wide variety of social questions.

FOR FURTHER READING

The most fundamental statement by Marx and Engels on human nature and society is *The German Ideology* (New York: International Publishers, 1947), written in 1846. Much has been written about what some commentators believe to be Marx's deep humanistic concept of man, expressed in youthful sketches and notes first published in the 1930s, a half-century after Marx's death. The *Economic and Philosophical Manuscripts of 1844* are now available in a number of editions, including the useful collection of T. B. Bottomore (ed.), *Karl Marx: Early Writings* (New York: McGraw-Hill, 1964). Collections of the thinking of Marx and Engels on society and social transformation include Robert Freedman (ed.), *Marxist Social Thought* (New York: Harcourt, Brace and World, 1968), and T. B. Bottomore (ed.), *Karl Marx: Selected Writings in Sociology and Social Philosophy* (New York: McGraw-Hill, 1964). Alfred G. Meyer, *Leninism* (New York: Praeger, 1962) includes an analysis of Lenin's ideas on social change in its opening chapters.

There are a number of worthwhile collections of readings on Soviet social policies and their impact: Cyril E. Black (ed.), *The Transformation of Russian Society* (Cambridge, Mass.: Harvard University Press, 1967); Alex Inkeles and Kent Geiger (eds.), *Soviet Society: A Book of Readings* (Boston: Houghton Mifflin, 1961); Alex Inkeles, *Social Change in Soviet Russia* (Cambridge, Mass.: Harvard University Press, 1968); Paul Hollander (ed.), *American and Soviet Society: A Reader in Comparative Sociology and Perception* (Englewood Cliffs, N.J.: Prentice-Hall, 1969); Allen Kassof (ed.), *Prospects for Soviet Society* (New York: Praeger, 1968); George Fischer (ed.), *Science and Ideology in Soviet Society* (New York: Atherton, 1969); and Alex Simirenko (ed.), *Soviet Sociology: Historical Antecedents and Current Appraisals* (Chicago: Quadrangle Books, 1966).

Soviet studies of Soviet society have been multiplying rapidly. A cross section of recent work is available in Stephen P. Dunn (ed.), *Sociology in the USSR* (New York: International Arts and Sciences Press, 1969). See also the periodical issued by the same publisher, *Soviet Sociology*. Translations of Soviet studies of man as worker, the single greatest emphasis of Soviet sociology, include G. V. Osipov (ed.), *Industry and Labour in the U.S.S.R.* (London: Tavistock, 1966), and A. G. Zdravomyslov et al., *Man and His Work: A Sociological Study* (New York: International Arts and Sciences Press, 1969).

Interviews of displaced persons from the Soviet Union after World War II yielded valuable information on the responses and attitudes of the Soviet populace during the 1930s. Two major works that resulted are Raymond

A. Bauer et al., *How the Soviet System Works* (Cambridge, Mass.: Harvard University Press, 1956), and Alex Inkeles and Raymond A. Bauer, *The Soviet Citizen* (Cambridge, Mass.: Harvard University Press, 1961).

On the subject of political socialization, training, and indoctrination, see the following: Gayle Durham Hollander, *Soviet Political Indoctrination: Developments in Mass Media and Propaganda Since Stalin* (New York: Praeger, 1972); Ellen P. Mickiewicz, *Soviet Political Schools* (New Haven, Conn.: Yale University Press, 1967); and Frederick C. Barghoorn, *Politics in the USSR* (2nd ed.; Boston: Little, Brown, 1972), chapters 4, 5, and 6. Two works on the role of the educational system delve into its psychological assumptions: Brian and Joan Simon, *Educational Psychology in the U.S.S.R.* (Stanford, Calif.: Stanford University Press, 1969), and Urie Bronfenbrenner, *Two Worlds of Childhood: U.S. and U.S.S.R.* (New York: Russell Sage Foundation, 1970). The role of the Komsomol and other channels for influencing the political education of young people are dealt with in Ralph T. Fisher, Jr., *Pattern for Soviet Youth* (New York: Columbia University Press, 1959) and Allen Kassof, *The Soviet Youth Program* (Cambridge, Mass.: Harvard University Press, 1965).

11

LAW, LIBERTIES, AND CONSTRAINTS

AMONG THE LEADING Bolsheviks, only Lenin possessed a legal education; and among the powerful and near powerful after Lenin's time, Andrei Vyshinsky stood virtually alone as a legal specialist, a second-echelon figure politically since he never sat on the Politburo or in the Secretariat. Lenin is remembered for two seemingly contradictory contributions to Bolshevik legal policy: his statements at the time of the Revolution that the proletariat would soon be able to dispense with the formalities of the law within its own ranks, and his initiative in getting the first comprehensive legal codes drawn up and enacted in 1922. In *State and Revolution*, he saw "popular justice" as a means of dispensing altogether with the formalities of the law:

> For when *all* have learned to administer and actually do independently administer social production, independently keep accounts and exercise control over the idlers, the gentlefolk, the swindlers and suchlike "guardians of capitalist traditions," the escape from this popular accounting and control will inevitably become so incredibly difficult, such a rare exception, and will probably be accompanied by such swift and severe punishment . . . , that the *necessity* of observing the simple, fundamental rules of human intercourse will very soon become a *habit*.[1]

The civil and criminal codes of 1922, and the judicial system made formal in the same year, could be reconciled ideologically with Lenin's prophecy in view of their relation to the NEP, which had begun the

---

[1] V. I. Lenin, *The State and Revolution* (Moscow: Foreign Languages Publishing House, n.d.), p. 163.

year before. Capitalism had been restored to the countryside and in restricted form to industry and trade. It had to be regulated according to capitalist norms, and hence the need for law codes and a fairly conventional hierarchy of courts. The real break with Lenin's early utopianism came in the 1930s, with the crystallization in both fact and Soviet Marxist theory of "socialist law," a new type of law whose function would be to regulate the affairs of a socialist society and economy. The conception of rights embodied in the early Soviet constitutions, far from being dropped as a feature carried over from bourgeois democracy, remained as part of the new law. Likewise individual property rights, hedged by many limitations which made them compatible with a socialized economy and which prohibited important types of private gain, were carried over into the new socialist law.

Since the 1930s, policy concerning the legal system, rights, and property relations has moved within the framework of these basic decisions. In spite of the many political incursions into the workings of justice that have received so much publicity abroad, the Brezhnev administration has sought to promote stability and regularity in the everyday dealings of Soviet citizens. The means by which the legal system is used today to promote social change are basically the same means that emerged in the early postrevolutionary period. Aside from the "antiparasite" legislation described later in this chapter, no radical new uses of the legal system have been initiated. But as a means of consolidating a socialist system and promoting positive human relationships, the Soviet legal system is worthy of attention today in spite of the manifest abuses that have attracted so much attention in the outside world.

THE SOCIALIST LEGAL ORDER

For several years after the Bolsheviks took power, it appeared that law and legal institutions had already been demolished in favor of a radically new system of resolving disputes. The "people's courts," inaugurated very soon after the coup, did away with the several legal professions altogether. Judges were elected for short terms, and each was assigned a pair of lay assessors by the local soviet. Lawyers and public prosecutors could be any persons not deprived of civil rights (e.g., not the former bourgeoisie and priests). The institution of preliminary investigation was retained, though performed for the time being by the judges themselves. The broad outlines of the old judicial system were still there, but the system was now turned over to ordinary citizens, who were expected to dispense a popularized justice in what was now more a neighborhood meeting than a court. Courts were bound by prerevolutionary laws, but "only insofar as those laws are not annulled by the revolution, and do not contradict the revolutionary conscience and revolutionary conception of right."[2] There was yet more of the flavor of the French Revolution in the "revolutionary tribunals" empowered to try a wide variety of acts declared to be counterrevolutionary, including profiteering and speculation. A "tribunal of the press" was set up to halt the publication of misinformation which could harm the revolutionary order.

Growing Formalization and Professionalization

From that point on, however, legal reform went in the direction of professionalization rather than further popularization. The great volume of cases, the lack of experience on the part of the amateur judges and prosecutors, and lack of explicit guidance from higher authorities all led step by step to the important legal reforms of 1922. The Commissariat of Justice, which had the task of overseeing the courts, was interested in seeing uniformity in court standards and operations. In 1920 it reformed the manner of selecting judges and holding sessions, organized the procurators as an independent professional staff, established a draft of ordinary citizens to act as legal counsel, and set up a department to act as a national appeals tribunal.

In 1922 the courts became a hierarchy independent of the Commissariat. The revolutionary tribunals were amalgamated with the regular courts, but specialized courts were established to deal with crimes affecting military affairs, transport, and labor relations. Procurators were formed into a hierarchy of their own, responsible at first to the courts. Lenin made a strong argument for rendering the Procuracy completely independent of the courts and government, except at the all-Union (national) level, as a way of assuring uniform application of the laws. Though it was ten years before this could be done, the principle of separateness has been one of the most consistent features of the Soviet legal system. The capstone of the new structure was the USSR Supreme Court, established in 1923.

In outward form the new legal system strongly resembled the French system, which in turn had served as a model for most of Europe, including Tsarist Russia. The norms of law were set forth in codes, which were subject to judicial interpretation only in a marginal way. Two lay assessors sat with every judge to form the court; the jury as used in systems of the English type did not exist. Courtroom procedure was informal, since the result did not turn on the intricacies of pleading, motions, cross-examination of witnesses, and the like. Most of the information used in the court was gathered by an investigating magistrate in a procedure quite apart from court sessions. Procedural guarantees similar to those

---

[2] The text of the decree of Dec. 7, 1917, is in James H. Meisel and Edward S. Kozera (eds.), *Materials for the Study of the Soviet System* (Ann Arbor, Mich.: George Wahr Publishing Co., 1953), pp. 28–30.

used in the West were set forth explictly: "No one may be deprived of freedom and placed in confinement except in cases provided for by law, and in a manner established by law."[3]

The Law as Educator

Three different goals of the Soviet system have competed for influence in development of laws and procedures. The first was—and is—the need for an orderly framework of rules and restrictions which permits ordinary citizens to go about their business with a minimum of friction. Precise boundaries of acceptable conduct guard both the individual and the state against incursions, and provide an exact mechanism for dealing with those that occur. The second need is for channels through which Soviet citizens can bring their wayward fellow men back within the limits of acceptable conduct *without* resorting to formal procedures. As in Lenin's statement at the beginning of this chapter, the class-conscious proletariat of the early years and the whole socialist society that later advances toward communism maintains its own spontaneous discipline. The third need, which may possibly mediate between the first two but may also conflict with both in some areas, is the role of the law as an educator. This function is described by Harold Berman as a central characteristic Soviet law from the very beginning:

> In the Soviet system . . . the educational role of law has from the beginning been made central to the concept of justice itself. Law still has the functions of delimiting interests, of preventing interference, of enforcing the will and intent of the parties—but the center of gravity has shifted. The subject of law, legal man, is treated less as an independent possessor of rights and duties, who knows what he wants, than as a dependent member of the collective group, a youth, whom the law must not only protect against the consequences of his own ignorance but must also guide and train and discipline. The law now steps in on a lower level, on what in the past has been a prelegal level. It is concerned with the relationships of the parties apart from the voluntary acts by which their alleged rights and duties are established; it is concerned with the whole situation, and above all, with the thoughts and desires and attitudes of the people involved, their moral and legal conceptions, their law-consciousness. Soviet law thus seeks not simply to delimit and segregate and define, but also to unite and organize and educate. The result is the creation of entirely new legal values within a framework of language and doctrine which otherwise appears conventional and orthodox.[4]

---

[3] Article 5 of the 1922 Code of Criminal Procedure of the Russian Republic.

[4] Harold J. Berman, *Justice in the U.S.S.R.* (New York: Vintage Books, 1963), pp. 283–84.

Early experiments to realize the last two needs, "popular justice" and educative roles, were soon overshadowed by the laws codes of 1922 and thereafter, and the building of a highly formal legal structue. However, some features of both "popular justice" and educative roles survived and were expanded in the Khrushchev period. Today as in the 1920s, judgeships are elective, trials are sometimes held in factories or on farms as a means of public instruction, and popularization of the legal system through literature, public lectures, and other media is promoted on a large scale. The role of the judge continues to be an active one: he (or she, since many lower-court judges are women) intervenes at any and every stage of the proceedings not only to bring new "angles" to light, but to educate courtroom spectators as well. Wrote the Chief Justice of the USSR Supreme Court in 1947:

> Trying the case in great detail, strictly observing the law, the court step by step discloses the whole picture of the crime or the civil dispute. It raises the explanations of the parties to a higher level, transforming the whole trial not into a spectacle, as the selfish bourgeois court does, but into a serious instructive school for educating those attending the session to observe and respect law and justice.[5]

The obligation borne by judges is shared by both prosecutors and defense attorneys; they too, in summarizing their cases, and encouraged to stress the general significance for the public of the particular problem at hand. Wrote the Chief Justice of the Latvian Supreme Court recently:

> The summations by both prosecutors and lawyers must contain a precise legal analysis of evidence, a legal evaluation of the acts of the accused; they must be statements by professionals talking to professionals . . . However, the summation is called upon to play a large role in the legal education of citizens. "Nowhere in daily life," said M. I. Kalinin [President of the Soviet Union, 1919–46] "is there as good a possibility for agitating for a cause as there is in court trials. But we still do not yet know how to exploit this as we should. . . . When you agitate, you must choose an appropriate example and proceed on the basis of concrete circumstances. The trial is precisely . . . the concrete example taken directly from life." . . .
> The judicial forum offers a rare opportunity to expose shortcomings and indicate ways of correcting them, proceeding on the basis of a real life situation, and to reveal vividly the mechanism of abuses, not just hypothesizing on their possible consequences, but already possessing knowledge of them in the form of regrettable "given circumstances." . . .[6]

In recent years there has been an effort to involve the public in the form of "public representatives" who are admitted to given cases for

---

[5] Ibid., p. 301.
[6] A. Likas, "Statements in Court," *Literaturnaya Gazeta*, July 4, 1973, p. 12.

the purpose of expressing the judgement of the groups or "collectives" which appointed them, usually the co-workers of the accused. Though they are styled "public defender" and "public accuser," a recent debate on their role in *Izvestiya* has stressed the view that they are not bound either to accuse or defend. Wrote a local procurator:

> The institution of public representatives for prosecution and defense has proven itself in practice. The public representatives express the opinion of their comrades; they are granted the rights of independent participants in the proceedings and are not assistants to the prosecutor or the defense attorney. It is important, in our opinion, to strive for a situation in which the public representative expresses the opinion of the public in court, an opinion based on universally acknowledged moral principles, and this opinion of the collective is taken by the court as an expression of the collective's will and conscience.[7]

Comrades' courts, the earliest and most durable form of "popular justice" outside the framework of the regular judicial process, were established in 1918 as an aid to military discipline, and the following year to improve discipline in the factories. Their functions and authority have varied over the years; their decline in the latter Stalin period was due partly to the fact that the petty violations they were empowered to deal with came increasingly under the purview of the regular system of criminal justice. Khrushchev revived them in 1959, giving them the power to require of defendants an apology, a fine up to 10 rubles, and damages to the injured party up to 50 rubles; they may also impose several forms of public censure, and propose to the defendants' employers that they be transferred or demoted, or to housing authorities that they be evicted. The purpose of the comrades' courts was set forth in the 1959 legislation:

> Comrades' courts are elected social agencies charged with actively contributing to the education of citizens in the spirit of a communist attitude toward work and toward socialist property, the observance of the rules of socialist community life, the development among Soviet people of a feeling of collectivism and of comradely mutual assistance, and respect for the dignity and honor of citizens. The chief task of the Comrades' Courts is to prevent violations of law and misdemeanors detrimental to society, to educate people by persuasion and social influence, and to create an attitude of intolerance toward any antisocial acts. The Comrades' Courts are invested with the trust of the collective, express its will and are responsible to it.[8]

---

[7] A. Basov, "The Public Representative in Court," *Izvestiya*, Oct. 27, 1972, p. 3. Translated in *Current Digest of the Soviet Press* 24 (Nov. 15, 1972), pp. 17–18.

[8] Berman, *Justice in the U.S.S.R.*, p. 289.

While the 1959 legislation was intended to cast the comrades' courts in the role of harbinger of the communist future, when the state as an organ of compulsion can be dispensed with altogether, the tendency in the 1960s pointed away from any expansion of "popular justice" by this route. Increasingly their procedures were brought into a well-ordered relationship with the procedures of the regular criminal and civil courts. While their educative function remains, because their judges are ordinary citizens and they meet at places of employment and residence where the offenses are committed, the norms by which they operate have become less the judgment of "collectives" and more those of an explicit legal framework.[9]

Contrary to the widespread impression in the West that there is little crime reporting in the Soviet press, there is actually a good deal of it. The bulk of the items concerning crime and criminal trials are designed to educate the Soviet public in the causes of crime, the defects in the upbringing of those who become criminals, the lax attitudes of ordinary citizens which sometimes contribute to commission of a crime, and the moral breakdown of criminals, their willful refusal to adhere to the norms of the society about them (or at least those norms which are officially promoted). The reports by Grigori Medynsky and Olga Chaikovskaya in *Izvestiya* and *Literaturnaya Gazeta* have sometimes attained a high, perceptive level of courtroom reporting, though always with the purpose of pointing out a moral.[10]

From Bourgeois to Socialist Law

The decision to establish a conventional European legal structure, though it may have begun with a "snowballing" of separate decisions in 1918–19, was a conscious, deliberate step in the early 1920s, and one supported by Lenin. It stands in glaring contradiction to Lenin's penchant for linking discipline and spontaneity in organizing the state and the economy. Here, in unexpected Bolshevik form, was the "middle ground" of orderly norms and procedures which properly belonged to the bourgeois era. To be sure, the substance of the laws included many new features specific to the Soviet system. But the great emphasis on orderly procedures, coupled with the building of specialized legal professions, seemed much more than simply a weapon to be used by the dictatorship of the proletariat and then dropped.

If we accept the arguments of a group of important legal experts of the 1920s, this seemingly bourgeois legal system was indeed a bourgeois

---

[9] See Albert Boiter, "Comradely Justice: How Durable Is It?" *Problems of Communism* 14 (March–April 1965), pp. 82–92.

[10] For translations of crime and courtroom reporting, see items in the "State and Law" section of *Current Digest of the Soviet Press.*

phenomenon, which could be dismantled with the arrival of socialism. Yevgeni Pashukanis, Pavel Stuchka, and others argued that there was no such thing as socialist law. Pashukanis argued that law rests on commercial transactions, even criminal law, where punishment may be regarded as "payment" for a crime. As long as the NEP prevailed, he said, as long as commercial exchanges were still legal, and crime still a sorry legacy from the capitalist era, bourgeois law must continue in a form adapted to Soviet conditions. Law in the Soviet system should be flexible enough to conform to changing political demands, and finally dispensed with altogether.

The lawyers and legal specialists of the 1920s were hard hit by the purges. By the end of the 1930s, many of them had been denounced, and their theories as well. A new Stalinist doctrine of law was set in their place by Andrei Vyshinsky, the USSR Procurator-General who made a name for himself as chief prosecutor in the show trials of the Great Purge. "Socialist law" and "socialist legality" were the watchwords that transformed a bourgeois institution into a Soviet one. In Vyshinsky's hands, the legal order now assumed a large place in the Soviet system. It was enshrined in the 1936 Constitution as a permanent feature of socialism, a guarantor of regularity and precision in the application of the state's awesome power. Vyshinsky's theory did not specify a "government under law," a government limited in its operation by legal principles and institutions. The legal order was first of all an instrument which channeled the power of the socialist state. It was also a means of using traditional institutions to enhance the authority of the still young Soviet political system.[11]

Perversely, the idea of a regular socialist legal order was being undermined while Vyshinsky was developing it. From 1934 on, extrajudicial procedures were used to mete out punishments for the most severe crimes, those involving charges of treason, sabotage, and other threats to the nation's security. Immediately after Kirov's assassination in December 1934, a decree aimed at "terrorist organizations and terrorist acts against representatives of the Soviet Government" provided swift investigation and trials, without the right of counsel or appeal.[12] Many cases were heard by special courts, particularly military courts and NKVD tribunals. The old Tsarist principle of "crime by analogy" was revived, under which acts not defined in the law codes could be treated as crimes if they equalled a crime in seriousness. Retroactive application of the laws was common. Vyshinsky also placed the burden of proof on the accused in trials for serious political crimes. Using a little-noticed provi-

---

[11] Vyshinsky's major exposition of this theory was a book he compiled in 1938, which has been translated under the title *The Law of the Soviet State* (New York: Macmillan, 1948).

[12] Decree of Dec. 1, 1934, *Izvestiya*, Dec. 5, 1934.

sion of the 1923 Code of Criminal Procedure, he applied in rigorous fashion the point that confessions were evidence of guilt, no matter how they were obtained. Finally, the NKVD began to deport and execute large numbers of people without trial. After the Great Purge ended, the changes it had wrought in the system of criminal justice remained essentially unchanged until Stalin's death.

Post-Stalin Reforms

The legal system as it stood in the early 1950s was a political liability to Stalin's successors. To the extent that it had been abused in order to inflict arbitrary punishment, it had ceased to be a true legal system; to the extent that the law had been circumvented altogther, it was relegated to a minor place in the political system.The Malenkov regime immediately began to correct some of the legal system's worst features, a development heralded by amnesty for many labor camp inmates in 1953. The Special Board of the Ministry of the Interior was abolished, the instrumentality set up after Kirov's assassination to punish "terrorists" without trial. The security police was stripped of its power to investigate crimes apart from supervision by the Procuracy. The courts were forbidden to conduct trials for anti-state crimes in the absence of the defendant. Military courts could no longer try civilians, except for charges of espionage.

The content of the laws and legal doctrines was as much in need of reform as the machinery of justice. These were dealt with in a complete rewriting of the nation's criminal codes, which began with publication of all-Union guidelines in 1958. These served as the basis for the new codes adopted by the Union Republics in the next few years, since the 1936 Constitution left both criminal and civil codes to their jurisdiction. Vyshinsky had promoted the doctrine that, in crimes against the state, the burden of proof lies with the accused, who must demonstrate his innocence. While the phrase "presumption of innocence" is not used, its content is there. Vyshinsky had also maintained that confessions represented conclusive evidence in themselves; and in view of the torture and threats which had been used to extract confessions in the Great Purge, this had made simple work of countless trials. The new codes returned to the original provisions of the 1920s that confessions must be corroborated by other evidence.

The category of "counterrevolutionary crimes" had been used to cover a wide variety of acts during the 1930s. The notorious Article 58 and 59 of the Criminal Code had been amended many times over so as to bring minor crimes into the circle of acts entailing either the death sentence or long imprisonment. Worst of all, Vyshinsky had inserted a "crime by analogy" provision, which made a counterrevolutionary act out of any circumstance that could be considered analogous to the many acts specified. The scope of all these crimes was now narrowed considerably, and their content made more precise. Now called "crimes against the state," they still include several provisions that can be (and have been) loosely interpeted, most notably "anti-Soviet agitation and propaganda," Article 70 of the Russian Republic's code. But at the time the new codes were adopted they were welcomed by Soviet legal specialists as a victory for the precision of legal norms.

The Procuracy, intended at its founding in 1922 to be the supreme guardian of the machinery of justice and the correct application of laws, received a new mandate in 1955 in the Statute on Procuracy Supervision. This agency, still an independent hierarchy responsible only to the USSR Council of Ministers, now received a blanket authorization to maintain ongoing checks and investigations in every agency of the government, so as to verify the legality of their acts. Among other things, this increased the value of the Procuracy's local offices as a place to which ordinary citizens could turn for redress of grievances against official acts.

"Popular Justice" Again

Side by side with these measures, Khrushchev promoted several types of "popular justice," the first major effort in this direction for many years. Among other things, he was attempting to demonstrate ways in which the formal mechanism of the state as an instrument of compulsion could be dismantled step by step, and its functions turned over to nongovernmental bodies operating not so much on the basis of exact rules as by virtue of their perception of the new communist morality. The "state of all the people" combined, therefore, means of compulsion with means of informal social control.

The comrades' courts of the old days were revived in the manner already described. More serious, from a legal point of view, was the antiparasite legislation enacted first in several of the Union Republics in the latter 1950s, then finally in the Russian Republic in 1961. This legislation enabled "people's assemblies," gatherings of one's co-workers or neighbors, to impose truly serious penalties on those whom they judge to be "parasites." The term was and is an ill-defined one, the more so because it includes a large variety of acts for which there were already criminal penalties. The 1961 law stated that

> . . . there are still individuals who are stubbornly opposed to honest work. Such people frequently hold jobs for appearance's sake while in actual fact living on unearned income and enriching themselves at the expense of the state and the working people or, although able-bodied, hold no job at all but engage in forbidden businesses, private

enterprise, speculation and begging, derive unearned income from the
exploitation of personal automobiles, employ hired labor and obtain
unearned income from dachas and land plots, build houses and dachas
with funds obtained by non-labor means, using for this purpose illegally
acquired building materials, and commit other antisocial acts. On the
collective farms such persons, enjoying the benefits established for collective farmers, avoid honest work, engage in home brewing, lead a
parasitic way of life, undermine labor discipline, and thereby harm
the artel's economy.[13]

The people's assemblies—sometimes mass meetings of thousands, as in the
antiparasite drive of 1963—were empowered to send parasites into exile
for two to five years; this did not mean a prison or labor camp sentence,
but rather the requirement of living in a remote (and usually unpleasant)
locality under police surveillance. Ordinarily these sentences had to be
ratified by local governments in order to come into force (in practice
by the local police), while the most serious ones went to the regular
courts.

The "popular" character of the antiparasite legislation was reduced
considerably in 1961 after a struggle of several years. During the years
1957–60, when such laws were adopted in most of the non-Russian republics, many Soviet jurists and legal specialists opposed them. Their most
potent argument was that national guidelines for new criminal legislation
adopted in 1958 stated explicitly that criminal punishment may be applied
only by judgment of a court. Khrushchev continued to press for extension
of the antiparasite laws, and enlisted the vigorous support of the Young
Communist League.[14] His victory in gaining a law for the Russian Republic in 1961 was only a partial one, for the most flagrant "parasites,"
those holding no job at all, now had to be dealt with by a regular court,
though without the procedural safeguards for normal cases. Undaunted,
Khrushchev launched several intensive antiparasite campaigns in the Russian Republic and elsewhere during his last years of power.[15]

For Khrushchev, "popular justice" was much more than just a way
of striking at people whose way of life was not a crime under the new
law codes, or a way of getting ordinary people involved in law enforcement. On the plane of ideology, it was meant as important evidence that
the state was beginning to wither away, for here state functions had

[13] Berman, *Justice in the U.S.S.R.*, pp. 291–92.
[14] The Komsomol's close relationship with the whole Soviet security apparatus
has long been assumed by foreign observers; its head during the 1950s, Alexander
Shelepin, became head of the KGB at the end of 1958, in the midst of this
debate. It is possible to infer that the KGB supported the antiparasite laws as
a ready way of dealing with nonconformists of different kinds who were not
clearly guilty of a crime.
[15] See Leon Lipson, "Hosts and Pests: The Fight Against Parasites," *Problems
of Communism* 14 (March-April 1965), pp. 72–82.

been transferred to nongovernmental bodies. The whole area of law enforcement is a critical one in the doctrine of the state, since Marx had described the state's main historical function as one of compulsion against classes. If compulsion can be reduced in one area after another, went the argument, it is because society has learned to manage its affairs without the crutch of force, and is able to deal with deviant behavior through persuasion and social pressure. If the "state of all the people" which Khrushchev proclaimed in 1959 was to be more than a slogan, the proof of its reality should be evident first of all in the means used to overcome deviant behavior.

"Popular justice" has a double edge: on the one hand, it involves people in the problems of their communities, and serves as a channel for creating a real public standard of conduct; on the other hand, it can be a channel for all kinds of popular prejudice and discontent, and can be manipulated so as to reinforce prejudice against nonconformists. Khrushchev, when he was obliged to show himself a stern proponent of "law and order," used the people's assemblies to underscore his wrath at the parasites.

A Conservative Trend

Since 1960, well before Khrushchev's removal, the trend of Soviet criminal law has been in the direction of stiffer penalties, extension of the definition of what is criminal, and withdrawal of the emphasis on popular justice. While national crime data are not published in any meaningful form, there are a number of indications that Soviet law-enforcement officials saw the consequences of the criminal code revisions as a crime wave. In 1961 and 1962, the death sentence as maximum penalty was reintroduced for six existing crimes and ten new crimes. The law forbidding currency speculation was made retroactive. The advocates of the presumption of innocence lost ground in a public debate over the application of this principle to the preliminary investigation. Those who urged that lawyers be admitted to the preliminary investigation along with their clients made no headway, nor did the proposal for jury trials, already rejected in the 1958 reforms, fare any better after Khrushchev's dismissal than it had before.

Popular justice was now de-emphasized. The comrades' courts and people's detachments continued, to be sure, though without the publicity or the ideological proclamations that had accompanied them in the early Khrushchev years. The people's assemblies were done away with altogether in 1965. The "parasite cases" were handed over to court jurisdiction in Moscow and Leningrad, though elsewhere local governments retained jurisdiction over them. The following year, the police was authorized

The Evolution of Soviet Politics

to impose its own fines for minor cases of hooliganism. Since these could not be appealed, this was one more offense removed from the jurisdiction of both regular courts and comrades' courts. Finally, as if to place the seal on this revival of legal conservatism, the central ministry in charge of regular police functions was revived in 1966 after a lapse of six years— Khrushchev had done away with it in 1960. It initially bore the name of Ministry for the Protection of Public Order (MOOP), as did the corresponding ministries in the Republics. But a few years later, in deference to this same legal conservatism, it was given back its old title of Ministry of the Interior (MVD).

The Brezhnev regime's campaign against political dissidents, real and suspected, has lately begun to erode some of the formal protection of the laws while adding little to the law's educative role, unless it be in a narrow political sense. The 1964 trial of the poet Joseph Brodsky for "parasitism" and the 1966 trials of the writers Andrei Sinyavsky and Yuli Daniel for "anti-Soviet agitation and propaganda" showed the readiness of courts to bend definitions to conform to political pressures. (Admittedly "parasitism" was always a woefully imprecise charge under the original antiparasite laws; the point here is that this was the first important application of it by a court.) These were the first in a long chain of trials involving dissent and protest, in which courts were equally compliant.[16]

The role of the three major law-enforcement agencies has cast further doubt on the quality of legal norms—the Procuracy, the KGB, and the regular police, now under the Minister of the Interior or MVD. The post-Stalin legal reforms did not give arrested persons the right to legal counsel until their cases came to court. The pretrial investigation, a Continental European institution that existed in Tsarist law and was incorporated into Soviet law, is intended to produce a report clarifying all aspects of a case, including mitigating and potentially exonerating circumstances. Consequently a document which itself is the result of what might be called a closed-doors trial is produced without the benefit of the defense counsel. Contrary to a widespread impression abroad, Soviet lawyers are members of a professional organization, the Collegium of Lawyers, and not servants of the state. That they too can be subject to political pressures is not difficult to imagine. But their role is a vital one, which can be of great benefit to the accused, and of which the lawyers themselves are justly proud. But the fact that the pretrial investigation is carried out in secret by a representative of one of the three main agencies—it can be any, depending on the nature of the crime—places the entire initiative in the hands of the state.

Ever since the 1958 reforms, the problem of the weight to be assigned

---

[16] See the many accounts in Abraham Brumberg (ed.), *In Quest of Justice: Protest and Dissent in the Soviet Union Today* (New York: Praeger, 1970).

to the pretrial investigation has cropped up again and again. A review of a professional book on the subject made the following observation:

> The opinion is often expressed in the literature that the truth (i.e., the individual's guilt) has already been established at the time of the indictment, that this truth is based with certainty on evidence obtained during the investigation and that the investigator is convinced of the individual's guilt, although he has not yet questioned him or verified the circumstances that he might cite in his defense.
>
> In our view, all of these propositions are mistaken, contradict the assumptions of the Soviet criminal process and may entail quite undesirable practical consequences. . . ."[17]

The view criticized here has most certainly contributed to the freedom of law-enforcement agencies to harrass dissidents without the possibility of a lawyer's intervening to test the legality of their conduct.[18] It has made the practice of placing dissidents or suspects in mental hospitals a simple one, a practice which is clearly on the increase and has received a good deal of deserved publicity in the West. While the Soviet law of criminal procedure includes careful provisions for dealing with mentally disordered defendants before trial and for determining sanity in court proceedings, the cases that have come to the attention of the outside world have involved commitment to psychiatric institutions without arrest, which leaves them outside the procedural safeguards.

THE PLACE OF RIGHTS

In chapter 7 we saw the Soviet leaders' inhibitions about making individual rights a major part of the new system. The new rights as a legal, constitutional phenomenon would be temporary; they, with the other paraphernalia of democracy, would reach full fruition under proletarian rule, only to wither away with the transition to communism. Until the 1936 Constitution, the full enjoyment of rights was denied to members of the former exploiting classes, whose definition in practice was a loose one. Since rights in the narrow legal sense are rights *against* the state or society, their use in the Soviet system would be marginal. Experiments with rights in the Russian Empire after 1860 had been quite limited, and their results unimpressive. Russian culture, which places so much emphasis on unity of feeling and action, provided little fertile soil for the idea of rights as precise and absolute claims against authority.

---

[17] Review by V. I. Kaminskaya in *Sovetskoye gosudarstvo i pravo*, no. 7 (July) 1973, pp. 148–49. Translation from *Current Digest of the Soviet Press* 24 (Jan. 17, 1973), p. 26.

[18] See the methods described by Andrei Amalrik, *Involuntary Journey to Siberia* (New York: Harcourt Brace Jovanovich, 1970), chapters 1–5. Amalrik, to be sure, refused to have a counsel in his trial later on.

Soviet rights fall into three broad categories: (1) the rights of expression and action, which include the rights traditional in the West,
plus a few uniquely Soviet touches described in chapter 7; (2) positive
social and economic rights; and (3) several rights directed against arbitrary conduct by law-enforcement agencies. The traditional rights, particularly those of expression and organization, are transformed in the
1936 Constitution to mean rights *for* citizen involvement in public affairs
under the tutelage of the Communist Party. State subsidies to nongovernmental organizations, and the Party's role as the "leading core" of all
state agencies and nongovernmental organizations, are intended to educate
and direct citizens in the proper use of their rights. The positive rights,
including the guarantees of employment, education, rest, and security
against disability and old age, are proclaimed by the Constitution to be
guaranteed by the economic and social system. The whole idea was to
take some of the formulations of rights customary in democratic constitutions, and transform them into vehicles for establishing directions of social
development, without handing the initiative to ordinary citizens by encouraging claims *against* the system. In the Constitution, such claims
are only three in number: freedom from arbitrary arrest, inviolability
of the home, and privacy of correspondence (Articles 127 and 128 of
the Constitution).

Expression and Assembly

The foreign press has given much attention, and rightly so, to judicial
and political inroads on the constitutional guarantees of expression and
assembly. The trials of writers and protesters for "anti-Soviet agitation
and propaganda" or similar crimes have placed Soviet policy makers
in a dilemma.[19] The political "edge" of the actions and manuscripts which
caused prosecution is regarded as a danger to the system. If the desired
political content of rights is held to be decisive, then there is no problem
in obtaining convictions. However, the legal system through which convictions must be obtained is one which stresses precise definitions and
orderly procedures. Placing the primary stress on exact use of the laws,
while it is unlikely to produce many acquittals, gives critics of "political
justice" a weapon to use in mustering support for those on trial. Here,
then, is one important consequence of Stalin's and Vyshinsky's decision
to build a full-blown *socialist* law instead of replacing the legal system
with "popular justice," or with some other kind of arrangement which
would reflect the transition to communist public discipline without courts
and lawyers.

Considering the number of dissidents who have been kept in mental

---

[19] This is Article 70 of the RSFSR Criminal Code.

hospitals rather than placed on trial, one might agree with some cynical observers that courts will be replaced by psychiatrists' offices in the communist future, thereby completing the "withering away" of the law. As long as the legal system remains, though, its procedures are potential weapons of protest against injustice. The single most fascinating development in this field was the recent establishment of the Committee on Human Rights by Andrei Sakharov, one of the country's most famous scientists, the "father of the Soviet hydrogen bomb." The four-man Committee's precarious existence rests on the determination of its members to make the Soviet Constitution's guarantees a reality. It rests equally on their conviction that the Soviet regime is now secure enough to be able to do this. In this sense, the Committee is representative of the vast bulk of protest that has come to the attention of the outside world. Far from proposing to dismantle the one-party system, they are urging Soviet authorities to realize their own professed ideals, which includes adhering strictly to their own laws—or to most of them, since some protests have been against particular laws.[20]

The Handling of Public Protest

The issue of legality, and particularly of the rights of citizens to protest illegality and to petition for changes in the laws, came sharply into focus in a series of trials that began in the mid-1960s. In 1966 two writers, Andrei Sinyavsky and Yuli Daniel, were convicted under the "anti-Soviet agitation and propaganda" law for works of theirs which had been published abroad under pseudonyms. Both received heavy sentences.[21] In January 1967 two small demonstrations in Moscow demanded the release of both men and revision of Article 70, under which they had been convicted. Four of the demonstrators were arrested, tried, and convicted of participating "in group activities that grossly violate public order," though the demonstrations themselves had been entirely peaceful. A year later Alexander Ginzburg, Yuri Galanskov, and two others were convicted under Article 70 for their underground literary doings, which had included a compilation of documents on the Daniel-Sinyavsky trial. The Soviet occupation of Czechoslovakia in August 1968 produced a protest demonstration on Red Square. Among the protesters were Daniel's wife and Pavel Litvinov, grandson of the Soviet foreign minister of the 1930s. A similar demonstration took place in Leningrad, and the defendants in both cases received several years of exile or prison.

Since that time protests and trials have continued without letup. The objects of the protests have varied; the early 1970s were marked by

---

[20] See the documents reproduced in Brumberg, *In Quest of Justice.*

[21] The record of this trial is in Max Heyward (ed.), *On Trial: The Soviet State Versus "Abram Tertz" and "Nikolai Arzhak"* (New York: Harper and Row, 1967).

a rise in protests concerning the status of national and religious minorities. A large volume of protest documents has been circulating in the Soviet Union, many of them addressed to high authorities. Underground newspapers have been on the rise in the 1960s and 1970s; the one best known abroad at present bears the dry title *Chronicle of Current Events,* and concentrates on presenting information about abuses of justice and efforts of protesters to make their voices heard.[22]

The theme which unites nearly all of this criticism is the need for the authorities to adhere to the Constitution and the laws in dealing with civil liberties cases. While protest has been aimed at some of the laws themselves, part of the objections have dealt with the issue of constitutionality, the nonconformity of one or another law to the Soviet Constitution. Vladimir Bukovsky, who was arrested in the January 1967 demonstration which demanded revision of Article 70, cited Article 125 of the Soviet Constitution in his defense. This article (see chapter 7) pledges assistance to free expression, including demonstrations, by providing printing equipment, the use of public buildings, and use of the streets—and Bukovsky, reciting the Article, interjected "Yes, streets, citizen prosecutor!"[23]

A secondary theme has been the attack on censorship, that is, on a long-established arm of the government whose legality may or may not be supported by the Soviet Constitution, depending how one interprets it. Alexander Solzhenitsyn, recent recipient of the Nobel Prize and beyond doubt the greatest living Russian author, argued the illegality of censorship in a 1967 letter to the Soviet Writers' Congress then in session, asking that the Congress discuss

> . . . the no longer tolerable oppression, in the form of censorship, that our literature has endured for decades and that the Union of Writers can no longer accept.
>
> Under the obfuscating label of *Glavlit* [Main Administration for Literary Affairs and Publishing] this censorship—which is not provided for in the Constitution and is therefore illegal, and which is nowhere publicly labeled as such—imposes a yoke on our literature and gives people unversed in literature arbitrary control over them. A survival of the Middle Ages, the censorship has managed, Methuselah-like, to drag out its existence almost to the twenty-first century.[24]

Another area of protest has been violations of proper court practice in the many trials involving rights issues. Denial of public access to the trials, except for a reliable handful of citizens, has occurred in some

---

[22] The first eleven issues of the *Chronicle,* organized by subject matter, are available in Peter Reddaway (ed.), *Protest and Dissent in the Soviet Union* (New York: American Heritage Press, 1972).

[23] *Problems of Communism* 17 (July-August 1968), p. 34.

[24] Brumberg, *In Quest of Justice,* pp. 245–46.

of the important cases. Refusal to hear key defense witnesses is another complaint. Unofficial protocols of the trials distributed by friends of the defendant have been among the most valuable underground documents, and the authorities have clearly attempted to stop this practice by barring unauthorized spectators from the courtroom.

The number of people involved in these cases is miniscule, and the cases themselves are but a tiny proportion of the courts' total case load. On the other hand, this handful of cases has been the first significant test of Article 70 and other provisions concerning freedom of public expression since the new criminal codes were drawn up in Khrushchev's early years of power. Law enforcement authorities have shown concern about these challenges by the way they have overreacted. There is hardly any possibility that courts could interpret constitutional freedom of expression otherwise than as they have so far. Not only are political pressures strong, but formal responsibility for interpetation of laws rests with the Presidium of the Supreme Soviet. As in many other European legal systems, even the highest courts in the land do not interpret laws or the constitution, but only apply them.

It is not, therefore, the possibility of more liberal court interpretations of the constitution that makes these cases significant, but the fact that the defendants and their supporters have been challenging the government on its own ground. By using the Soviet Constitution as the basis of challenge, this small group of dissenters has been able to attract the support of prominent people in nonpolitical areas, first of all among scientists. This makes its position different from that of dissenters in the last century: 19th-century radicals had to challenge the Tsarist system to change its laws rather than live up to them.

The Positive Rights

Of the four economic and social rights set forth in the 1936 Constitution, three have been dealt with systematically in laws: the right to rest and leisure, the right to education and the right to support in old age and in the event of disability. The status of the right to work must be sought in a variety of regulations and administrative practices. The constitutional articles themselves (see appendix I, Articles 118–121) make a strange impression at first, especially if one is used to the norms of Anglo-American law. It appears that the only guarantee of these rights lies in the citizen's trust that the Soviet system is able to provide all these benefits, not in legal recourse against the state.

The major problem with these rights in the past had not been their lack of precision, but the absence of judicial recourse in cases where they were denied. For example, it was not until the Brezhnev administration that collective farmers were brought under the social security system.

Interestingly, the original land law of 1918 provided that all farmers, including individual proprietors, were to receive pensions and disability payments at the expense of the state. This was never put into operation and lapsed at the time of collectivization, when the new collective farms were directed to form their own social insurance pools.

Another problem with positive rights is the lack of direct, effective channels for remedying wrongful acts of officials. Ordinarily the channels open to the individuals are to file a complaint with the offending agency itself and to report the facts to the local public prosecutor, who can take a variety of remedial steps. The prosecutor's action can be quite effective, but he is under no obligation to act. Administrative courts and formal agency tribunals for reviewing complaints by individuals are nonexistent. What actually happens in cases like this is that the wronged citizen goes from official to official in different hierarchies, including the Party, until he finds one who can straighten things out.[25]

The Right and Duty to Work

The right to work, Article 118 of the Soviet Constitution, comes first in the list of rights and duties, but it is the least clear. Article 12 makes labor a duty as well, or more precisely "an obligation and a matter of honor for every able-bodied citizen." No comprehensive laws have been passed concerning the right to work. There have been state employment agencies: *Orgnabor* in the Stalin era and, since 1967, the Committee for Utilization of Labor Resources. These, however, have been more of an administrative convenience than a means of guaranteeing a right. Oddly enough, it was not until the Khrushchev era that there were laws spelling out the duty to work. By the early 1960s the antiparasite legislation of the Union Republics had filled this gap, though not completely, since the definition of "parasite" was so unclear. Only in 1970 was a comprehensive law finally enacted which gives local governments the authority to assign idlers to whatever regular jobs are available and provides up to a year of imprisonment for refusing to take a job.[26]

Unemployment officially vanished from Soviet statistics around 1930, and with it the concept of unemployment compensation. The topic did not reappear in legislation until the early 1970s, when provision was made for short-term technological unemployment. Job shortages had long been a *local* problem, however, in some areas of the country. The western periphery of the Soviet Union has received comparatively little industrial investment, partly for security reasons, and small towns generally have

---

[25] See the author's article on this subject, "Citizen Versus Administration in the USSR," *Soviet Studies* 17 (October 1965), pp. 226–37.

[26] Decree of Feb. 25, 1970. *Current Digest of the Soviet Press* 22 (May 19, 1970), p. 32.

been neglected by planning agencies and ministries in locating their new enterprises. These areas have experienced a population outflow, but, even so, there is an annual problem of finding work for graduates from secondary schools and technical schools. Every spring the Soviet press carries numerous articles on this problem and what is being done about it.

The system of assigning graduates to jobs for an obligatory three-year period has evoked much criticism abroad as a limitation on individual freedom. The Soviet Constitution does not list choice of employment among its various rights. The assignment system applies not only to universities and instititutes, but to technical schools and vocational training schools also. Actually, assignments are less of a restriction than at first appears. Those who graduate with high marks, or with military service or labor experience, get a preference in job choice. To the extent possible, jobs are offered to graduates in the area of their formal residence—that is, where their internal passports are registered. (This is sometimes not possible, however, and whole classes can be assigned to remote areas.) No criminal penalties are imposed for leaving one's job assignment before the three years are up, except that those who remain jobless are apt to be prosecuted under the antiparasite laws. The 1940 law which forbade job-leaving without permission, a war emergency measure, was dropped quietly in 1956 and probably had not been enforced for several years before that. While regulations forbid employers to hire job-leavers, they usually ignore this if they are in need of labor.

The most significant indicator of freedom and restrictions in job choice is the way Soviet authorities have attempted to deal with the problem of high labor turnover. The early years of the Soviet industrialization drive in the 1930s were also a period of very high labor turnover. The greatly increased wage differentials that were introduced in 1931 were justified by Stalin mainly as an effort to lower the turnover rate (though other motives were certainly present as well). After this failed to solve the problem, restrictions were applied which eventually became law. John Scott's firsthand account of the experience of Magnitogorsk noted that, in the first two years following Stalin's speech, administrators and foremen simply refused to let workers go, even though they supposedly had a right to quit after giving 15 days' notice. The trade unions were of no help, since they feared being criticized for failing to combat labor turnover. These abuses, said Scott, were stopped in 1936, but they began again in 1938. In 1940 a government decree forbade all Soviet workers to leave their jobs without permission.[27]

Today industrial job-changing is still a problem for the economy; newspaper articles often deal with the problem of excessive labor turnover. In many areas and situations, job-changing is made difficult by

---

[27] John Scott, *Behind the Urals* (Boston: Houghton Mifflin, 1942), p. 75.

administrative regulations, refusal of residence permits, housing scarcities, and threats to the career advancement of younger people whose job records show frequent changes. However, the way in which the job-changing problem is discussed in the Soviet press, and the many sociological investigations of it, all indicate that the use of incentives is today the primary means for increasing employment stability. Studies of the causes of high labor turnover have pointed increasingly to living conditions as the most important single factor—availability of housing, quality and dependability of the supply of food and other consumers' goods, and the level of social services, such as day care for working mothers.[28]

REGULATION OF PROPERTY

The Soviet leaders had a number of choices open to them in organizing distribution and in regulating possessions. The major ideological restriction was Marx's assumption that the means of production would no longer be owned individually. Property may be held and used by individuals as long as it is not used to exploit the labor of others, according to the *Communist Manifesto*. From this requirement flows the distinction recognized specifically in Soviet law, between "individual property" and "private property," the latter defined as property unrestricted as to use, and hence prohibited.

Beyond this basic prohibition, ideological constraints on the organization of property were few. But as in so many other areas of choice, the choices which the early Bolshevik leaders faced here were greatly restricted by immediate problems. Laws and policies which appeared to embody progress toward the communist future were often crisis measures, and these were reconciled with ideology as best as possible.

Land

In the early postrevolutionary years, the land problem overshadowed all other property problems. The Decree on Land, passed immediately after the Bolsheviks came to power, abolished private property in land in the Marxian sense, and provided a flexible system of land use by individuals. All persons desiring to cultivate the land with their own labor had a right to the use of land; the forms of land tenure were left to each village; household gardens in both country and city were left to the use of those currently in possession of them; all commercial transactions in land were prohibited; the state took over management of all mineral wealth and important forest lands, as well as the large specialized estates; and the state was to act as apportioner of land. Inheritance of

---

[28] See the author's *Soviet Social Policies* (Homewood, Ill.: Dorsey Press, 1970), pp. 142–56.

the land was recognized indirectly: when a farmer died or left the land, it technically reverted to the state, but both near relatives and persons designated by the former land user had a preferential right to it. These were eminently sensible arrangments, and three years later they formed the basis for the period of truce in the countryside under the NEP policies. A supplementary decree of February 1918 gave preference to collective farms in apportioning land, but left several options open as to the type of collective farm.

There is no reason why Karl Marx should not have been satisfied with mixed possession of the land, since it did not contradict his conditions for property management under communism. From the beginning, the Soviet leaders left no doubt that they regarded collectivized agriculture as more efficient and somehow "more socialist" than individual holdings. On the first count, Marx might have agreed that there was a case for collectivization. In chapter 2 we saw the actual motives for collectivization, and the fact that the most urgent motive stemmed from the peasants' capacity to withhold grain from the market. Underlying the leaders' anxiety at this phenomenon was a deeper anxiety: individual possession of the land, even without the use of hired labor or the ability to buy and sell land, was promoting a private property mentality which was at the root of agrarian resistance to the regime's demands.

Housing

This same anxiety has been responsible for most of the fluctuations of personal property rights in other areas. Land use and home ownership in the cities and towns have pursued a zigzag course whose limits were determined by economic advantage on the one hand and uneasiness about the "private property mentality" on the other. In 1918, a large part of privately owned urban housing was nationalized, and severe restrictions were placed on the capacity of individuals to own and inherit housing. The NEP brought a relaxation of this policy, which permitted individuals to buy and build housing on land leased from local governments. The 1936 Constitution placed formal legal protection on home ownership.

In 1948, in the wake of World War II, a decree encouraged private housing construction as a measure to relieve the nation's terrible housing shortage: critical enough during the 1930s, the lack of housing space had become a disaster as the result of wartime destruction. Every Soviet citizen now enjoyed the right to buy or build a house of up to five rooms on any plot of land assigned by local governments, in the country as well as in urban areas. Houses could now be owned without time limit (the 1922 legislation caused them to revert to the state after 49 years), and could be inherited. As in the past, the right to an individually owned dwelling was interpreted to mean ownership of one house (vacation cottages excepted); ownership of two or more could only mean that one was rented for profit. The same principle applied to apartment dwellers: possession of a state or cooperative apartment plus a house was considered a means of unjustified enrichment.[29]

The Khrushchev Period: Concern and Restrictions

Khrushchev continued all these provisions, which were given greater permanence by being included in the civil law codes of the early 1960s. A decree of 1959 fostered individual construction by ordering construction suppliers to furnish individual builders with building materials and components.[30] Early in the 1960s the government launched a campaign for organizing cooperatives to purchase apartment buildings. Apartments cost anywhere from 2,000 to 8,000 rubles, the price varying with size, but even the cheapest were well over the average annual wage, and the down payment was originally 50 percent. Since then the terms have been eased and the cooperatives have become plentiful, even if available mainly to the better-paid Soviet citizens.

After 1960, Khrushchev and other leaders became concerned about the many houses that were being built by people who did not seem to have the money for such a large undertaking. Officials were diverting labor and materials from state construction organizations to build expensive homes for themselves, ordinary citizens were using money they made in illicit pursuits to do the same. A 1962 law provided for confiscating houses that had been built with unearned income.[31] Trials held under this law placed the burden of proof on the home owner, who was obliged to show that he had not used unearned income to build or buy his house.[32] Another sour note was a 1961 decree halting the assignment of individual garden plots to city dwellers, plots usually grouped on the outskirts of a city or town, and providing an important supplement to the diet of those who worked them.[33] The last years of the Khrushchev regime, in fact, saw policy moving in the direction of restricting personal efforts for personal gain. Khrushchev promoted automobile rental services as a way for the Soviet Union to enter the mass automobile era, without letting the cost of buying and maintaining a car become a major goal for the individual (as it must be, since even the smaller cars cost over

---

[29] The 1922 and 1948 decrees can be found in Meisel and Kozera, *Materials for the Study of the Soviet System*, pp. 139–41 and 418.

[30] Decree of the USSR Council of Ministers of Aug. 29, 1959. *Spravochnik partiinogo rabotnika, vypusk 3* (Moscow: Gospolitizdat, 1961), pp. 392–95.

[31] *Vedomosti Verkovnogo Soveta SSR* 1962, no. 16.

[32] See Samuel Blombergen, "Personal Property: Downward Trends," *Problems of Communism* 14 (March-April 1965), p. 46.

[33] Decree of the USSR Council of Ministers of September 18, 1961. *Spravochnik partiinogo rabotnika, vypusk 4* (Moscow: Gospolitizdat, 1963), p. 372.

twice the average annual wage). Collective vacation resorts were stressed, and the building of private summer cottages discouraged. Here, in fact, was one of the areas in which Khrushchev's initiative and influence never abated, even though he was experiencing reverses in other policy areas.

The Brezhnev Period: Stability for the Present

The Brezhnev administration very quickly reversed this trend after 1964. The restrictions on urban garden plots were lifted, including a regulation of the 1950s taxing livestock owned by city dwellers. Collective farmers were offered long-term mortgages to enable them to build individual houses, a far cry from Khrushchev's "argo-city" proposal for housing them in apartments and thereby making it harder for them to cultivate their all-important private plots. The way was cleared for growth of private automobile production, and consumer credit put in its first appearance. While pressing its campaign to catch and prosecute people who were getting their money in illegal ways, the post-Khrushchev regime showed itself far less concerned than its predecessor about the individual use and enjoyment of worldy goods.

The present state of personal property rights is one of security mixed with elements of insecurity. Articles 7, 9, and 10 of the 1936 Constitution have been reaffirmed in various laws of the post-Stalin era, an important consideration in view of the Constitution's declaratory nature. Article 7 guarantees the private plots of collective farmers. Article 9 permits private enterprise by farmers and artisans while forbidding the use of hired labor, and Article 10 covers individual property generally:

> The personal property right of citizens in their incomes and savings from work, in their dwelling houses and subsidiary home enterprises, in articles of domestic economy and use, and articles of personal use and convenience, as well as the right of citizens to inherit personal property, are protected by law.

The main source of insecurity is the threat of prosecution for using individual property for private gain. The 1961 civil law guidelines state flatly that individual property of citizens may not be used as a source of unearned income. The borderline between what is legal and what is not is thin in places, and in the past it has varied with the political winds. Country dwellers, whether they are collective farmers or not, may usually sell the surplus from their garden plots, but a city dweller who does the same thing may fall under suspicion. Selling one's personal possessions is legal, and there are commission stores to promote such sales; but selling a large quantity of clothes or anything else may be regarded as foridden commerce.

Official anxiety about the "private property mentality" has abated for the present, but it is a long-standing concern of Soviet political leaders and could easily bring more attacks on property in the future. The potential threat is not the abolition of Article 10, whose principles offer a commonsense way of organizing individual use of property, and save the state what would otherwise be a terribly complex job of apportioning goods to people. Instead, the threat comes from the possibility of a narrow interpretation of property rights, which would undermine the psychological security which they are intended to support.

However, there are no present signs that the Brezhnev administration is moving toward property restrictions in an effort to promote general social change. Judging by the swiftness with which it removed Khrushchev's restricions on the use of garden plots by city dwellers, the new regime's intention appeared to be that of assuring Soviet citizens that their property is secure. This was also a response to the disastrous harvest of 1963—private plots have played a singificant role in the nation's food supply. The popularity of cooperative apartments and the significant increase in private automobile sales have offered a way of returning rapidly growing private savings to the economy. During the 1960s, disposable money income doubled, and individual savings accounts nearly quadrupled.[34] The confiscation of savings in 1947, thinly disguised as a currency reform, still lurks in the memory of the older generation. Promotion of individual savings, the stability of inheritance laws, and the production of more private automobiles, better-quality apartments and other major consumption items have all served to provide reassurance on this score. All this will not prevent future Soviet leaders from attacking whatever they consider to be excessive personal wealth. At present, however, there appears to be little gain in mounting any kind of major campaign for property restrictions. Social stability rather than social change remains the goal of property laws.

EVOLUTION OR DEGENERATION?

It is all too easy to permit the arbitrary abuse of Soviet law for political reasons to obscure its basic path of evolution, and the lessons it bears for noncommunist legal systems. Of the three functions of the law outlined at the beginning of this chapter, the most distinctive developments for the Soviet system as a whole have taken place within the educative function. This function has been well reconciled with the function of the law as regulator, except that in an area which foreigners regard as very critical, that of freedom of expression and organization, the precise norms which characterize the law's regulatory function are lacking. One

---

[34] David W. Bronson and Barbara S. Severin, "Consumer Welfare," in *Economic Performance and the Military Burden in the Soviet Union* (Washington, D.C.: U.S. Government Printing Office, 1970), p. 99.

might say, in fact, that it is precisely the Soviet leaders' strong awareness of the law's educative role that has led them to approve "educative" measures which are so arbitrary or repressive that they tend to undermine this role. Give an educative type of law, the temptation to use it for short-term political gain is enormous.

Under the constant pressure of immediate political demands, any form of law will degenerate according to what is demanded of it, as Soviet law did during and after the Great Purge. While it remains to be seen what effect the expanded penalties of the 1960s will have, or the procedural abuses that have accompanied the much-publicized trials of dissidents, so far these are partial incursions which have left many other areas of the legal system untouched. This is clearly an unfinished story. If the indubitably positive features of Soviet law could be rescued from the ruins of the Vyshinsky era, then there is hope that a legally more enlightened leadership than the present one will go on building where the reformers of the latter 1950s were compelled to leave off.

FOR FURTHER READING

The best introduction to the Soviet legal system, though now somewhat dated, is Harold J. Berman, *Justice in the U.S.S.R.* (New York: Vintage Books, 1963). It is outstanding in comparing Soviet legal principles and procedures with those of Tsarist Russia, the Continental legal tradition generally, and Anglo-American law. More recent surveys include E. L. Johnson, *An Introduction to the Soviet Legal System* (New York: Barnes and Noble, 1970), and Robert Conquest (ed.), *Justice and the Legal System in the U.S.S.R.* (New York: Praeger, 1968). More specialized is Samuel Kucherov, *The Organs of Soviet Administration of Justice: Their History and Operation* (Leiden: E. J. Brill, 1970).

Soviet descriptions of Soviet law include P. S. Romashkin (ed.), *Fundamentals of Soviet Law* (Moscow: Foreign Languages Publishing House [1962]), V. M. Chkhikvadze et al., *The Soviet State and Law* (Moscow: Foreign Languages Publishing House, n.d.), and V. M. Chkhikvadze, *The State, Democracy and Legality in the USSR* (Moscow: Foreign Languages Publishing House, n.d.).

Translations of currently valid Soviet legal codes and related official documents may be found in the following: Harold J. Berman (ed.), *Soviet Criminal Law and Procedure: The RSFSR Codes* (Cambridge, Mass.: Harvard University Press, 1966); Harold J. Berman and John B. Quigley (eds.), *Basic Laws on the Structure of the Soviet State* (Cambridge, Mass.: Harvard University Press, 1969); and John N. Hazard and Isaac Shapiro (eds.), *The Soviet Legal System: Post-Stalin Documentation and Commentary* (2nd ed.; Dobbs Ferry, N.Y.: Oceana, 1969). Three periodicals carry translations of recent laws, codes and commentaries: *Soviet Government, Soviet Statutes and Decisions,* and *Current Digest of the Soviet Press.* The first two are published by the International Arts and Sciences Press in White Plains, N.Y., and the

Current Digest by the American Association for the Advancement of Slavic Studies.

Two absorbing accounts of Soviet law in action, based on firsthand observation, are B. A. Konstantinovsky, *Soviet Law in Action: The Recollected Cases of a Soviet Lawyer* (edited by H. J. Berman; Cambridge, Mass.: Harvard University Press, 1953), and the more recent account by an American observer, George Feiffer, *Justice in Moscow* (New York: Simon and Schuster, 1964).

Two interesting volumes deal with the evolution of Soviet law in its relationship to theory and social questions, during the Lenin and Stalin eras: John N. Hazard, *Law and Social Change in the U.S.S.R.* (London: Stevens, 1953), and Rudolph Schlesinger, *Soviet Legal Theory: Its Social Background and Development* (New York: Oxford University Press, 1945).

12

SOCIAL STRATIFICATION

UNTIL THE MIDDLE of the present century, the Soviet Union, the United States, and the world's other industrial nations seemed to be forging homogeneous societies. Urbanization, geographical mobility, mass communications, and occupational roles geared to ability all served as a social "meat grinder," obliterating old distinctions. New distinctions might arise, but these would lack permanence. The formal value systems of both East and West reinforced this view: Soviet Marxism predicted the obliteration of all social and national distinctions; American political rhetoric and formal education supported the doctrine of truly equal opportunity for all, plus the idea of an inexorable "melting pot" which would put an end to differences of national origin. Both value systems assumed that even if distinctions persisted for a time they would not form barriers to individual choice.

In both the Soviet Union and the United States, these expectations have materialized far more slowly than was believed earlier in the century. In the case of ethnic and national feelings, the "melting pot" trend is in doubt. The parts of the American value system which promoted it have been virtually dropped. The opportunities for economic and occupational mobility must be viewed in the light of persisting and growing disparities of income, together with barriers to low-income groups. In the Soviet Union, an ever larger proportion of protest actions have been those by non-Russians on behalf of their nationalities. Disparities of income have been reduced in the post-Stalin era, but some large problems remain. There is still a question, for example, to what extent it will be possible to give collective farmers and their children opportunities truly equal with those of the urban population. University admissions are another problem: to what extent will higher education continue to create distinctions of rewards, feelings, and associations?

Problems arising from national differences in the Soviet Union are far more in evidence today than problems having to do with classes, status, rewards, and opportunity. But the latter have generated a good deal of open discussion during the whole post-Stalin period. Sociological studies of the 1960s and 1970s have thrown light on problems of stratification. The fact that they are now dealt with openly, while at the same time research in questions of national identity are still treated gingerly, may be evidence that Soviet policy-makers consider that solutions to the remaining problems of stratification are in sight.

INDUSTRIALIZATION AND STRATIFICATION

Did the Soviet Union have to promote stratification in order to become a major industrial power? Does building any modern industrial economy necessarily heighten stratification? Was a choice open here? Alex Inkeles maintains that the basic trend has been to reduce inequalities of every type; Stalin's renewal of differentiated rewards in 1931 was but an episode in a long-term movement toward reducing the disparities. This has been accompanied, he maintains, by reductions in the distance between top and bottom in the "stratification subsystems" other than income, which include status, power, and knowledge. In a modern society, the position an individual occupies on any one of these scales, high, middle or low, is likely to be the position he occupies on all the scales; this was not true of traditional, preindustrial societies. In all these scales, the distance between top and bottom is reduced as a society becomes modern, and this is proving to be the case in the Soviet Union too.[1]

Those who consider that totalitarian rule sharply distinguishes the Soviet experience with modernization from the experience of the Western industrial nations also tend to assume the manipulability of social relationships under totalitarianism. Robert Feldmesser maintains that Soviet rule has meant not only the destruction of classes but the use of relationships among strata to suit political needs. In this view, studying class relationships is useful mainly for understanding the ruling stratum's political demands. It cannot be used to build a general theory of social groupings in modernizing societies.[2] The now classic explanation of totalitarian rule, that of Carl Friedrich and Zbigniew Brzezinski, does not even include social stratification among the many instruments used by totalitarian rulers.[3]

[1] Alex Inkeles, *Social Change in Soviet Russia* (Cambridge, Mass.: Harvard University Press, 1968), chapter 7.

[2] Robert A. Feldmesser, "Social Classes and Political Structure," in Cyril E. Black (ed.), *The Transformation of Russian Society* (Cambridge, Mass.: Harvard University Press, 1967), pp. 235–52.

[3] Carl J. Friedrich and Zbigniew K. Brzezinski, *Totalitarian Dictatorship and Autocracy*, 2d ed. rev. (New York: Praeger, 1966).

As a warning about the assumption that modern industrial nations are producing fairly homogeneous societies, one should consider the development projected in Michael Young's *Rise of the Meritocracy*. This portrays an English society of the future organized strictly according to ability and performance. All persons of high talent have been put into the professional and managerial jobs which require talent; all the rest are "technicians," performing the routine tasks. Everyone gets absolutely the same pay, except that the managerial and professional group requires lavish fringe benefits in order to sustain its high-quality performance. In the end, however, stable classes reassert themselves, since the self-renewal of occupational strata proves to be a less objectionable way of maintaining the system.[4] Soviet higher education, in its relation to occupational strata, certainly has some of the potential for bringing Soviet society to such a pass. It may turn out that as differences in income are reduced, differences in occupation and status will become more rather than less important. The desperate urge of such a large proportion of Soviet young people to get into the universities can hardly be explained merely in terms of income rewards and other material benefits.

Soviet society today provides at least some evidence in support of all these theories: (1) its stratification is reinforced by the correspondence of the "subsystems"—income, status, power, and knowledge; (2) its strata are fluid enough to be subject to economic and political manipulation; and (3) its educational and job-placement systems may be viewed as a "meritocracy" in the making. The first may be regarded as the consequences not just of modernization, but of a conscious effort to spur modernization by erasing all social distinctions which do not promote it. The manipulability of strata may be regarded as having both economic and political usefulness: it channels human resources where they are most needed. Manipulation can also prevent the formation of closely knit occupational groupings which might seek an autonomous political role. The "meritocracy" principle, enforced in an elementary way by the Soviet higher education system, had both an economic and political origin also. It was a known and reliable way of producing technological skills, and it kept the loyalty of newly skilled managers and engineers by offering status and material rewards.

IS THERE A RULING CLASS?

Accusations that the Soviet Union promotes its own class system have come from many quarters. Various definitions of "class" are used to support the accusation, and Stalin is usually identified as the factor most responsible for building up the class system. Trotsky, after his expulsion

---

[4] Michael Young, *The Rise of the Meritocracy* (Baltimore: Penguin Books, 1961).

from the Soviet Union, accused Stalin of having fostered gross inequalities worthy of capitalism. Stalin, he said, had set up the new bureaucracy as a ruling class that has amassed power unprecedented in the history of classes.[5] Milovan Djilas, a top Yugoslav communist leader who was demoted and imprisoned during the 1950s for his unorthodox writings, made a more refined critique in *The New Class*.[6] Starting with the contention that the means of production in the Soviet Union (and in Yugoslavia of the early 1950s) were in fact controlled solely by the top Party leadership, he identified the Party bureaucracy as a class by virtue of this control. This definition was narrower than that of Marx, who had described the bourgeoisie as a whole complex of strata, from political leaders and the captains of industry down to small shopkeepers and white-collar employees. Djilas conceded that it was difficult to draw any firm line between the Party bureaucrats and other administrators, who share the Party's function of management in a subordinate way and who enjoy some of the privileges of Party functionaries. That is, the "new class" is not set apart clearly by its hierarchical status, and to this extent fails to meet one modern sociological criterion of class. What Djilas did stress was the Party bureaucracy's domination of the economy: it controls not only the means of production, but also distribution, working conditions, and economic planning.

Feldmesser, already referred to, argues that there is not, and cannot be, a hierarchy of classes. In Feldmesser's definition, a class must not only occupy a hierarchical position, but must also serve as the main reference group for its members. It does this by possessing unique norms and by enforcing obedience to these norms by its members. Lenin created his own reference group by using ideological conviction rather than class origin as the criterion for eligibility to the Party. The Party's norms are not sharply distinguished from the norms of the many suborganizations and subcategories which it has created. Interviews with refugees from the Soviet Union following World War II showed that most values, particularly these concerning the overall structure of the Soviet system, were widely shared among different social strata; this included negative as well as positive judgments on the system. Consequently, says Feldmesser, the ruling group, however defined, is set apart from the rest of society because it commands and controls the means to enforce its commands. This is a totalitarian characteristic: a top stratum ruling over social strata which are not classes. They cannot be classes because they are prevented from becoming primary reference groups, developing autonomy, or enforcing norms of their own. In such a system, concludes Feldmesser,

---

[5] Leon Trotsky, *The Revolution Betrayed* (New York: Merit Publishers, 1965), chapters 6 and 9.

[6] Milovan Djilas, *The New Class* (New York: Praeger, 1954).

. . . no group, other than the political leaders themselves, can be permitted to acquire a material or social basis of support strong and stable enough to allow it to regulate the composition and behavior of its own membership.[7]

Class attitudes may be more important than the question of whether this or that stratum corresponds to a sociological definition of class. If group attitudes having the intensity of the older class attitudes persist in spite of lessening differences among social strata, Soviet progress toward a nonstratified society is still in question. The study of wartime refugees from the Soviet Union, mentioned above, showed that these attitudes were strong and pervasive in the 1930s. There was a strong dislike of the Party by non-Party members in all strata, and mistrust of the intelligentsia (defined as nonmanual workers) by ordinary workers and farmers.[8] This is not surprising in view of the policies of the 1930s: for the peasantry, forced collectivization, high demands, and a depressed standard of living; for the intelligentsia and the upper strata of nonmanual workers, a new recognition and increasing rewards.

THE INTELLIGENTSIA

Soviet sociology, a new but burgeoning academic field, has conducted few surveys which deal directly with attitudes of various strata of society toward other strata. However, enough information has come to light about career attitudes to form a coherent picture of what appears to be the single most important social cleavage: the distinction between those with a higher education and those without it. This does not, of course, correspond to the difference between nonmanual and manual occupations, since no higher education is required for many white-collar occupations. In the early decades of Soviet history, a far larger proportion of those considered intelligentsia did not have a higher education than is the case today. In any case, the occupational definition is the one most consistently used in ideological and sociological writings in the Soviet Union, no matter whether the more humble white-collar occupations are included.

Studies of Stratification

With this definition in mind, one may draw the following conclusions from sociological surveys, legislation, policy statements, and press com-

---

[7] Feldmesser, "Social Classes and Political Structure," p. 252. The survey of refugees is contained in Alex Inkeles and Raymond A. Bauer, *The Soviet Citizen: Daily Life in a Totalitarian Society* (Cambridge, Mass.: Harvard University Press, 1961).

[8] Inkeles and Bauer, *The Soviet Citizen*, ch. 5.

mentary in the 1950s and early 1960s: (1) occupations filled by the intelligentsia are almost universally regarded as more desirable than other occupations; and (2) it is the sons and daughters of the intelligentsia who have the best chance of filling these occupations, and the children of agricultural workers the worst chance. In 1965, a sociological study of secondary school graduates in Novosibirsk Province showed both of these points vividly; part of the results is shown in Table 12–1.

TABLE 12–1
Personal Plans of 1963 Graduates of Secondary Schools
in Novosibirsk Province, and Their Realization,
by Occupation of Parents
(in percentages)

Occupation of Father (or of Mother, if no Father Present)	Intention			Realization		
	Work	Combine Work with Study	Study Full Time	Worked	Combined Work with Study	Studied Full Time
Urban professional†.	2	5	93	15	3	82
Rural professional	11	13	76	42	–	58
Industrial and construction workers	11	6	83	36	3	61
Transport and communications workers	–	18	82	55	–	45
Agricultural workers	10	14	76	90	–	10
Workers in trade and services	9	15	76	38	3	59
Others	12	38	50	63	12	25

*This was a 10 percent sample of the larger study, or about 900 graduates.
. †This is a translation of the Russian term *intelligentsiya*, which in this context is probably a bit broader than "professional."
Source: V. N. Shubkin, "Youth Enters Life," *Voprosy filosofii*, no. 5 (May) 1965, p. 65. A full translation of this most interesting article is available in *Current Digest of the Soviet Press*, vol. 17 (August 18, 1965), pp. 3–9.

At about the same time, a sociologist in Sverdlovsk produced an investigation of the social origins of the intelligentsia there. The study showed first of all that the children of the intelligentsia occupied more than their share of places in the universities and institutes, measured against the proportion of intelligentsia in the area's population and in national census figures. At the time the survey was done, about 4 percent of the nation's labor force possessed a higher education. At the Urals University, the proportion of children of the intelligentsia ranged from 58 percent in physics (the most prestigious academic specialty) to 11 percent in economics. However, between the beginning (in 1958) of Khrushchev's campaign for democratizing higher education and the year of the survey (1964), the proportion of workers' children in the entering classes of the city's largest institute rose from 34 to 49 percent; nationally about 58 percent of the 1964 labor force was in occupations not associated with agriculture or the intelligentsia. The survey's author identified the factors which gave the children of the intelligentsia such an advantage: parents' income, education, and occupation, and the chance of attending big-city schools. In city schools the facilities, level of instruction and overall stimulation are better than in small town and rural schools.[9]

Building the status and privileges of the intelligentsia had been Stalin's work. Mass recruitment of specialists into the Party, ideological elevation of the term "intelligentsia," expansion of higher education, and the heightening of specialists' rewards had all created this. Higher education during the 1930s has been reshaped to meet the demands of the economy. From then on, admissions were conducted according to nationally standardized examinations, and the number of students admitted in each specialty was determined centrally. For a country so desperately in need of specialists, this stringent control of educational goals was understandable. An unexpected feature was the introduction in 1940 of tuition not only for higher education, but for the final years of secondary education as well; it was all the more surprising because the 1936 Constitution had guaranteed free tuition at all levels. Tuition levels were so low, however, that it is hard to see what purpose they served; they were abolished in 1956.

Khrushchev Tries to Reshape the Intelligentsia

A big problem that Khrushchev faced was a growing unease among Party leaders about the extent to which the occupational status of the intelligentsia was breeding undesirable social distinctions. Their concern stemmed partly from a major point of Soviet Marxism, the progressive obliteration of social (if not occupational) distinctions; and it was due partly to a growing awareness of the hostility that would continue to grow among the nonintelligentsia unless decisive steps were taken to lessen these distinctions. Furthermore, Party officials may have supported an easing of the "education barrier" because of their own situation. At the end of the 1950s and early 1960s, when Khrushchev's educational reforms were just going into effect, only 44 percent of the approximately

---

[9] M. N. Rutkevich, "Social Sources of the Replenishment of the Soviet Intelligentsia," *Voprosy Filosofii*, no. 6 (June 1967), pp. 15–25. There is a condensed translation in *Current Digest of the Soviet Press* vol. 19 (September 20, 1967), pp. 14–17.

300 top Party officials possessed a higher education. At the very top, taking the Politburo and Party Secretaries together, the proportion having a higher education rose above 50 percent only after Stalin's death.[10] Khrushchev himself, a coal miner from the age of 15, a capable mine technician later on, had flirted only briefly with higher education at Moscow's Industrial Academy (in 1929–30) before moving yet another step up the Party's bureaucratic ladder.

The intelligentsia owed much to the Party and its leaders; with a few exceptions, its political loyalty was not in question. The real problem was that de-Stalinization was interpreted by many to signal the end of the intelligentsia's privileged position. Furthermore, top economic administrators were discovering that the universities and institutes were turning out young specialists whose knowledge was very theoretical. Graduates were reluctant to "get their hands dirty" learning about production; sometimes they contrived to evade work assignments to the places they were most needed. The number of secondary school graduates seeking admission to the universities and institutes was growing alarmingly. In 1950, there were 242,000 fresh secondary school graduates and 228,000 places offered for full-time study in higher education, not to mention the far less preferable evening and correspondence divisions of higher education, which offered a further 121,000 places. Five years later, there were five secondary school graduates for every full-time place offered in higher education. Even the technicums—intermediate technical training schools—could not handle the overflow. Not only did this disappoint expectations, but it meant that the school system was turning out a surplus of graduates with no labor skills and little desire to acquire any. Small wonder that many parents kept their children at home after graduation. They hired tutors in an effort to get their offspring into the top fifth of the entrance examination scores the following summer; some used political influence to get them admitted.[11]

In chapter 10 we noted Khrushchev's efforts to create respect and understanding for manual labor through the educational system. The larger purpose of his 1958 proposals, of which labor education was but one facet, was to do away with the role of university admissions as a one-way threshold into a privileged world. His original proposal, that of April 1958, would have done away with full-time education altogether from the ninth grade to the third year of higher education. Obligatory

[10] George Fischer, *The Soviet System and Modern Society* (New York: Atherton, 1968), p. 37, and Zbigniew Brzezinski and Samuel P. Huntington, *Political Power: USA/USSR* (New York: Viking Press, 1965), p. 161. Fischer's study included Party secretaries down to the province level, for 1958 and 1962; however, educational backgrounds were known for only 82 percent (1958) and 88 percent (1962) of the individuals in the posts surveyed.

[11] See Robert J. Osborn, *Soviet Social Policies* (Homewood, Ill.: Dorsey Press, 1970, pp. 95–98.

education would be increased from seven to eight years; at the end of the eighth year, at age 15 or 16, those who wished to complete their secondary education in the regular academic track would have to do so in evening schools. Those with no ambition or ability to follow the academic track could enter the already existing system of vocational training schools and technicums, many offering evening programs. Evening education was nothing new—the *rabfak* or "workers' schools" had played quite a role in the 1930s, though they had declined since that time. Now these would be revived as "Schools of Working and Rural Youth," which would combine general education with vocational and technical training.

Had this part of Khrushchev's plan been realized, it would have created a very different type of university entrance procedure. Prospective students would be judged on the basis not only of their scores on the entrance examinations, but of recommendations from their place of work—the local trade union committee, the Komsomol unit, and management itself. Those who did not gain entrance to higher education would already have a trade; or at least they would be in the process of learning one. The technicums and vocational schools would still be open to them, and also higher education via correspondence courses. The lucky minority which gained entrance to the universities and institutes would continue working full time for a year or two, studying in evening courses; later on they would be released from work two or three days a week. Only in their last two years would they study on a full-time basis.

Had these proposals been put into effect, it is not certain they could have changed the pattern of university admissions. Disparities of ability would still be strongly influenced by family circumstances. It would (and will) be a long time before rural and small-town schools are brought up to the level of city schools. It would have taken a quota system of admissions to guarantee equal access for the sons and daughters of collective farmers. The actual reform passed in December 1958 left full-time education in effect. The secondary schools were now decked out with the three adjectives "general education, labor, and polytechnical." They were pledged at least to acquaint their students with production processes and to instill a respect for labor; their ten-year program was lengthened to 11 years to permit this. Universities were to take work experience into account in deciding on admissions, though in what manner was not specified.

The 1958 reform did accomplish some useful things. At some universities and institutes, the proportion of matriculants from families of workers and farmers increased markedly. Some secondary schools were able to give their students experience in production processes. But resistance from officials in the school system and higher education first minimized the impact of the reforms, then secured their abolition piece by piece.

By the time Khrushchev departed from the political scene, little if anything was left of them.

The Limits of Choice

In a real sense, the Khrushchev program's failure was a direct consequence of Stalin's decision around 1930 to build up a conventional European university system to supply the nation's economy with specialists. Along with this move went a further decision to accept the kind of stratification in the universities were bound to produce. The decision was a pragmatic one; ideology had to be readjusted to suit necessity, which was what Stalin did at the 1939 Party Congress in praising the intelligentsia and according it a special place in the system. By the 1950s, higher education's conventional methods and values were well established and strongly supported by the entire educational system. The status of education itself was closely linked to the status of its most valued product, the graduate of a university or institute. The threat which Khrushchev's reforms posed to the educational system was enormous; but educational administrators were able to ward off the reforms' worst impact.

Outside of the regular educational system, only the Communist Party offers an approach which can be called unconventional. The system of Party schools, including the prestigious Higher Party School in Moscow, offer programs geared to the needs chiefly of Party apparatus workers at the time they most need such programs. Khrushchev's principle was embodied in this system long before he rose to prominence: he believed that higher education should be open to those who have already proven themselves in a field of work and are ready to increase their effectiveness at work by increasing their special knowledge. However, not even Khrushchev proposed entrusting specialists' education to the employers themselves; the Party's internal school system is hardly a feasible model today for the rest of the school system. A nonconventional educational structure, one which would at least blur the sharp dividing line created by the university entrance examinations, might possibly have emerged from Lunacharsky's experiments of the 1920s. Once there was great pressure to turn out specialists, prerevolutionary educational methods were resurrected and quickly adapted to Soviet needs. Ever since the watershed period of the 1930s, Soviet leaders have had to live with this decision, and in recent years it has produced its share of official discomfiture.

WORKERS' OPPORTUNITIES AND MOTIVATION

Looking back on the abortive Khrushchev reforms from the perspective of the 1970s, it is easy to dismiss them as a naive effort to get rid of an awkward social division by undermining education itself. Since

Khrushchev's wage reforms have created a situation in which many skilled workers earn more than even middle-level engineers, one wonders why he was not content with altering the reward system. However, events of the Brezhnev era have justified Krushchev's concern. The same problems to social difference with which he attempted to deal have been the object of much discussion and some administrative action, which so far has produced very modest results. An annual flood of press items, which comes to a peak as university entrance examinations get under way in August, testifies to the high social status of jobs held by the intelligentsia. It testifies also to the unwillingness of many young people (and their parents) to content themselves with the worker's lot as a matter of deliberate choice. The secondary schools still have not been doing an adequate job of creating respect for manual labor, let alone providing their students with some direct experience of it. The technicums remain something of a stepchild of the Ministry of Higher Education, and the vocational schools—which are in a system of their own—still have a long way to go to remove their "dead end" stigma.

The director of the Leningrad Machine-Building Combine recently described the great problems his group of plants was experiencing in recruiting young people for ordinary workers' jobs. Almost no graduates of the eight-year and ten-year schools in Leningrad apply for factory work, and so the plants were obliged to recruit dropouts (who constitute over a third of newly hired workers) and to rely on the influx of young people from the countryside; and even the latter source has been drying up. The drive to get into nonmanual occupations has outstripped the economy's present need for these occupations. For this, the structure of the educational system itself is at fault:

> People often say that schools and parents mistakenly encourage young people chiefly to get into higher education, but on the other hand there are objective causes which support teachers and parents in these admonitions. If you inquire into the origin of this constant advice, you come to the following conclusions: First, the ratio of development between higher and vocational education is set incorrectly. Higher education gets a clear preference, which is not justified by economic needs. Secondly, training in vocational schools has seriously deteriorated; in particular, the length of instruction has been shortened too much. Thirdly, the secondary schools are run in a way that they still devote insufficient attention and energy to educating their pupils in respect for labor.[12]

Ironically, the steps undertaken in the Brezhnev era to provide better motivation and status for manual occupations may actually increase the number of applicants seeking admission to higher education. For one

---

[12] G. Kulagin, "Work and the Worker," *Literaturnaya Gazeta*, July 23, 1969.

thing, there has been a drive to enable young workers to complete their secondary school education by expanding the evening schools. The vocational schools, since 1967, have been attempting to make their courses more acceptable by offering the trainees the chance of finishing their secondary education while they are learning a trade. One purpose of this program is to increase the number of applicants to the technicums. However, the same trainees can just as well take their chances on the higher education entrance exams along with all the other young people. Cram courses to prepare applicants for the tough university entrance examinations have been multiplying, under different names and auspices. Evening and correspondence courses to this end have been sponsored by universities themselves. In at least one case, a technical institute agreed to operate a one-year school for full-time study, in which workers from a group of enterprises which financed the school could make up for their often faulty education by spending this year of preparation for the examinations. Many enterprises have programs of sponsoring their more promising workers for admission to the universities.

One type of proposal, however, was dropped after a year of press debate: several universities discussed the possibility of admitting, on a trial basis, promising students who were not able to pass the entrance examinations because of inferior schooling, first of all students from rural areas, but also young workers who had finished secondary school at night. Here orthodoxy prevailed—the Ministry of Higher Education did not intend to fill any of its valuable student places with probable risks. What was done, in the fall of 1969, was to turn the cram courses into a national system under the aegis of the Ministry of Higher Education. Since well-to-do families are able to hire tutors, the Ministry contended that similar assistance should be made available to the children of manual workers, and all young people working at manual occupations.[13]

THE CASE OF THE FARMERS

If it is true that the Soviet regime is able to manipulate social relationships at will, the status of the collective farmers, and to a lesser extent all the lower-paid agricultural workers, forms an important test case. Karl Marx had assumed that central economic planning could simply wipe out the distinction between agricultural and nonagricultural pursuits. In the *Communist Manifesto*, besides calling for "establishment of industrial armies, especially for agriculture," he prophesied that the whole difference between city and country would vanish. Agriculture and industries would be combined somehow, and the population would be more equally distributed. Some Soviet city planners of the 1920s forsaw a

---

[13] Osborn, *Soviet Social Policies*, pp. 128–30.

linear pattern of urban development which would send long fingers of cities reaching into the countryside, bringing both Bolshevik ideas and urban living conditions to the countryside. Such ideas were swept aside with the beginning of collectivization, and it was not until the end of the Stalin era that fresh ideas for transforming the peasantry as a class could be discussed.

Khrushchev's Solutions

Khrushchev, who even before Stalin's death had staked his political career on improving both agriculture and the lot of the farmers, undertook to make good on Marx's promise. He had been forced to retract his 1951 proposal for "agro-cities" the day after it appeared in print, but once in power he pursued a modified version of it. In 1951 he had maintained that the amalgamation of collective farms, then in progress, would make it possible to provide large and well-equipped residential centers for the farmers. He stressed the "city" of "argo-city": the farmer must be provided with everything the city dweller has.[14]

At the time Khrushchev's article appeared, the agro-city idea had been under discussion within the Party officialdom for over a year. Plans for some 50,000 agro-cities lay on the drawing boards, and a prototype city had already been built in the Ukraine in 1949, while Khrushchev still headed the Ukrainian Party. The press attacks which followed Khrushchev's retraction of his *Pravda* article stressed the disruption of agricultural production which building the agro-cities would entail—the farmers were to provide the construction labor themselves, for one thing. But the criticisms also dealt with the proposal to reduce the role of the traditional garden plot, so essential to the diet, well-being and income of the farm family. Under Khrushchev's proposal, these plots would be removed to the outskirts of the new agro-cities. Not only would tending them be more difficult, especially the care of such livestock as the farm household was permitted, but the last distinctive part of the individual farm would vanish. Khrushchev's article was a last-ditch defense of his belief that the farmers were fully capable of accepting urban ways:

> Some architects consider it best to construct settlements of individual single-family dwellings. They follow the contention that the collective farmers have supposedly been accustomed to individual houses, and this, they say, belongs to the collective farmers' psychology. These comrades are profoundly mistaken. It is wrong to think that once people live in the country in individual houses they cannot renounce this habit. It is we who should renounce our old views on the village and on the collective farmers. The present-day collective farmer is capable

[14] *Pravda*, March 4, 1951. The retraction stating that Khrushchev's article had been published merely for the purpose of discussion appeared on March 5.

of understanding all that is best, of rapidly evaluating all that is advanced, and of appraising the advantages of the new if it is convenient for living.[15]

After he came to power, Khrushchev continued to promote the amalgamation of collective farms, together with the expansion of the system of state farms (*sovkhozy*). By 1964, there were 10,000 state farms as against 38,000 collective farms. As the acreage of the collective farms decreased, the acreage of the state farms increased, and in 1970 surpassed that of the collective farms. However, the ideological pronouncements of the Khrushchev period carefully stopped short of predicting that collective farms would be turned into state farms in any short span of time. Rather, the two forms would merge in the distant future in a form of property that is neither state nor collective, but "social property." This would provide Marxian basis for eliminating the last class distinctions:

> Under socialism, as is known, there still are classes—the working class and the peasantry. This is due to the existence of two forms of social property, to the preservation of differences between town and country, to the existence of different forms of distribution of material wealth.[16]

The whole matter of private plots was passed over in silence in policy statements, save for the prediction that one day they would become unnecessary and be dropped voluntarily. The agro-city proposal was now offered not as any sudden transformation of rural life, but as the end result of natural development of rural population centers. The Brezhnev regime, which has not been inclined to multiply ideological pronouncements in any field, has added little to the Khrushchev-era statements. Its willingness to pour vastly greater investments into agriculture, and its practical steps toward improving rural incomes and fringe benefits (see chapter 3) speak more clearly than any new ideological developments possibly could.

Persisting Problems

About the Soviet farmers as a class or stratum we have much less satisfactory information than we do about the intelligentsia and the industrial workers. Even the young discipline of Soviet sociology has not devoted nearly the attention to the countryside that it has to factory life

---

[15] Ibid. Translation from James H. Meisel and Edward S. Kozera (eds.), *Materials for the Study of the Soviet System* (Ann Arbor, Mich.: George Wahr Publishing Co., 1953), p. 576.

[16] *Fundamentals of Marxism-Leninism* (Moscow: Foreign Languages Publishing House, n.d.) p. 809.

and the urban world. Foreign visitors have a good deal of contact with the Soviet intelligentsia, and occasional contact with urban workers, but it is rare that a foreigner gets more than a tourist look at the farms. Therefore any statements about the farmers must be made with unusual caution.

As to income, the Minister of Agriculture stated in 1970 that rural incomes, including those of workers on the state farms, were about 15 percent lower than urban wages.[17] This seems just a bit optimistic in the light of other evidence. Introduction of minimum wage legislation and social security benefits has improved rural cash incomes vastly over their level at the time of Stalin's death. In 1968, state farmers were earning (exclusive of income from private plots) 92 rubles monthly as against an urban wage average of 112 rubles. But collective farmers' earnings, by one estimate, were recently between 15 and 25 percent below those of state farmers.[18]

As to status of the occupation of collective farmer or agricultural worker, the main evidence is available in the form of press items and occasional sociological surveys concerning the constant drain of young people from the farms. The writer knew quite a number of university students who had come from collective farms, and while their love of the countryside was genuine, all considered that they had "made it" out of the farms and would never return to them in any job capacity. As to what causes other young people to stay or to return, Soviet sociologists have yet to make a comprehensive study. The most important overt limitations on the status of farmers have to do with their mobility. Most were not included in the internal passport system that was introduced in the 1930s. Those who did not leave as young people found their ability to leave later made difficult or blocked outright. Also, the absence of an internal passport can be quite a handicap in ordinary travel within the Soviet Union.

We saw earlier the limited access of rural youth education. While many do "make it" to the best universities and good jobs, most are handicapped by the poor quality of rural schools. This disparity in school quality is due to a variety of factors: lower investments, the unwillingness of teachers' institute graduates to go to the villages, and the difficulties— incredible in Western eyes—of transporting village children to and from school. The transportation difficulties, which come not so much from a lack of vehicles as from an abysmal lack of paved roads, have made it necessary to construct boarding facilities. These increase the per-pupil costs of education severalfold, and cannot possibly be extended to cover

---

[17] Roy D. Laird, "Prospects for Soviet Agriculture," *Problems of Communism* 20 (September–October 1971), p. 34.

[18] David Lane, *Politics and Society in the USSR* (New York: Random House, 1971), p. 400.

the entire rural secondary school population. All this accounts for the discouraging result, for young people from the farms, of the Novosibirsk study cited earlier. Of secondary school graduates who were sons and daughters of agricultural workers, whether from collective or state farms, 90 percent wished to continue studying, but only 10 percent realized this ambition. For the children of industrial and construction workers, the proportions were 89 and 61 percent respectively—that is, the great majority realized at least the goal of entering higher education or the technicums.

In spite of many individual improvements in their situation in recent years, Soviet farmers as a group continue to rank low in income, status, education, and power. It remains to be seen to what extent the recent improvements in income will be accompanied by improvements in the other three categories.

DECISIONS AND MOTIVES

Until Khrushchev's time, the decisions that most strongly affected stratification were based on short-term economic and political needs, rather than on long-term goals of social change. The exceptions to this were those of the first ten years after the Revolution, when the "left communists" were appeased for the time being in certain areas. These included the opening up of the educational system (including, for example, abolition of examinations in higher education) and the narrowed wage and salary differentials that prevailed until the First Five-Year Plan. However, even Lenin's agreement to the wage policies of the 1920s may be seen as an effort to maintain the cooperation of the trade unions, some of whose officials had supported opposition platforms within the Party in 1920–21. Stalin's wage policy served as a lever for allocating labor resources and a means of rewarding the most loyal segments of the proletariat; his economic pillage of the countryside, which resulted in low rewards and status for the peasantry for three decades thereafter, solved his immediate economic and political problems in the manner described in chapters 1 and 2; his promotion of quasi-elitist educational policies, and the social and economic stratification which this supported, grew out of the economy's pressing need for specialists, and to a lesser extent from the desirability of perpetuating the rewards given to the new officialdom by conferring them on their sons and daughters as well.

Khrushchev's campaign for reducing differences in strata had its short-term motivations as well, but among his motives was that of playing the role of leader of progress toward a new form of society in which distinctions between strata would at least be greatly reduced. His educational reforms of 1958 attempted to combine this goal with the goal of making secondary and higher education better adapted to the needs of a mature industrial economy. The new wage policies effected in 1956–59 were an effort to bring the lowest wage categories up to a tolerable level, and thereby to eliminate one of the worst features of Stalin's wage system. Khrushchev's largely unsuccessful efforts to eliminate glaring examples of privilege among the officialdom and the intelligentsia formed one kind of bid for wider support of his de-Stalinization campaign and an aid to the legitimacy of his administration. In short, this was an effort to gain political support by moving in the direction of professed Soviet Marxist ideals concerning society, in a series of well-publicized campaigns which stressed indirectly the ways in which Stalin had neglected these ideals.

The Brezhnev-Kosygin administration, while not abandoning these ideals, has moderated the policies which Khrushchev set in motion. In the case of educational opportunity, it cancelled Khrushchev's reforms altogether but sought to achieve his major goals by encouraging a degree of diversity and experimentation, for example in the admission of educationally disadvantaged students (e.g., those from rural schools) to higher education by way of special preparatory programs. The wage "floor" has been raised further, but without reducing the essential character of wage and salary differentials. In short, the present Soviet leaders have shared Khrushchev's view of the present political necessity of making progress toward certain key social goals; but they have sought to achieve this progress without antagonizing the portions of the intelligentsia which had earlier felt threatened by it, a strategy which today involves serious compromises.

FOR FURTHER READING

Studies of stratification in Soviet society must be sought in a variety of articles and chapters in books. Historical and contemporary surveys of the question include the following: Robert A. Feldmesser, "Social Classes and Political Structure," in Cyril E. Black (ed.), *The Transformation of Russian Society* (Cambridge, Mass.: Harvard University Press, 1967); David Lane, *Politics and Society in the USSR* (New York: Random House, 1971), chapter 12, "Social Stratification"; and Paul Hollander, *American and Soviet Society: A Reader in Comparative Sociology and Perception* (Englewood Cliffs, N.J.: Prentice-Hall, 1969), Part III, "Social Stratification."

The experience of Soviet citizens with social stratification during the Stalin era is dealt with in the analysis of interviews with displaced persons from the Soviet Union after World War II, in Alex Inkeles and Raymond A. Bauer, *The Soviet Citizen: Daily Life in a Totalitarian Society* (Cambridge, Mass.: Harvard University Press, 1961) chapters 4 and 13. See also Alex Inkeles, "Social Stratification and Mobility in the Soviet Union, 1940–1950," *American Sociological Review* 15 (1950), pp. 465–79.

The purposes and impact of the 1958 education reforms, as they related to stratification and mobility, are discussed in George Z. F. Bereday and Jaan Pennar (eds.), *The Politics of Soviet Education* (New York: Praeger, 1960). For developments during the 1960s see Robert J. Osborn, *Soviet Social Policies: Welfare, Equality and Community* (Homewood, Ill.: Dorsey Press, 1970), chapter 4, and Raymond Poignant, *Education and Development in Western Europe, the United States, and the U.S.S.R.: A Comparative Study* (New York: Teachers College Press, 1969).

Recent Soviet studies of educational aspirations and mobility include M. N. Rutkevich (ed.), *The Career Plans of Youth* (New York: International Arts and Sciences Press, 1969), and V. N. Shubkin, "Youth Enters Life," *Current Digest of the Soviet Press* 17 (August 18, 1965), pp. 3–9. For other Soviet commentaries see Fred Ablin (ed.), *Education in the U.S.S.R.* (2 vols.; New York: International Arts and Sciences Press, 1963), and the periodical *Soviet Education*, likewise published by the International Arts and Sciences Press.

On the history of wage and salary differentials, see Abram Bergson, *The Structure of Soviet Wages* (Cambridge, Mass.: Harvard University Press, 1944); Murray Yanowitch, "The Soviet Income Revolution," *Slavic Review* 22 (December 1963), pp. 683–97; Osborn, *Soviet Social Policies*, chapter 5; and Robert Conquest (ed.), *Industrial Workers in the U.S.S.R.* (New York: Praeger, 1967), chapter 2.

On the status of Soviet farmers, see David W. Bronson and Constance B. Krueger, "The Revolution in Soviet Farm Household Income, 1953–1967," and Alexander Vucinich, "The Peasants as a Social Class," both in James R. Millar (ed.), *The Soviet Rural Community* (Urbana, Ill.: University of Illinois Press, 1971), pp. 214–58 and 307–24. The history of the Russian peasantry as a class is summarized in Lazar Volin, "The Russian Peasant: From Emancipation to Kolkhoz," in Black, *The Transformation of Russian Society*, pp. 292–311.

Soviet research on the problem of occupational prestige is examined in Murray Yanowitch and Norton T. Dodge, "The Social Evaluation of Occupations in the Soviet Union," *Slavic Review* 28 (December 1969), pp. 619–43.

13

NATIONS AND FEDERALISM

The young Soviet regime's most difficult policy areas were those in which enormous practical problems were attended by the need for radical adaptation of Marxist prophecies to circumstances that Marx had not foreseen. The decision to build a socialist order in spite of the failure of a European proletarian revolution was of this kind, one which compelled a socialist regime to squeeze from the population the sacrifices that capitalism should have exacted instead. If any other problem approached this in magnitude, it was most certainly the decision to build a multinational political system out of the nationalities of the former Russian Empire. Here also the policy was premature by Marx's own standards, since the majority of the non-Russian nations were just then entering a phase of growing nationalism which Marx held to be characteristic of the early bourgeois period. Moscow's problems in dealing with these many nationalisms, including the nationalism of the Russians themselves, have persisted to this day. It was the early decisions concerning federalism and the status of national cultures, which have been upheld to this day, that virtually guaranteed future conflicts.

THE MULTINATIONAL EMPIRE

From a Marxist point of view, Russia in the early 20th century was even less likely to produce a proletarian movement among the 56 percent of its population that was non-Russian than among the ethnic Russians. The Russian Empire's proletarians, defined as industrial workers and those in industry-related wage employment, not only were a small minority of the population, but were mainly Russians. There were also small proletarian elements among the Latvians, Armenians, Poles, Finns, and Jews.

FRANZ JOSEF LAND

BARENTS SEA

NOVAYA

ZEMLYA

KARA SEA

BALTIC SEA

KARELIAN A.S.S.R.

23 3 Tallin
Vilnius Riga 2 1

Minsk

BYELORUSSIAN
S.S.R.

Kishinev

Kiev

RUSSIAN

Moscow

KOMI
A.S.S.R.

UKRAINIAN S.S.R.

4

SOVIET

FEDERATED

BLACK
SEA

5

6 7

8 9

10

11

12

13
17 14
16 Tbilisi 15

Yerevan

19 18

20 21

Baku

CASPIAN SEA

22

KAZAKH S.S.R.

TURKMEN S.S.R.

UZBEK S.S.R.

Ashkhabad

Frunze

Alma-Ata

Tashkent

KIRGHIZ S.S.R.

TADZHIK S.S.R.

Dushanbe

1. Estonian S.S.R.	13. Kabardino-Balkar A.S.S.R.
2. Latvian S.S.R.	14. North Osetian A.S.S.R.
3. Lithuanian S.S.R.	15. Chechen-Ingush A.S.S.R.
4. Moldavian S.S.R.	16. Adzharian A.S.S.R.
5. Mordvin A.S.S.R.	17. Georgian S.S.R.
6. Chuvash A.S.S.R.	18. Daghestan A.S.S.R.
7. Mari A.S.S.R.	19. Armenian S.S.R.
8. Tatar A.S.S.R.	20. Nakhichevan' A.S.S.R.
9. Udmurt A.S.S.R.	21. Azerbaidzhan S.S.R.
10. Bashkir A.S.S.R.	22. Karakalpak A.S.S.R.
11. Kalmyk A.S.S.R.	23. Kaliningrad Province of the
12. Abkhazian A.S.S.R.	R.S.F.S.R.

Source: **George Kish,** *Economic Atlas of the Soviet Union,* 2d ed. rev. (Ann Arbor, Mich: University of Michigan Press, 1971), p. 4. By permission of the University of Michigan Press.

CHUKCHI SEA

WRANGEL IS.

SEVERNAYA ZEMLYA

NEW SIBERIAN IS.

LAPTEV SEA

BERING SEA

YAKUT A.S.S.R.

REPUBLIC

SOCIALIST

SEA OF OKHOTSK

SAKHALIN IS.

KURIL IS.

BURYAT-MONGOL A.S.S.R.

SEA OF JAPAN

•   Republic Capitals

▬▬▬   International Boundaries

────── Boundaries of Soviet
          Socialist Republics (S.S.R.)

········ Boundaries of Autonomous
          Soviet Socialist Republics
          (A.S.S.R.)

MILES   0   250   500   750   1000

The many other non-Russian nations farmed, fished, hunted, and pursued the ancient occupations of preindustrial cities. Their historical experiences were very diverse, and they stood at different stages of cultural development. Some of these nations could look back on a glorious national past in the form of feudal kingdoms: these included the Poles, the Lithuanians, the Georgians, the Tatars, and some of the Turkic peoples of Central Asia. Others, including many ethnic groups of Siberia, had not even progressed to the point of a written alphabet or to territorial organization as a nation. Some had spawned a small bourgeoisie in the form of wealthy merchants or small peasant proprietors; others had a distinctly feudal society. What they all shared was the experience of Russian domination and third-class citizenship. Nationalities were recognized mainly as linguistic categories for the benefit of the national census. National cultural aspirations, where they existed, were usually met with repression; of national independence there could be no talk; autonomy in local administration had been granted only to Finland, a special case, and to certain rulers in Central Asia; Georgia's strong cultural autonomy was tolerated.

Some of the non-Russian nations appeared to be on the eve of an upsurge in national feeling at the turn of the century. If, according to Marx, nationalism is a means whereby a rising bourgeoisie can shatter the bonds of feudal rule which have restrained it, the non-Russians of the Empire had a potent weapon to use when the opportunity arose. An important part in the 1905 disturbances was played by non-Russians; in every major non-Russian area, including even the Buryat Mongols and Yakuts in eastern Siberia, there was a movement for political autonomy and the recognition of national rights.

Many of the non-Russian parties that suddenly emerged from a semi-underground existence in 1905 made specific demands. In the Ukraine, the People's Party wanted nothing less than independence, while three other parties would have settled for local autonomy and a Ukrainian parliament. The Polish National Democrats, who held about 50 seats in the first two State Dumas, tried to introduce legislation for Polish autonomy; the left-wing Polish parties stressed coordination of the revolutionary movement with other left-wing parties of the Empire. There were analogous movements in the three Baltic nations, also in Georgia, Armenia, and Finland. Only the Finns made any concrete gains, in this case somewhat enlarging the autonomy they already enjoyed. Among Russian Jews there were both Zionist and anti-Zionist organizations, plus some smaller groups which embraced both Zionism and socialism. The All-Russian Moslem League, formed in 1905, failed to create agreement on joint political aims for the Empire's numerous and geographically scattered Moslem nationalities, but it did press for autonomy in cultural matters.

In most of the major non-Russian nations, there was a debate over whether to stress national goals (independence or autonomy) or to cooperate with other nationalities in pressing for political and economic changes. If cooperation could bring about these changes—whether reform or revolution—was not the stress on national goals narrow and self-defeating? Most of the Marxist and leftist parties struck a compromise on this issue by coupling a program for a general revolution by all nations of the Russian Empire with demands for autonomy within a future federation.

This choice had potentially sweeping implications for the future of Russia and the Russians. The Russians themselves were an ethnic minority in their own Empire, constituting (according to the 1897 census) only 44 percent of a total population of 125 million. Three quarters of the population was Slavic, including 22 million Ukrainians, 6 million Byelorussians, and 8 million Poles. Jews, Kazakhs, Tatars, and Kirghiz numbered several million each; others whose numbers exceeded the one-million figure were Azerbaidzhanians, Armenians, Lithuanians, Latvians, Germans, Moldavians, Mordvins, and Bashkirs. Altogether the Empire's census recognized some 126 linguistic groups, and the actual ethnographic figure far exceeded that number.[1] A truly federal structure could have ended ethnic Russian domination of this vast territory; secession by the major non-Russian nations not only would have reduced the territory considerably, but would have cut off the Ukraine's rich soil, Baku's oil, Central Asia's cotton and silk, Poland's coal, and some vital access routes to the outside world. Much of Russia's recent wealth had been built on its domination of the non-Russian areas. Its routes of access to the outside world led through non-Russian areas; an independent Ukraine, for example, would control the key commercial port of Odessa. Concerted action by the other great powers to wrest the non-Russian areas from Moscow's control could reduce the remaining ethnic Russia to a second-rate power. The result would be hardly different if the non-Russian nations were to become independent by their own efforts. Either they would have to seek the protection of foreign powers in order to forestall eventual Russian reconquest (e.g., Poland under France's protection in the 1920 war with Soviet Russia, and thereafter); or else these same foreign powers, in order to protect and expand their investments, would move in uninvited to establish protectorates. In short, Russia's place in the world depended heavily on its ability to retain control of most of the ethnically non-Russian areas.

THE ALTERNATIVES

What, then, were the alternatives to continuing the Russian Empire's policy of absolute dominion over the non-Russians? The evolution of

---

[1] See the table in David Lane, *Politics and Society in the USSR* (New York: Random House, 1971), p. 431. Since the 1897 census defined nationalities by language only, the ethnographic figure for many groups was somewhat larger.

Soviet federalism is usually discussed in terms of Marxist theory, because those who made the decisions were Marxists. Ironically, although Lenin and Stalin are associated with a policy of reunifying the former Empire's territory at all costs, both Marx's own thinking and Lenin's original slogan of national self-determination were entirely compatible with granting national independence. Assuming, as both Marx and Lenin did, that the coming proletarian revolution would embrace much of Europe, a proletarian-ruled Russia could survive, even stripped of its non-Russian areas, with help from Germany and elsewhere. However, none of the major Russian-dominated political movements of the prerevolutionary years actually favored breaking up the Russian Empire. Among the non-Russians, opinion at the turn of the century and in 1905 was divided on the whole matter of independence, partly because independence might mean simply delivering one's self into the hands of another great power.

In the wake of the 1905 revolution, the Constitutional Democrats (Kadets) came forth with a proposal for cultural autonomy and the removal of all ethnic discrimination. While they supported autonomy for Finland and Poland, the Kadets rejected federation on the ground that ethnic Russia would far outweigh the other national units. If adopted, the Kadet program might have reconciled many of the non-Russian nations to their status in the Russian Empire. In any case, the Kadets did little to raise the national question in the Duma, and in fact a portion of their membership was opposed even to this limited program.[2]

The Social Revolutionaries, by contrast, were quite interested in the national question. They enjoyed the support of socialists among the national minorities, and in 1905 came out unequivocally in favor of federation:

> A democratic republic with broad autonomy of regions and communities (*obshchiny*) both urban and rural; and widest possible application of the federal principle to the relations among the individual nationalities; the recognition of the native languages in all local, public, and state institutions . . . ; in areas with a mixed population, the right of every nationality to a part of the budget devoted to cultural and educational purposes, proportionate to its number, and to the disposal of such funds on the bases of self-rule.[3]

Unfortunately, the Social Revolutionaries too were divided on this proposal, and many members were opposed to a clause promising the "unconditional right to self-determination."

The actual options of 1917 were a good deal narrower than those of 1905. The Provisional Government hedged on the whole issue of inde-

---

[2] See the excerpts from the text of the January 1906 proposals in Richard Pipes, *The Formation of the Soviet Union*, rev. ed. (New York: Atheneum, 1968), p. 29.

[3] Ibid., p. 31.

pendence and autonomy, deferring it for consideration in the Constituent Assembly. But its promise of independence for Poland and Finland undermined this stance, and probably served to hasten the Ukrainian Rada's steps toward independence. More than anything else it was the Bolshevik seizure of power which gave impetus to those national movements which were still debating independence. Either they opposed remaining together with a Bolshevik Russia, or they believed that Lenin was offering national self-determination at face value.

In 1917, therefore, when independence had become a real option for the major non-Russian nations, the only strategy which might have kept them voluntarily united with Russia was federalism on liberal terms *plus* an international motive to make a Russian connection more desirable than whatever the alternative connections were. Armenians and Georgians, for example, would still be likely to prefer alliance with Russia to domination by Turkey. For Poland and Finland, on the other hand, Allied support together with the removal of any kind of German threat (indeed, German support was welcomed by the Finnish White forces) made it very unlikely that the Russians could devise any similar kind of motive. For the Ukraine, it would have been equally difficult to devise a motive, save possibly for offering the reconquest of Galicia (the western Ukraine) from Poland as the reward of federation with Moscow.

MARX ON NATIONHOOD

Marx and Engels held that neither nations nor nationalism had existed before the modern, postfeudal age. These were specific products of the bourgeois era. They became weapons in the hands of the rising bourgeoisie, which took the fact of ethnic differences and turned it into a holy principle. This principle made an effective weapon against the feudal order, and it had the advantage of being all-embracing with respect to classes: it appealed to all classes within a given nation, hence served as a powerful call for political unity. Even where absolutist rulers had used a type of nationalism to support their rule, as in England and France, the bourgeoisie took matters a step further: nations alone could legitimize rulers, not divine right or feudal grants of power. Once in power, said Marx, the bourgeoisie made nationalism an important part of its "superstructure," the whole system of institutions, beliefs, and culture which was used to support an economic system, in this case capitalism. Because the bourgeoisie ascribed power to the entire nation, it also supported doctrines of political equality and representative government. These in turn formed a convenient mask of solicitude for human rights. They diverted attention from the way in which the capitalist economy was building an enormous exploited class of proletarians, and was intensifying its exploitation of them.

The bourgeoisie did not face reality in appealing to industrial workers with its nationalism, said Marx. The industrial proletariat was a nation apart, a people excluded from participating in the national culture. Its world was restricted to the factory and the factory town; it received little education; it had little leisure with which to acquaint itself with the lives of its fellow countrymen in other walks of life. Peasants, at least, imbibed the traditions of their forefathers, which were a part of the national culture. But the proletariat lived in a new world. This world was oppressive and debasing, offering no escape for its inhabitants save the path of revolt. Yet this very oppression, according to Marx, was shaping a new kind of man and a new culture.

Up to this point, one cannot fault Marx's reasoning, considering the times he lived in. Numerous official investigations in England provided data for his conclusions, beginning with the reports of the Factories Inquiry Commission in 1833. The novels of Émile Zola are in a sense firsthand reports which support Marx. Friedrich Engels, at the very outset of his lifelong collaboration with Marx, wrote a detailed and most impressive study of the English working classes, in which he observed:

> In the circumstances it is not surprising that the working classes have become a race apart from the English bourgeoisie. The middle classes have more in common with every other nation in the world than with the proletariat which lives on their own doorsteps. The workers differ from the middle classes in speech, in thoughts and ideas, customs, morals, politics and religion. They are two quite different nations, as unlike as if they were differentiated by race.[4]

From this judgment, Marx drew an international political conclusion: the proletariat of one country is essentially like the proletariat of every other country. Hence nationalisms cannot divide the proletariat. Proletarians can cooperate across national boundaries and coordinate their political activities, since nothing divides them as the bourgeoisie is divided. Given a proper mechanism for coordination, the proletarian revolution can and must be international, giving way to a huge transnational society in which national differences will ultimately vanish. Said the *Communist Manifesto:*

> The workingmen have no country. We cannot take from them what they do not have. Since the proletariat must first of all acquire political supremacy, must rise to be the leading class of the nation, must constitute itself *the* nation, it is to this extent national itself, though not in the bourgeois sense of the word.
>
> National differences and antagonisms among peoples are daily more and more vanishing, owing to the development of the bourgeoisie, to

---

[4] Friedrich Engels, *The Condition of the Working Class in England* (Stanford, Calif.: Stanford University Press, 1958), p. 139.

freedom of commerce, to the world market, to uniformity in the mode of production and in the conditions of life which it entails.

The supremacy of the proletariat will cause them to vanish still faster. . . .

In proportion as the exploitation of one individual by another put to an end, the exploitation of one nation by another will also be put to an end. In proportion as the antagonism among classes within the nation vanishes, the hostility of one nation to another will come to an end.[5]

THE DILEMMA OF SELF-DETERMINATION

Should Marxists support movements for national independence and autonomy? There were several possible approaches. National Marxist parties could follow the formula Marx prescribed for German communists in 1849 by helping each bourgeoisie complete its own nationalist revolution. This would strengthen left-wing forces—one could not yet speak of an industrial proletariat—and prepare them for a future proletarian struggle. A more direct route to power would be Marxist support of national aims simply as a tactic for ending Tsarist rule, followed by a coordinated strategy of Marxist parties throughout the former Empire to end bourgeois rule as soon as possible. A big question here, one which was important to Lenin, was whether these national aims embraced political independence, or only political or cultural autonomy. A third possibility was to concentrate on the class conflict only.

Marx's own stand on national independence movements turned on the capacity of any given movement to promote the proletarian revolution. He was against national independence movements among the smaller nationalities; from his own observations on the many small states of pre-Bismarckian Germany, he concluded that the proletariat would be most effective politically in large states. He recognized the value of national independence movements in threatening Europe's multinational empires; but his support for them varied from one situation to the next. In 1870 he urged Russian socialists to work for the independence of Poland; this, among other things, would assist in the eventual overthrow of the German government. Later in the 1870s he advised Polish socialists to delay their demands in order not to work against the revolutionary situation which Marx believed had arisen in Russia.[6]

What of the nations of the Russian Empire in the event a Russian-led proletariat revolution succeeded? Few Russian Marxists believed the revo-

---

[5] Translation adapted from Lewis S. Feuer (ed.), *Marx and Engels: Basic Writings on Politics and Philosophy* (New York: Anchor Books, 1959), p. 26.

[6] Robert Conquest (ed.), *Soviet Nationalities Policy in Practice* (New York: Praeger, 1967), p. 15.

lution could happen soon. Still, the very possibility created a new set of problems. Would these nations be free to separate and go their own ways? Would the Russian proletariat assume some kind of tutelage over them and guide them toward socialism? Was some kind of federation desirable or possible? If non-Marxist nationalist parties gained control of the non-Russian nations, should they be overthrown? During the disturbances of 1905, national independence under nationalist (nonsocialist) auspices loomed as a real possibility.

In 1917, independence was within the grasp of these nations well before the Bolshevik seizure of power. For example, in the summer of 1917 the Ukrainian Rada (Council) had declared self-determination for the Ukraine, but without separating from Russia at that point. The Bolshevik coup made a decision on national independence imperative for some of the nationalities: the Ukrainian Rada for the moment cooperated with the Bolsheviks; the Byelorussian National Congress declared its land's independence; Georgians and Armenians cooperated to form a provisional Transcaucasian government; independence movements quickly gained the upper hand in Finland, the Baltic states, and Poland, though the latter two were still under German occupation. The disintegration of Russia as a political unit was no longer just a fear of Lenin's, but a reality.

Lenin's Strategy

While many Russian socialists were talking of autonomy and federation as solutions to the national question, Lenin took a radical stand for the right of national self-determination. By this slogan he meant nothing less than the right of nations to secede and form their own governments. Alongside the right of seccession, he urged rights for national minorities in other contexts as well: the abolition of disabilities based on nationality, the right to education in one's native language, and linguistic equality in other contexts. The statement of national rights was only half of his thinking, however; *how* these rights should be used was another matter. Using the right of self-determination to secede and form an independent state may or may not be expedient; in any case, said Lenin, this choice must be subordinated to the requirements of the class struggle.

In the Russian Empire, the slogan of self-determination was useful to Lenin primarily for helping complete the bourgeois-democratic revolution. Whether national separation would help do this was a question to be determined in each individual case. As for minority rights, these did not mean promotion of national cultures. Lenin had been arguing this point with the Austrian Social Democrats, who sought support from the non–German-speaking majority of the Austro-Hungarian Empire by promoting cultural autonomy as such: "A struggle against any national oppression—unreservedly yes. A struggle on behalf of any national development, of 'national culture' in general—unreservedly no."[7] At the Second Party Congress in 1903 Lenin had vigorously opposed autonomous status within the party for the Jewish *Bund*, among other things because it would necessarily stress the Jewish cultural identity, since the Jews lacked a compact ethnic territory within the Russian Empire. Finally, since big states are the best setting for capitalism to complete its work and the proletariat to organize in great masses, Lenin held that bigness is to be promoted and movement toward national separation to be resisted.

Independence, Autonomy, or Solidarity: The Socialist Debate

Lenin's views on the national question had been incorporated into the 1903 Party Program. At the time they had provoked little debate; this was not one of the issues that divided Bolsheviks and Mensheviks. A decade later, many Mensheviks were beginning to recognize nationalism as a general positive force and to give it a definite place in their programs. The Austrian socialist leaders had come out in defense of nationalism, and the powerful Georgian Mensheviks were attracted by the idea. There was a challenge from the opposite ideological direction as well: Rosa Luxemburg, the famous Polish socialist, had stirred up a good deal of debate with her doctrine of strict, uncompromising internationalism. While she was not as rigid in her deprecation of national aspirations as were some of her supporters, "Luxemburgism" was gaining quite a following in Eastern Europe in the 1900s.

Lenin's problem was one not only of present strategy, but also of the proposed structure of a future socialist state. The Mensheviks and a number of national parties saw cultural autonomy in a federal state as the solution. To Lenin this was anathema because it would promote national cultures at a time when they ought to be on the wane, giving way to a single proletarian society. If socialists became involved in promoting nationhood itself, they would open a door for continued bourgeois rule. From the point of view of revolutionary strategy, cultural autonomy was a reformist goal which could only undermine a united proletarian effort. In national areas where most of the people to whom Lenin wished to appeal were peasants rather than proletarians, and as peasants a prey to nationalist appeals, the cry for cultural autonomy was a doubly dangerous move.

The Bolsheviks at this point were carrying on their work in various cities of the Austro-Hungarian Empire—Prague, Vienna, Krakow. In recent decades these had been the scene of powerful bids for cultural autonomy by the major nationalities of that ramshackle empire. All around him, Lenin saw bourgeois-led nationalist parties making great

---

[7] Ibid., p. 17.

strides; he feared that triumphant nationalism would delay working-class action by decades. As a Marxist, Lenin could have accepted these developments with equanimity: the bourgeoisie must triumph before bourgeois society can give birth to its own proletariat, and nationalism is the immediate vehicle of this triumph. But Lenin the strategist, the "compulsive revolutionary," was forever seeking shortcuts through history. Deflating bourgeois nationalism before it was firmly established, lest it infect the workers and peasants, was one such shortcut.

Stalin on the National Question

Lenin chose none other than Stalin to defend his position. Stalin's *Marxism and the National and Colonial Question* (1913) remains today a basic piece of Soviet doctrine on the national question. This reiterated Lenin's doctrine of national self-determination and made certain other points explicit. It conceded the need for federalism as a temporary political phase, while stressing the unitary state as the only true proletarian state. The Austrians had accepted the idea of *extraterritorial* nationalism, that is, the recognition of nations as nations, whether they occupied a compact national area or not. To counter this demand, Lenin proposed *regional* rather than *national* autonomy. That is, autonomy would come in the form of multinational geographical subdivisions, not in the form of a special place for nationalities as such. This would serve to discourage the growth of nationalism, and it took account of the great mixing of nationalities in Eastern Europe, the Caucasus, and elsewhere, which made it impossible to create geographical units on a strictly ethnic basis. This point was to prove very important in the Soviet concept of federalism. Within the framework of regional autonomy, the rights of all national minorities would be guaranteed, particularly the use of their languages. Given these rights, the demand for a separate political status will dry up. The Party must be a unitary one, wrote Stalin, but here too a certain regional autonomy may be recognized. This decision dates from 1903, actually: the Jewish *Bund's* walkout from the Second Party Congress occurred first of all over the issue of a federalized party.

In a way, Lenin was right in regarding nationalism as a virus capable of destroying socialist unity. The outbreak of World War I promptly shattered the Second International, most of whose constituent parties elected to support the war effort of their respective governments; only in Russia and Serbia did socialist parties oppose the war. Socialist debates over the role of nationalism went on. Lenin after 1914 became convinced that nationalism in Europe was on the way out, that class struggles would be carried on within great multinational states and across international boundaries. He did predict that nationalism could strike a blow against all the colonial powers in their colonial holdings, and he did not exclude the possibility that wartime conquests or renewed despotism after the war would evoke resistance of a nationalist type. Nationalism for Lenin was a force to be exploited at a given time, not a deep-rooted social reality to be treated as such.

Lenin returned to Russia in April 1917 bearing the same doctrine of extremes which he had written into his Party's first program: self-determination and independence on one hand, a unitary workers' state on the other; nationalism as a vital political force, supranational classes as the result. Once in power, he quickly improvised a middle ground: federation as the constitutional form, national cultures with proletarian content as the social goal. But the original program left its imprint on Soviet policies both at home and abroad, in the form of blind spots regarding nationalism, an inability to cope with some of the central questions posed by the many non-Russian nations.[8]

THE BOLSHEVIK DILEMMA AFTER 1917

The Decree on Peace, the Bolsheviks' first official act in 1917, interpreted "peace without annexations" to mean self-determination by open referendum after the complete withdrawal of foreign troops. The Declaration of the Rights of the Peoples of Russia, issued a week later, stressed the point that self-determination included the option of national independence. The Declaration also called for "the free development of national minorities and ethnic groups inhabiting the territory of Russia," which suggested that national cultural development would be at least indulged.

For a time after the Bolsheviks took power, their relations with the non-Russian peoples were a matter of theory and propaganda only, for most of these areas lay beyond Bolshevik control. The Ukraine, Byelorussia, and Poland had been handed to the Germans in the Brest-Litovak treaty of March 1918; Finland had already declared its independence; German-supported White (i.e., anti-Bolshevik) forces conquered the Baltic states and ultimately brought independence to them; British and French forces intervened in the Ukraine and Transcaucasia in support of White forces there; other White forces controlled much of Siberia, and the Japanese occupied parts of the Russian Far East until 1922.

The Bolshevik victories of 1919 and 1920, which brought the Civil War to an end, raised a critical problem: Was the Red Army coming as a proletarian conqueror, or to uphold national self-determination regardless of its political auspices? Poland, the Baltic states, and Finland had become independent and gone their own ways; their new governments were anti-Soviet; and Moscow had acquiesced in the new situation

---
[8] See the analysis of the evolution of Lenin's thinking in Pipes, *The Formation of the Soviet Union*, chapter 1.

in signing the Treaty of Riga in 1921 (though not until after a brief Soviet-Polish war, which the Poles had launched, had brought Soviet troops almost to Warsaw before they were repulsed). If, on the withdrawal of foreign troops from the south in 1920, nationalist parties gained the upper hand in the Ukraine, Georgia, Armenia, and Central Asia, must Moscow acquiesce in the independence of these nations too, under nonsocialist governments? If not, what kind of strategy other than outright conquest would bring them into the Bolshevik orbit?

It is not surprising that Lenin altered his position on national self-determination somewhat, though one may argue that it was the application of his theory that was altered rather than the theory itself, whose consistency Lenin defended to the last. Federalism, in any case, was a departure from Lenin's prerevolutionary idea, whether it represented a change of theory or only a strategy. The last major undertaking of Lenin's career was supervising the preparation of the USSR Constitution of 1923, which created a federation of socialist republics. Lenin's office in the Kremlin, restored today as it was when illness last took him from his desk, was decked out with maps on which the location of ethnic groups had been pencilled in great detail. This effort represented the compromise he was offering to the many national minorities at the close of several years of bitter strife with them.

Moscow's Strife with the Nationalities

The Bolshevik regime took prompt action to see to it that national self-determination worked in favor of reunification. In the Ukraine, the Rada's first move was not toward national independence, but toward a federation with Moscow. A temporary coalition between the Rada and local Bolsheviks at the time of the Bolshevik coup soon disintegrated over a variety of issues. The Rada then arrested the local Bolshevik leaders, and Lenin delivered an ultimatum threatening war if the Rada persisted in its noncooperation. In January 1918 the Rada proclaimed the Ukraine's independence, and there followed two years of chaotic warfare ending in Bolshevik conquest. During this time the Bolsheviks not only had failed to find allies in much of the Ukraine, but were hard pressed to build any kind of Bolshevik organization there which might justify their presence. In Byelorussia, the National Congress which had gathered in Minsk was overthrown by pro-Bolshevik troops acting on Moscow's orders, in December 1917. While the Byelorussian nationalist movement was weak, it was of no less concern to Lenin than the strong movements elsewhere.

A Transcaucasian authority was set up immediately after the Bolshevik coup; dominated by the Georgian Mensheviks, it included Armenian and other local representatives. Lenin did not even try the kind of political maneuvering that had been used against the Ukrainian Rada. A Bolshevik coup was planned for early December 1917, using local military units loyal to the Bolsheviks. This was thwarted, the Bolshevik Party was outlawed, and in April 1918 the Transcaucasian Federation proclaimed itself an independent state. In Central Asia and other Moslem areas, Lenin's government pursued a dual policy which combined the destruction of indigenous organizations resisting Bolshevik rule with alliances with nationalists willing to cooperate. Among ethnic Russians in Central Asia, who had lived there for some decades as a privileged colonial elite, the Bolsheviks found many who were willing to help establish Soviet power as a way of countering the threat of rising nationalism among the Moslems.

Of the Russian-ruled nations which succeeded in becoming independent, none did so without first resisting an effort by the Soviet regime to establish a Soviet-oriented government. The military conflicts which made these efforts possible were not primarily the Bolsheviks' doing. But Lenin and his commanders pressed their military operations further than self-defense alone required, and their political intent was plain. Poland, whose independence the Soviets had recognized in 1918, pursued a belligerent policy to extend its eastern frontiers at the expense of Russia. But the Soviet drive to the gates of Warsaw in 1920, in a war begun by the Poles, was nothing less than an effort to topple Pilsudski's new government and put a Soviet type of regime in its place.

Lithuania, Latvia, Estonia, and Finland had all proclaimed independence in 1917 and early 1918. The Baltic states were then surrendered to German occupation by the Treaty of Brest-Litovsk, in March 1918. Immediately after Germany's surrender to the Western Allies the following November, Bolshevik forces invaded all three states. The threat to Soviet rule from this direction was a real one: General Yudenich commanded a White army which tried to take Petrograd, and with Allied approval German troops were used to oppose the Bolsheviks for some months after the German surrender. But the Soviet government had more at stake than defense of the territory it already held: it openly proclaimed its intention of setting up Soviet republics in place of the German-supported nationalist governments. It was active Allied support for the new Baltic governments that tipped the balance in favor of their independence, a factor lacking in the Ukraine, Transcaucasia, and elsewhere. By the end of 1919 Soviet troops had withdrawn from Latvia and Estonia, while the hasty Russian recognition of independent Lithuania in the summer of 1920 was a stratagem to aid Moscow's brief war with Poland.

As for Finland, Lenin's seemingly generous grant of independence at the end of 1917 looks a good deal less generous when one considers the circumstances. A civil war was already brewing in Finland, and the "Red" forces were strongly Bolshevik-oriented and in a good position for conquest. It was with Soviet support that the Finnish communists overran Helsinki and the south; the Soviets declared war over the Karelian issue in 1919, and only the help of German troops restored the Finnish nationalist regime to power. Not until 1940 did Moscow succeed in claiming the Baltic states as its own, this time with German collusion. The Finns at the same time (November 1939) chose to fight rather than yield. A Soviet effort to recognize a Finnish communist regime during the hostilities met with no popular response, and Stalin after the Finnish defeat contented himself with a large slice of Finnish territory.

We saw in chapter 4 that the February 1921 invasion of Georgia, to which Lenin agreed after much doubt and hesitation, later became the cause of Lenin's warning against "Great-Russian chauvinism" and a major reason for his dictating the "Testament" and attempting to remove Stalin as General Secretary. The Georgian Menshevik regime was strong and popular, and Georgian Bolsheviks very weak. Moscow's recognition of an indpendent Menshevik Georgia in the treaty of May 1920 had been not only a practical compromise for the moment, but the first step toward subversion of the new regime in Tbilisi, since the Georgians were obliged under the treaty to release the Georgian Bolsheviks from prison. Lenin's hesitations sprang not from his reluctance to impose a solution by force, but from the international complications which might result, particularly in the negotiations then in progress with Kemalist Turkey. His later attack on Stalin and Ordzhonikidze sprang not from their having organized the invasion, but from the brutal treatment of the Menshevik leaders which resulted. Lenin, well aware of Ordzhonikidze's callous treatment of both Azerbaidzhan and Armenia, urged him in the wake of the invasion to seek a compromise with the Mensheviks, but in vain.[9]

Ultimately, the political fate of every major national area was settled by force of arms. It must be said that in many areas resistance was carried on primarily by White Russian forces which were ethnically Russian, and whose commanders were uncompromisingly hostile to the strivings of the non-Russians whose soil they temporarily occupied. But without Bolshevik victories in the Civil War and the presence of the Red Army, a different combination of forces would have ruled these nations than the small groups loyal to the Bolsheviks.

Lenin's career was one interlaced with both tragedy and irony. The uncompromisingly radical theoretical positions which he proclaimed before the Bolshevik seizure of power, which in all sincerity he tried to maintain after he was in power, led to situations which could be resolved only by the use of force. Lenin was not one to spare force

---

[9] Ibid., pp. 234–41.

when Bolshevik rule was threatened; yet using force to save his regime led to further uses of force to settle political disputes which did not necessarily threaten it. Ultimately this process led to the forcible settlement of most national questions in Moscow's favor.

Self-Determination by the Working Classes Only

Bolshevik proclamations probably had little effect on what was happening in the non-Russian areas. But Lenin's self-determination slogan may have encouraged nationalist forces to declare their nations independent. In any case, the Bolshevik leaders were deeply disturbed at the almost immediate breakup of old Russia. Intervention for the purpose of stemming this tide would have to be carried out under new slogans and perhaps with amended doctrines. Stalin had been placed in charge of the Commissariat for Nationalities at the time Lenin formed his cabinet in November 1917, and so the task logically fell to him. At this point it suddenly came to light that a number of Lenin's colleagues from among the "left" communists thought his doctrine of self-determination dangerous. Just a month after the Bolshevik coup, Stalin countered this challenge by stating that the new regime would recognize national independence "upon the demand of the working population of such an area." Later on he stated flatly that self-determination must be limited "by granting it to the toilers and refusing it to the bourgeoisie." Self-determination should be "a means of fighting for socialism."[10] Bourgeois self-determination was appropriate only for the underdeveloped world.

Lenin yielded no ground to the "left" on this question until 1919, when a new Party Program was drawn up and the self-determination issue had to be resolved somehow. The solution was a neat one which left the door open to differential treatment of different nations. The Party, from now on, would act according to the level of historical development of any given nation. For a nation evolving from feudalism (meaning absolutism as well) to bourgeois democracy, bourgeois nationalism could be recognized; for a nation evolving from bourgeois democracy toward socialism, the only valid self-determination was that exercised by the proletariat, or the working classes generally. Recall, in this connection, the Bolsheviks' penchant for recognizing "telescoped history," interpreting political developments which Marx would have regarded as premature as valid historical movements. The Bolshevik regime could now declare any pro-Bolshevik seizure of power anywhere to embody evolution from bourgeois democracy toward socialism. How, otherwise, could Bolshevik rule be justified in an area such as Central Asia, which

---

[10] Ibid., p. 109.

aside from its "colonial" Russian enclaves was a group of nations still thoroughly immersed in its own brand of feudalism?

FEDERALISM AS A SOLUTION

The second change of strategy, one which Lenin agreed to more readily than the change in self-determination, was the acceptance of a form of federalism. Lenin's pet doctrine of "regional federalism," which de-emphasized national identity, had no political appeal. As Bolshevik regimes were being set up in one national area after another—though the fate of many had to await the end of the Civil War—the idea of uniting them in a federation of nations suddenly seemed a logical course after all. Simultaneously with the Bolshevik attack on the Ukraine in January 1918, Lenin drafted a statement proclaiming federal union between a Soviet Ukraine and Soviet Russia (which was not made formal, actually, until the 1923 Constitution). A resolution passed by the Congress of Soviets in the same month declared Soviet Russia itself to be "a free union of free nations," and "federation of Soviet national republics."[11] Six months later, the Constitution of the Russian Socialist Federal Soviet Republic became law.

The Russian Republic as a Federation

Almost nothing in this document suggested a federal structure, save for one article which provided for "autonomous regional unions" and for "regions with special usages and national characteristics." Their governmental organs would be identical to those of other local governments, but they would enter the RSFSR "on a federal basis." Between 1919 and 1922, eight Autonomous Republics, ten Autonomous Regions, and one "Toilers' Commune" (Karelia) were formed. They came into being by central decree, and they were endowed with few special rights or distinguishing features. The Autonomous Regions were subject to the same constitutional provisions as ordinary provinces. They exercised their autonomy exclusively in the realm of local government functions, including education, public health, and social security. In this respect they bore some resemblance to the zemstvos of Tsarist Russia, which likewise had busied themselves with local welfare without having a voice in larger governmental affairs. From 1920, when Stalin returned to active leadership of the Commissariat of Nationalities, this Commissariat assumed extensive jurisdiction over the affairs of these 19 federal units, opened branch offices in all of them, and assembled representatives chosen by

---

[11] Ibid., p. 111.

them in a new body called the Council of Nationalities. With the adoption of the USSR Constitution in 1923, the Commissariat was abolished, while the Council of Nationalities became the second chamber of the new federal Central Executive Committee.

The Process of Unification

By 1923 the other Soviet Republics were already joined to the Russian Republic both in fact and through a number of statutes. Ties with the Ukraine came first, and these formed a model for the rest. In 1919, when it was at last possible to maintain a Bolshevik regime in Kiev, the two Republics merged administration of military affairs, economic management, foreign trade, communications, railroads, and labor. Some 30 members of the Ukrainian Central Executive Committee were included in the Rusian CEC. In December 1920 these arrangements were embodied in a treaty, which in effect handed over to the RSFSR the commissariats responsible for these fields, in return for recognition of the Ukraine as a sovereign republic. The Ukraine retained its Commissariat of Foreign Affairs and could maintain relations with foreign powers. Similar arrangements were made with Byelorussia. In 1920 and in 1921, treaties were signed with Azerbaidzhan, Georgia, and Armenia. Ordzhonikidze, meanwhile, as head of the Party's Moscow-directed Caucasian Bureau, had set to work merging the commissariats of the three Transcaucasian republics in preparation for a Soviet Transcaucasian Federation, an idea opposed even by the local Bolshevik leaders in all three. The leaders of these republics lost no time making use of their formally sovereign status. The Ukraine and Georgia sent representatives along with Lenin's Commissar for Foreign Affairs (Chicherin) to discuss the Turkish Straits problem at the Lausanne Conference of 1923. Azerbaidzhan established relations with no less than six foreign countries.

On the surface, the USSR Constitution of 1923 was the next logical step, a measure to formalize the centralized administrative relationships that Moscow had insisted on, while granting enough to the republics to satisfy their leaders' demands for status in the new federation. But like so many of the other measures we have already examined, this too was a response to a crisis. The Bolshevik leaders of the Ukraine, headed by Mikola Skrypnik, were protesting Moscow's high-handed management of Ukrainian affairs. The Georgian party, though it was the beneficiary of Ordzhonikidze's invasion and defeat of the Mensheviks, was now threatened with the plan for a Transcaucasian Federation, designed explicitly to cut down its power. In Central Asia, the spreading Basmachi revolt served as proof to local communist leaders there that Moscow's policy of invasion and repression was creating a dangerous situation. In all these areas, therefore, loyal Bolshevik leaders were finding that policies imposed by Moscow were endangering their own positions and possibly endangering Soviet rule itself.

The USSR Takes Shape

The USSR Constitution, Lenin's last contribution to building his political system, was both a reworking of practical relationships among the republics and a symbol of compromise between Party leaders in Moscow and those in the non-Russian areas. In the end, some administrative concessions were made to the Ukrainian leaders; the Transcaucasian Federation was dissolved into its three constituent republics; and, in Central Asia, concessions to Moslem ways and institutions helped end the Basmachi uprising.

Moscow had to make other concessions in the terms of the new constitution as well. It was Stalin who got the job of supervising the drafting process. The first project he submitted was opposed by Lenin because of its extreme centralization, and had to be scrapped altogether. What Stalin intended to do was simply to incorporate these five republics into the RSFSR; a hard-line centralist, he saw no reason why the Ukraine, Georgia, and the rest should enjoy greater powers than the very minimal powers given to the Tatars, Kirghiz, or Yakuts. This would have undone the system of federal (and pseudofederal) arrangements which Lenin had built up. More important, it would have added the symbolism of Russian hegemony to the already emerging reality of this hegemony. The Georgian party leadership voted flatly against the draft; the Byelorussians said they would settle for nothing less than what the Ukraine received, and a bit later the Ukrainians too protested the threat to their status as a republic.

The second draft constitution provided for an entirely new level of government embracing as equals the RSFSR and the other Republics. The top organs were the same as those in the RSFSR Constitution, but bore the designation "USSR": the Congress of Soviets of the USSR, the Central Executive Committee (CEC) of the USSR, and the Council of People's Commissars of the USSR. The main difference was that the CEC at this level was bicameral, consisting of a Federal Soviet of 371 members, and a Soviet of Nationalities having five representatives from each Union Republic and one from each Autonomous Republic. Each chamber selected its own Presidium, and the two chambers acting jointly constituted the Presidium of the CEC, whose functions we noted in chapter 7. The idea of bicameralism was strongly opposed by most Bolshevik leaders, including Stalin; consequently it was not a part of Stalin's second draft. Stalin changed his mind only when he realized that the second chamber would be none other than the Council of Nationalities, which he had organized and staffed himself.

The powers assigned to the new USSR Government confirmed the existing state of affairs, the one important change being that the member republics were no longer competent to have their own diplomatic or trade relations with foreign countries. The two categories of commissariats had their inception here. The strictly centralized commissariats, later designated "All-Union Commissariats" in the 1936 Constitution, covered foreign affairs, military affairs, foreign commerce, transport, and communications. The commissariats which entrusted the execution of their policies to their counterparts in the republic governments, designated "Union-Republic Commissariats" in 1936, included those administering finances, labor and supplies, plus the Supreme Economic Council, the Workers' and Peasants' Inspectorate, and—occupying its own special Chapter in the constitutional text—the Unified Political Administration or OGPU. Republic commissariats without counterparts at the USSR level included those dealing with agriculture, justice, the ordinary police, education, health, and social security.

The Non-Russian Bolsheviks Protest

The second draft provoked an explosion among the Georgian leaders, the supposedly loyal faction that had replaced the deposed Mensheviks in 1921. Unlike Stalin's first draft, it proposed to reestablish the Transcaucasian Federation, merging Georgia, Armenia, and Azerbaidzhan in a single unit. This was plainly nothing less than a constitutional vehicle for legitimizing Moscow's already very firm grip over the fractious Georgians. Now even those Georgian leaders who had supported Lenin's centralism to the hilt protested. Lenin, irritated by their insubordination, took Stalin's part; the entire Georgian Central Committee resigned, to be replaced by Ordzhonikidze's compliant young appointees, who then approved the draft.

The last gasp of opposition came to a head at the 12th Party Congress in April 1923, where the simmering nationality disputes burst into the open. Stalin, as we saw in chapter 4, succeeded in sidestepping the impact of Lenin's "Testament," whose attack on Stalin was a direct response to the way he had handled the Georgian problem. The Ukrainian leader Rakovsky, who earlier had been an extreme centralizer, attempted to cut back the functions assigned to the new USSR Government. A move in this direction had the support of a memorandum from Lenin himself. Rakovsky's draft would have retained diplomatic status for the republics, plus a separate citizenship and control of armed forces and foreign trade. Rakovsky proposed further that only the four Union Republics should elect deputies to the Council of Nationalities, since otherwise this body would be dominated by the RSFSR. An alternate and more sweeping solution to the last problem was put forth by the Georgian delegation, whose amendments would have stripped all the Autonomous Republics from the RSFSR and had them enter the USSR as separate Union Republics. All these moves were doomed to failure in a conclave packed with Stalin's supporters. Ten days after Lenin's death, at the end of January 1924, the Second All-Union Congress of Soviets placed the final stamp of approval on this highly centralized federation.

Stalin's Constitution of 1936

At this point, one could almost write "et cetera" to the evolution of Soviet federalism. While the treatment of nationalities as such has a history of its own, still far from finished as of the 1970s, the governmental framework of federalism has changed little. Unlike the 1923 Constitution, which reflected a crisis over federal concepts, the "Stalin Constitution" of 1936 embodied only Stalin's desire to place the stamp of his regime on the governmental system, to announce the advent of socialism, and to reaffirm Soviet-style democracy and federalism at a time when Moscow's policies were casting more doubt than ever on both. It spelled out relations between Moscow and the Union Republics in much greater detail than had its predecessor a dozen years earlier, but essentially nothing was changed. By setting forth the structure of the Union Republics and Autonomous Republics at great length, it eliminated the possibility of local experiments. As to functions, the USSR Government received some additional areas of competence, including state security, state insurance, some agricultural functions, and the capacity to pass basic legislation on civil and criminal codes, family law, and natural resources.

The Union Republics numbered 11 in 1936. Central Asia had been given heightened status by being assigned four full Union Republics: Kirghiz, Tadzhik, Turkmen, and Uzbek. Stalin, having attempted "regionalism" as a solution for Transcaucasia, now shunned it in Central Asia, since it might have provided an entering wedge for Pan-Turkism or Pan-Islamism among nations closely related by language, customs, and religion. Kazakhstan had become a sprawling republic of very mixed population. Transcaucasia, once the Georgian protests had been suppressed, was broken up once again into its three components. The Nazi-Soviet pact of 1939 resulted in territorial acquisitions the next year, which were promptly incorporated as four new Republics: Estonia, Latvia, Lithuania, and Moldavia. At the same time, the Karelian Autonomous Republic was elevated to Union status as the Karelo-Finnish Republic, obviously in preparation for the addition of neighboring Finland itself. Khrushchev in 1956 demoted it to its original role as the Karelian Autonomous Republic, a gesture of good will to Finland. This resulted in the present total of 15 Union Republics. The Autonomous Republics, Autonomous Provinces, and National Areas were created to give formal status to the small national groups they embrace and to provide an administrative setting for use of local languages and the recognition of national cultures. Otherwise the first two types are very much like ordinary provinces in the way they are integrated into the constitutional structure, and the National Areas are like districts. (See Diagram 13–1 for the distribution of these units.)

FEDERALISM IN A CENTRALIZED ECONOMY

The 1936 Constitution marked a high point of centralization of three types: the number of functions accorded to the central government, central supervision over the Union Republics, and multiplication of lines of command leading directly from Moscow to economic units and local governments. This last feature of the Constitution was reinforced further by the multiplication after 1936 of central ministries, roughly half of which were of the all-Union type, thus quite separate from the Republic governments. The only exceptions to this trend were purely symbolic and introduced for diplomatic reasons: in 1944, during World War II, the Union Republics were accorded the right to conduct their own foreign relations and to create their own military forces.

One motive—and probably the main motive—for the Republics' new diplomatic status came to light at the Dumbarton Oaks and Yalta Conferences, where the Soviet representatives sought international status for their 16 Union Republics, including seats in the U.N. General Assembly. Moscow ultimately settled for two extra U.N. seats, those for the Ukraine and Byelorussia. Aside from the active participation of Ukrainian and Byelorussian delegations in the various U.N. bodies, and the fact that they have signed some major international treaties, none of the Union Republics has established formal diplomatic relations with foreign countries. The constitutional provision for republic armed forces, which could have led to a revival of the national military units that had existed in the 1920s and 1930s, was neglected after World War II.

During the de-Stalinization campaign of the latter 1950s, excessive centralization figured as one of Stalin's sins, albeit a minor one. The 1957 reform of economic administration, for which Khrushchev had fought so insistently, transferred a good many economic functions to the Union Republics' jurisdiction. Each republic received its own Regional Economic Council, and the heads of the republic governments were now made ex officio members of the USSR Council of Ministers. In this and later measures, the republics were granted more discretion in economic planning, in the allocation of budgetary resources within their own boundaries, and in the use of surplus resources. But the main instruments of central economic control remained: central economic plan-

DIAGRAM 13–1
The Federal Structure and Lesser National Governmental Units

Union Republics (with date of establishment)	National Governmental Units Subordinated to the Union Republics		
	Autonomous Republics (ASSRs)	Autonomous Provinces	National Areas
Armenian (1920)			
Azerbaidzhan (1920)	Nakhichevan	Mountain Karabakh	
Byelorussian (1919)			
Estonian (1940)			
Georgian (1921)	Abkhazian	South Ossetian	
	Adzharian		
Kazakh (1936)			
Kirghiz (1936)			
Latvian (1940)			
Lithuanian (1940)			
Moldavian (1940)			
RSFSR (Russian) (1917)	Bashkir	Adygei	Agin Buryat
	Buryat	Karachai-Cherkes	Chukotski
	Chechen-Ingush	Khakas	Evenk
	Chuvash	Jewish	Henet
	Daghestan	Mountain Altai	Kanty-Mansiiski
	Kabardino-Balkar		Komi-Permyatski
	Kalmyk		Koryak
	Karelian		Taimyr
	Komi		Ust-Ordyn-Buryat
	Mari		Yamal-Nenet
	Mordvin		
	North Ossetian		
	Tatar		
	Tuvin		
	Udmurt		
	Yakut		
Tadzhik (1929)		Mountain Badakhshan	
Turkmen (1924)			
Ukrainian (1917)			
Uzbek (1924)	Karakalpak		

ning, the single all-Union budget, and the same Party centralism that had existed from the early 1920s on.

In the early 1960s, the decentralization trend was reversed. While Khrushchev was still in power, the republic Regional Economic Councils were subordinated directly to a new central body, the Supreme National Economic Council, a superagency to end all superagencies. The four Central Asian republics—the Kirghiz, Uzbek, Turkmen, and Tadzhik SSR's—were placed under a single regional Regional Economic Council, and other economic agencies covering the entire area were set up in what was certainly a move to create a single economic unit. These moves were accompanied by attacks on "localist tendencies," attacks directed both at Central Asia and at other non-Russian republics.[12]

Abolition of the system of Regional Economic Councils in 1965, the first year of the Brezhnev-Kosygin administration, meant some reduction in administrative control over the economy on the part of the republics. Until the merger of the councils in Central Asia, nearly all the republics had possessed their own individual councils, attached to the Union Republic's government in each case. (The Ukraine was divided among several councils, however.) Reestablishment of Stalin's old system of central ministries removed a number of production branches from the republics' purview altogether. Certain important branches were placed under ministries in the Union-Republic category, however: metallurgy, electric power, the chemical industry, heavy industrial construction, and oil extraction and refining. At the end of the Stalin period, all these branches had come under all-Union ministries. Whatever may have been the administrative reasons for placing them in the Union-Republic category a dozen years later, from a political point of view this was a concession to the status of the republic governments.

In 1973 the republics' administrative integrity was seriously threatened by division of the entire nation into seven regions for the purpose of economic planning. From 1962 on, there had been 18 such regions, 14 of which followed the boundaries of the non-Russian republics, and four subdivided the huge Russian Republic. Now the three Baltic republics and Byelorussia were grouped in a single region together with most of European Russia; the Ukraine, Moldavia, and the three Transcaucasian republics were grouped with an area of the Russian Republic north of the Caucasus; and the four Central Asian republics were brought together.[13] While this reorganization concerns planning and not administra-

---

[12] Conquest, *Soviet Nationalities Policy in Practice*, pp. 126–27.

[13] Kazakhstan, not formally classified as "Central Asian," retained its own planning boundaries, and the remainder of the Russian Republic was divided into the Volga-Urals, Siberia, and the Far East. See the two articles justifying the new planning regionalization by the economist Viktor Kistanov, translated in *Current Digest of the Soviet Press* 25 (March 28, 1973), pp. 1–7.

tion of the economy, it does mean the end of any possible emphasis on further economic integration of the republics individually. In December 1972, in a speech commemorating the 50th anniversary of federation, Brezhnev indicated clearly that the republics could no longer justify their claims to economic investment as republics:

> It is also obvious that we must give some thought to the most rational location of productive forces in the country. Now, when the task of evening out the level of economic development of the national republics in our country has been accomplished in the main, it is possible for us to approach economic questions primarily from the standpoint of the interests of the economy as a whole, of improving the efficiency of the U.S.S.R.'s entire national economy—needless to say, with consideration for the specific interests of the Union and autonomous republics.[14]

Indigenization and Persecution

In order to make even this very limited federalism a reality, there had to be massive recruitment of non-Russians for governmental posts. The same was true for the Party, since the ratio of Party members to population was much lower initially among non-Russians than Russians. Part of the heritage of Tsarism was the circumstance that average educational levels were lower among most non-Russians than among Russians; also, relatively few non-Russians held the kind of jobs that might have prepared them for responsibility in the Soviet system. The campaign of "indigenization," as it was called, proceeded slowly in the 1920s in spite of a serious effort by the Party to recruit and train non-Russians. The armed forces recruited some 17 national divisions from among the larger nationalities, plus a number of smaller units.

"Indigenization" had clear advantages for the stability of the Soviet system. Without it, the old colonial relationships between Russians and non-Russians would continue, regardless of governmental forms. Also, since the non-Russian areas were among those least touched by the ideology of the new regime, involving their populations in both Party and state was probably the most effective means of political socialization. Finally, if any progress were to be made toward a single proletarian culture, the non-Russians must first be drawn out of their traditional cultures and into the mainstream of the new system. Until the mid-1930s, the fact that non-Russians held in some cases less than 10 percent of the posts in the republics that bore their names was not due to Moscow's fear of increasing their proportion. Rather, it resulted first from the intrinsic difficulties of recruitment and training, and secondarily from the

[14] *Pravda*, Dec. 22, 1972. Translation from *Current Digest of the Soviet Press*, 24 (Jan. 17, 1973), pp. 17–18.

old and widespread attitude among Russians that their nation's leadership was natural and desirable. During these years, Stalin himself fulminated against mainifestations of "Great-Russian chauvinism" in both Party and state.

The 1930s and the World War II period dealt a number of blows to the hopeful growth of local leadership and talent. Collectivization and the Great Purge struck especially hard at the non-Russians. Most particularly, collectivization embittered relations between Moscow and the top national leadership in many republics. Those who protested in some way in the early 1930s were certain to be purge victims in the latter 1930s, not to mention the leaders who had fought for their republics' autonomy in the early 1920s. Indigenization was halted in the Ukraine and Byelorussia, which underwent Party purges from 1933 on; Mikola Skrypnik, who had resisted centralization in 1923 but had cooperated loyally with Moscow thereafter, committed suicide in protest. Accusations of "bourgeois nationalism" were hurled at many loyal non-Russian Party officials who, having been recruited to administer their various nations, had developed some pride in their national republics as a result. The 1937 purges decimated the Party bureaucracy in many of the Soviet Republics, and some of their top figures appeared beside Bukharin in the "anti-rightist" show trial of 1938.

The wartime deportations of entire nations to the east were in part a precautionary measure, in part an overreaction to actual collaboration with the Germans, and in part simply a settling of old scores and the elimination of old nationality problems. Deportations of non-Russians from the country's western border areas began in the late 1930s. The areas annexed in 1940 suffered particularly, especially the three Baltic nations, since their loyalty was naturally suspect. The Volga Germans were deported in 1941 for about the same reasons that Japanese-Americans were deported from California. In 1943–44 the Crimean Tatars were sent to Kazakhstan, and the Kalmyks plus a number of small North Caucasian nations, the Chechens, Ingushi, Karachai, and Balkars, suffered a similar fate. Their republics were wiped off the map. Large numbers of Ukrainians found themselves in Siberian labor camps as a result of the welcome which parts of the Ukraine had accorded to the German troops, whom they mistakenly regarded as liberators.[15]

In one way or another, a whole generation of non-Russian national leaders which Moscow had urgently needed was killed, imprisoned, or cast out of political life. World War II marked the crest of the Russian nationalist revival which Stalin had inaugurated in 1934. The reduced emphasis on Russian nationalism after 1946, and the official effort to revive ideology as a force, offered some hope of a larger and more secure

[15] This grim story is detailed in Robert Conquest, *The Soviet Deportation of Nationalities* (New York: St. Martin's Press, 1960).

role for the non-Russians nations and their republics, even if it did not augur well for promoting national cultures. But Stalin's last years saw purges directed against the leaders of a number of republics. Estonia was hit in 1949–50, amid charges of bourgeois nationalism, kulak conspiracies, and plots by the former bourgeoisie to restore capitalism. Latvian and Lithuanian leaders, anxious about their own positions, joined in the chorus of attacks on real or alleged anti-Soviet plots in their nations. The Ukraine was the scene of organized guerilla and underground activities which continued for several years after the end of World War II, particularly in the newly acquired Western Ukraine (Galicia). That Stalin was still mistrustful of the Ukraine we know from Khrushchev's secret speech in 1956; but the Ukrainian Party leadership escaped serious consequences (Khrushchev himself was the Party leader there from 1938 to 1948) by squelching local efforts to gain greater autonomy. A sweeping Party purge in Georgia at the end of 1951 represented an effort to undermine Lavrenti Beria's power base there, rather than a struggle over the issue of autonomy. But the continuing importance of control over Georgia testified to an ever-present danger of what a cohesive Georgian leadership might undertake to do.

After Stalin's death, the issues of national identity and of autonomy within the federal system were argued and fought over on a different plane. Not often were they connected with high-level political struggles; the Georgian leadership changes of 1973 are a possible exception. Instead, there was a complex pattern of local struggles over language, cultural manifestations, population policy, and the details of federalized administration. As chapter 14 will show, the problems in these areas are not likely to be resolved soon.

The Non-Russian Share in the Ruling Strata

In the early years of Soviet rule, recruitment of non-Russians in the Party was hampered by the fact that the non-Russian nations were predominantly rural. Some of these, particularly the Central Asian nations, had social structures and controls capable of inhibiting young people from joining the Party. That is, social circumstances prevailing within most non-Russian nationalities were those which even among Russians hampered recruitment efforts. The Transcaucasian nations, thanks largely to Georgia's large Social-Democratic movement, furnished far more than their share. In the 1920s, Party leaders made a very determined effort to bring non-Russians into the Party, with success only in some cases. This meant, among other things, accepting a far higher ratio of applicants with peasant backgrounds than was considered desirable for the Party membership as a whole. The latter 1930s and the 1940s saw a statistical deterioration of the non-Russians' position, except for the Georgians and

ians, whose position improved. From the 1950s on, the trend had n the direction of redressing the imbalances.[16]

e disparities in Party membership ratios as compared with national-tios in the population are still noticeable. In 1965, 51 out of every Soviet citizens were Party members. For Russians, the ratio was and this figure was topped only by the Georgians (65) and Armenians). The Ukrainians, Byelorussians, and Azerbaidzhanians could each im 44, and most of the other nationalities fell in the range of 33 to , the Moldavians trailing all the rest with 17, or one third of the national verage.[17] Figures on the composition of the Communist Parties of the various republics reflect the overall membership ratios. For example, in the Uzbek Republic in 1959, 62.1 percent of the population was Uzbek, but only 49.5 percent of the Uzbek Communist Party's membership. However, a variety of figures show that the degree of "indigenization" in Party membership was increasing during the 1960s.[18]

Data on the national composition of the leading political strata offer a mixed picture. Of the 16 full members of the Politburo after the April 1973 changes, there were four Ukrainians, a Byelorussian, a Latvian, and a Kazakh; among the seven alternates were a Byelorussian and an Uzbek. Of these ten non-Russians, four headed the parties of their Republics (the Ukrainian, Byelorussian, Kazakh, and Uzbek parties). During the 1960s and early 1970s, if one regards the Politburo and Secretariat as a single unit, Russians have consistently held about 60 percent of the places. Among the full members of the Central Committee, the ratio has been 58 percent, the remaining nationalities having a share of seats roughly in proportion to their share of the population, with some minor divergences (e.g., there should be one Latvian, but instead there are two; there should be two each from the Azerbaidhzanians, Lithuanians, and Moldavians, but each has only one seat).[19] The Russian preponderance on the USSR Council of Ministers has been higher: it was two thirds in Khrushchev's last years, and 72 percent following Khrushchev's removal, due to the addition of a number of new ministers because of the Brezhnev's restoration of the ministerial system.[20]

A striking feature of political leadership of the 15 republics is the number of cases in which the republic Party's second in command is a Russian or Ukrainian. During the 1960s and early 1970s, this arrangement has prevailed in the parties of ten of the 12 non-Slavic republics,

[16] T. H. Rigby, *Communist Party Membership in the U.S.S.R., 1917–1967* (Princeton, N.J.: Princeton University Press, 1968), pp. 365–76.

[17] Ibid., pp. 378–79.

[18] Ibid., pp. 390–99.

[19] Yaroslav Bilinsky, "The Rulers and the Ruled," *Problems of Communism* 16 (September-October 1967), p. 23.

[20] Ibid., p. 25.

the exceptions being Armenia and Estonia. In six o
first deputy chairman of the government has been a R\
all five Central Asian Republics, plus Moldavia, fall
The number of cases in the Khrushchev and early \
in which the top indigenous leaders were removed from o
suggests two things: something of a figurehead status for
and a halt to their probable efforts to recruit their fellow
into leading positions faster than Moscow considered desirable.

To the extent that the Soviet leadership succeeds in promoti\
tion-mixing through migration, there is likely to be a process \
digenization" in Party and government posts. The following int
item was reported from a conclave of Party activists in Georg

> . . . I[t] was noted at the *aktiv* meeting that in Abkhazia a half-bak\
> "theory" according to which responsible posts should be filled onl\
> by the representatives of the indigenous nationality has gained a certain\
> currency. The authors of this theory forgot that all residents of a
> particular republic, regardless of their national affiliation, are exponents
> of the statehood of the republic in question and its builders in all
> fields of the national economy and culture. Of course, every national
> republic has local cadres that have grown up during the years of Soviet
> power. This is a great achievement of the Communist Party. But no
> one has been given the right to ignore the national composition of
> the population or to disregard the continual exchange of cadres among
> nations and the interests of all nationalities.[22]

Only in the USSR Supreme Soviet have the non-Russians had considerably more than their share of posts, over 55 percent as compared with
their population ratio of approximately 46 percent. This is easily explained
by the system of representation in the Council of Nationalities: 32 deputies from each Union Republic, regardless of population, and similarly
11 from each Autonomous Republic, five from each Autonomous Region,
and one from each National Area. Nothing prevents Russians from being
elected as deputies from non-Russian units, and many are, but the overall
effect is proportionate overrepresentation of the non-Russians.

The whole pattern of top personnel selection by nationality strongly
suggests that a quota system is in effect. Today it works to the slight
advantage of Russians in most cases, but its tendency is toward position-
holding strictly in proportion to the population. It has cut down the
role of Georgians and Armenians, and it has been bringing up the role
of most of the rest, some of which still lag far behind. An informal
system of nationality representation on the top organs in proportion to
population offers an advantage in symbolism with no corresponding
liability. However, Soviet Marxist doctrine still maintains, just as the

---

[21] Ibid., pp. 20–22.
[22] *Zarya Vostoka*, April 27, 1973. Translation from *Current Digest of the Soviet Press* 25 (May 16, 1973), p. 5.

early Bolsheviks did from the 1903 Party Congress on, that the Party is unitary and not federal; its articulation in national components is a territorial solution to the problem of dividing responsibilities and not a nationality-based solution. Consequently the top leadership also has an interest in keeping the quota system informal and flexible.

Jews were greatly overrepresented in the Party's membership in the early decades of Soviet rule. Urban orientation, a higher than average educational level, and the experience of meeting political obstacles to advancement all made the Russian Empire's Jews a likely recruiting ground for radical organizations. It is also noteworthy that several non-Russian nationalities of the Empire's western periphery, living on territory that was also the "Jewish pale of settlement" under Tsarist laws, provided more than their share of recruits—the Poles and the Baltic peoples. All these nationalities provided a high proportion of the early Bolshevik leaders. Three of the original (1919) Politburo of seven were Jews: Trotsky (Bronstein), Kamenev (Rosenfeld), and Zinoviev (Apfelbaum). In the mid-1920s, Jews comprised over 4 percent of Party members but were 1.8 percent of the population. Since that time, no comprehensive data have been made public on Jewish Party membership. Partial data indicate that after World War II the Jewish ratio fell somewhat, so that by the 1960s the proportion was something like 1.5 or 1.7 percent, while Jews constituted about 1 percent of the population.[23] There has been a notable absence of Jews in high places during the post–World War II period. Kaganovich was the last Jew on the Politburo; he was expelled by Khrushchev in 1957. Otherwise only Veniamin (Benjamin) Dymshits remains anywhere near the top, the only Jewish Central Committee member or alternate, also the only Jew on the Council of Ministers. (A strict membership-to-population ratio on the Central Committee would require two full members and either one or two alternates.) Jews have been underrepresented on the Supreme Soviet as well, with five deputies instead of the 15 that would be in keeping with their proportion of the population.

THE SOVIET CHOICES

Shortly before Marx's death, Engels voiced an important reservation about nations and revolution:

One thing alone is certain: the victorious proletariat can force no blessings of any kind upon any foreign nation without undermining its own victory by so doing.[24]

[23] Rigby, *Communist Party Membership in the U.S.S.R., 1917–1967*, pp. 373–74, 383–88.

[24] Letter of Engels to Karl Kautsky, Sept. 12, 1882. Karl Marx and Friedrich Engels, *Selected Works* (New York: International Publishers, 1968), p. 688.

Lenin would most likely have undermined his own precarious regime had he followed this injunction. If his version of national self-determination and federalism had been applied to the situation of the Russian Empire in 1905, they might very well have succeeded without the use of force, subterfuge, and broken treaties. But the situation in which Lenin completed the fashioning of his policies concerning nationhood was one in which all the good options had vanished—vanished, that is assuming it was the objective to keep most of the nations of the defunct Empire together in voluntary union.

By 1918–19, independence dominated the politics of the major non-Russian areas; even socialists of most stripes were convinced that socialism was very compatible with independence from Moscow; foreign governments had demonstrated in practice their readiness to exploit anti-Russian discontent in order to protect their investments or build their spheres of influence; and by 1920 or 1921, all real hope of a proletarian revolution in Europe had faded, an event which would have been necessary to guarantee the survival of a Bolshevik Russia stripped of its vast non-Russian territories. For all of Lenin's displeasure at the high-handed strategy of Ordzhonikidze and those like him, it was none other than Lenin who led the new regime into a position where force would have to be the midwife of whatever solution might be found for the national problem. Everthing that has developed since that time has been an effort to make an imposed solution palatable and by whatever means to set aside the original causes of discontent with the solution.

FOR FURTHER READING

The thinking of Marx and Engels on the future of nations is summarized in Solomon F. Bloom, *The World of Nations* (New York: Columbia University Press, 1941). Lenin, who likewise left no systematic theoretical statements on the national problem, is dealt with in Alfred D. Low, *Lenin on the Question of Nationality* (New York: Bookman Associates, 1958). See also Alfred G. Meyer, *Leninism* (New York: Praeger, 1962), chapter 7 ("Nationalism"). A useful collection of Stalin's writings on the subject is Joseph Stalin, *Marxism and the National Question: Selected Writings and Speeches* (New York: International Publishers, 1942). Klaus Mehnert, *Stalin Versus Marx* (London: Allen and Unwin, 1952) offers a highly critical interpretation of Stalin's adopted Great-Russian nationalism.

A detailed, highly valuable study of the origin of Soviet federalism is Richard Pipes, *The Formation of the Soviet Union: Communism and Nationalism, 1917–1923* (New York: Atheneum, 1968). The further course of federal relations is traced in Robert Conquest (ed.), *Soviet Nationalities Policy in Practice* (New York: Praeger, 1967). See also various items in *Problems of Communism* 16 (September-October 1967), a special issue devoted to nationality questions. For a brief survey of the formal institutions of Soviet federalism, see Karel Hulicka and Irene M. Hulicka, *Soviet Institutions, the Individual and Society* (Boston: Christopher, 1967), chapter 4 ("Soviet Federalism"). A now dated but still useful volume of documentation is R. Schlesinger (ed.), *The Nationalities Problem and Soviet Administration* (London: Routledge and Kegan Paul, 1956), containing a variety of Soviet writings on the subject.

14

NATIONAL AND RELIGIOUS IDENTITY

MARX'S ORIGINAL DOCTRINE of nationalism foresaw the extinction of national identity and feeling among the proletariat while capitalism still held sway: "The workingmen have no country." In his later years he became increasingly concerned with the persistence of nationalism among the lower classes, as for example the English workers' acquiescence in their country's oppression of Ireland. Lenin, by contrast, had to cope with the persistence of national identity and nationalism as a *post*-revolutionary phenomenon. This meant, first of all, that the idea of the tenacity of national feelings had to be incorporated into Soviet Marxism together with the idea that nations would die a natural death under socialism. Secondly, it meant that the idea of *managing* national feelings had to be incorporated into the new regime's social strategy. There were at least two compelling reasons why the Bolshevik regime could not simply let national feelings find their own path to self-extinction: the centuries-old hatred of non-Russians for Russians had to be dealt with as an immediate problem, and hostile political forces both inside and outside the country must not be permitted to exploit national feelings as a means of toppling Soviet rule.

In order to cope with these problems, nations as such must be accorded status, respect, and a degree of freedom to manifest themselves and develop. For this practical necessity, Lenin found a Marxist justification: a historical development must run its course and develop its full potential before it gives way to another stage of development. Thus Lenin had also justified the New Economic Policy in 1921: the potential of capitalism must be permitted to develop more fully in order to complete capitalism's historical mission of building the economic basis of socialism. But like capitalism under the NEP, national cultures and feelings would develop under proletarian auspices, hence within well-defined limits in order to forestall any danger they might pose to the new regime.

The history of national cultures under Soviet rule is intricate and many-faceted. At its best, it brought a genuine feeling of national self-respect to many peoples who before the Revolution could not have dreamed of such recognition. At its worst, it could mean mass deportations (in the World War II period) and the obliteration of national leadership in the Great Purge and lesser purges. In the 1920s Stalin coined the watchword "national in form, proletarian in content" as a general criterion for separating the desirable from the undesirable, and the permissible from the impermissible. In practice, it proved to be a very foggy sort of criterion, and was used to justify every kind of incursion and restriction on national cultures. Similarly, the idea of many national cultures' gradually merging into a single socialist culture raised as many policy problems as it answered. It was greatly complicated by Stalin's elevation of Russian nationalism, from 1934 on, which was coupled with the assumption that the new international culture would be permeated with specifically Russian features, first of all the Russian language.

The application of these policies has given rise to countless disputes in the field of literature and the fine arts, the interpretation of national histories, and the use of languages. These have become more or less permanent cultural battlegrounds simply because not only Stalin, but the post-Stalin regimes, have regarded all national manifestations with great wariness. Culture, in Soviet Marxism, is part of politics, and hence Moscow has intervened repeatedly in what might otherwise have been the squabbles of intellectuals.

Demographic issues, by contrast, were not the subject of open policy battles in the Stalin era, or until the 1960s. However, official statements of recent years show the resistance to the government's population policies is today a matter of increasing concern. Encouragement of labor migration among the 15 Union Republics is presented today as promotion of the "drawing together" of national cultures, their watering down as distinct ethnic units. There has likewise been recent discussion of economic equality among the republics, including official rebuttals of charges that inequalities persist today. Culture, history, languages, demography, and economic development—such are the areas in which the Soviet regime has sought to create conditions for the ultimate dying-out of national differences.

NATIONALISM AND NATIONAL CULTURES

For the Bolsheviks of Lenin's time and the 1920s, the new proletarian order meant a rejection of the Russian past. The Russian Empire was interpreted as an oppressor of all who inhabited it, and the Tsars as pitiless despots. The writing of history was dominated by Michael N. Pokrovsky, who had joined the Bolsheviks in 1905 and as a political emigré had written a *History of Russia* demonstrating the evils of Russian rule. After the Revolution he was held in high honor and elected to the Party Central Committee; his *History* became the bible of every Soviet historian.

Those oppressed by Tsarism included the non-Russian nationalities, which after the Revolution rose to claim the status of full nationhood which had been so long suppressed. The Bolsheviks' problem was to place limits on both continued Russian ethnic domination and unacceptable manifestations of nationalism among the non-Russians. The Russian proletariat was advertised by Moscow as the leader and big brother of the much weaker revolutionary forces among the nationalities; but Lenin and Stalin referred again and again to the dangers of "Great-Russian chauvinism." Lenin warned in 1919 that

> . . . in the question of nationality it is not possible to proceed from the assumption that economic unity is necessary at any price. Necessary, of course, it is. But we must attain it through propaganda, through agitation, through a voluntary union. The Bashkirs distrust the Russians, because the Russians are at a higher level of civilization and have used their civilization to rob the Bashkirs. Consequently . . . the name Russian means oppressor to the Bashkirs. . . . We must take this into account, we must combat it. But that takes a long time. We cannot get rid of it by decree. We must go to work on it very cautiously. Above all, such a nation as the Russian who has aroused a wild hatred in all other nationalities must be particularly cautious. We have only now learned to manage better, and even that only some of us. There are still many communists who demand "uniform schools" and accordingly no instruction to be given except in Russian. In my view a communist who thinks in that way is a pan-Russian chauvinist. The tendency still exists in many of us and we must wrestle with it.[1]

Stalin at the 1923 Party Congress added an important qualification about combating Russian chauvinism:

> When it is said that the fight against Great Russian chauvinism must be made the cornerstone of the national question, the intention is to indicate the duties of the Russian Communist; it implies it is the duty of the Russian Communist himself to combat Russian chauvinism. If the struggle against Russian chauvinism were undertaken not by the Russian but by the Turkestani or Georgian Communists, it would be interpreted as anti-Russian chauvinism.[2]

---

[1] From Lenin's closing speech to the 8th Party Congress, March 19, 1919. Translation from Hans Kohn, "Soviet Communism and Nationalism: Three Stages of A Historical Development," in Edward Allworth (ed.), *Soviet Nationality Problems* (New York: Columbia University Press, 1971), p. 53.

[2] Quoted in Robert Conquest (ed.), *Soviet Nationalities Policy in Practice* (New York: Praeger, 1967), pp. 53–54.

The non-Russians were encouraged by the new federal system and official doctrine to assert their rights as nations, even to bring their nationhood to full flower in preparation for the eventual disappearance of both national and class differences. Stalin, as Commissar of Nationalities as well as later on, promoted the study of the country's 180 nationalities in order to determine which national characteristics and traditions should be encouraged, and which discouraged or suppressed. National histories and folklore, in some cases unwritten, were examined to discover events and heroes which embodied useful concepts. The use of national languages was promoted, even at great trouble and inconvenience.

Among some of the larger nationalities, intellectuals and even communist leaders took advantage of their newly respectable nationalism to assert their cultural independence of Moscow. In the Ukraine, Mykola Khvylovy in 1925 denounced Moscow's interference and preached a separate Ukrainian path to communism. The Ukraine's commissar for education protested to Stalin that Moscow was delaying the campaign for "Ukrainization." A prominent Ukrainian economist, Michael Volobuyev, asserted that the Ukraine and other non-Russian areas were being exploited for Moscow's benefit.

Toleration of nationalism in such forms continued until 1930. At the 16th Party Congress held that year, Stalin defended the development of national cultures against demands from Russians within the Party that it was time to establish a single international culture. The harbinger of a changed policy came at the end of 1930 in the form of an attack by Stalin on the Ukrainian poet Demyan Bedny, whom he accused of attempting to discredit the Russian proletariat. Between 1930 and 1933 the Ukrainian leaders who had attempted to combine nationalism, communism, and loyalty to the Soviet federation (if not always to Moscow's policies) had been driven out. Michael Khrushevsky, author of what remains today a basic history of the Ukraine, was exiled to Russia; Shumsky, the education chief, vanished in 1933, and Khvylovy committed suicide the same year. The historical section of the Ukrainian Academy of Sciences, which had shaped a positive view of Ukrainian history (one not necessarily out of keeping with Moscow's views up to that time) was disbanded.

Russian Nationalism

The foundation for a resurrected Russian nationalism was laid in 1929, five years before it was abruptly made respectable. The concept of a "socialist nation," which Stalin introduced in an essay written that year, was analogous to that of the "socialist state" in that, according to Marx's picture of the future, neither nations nor states would be characteristics of socialism. On the contrary, both were at most holdovers from the bourgeois era, the state because it would be needed briefly to complete class conquest, and the nation because whatever national feelings are present at the time of the revolution would not vanish immediately. The "socialist nation" described by Stalin is one led by the proletariat rather than the bourgeoisie. Since the proletariat is international as well as national, its aspirations as a nation differ fundamentally from national aspirations of the past.[3] In this manner, a qualified continuity of national consciousness and feeling was established between the capitalist and socialist periods. This link opened up a new possibility for using national feeling: certain elements of the nationalisms of the past could be rehabilitated and made to serve the present.

In chapter 1 we saw Stalin's refusal in 1931 to slacken the pace of economic development. In itself, this was no surprise to the economic administrators whom he was addressing. His justification, however, must have come as a total shock:

> To slacken the tempo would mean falling behind. And those who fall behind get beaten. But we do not want to be beaten. . . . One feature of the history of old Russia was the continual beatings she suffered because of her backwardness. She was beaten by the Mongol Khans. She was beaten by the Turkish beys. She was beaten by the Polish and Lithuanian gentry. She was beaten by the Japanese barons. All beat her—because of her backwardness, cultural backwardness, political backwardness, agricultural backwardness. They beat her because to do so was profitable and could be done with impunity. You remember the words of the pre-revolutionary poet [Nekrasov]: "You are poor and abundant, mighty and impotent, Mother Russia." Those gentlemen were quite familiar with the verses of the old poet. They beat her, saying: "You are abundant," so one can enrich oneself at your expense They beat her, saying "You are poor and impotent," so you can be beaten and plundered with impunity. . . .
>
> We are fifty or a hundred years behind the advanced countries. We must make good this distance in ten years. Either we do it, or we shall go under.[4]

Mother Russia! Such an appeal had no precedent in the 14 years the Bolsheviks had ruled Russia. The events of the next few years showed it to have been a "trial balloon" with whose impact Stalin was well satisfied.

In May 1934 Stalin and Molotov signed a decree condemning utterly Pokrovsky's negative interpretation of the Russian past. (Pokrovsky, providentially, had died two years before; after a state funeral, his ashes were placed in the Kremlin wall.) Russian history was now rewritten, for the second time in two decades. Most important, certain rulers and

---

[3] J. Stalin, *Works*, vol. 12 (Moscow: Foreign Languages Publishing House, 1956), pp. 355–56.

[4] Ibid., vol. 13, pp. 40–41.

policies were identified as "progressive" in the Marxist sense—that is, they hastened the advent of future class formations in decisive fashion. These included policies of centralization, economic modernization, territorial expansion, and the destruction of feudal privilege. No longer were Ivan the Terrible and Peter the Great looked upon as bloody tyrants, and Russian aggrandizement at the expense of neighboring nations was now looked upon as ultimately beneficial for the latter. Books containing the earlier Bolshevik interpretation of Russian history were withdrawn from libraries and schools. In the same year that Pokrovsky was condemned, Stalin personally vetoed publication in the Party's theoretical journal of a recently discovered article by Engels, written in 1890. The problem was that the article was about Tsarist foreign policy of that period, and it described Russia as the imperialist villain among the European powers.[5] The year 1934 also saw the term *rodina* or "homeland" used in official speech for the first time since the Revolution; a *Pravda* editorial went to great lengths to justify its use. The new perspective on history was epitomized in Sergei Eisenstein's 1938 film *Alexander Nevsky*. This glorified, rather in Hollywood fashion, the struggle of a famous 13th-century Prince of Novgorod against the Livonian knights.

The 1934 decree condemning Pokrovsky had serious consequences for non-Russian writers and historians, the chief custodians of their nations' cultures. For writers, the relatively permissive policies of the 1920s had already come to an end in 1932 with the abolition of the Russian Association of Proletarian Writers (RAPP), which had included some partly autonomous non-Russian branches. It was replaced by the highly centralized, politically controlled Union of Soviet Writers. The 1930s saw an earnest effort by non-Russian writers and poets to produce works on approved contemporary themes. These now included literary recognition of the Great Russians as cultural leaders of the non-Russians in the past as well as the present. The demand that fell hardest, however, was that the political past of the non-Russian nations had to be treated negatively, even after glorification of some of the Russian Tsars was being encouraged.

Nationalism in World War II

From 1939 on, when Russia stood under a growing threat of war, to the bitterly won Soviet victory over Nazi Germany in 1945, the nationalist revival bore even stranger fruit. Pan-Slavism, the 19th-century idea of Slavic blood-brotherhood, received official blessing very soon after the German invasion. Relations between the Kremlin and the long-persecuted Russian churches suddenly improved when most of the latter gave

---

[5] I. V. Stalin, *Sochineniya*, vol. 1 (14) (Stanford, Calif.: The Hoover Institution, 1967), pp. 2–10.

their full moral support to the war effort. In 1943 Stalin received all three Orthodox Metropolitans in the Kremlin. Within less than a week the Russian Orthodox Church, an institution strongly identified with Mother Russia one and indivisible, had been permitted to reestablish its Holy Synod and elect a Patriarch, as in times of old. A church leader spoke of the Church's "sacred hatred against the fascist robbers" and called Stalin "our common Father Iosif Vissarionovich."[6]

What made foreign observers wonder whether the days of Soviet Marxism were numbered was Stalin's dissolution of the Third Communist International, the "Comintern," in the spring of 1943. Since the early years of the Revolution this had been the formal international body for promoting the world proletarian revolution which Marx had predicted. True, the International as such had accomplished little during the intervening years, and those of its functions which were still of value to Moscow were carried on as before, Comintern or no. The dissolution was a gesture to allay some nagging doubts of the Western democracies, Russia's wartime allies. Six months later, Stalin had his first meeting with Roosevelt and Churchill, in neighboring Iran, to coordinate wartime strategy. Never before had he met or conferred with the heads of the great capitalist powers. The Soviet Union, it seemed to many observers at that time, had become plain old Russia again, nationalist and conservatively imperial. In view of Russia's need for Western support, Stalin's offhand scrapping of the Comintern reminds one of Napoleon's efforts to join the family of European monarchies by divorcing his parvenue French wife for an Austrian princess.

In 1945, just after Hitler's defeat, Stalin at a victory celebration offered a well-publicized toast to the *Russian* people. Then as now, ethnic Russians were less than 55 percent of the total Soviet population. In this brief speech Stalin was not only elevating them above national minorities large and small, but also throwing a barb at those non-Russians who, rightly or wrongly, had been accused of collaboration, and in some cases deported eastward as entire nations:

> I should like to drink to the health of our Soviet people . . . and first of all to the health of the Russian people . . . because it is the most outstanding nation of all the nations forming the Soviet Union. . . . It has won in this war universal recognition as the leading force in the Soviet Union among all the peoples of our country. . . . The confidence of the Russian people in the Soviet government was the decisive force which ensured the historic victory over the enemy of mankind—fascism.[7]

[6] Walter Kolarz, *Religion in the Soviet Union* (New York: St. Martin's Press, 1961), pp. 48–51.

[7] Quoted in Hans Kohn, *Pan-Slavism: Its History and Ideology* (New York: Vintage Books, 1960), p. 297. By permission of Harvard University Press.

Nationalism and Ideology Mix

Yet those who prophesied the end of Soviet Marxism were proven wrong during the Stalin's last years. From 1946 on, nationalist symbols were played down, though by no means abolished. A fresh emphasis was placed on ideological purity in all spheres of life. One must bear in mind that "ideological purity" here refers to a Marxism embracing some peculiar Russian and Stalinist amendments. Years before, Stalin had created a very convenient ideological short circuit when he claimed that support of the Soviet Union was the supreme obligation of communist parties everywhere, no matter what their local needs. Promoting the coming world revolution, therefore, did not necessarily mean supporting foreign parties and movements that were eager to get on with the job. Nevertheless, the late 1940s saw a return to Soviet Marxism as the supreme justification of material sacrifices and the renewed industrialization drive. The interpretation of Isaac Deutscher is of interest here:

> We have seen that the two policies, the nationalist and the revolutionary, clashed on crucial points. Stalin did not, nevertheless, make a clear-cut choice between the two; he pursued both lines simultaneously; but whereas the nationalist one predominated during the war, the revolutionary one was to gain momentum after the war.[8]

Stalin's appeal to national unity via the Russian past, though it could be reconciled in a rough-and-ready fashion with the rest of Soviet Marxism, was an indirect confession of the regime's failure to create a new Soviet identity to replace separate national identities. The return to Russian nationalism may have been prompted partly by the fierce opposition to collectivization in the Ukraine and certain other non-Russian areas. Stalin's mistrust of the non-Russians deepened during the 1930s, and reached a climax with the wartime deportations. Russian nationalism became, for the time being, a substitute appeal to unity which attempted to compensate for the political, social, and national divisions promoted by Stalin to achieve his goals.

Interpreting National Histories and Cultures

If the World War II period had seen the height of the Russian nationalist revival, it had also been a period of cultural liberalism, at least by comparison with the decade of the 1930s. In 1946, when Zhdanov condemned the fruits of this liberalism and called for ideological conformity in every sphere, the axe fell on national cultural expression as well. This began with a major attack on some leading Ukrainian writers

---

[8] Isaac Deutscher, *Stalin: A Political Biography* (New York: Oxford University Press, 1949), p. 552.

The Evolution of Soviet Politics

as well as on the head of the Ukrainian branch of the Union of Soviet Writers, who was dismissed as a "prisoner of bourgeois nationalism." Frequently these attacks criticized the failure of a writer, poet, or even composer to stress the historic friendship of his people for the Russian people, and the debt they supposedly owed to Russians. For example, a work by a Turkmen poet was criticized for having

> glossed over the historical fact that only annexation by Russia had saved the Turkmen people from age-long slavery and complete ruin, and that thanks only to the October Socialist Revolution and the Soviet régime were the Turkmen people able to begin a new life and to achieve great success in economic and cultural development.[9]

A biography of the famous 19th-century Ukrainian poet Taras Shevchenko was attacked for failing to point out that his political views were derived from the well-known Russian radicals of the same era. A Georgian composer's opera about the Civil War period in the Caucasus, Vano Muradeli's *The Great Friendship*, first performed in 1947, became the target of a Central Committee resolution. This expressed outrage at the opera's suggestion that Georgians and other Caucasian peoples had initially been hostile to the Russians during the Civil War.[10]

The theme of the benefits of Russia's annexation of the non-Russian nations was strongly emphasized during the last years of Stalin's rule. The union of the Ukraine with Russia in 1654, for example, was treated as the very cornerstone of the Ukraine's subsequent progress. The 250 years of Tsarist oppression and national discrimination that followed were ignored, and the tercentenary of union was celebrated in 1954 with much fanfare. The conquest of Central Asia in the latter 19th century, the conquest of the northern Caucasus earlier, and the union of Georgia and Russia in 1801 were dealt with similarly.

With this emphasis on Russian hegemony went a deprecation of national heroes, real or legendary. During Stalin's last years the national epics of the Moslem nations were attacked as alien to the very cultures that had produced them. The Buryat Mongol epic *Geser* fell under Moscow's ban because the mythical Geser was in reality Genghis Khan. The Azerbaidzhanian epic *Dede Korkut* was termed "an instrument for Pan-Turkic and other bourgeois propaganda." Several other epics fared similarly.[11]

Khrushchev's de-Stalinization campaign provided the impetus for tem-

[9] Conquest, *Soviet Nationalities Policy in Practice*, p. 66.

[10] The text of this resolution, which attacked other tendencies in contemporary Soviet music as well, is in James H. Meisel and Edward S. Kozera (eds.), *Materials for the Study of the Soviet System*, 2d ed. (Ann Arbor, Mich.: George Wahr Publishing Co., 1953), pp. 414–18.

[11] Conquest, *Soviet Nationalities Policy in Practice*, pp. 66–70.

pering the extreme condemnation of these aspects of national cultures. Only a few months after the 20th Party Congress (1956), the Union of Soviet Writers promoted the rehabilitation of the national epics just mentioned, together with traditions and literary works of other nations which had likewise been attacked. Simultaneously, in the summer of 1956, a conference of Ukrainian historians supported views that had been condemned for the past quarter-century. Steps were taken to modify the official Russophile view of the 1654 union with Russia; the contributions of the gentry and of bourgeois historians to Ukrainian historiography were recognized once more; and one historian even raised the highly sensitive question of Ukrainian opposition to the Bolsheviks in the Civil War:

> A serious lacuna is that in recent historical works nobody has posed the question about [Russian] great power chauvinism in the Ukraine and the great damage which it inflicted upon the cause of fighting Ukrainian bourgeois nationalism, the cause of constructing a sovereign Ukrainian Soviet State.[12]

From the mid-1950s until the present, there has been a constant interplay between the Party's demands concerning the use of national cultures and history, and efforts by local officials, writers, and scholars to maintain a coherent, positive interpretation of their cultures. Attacks on what Party officials claimed was resurgent bourgeois nationalism resumed in 1959. While these attacks have come in the form of press campaigns and public statements coordinated over a period of several months each, hardly a year has passed without public criticism of nationalism in some form. The perennial problem for local officials and intellectuals in the non-Russian republics is to test which parts of their national cultures can be made acceptable. To take one example, the Kirghiz poet Tynystanov, whose writings had been condemned under Stalin but admitted to favor after 1956, was praised in 1960 by a lecturer at the Kirghiz State University as the founder of Kirghiz Soviet literature. The lecturer was then attacked for having "interpreted the civil rehabilitation of K. Tynystanov as an amnesty for his nationalist views."[13] A more recent example from the same republic was an attack by the chief of the Kirghiz Communist Party on local poets who devoted too much attention to glorifying their nation's spectacular mountain scenery, making them "a fetish, a subject to be revered as a deity."[14]

---

[12] From an article by N. Suprunenko, quoted in Yaroslav Bilinsky, *The Second Soviet Republic: The Ukraine After World War II* (New Brunswick, N.J.: Rutgers University Press, 1964), p. 207.

[13] Conquest, *Soviet Nationalities Policy in Practice*, pp. 68–69.

[14] Theodore Shabad, "Odes to Snowy Peaks Irk a Soviet Official," *New York Times*, July 15, 1973.

Toward a Homogeneous Culture

Authoritative recent statements on the future of Soviet nationalities point toward their fusion at some point into a common culture. The 1961 Party Program stated that "under socialism the nations flourish and their sovereignty grows stronger." Nevertheless, it established that the boundaries between the republics "are increasingly losing their former significance," and that events are leading toward "a greater social homogeneity of nations" by way of "common communist traits in their culture, morals and way of living." The Party Program marked the beginning of a new phase of development in the Soviet Union's history, that of "full-scale communist construction," and during this period "the nations will draw still closer together until complete unity is achieved." However, the Program warned that "the obliteration of national distinctions, and especially of language distinctions, is a considerably longer process than the obliteration of class distinctions."[15] A decade later, Brezhnev had the following to say at a Supreme Soviet meeting commemorating the 50th anniversary of the agreement to form a federal system (1922–72):

> The further drawing together of the nations and nationalities of our country is an objective process. The Party is against the forcing of this process—there is no need for this, since the process is dictated by the entire course of our Soviet life. At the same time, the Party regards as impermissible any attempt whatsoever to hold back the process of the drawing together of nations, to obstruct it on any pretext or artificially to reinforce national isolation, because this would be at variance with the general direction of the development of our society, the Communists' internationalist ideals and ideology and the interests of communist construction.
>
> Lenin spoke out very clearly on this score: "The proletariat cannot support any reinforcement of nationalism—on the contrary, it supports everything that helps to obliterate national distinctions and to remove national barriers, everything that makes the ties between nationalities closer and closer."[16]

If the frequency, tone, and content of public attacks on nationalism may be taken as an indication of how Soviet leaders view their progress—

---

[15] Jan F. Triska (ed.), *Soviet Communism: Programs and Rules* (San Francisco: Chandler, 1962), pp. 107–109.

[16] L. I. Brezhnev, "On the 50th Anniversary of the Union of Soviet Socialist Republics," *Pravda*, Dec. 22, 1972. Translation from *Current Digest of the Soviet Press* 24 (Jan. 17, 1973), pp. 9–10. The actual event which determined the timing of the anniversary celebration was the convoking of the First Congress of Soviets of the USSR, Dec. 30–31, 1922. The Central Executive Committee of the USSR approved the draft Constitution the following July, and it was ratified by the Second All-Union Congress of Soviets on Jan. 31, 1924, just ten days after Lenin's death.

or lack of it—toward the obliteration of national distinctions, nationalism is regarded with as much concern in the 1970s as it was in the 1960s or 1950s. The Brezhnev administration appears to regard the 1961 Party Program as fully valid in its promise to merge the Soviet nationalities into a single international culture, even though other parts of the Program have been deemphasized. If the Program's prophecy about the "obliteration of national distinctions" is seldom repeated, the trends which lead in that direction are strongly supported.

The federation anniversary in 1972 was followed by a vigorous campaign of newspaper articles and statements by public figures, including most notably the Party leaders of the Union Republics, all calling for a drive to build the internationalist features of the non-Russian republics, and at the same time flaying negative manifestations of nationalism. Reporting on progress in his republic, the head of the Moldavian Communist Party attacked a number of Moldavian writers, summarizing their errors thus:

> It must constantly be remembered that attempts to lead literature and the arts away from ideological conviction and into abstraction and national narrow-mindedness are launched from various positions. Here one finds people trying to capitalize on the "sanctity" of the nation's cultural heritage, playing on feelings of allegiance to "the homeland's past," a fawning before religion, a melancholy longing for thatched roofs and peasant ceremonies, etc. National narrow-mindedness, alienation and exclusiveness are manifested in a good many forms, but their essence is the same. They all reflect an attempt to preserve and revive nationalistic prejudices, to cultivate autarky and parochialism, to weaken the unity and internationalist convictions of Soviet people. These tendencies are alien to the interests of the Moldavian people; they distract some people, especially young people, from active participation in sociopolitical life, impede the development of communist consciousness and the formation of new traditions and ceremonies and create conditions for the operation of illegal sectarians and other hostile elements. . . .[17]

The head of the Turkmen Communist Party found many faults in his republic having to do with national narrowness. Education in socialist internationalism had been neglected in higher education, he reported, where "certain students do not understand the internationalist essence of our social system or the fact that the Turkmen Republic's achievements are the result of the joint efforts of all the Soviet peoples." What remains of the Islamic faith is still a danger, since it "plays the role of 'custodian' of reactionary national customs and traditions, stirs up feelings of national exclusiveness and serves as a cover for nationalism." Writers on the re-

---

[17] *Sovetskaya Moldaviya*, April 27, 1973. Translation from *Current Digest of the Soviet Press* 25 (May 16, 1973), pp. 9–10.

mote past of the Turkmen people "in defiance of the truth, create portraits of the Khans that exaggerate the enlightened aspects of their lives and play down their antipopular activity."[18]

Similar reports came from nearly all of the other Union Republics, with local variations: in the Ukraine, Zionism was mentioned alongside bourgeois nationalism as a major force to be overcome. The First Secretary of the Armenian Party warned against the ideological inroads of the Dashnaks, the major political organization of Armenian emigrants; speakers at a Georgian Party conclave mentioned the narrow nationalism of the smaller nationalities within Georgia as a negative force.[19] The ritual character of these reports and statements is evident: they are intended as proof that the various Party organizations in the republics are responding energetically to the demands put forth by Brezhnev, Masherov, and other speakers at the federalism anniversary in December 1972. But there is more than ritual in the overall pattern of the Brezhnev regime's drive to promote internationalism, defined in this context as development of common characteristics among the Soviet nationalities. Language policy and demographic mingling are today being used with very serious intent as the chief practical means of fusing many cultures into a single culture.

LANGUAGE POLICY

What was done for the non-Russian languages under Lenin and through the 1920s was very significant in providing a basis for continued national identity, even if this was not Lenin's intention for the long run. In a number of cases, the very recognition of local languages for official use and as a medium of instruction was itself an enormous concession. The Tsarist regime had pursued a policy of selective Russification, which had affected the Ukraine and Byelorussia particularly. For some of the nations of Siberia, only some of which had been affected by Russification, it meant a totally unprecedented recognition and the introduction of an alphabet. In Transcaucasia, linguistic recognition did not represent a great change, particularly because the Armenians and Georgians could look back on a rich store of written culture which antedated that of Russia by centuries. Central Asia, too, possessed a written culture and a linguistic identity that had been scarcely affected by Tsarist policy. St. Petersburg had not sought to transform these tightly knit non-Slavic cultures, concerning itself rather with breaking political opposition.

---

[18] *Turkmenskaya Iskra*, April 3, 1973. Translation from *Current Digest of the Soviet Press* 25 (May 16, 1973), p. 10.

[19] These reports are available in *Current Digest of the Soviet Press* 25 (April 11, 1973) and 25 (May 16, 1973).

Goals of Language Policy

Policy concerning the content and evolution of the non-Russian languages has served several purposes. Literacy was a major goal in the 1920s and 1930s, which meant that written languages had to be made accessible, and in some cases a system of writing devised where none was present. Another goal was to use language as one means for distinguishing many non-Russian cultures from related cultures abroad. Tadzhik was made distinct from Persian, Karelian from Finnish, and Moldavian (after 1940) from Romanian. A third goal was to use non-Russian languages as a vehicle for supporting the spread of Russian as a second language. In Central Asia, the introduction of a Latin alphabet in place of Arabic writing was designed to remove these cultures one step further from the Moslem world outside Soviet borders. In 1937, Latinization was abandoned, and the Cyrillic alphabet introduced instead, partly in order to ease the learning of Russian. In many languages, Russian loan words were introduced in large numbers, while loan words from other languages were rooted out (e.g., Arabic and Persian terms from Uzbek). A fourth goal was to make the non-Russian languages viable for use in scientific and technological communication. During the 1920s, Moscow had promoted the modernization of these languages to this end, using indigenous roots wherever possible. In the 1930s, however, a drive was begun to use Russian loan words instead, and this policy has continued to the present day.

Extent of the Use of Russian

Among the most interesting census data are the figures showing what proportion of each nationality regards the national language as its native tongue. Unlike Tsarist census figures, which defined nationalities as linguistic groups, Soviet censuses have separated ethnic from linguistic identification. In 1926, Russians comprised 54 percent of the USSR population by nationality, but 58.5 percent of the population designated Russian as its native language; that is, 4.5 percent stated that linguistically they had been Russified. In 1959 this had risen to 4.8 percent, and in 1970 to 5.4 percent. While on the surface these figures suggest that Russification is proceeding only very slowly, one must consider that some 20 million non-Russians were added through territorial expansion in the 1940s (the Baltic countries, eastern Poland, northern Bukovina, Bessarabia, and Tannu Tuva). This helps explain the fact that the number thus Russified has doubled in the same period, from 6.5 million in 1926 to 13 million in 1970. Meanwhile the number of those using non-Russian languages as their primary tongue has risen from 60 to 100 million. In a number of nationalities, the proportion of those adhering to their native language has actually increased: among Georgians, for example, from 96.5 percent in 1926 to 98.4 percent in 1970, though the trend has been slightly downward since the 1959 census. The Ukrainians and Byelorussians have shown a slight trend toward Russification during the 1960s (87.7 to 85.7 percent and 84.2 to 80.6 percent, respectively) while the Central Asians have stayed consistently above 98 percent and the three Baltic peoples above 95 percent, with no sign of a downward trend.[20]

In recent years much official attention has been given to promoting Russian as the "inter-nationality language of multi-lingual Soviet society," a formulation which leaves room for the continued existence of the non-Russian tongues, while elevating Russian as the common medium of expression. Presumably Russian will be the language of the distant future, when there will remain only a single Soviet people instead of nationalities. An important question here, apart from the question of doctrine, is the extent to which Soviet policies have deliberately extended the use of Russian beyond what would have happened without any particular pressure from Moscow. Russian would doubtless have remained the lingua franca of the Soviet Union in any case. The spread of industries and urbanization to non-Russian areas also promoted the use of Russian, since during the early stages of industrialization (in both the Witte period and the early Five-Year Plans) the importation of Russian specialists and skilled workers was the quickest way of providing this kind of manpower. Also, the fact that many languages do not develop an indigenous terminology of science and technology may be the result of circumstances other than linguistic suppression.

Language Use in the Schools

Some policies have definitely encouraged both the spread of Russian as a lingua franca and the eventual adoption of Russian as a first language. The 1958 education reform proposed that the parents of schoolchildren be given the choice between Russian and the local non-Russian language as a medium of instruction. Whichever they chose, their children could also study the other in regular language classes. This idea was the subject of vigorous debate, and the choice was then left to the individual Republics, almost all of which opted for this plan. Except for Central Asia, there was opposition to this plan in most of the major non-Russian Republics. There the fear was that the plan offered an entering wedge by which Russian would supplant local languages, the latter remaining optional. Up to that time, over 60 non-Russian languages had been used at the primary level, their number and use decreasing at the secondary

[20] Richard Pipes, "The Forces of Nationalism," in Paul Hollander (ed.), *American and Soviet Society: A Reader in Comparative Sociology and Perception* (Englewood Cliffs, N.J.: Prentice-Hall, 1969), pp. 313–15.

level, and Russian predominating in higher education. The major consequence of this debate was that it led later to measures for the obligatory
study of Russian in all schools. Russian schoolchildren living in non-Russian areas have no similar obligation to study the local language. Russians
generally have shown little inclination to learn the non-Russian languages.

The language issue is a very live one today. The 1958 reforms were
followed by sharp debates over the use of the non-Russian languages.
A 1959 purge in Latvia was occasioned partly by the insistence of some
local officials on compulsory study of Latvian. A meeting of the Ukrainian
Academy of Sciences in 1964 saw the defeat of proposals that the use
of Ukrainian be extended. Educational reforms during the Brezhnev period have been accompanied by renewed debate over the school language
policy. A new draft law on education, published for discussion purposes
in the spring of 1973, continued the 1958 policy by specifying "instruction in one's native language or another language of the peoples of the
USSR, and freedom of choice in the language of instruction." In secondary education, parents are given the right, in the draft, to select
for their children a school "with the appropriate language of instruction."
Students are to have the opportunity to study, in addition, another of
the languages spoken in the Soviet Union.[21]

Rights are one thing, policy and administrative practices another. The
1961 Party Program, after specifying complete freedom of choice in
language use, including selecting a language of instruction for one's children, had the following to say about policy:

> The voluntary study of Russian in addition to the native language
> is of positive significance, since it facilitates reciprocal exchanges of
> experience and access of every nation and nationality to the cultural
> gains of all the other peoples of the USSR, and to world culture.
> The Russian language has, in effect, become the common medium of
> intercourse and cooperation among all the peoples of the USSR.[22]

P. M. Masherov, head of the Byelorussian Party, a Politburo member,
and today one of the Party's chief spokesmen on nationality relations
wrote a major article on the eve of the 1972 federation anniversary which
emphasized the need for making knowledge of Russian universal in the
Soviet Union. This is necessary, he stated, for anyone who wishes to
be among the "creators of communist civilization":

> Obviously, one important task consists in creating in all the country's
> republics conditions facilitating and stimulating as much as possible
> the working people's mastery of the Russian language, along with their
> own native tongues. From this standpoint, a correct orientation on
> the part of the Party, state and public organizations, the family and

---

[21] *Izvestiya*, April 5, 1973.

[22] Triska, *Soviet Communism*, p. 109.

the school, as well as extensive and painstaking work to expand the training and improve the qualifications of the requisite cadres of pedagogues and philologists and to improve the quality of teaching of the Russian language in national schools, are equally necessary.[23]

One example of this policy in practice is a recent campaign in Azerbaidzhan both to improve the teaching of Russian, and to extend the use of Russian as a language of instruction. "As of 1970," a press item reported, "the teaching of Russian was introduced everywhere beginning with the first grade and, the voluntary principle notwithstanding, there has not been a single case yet of unwillingness or refusal to study Russian." Steps were taken to train more Russian language teachers. Formerly a local pedagogical institute trained teachers to give instruction in both the Russian and Azerbaidzhan languages, but this program reverted to Russian only in 1970. In higher education, in the technicums (specialized secondary schools) and in vocational schools, Russian is already the predominant language. But the head of the Azerbaidzhan Communist Party reported in the spring of 1973 that many instructors in these institutions still had a poor command of Russian. He stressed the use of television and radio as a means of promoting knowledge of Russian among the population generally.[24]

In sum, while the Soviet regime has done much to promote the non-Russian languages, it has also sought to create a setting in which the use of Russian will spread by stages, ultimately at the expense of the others. This has created enough resistance among many non-Russians to make language policy into a source of continued concern on both sides.[25]

DEMOGRAPHIC DEVELOPMENTS AND POLICY

Tables 14–1 and 14–2 speak eloquently of several trends and relationships. A declining birth rate among the Slavic nationalities stands in sharp contrast to the rapid increase of some of the non-Slavs, notably the Central Asians (Uzbeks, Tadzhiks, Turkmens, and Kirghiz) and the Kazakhs. The slight Russian majority in the USSR population is decreasing rather

---

[23] P. Masherov, "On Certain Features of Nationality Relations in the Conditions of Developed Socialism," *Kommunist*, no. 15 (October) 1972, pp. 15–33. Translation of this passage from *Current Digest of the Soviet Press* 24 (Dec. 13, 1972), p. 5.

[24] L. Tairov, "In the Language of Brotherhood," *Pravda*, October 28, 1972; report by G. A. Aliyev in *Bakinsky Rabochy*, April 20, 1973. Translation in *Current Digest of the Soviet Press* 24 (Nov. 22, 1972), p. 23, and 25 (May 16, 1973), p. 7.

[25] Developments of the 1950s and 1960s are summarized in Jacob Ornstein, "Soviet Language Policy: Continuity and Change," in Erich Goldhagen (ed.), *Ethnic Minorities in the Soviet Union* (New York: Praeger, 1968), pp. 121–46.

TABLE 14-1
National Composition of the Soviet Population
in 1959 and 1970
(in millions)

Nationality	1959 Census		1970 Census	
	Number	Percent of Total	Number	Percent of Total
All Nationalities.	208.8	100.0	241.7	100.0
Russians	114.1	54.6	129.0	53.4
Ukrainians	37.3	17.8	40.1	16.7
Uzbeks	6.0	2.9	9.2	3.8
Byelorussians	7.9	3.8	9.1	3.7
Tatars	5.0	2.4	5.9	2.4
Kazakhs	3.6	1.7	5.3	2.2
Azerbaidzhanians	2.9	1.4	4.4	1.8
Armenians	2.8	1.3	3.6	1.5
Georgians	2.7	1.3	3.2	1.3
Moldavians	2.2	1.1	2.7	1.1
Lithuanians	2.3	1.1	2.7	1.1
Jews	2.3	1.1	2.2	0.9
Tadzhiks	1.4	0.7	2.1	0.9
Germans	1.6	0.8	1.8	0.8
Chuvash	1.5	0.7	1.7	0.7
Turkmenians	1.0	0.5	1.5	0.6
Kirghiz	1.0	0.5	1.5	0.6
Latvians	1.4	0.7	1.4	0.6
Mordvinians	1.3	0.6	1.3	0.5
Bashkirs	1.0	0.4	1.2	0.5
Poles	1.4	0.7	1.2	0.5
Estonians	1.0	0.4	1.0	0.4

Source: *Pravda*, April 17, 1971. A full table in translation is available in *Current Digest of the Soviet Press*, vol. 23 (May 18, 1971), pp. 14–18. Percentage data have been computed. Omitted are data on nationalities numbering less than 1 million, 69 in number, plus a residual figure for very small national categories.

than increasing. This trend is likely to continue in spite of Moscow's current campaign to increase births generally. Nationally, Soviet population growth has declined from a postwar (1950) 17 per thousand annual increase to below 9 per thousand at the end of the 1960s. Meanwhile the rates for the four Central Asian republics and for Armenia have remained between double and triple the latter national rate.[26] The many calls for an increased Soviet birth rate, which have appeared frequently in the Soviet press during the early 1970s, can be interpreted partly as a campaign to increase the birth rate of Russians and of Slavs generally.

[26] Ellen Mickiewicz (ed.), *Handbook of Soviet Social Science Data* (New York: The Free Press, 1972), p. 51. *Narodnoye khozyaistvo SSSR v 1967 g.* (Moscow: Statistika, 1968), pp. 40–41.

TABLE 14–2
Population of the Union Republics and Their National Composition,
1959 and 1970

Republic and Nationalities	1959 Census		1970 Census	
	Number	Percent of Total	Number	Percent of Total
Russian.	117.5	100.0	130.1	100.0
Russians	97.9	83.3	107.7	82.8
Tatars	4.1	3.5	4.8	3.7
Ukrainians.	3.4	2.9	3.3	2.6
Chuvash	1.4	1.2	1.6	1.3
Bashkirs	1.0	0.8	1.2	0.9
Mordvinians	1.2	1.0	1.2	0.9
Peoples of Daghestan.	0.8	0.7	1.2	0.9
Ukrainian	41.9	100.0	47.1	100.0
Ukrainians.	32.2	76.8	35.3	74.9
Russians	7.1	16.9	9.1	19.4
Byelorussian.	8.1	100.0	9.0	100.0
Byelorussians	6.5	81.1	7.3	81.0
Russians	0.7	8.2	0.9	10.4
Uzbek	8.3	100.0	12.0	100.0
Uzbeks.	5.0	61.1	7.7	64.7
Russians	1.1	13.5	1.5	12.5
Kazakh.	9.2	100.0	12.8	100.0
Kazakhs	2.7	29.8	4.2	32.4
Russians	3.9	43.2	5.5	42.8
Georgian	4.0	100.0	4.7	100.0
Georgians	2.6	64.3	3.1	66.8
Armenians.	0.4	0.5	11.0	9.7
Russians	0.4	10.1	0.4	8.5
Azerbaidzhan	3.7	100.0	5.1	100.0
Azerbaidzhanians.	2.5	67.5	3.8	73.8
Russians	0.5	13.6	0.5	10.0
Armenians.	0.4	0.5	12.0	9.4
Lithuanian.	2.7	100.0	3.1	100.0
Lithuanians	2.2	79.3	2.5	80.1
Russians	0.2	8.5	0.3	8.6
Moldavian	2.9	100.0	3.6	100.0
Moldavians	1.9	65.4	2.3	64.6
Ukrainians.	0.4	14.6	0.5	14.2
Russians	0.3	10.2	0.4	11.6
Latvian.	2.1	100.0	2.4	100.0
Latvians	1.3	62.0	1.3	56.8
Russians	0.6	26.6	0.7	29.8
Kirghiz	2.1	100.0	2.9	100.0
Kirghiz.	0.8	40.5	1.3	43.8
Russians	0.6	30.2	0.9	29.2
Uzbeks.	0.2	10.6	0.3	11.3
Tadzhik	2.0	100.0	2.9	100.0
Tadzhiks.	1.1	53.1	1.6	56.2
Uzbeks.	0.5	23.0	0.7	23.0
Russians	0.3	0.3	13.3	11.9
Armenian	1.8	100.0	2.5	100.0
Armenians.	1.5	88.0	2.2	88.6
Russians	0.06	3.2	0.07	2.7

TABLE 14–2 (*Continued*)

Republic and Nationalities	1959 Census		1970 Census	
	Number	Percent of Total	Number	Percent of Total
Turkmenian	1.5	100.0	2.2	100.0
Turkmenians	0.9	60.9	1.4	65.6
Russians	0.3	17.3	0.3	14.5
Estonian	1.2	100.0	1.4	100.0
Estonians	9.0	74.6	9.0	68.2
Russians	0.2	20.1	0.3	24.7

Source: *Pravda*, April 17, 1971. A full table in translation is available in *Current Digest of the Soviet Press*, vol. 23 (May 18, 1971), pp. 14–18. Figures are rounded to the nearest 100,000. Only those nationalities are shown which either numbered over 1 million in either year, or comprised over 10 percent of the population of a republic in either year. Figures for the Russian population are shown in every case.

Intermarriage

Brezhnev in his major address on the 50th anniversary of federation noted with approval that "the number of mixed marriages in the country is growing—the figure is in the millions."[27] Data on intermarriage among the nationalities are available only in certain forms, but from what has been published there emerges a picture of considerable intermarriage, occurring at an increasing rate, but with striking national variations.

In the mid-1960s the national rate was 102 mixed marriages per thousand, the highest rates being in Latvia (158) and the Ukraine (150).[28] The lowest rate was in Armenia (32). Not unsurprisingly, the proportion was found to be far higher for urban than for rural populations, and higher in large cities than in smaller communities. Urban mixed marriages for the USSR were 151 per thousand as against 58 for the countryside. Figures from selected Soviet cities show that the proportion of mixed marriages occurring each year has risen significantly in some cases: in Tashkent, capital of the Uzbek Republic, from 0.7 percent in 1937 to 20 percent in 1959, for example.[29] Because of the incompleteness of data, it is impossible to tell what proportion of these marriages cross the sharper racial lines, particularly in the case of marriages between Slavs and Central Asians. For example, in the mid-1960s the writer was told in

[27] *Pravda*, Dec. 22, 1972. Translation from *Current Digest of the Soviet Press* 24 (Jan. 17, 1973), p. 8.

[28] Yaroslav Bilinsky, "Assimilation and Ethnic Assertiveness Among Ukrainians of the Soviet Union," in Goldhagen (ed.), *Ethnic Minorities in the Soviet Union*, pp. 156–57.

[29] A. I. Kholmogorov, *Internatsionalnye cherty sovetskikh natsii* ("International Features of Soviet Nations") (Moscow: "Mysl," 1970), pp. 82–90.

Samarkand that such marriages were a rarity; but in Tashkent, a much larger city, they were certainly no longer a rarity.

Mixing through Migration

Population movements are a matter of serious concern, because they offer the quickest path to the spread of the Russian language and culture. The movement of Russians into the major Ukrainian cities, a phenomenon which began long before the Revolution, has resulted in the predominant use of Russian in these cities, including an increase in the number of Ukrainians whose primary language is now Russian.[30] Table 14–2 shows the extent to which the Russian population of the Ukraine has been increasing—28 percent in slightly over a decade. The preponderance of Russians in Kazakhstan is an old phenomenon, though recently it has been offset somewhat by the high Kazakh birth rate. The Kazakhs' enormous geographical dispersion, a heritage of their nomadism of past centuries, paved the way for this dilution through immigration. The Russian influx into all three Baltic republics has created a good deal of social friction there, and this has been one factor spurring a series of recent protest actions. Another kind of concern about the nationhood of the non-Russians has been the extent of emigration from the non-Russian areas, the result in most cases of manpower needs, and effected partly through the job assignment system for university and school graduates. One wonders, for example, whether the decline of Ukrainians in the Russian Republic is due to Russification in the form of young people's identifying themselves as Russians when their internal passports are drawn up.

As with trends in language use, the big question here is the extent to which the Soviet regime has promoted the dilution of ethnic distinctness through population movements. The pattern of Russians moving out into the non-Russian areas was well established before the Revolution. In the 1920s and 1930s there was every reason to bring Russian specialists and skilled workers to the new industrial projects outside the Russian Republic, local skills being in short supply or completely unavailable. At the time, this trend was publicized as a campaign by the Russian proletariat to come to the aid of working people in the non-Russian areas, and much was made of the Russian workers' role as a key factor in transforming the economy and society of the other nationalities. Since the Khrushchev era, and very markedly in the Brezhnev period, the emphasis has been on population exchanges in all directions, a trend which is bringing about a new social entity, the "Soviet people." Masherov,

---

[30] Bilinsky, "Assimilation and Ethnic Assertiveness Among Ukrainians of the Soviet Union," pp. 159–60.

in the 1972 statement quoted earlier, was specific about the means to accomplish this:

> It is noteworthy that the composition of the populations of the Soviet republics, owing mainly to the action of the principles of internationalism, the expansion of production ties and exchanges of cadres of workers and specialists, is becoming more and more multinational, with a simultaneous absolute increase in the number of residents belonging to the indigenous nationalities. Data from the census of 1970 indicate that the population of the Central Asian republics and Kazakhstan increased by 1,200,000 people in the preceding years through the arrival of people from other parts of the country. In the same period, the number of Byelorussians in the Ukraine increased by 95,000, while the number of Ukrainians in Byelorussia went up by 58,000. The intensification of the multinational composition of all areas of the U.S.S.R. is a logical and progressive phenomenon. The preservation of the population's national homogeneity through artificial measures would contradict the objective processes of the social and economic development and drawing together of the socialist nations. . . .[31]

Observers of the Soviet scene sometimes make the distinction between "Russification" and "Russianization." While Russification means the ultimate linguistic, cultural, and (eventually) ethnic extermination of this or that non-Russian people, Russianization means the adoption of Russian as a much-used second language by non-Russians, plus their adaptation to Russian culture and social norms and expectations, without renouncing their ethnic identity altogether. It is reasonable to conclude that the policy of promoting the "drawing together" of nations by manipulating population movements would result in a Russianized population, if carried far enough. What, for example, will happen to Kazakh culture and the Kazakh language if the influx of Russians and Ukrainians into that Republic continues? While the high Kazakh birth rate had increased the Kazakhs' share in the total population by a few percentage points in spite of the influx, population mixing in the cities plus intermarriage cannot but threaten the Kazakh national identity. From the official Soviet point of view, both the mixing and the change of identity are to be welcomed. Said Brezhnev in 1972:

> The more intensive the economic and social development of each national republic is, the more pronounced the process of the internationalization of all our life becomes. For example, take Soviet Kazakhstan, which is growing rapidly. Along with the Kazakhs, millions of Russians and hundreds of thousands of Ukrainians, Uzbeks, Byelorussians, etc., are now living there. Kazakh culture is developing and becoming richer as it increasingly absorbs the best elements of Russian,

---

[31] Masherov, "On Certain Features of Nationality Relations in the Conditions of Developed Socialism," p. 4.

Ukrainian and other cultures. Is this good or bad? We Communists
confidently reply: It is good, very good![32]

THE ROLE OF ECONOMIC POLICY

Foreign travellers in the non-Russian republics sometimes meet non-
Russians who claim that their republics or national areas are exploited
economically: Moscow takes out more than it puts back in. There are
Ukrainians who maintain that their important mining and heavy industry
have contributed much but reaped fewer rewards than the Russian Republic's industries; some Georgians say that while their prosperous republic was treated fairly by Stalin, Khrushchev turned the tables against
it economically in his desire for vengeance against Stalin's memory. While
even Soviet studies of the question have noted differences in the level
of prosperity as among the Union Republics, it is difficult to demonstrate
conclusively, and as a general statement, the charge that Moscow has
treated the non-Russian republics as economic colonies. Also, since there
are no comprehensive data on individual incomes and living conditions
by *nationality*—and income data generally occur only in small samples
used in various studies and reports—there is no basis for drawing conclusions about the prosperity of Russians as opposed to non-Russians.

If one considers economic improvement as an indicator of how Moscow
is treating the non-Russian nationalities, then one must also consider
whether certain kinds of improvement are actually undermining a nationality's noneconomic characteristics—traditional culture, demographic
homogeneity, use of the native language, and others. One study of the
Lithuanian economy, highly critical of Soviet aims and methods, came
to precisely this conclusion about the industrialization of Lithuania. The
program of pushing industrialization in Lithuania, during the 1950s, at
a rate far above that for the Soviet Union as a whole, and in a republic
without the labor or material resources for this, can be interpreted only
as an effort to colonize Lithuania with Russians, according to this study.[33]

Equality and Disparities

Another study surveyed changes in the Union Republics during the
1950s and 1960s according to a list of 23 indices. These included data
on agricultural output, distribution of electric power, medical facilities,

---

[32] *Pravda*, Dec. 22, 1972. Translation from *Current Digest of the Soviet Press*
24 (Jan. 17, 1973), p. 8.

[33] Pranas Zunde, "Lithuania's Economy: Introduction of the Soviet Pattern,"
in V. Stanley Vardys (ed.), *Lithuania Under the Soviets* (New York: Praeger,
1965), pp. 141–69.

housing space and construction, educational enrollments, books published, and membership in the Party, Young Communist League, and trade unions. This was an attempt to discover whether certain republics were favored above others during this time span, in terms of overall welfare, cultural level, and political activity. The study concluded that, for the most part, the republics were changing in a similar manner during these two decades. Whatever inequalities existed at the beginning of the 1950s, therefore, remained two decades later. But beyond this fact, a pattern of discrimination was not present.[34]

Almost every kind of economic difference among the 15 republics can be assigned causes other than deliberate discrimination, although this is not to say that discrimination itself has not also been a cause. If the Russian Republic appears to have received more industrial investment than its share of the population indicates it should have, one must consider its enormous resources, and whether or not exploiting a given resource is advantageous compared with trying to get the same result in another republic. Lower-than-average industrial earnings in a given republic necessarily reflect differences in the "mix" of industries as among republics. The non-Russian republics generally have a higher proportion of light and food industries than does the Russian Republic, and wages in these industries are below the average industrial wage. Also, nearly all the areas for which the currently very high hardship wages are paid lie within the Russian Republic (northern and eastern Siberia). Differences in budget allocations for housing reflect differences in housing needs, climatic factors, differing construction costs per square meter, and the planned expansion of cities (or the building of new cities) because of industrial location policies.

Here are a few figures from a detailed study of this question: In 1965, average monthly wages for all except collective farmers were on the average 6.4 percent lower in the non-Russian republics than in the RSFSR; however, they had been 17.4 percent lower in 1940. Average per capita income taxes for 1960–65 were lower in all the non-Russian republics save for Latvia and Estonia, where they were 5.1 percent and 17.7 percent higher, respectively. The Ukrainian Republic came next after the RSFSR on this same scale, but well below it, with 77.90 rubles collected for every 100 rubles in the RSFSR. The other republics ranged below this, down to Moldavia, with 39.4 rubles. A computation of per capita disposable income showed exactly the same pattern: With the RSFSR set as 100.0 of the index, the Ukraine came next after it with 79.4; Moldavia, Azerbaidzhan, and Tadzhikstan stood lowest (55.7, 55.3, and 55.3, respectively); and Estonia and Latvia were well ahead (124.6

---

[34] Ellen Mickiewicz, "Uses and Strategies in Data Analysis of the Soviet Union: Cleavages in Industrial Society," in Mickiewicz, *Handbook of Soviet Social Science Data*, pp. 35–40.

and 115.8).[35] A Soviet study of some of these same indices agreed that the variation in actual wages was around 6 percent in the 1960s. After superimposing other indices to compensate for the different "mixes" of industrial branches and occupations, the study reduced the earnings difference and other differences statistically, in some cases to insignificant variations only.[36] The "index game" is a favorite sport of both Soviet and foreign economists in comparing Soviet performance with that of the other industrial nations. In cases such as this it all depends on whose indices one prefers.

As regards the income of collective farmers, a study by two British economists showed the farmers of Central Asia and Transcaucasia to have been vastly better off than those of European Russia and the Ukraine. Not all farmers in these two areas shared this prosperity, but those who did had earnings well above those of industrial workers. Today the advantaged position of these two areas remains, but the difference is considerably narrower. In 1950, for example, Central Asian collective farmers were receiving an average cash income nearly five times that of the Soviet average, while in 1958 it was 125 percent higher than the Soviet average.[37]

This same study showed that the two areas (Central Asia and Transcaucasia) have been contributing less than the average amount per capita to Soviet budgetary revenues. They have been permitted to keep a greater than average proportion of the revenues raised on their territories, and these have gone into both economic and social development. This was probably true even in Stalin's time, although the figures of that era do not form definite proof.[38] The non-Russian Slavic areas—the Ukraine and Byelorussia—have not enjoyed similar advantages.

Comparisons between the Transcaucasian and Central Asian Republics on the one hand, and adjacent regions of non-Soviet Asia on the other, are favorable to the Soviet Union on almost any count: Soviet Armenia versus Turkish Armenia, Soviet Azerbaidzhan versus Iranian Azerbaijan, and the Central Asian republics versus Afghanistan and northeastern Iran. The Soviet areas have developed more rapidly than their non-Soviet counterparts in both consumption and social services.

While there are definite regional differences in prosperity and resource allocations, some of these are to the advantage of the non-Russian repub-

---

[35] Vsevolod Holubnychy, "Some Economic Aspects of Relations Among the Soviet Republics," in Goldhagen, *Ethnic Minorities in the Soviet Union*, pp. 94, 95, and 97.

[36] V. Zlatin and V. Rutgaizer, "Comparison of the Levels of Economic Development of the Union Republics and Large Regions," *Problems of Economics* 12 (June 1969), pp. 3–24.

[37] Alec Nove and A. J. Newth, *The Soviet Middle East: A Communist Model for Development* (New York: Praeger, 1966), p. 103.

[38] Ibid., pp. 95–97.

exploitative systems; their use has been to reconcile the oppressed to their oppression and to give hope to those for whom there is no hope in the existing situation.

While Marx left no indication whether the proletariat should simply crush religion or let it die a natural death after the revolution, the Bolsheviks' first impulse was the former. But practical reasons dictated an accommodation. The Russian Orthodox Church had been an official religion, which had claim to important social functions (marriage and education) and served political purposes. The suppression of the 1905 disturbances was assisted by the so-called "Black Hundreds," Church-led campaigns which sought to intimidate the countryside. However, Russian Orthodoxy as a state church had performed at least two functions which the Soviet regime was to find useful later on: it served to whip up patriotism in time of war, and it guarded its near-monopoly position carefully against the inroads of Catholicism (on the Empire's western periphery), schismatic Orthodox groups, and protestantism. Therefore, as long as it remained inadvisable for the Soviets to disband all religious organizations by force, some kind of regulation of relations *among* religions was necessary. This goal was pursued in addition to that of establishing a strictly limited domain for religious practices within Soviet society.

These policies did not come fully into their own until after World War II, when, as we saw earlier, the Russian Orthodox Church turned out to be a useful aid to Russian patriotism. An accommodation between State and Church which had been worked out in the 1920s was threatened in the 1930s by an active state-sponsored campaign against religion, notably through the "League of the Militant Godless," organized in 1929. Churches were closed, religious processions and observances were subjected to attacks, and Sunday was abolished as a universal day of rest in favor of a rotating weekly holiday, a system which lasted only up to 1940. During World War II, the accommodation of the 1920s was reaffirmed, spelled out in greater detail, and in some respects amended to the benefit of the Church. Other religious bodies profited too, though not quite to the same extent: these were the Georgian and Armenian Orthodox Churches, the Old Believers (Orthodox schismatics whose movements date from the 17th century), Islamic bodies in Central Asia, and major protestant groups, two of which united in 1944 to form the "All-Union Council of Evangelical Christians and Baptists." The position of the Jewish synagogues improved only slightly and temporarily, soon to worsen under Stalin's anti-Semitic campaign. Roman Catholicism fared badly after the war for several reasons: its allegiance to a foreign authority, during a time when Soviet press attacks referred to the Vatican as "the Catholic branch of the State Department"; the fact that a large proportion of Catholics resided in the western areas which were acquired by the Soviet Union in 1940, then lost to the German invasion, and finally reconquered in 1944–45; and the centuries-old rivalry between the Russian Orthodox Church and Catholicism in these same areas.

While the position of the major religious bodies became somewhat easier in the 1950s, after Stalin's death, Soviet policies have fluctuated only within narrow limits. Considerably better coordination of policy was achieved by setting up (in 1943) two state offices which maintain permanent liaison with the "recognized" religious bodies: the Council for the Affairs of the Orthodox Church, and the Council for the Affairs of Religious Cults, an arrangement which reflects the primacy of Russian Orthodoxy in the eyes of Soviet policy-makers. The determinants of Soviet policies today fall into several broad categories: containment of religious practices, ideological combat, publicity use of religion, and the separation of religious from national identities.

Containment

Within less than three months after the Bolsheviks came to power, they had stripped the churches of their civil law functions (marriage and registration of civil status), proclaimed freedom of conscience, forbidden religious instruction in all general-education schools, public and private, and nationalized all property of religious organizations, allowing them to continue using it at the state's discretion.[44] Aside from the curious provision making the state the custodian of all church property, the early laws followed a strict line of separating church and state. They subjected religious organizations to the same regulations that govern other private organizations, and omitted all reference to religion in state documents (hence the absence of census figures on religion).

In later legislation, Soviet authorities sought to contain the influence of religious bodies rigorously by restricting their influence to their existing membership. While the 1918 Constitution guaranteed freedom of both religious and antireligious propaganda, the 1936 Constitution spoke only of freedom of religious *worship*. A law of 1929 stripped religious associations of almost every capacity that might enable them to grow and thrive: they could not be legal entities; they were forbidden to use the property assigned to them for any but religious purposes; they could not give material assistance to their members; they could not rent premises for religious meetings; only books necessary for worship could be kept in their places of worship; no central funds for collecting gifts were allowed; and finally, in a provision that must be read to be believed, religious bodies could not "organize for children, young people, and women special prayer or other meetings, or generally meetings, circles,

---

[44] Decrees of Dec. 31, 1917, and Jan. 29 and Feb. 5, 1918. Translations are available in Meisel and Kozera, *Materials for the Study of the Soviet System*, pp. 39–43, 62–64.

groups, or departments for biblical or literary study, sewing, working or the teaching of religion, and so forth, or organize excursions, children's playgrounds, public libraries, or reading rooms, or organize sanatoria and medical assistance."[45]

The whole idea, therefore, was to turn religion inward, to isolate it from the world about it. This law is in effect today. It is impossible to know, of course, to what extent the present "inwardness" of Soviet religious bodies is the result of this compulsion, and to what extent the inwardness might have evolved anyway, particularly in the case of the Russian Orthodox Church. Containment also meant, in Stalin's time, the virtual cutting off of association with coreligionists in foreign countries. This type of restriction was relaxed somewhat in Khrushchev's time, and in some contexts foreign contact was encouraged for publicity reasons (see below). All the "approved" religions save for Judaism have profited from this policy; to date, Soviet synagogues have not received permission to form a national association which might represent them in world Jewry.

Another function of containment has been to discourage revolt by believers against their own leadership, some of whom may rightfully be accused of having compromised their organizations. A large-scale revolt within the ranks of the Evangelical Baptists in the early 1960s resulted from the denomination leaders' failure to protest a 1960 directive; the directive, which came to the attention of the outside world through unofficial channels, ordered the Baptists to stop proselytizing altogether, and particularly to bar children of school age from worship services. The leader of the schism received a heavy prison sentence in 1962, but the dissenters continued to gain followers, and they maintain their position to this day.[46]

In the case of sects imported from the West, notably the Pentacostals and Jehovah's Witnesses, containment has meant nonrecognition and persecution. These denominations must operate clandestinely, and appear to have done so successfully up to now. The Soviet press has treated them, predictably, as vehicles of capitalist subversion. Besides leading an underground existence, they partake of the Roman Catholic Church's sin of being subordinate to religious bodies whose headquarters lie outside the communist world.

Ideological Combat

The old League of the Militant Godless, which lapsed during World War II, was resurrected afterward with a different title and a more

---

[45] RSFSR Decree of April 8, 1929. Translation from Meisel and Kozera, *Materials for the Study of the Soviet System*, pp. 179–80.

[46] Michael Bourdeaux, "Reform and Schism," *Problems of Communism* 16 (September–October 1967), pp. 110–14.

refined approach. The "Knowledge" Society, as it is known today, has a membership of over a million who participate in a nationwide lecture program, only a part of which is aimed against religious belief. Local Komsomol organizations have frequently taken part in harrassing religious observances, often more crudely than higher authorities think desirable, according to a variety of press items. The writer was among a crowd of the curious outside a Moscow church during a midnight Russian Easter service. Not only were several agitators circulating among the crowd to spot the believers and engage them in quiet debate on religion, but a group of young people was holding a loud guitar concert on the crowd's fringes, unmolested by the militia. Novels and plays have dealt with religious beliefs, sometimes with considerable understanding.[47]

In the past, a main focus of ideological attack was on the negative effects of religion on everyday life and individual well-being. Fanatical old women forbidding their grandchildren to join the Young Pioneers or attend atheist schools, Moslem families punishing daughters who had the temerity to want careers, village priests denouncing the atheist officials who had come to collectivize the farms—all these made ready targets. Today the focus has shifted to anything that resembles an effort to make religion relevant and credible in the modern world. A growing curiosity about religious concepts among the Soviet intelligentsia has proven particularly disturbing to Soviet authorities. The literature of the "Knowledge" Society, and the educated clientele many of its lectures are now aimed at, are evidence of this concern.

The Publicity Use of Religion

Visitors to the Soviet Union who wish to visit a church, synagogue, or mosque can usually do so freely. In fact, the houses of worship that remain in operation are there to some extent for the benefit of the outside world. The Soviet Government is understandably anxious to convey the impression that religion in the Soviet Union is dying a natural death but is in no way suppressed. Visitors are struck first of all by the predominance of the elderly in most congregations. If they inquire a bit into the activities of any given house of worship, the "inwardness" already mentioned may come as a shock: no autonomous social gospel, no outreach programs, and little awareness of changes in religious doctrine abroad. An uninformed visitor is very likely to conclude that the congregations are on their last legs and are unconcerned about building their membership by making religion more relevant to the world around them. The only circumstance that contradicts this impression somewhat is that some churches are so crowded for their services that many worshippers must

---

[47] For a detailed survey of antireligious propaganda, see Kolarz, *Religion in the Soviet Union*, chapter 1.

stand. While this testifies to the loyalty of their congregations, it is also a consequence of the number of churches and synagogues that have been closed, from the distant revolutionary past tp recent years.

Religious leaders have frequently spoken out on international issues and attended international conferences of various kinds, all with the Soviet Government's approval and in support of official positions. Soviet Moslem leaders, for example, have made many statements in support of Soviet policy in the Middle East, some of them broadcast for foreign consumption. The annual pilgrimage to Mecca, halted in Stalin's last years, was resumed after his death to the extent of sending a rather high-level Moslem delegation each year, likewise armed with approved public statements on a variety of issues. After 1945, Patriarch Alexis of the Russian Orthodox Church undertook a different kind of campaign: with the Soviet Government's full support, he spent a number of years pressing the claims of the Moscow Patriarchate among Orthodox churches abroad, and he established its jurisdiction over some of them. From 1949 on, Russian Orthodox delegations were prominent in communist-dominated international peace conferences. The Baptists have followed the latter path on a more modest scale, and from 1955 on have sent delegates to congresses of the Baptist World Alliance.

Religions and National Identities

Since the late 17th century there had been no separate Orthodox organization for the Ukraine and Ukrainians. During the Russian Civil War, while the Ukraine was in the hands of Simon Petlyura's nationalist government, a Ukrainian Autocephalous Church was formed which lasted until it fell victim to official persecution in 1930. While the Church was strongly nationalist in its political orientation, it shared the belief of many "left" Ukrainian communists of the 1920s that nationalism and communism are fully compatible. Accordingly it supported many of the specific aims of the young Bolshevik regime and received Moscow's support in turn, among other things for an attempt to bring Ukrainian emigrés in North America under its jurisdiction. Later in the decade the Church was obliged to make substantial concessions to the regime in order to preserve its existence, including a purge of many of its clergy. Finally, under severe pressure, its leaders signed a confession of counter-revolutionary activity, and the hopeful experiment came to an end. A Byelorussian Autocephalous Church, less nationalistic than its Ukrainian neighbor, nevertheless suffered the same fate, as did the Estonian Church after World War II. In the European USSR, only the Latvian Autocephalous Church has survived and fared relatively well.[48]

---

[48] Ibid., chapter 3.

Soviet leaders are understandably reluctant to see religious organizations used as a spur to national feeling; the experiences of Soviet Jews after 1948, mentioned earlier, show how sensitive a point this is with Moscow. The Georgian Orthodox Church, abolished as a separate ecclesiastical jurisdiction in the wake of Russia's annexation of Georgia at the beginning of the 19th century, sprang to life again in 1917. From the time of the Soviet military conquest of Georgia in the early 1920s, it suffered far more official persecution than did the Russian Orthodox Church. Travellers in modern Georgia are invariably struck by the high number of ruined and converted churches, a by-product of the struggles of the 1920s and 1930s. While the Church's position improved in the wake of World War II, its position is weaker than that of the Armenian Church. The latter, while going through some of the same experiences as Orthodoxy elsewhere, enjoyed the advantage that Soviet recognition of the Armenian identity and culture necessarily meant recognizing the Church's powerful historical role. Also, while three quarters of the Armenian Church's members live outside the Soviet Union, its head, the Catholicos of Echmiadzin, lives in Soviet Armenia; this made the Church a potentially useful instrument in certain foreign dealings. Consequently the Armenian Church has been accorded a special deference, and has been able to bolster its organization where other religious bodies have seen their positions eroded more and more. Today, as in the past, even many a good Armenian communist observes Church holidays, not usually by attending services, but among family and friends: the Church, Armenia's ancient bulwark through long centuries of occupation and persecution, must be given its due.

Among the Moslems of Central Asia, the Caucasus, and elsewhere, the Soviets encountered two special problems in dealing with Islam. First, Islam represented the overriding unity of these national groups; its main centers of leadership lay beyond Soviet borders, and in the 19th century Islamic solidarity had served as a symbol of resistance to Russian invasion of the Caucasus and Central Asia. Secondly, Islam is much less an organization and much more a total way of life than is the case with any but the most fanatical offshoots of Orthodoxy. Soviet leaders and officials, ever slow to incorporate cultural understanding into their policies, were under the illusion that in the early decades they had dealt Islam a mortal blow, whereas they had done only surface damage. The breaking up of Central Asia into four republics was one of Moscow's few really well-designed measures. Otherwise the maddening slowness with which the wearing of the veil, the daily prayer routines, and a host of other practices diminished was a measure of Russian incapacity to meet Islam on its own ground. Today the peoples of Central Asia appear to have adapted well to Soviet demands and the outlook of the 20th century; Islam as a formal religion appears a skeleton, hardly capable of causing anxiety for Moscow. But appearances may be deceptive. In spite of post-Stalin improvements in the psychology of antireligious efforts among the population of Moslem background, the old way of life has sought channels of survival less visible than those of the past, and more difficult to root out.

SOVIET JEWS: A SPECIAL CASE

Soviet Jews have posed several dilemmas for Soviet policymakers because they embody a mixture of characteristics which Moscow is used to dealing with separately. These include the Jewish claim to recognition as a nation without a traditional national area, the identification of many Soviet Jews—we do not know what proportion—with Israeli nationalism, the Jews' urban concentration and high educational level, the historical identity of Jews as a religion just as much as a nation, and the fact that only a minority claims Yiddish as its first language. Compounding these problems of official policy is a long history of virulent Slavic anti-Semitism, promoted by the Tsars for their own purposes, and by Stalin in his last years as a response to Israel's claim to Jewish loyalties after 1948.

The territorial concept of national autonomy, as it evolved between the Revolution and the 1923 Constitution (see chapter 13), offered a framework for making concessions to national aspirations without actively building national cultures. There was, of course, a good deal of "active building" of non-Russian cultures. The trouble with promoting Soviet Jewish culture was that it meant promoting a national culture as such rather than only the *right* to national cultural expression. Since Jews lack a territorial base within the Soviet Union, culture alone forms the basis of their identity. An effort to solve this problem by creating a Jewish region in the Soviet Far East was doomed to failure from the beginning.

Promoting Jewish secular culture while undermining Judaism created another policy dilemma, though less serious than the dilemma of cultural autonomy. Secularization of the Jewish community had been going on under Tsarist and Soviet rule just as it had elsewhere in Europe. The danger was one which Moscow had encountered in promoting Armenian culture: it would be absurd to try to erase from Armenian history the central role of the Armenian Orthodox Church, hence important concessions were made in this area. With Soviet Jews, there was some possibility that the synagogues might once again become the chief focus of Jewish cultural identity.

The Revolution, partly because it abolished the old legal restrictions on Jews, marked the beginning of a rising trend toward Jewish assimilation in Russian culture. This manifested itself partly in the movement of many Jews from their old small-town enclaves to the big cities and industrial centers, and partly in a great increase in mixed marriages. By the beginning of World War II, it appeared the Soviet Jews were well on their way to voluntary assimilation. The war changed everything: the Nazi extermination policy, the establishment of Israel, and Stalin's consequent attacks on Soviet Jews all laid the foundation for a resurgent Jewish identity, which has been widely shared by Jewish young people, and not only by the older generation. Israeli military victories in 1956 and 1967 have promoted this movement.

One major aspect of Soviet policy has been to limit the feelings of kinship which some of its border minorities may still harbor for their ethnic brothers (or near-brothers) across the border. Thus, the Moldavians are encouraged in various ways to regard their culture as distinct from that of Romanian Moldavia, even though Romania is part of the socialist bloc. Moscow has also tried to promote the idea that emigrés in distant lands, whether Russians or non-Russians, have cut themselves off from their socialist homeland and should be condemned for having done so, instead of being regarded as brothers living abroad. Soviet Jews in 1948 suddenly found themselves with a homeland abroad, if they chose to identify with it.

This new identity offered an alternative to assimilation. Jewish demands, instead of focusing primarily on the need for more recognition of the Jewish cultural identity, focused instead on the right to emigrate. In the latter 1960s and early 1970s, this demand was promoted by a wave of demands from other sources for the recognition of basic rights generally. Andrei Sakharov's Committee on Human Rights was a noteworthy product of this period, as was the petition on behalf of the 300,000 Crimean Tatars for permission to return to their Crimean homeland from their places of resettlement in Central Asia. But the fact that the primary demand from among Soviet Jews—that is, from those Jews who chose to make a demand of some kind—was for emigration offered Soviet policy-makers a possible course of action: a minority of the most active and most troublesome would be permitted to emigrate, while enormous barriers to emigration would deter the majority. This would serve to "decapitate" the Israel-oriented movement. It would also allay the fears of Arab governments, which were already concerned that permission for Jews to emigrate would both give Zionism everywhere a further impetus and supply Israel with more well-trained specialists. But in fact far more than just a small stratum of Jewish activists has been permitted to emigrate.

The "head tax," imposed in August 1972 and then suspended (at least for the moment) in the spring of 1973, was one part of the means by which this complex policy was initiated; legal harrassment and outright refusal to grant emigration visas to some have also been used. Under this decree (which was not made public until five months after its adoption) persons having a higher education were required to reimburse the state for the cost of their education, an average of 8,000 rubles, or more than five times the average annual wage. This was intended both to reduce the number of actual emigrations of highly educated Jews to a small trickle and to give authorities the option of removing those considered troublemakers by waiving the tax selectively.

SOME CONCLUSIONS

The Soviet system has thus far succeeded in its "middle-range" objectives concerning social strata, ethnic groups and religious bodies. While all of them still pose problems for the policy makers, it does not appear that even the groups with the strongest potential for pressing their demands—some of the non-Russian nationalities—are able to convert these demands into outright resistance. The regime's success must be viewed against a history of dealing with groups which has at times involved massive force: the closing of churches, collectivization, armed struggle against nationalist movements in the early years, deportation of certain nations in the World War II period, Stalin's persecution of Jews, the battle against Ukrainian insurgents after World War II, and the decimation of non-Russian Party leadership in the 1930s. Strict administrative measures continue to regulate the behavior of certain groups and categories. Examples are restrictions on the movement of the rural population through the internal passport system, and regulation of group expression through censorship (e.g., certain expressions of national pride and tradition, and the ban on religious proselytizing). At the same time, enough incentives are offered for compliance with the regime's wishes that nearly all groups maintain a high degree of cooperation with the system around them.

The Soviet leaders are confronted with two basic kinds of problems in managing their society. The first is that demands by one or several social categories are likely to produce demands by others; yielding to one demand may make it harder to resist the next. There is every probability, for example, that the Crimean Tatars' demands in the early 1970s for repatriation to their native Crimea were encouraged by the success (perhaps temporary) of Soviet Jews in opening channels for a limited flow of emigrants to Israel. The spread of organizational revolt among the Baptist rank and file doubtless influenced a parallel development in the Russian Orthodox Church.

The second problem is that nationalities, religions, and social strata do not appear to be moving in the direction of—respectively—assimilation, natural death, and uniformity. Up to now, the Soviet regime can claim to have arrived at a "middle stage" in realizing Marx's prophecies concerning society. From this point on, realization of the ultimate Marxian prophecies seems quite unlikely, at least if one is reckoning in decades rather than centuries. The difficulty is not that of reconciling ideology with reality, which has been done often, but the pursuit of present ideological guidelines by applying increasing pressure. The inadequacy of much of Soviet Marxism as a set of guidelines for shaping social relations may reinforce some blind spots and wrong assumptions long prevalent among Soviet policy-makers. This could lead again to the use of widespread compulsion, just as happened at various points during the first three decades of Soviet rule.

FOR FURTHER READING

The condition and development of the national minorities under Lenin and Stalin, plus some background from Tsarist times, are set forth in comprehensive fashion in Walter Kolarz, *Russia and Her Colonies* (New York: Archon Books, 1967). A number of different disciplines are brought to bear on recent nationality problems and developments in Edward Allworth (ed.), *Soviet Nationality Problems* (New York: Columbia University Press, 1971). Other surveys include Erich Goldhagen (ed.), *Ethnic Minorities in the Soviet Union* (New York: Praeger, 1968), and Robert Conquest (ed.), *Soviet Nationalities Policy in Practice* (New York: Praeger, 1967).

A large number of studies of individual nationalities and groups of nationalities have appeared in the 1960s and 1970s. On the Ukraine, see John A. Armstrong, *Ukrainian Nationalism* (New York: Columbia University Press, 1963), Yaroslav Bilinsky, *The Second Soviet Republic: The Ukraine After World War II* (New Brunswick, N.J.: Rutgers University Press, 1964), and Robert S. Sullivant, *Soviet Politics and the Ukraine, 1917–1957* (New York: Columbia University Press, 1962). The one major work on Byelorussia thus far is Nicholas Vakar, *Belorussia* (Cambridge, Mass.: Harvard University Press, 1956). The Baltic nations have not been treated comprehensively, with the exception of V. Stanley Vardys (ed.), *Lithuania Under the Soviets* (New York: Praeger, 1965). Transcaucasia, with the exception of Azerbaidzhan, is dealt with in D. M. Lang, *A Modern History of Soviet Georgia* (New York: Grove Press, 1962), and Mary Matossian, *The Impact of Soviet Policies in Armenia* (Leiden: E. J. Brill, 1962).

There is a very full literature on Soviet Central Asia. Major titles include: Edward Allworth, *Central Asia: A Century of Russian Rule* (New York: Columbia University Press, 1966); Elizabeth E. Bacon, *Central Asians Under Russian Rule: A Study in Culture Change* (Ithaca, N.Y.: Cornell University Press, 1967); Alec Nove and J. A. Newth, *The Soviet Middle East* (New York: Praeger, 1966); Teresa Rakowska-Harmstone, *Russia and Nationalism in Central Asia: The Case of Tadzhikstan* (Baltimore: Johns Hopkins Press, 1969); Michael Rywkin, *Russia in Central Asia* (New York: Collier Books, 1963); and two works by Geoffrey Wheeler, *The Modern History of Soviet Central Asia* (New York: Praeger, 1964) and *Racial Problems in Soviet Muslim Asia* (2d ed.; New York: Oxford University Press, 1962).

There are also some revealing studies of Russian nationalism and the Russian national character, including: Frederick R. Barghoorn, *Soviet Russian Nationalism* (New York: Oxford University Press, 1956), Wright Miller, *The Russians as People* (New York: Dutton, 1961), and Leonid Vladimirov, *The Russians* (New York: Praeger, 1967). See also Lowell Tillett, *The Great Friendship: Soviet Historians on the Non-Russian Nationalities* (Chapel Hill, N.C.: University of North Carolina Press, 1969).

The best and most comprehensive survey of religions in the Soviet Union, though now somewhat dated, is Walter Kolarz, *Religion in the Soviet Union* (New York: St. Martin's Press, 1961). Two substantial items on the Russian Orthodox Church are Michael Bourdeaux, *Patriarch and Prophets: Persecution of the Russian Orthodox Church Today* (New York: Praeger, 1970), and John Shelton Curtiss, *The Russian Church and the Soviet State* (Boston: Little, Brown, 1953). On protestantism, see Steve Durasoff, *The Russian Protestants: Evangelicals in the Soviet Union, 1944–1964* (Cranbury, N.J.: Fairleigh Dickinson University Press, 1971). Although there is still no one comprehensive work on Judaism in the Soviet Union, the standard background book on Soviet Jews remains Solomon M. Schwarz, *The Jews in the Soviet Union* (Syracuse, N.Y.: Syracuse University Press, 1952). See also chapter 12 of the Kolarz book, "The Secularisation of Soviet Jewry." Islam is covered in Alexandre Bennigsen, *Islam in the Soviet Union* (New York: Praeger, 1967), and Serge A. Zenkovsky, *Pan-Turkism and Islam in Russia* (Cambridge, Mass.: Harvard University Press, 1960); see also the works on Central Asia.

Protests from Soviet citizens against one or another aspect of nationality policy are given in Abraham Brumberg (ed.), *In Quest of Justice: Protest and Dissent in the Soviet Union Today* (New York: Praeger, 1970), pp. 183–213. Documentation of protest in the Ukraine is given in *The Chornovil Papers* (New York: McGraw-Hill, 1968) and Ivan Dzyuba, *Internationalism or Russification? A Study in the Soviet Nationalities Problem* (London: Weidenfeld and Nicolson, 1968). Expressions of dissent against religious policies are provided in the Brumberg volume, pp. 214–44.

CONCLUSION

PROGNOSES ABOUT THE FUTURE of the Soviet system cover every degree of optimism and pessimism, from unswerving progress toward the regime's stated goals to utter collapse of the system. The 1961 Party Program concluded as follows:

> The Party proceeds from the Marxist-Leninist proposition: History is made by the people, and communism is a creation of the people, of its energy and intelligence. The victory of communism depends on people, and communism is built for people. Every Soviet man brings the triumph of communism nearer by his labor. The successes of communist construction spell abundance and a happy life to all, and enhance the might, prestige and glory of the Soviet Union.
>
> The Party is confident that the Soviet people will accept the new Program of the CPSU as their own vital cause, as the greatest purpose of their life and as a banner of nation-wide struggle for the building of communism. . . .[1]

Andrei Amalrik, the historian and political dissident, charted several different routes by which he expects the Soviet political order to collapse altogether:

> Summing up, it can be said that as the regime becomes progressively weaker and more self-destructive it is bound to clash—and there are already clear indications that this is happening—with two forces which are already undermining it: the constructive movement of the "middle class" (rather weak) and the destructive movement of the "lower classes," which will take the form of extremely damaging, violent and

---

[1] Translation from Jan F. Triska (ed.), *Soviet Communism: Programs and Rules* (San Francisco: Chandler, 1962), p. 129.

478

irresponsible action once its members realize their relative immunity from punishment.[2]

Andrei D. Sakharov, the famous Soviet physicist and recently an outspoken promoter of political reform, foresees the Soviet Union on a course of liberalization which will lead it toward "convergence" with the Western democracies, by stages:

> In the first stage, a growing ideological struggle in the socialist countries between Stalinist and Maoist forces, on the one hand, and the realistic forces of leftist Leninist Communists (and leftist Westerners), on the other, will lead to a deep ideological split on an international, national, and intraparty scale.
>
> In the Soviet Union and other socialist countries, this process will lead first to a multiparty system (here and there) and to acute ideological struggle and discussions, and then to the ideological victory of the realists, affirming the policy of increasing peaceful coexistence, strengthening democracy, and expanding economic reforms. . . .
>
> The author, incidentally, is not one of those who consider the multiparty system to be an essential stage in the development of the socialist system or, even less, a panacea for all ills, but he assumes that in some cases a multiparty system may be an inevitable consequence of the course of events when a ruling Communist party refuses for one reason or another to rule by the scientific democratic method required by history.[3]

Zbigniew Brzezinski, an American specialist on communist affairs, sees the Soviet leadership confronted with a choice between reform and "degeneration":

> . . . [T]he effort to maintain a doctrinaire dictatorship over an increasingly modern and industrial society has already contributed to a reopening of the gap that existed in prerevolutionary Russia between the political system and society, thereby posing the threat of the degeneration of the Soviet system.
>
> A political system can be said to degenerate when there is a perceptible decline in the quality of the social talent that the political leadership attracts to itself in competition with other groups; when there is persistent division within the ruling elite, accompanied by a decline in its commitment to shared beliefs; when there is protracted instability in the top leadership; when there is a decline in the capacity of the ruling elite to define the purposes of the political system in relationship to society and to express them in effective institutional terms; when there is a fuzzing of institutional and hierarchical lines of command, resulting

---

[2] Andrei Amalrik, *Will the Soviet Union Survive Until 1984?* (New York: Harper & Row, 1970), pp. 41–42.

[3] Andrei D. Sakharov, *Progress, Coexistence and Individual Freedom* (New York: Norton, 1968), pp. 81–82.

in the uncontrolled and unchanneled intrusion into politics of hitherto politically uninvolved groupings.[4]

The Soviet leaders, whose system is showing signs of degeneration, could save themselves from its consequences by certain reforms: opening the ranks of top leadership to talent from various fields other than professional politics, institutionalizing a chief executive for the sake of stability, and providing an institutionalized arena for mediating group interests. Either way, says Brzezinski, the system must undergo change.

Those observers who subscribe to the "totalitarian model," or a variant of this such as the "administered society," foresee continued stability of the present system based on its ability to undercut pressure for change:

> Most important is the fact that, during almost half a century of Communist rule, the possibilities for alternative institutional forms have been largely wiped out. Even were the will to democratic or pluralistic institutions substantially present—and it is not—it is highly doubtful that the resources currently available by way of formal structures, source philosophies, or practical experience would go very far. The Bolshevization of a society, if it goes on long enough, is an irreversible process, because it is so intense and so total that it indelibly alters not only earlier institutional forms, but the entire pattern of a population's expectations of reasonable and workable alternative possibilities for social order.[5]

In direct contradiction to this "pessimistic" view is that of Richard Lowenthal, who sees the political systems of the communist nations generally on the defensive because of the societies and economies they have built:

> Yet though the totalitarian institutional framework has in the main been preserved, the basic relation between the political system and the development of society has been reversed. Formerly the political system was in command, subjecting an underdeveloped society both to forced development and to a series of revolutions from above. Now the political system has to respond to the pressures generated by an increasingly advanced society. Formerly the Communist political superstructure was concerned with forcibly transforming the system's economic and social basis, contrary to the generalizations derived by Karl Marx from the evolution of the industrial society in the West. Now, the economic and social basis of the countries under Communist rule, having reached a state of development comparable to that of the modern West, is begin-

---

[4] Zbigniew Brzezinski, "The Soviet Political System : Transformation or Degeneration," *Problems of Communism* 15 (January–February 1966), p. 14.

[5] Allen Kassof, "The Administered Society: Totalitarianism Without Terror," *World Politics* XVI:4 (July 1964), p. 574. Copyright © by Princeton University Press; reprinted by permission.

ning to transform the political superstructure in the familiar manner described by the Marxist interpretation of history.[6]

CHANGES IN THE POLITICAL SYSTEM

The prophets of both change and stability focus their attention on particular characteristics of the Soviet political system which they regard as the most important ones. It is important to decide first of all whether they are discussing the same characteristics. A change from a one-party system to a multi-party system is hardly of importance if a dominant party remains which keeps the rest in subservient roles, or if all the parties are restricted in a manner which prevents their effecting change in other areas of the system. The abolition of censorship, which most observers agree would be a politically significant change in itself, may have little effect on other parts of the system if the means of mass communication continue to be owned and coordinated by the state. A one-party system, on the other hand, may undergo fundamental change if the party becomes the arena of factional interplay that brings policy disputes out into the open, where the party rank and file is able to influence decisions. Or, conceivably, administrative decentralization could proceed to the point where territorial units become effective vehicles for local influence over central decisions. That is to say, changes in certain overt features may not necessarily lead to "change" in a large sense, while important processes can change without requiring fundamental change in the overt characteristics.

It is the second kind of change that is most frequently the topic of debate among observers of Soviet politics: the gradual change in personnel, attitudes, and ways of making decisions that occurs within seemingly unchanging institutions. Much has been written, for example, about the change in Party leadership from the "Old Bolsheviks" to the *apparatchiki*—those trained in the Party's bureaucracy—to experts who have gained their experience at least partly outside the Party.[7] The declining use of arbitrary police power is likewise the subject of debate among observers who all agree that the massive police apparatus is still present, but disagree on its political role. The role of the Party, and its capacity to make and enforce decisions in the face of many pressures and crosscurrents within the system, is another major topic of discussion. Some believe

---

[6] Richard Lowenthal, "Development vs. Utopia in Communist Policy," in Chalmers Johnson (ed.), *Change in Communist Systems* (Stanford, Calif.: Stanford University Press, 1970), p. 112.

[7] See for example the article by Richard Lowenthal, cited above, in Johnson, *Change in Communist Systems*, pp. 33–116, and in the same volume H. Gordon Skilling, "Group Conflict and Political Change," pp. 215–34. For a projection of his hypothesis as concerns the East European regimes, see Ghita Ionescu, *The Politics of the European Communist States* (New York: Praeger, 1967).

that the Party leadership wields an effective instrument for doing this; others think that the Party's role has become diffuse to the point of producing a crisis of identity, possibly accompanied by a crisis of legitimacy.[8]

The concepts developed by political scientists to describe systemic change, as they may apply to the problem of change in the Soviet Union, offer a useful vocabulary but little else. The input-output scheme, an interesting way of classifying events that relate to the political system, is useful only if we can detect specific links between the demands that constitute "input" and the decisions that result from it. As we have seen, specialists on the Soviet system disagree on what kind of "input" comes from Soviet society and political structures, also on whether it is making itself felt in the decisions coming from the Kremlin. "Social mobilization," "political mobilization," "interest aggregation," "political communication," and related concepts have been used with good effect as a way of describing changes in the politics of the underdeveloped world, and they are equally useful in describing the techniques used by Moscow in the 1920s and the early 1930s. However, once mobilization of a particular kind has been accomplished and certain other kinds of social and political mobilization have been stopped and reversed, a new vocabulary is needed to describe possible lines of development from that point on. Writers on political development have dealt with the proposition, for example, that multi-party systems undergoing modernization are less stable than those with one-party systems.[9] But what can be said of one-party systems ruling thoroughly modernized societies? As the quotations above suggest, there is disagreement not only about the idea, but also about what is actually happening (or not happening) to Party rule in the Soviet Union and other modern one-party states.

Analysts of Soviet politics in recent years have been most persuasive when they have undertaken to demonstrate partial hypotheses and individual descriptive statements. As an example of the latter, a study by George Fischer demonstrated a trend in favor the appointment of "dual executives" to top Party posts, meaning persons whose careers include extensive work in both the Party and nonparty technical posts.[10] However, as Fischer himself concedes, it is not at all certain what this trend portends for the Soviet system as a whole: it is an advantage for maintaining one-party rule, but by itself it could not prevent other trends from undermining this rule. As an example of a partial hypothesis—partial

---

[8] See for example Erik P. Hoffman, "Role Conflict and Ambiguity in the Communist Party of the Soviet Union," in Roger E. Kanet (ed.), *The Behavioral Revolution and Communist Studies* (New York: The Free Press, 1971), pp. 233–58.

[9] This is proposed in Samuel P. Huntington, "Political Development and Political Decay," *World Politics* 17 (April 1965), pp. 386–430.

[10] George Fisher, *The Soviet System and Modern Society* (New York: Atherton, 1968).

in the sense of predicting one type of change without venturing to predict others—a study of the 1958 education reforms proposed (among other things) that "the more modern the society, the more dependent it is on technical expertise, which in turn improves the prospects that groups may influence policy when higher powers seek their judgment."[11] Even if one could demonstrate this trend over a period of time in a number of one-party systems, predicting its further effects is highly problematic. If such a trend alarmed the leaders of a given country, would they not seek ways of using expertise which do not entail an increasing political influence for groups? The "dual executive" development may be regarded, among other things, as just such a step.

All things considered, we are not in a position to demonstrate general propositions concerning the future of the Soviet system. At most, we can develop a range of possibilities and test them against very incomplete evidence, also against the informed guesswork of people with a detailed knowledge of Soviet politics. The point hardly needs belaboring that prognoses about any modern society are nearly as problematic, the main difference being that in some of the noncommunist industrial nations we possess much fuller information about the society, public feeling, and the actual workings of political structures.

IDEAS OF CHANGE

Those who foresee changes in the Soviet system, whether they advocate the "convergence" notion or not, nearly always picture the Soviet system yielding to pressures which carry it a certain distance in the direction of the noncommunist democracies. Each idea of this kind rests on the presumed incompatibility of two or more components of the system. Unfortunately, at the present level of our knowledge, most of these "negative linkages" can neither be proved nor disproved. It is easier to find fault with their logic than to gather data in support of them. In any case, some of the more familiar prophecies deserve a brief look.

"An Educated Populace Will Eventually Demand Democracy"

The assumptions contained within a statement such as this are so questionable by themselves that we must suspend judgment on it, at least, for want of information. The idea that truly enlightened people will agree on a particular basis of government is a bold assumption about human nature. Andrei Sakharov (above) supports this notion, and it is one of the chief roots of the convergence idea. Plato's *Republic* should

---

[11] Joel J. Schwartz and William R. Keech, "Group Influence and the Policy Process in the Soviet Union," *American Political Science Review* 62 (September 1968), pp. 840–851.

stand as a warning: Highly intelligent and well-informed people can just as easily conclude that they are custodians of the truth on behalf of the less intelligent majority, and hence they may reasonably decide not to let the latter make political decisions.

The statement assumes further than any kind of full education will lead those who receive it to perceive certain truths about man and society. Does a technical education, for example, "spill over" into education about man and government? For some, yes—one thinks of all the Soviet scientists who have advocated political freedom and the expansion of democracy in the Soviet Union. As for the majority of the Soviet intelligentsia— let alone those of lesser educational accomplishments—the evidence is fragmentary and points in both directions. Some foreign observers regard the intelligentsia as that segment of Soviet society which has "sold out" to the system by accepting privileges in return for loyal service.

Next, the statement assumes that, in a country such as the Soviet Union, state-sponsored education will necessarily fail in one of its major aims. Instead of creating loyal citizens, Soviet education in this view is actually opening their eyes to ideas it attempts to shut out. This notion simply underestimates the capacity of a state which dominates its society's means of communication to educate its society for conformity. To be sure, the accounts of foreign visitors and the evidence shown in privately circulated writing provide plenty of examples of Soviet education's backfiring in its political effort. However, one has little difficulty meeting well-educated people who accept fully the political ideas that are offered to them via education. In the writer's experience, while even those who generally accept what they are taught do not by any means accept everything, they appear to be the overwhelming majority. And finally, the Soviet intellectuals who admire Western political ideals often separate the demand for personal freedoms from demands for political freedoms and a different political structure. Among such people, skepticism about two-party and multi-party systems is widespread. If they were granted the kind of individual freedoms they desire, would they use these freedoms to press for a political restructuring? This might conceivably happen, but as a prediction it is risky.

"A Consumption-Oriented People Will Demand Democracy"

This statement looks flimsy even on the surface, without inquiring into the secondary assumptions it contains. Bread and circuses will sooner reconcile the citizen to the existing order than impel him to press for change. However, one recalls the demands of much of the French bourgeoisie at the time of the French Revolution: business-oriented people who were already doing well used the revolutionary crisis as a setting for making demands for a new system, which would enable them to do even better. The Soviet system, however, offers no comparable linkage between individual prosperity and the introduction of a democratic order, except that a greater public voice in government might result in pressure to orient economic priorities more toward consumption.

A more plausible kind of statement is that a government which encourages high private consumption as a goal may also be encouraging a "privatization" of individual lives, a turning away from the system's demands for effort and sacrifice. To this extent, consumption can and does subvert certain kinds of official demands for individual commitment. It may be that some of those whose lives have become "privatized" see a democratic order as a guarantee that the state will not in the future invade their lives or threaten their prosperity without good reason. But to show that a large number of prosperous Soviet citizens will react this way is a dubious undertaking, which at least must wait for a great deal of future evidence.

"Any Modern System Breeds Interest Groups"

The economic debates of the post-Stalin period convinced some analysts that "interest groups" of some kind—and even defining them posed problems—were now an important part of the policy-making process. In the 1960s, some analysts of Eastern Europe had come to this same conclusion concerning those countries.[12] However, a phrase that describes well-established institutions in the Western democracy is likely to be misleading as a "handle" for group phenomena in Soviet politics. From the Party's very beginning in 1903 to the present day, the top leadership has produced informal groupings on specific issues. At the next lower level, spokesmen for institutions of Soviet rule—for example, the Ministry of Defense or the State Planning Committee—often take sides openly on issues that affect their work. Whether there is a third level of interests in the form of broad social categories, such as collective farmers or industrial workers, is hard to say, aside from the institutions (e.g., trade unions) that profess to speak on their behalf.

However, a political system does not have to be modern, or an economic system industrialized, in order to produce factions in the top leadership, or institutionally based interests. Also, there is at present no indication that the Soviet system is on the point of producing many interest groups in the Western sense, meaning formal organizations, acting singly or in coalitions, that have arisen independently and openly promote causes that may be opposed by the political leadership. In fact, the Soviet political system seems admirably equipped to prevent this.

---

[12] See H. Gordon Skilling, "Interest Groups and Communist Politics," *World Politics* 18 (April 1966), pp. 435–51, and Ionesco, *The Politics of the European Communist States.*

The statement does contain a residuum of truth. The more complex a society and economy, the more issues will arise which the political leadership must deal with somehow. The top leadership becomes the recipient of an increasing flow of demands, the most important of them coming from the growing array of institutions which they rule. It is likely that the leadership will find it useful to promote separate institutional points of view, since this will clarify issues and give the leaders a greater range of options when the time comes to make a decision. Informal groupings among the top leaders also serve a purpose, since the political dimensions of pending decisions must be clear before it is expedient to proceed. The leaders will very likely share the concern that this process not divide them in a way that paralyzes action or produces destructive political vendettas. They will also share the resolve not to permit the institutions they deal with to gain any kind of political autonomy. Debate and bargaining, therefore, are encouraged to the extent that they are useful. But to note this development, and then use it to project a trend toward autonomous interest groups and open bargaining among well-organized groups over even the most sensitive political issues, is to apply a Western concept unthinkingly to a very different sort of setting for interests.

"Ending Political Repression Would End One-Party Rule"

A statement like this is typical of many which suggest that the major characteristics of the Soviet system must stand or fall together. There is a further suggestion that because of the great interdependence of characteristics, the system either stands firm as it is or else falls with a great crash; therefore evolution by stages to a difference set of characteristics is ruled out. Repression in this case means the absolute ban on competing political movements, plus control of communications and the use of arbitrary measures against individuals to this end.

Elsewhere in the world, parties have maintained their predominance by a variety of means which do not necessarily involve repression. Mexico's Revolutionary Institutional Party has long served as the archetype of one-party predominance within a multi-party system, its position anchored mainly by the way its functions are interwoven with those of the state administration, the trade unions, and other organizations. One might argue that its actual functions are modest by comparison with the Communist Party in the Soviet Union, particularly that it has no similar grip on the nation's economy and cultural life. In spite of this, its position in the Mexican political system has been hardly less secure.

It would be hard to put together an argument that the particular means which the Party uses to assure its political monopoly are the only ones sufficient for the purpose. This would involve some risky judgments about political culture in the Soviet Union, together with an even riskier prognosis that even a small breach in the Party's position would endanger its entire place in the system. The fact that today's Party leaders view the political efforts even of very small dissident groups as a matter of serious concern tells us something about the leaders' own political culture. But it tells us little about the actual possibility of a rivulet of dissent turning into a torrent.

Here is an example of an area of political concern in which the Soviet leadership is inhibited from making choices by the decisions of the distant Soviet past. Lenin's concept of the Party, his struggle against the Mensheviks, his unhappy experience in a coalition with one wing of the Social Revolutionaries, and the events that led up to the Resolution on Unity—all these were enshrined in Soviet Marxist ideology, and they have effectively restrained the post-Stalin leaders from making room for unorthodox political views.

"Nationalism Will Prove Stronger than Communism"

Statements about resurgent nationalism can be assigned several meanings. One meaning is that the leaders' goals will ultimately revert to traditional national goals, to the exclusion of further goals derived from Marxism which prove incompatible with this change. Another meaning is that the population will demand a restoration of old national goals, eventually forcing the leaders to retreat from parts of Marxism. A third meaning, which applies to a multi-national communist system, is that the several nationalities will demand satisfaction of their national aspirations before all else, likewise forcing a retreat by the leadership.

As to the first meaning, some of the Tsars' most important goals have already been realized, leaving the Soviet leadership the option of setting itself further objectives as it sees fit. Economically and militarily the nation has again become a first-rate power. The Tsars' long-standing concern for security against the European powers has been realized in the form of a permanently divided Germany and a Soviet-oriented East European bloc. For a country that three-quarters of a century ago was unable to compete for influence in areas beyond its territorial periphery, the Soviets have exceeded the Tsars' wildest dreams through trade, aid, diplomatic initiatives, and party-to-party relationships in Asia, Africa, and Latin America. Only in the emergence of a powerful China and in failure to gain control of the Turkish Straits has Moscow suffered defeats as measured against the objectives of the Russian Empire. In its international stance, at least, the Soviet Union, far from being the prisoner of traditional objectives, has realized them to the extent of being free to mold new policies, no matter whether they are derived from Marxism or from other considerations.

The second meaning, popular demand for restoration of national goals, has thus been met also. We saw in chapter 14 how the Stalin regime appealed to traditional Russian national feeling in the 1930s and 1940s, when it badly needed support, and how Russian history was rewritten a second time in support of this appeal.

The third meaning, that of demands by the non-Russian nations, is by far the most interesting, but also the hardest to make judgments about. The central importance of the national question in Yugoslavia suggests that the same development is not inconceivable in the Soviet Union. However, the potential for an open resurgence of national feelings similar to the feelings of the Croats in Yugoslavia will probably become known only when a crisis of some kind gives free rein to their expression. From the materials of the underground press in the Soviet Union it appears that national feeling has been on the increase in recent years. Pressure on the part of the regime to undermine this feeling is likely to backfire in the long run. In any case it appears that nationalism among the separate nationalities has not been on the wane in spite of ideology-based forecasts about its disappearance. Whether this fact makes nationalism "stronger than" the Soviet regime is hardly a meaningful question. What is most important at present is that the Soviet regime will have to reckon with strong national feelings for the indefinite future.

"Economic Decentralization Would Weaken One-Party Rule"

A statement like this is based on two specific occurrences: the resistance of much of the Soviet Party bureaucracy to some implications of the 1965 economic reform, and the Yugoslav experience in cutting back the Party's authority over economic management in the 1950s and subsequently. In chapter 9 we saw that the 1965 reform offered somewhat more autonomy to enterprise directors and consequently threatened to reduce the role of Party officials in transmitting orders, negotiating between enterprises and their ministries, and issuing orders of their own. The Yugoslav leaders in the wake of the 1950 reforms drew the conclusion that the League of Communists (the Yugoslav party) could prepare for its own dismantling in the not-too-distant future; this was an important message of the League's 1958 program which deeply disturbed the Soviet leaders.

The big question here is whether cutting back certain important Party functions in economic management would weaken the Party's position generally. The Yugoslav example proves little, since the decision to relegate the League to the background in the economy was taken independently of the economic reforms themselves. The fact that many Soviet officials in the 1960s felt a threat to their roles does not prove that the Party's overall role in the economy was threatened. (The partial character of the reforms and the halting, grudging way they have been put into operation have apparently calmed the fears of these officials for the time being.) Had the reforms been thoroughgoing, giving the enterprises an autonomy like that in Yugoslavia, Party management of their affairs might easily have become more important rather than less so. In fact, it is more than likely that any further steps toward autonomy in economic management would be limited in practice by a much closer Party watch over management. Were the Party to drop its role in management, and instead confine itself to personnel questions and political education, the personnel function in itself could be enough to leave the Party with a decisive voice in management. Finally, it would be hard to prove that a reduced role for the Party in the economy would mean a reduced role in other areas of Soviet life.

PAST AND FUTURE CHOICES

A major purpose of this book has been to emphasize political choices and how they were made. If there is any overall conclusion that may be drawn from the choices that we have reviewed, it is that most of them did not proceed logically and inexorably from the situations which made choice necessary. The logic of these choices consisted only in the fact that they were efforts to deal with actual problems, in situations where "muddling through" or trying to avoid choices would have been an inappropriate response by almost any standards. In chapter 1, as we saw, the choice was not that of proceeding with a program of further industrialization, for this was already agreed on at the time the Great Debate began. Within this area of agreement, the specific choices that finally emerged can be called highly arbitrary. Similarly, there was nothing inexorable about the bureaucratization of the Party as it was described in chapter 6. A very different Party could have emerged from this period. Here the area of initial agreement was that the Party should serve as the political brain and nerves of the Soviet system. The specific solution to the problem of disarray and localism in Party ranks need not have been the particular command structure which Stalin presided over from 1922 on. To take yet another example, the Soviet state structure was not by any means fated to inherit the characteristics of Tsarist bureaucracy. Lenin might conceivably have tried to dismantle the old state structure entirely, as he had prophesied in *State and Revolution*. The fact that he and others seized on traditional Russian solutions to many administrative problems reflects only their willingness to cope with emergencies by using types of structures that had worked in the past.

A second conclusion is that the important choices, once they had been made, proved very hard to alter in later decades, even when the Soviet leaders had much to gain by changing them. The priority for heavy industrial investment, the low estate of the collective farms, Stalin's decision to elevate the intelligentsia in Party ranks, the centralist solution to the problem of federalism, the use of high reward differentials—these and nearly all the other decisions we have seen in this book were tinkered with repeatedly, or reformed only by timid stages, or altered in sweeping policy statements, only to revert to their former condition after a period of experimentation. Fundamental changes in some of these early decisions have been occurring in recent years, though by stages—parity for consumer-related investment after 1967, and important changes in the welfare of the farmers from 1965 on. But each change has been made at the cost of an enormous struggle against the inertia of much of the leadership, the officialdom, and even categories of ordinary citizens whose reactions were rooted in the acceptance of past decisions.

Are the present leaders prisoners of the Soviet past? Their deference to Lenin's political system, and to most of Stalin's major additions to it, is much more than just the desire to preserve the continuity of Soviet Marxist ideology. The behavior of the Brezhnev regime, particularly, lends some weight to one aspect of the much-criticized theory of totalitarian rule. The regime's aversion to changing any major characteristics of the system and its sharp reaction even to small challenges to the system's integrity all suggests that it sees Soviet rule threatened by a possible change in any single characteristic. The scrapping of a proposed reform of the Soviet Constitution in the latter 1960s is one clear indication of this. The changes would not have been earth-shaking in any case, but the very idea of opening the door to reform proposals of a kind which would justify a major constitutional revision proved unacceptable to the Kremlin after 1968.[13]

Russia's experience with political reform in the present century suggests that the Soviet leaders' aversion to change is prudence rather than unthinking rigidity. Twice before the Bolshevik seizure of power, and at least once after the Soviet regime was well established, reforms led to "snowballing" of demands for further reforms: in 1905, early 1917, and in 1945–46, in the immediate wake of World War II, when many Soviet citizens assumed that wartime concessions would be carried over into peacetime. Perhaps one should add the years 1957–59, when Khrushchev's reform proposals aroused demands in specific areas. Regimes which make concessions in one direction must be prepared for demands for similar treatment from every other direction as well.

Because of the age of the present Soviet leadership, it is likely that the majority of the Politburo and Secretariat will have been replaced

---

[13] See Jerome M. Gilison, "Khrushchev, Brezhnev and Constitutional Reform," *Problems of Communism* 21 (September-October, 1972), pp. 69–78.

by the end of the 1970s or the early 1980s. Their successors will be men who have come up through the ranks of the Party as the most important part of their careers, although an increasing number of them will have had experience in the upper levels of economic administration as well. On the surface of things, one may well conclude that the present regime's outlook will be inherited by its successors, even if the latter will be more disposed to make pragmatic adjustments in the political system. What we cannot know is whether among the younger leaders there is a potential Dubček, or at least another Khrushchev, a man of originality and ability, capable of biding his time on important new ideas until he is in a position to advocate them openly. The choices open to reformers and potential reformers among Soviet leaders in the post-Stalin era have been narrower than the outside world has supposed, for reasons which have been set forth in this book. But this prospect has been changing over the years; and one may hope that the alternatives from which future Soviet leaders are able to choose will be happier ones than those confronted by their predecessors.

The immediate consequences of the basic decisions we have reviewed in this book have much about them that from a Western view is negative. For this reason it can hardly be stressed enough that in many of these cases *all* the options had bad things about them. Even those options which could have led Russia in the direction of the democratic European systems might well have required compensating measures leading back in the direction of dictatorship. Today, at least, the Soviet regime is at the point where it can afford both consumer prosperity and other resource-consuming undertakings, whatever they may be. It is dealing with a well-educated populace which is no less amenable to reason and persuasion than the people of the modern nations generally. It has developed a large array of political institutions to help direct the nation's energies, even if the potential of many institutions has suffered deliberate neglect. The Bolsheviks of the Revolution and Civil War, were they alive today, could only envy the variety of choices open to their successors a half-century later. One can only hope that the successors of the narrowly cautious Kremlin leaders of today will come to power with a breadth of vision corresponding to their opportunities.

SYNOPSIS OF RUSSIAN AND SOVIET HISTORY FROM 1890

1890–1905

Political. Russia had had no national representative institutions since the 17th century; the Senate was a body of high-level officials appointed by the Tsar, and the Tsar's ministers did not form a cabinet in the modern sense. The Tsar ruled as "Emperor-Autocrat," and his rule was supported by a well-developed bureaucracy (though in many ways inefficient), tightly controlled from St. Petersburg. The Zemstvos had been formed in the 1860s, local self-governing assemblies with limited functions and powers, their activity hedged about by the prerogatives of the state bureaucracy. Nicholas II (reigned 1894–1917) had inherited the autocratic convictions of his father Alexander III, but not the latter's firmness.

Agitation for change in the 1890s came from the liberal nobility that had supported the Zemstvos; these nobles now wanted a national Zemstvo organization. Liberals, intellectuals, and Zemstvo workers formed the Union of Liberation (1903) to demand a liberal constitution. The Social Revolutionary Party (SRs) was organized in 1901 as successor to the old *narodnik* (Populist) movement. The Russian Social Democratic Labor Party, the first national Marxist organization, had held its first congress in 1898. It was re-formed among Russian Marxist emigres in Europe by Lenin in 1903, splitting into Bolshevik and Menshevik wings at that point. Its influence remained small by comparison with that of the SR's.

Economic. Russia in 1890 was an overwhelmingly agricultural and peasant nation, a major grain exporter, and an importer of manufactured goods from Western Europe. Industrialization had received some impetus from the 1860s on, and a major railway system was being constructed. Plans for the Trans-Siberian Railroad to the Pacific coast were adopted in 1890. Russia was heavily dependent on foreign loans and investments for nearly all industrial development, and was a major debtor nation. Though private enterprise was encouraged, the Russian government was directly involved in every major economic undertaking.

A major industrialization program was begun under supervision of Sergei Witte, the Minister of Finance (served 1892–1903). Railway construction was pushed at a rapid rate, foreign investors were encouraged, and large loans were floated abroad, particularly in France. Exports had to be increased and more taxes raised, so that the burden of industrialization fell heavily on the large landowners and even more on the peasants. Protests against this policy, and protests from other quarters about Witte's opposition to the Far Eastern policy (see below) led to Witte's dismissal in 1903 and to subsequent moderation of the industrialization drive.

The lot of the peasantry had in some ways become worse after the Emancipation (the end of serfdom in 1861). Reparations dues were heavy, landless peasants were increasing in number, and the bulk were still bound to the village communes. The repartitional commune was an ancient institution that now became a device for collecting taxes and reparations. From the 1880s on, the government took steps to replace communal with private ownership, though the transformation promised to be a long process. A terrible famine occurred in 1891–92.

Foreign Relations. Russia's long-standing policy of cooperation with Germany and Austria had come to an end in the 1890s because of Germany's alarming military growth, conflicts with Austria-Hungary over influence in the Balkans, and German's policy of supporting Austro-Hungarian claims (from 1879). Negotiations during 1891–94 led to a Franco-Russian military convention pledging each country to support the other in the event of war with Germany. Diplomatic conflicts with Britain over influence and claims in Asia (Iran, Central Asia, China) blocked any similar arrangement with that nation.

Far Eastern problems dominated Russia's foreign relations thereafter. An important section of the Trans-Siberian Railroad led across Manchuria. Over strong British objections, Russia forced China to cede a base on the Yellow Sea (Port Arthur) and a railroad spur leading to it. The Boxer Rebellion (1900) led to Russian military occupation of Manchuria and to Russian attempts to extract further concessions from China and the European powers as the price of withdrawal.

A Russian attempt to assert claims in northern Korea led to the outbreak of war with Japan (February 1904). The Japanese defeated Russian forces decisively at Port Arthur (January 1905) and sank most of the Russian expeditionary fleet before it could aid Russian land forces (Tsushima, May 1905). This war endangered the Franco-Russian alliance and solidified that Anglo-Japanese alliance. Russia negotiated for an alliance with Germany, intending to draw France in as well. The Björkö

Treaty, signed by the Russian and German Emperors (July 1905) was cancelled because of the objections of Russian statesmen and because of French refusal to join.

The 1905 Revolution. A rising wave of political demands, strikes, and unrest coincided with Russian military defeats to produce an unprecedented series of demonstrations and disorders. A procession of workers to the Winter Palace to lay demands before the Tsar was fired upon ("Bloody Sunday," January 22, 1905). Minor concessions by the government did nothing to stem the unrest, which now included mutinies in the armed forces, nationalist outbreaks in the non-Russian areas, peasant violence against landowners, and ultimately (October 20–30, 1905) a successful general strike. The October Manifesto (October 30) promised a representative institution in the form of the State Duma. By yielding to the demands of the moderate liberals, this offer split the liberal camp into the "Octobrists" who were satisfied with the concessions, and the "Kadets" (Constitutional Democrats) who sought a British-style parliament and limited monarchy.

Marxist Socialists played a minor role in 1905. The St. Petersburg Soviet (Council) grew out of a strike committee, and was headed briefly by Trotsky. A Bolshevik-inspired workers' insurrection in Moscow (December 1905) came late and had little effect on events.

1905–1917

Political. Witte, skeptical of the reforms, was appointed Russia's first Prime Minister at the time of the October Manifesto (1905). He was dismissed on the eve of convocation of the First Duma (May 1906) and replaced first by an old-line bureaucrat, then (in June) by the conservative but dynamic Peter Stolypin (served 1906–11). The lower house of the Duma, elected under a liberal suffrage law, was dominated by the Kadets. The Fundamental Laws promulgated at this time severely restricted the Duma's powers and preserved the principle of autocracy. The Kadet leaders challenged the Tsar's ministers concerning the Duma's powers, and in July the Tsar dissolved the Duma. A public appeal by the Kadet leaders (the Vyborg Manifesto) found little response. The Second Duma (March–June 1907) was likewise Kadet-dominated, though the radical parties were now strong enough to disrupt Kadet efforts to cooperate with the Tsar's ministers. This led to a second dissolution and to a new electoral law, which greatly reduced representation of the radical parties and national minorities. The Third Duma (1907–12) and Fourth Duma (1912–17) were dominated by conservatives, who nevertheless cooperated with Stolypin in a moderate reform program (Zemstvo reform, education, police reorganization, social insurance, etc.). In some cases the Duma functioned effectively as investigator and critic of the government (investigation of the Lena goldfield massacre of 1912, and criticism of Rasputin).

Repression of dissident groups was carried on from 1906. For socialists and radicals generally, it was a time of demoralization and little activity. Leftist leaders were hunted down, and were exiled to Siberia (Stalin) or compelled to remain abroad (Lenin, Trotsky). But, beginning in 1912, there was a rising wave of industrial strikes and urban unrest which ended only with the outbreak of war in 1914.

Economic. The peasantry had been the main victim of Witte's industrialization program. This program was now moderated, and Stolypin's policies permitted peasants to withdraw from their communes and become independent proprietors. Agriculture prosperity and exports rose somewhat. Railroad construction was cut back, subsidies to industries were cut, and industrial syndicates maintained high prices. The economy's generally satisfactory progress ended during World War I, which revealed its vulnerability: dependence on foreign equipment, transport bottlenecks, and declining agricultural output due to shortages of manpower, draft animals, and fertilizers.

Foreign Relations. Growing concern over the power of Germany led Britain and Russia to settle their differences in Asia. The Anglo-Russian entente (August 1907) divided Persia into spheres of influence, settled some lesser problems, and offered Russia the hope of a more favorable arrangement in the Turkish Straits. A series of agreements with Japan (1907, 1910, 1912, and 1916) dealt successfully with the problem of spheres of influence in the Far East. Russia maintained its position in northern Manchuria and sought to increase its influence in Outer Mongolia and Sinkiang (western China).

In Europe, Russia was increasingly involved in the tangled affairs of the Balkans, rivalry over which involved the great powers. After the annexation of Bosnia and Herzegovina by Austria-Hungary (October 1908) Russia attempted unsuccessfully to unite the Balkan countries and the Ottoman Empire against further Austrian penetration. It was equally unsuccessful in gaining a revision of the Straits regime in return for guaranteeing the Turks against attack (fall, 1911). Russia supported Serbian territorial claims in the wake of the First Balkan War (October 1912–May 1913), but without result.

World War I. Germany and Austria declared war on Russia (August 1 and 6, 1914) as a consequence of Russian mobilization in support of Serbia. Russian forces suffered serious defeats in East Prussia (Battle of Tannenberg, August 1914) and in Galicia (May 1915). The only major Russian success was the Galician offensive of June–September 1916, which nevertheless stopped short of its most important objectives. The Russian war effort was hampered by outmoded equipment and military doctrines, as well as by enormous problems of supply and war production.

The beginning of the war saw an outburst of public patriotism. Hopes were focused on the possibility of seizing Constantinople and the Turkish Straits as the reward of victory; the secret Treaty of London (April 1915) with England, France, and Italy would have accomplished this by breaking up the entire Ottoman Empire. Russian defeats contributed to high-level dissension (dismissal of War Minister Sukhomlinov and Grand Duke Nicholas, the commander-in-chief, in 1915). Representatives of the Duma and Zemstvos were given a direct role in war mobilization problems, but the Tsar refused to consider demands from a progressive Duma bloc for a new ministry which would have the nation's confidence. Domination of the royal family by the adventurer–monk Rasputin and the appointment of arch-conservative Stürmer as prime minister (February 1916) contributed to disaffection among those who had supported the Tsar's conduct of the war. Duma leaders warned of disaster unless there were a radical change in government policies (November 1916). Rasputin was murdered by a group of aristocrats (December 1916). Food supplies dwindled, and public disaffection grew.

The Russian Revolution, 1917. Spontaneous antiwar demonstrations in St. Petersburg, beginning on March 8, were sparked by food shortages and war-weariness. The movement spread rapidly and was joined by parts of the local army garrisons. Most of the Tsar's ministers were arrested. On March 15 the Tsar abdicated in favor of his brother, who refused the position. The Duma met to form a Provisional Government under Prince Lvov. On March 12 the Soviet of Workers' and Soldiers' Deputies was formed by radicals who occupied rooms in the same palace where the Duma met, and who claimed political control over the acts of the Provisional Government. Kadets and Octobrists dominated the original Provisional Government; Mensheviks and SR's ruled the Soviet. The growing strength of the left-wing parties enabled them to claim 6 of 16 cabinet seats in May. In July, following the failure of the Galician offensive and a Bolshevik demonstration, socialists gained 11 of 18 seats. Alexander Kerensky, an SR with influence in other socialist groups, became Prime Minister.

The peace issue was exploited by the Bolsheviks, initially a small minority. The Provisional Government was pledged to continue the war against the Central Powers, and Mensheviks and SR's compromised themselves on this issue by sharing rule. Lenin arrived from Switzerland on April 16 and at once called for a political drive to seize power. The Bolsheviks were not supported by other left-wing parties on this issue. Their July demonstration capitalized on continuing military defeats, but also brought persecution on their heads; Lenin went into hiding.

In September, the attempt of General Kornilov to seize power by bringing troops from the front was thwarted with Bolshevik assistance. The Bolsheviks, a minority in the First All-Russian Congress of Soviets

(June), had been gaining strength in various soviet elections; they had also been arming themselves openly. Lenin with some difficulty persuaded the Bolshevik Central Committee to organize a power seizure. This was carried out on the night of November 6–7, culminating in seizure of the Winter Palace and arrest of the ministers of the Provisional Government. Lenin gained approval for this act at the Second Congress of Soviets, then in session and having a Bolshevik majority. The Congress elected a Council of People's Commissars (or cabinet) headed by Lenin and consisting exclusively of Bolsheviks (a few left-wing SR's were added later).

1917–1921

Political. The All-Russian Congress of Soviets, and the entire system of soviets down to the local level, was transformed by stages into an instrument of government, formalized in the Constitution of the Russian Soviet Federated Socialist Republic (RSFSR) (June 1918). Opposition parties were banned soon after the Bolsheviks took power, and their newspapers were closed. The *Cheka*, the first security police, was established in order to suppress opposition elements (December 1917). A coalition with left-wing elements of the Social Revolutionaries continued to the summer of 1918, when the Bolshevik program of grain seizures ended all cooperation and led the Bolsheviks to proscribe the SR's as well. SR agitation against the peace treaty with Germany, and assassination of the German ambassador by an SR member (July 1918) also played a role.

The Bolshevik regime fulfilled the Provisional Government's promise to hold elections to a Constituent Assembly (November–December 1917) to write a Russian constitution. The SR's elected a decisive majority of delegates. The Assembly met for three days, under SR leadership, then was closed down by the Bolsheviks.

Waging the Civil War, and mobilizing resources for it, became the new regime's main problem. The 8th Party Congress (March 1919) elected the first Politburo, approved a Party Program charting the nation's course to socialism, and affirmed the principle of Party political leadership over the governmental structure of soviets. During the Civil War Trotsky was Commissar of War, Stalin Commissar for Nationalities, and both were Politburo members. In spite of strains, the leaders remained united as long as the existence of their regime was under threat. Mensheviks remained strong in parts of the governmental structure and particularly in the trade unions. The government of independent Georgia was Menshevik-dominated. The SR's, though no longer legal, were still a force.

Economic. The "Decree on Land" (November 1917) nationalized all agricultural land, confiscated the land of large landowners, but did not restrict forms of land tenure for the mass of peasants, except to forbid its sale and purchase. Banks were seized, and the entire economy was declared socialist property in an effort to deal with the food shortage and maintain production (December 1917). Simultaneously the Supreme Economic Council was established as overall economic coordinator. The national debt was repudiated (January 1918). A system of Workers' Control was set up in order to promote production and keep a proletarian watch over the capitalist managers (November 1917). Its failure contributed to the decision to take the larger enterprises under direct state management (June 1918), and ultimately the smaller enterprises as well. Workers were obliged to join government-approved trade unions, and compulsory labor service was used in some cases. Through rationing and the use of consumer cooperatives the government supervised food distribution. Foreign trade was nationalized (April 1918) but was of small importance because of the Civil War and the Allied blockade (until 1920).

"War Communism" was in force from the summer of 1918 to the end of 1920. In industry and the cities, it meant direct government supervision of production and distribution through the Supreme Economic Council and specialized agencies (Trotsky's Central Transport Commission). In the countryside, it meant forced grain collections to feed the cities and the armies, supported by a policy of inciting the poor peasants against the well-to-do (the "Committees of the Poor").

Foreign Relations and the Civil War. The Bolsheviks' "Decree on Peace" (November 1917) called for an end to World War I without annexations or indemnities. Negotiations began with the Central Powers, who demanded territorial changes (December 1917). The Treaty of Brest-Litovsk (March 1918) required the Bolsheviks to abandon Poland, the Ukraine, the Baltic states, Finland, and the Transcaucasian nations, all of which proclaimed their independence. Opposition to Bolsheviks by Russian army commanders and Cossacks led to warfare early in 1918, lasting until 1920. The "White" (anti-Bolshevik) forces fought in the Ukraine (under Denikin and Wrangel), the Baltic area (Yudenich), and the Urals (Kolchak). Most of these forces were defeated by the end of 1919; Wrangel hung onto the Crimea until the end of 1920.

Allied landings on Russian soil began in 1918. They were carried out by different countries for different reasons, though all gave support of some kind to the White forces. American and British forces occupied Murmansk and Archangel to protect war material. French forces landed in Odessa and gave direct support to Denikin. The British occupied Baku and the Caucasus, partly to protect investments in the area. The Japanese occupied parts of the Russian Far East, in the hope of gaining long-term concessions. After the surrender of the Central Powers (November 1918) German troops were employed to help defeat the Bolsheviks and their allies in the Baltic states and Finland, which gained their independence as a result. Foreign troops were withdrawn by 1920, except for the Japanese, who withdrew in 1922 under American pressure. Newly independent Poland invaded the Ukraine (April 1920); the Polish forces were repulsed by the Red Army, which almost took Warsaw but was repulsed in turn (August–September 1920). The war ended with an agreement (October) giving Poland large territories on the east and leading to a treaty the next year. The Ukraine, Byelorussia, and the Caucasian nations became Soviet Republics, but were not formally federated with the Russian Republic until 1922.

Russia, having concluded a separate peace with Germany, was not a party to the Versailles Conference (January–June 1919). During the Conference the Western powers tried unsuccessfully to mediate the Russian conflict. All were concerned about investments, Russian debts, and Bolshevik propaganda; they imposed a blockade, which ended in 1920 when Britain negotiated a trade agreement.

The Third Communist International was founded in Moscow (March 1919) to coordinate the spread of communism. Soviet-dominated, it was politically ineffective and at the same time was a serious obstacle to Moscow in establishing diplomatic relations with Europe and the world. Aside from several short-lived socialist regimes and attempted uprisings (1919 to 1923), the hoped-for spread of revolution to Europe did not take place.

1921–1929

Political. An anti-Bolshevik uprising on Kronstadt, in the Gulf of Finland, was suppressed (February–March 1921). The overthrow of the Menshevik-dominated regime in Georgia in the same year, and suppression of a Central Asian revolt later in the decade, marked the end of organized antigovernment hostilities. The several Soviet Republics—Russia, the Ukraine, Byelorussia, and Transcaucasia—were formally united (December 1922) as the Union of Soviet Socialist Republics.

The 10th Party Congress (March 1921) approved the New Economic Policy (see below) and prohibited formal political factions within the Party. Stalin was appointed General Secretary of the Party (March 1922) and from then on built his personal power through control of the growing Party bureaucracy. During Lenin's final illness (May 1922–January 1924) a "triumvirate" of Stalin, Zinoviev, and Kamenev ruled the country. After Lenin's death, Stalin argued for the building of "socialism in one country" against Trotsky and the Left (1924–25). The "Great Debate" over the tempo and strategy of economic growth provided the setting for leadership struggles (1924–28). Trotsky, Zinoviev, Kamenev, and others formed a united opposition to Stalin, and organized demonstrations demanding more intensive industrialization (1926). All three leaders were removed from the Politburo and other leading posts (1926–27); Trotsky was exiled to Alma-Ata (1928) and expelled from the country the next year. The leaders of the Right—Bukharin, Rykov, and Tomsky—hitherto supported by Stalin, now clashed with him (1928). They moved toward a common front with the defeated leaders of the Left and in turn were removed from their leading posts as the First Five-Year Plan began.

Economic. War Communism was abandoned in 1921 and replaced by the New Economic Policy (NEP) (1921–28). Small enterprises and trade returned to private ownership, under certain restrictions; larger enterprises were organized as autonomous but state-supervised "trusts." Individual plots were now secured to peasant households, with acreage restrictions and prohibitions on sale and purchase of land. Prewar peasant communes were restored spontaneously in much of the countryside. A tax in kind replaced requisitioning. A serious famine occurred in 1921–22. Industrial recovery was slow; the 1913 level of production was reached only in 1927.

Difficulties in motivating peasants to market sufficient agricultural products were acute in the "scissors crisis" of 1923–24 and again in 1927–28, when the Soviet Union was obliged to import grain. Foreign trade was well under the prewar level, and showed an adverse balance throughout the period. Large foreign loans to pay for industrialization were no longer available. The "Great Debate" of 1924–28 pitted "Right" against "Left"; the former advocated building peasant prosperity first as the basis for massive industrialization; the latter urged a high tempo of industrialization at the expense of the peasants.

Foreign Relations. With the end of the Civil War and withdrawal of the Allied blockade (1920–21), the Soviet regime sought diplomatic relations with the major powers and the border states. Treaties of 1921 recognized the independence of Poland, Finland, and the Baltic states, and established relations with Turkey, Iran, and Afghanistan. A trade agreement with Great Britain in 1921 paved the way for establishing diplomatic relations in Britain and most of the remaining European powers. Russia took part in the Genoa Conference (1922), called in order to settle claims and debts arising from World War I; at the Conference, the Soviets and Germany concluded a surprise agreement (Treaty of Rapallo) for mutual protection with regard to foreign claims. A secret agreement had already been negotiated between the Soviets and the German military, to enable Germany to circumvent the Versailles Treaty's military limitations in return for helping build the Soviet army. At the Lausanne Conference (1923), the Soviets failed to gain the protective Turkish Straits settlement they sought. A Soviet delegation took part in international disarmament negotiations (1927–33). Comintern propaganda was sometimes an obstacle to normal relations; relations with Britain were severed in 1927 for a time. Long negotiations with the Chinese government produced a treaty (1924) which supported China's integrity but reestablished Soviet rights in Manchuria. Negotiations with the Chinese nationalist movement (Sun Yat-sen, Chiang Kai-shek) in southern China produced a political agreement which merged the small Chinese Communist forces with the nationalists and brought Soviet advisers and aid for the Great Northern Campaign (1926). Chiang's slaughter of his Chinese Communist allies ruptured relations (1927). Relations were established with Japan in 1925.

1929–1934

Political. Stalin's triumph over both Left and Right was sealed with his setting economic goals (1929) even more extreme than what the Left had advocated. Leaders of the Left were readmitted to lesser posts, except for the exiled Trotsky; those of the Right were made to recant their "errors" at the 16th Party Congress (1930), and were likewise given less important posts. The reconstituted Politburo, though consisting largely of men whose careers Stalin had promoted, probably disagreed with Stalin on a number of policies. In 1932–34 some of them urged moderation in the economic tempo, collectivization, and the punishment of former deviationists.

Sabotage trials began in 1928; leading ex-Mensheviks were tried and sentenced in 1931. Routine Party purges (withdrawal of membership) were carried out in 1929–30 and 1933–34. Several plots among Party officials to remove Stalin were discovered during 1930–33 (the Riutin affair, 1932). Stalin's position was somewhat shaken in 1932–33 because of high-level discontent with his extreme policies, the famine and suffering among the peasantry, and his wife's suicide. Rise of Sergel Kirov, head of the Leningrad Party organization, was also a factor; he was acclaimed at the 17th Party Congress in 1934, and may have received the support of those urging moderation.

Conformity was imposed in many areas of national life. Trade unions were reoriented to help speed production and maintain labor discipline. Artists and writers were placed under state-sponsored organizations and required to conform to "socialist realism." Religious bodies were subjected to a new wave of persecution.

Economic. Stalin abruptly raised the industrial goals of the First Five-Year Plan (1928–32) in the spring of 1929, and the same fall pressed the collectivization drive much faster than any had proposed. The tempo of collectivization was moderated in the spring after Stalin accused some officials of being "dizzy with success," but it was pressed relentlessly in the early 1930s, ending with nearly total collectivization. The "kulaks" (about 5 million well-to-do peasants) were rounded up and deported to other parts of the country. There was famine in 1932–33, partly the result of economic dislocation; peasant deaths numbered in the millions, the Ukraine being particularly hard hit. Slaughter of livestock by recalcitrant farmers was another disaster. Resources were concentrated on gigantic industrial projects, which were pushed to completion amid both enthusiasm and sacrifices. The Five-Year Plan was declared completed at the end of 1932, ahead of schedule, though a number of important goals had not been met. The Second Five-Year Plan (1933–37) at first continued the high industrialization tempo, but was moderated at the 1934 Party Congress. A new emphasis on armaments from 1934 on was occasioned by Hitler's rise to power in Germany, and Japan's expansion in the Far East.

Foreign Relations. An agreement with China brought an end to a period of dispute over use of the Chinese Eastern Railway (in Manchuria) (1929). Japanese occupation of Manchuria (1931–32) was followed by tension and incidents between the two countries, the most serious occurring on the borders of Outer Mongolia, since 1924 a virtual Soviet protectorate. Establishment of diplomatic relations with the United States in 1933 (the first year of the Roosevelt administration) was sought to help contain further Japanese expansion. The Litvinov Protocol (February 1929), signed in Moscow by the Soviet Union, Poland, Estonia, and Rumania, linked the Soviet Union to the Kellogg-Briand Pact of the previous year, a pledge to renounce war. Separate nonaggression pacts were concluded in 1932 with Poland, Estonia, Latvia, and Finland, partly a means of securing the country's European borders in view of tension in the Far East. France, dropping its harsh anti-Soviet stand for the first time since the Revolution, signed a similar pact with the Soviets (November 1932). The establishment of the Nazi regime in Germany (January 1933) did not immediately alter the cooperative Soviet-German relations. But in 1934, as a precaution, further nonaggression pacts were concluded with Poland and the Baltic states, and there were agreements in the same year with Czechoslovakia and Romania, the Soviets recognizing Romania's jurisdiction over Bessarabia. The Soviet Union joined the League of Nations at about the same time as Germany left it (September 1934), an indirect affirmation of its anti-Nazi position.

1934–1939

Political. The assassination of Kirov (December 1934), probably instigated by Stalin, was used as a pretext for launching the Great Purge. Zinoviev, Kamenev, and others were tried for treason (January 1935) and given prison sentences. The next year they were again put on trial (August 1936) as Trotskyites, on the basis of fabricated evidence; 16

of the group were executed. Another group of 13 (including Pyatakov and Radek) was executed after a similar trial (January 1937, Pyatakov and Radek included), and in March 1938 the old Right leaders (Bukharin, Rykov, and others) suffered the same fate. A group of top military leaders (Marshal Tukhachevsky and others) was tried in secret on fabricated charges of treason and executed (June 1937).

The Purge affected the rest of the Party as well. Two thirds of the 1934 Central Committee was executed, and over half the delegates to the 1934 Congress were charged with crimes. Leaders in the non-Russian areas were particularly hard-hit. Mass expulsions from the Party paved the way for fresh recruitment and promotions; persons with managerial and technical skills were favored. The Party's leadership and membership were stabilized at the 18th Party Congress (March 1939). The security police (NKVD) became a formidable instrument. Ordinary citizens fell victim to the purges; the labor camp population numbered in the millions, probably reaching over 10 million at its height.

The Soviet Constitution of 1936 ("Stalin Constitution") preserved the basic structural features of previous constitutions. It was the first national constitution to include political, economic, and social rights, and the first to mention the Communist Party. The old Supreme Economic Council was broken up into central commissariats (ministries) for branches of the economy, which grew in number. The central governmental organs (now the bicameral Supreme Soviet, and its Presidium) remained rubber-stamp bodies; local government was neglected.

Economic. The Second Five-Year Plan (1933–37) moderated the pace of heavy industrial growth; there were some concessions to light industry and consumption. Military-related industries were favored due to German rearmament and the rise of war tensions. Collectivization was completed; a Model Charter was issued (1935) to maintain a standard organization on the farms. Machine-Tractor Stations (MTS) were set up to allocate scarce mechanized equipment, control output, and keep a political watch. Agricultural production rose; the bountiful harvest of 1937 spurred official optimism.

Labor was spurred by "Stakhanovism," the use of competition to increase productivity norms; wage differentials were used as incentives; piecework prevailed in the reward system. Controls over labor became ever more stringent. Collective bargaining was abolished in 1933, penalties for absenteeism were severe, and from 1940 on jobs were frozen.

Foreign Relations. Soviet policies during this period were motivated by fear of rising German power, and particularly in 1937–39 by failure of Britain and France to stand firmly against the expansion of Germany, Italy, and Japan. A defensive alliance with France (May 1935) included a Soviet pledge to go to the aid of Czechoslovakia if France did the same. Soviet leaders were made skeptical by the failure of Britain and

France to take action against the Italian invasion of Ethiopia (1935), German rearmament (1935), and German occupation of the Rhineland (1936). In the Spanish Civil War (1936–39), the Soviets supplied volunteers and considerable aid to the Republican side against the Falange, which in turn was aided by the Fascist powers. The scale of Soviet aid in Spain was cut back sharply after less than a year. At the Munich Conference (September 1938) Britain and France yielded to Hitler's territorial claims on Czechoslovakia, a step perceived by Moscow as an effort to turn German expansion eastward. Negotiations between Moscow and the two Western powers for a joint security program were carried on with hesitation and mistrust on both sides, and ended abruptly with the German-Soviet pact of August 1939. In the Far East, large-scale fighting broke out between Soviet and Japanese forces near the Mongolian border (July–August 1938), but a compromise ended the conflict, which was a Japanese test of Soviet strength.

The 7th Comintern Congress (July–August 1935) called for a "united front" strategy to halt the rise of fascism. Since 1928, communist parties had been forbidden to cooperate with other parties of the left, and had been directed to support the policies of governments opposed to the fascist powers. The actual impact of this policy was not great, except that it made Soviet relations with the Western democracies easier.

1939–1945

Political. The Soviet leadership remained stable during the World War II period. Stalin assumed the post of head of government (1940) in addition to his Party posts. Party membership swelled by almost two million during the war years, while at the same time the Party's functions declined; there were no Party congresses or conferences from 1941 to 1952. In the armed forces, the system of Party controls was subordinated to the regular command structure.

Important concessions were made to public opinion in an effort to forge national unity. Official promotion of Russian nationalism, reintroduced to some degree in the 1930s, reached its height during the war. The Orthodox Church and other religious bodies gave their support to the war, and in return received a degree of recognition and protection after two decades of persecution. Literature and the arts were liberated from narrow ideological controls, provided they supported the war effort.

Some non-Russian nationalities became political victims during this period. Seven nationalities were resettled en masse in Siberia and Central Asia because of suspected disloyalty (Volga Germans, Crimean Tatars, Kalmyks, and four small Caucasian nationalities). There were deportations from the western Ukraine and the Baltic states, where the German invasion had been initially welcomed by some. The system of labor camps remained intact through the war period.

Foreign Relations. German-Soviet pact of August 1939 surprised the world. Publicly, each of the two powers pledged neutrality if the other were attacked. Secret agreements divided most of Eastern Europe into zones of influence. Two weeks after the German invasion of Poland, Soviet troops occupied Eastern Poland, which was annexed to the Soviet Union. Territorial demands on Finland resulted in the "Winter War" (November 1939 to March 1940); at the end, Finland ceded much of Karelia to the Soviet Union, and granted it a naval base on Finnish territory, though Finland itself was not occupied. Pressure on the Baltic states by Moscow in 1940 was followed by Soviet occupation and by annexation to the Soviet Union (July 1940). Similar pressure on Rumania ended with Soviet annexation of Bessarabia (June 1940). Disputes with Germany over other claims and military movements remained unresolved. In the Far East, a second major border incident with Japan was settled during the invasion of Poland (September 1939). The Soviet Government continued its support of the Chinese Nationalist Government against the Japanese invasion, but was able to conclude a neutrality pact with Japan (April 1941).

World War II. The German invasion of June 1941 was not expected by Stalin, who had ignored warnings from the Western powers. Soviet forces were unprepared; by October the German forces had seized much of the European USSR and came close to taking Moscow, but were repulsed in the war's first major battle. A winter offensive (January–May 1942) against the Germans ended the threat to Moscow and regained some territory, but a German counteroffensive completed the conquest of the Ukraine, crippling Soviet food production and threatening oil supplies in the North Caucasus and Baku. Leningrad was under seige for much of the war. Britain promised all possible aid soon after the invasion, and the United States offered massive supplies (Lend-Lease Agreement). Moscow maintained neutrality with regard to Japan throughout the war, until after the defeat of Germany. The Battle of Stalingrad (November 1942–January 1943) crushed an enormous German force and proved to be the turning point of the invasion. A Soviet offensive in 1943 retook the North Caucasus and the eastern part of the Ukraine, though a summer counteroffensive (July 1943) by the Germans delayed the Soviet drive. Between the fall of 1943 and the end of 1944 Soviet forces recaptured all Soviet territory and pushed into Eastern Europe. Finland and Rumania surrendered in August 1944, and Bulgaria the next month after a Soviet declaration of war. Poland was taken from the Germans in January 1945. Soviet and American troops made contact on the Elbe River in April, and in May Soviet troops took Berlin as Germany surrendered unconditionally. Wartime cooperation with the

United States and Britain was made difficult by Soviet objections to the Western delay in opening a second front in Northern Europe (which was not done until June 1944) and much more by differences over the future status of Germany and Eastern Europe. The dispute over the composition of a postwar Polish government was a particularly serious matter, which ended with a coalition dominated by the Soviet-sponsored Lublin Government. "Big Three" conferences (Stalin, Churchill, and Roosevelt) at Tehran (November 1943–January 1944) and Yalta (February 1945) resolved many postwar issues but left others not clearly resolved. The Potsdam Conference (July–August 1945) attended by Stalin, Truman, Churchill, and later Attlee in Churchill's place confirmed the division of Germany into zones of occupation and pledged the powers to take steps toward a single German government and a peace treaty fixing the status of Germany. In August 1945 the Soviet Union declared war on Japan, in keeping with its agreement at the Yalta Conference. Soviet troops quickly overran Manchuria; Japan surrendered in September. Soviet and American forces occupied Korea, their areas divided by the 38th parallel, according to decisions at the Yalta and Potsdam conferences. They were pledged to help Korea establish a united democratic government.

1945–1953

Political. Stalin's strong autocratic rule continued undiminished up to his death, a rule exercised more through his personal secretariat than through the Party; even the Central Committee met seldom. The 19th Party Congress (October 1952) was the first in 13 years. High-level conflicts manifested themselves after the death of Stalin's heir apparent Andrei Zhdanov (August 1948), whose followers were then purged by Georgi Malenkov, another Politburo member. Top economic planner Voznesensky was arrested (March 1949). Stalin took steps to limit the power of security chief Lavrenti Beria by allowing him only partial control of the security apparatus, also by purging his political protégés (1951–52). Another major purge was foreshadowed by the arrest of doctors charged with murdering Zhdanov (the "doctors' plot," January 1953), but was cut short by Stalin's death.

The end of wartime liberalism was announced in statements by Zhdanov (from August 1946). Stricter ideological controls were imposed on Soviet culture; foreign influences were attacked, and Russian nationalism somewhat toned down. Official anti-Semitism was a response to the establishment of Israel (from 1948), and included some executions of Soviet Jews. The power of the security police continued undiminished; many ordinary citizens and lesser officials were arrested from 1949 on, and the labor camp system continued as before.

Economic. Much of the European USSR was devastated by war; entire cities had been razed, half the rail network destroyed, and between 15 and 20 million persons had been killed. The Fourth Five-Year Plan (1946–50) concentrated on reconstruction, continuing the prewar priority for heavy industry at the expense of light industry and consumers' goods, including agriculture. The Fifth Five-Year Plan (1951–55) embodied the same priorities. By the time of Stalin's death (1953), coal, steel, and oil production was roughly twice that of the prewar (1940) level, and electric power output had nearly trebled.

Strict discipline and controls were imposed in the agricultural sector, whose organization had been disrupted by the German invasion. Under Politburo member A. A. Andreyev, the new Council on Collective Farm Affairs enforced compulsory farm labor requirements and collectivized the newly acquired territories on the west. Andreyev was dismissed (February 1950) for promoting the small "link" work teams. Khrushchev, now a Party Secretary, pressed for reforms. Efficiency was promoted by using the much larger "brigades" and reducing the number of collective farms through amalgamation. Farm work incentives remained low, and a serious technological lag persisted in agriculture.

Foreign Relations. Disagreements between the Soviets and the Western powers over the future status of Germany and over Soviet political manipulation in Eastern Europe marked the opening stage of the "Cold War." The only concrete progress was the signing of peace treaties for Italy and the smaller defeated powers (Hungary, Rumania, Bulgaria, and Finland) (February 1947). Negotiations over the future of Germany bogged down over a variety of issues (reparations, boundaries, plans for reunification, and economic restoration). After 1947 no further progress was possible.

In Eastern Europe, Soviet-oriented governments came to power as the result of Soviet pressures and management. In Yugoslavia, Tito's indigenous communist movement was strong enough to retain power in its own right; it had waged active resistance to German forces. By 1948, all of Eastern Europe save Greece and Finland was ruled by Soviet-oriented governments, which socialized their economies and introduced one-party rule, styling themselves "people's democracies." In 1946 the Soviets proclaimed the existence of a whole "camp of socialism," later embodied in the Cominform (1947) a partial resurrection of the defunct Comintern, and the Council of Mutual Economic Assistance (1949), a weak agency until well after Stalin's time. In 1948 Yugoslavia broke with the Soviets over the latter's tactics of domination; it turned to the West for aid without altering its form of rule.

Soviet diplomatic pressure on Turkey for a Soviet role in policing the Turkish Straits, and for territorial concessions, evoked an American response in the form of military and economic aid (1946), the "Truman doctrine," which covered Greece as well because of the civil war there. The Western powers, alarmed at what they perceived as a threat of Soviet political advances in Europe, sought security in military and economic cooperation: the Brussels Pact (1947), the Marshall Plan (1947), and the NATO alliance (1949). The Soviet blockade of Western land access to Berlin, which was inside the Soviet Zone but under four-power rule, was probably an attempt to disrupt these efforts (April 1948–May 1949).

In Manchuria, the Soviets rendered some assistance to the Chinese Communists in 1945–46, but did not anticipate the swift Chinese Communist victory (1949) or give any active help in the latter stages. Prolonged negotiations between Stalin and Mao in 1950 produced a mutual assistance treaty, apparently after a debate over Soviet retention of old extraterritorial privileges in China and over the amount of Soviet aid. The Soviets had promoted a one-party socialist regime in North Korea, and Soviet and American negotiations became deadlocked over the manner of Korean reunification. Soviet arms shipments in the spring of 1950 helped the North Koreans to launch an invasion of South Korea (June). Chinese and not Soviet forces went to the aid of the North when U.S. and South Korean forces overran most of it. The war became stalemated near the 38th parallel, armistice negotiations were begun (June 1951), but dragged on inconclusively for two years, until after Stalin's death.

Stalin agreed in 1944 to setting up the United Nations, but was unenthusiastic about it; Soviet participation was restricted largely to the central U.N. organs until after Stalin's death. Disarmament negotiations made little progress in the Stalin era. The Soviet Union was rapidly building a nuclear capacity; the first atomic device was exploded in 1949, and the first hydrogen device in 1953, ahead of the first American test. The Korean war was the immediate occasion of a major Soviet arms buildup.

1953–1955

Political. Malenkov took Stalin's place as head of government immediately after the latter's death (March 1953) but a week later gave up his post as a Party Secretary, which suggested an intentional limit on his power. "Collective leadership" was exercised by an informal but well-publicized triumvirate of Malenkov, Molotov, and Beria. The post of General Secretary was not filled; instead, Nikita Khrushchev was named First Secretary six months later (September 1953). Beria, who was probably plotting to seize power, was soon arrested (June 1953), tried in secret, and executed. In 1954 Malenkov was in conflict with other Politburo (Presidium) members, particularly over his favoring of consumer priorities. He was obliged to resign as head of government (February 1955) but retained his Politburo seat.

Cautious relaxation was introduced in a number of spheres. Amnesty was granted to many political prisoners; the "special tribunals" of the security police were abolished. Writers questioned the political controls over cultural life (Ilya Ehrenburg, *The Thaw*), and were under attack for doing so.

Economic. Malenkov challenged Stalinist economic dogma by urging that growth of consumers' goods output keep pace with growth of heavy industry (August 1953). His public campaign to this end later (fall of 1954) became an issue on which other leaders (including Khrushchev) attacked him. Khrushchev criticized sharply the condition of Soviet agriculture and recommended decisive changes. A campaign for ploughing the "Virgin Lands" (Kazakh steppe) for grain production began in 1954. Higher prices were paid for collective farm output, but increased work norms and controls were also introduced. Khrushchev revealed that the supply of livestock was below that of Tsarist Russia before World War I. The Malenkov period spurred criticism of economic policies and performance, and brought basic issues out into the open.

Foreign Relations. The Malenkov period was one of limited initiatives only, the leaders being preoccupied by internal problems. A brief workers' revolt in East Germany (June 1953) and political problems in other East European nations also limited the Soviet capacity to act. The possibility of a West German army's participating in a joint West European defense force spurred Soviet counterproposals at a foreign ministers' conference (January 1954); Moscow proposed a neutralized Germany, withdrawal of all foreign troops, and accomplishment of reunification by existing German provisional governments (established in 1949 in both halves). Moscow also agreed to resume disarmament negotiations in earnest. In the Far East, Soviet influence was used to bring about an armistice in Korea (July 1953), and to facilitate an agreement on the conflict in Indochina following the French defeat there (July 1954). Certain Chinese Communist grievances against Soviet policy were dealt with in a visit by Khrushchev and Bulganin to Peking (October 1954); the Soviets promised to evacuate the naval base at Port Arthur and to end the domination they had exercised over certain important Chinese enterprises under the guise of "joint-stock companies."

1955–1960

Political. Bulganin was named prime minister in Malenkov's place (February 1955), but Khrushchev established himself as the most important political leader. The first challenge to his rule was from Molotov, who as Foreign Minister opposed many of Khrushchev's policy initiatives of 1955 (see below). At the 20th Party Congress (February 1956) Khrushchev denounced Stalin's crimes and arbitrary leadership in the 1930s and subsequently, in a secret speech. The speech was meant to undercut Khrushchev's present rivals, who had served with him under Stalin. Khrushchev's plan for decentralization of economic management (see below) became the main battleground for those who challenged him, including Molotov, Mikoyan, and Kaganovich. Outvoted in the Politburo (May 1957), Khrushchev called the Central Committee, which after a week's debate (June 22–29) supported his plan. His three rivals (the "anti-Party group") were ousted from the Politburo. In February 1958 Khrushchev replaced Bulganin as head of government, thereby occupying the two posts Stalin had held from 1940.

Khrushchev's power was at its height during 1957–60, and he used it to launch new programs: a new emphasis on consumers' goods, radical improvement in supplying new housing, reform of education, local government reforms, an increased role for Party organizations, the updating of Soviet Marxist ideology, and others. At the 21st Party Congress (January–February 1959) he declared that the nation was advancing toward full communism. Cultural and intellectual freeedom increased somewhat, but limits were imposed to bar a fundamental change (prohibition of Pasternak's *Doctor Zhivago*). Serious legal reforms were undertaken, many victims of Stalin-era repression were rehabilitated, and Khrushchev pledged no return to such practices.

Economic.   The Sixth Five-Year Plan (1956–60) was the only plan explictly abandoned in peacetime; the Seven-Year Plan (1959–65) took its place when many of its goals were found unrealizable. Debate over this change (1956–57) was connected with Khrushchev's proposal for abolishing the many central ministries which ran the economy and for using new Regional Economic Councils in place. The reform was adopted in May 1957.

More adjustments of agricultural prices and the farms' decision-making powers produced a modest improvement in output during this period, but well below official expectations. Abolition of the Machine-Tractor Stations placed collective farms under the necessity of paying for equipment purchases and repairs. This, together with numerous reorganizations and limits on farmers' private plots, hampered agricultural growth.

Wage reforms raised the lowest wage categories to a tolerable minimum and reduced overall wage differentials somewhat. Some restrictions on labor mobility were removed. State housing construction increased rapidly, and private housing construction was encouraged. Social services were improved. Levels of consumption increased perceptibly, though in many respects not to the extent planned.

Foreign Relations.   Khrushchev's many initiatives of 1955 had been prepared by tentative steps in 1953–54. In May, Moscow signed a peace treaty with Austria, neutralizing that country. In the same month Khrushchev and other leaders made a visit of reconciliation to Yugoslavia, although the latter did not subsequently join the Soviet bloc's organizations. The Cominform was abolished in deference to Yugoslav wishes. Disarmament negotiations suddently went into high gear (May 1955), though after agreement seemed near on many important points, the United States requested a delay until fall. The Warsaw Pact was formed as a response to West German entry into NATO, and East Germany became a sovereign state at the same time, though no German peace treaty existed. The Soviets agreed to a meeting of the great power heads of state at Geneva (July), including the United States, Britain, and France. The meeting produced no specific agreements on the German question, disarmament, and other major issues, but it symbolized a new era of negotiation.

Stalin's old demands on Turkey were dropped in 1955. Foreign aid to the underdeveloped world, including large-scale military aid in some cases, was begun dramatically with arms shipments to Egypt (September 1955). A tour by Khrushchev and Bulganin to South Asia (December) highlighted Soviet aid negotiations there. Khrushchev dropped the old "two camps" thesis of 1946, and instead called the nonaligned nations a "zone of peace" with friendly ties to the communist world. The "peaceful coexistence" slogan was used from 1955 on, a call for nonmilitary competition among different systems in which Soviet leaders asserted history was on their side.

The de-Stalinization speech led directly to problems in Eastern Europe in 1956. Since 1953, Moscow's grip on these countries had been relaxed somewhat, and local leaders had been shifted accordingly. The de-Stalinization drive fanned long-smoldering unrest, which erupted in the Poznan riots in Poland (June) and even more serious riots in Hungary (October). The Polish problem was solved with Gomulka's return to power (October) and a temporary liberalization; a swift leadership change in Hungary (the Nagy regime) led to the new government's declaration of independence and neutrality, which in turn caused the Soviets to overthrow Nagy in a massive tank invasion (November). Though Yugoslavia approved of the invasion, Soviet-Yugoslav relations became worse during the remainder of the 1950s, and Yugoslav ideological changes were considered by Moscow dangerous to socialist unity ("revisionism").

In November 1958 the Soviet Union demanded a revision of the status of Berlin, setting a six-month ultimatum and threatening direct action which could lead to war. The ultimatum was extended to permit a visit by Khrushchev to the United States for consultation with President Eisenhower (September 1959). A return visit by Eisenhower was planned for 1960.

Disagreements with China became serious during these years, though they were not yet made public. The Soviet leaders disapproved of China's risky economic drive (the "Great Leap Forward," 1958–60) fearing an expensive Soviet economic rescue operation. Moscow likewise refused to support China's policy of increasing tensions with the United States in the Formosa Straits crisis (1958). The Chinese leaders were mistrustful of negotiations between Moscow and Washington.

The Soviets continued intense development of a missile arsenal and nuclear warheads, a form of defense strongly promoted by Khrushchev. In spite of the Soviet demonstration of missile capabilities in orbiting the world's first earth satellite (October 1957), the Soviets remained well behind the United States. An informal nuclear testing moratorium between the two countries began in 1958 and lasted three years. Soviet conventional ground forces were reduced, and construction of nuclear-powered submarines was begun.

1960–1964

Political. The U-2 incident and its aftermath (May 1960—see below) triggered action by those leaders who opposed certain changes, including the denigration of Stalin. Personnel changes brought the opponents to the fore (Kozlov, Suslov) and demoted or sidetracked Khrushchev's strongest supporters (Brezhnev left the Party Secretariat). Khrushchev suffered reverses on certain policies, but was capable of strong counter-attacks. With his pro-consumer policies under criticism, at the 22nd Party Congress (October 1961) he attacked the "metal eaters" who wanted to return to the old Stalinist priorities. He castigated Stalinism once more (removal of Stalin's body from the Red Square mausoleum). When advocates of economic recentralization made inroads into Khrushchev's 1957 system, he responded by placing the Party more directly in charge of the economy than ever before (December 1962). He dealt with the impact of the Cuban missile crisis (October 1962) by signing the test ban agreement (July 1963), and countered the bad harvest of 1963 by a drive for fertilizer production, a consumer-oriented priority.

There were changes in the direction of stricter legal, social, and cultural policies. "Economic crimes" were broadened in scope, and use of the death penalty expanded for these and other crimes. Khrushchev promoted anti-Stalinist writings (Yevtushenko, Solzhenitsyn, Tvardovsky) but later criticized some of the writers he had supported. His blast at modern art (December 1962) was an attempt to appease Party conservatives.

Economic. There was a distinct shift of emphasis to heavy industry and defense industry; growth in consumers' goods was cut back. Certain industrial gains were impressive, but weak spots remained in evidence. Public discussion of reform of enterprise management and incentives began, but a reform law came only after Khrushchev's removal. Agricultural output grew very slowly, far behind the Seven-Year Plan's goals. This was due partly to Khrushchev's growing preference for panaceas (e.g., abandoning grassland rotation), partly to his growing restriction of farmers' private plots, and partly to his many administrative reorganizations. The poor 1963 harvest necessitated grain imports from the United States and elsewhere. The 1964 harvest was good, however.

Foreign Relations. The U-2 incident (American spy plane shot down over Russia) and the public interpretation that Khrushchev put on it obliged him to call off the Paris summit conference angrily; he also cancelled Eisenhower's return visit to the Soviet Union. Overall hardening of Soviet policies vis-à-vis the West was accompanied by increased defense appropriations. Nuclear testing was resumed (August 1961). The increased flow of refugees from East Germany (the GDR) via the Berlin "escape hatch" was abruptly cut off by the building of the Berlin wall (August 1961), an event followed by extreme tension between the United States and the Soviet Union. Still, Moscow did not move to make good its ultimatum on Berlin, and finally a treaty of 1964 with the GDR quietly dropped the threat.

The emplacement of Soviet missiles on Cuba led directly to Soviet-American confrontation in the Cuban missile crisis (October 1962). An American "missile blockade" raised the possibility of war, until Moscow agreed to remove the missiles. Having failed to redress the persisting missile balance in this fashion, Khrushchev turned to negotiation, and in the summer of 1963 signed an international nuclear test ban agreement. He also embarked on a campaign to improve relations with Western Europe, including West Germany. Opposition to Khrushchev's trip to West Germany contributed to his political downfall.

Relations with China deteriorated rapidly, and in 1963 the muted exchanges of recriminations became open accusations. Soviet aid programs had been withdrawn by 1960, and trade fell to a low level. Khrushchev moved toward isolating China by making preparations for an international communist conference such as those of 1957 and 1960; this too may have contributed to his removal. Moscow was also having difficulties with Cuba during this period, having launched a massive aid program after the United States broke off diplomatic and economic ties in 1960–61. Soviet leaders feared Castro's intentions of using aid to promote revolutions elsewhere in Latin America instead of stabilizing his economy.

1964–1970

Political. Khrushchev was removed from his posts at a brief Central Committee meeting (October 1964), in a plot coordinated by Suslov, which included some of Khrushchev's former supporters. Brezhnev became First Secretary (after 1966 redesignated General Secretary) and

The Evolution of Soviet Politics

Kosygin head of government. Collective leadership was reaffirmed, and Khrushchev was charged with arbitrary and erratic leadership. Khrushchev's 1962 Party reorganization (industrial and agricultural hierarchies) was cancelled; old structures and personnel were restored (December 1964). Most officials in charge of mass media and propaganda were replaced; otherwise changes in top posts were few (reduction of Alexander Shelepin's power, 1965). Tensions were evident over particular issues, but there was no major factional strife like that of the 1920s or 1950s. Resource allocation continued to be the main subject of dispute.

The image and policies of Stalin were rehabilitated selectively, as a concession to leaders and others who opposed Khrushchev's version of de-Stalinization. There was a new emphasis on "law and order" (resurrection of the federal Ministry of Internal Affairs, 1966). Political dissidents and unorthodox writers received harsh treatment; the conviction of the writers Daniel and Sinyavsky (1966) was the first in a chain of trials of dissidents.

Economic. Reform of economic management, under debate since 1962, was finally approved (May 1965) for gradual introduction. Enterprises were given more autonomy and a more rational group of performance indicators. At the same time, Khrushchev's Regional Economic Councils were abolished and the former system of central ministries was reinstated. The reforms had only limited results for increased efficiency, and close supervision by ministries and the Party limited managerial autonomy. The continued decline of economic growth rates troubled Soviet economic planners.

Despite many persisting problems, benefits to consumers increased substantially. During the Eighth Five-Year Plan period (1966–70), consumer oriented investment increased at a faster rate than producer-oriented investment. The economic dogma that had supported the opposite relationship was quietly set aside. Collective farmers were given a guaranteed money wage for the first time and were brought under the social security system. The wage reforms of the latter 1950s were carried further, with raising of the lower wage rates and a steadily increasing average wage.

Foreign Relations. Two of Khrushchev's major policy drives were set aside immediately after his removal: a planned rapprochement with West Germany, and efforts to have the Chinese leaders formally condemned by the other communist nations. The idea of loosening the NATO alliance through approaches to the Western powers individually was applied to France, however, and accorded with De Gaulle's policy of limiting NATO obligations. In 1966 Moscow revived the idea of an all-European security system, which it continued to pursue into the 1970s.

The Brezhnev regime in 1965 renewed the arms drive of the beginning of the 1960s and reversed Khrushchev's program for reduction of conventional ground forces. American acceptance of the idea of nuclear parity placed arms control negotiations on a new footing; peripheral issues were dealt with first, in the ban on nuclear weapons in outer space (1967) and the nuclear nonproliferation treaty (1969). Massive American involvement in the Vietnam war (from 1965) was answered by a Soviet commitment to supply Hanoi with modern defensive weaponry. The Soviet Union shunned direct involvement in Southeast Asia, and continued negotiations with the United States in several areas.

In Eastern Europe, the Soviet Union sought approval for a political organ to coordinate the policies of the communist bloc (September 1965). This failed because of Romanian objections, but military coordination was increased in several ways (more joint maneuvers, standardization of weapons). West Germany's interest in abandoning its diplomatic boycott of Eastern Europe led to Soviet efforts to forestall German establishment of relations; Bonn recognized Romania. Fears of West German economic and political penetration formed part of the Soviet motives for invading Czechoslovakia (August 1968). More important was the Soviet fear that speedy internal liberalization by the Dubček administration (from January 1968) would spread to the rest of the communist bloc. The "Brezhnev doctrine" (September 1968) established the Soviet right to intervene in other communist nations to safeguard bloc solidarity; this was reaffirmed at a conference of world communist parties (July 1969), the first large-scale gathering of this kind since 1960.

Defeat of Egypt and Syria in the 1967 Arab-Israeli war was a blow to Soviet prestige in the Middle East. Moscow rearmed Egypt thereafter to make up for losses in the war, but did not encourage the intention of Sadat (Nasser's successor) to seek another conflict. The rapidly growing Soviet navy made its presence felt in the Eastern Mediterranean, and to a limited extent in the Indian Ocean also. The Soviet Union acted as a mediator in the India-Pakistan conflict of 1965 (Tashkent conference, January 1966), partly in order to reduce Chinese influence in South Asia, especially its links with Pakistan.

In Asia, Africa, and Latin America, the Soviet Union confirmed its preference for working through established governments rather than revolutionary movements. Cuba, highly dependent on its economic relations with the Soviets, was dissuaded with some effort from providing major support to revolutionary movements in Latin America (e.g., Venezuela in 1966). Economic and military aid to the underdeveloped world was increased sharply during this period.

Hostile polemics between Moscow and Peking were resumed in 1965. Diplomatic relations were not severed, but remained at a standstill during China's "Great Cultural Revolution," its internal political battles of 1966–69. A massive Soviet military buildup was promoted along the Chinese frontier. The main field of active competition between the two countries was the underdeveloped world, where the key governments preferred to have relations with both. Frontier incidents on the Amur River in 1969 led to unsuccessful efforts to negotiate such disputes.

1970–1973

Political. Brezhnev's image and personal leadership were emphasized, but he apparently avoided the arbitrary decision-making of Khrushchev's last years. Podgorny, the titular chief of state, was named second after Brezhnev in political ranking in 1971; Kosygin was now third, but remained as head of government. At the 24th Party Congress (April 1971) the emphasis was on compromise, stability, and increased Party involvement in the economy. A check on the performance of all Party members was announced, a step to weed out passive elements.

The first major leadership reshuffling under Brezhnev came in April 1973. The importance of foreign policy and the political weight of security and military forces were recognized in Politburo appointments of Gromyko (Foreign Minister), Grechko (Defense Minister), and Andropov (head of KGB, the security police). Those leaving the Politburo had already been demoted in their other assignments for various probable reasons: Voronov (agricultural failures), Shelest (opposed accommodation with the West), and Mzhavanadze (scandals and excessive nationalism in Georgia).

The hard line in law enforcement and cultural activity established in the latter 1960s continued. A particular target was manifestations of nationalism, particularly in the Ukraine and Georgia.

Economic. The Ninth Five-Year Plan (1971–75) was the first to embody a faster growth rate for consumer goods than for producer goods. Production of automobiles for private use was an important feature of planned consumer output. Imports of consumers' goods increased sharply. Problems of management and efficiency remained serious. The 1965 reforms not having fulfilled their promise, further reorganizations were undertaken in the spring of 1973: enterprises were grouped in "production associations," shifting management to the middle level between production units and central ministries; planning was reorganized in a seven-region system which ignored the boundaries of the 15 Union Republics. A bad harvest in 1972 necessitated grain purchases abroad. Transformation of collective farms into state farms continued.

Foreign Relations. The coming to power of the Brandt regime in West Germany (1969) and the readiness of the new Nixon administration to expand disarmament and security negotiations paved the way for a long-sought settlement of Central European problems. While no German peace treaty was drawn up, West German treaties with the Soviet Union (August 1970) and Poland (December 1970) settled de facto the problem of Bonn's legal claims to territories in the east. The status of West Berlin was then regulated by negotiations between the two Germanies, which constituted de facto mutual recognition (December 1972).

Arms limitation negotiations with the United States led to an agreement on the risk of accidental war (September 1971), limitation of antiballistic missle systems, and an interim agreement on offensive strategic weapons, the last two signed during Nixon's visit to Moscow (May 1972). Negotiations on mutual reduction of troop levels in Europe were taken up. The all-European security conference, urged by Moscow since 1966, opened in Helsinki in July 1973.

A trade agreement with the United States (October 1972) accompanied an upsurge of interest in trading with the West. Imports of sophisticated technology loomed large in Soviet motives, as well as keeping open the channels for advantageous grain purchases in years of inadequate harvests (1972 was the latest). The visit of Brezhnev to the United States (June 1973) symbolized the Soviet search for a cooperative relationship. Soviet concern over the American-Chinese rapprochment (Nixon visit to Peking, March 1972) was a major factor in seeking this.

While continuing to supply arms to North Vietnam, Soviet leaders quietly urged Hanoi to seek peace through compromise. In South Asia, Moscow supported India in the India-Pakistan war over East Pakistan (November–December 1971), and became an important supplier of arms to India. Economic aid to Pakistan has served to promote the Soviet role as a mediator in the continuing conflict in South Asia. In the Middle East, treaties with Egypt (1971) and Iraq (1972) embodied the Soviet policy of providing a military supportive role without making a firm commitment to action. Egypt's sudden ousting of Soviet advisers (July 1972) was motivated partly by the Soviet refusal to provide certain types of offensive armaments.

Appendixes

Appendixes

Appendix 1

CONSTITUTION OF THE UNION OF SOVIET SOCIALIST REPUBLICS*

I. THE SOCIAL STRUCTURE

Article 1. The Union of Soviet Socialist Republics is a socialist state of workers and peasants.

Article 2. The Soviets of Working People's Deputies, which grew and became strong as a result of the overthrow of the power of the landowners and capitalists and the victory of the dictatorship of the proletariat, is the political foundation of the USSR.

Article 3. All power in the USSR belongs to the working people of the city and country as represented by the Soviets of Working People's Deputies.

Article 4. The economic foundation of the USSR is the socialist economic system and the socialist ownership of the means of production, firmly established as a result of abolition of the capitalist economy, of private ownership of the instruments and means of production, and of the exploitation of man by man.

Article 5. Socialist property in the USSR exists either in the form of state property (belonging to the whole people) or in the form of cooperative and collective-farm property (the property of collective farms or cooperative societies).

Article 6. The land, its minerals, waters, forests, mills, factories, mines, rail, water and air transport, banks, means of communication, large state-organized agricultural enterprises (state farms, machine-tractor stations, etc.), as well as municipal enterprises and the bulk of housing in cities

---

* Ratified Dec. 5, 1936, as amended to July 1, 1973.

and industrial localities, are state property, that is, they belong to the entire people.

Article 7. The enterprises of collective farms and cooperative organizations, together with their livestock, buildings, implements and goods produced, are the common, socialist property of the collective farms and cooperative organizations.

Every collective farm household, in addition to its basic income from the collective farm, has for its own use a small plot of land attached to the house and, as its own property, a dwelling house, livestock, poultry, and minor agricultural implements, in conformity with the Collective Farm Charter.

Article 8. The land occupied by the collective farms is assigned to them for their use free of charge and for an unlimited time; that is, in perpetuity.

Article 9. Alongside the socialist economic system, which is the predominant form of economy in the USSR, the law permits small private undertakings of individual peasants and artisans based on their own labor and precluding the exploitation of the labor of others.

Article 10. The personal property right of citizens in their incomes and savings from work, in their dwelling houses and subsidiary home enterprises, in articles of domestic economy and use, and articles of personal use and convenience, as well as the right of citizens to inherit personal property, are protected by law.

Article 11. The economic life of the USSR is determined and directed by the state economic plan for the purpose of increasing the wealth of society, steadily raising the material and cultural level of the working people, and strengthening the independence of the USSR and its defense capacity.

Article 12. Work in the USSR is an obligation and a matter of honor for every able-bodied citizen, in accordance with the principle: "He who does not work shall not eat."

The principle applied in the USSR is that of socialism: "From each according to his ability, to each according to his work."

II. THE STATE STRUCTURE

Article 13. The Union of Soviet Socialist Republics is a federal state, formed on the basis of a voluntary union of Soviet Socialist Republics with equal rights:

Russian Soviet Federated Socialist Republic
Ukrainian Soviet Socialist Republic
Byelorussian Soviet Socialist Republic

Uzbek Soviet Socialist Republic
Kazakh Soviet Socialist Republic
Georgian Soviet Socialist Republic
Azerbaidzhanian Soviet Socialist Republic
Lithuanian Soviet Socialist Republic
Moldavian Soviet Socialist Republic
Latvian Soviet Socialist Republic
Kirghiz Soviet Socialist Republic
Tadzhik Soviet Socialist Republic
Armenian Soviet Socialist Republic
Turkmenian Soviet Socialist Republic
Estonian Soviet Socialist Republic

Article 14. The jurisdiction of the Union of Soviet Socialist Republics, as represented by its higher organs of state power and organs of state administration, includes:

a. representation of the USSR in international relations; the conclusion, ratification and denunciation of treaties of the USSR with other states; the establishment of general procedure governing the relations of the Union Republics with foreign states;

b. questions of war and peace;

c. admission of new republics into the USSR;

d. control over the observance of the Constitution of the USSR, and ensurance of conformity of the Constitutions of the Union Republics with the Constitution of the USSR;

e. approval of changes in boundaries between Union Republics;

f. approval of the formation of new Autonomous Republics and autonomous regions within Union Republics;

g. organization of the defense of the USSR, direction of all the Armed Forces of the USSR, establishment of guiding principles governing the organization of the military formations of the Union Republics;

h. foreign trade on the basis of a state monopoly;

i. state security;

j. approval of the economic plans of the USSR;

k. approval of the consolidated state budget of the USSR and of the report on its implementation; establishment of taxes that go to the Union, Republic and local budgets;

l. administration of banks and industrial, agricultural and trading enterprises and institutions under Union jurisdiction; general direction of industry and construction under Union-Republic jurisdiction;

m. administration of transport and communications of all-Union importance;

n. direction of the monetary and credit system;

o. organization of state insurance;

p. concluding and granting of loans;

q. establishment of guiding principles of land tenure and of the use of mineral wealth, forests and water;

r. establishment of guiding principles in the spheres of education and public health;

s. organization of a uniform system of economic accounting;

t. establishment of the fundamentals of labor legislation;

u. establishment of the guiding principles of legislation on the judicial system and judicial procedure and the guiding principles of civil, criminal and corrective labor legislation;

v. legislation on Union citizenship; legislation on the rights of foreigners;

w. establishment of the guiding principles of legislation on marriage and the family;

x. issuance of all-Union acts of amnesty.

Article 15. The sovereignty of the Union Republics is limited only in the spheres defined in Article 14 of the Constitution of the USSR. Outside of these spheres each Union Republic exercises state authority independently. The USSR protects the sovereign rights of the Union Republics.

Article 16. Each Union Republic has its own Constitution, which takes into account the specific features of the Republic and is drawn up in full conformity with the Constitution of the USSR.

Article 17. The right freely to secede from the USSR is reserved to every Union Republic.

Article 18. The territory of a Union Republic may not be altered without its consent.

Article 18-a. Each Union Republic has the right to enter into direct relations with foreign states and to conclude agreements and exchange diplomatic and consular representatives with them.

Article 18-b. Each Union Republic has its own Republic military formations.

Article 19. The laws of the USSR have the same force within the territory of every Union Republic.

Article 20. In the event that a law of a Union Republic diverges from a law of the Union, the Union law shall prevail.

Article 21. A single Union citizenship is established for citizens of the USSR.

Every citizen of a Union Republic is a citizen of the USSR.

Article 22. The Russian Soviet Federated Socialist Republic includes the Bashkir, Buryat, Daghestan, Kabardin-Balkar, Kalmyk, Karelian, Komi, Mari, Mordvin, North Ossetian, Tatar, Tuva, Udmurt, Chechen-Ingush, Chuvash, and Yakut Autonomous Soviet Socialist Republics; and the Adygei, Gorno-Altai, Jewish, Karachai-Cherkess, and Khakass Autonomous Regions.

Article 23. Repealed.

Article 24. The Azerbaidzhanian Soviet Socialist Republic includes the Nakhichevan Autonomous Soviet Socialist Republic and the Nagorny Karabakh Autonomous Region.

Article 25. The Georgian Soviet Socialist Republic includes the Abkhaz and Adzhar Autonomous Soviet Socialist Republics and the South Ossetian Autonomous Region.

Article 26. The Uzbek Soviet Socialist Republic includes the Kara-Kalpak Autonomous Soviet Socialist Republic.

Article 27. The Tadzhik Soviet Socialist Republic includes the Gorny Badakhshan Autonomous Region.

Article 28. Resolution of questions pertaining to the regional or territorial administrative division of the Union Republics comes within the jurisdiction of the Union Republics.

Article 29. Repealed.

III. THE HIGHER ORGANS OF STATE POWER OF THE UNION OF SOVIET SOCIALIST REPUBLICS

Article 30. The highest organ of state power in the USSR is the Supreme Soviet of the USSR.

Article 31. The Supreme Soviet of the USSR exercises all rights vested in the Union of Soviet Socialist Republics in accordance with Article 14 of the Constitution, insofar as they do not, by virtue of the Constitution, come within the jurisdiction of organs of the USSR that are accountable to the Supreme Soviet of the USSR: the Presidium of the Supreme Soviet of the USSR, the Council of Ministers of the USSR, and the Ministries of the USSR.

Article 32. The legislative power of the USSR is exercised exclusively by the Supreme Soviet of the USSR.

Article 33. The Supreme Soviet of the USSR consists of two chambers: the Soviet of the Union and the Soviet of Nationalities.

Article 34. The Soviet of the Union is elected by citizens of the USSR voting by electoral districts on the basis of one deputy for every 300,000 of population.

Article 35. The Soviet of Nationalities is elected by citizens of the USSR voting by Union Republics, Autonomous Republics, Autonomous Regions, and National Areas on the basis of 32 deputies from each Union Republic, 11 deputies from each Autonomous Region, and one deputy from each National Area.

Article 36. The Supreme Soviet of the USSR is elected for a term of four years.

Article 37. The two chambers of the Supreme Soviet of the USSR, the Soviet of the Union and the Soviet of Nationalities, have equal rights.

Article 38.   The Soviet of the Union and the Soviet of Nationalities have equal powers to initiate legislation.

Article 39.   A law is considered adopted if passed by both chambers of the Supreme Soviet by a simple majority vote in each.

Article 40.   Laws passed by the Supreme Soviet of the USSR are published in the languages of the Union Republics over the signatures of the Chairman and Secretary of the Presidium of the Supreme Soviet of the USSR.

Article 41.   Sessions of the Soviet of the Union and of the Soviet of Nationalities begin and end simultaneously.

Article 42.   The Soviet of the Union elects a Chairman of the Soviet of the Union and four Vice-Chairmen.

Article 43.   The Soviet of Nationalities elects a Chairman of the Soviet of Nationalities and four Vice-Chairmen.

Article 44.   The Chairmen of the Soviet of the Union and the Soviet of Nationalities preside at the sessions of the respective chambers and are in charge of their internal procedures.

Article 45.   Joint sessions of the two chambers of the Supreme Soviet of the USSR are presided over alternately by the Chairman of the Soviet of the Union and the Chairman of the Soviet of Nationalities.

Article 46.   Sessions of the Supreme Soviet of the USSR are convoked by the Presidium of the Supreme Soviet twice a year.

Special sessions are convoked by the Presidium of the Supreme Soviet of the USSR at its discretion or on demand of one of the Union Republics.

Article 47.   In the event of disagreement between the Soviet of the Union and the Soviet of Nationalities, the question is referred for settlement to a conciliation commission formed by the chambers on a parity basis. If the conciliation commission fails to arrive at an agreement, or if its decision fails to satisfy one of the chambers, the question is considered for a second time by the chambers. Failing agreement between the two chambers, the Presidium of the Supreme Soviet of the USSR dissolves the Supreme Soviet of the USSR and orders new elections.

Article 48.   The Supreme Soviet of the USSR at a joint session of the two chambers elects the Presidium of the Supreme Soviet of the USSR, consisting of a Chairman of the Presidium of the Supreme Soviet of the USSR, 15 Vice-Chairmen (one from each Union Republic), a Secretary of the Presidium and 20 members of the Presidium of the Supreme Soviet of the USSR.

The Presidium of the Supreme Soviet of the USSR is accountable for all its activities to the Supreme Soviet of the USSR.

Article 49.   The Presidium of the Supreme Soviet of the USSR:

a.   convenes the sessions of the Supreme Soviet of the USSR;

b.   issues decrees;

c. gives interpretations of the laws of the USSR which are in force;

d. dissolves the Supreme Soviet of the USSR in conformity with Article 47 of the Constitution of the USSR and orders new elections;

e. conducts popular referendums on its own initiative or on the demand of one of the Union Republics;

f. annuls decisions and orders of the Council of Ministers of the USSR and of the Councils of Ministers of the Union Republics if they do not conform to law;

g. in the intervals between sessions of the Supreme Soviet of the USSR, appoints and removes Ministers of the USSR on the recommendation of the Chairman of the Council of Ministers of the USSR, subject to subsequent confirmation by the Supreme Soviet of the USSR;

h. institutes orders and medals of the USSR and establishes titles of honor of the USSR;

i. awards orders and medals and confers titles of honor of the USSR;

j. exercises the right of pardon;

k. institutes military titles, diplomatic ranks, and other special titles;

l. appoints and removes the high command of the Armed Forces of the USSR;

m. in the intervals between sessions of the Supreme Soviet of the USSR, proclaims a state of war in the event of an armed attack on the USSR, or when necessary to fulfill international treaty obligations providing for mutual defense against aggression;

n. orders general or partial mobilization;

o. ratifies and denounces international treaties of the USSR;

p. appoints and recalls plenipotentiary representatives of the USSR to foreign states;

q. receives credentials and letters of recall of diplomatic representatives accredited to it by foreign states;

r. proclaims martial law in individual localities or throughout the USSR in the interests of the defense of the USSR or of the maintenance of law and order and the security of the state.

Article 50. The Soviet of the Union and the Soviet of Nationalities elect Credentials Commissions to verify the credentials of the members of the respective chambers.

On the recommendation of the Credentials Commissions, the chambers decide whether to recognize the credentials of deputies or to annul the election of individual deputies.

Article 51. The Supreme Soviet of the USSR, when it considers it necessary, appoints commissions of investigation and audit on any matter.

It is the duty of all institutions and officials to comply with the demands of such commissions and to submit to them all necessary materials and documents.

Article 52. No member of the Supreme Soviet of the USSR may be prosecuted or arrested without the consent of the Supreme Soviet of the USSR, or, when the Supreme Soviet of the USSR is not in session, without the consent of the Presidium of the Supreme Soviet of the USSR.

Article 53. Upon the expiry of the term of office of the Supreme Soviet of the USSR, or upon its dissolution prior to the expiry of its term of office, the Presidium of the Supreme Soviet of the USSR retains its powers until the newly elected Supreme Soviet of the USSR has elected a new Presidium of the Supreme Soviet of the USSR.

Article 54. Upon the expiry of the term of office of the Supreme Soviet of the USSR, or upon its dissolution prior to the expiry of its term of office, the Presidium of the Supreme Soviet of the USSR orders new elections to be held within a period not exceeding two months from the date of expiry of the term of office or dissolution of the Supreme Soviet of the USSR.

Article 55. The newly elected Supreme Soviet of the USSR is convoked by the outgoing Presidium of the Supreme Soviet of the USSR not later than three months after the elections.

Article 56. The Supreme Soviet of the USSR, at a joint session of the two chambers, appoints the Government of the USSR, which is the Council of Ministers of the USSR.

IV. THE HIGHER ORGANS OF STATE POWER OF THE UNION REPUBLICS

Article 57. The highest organ of state power in a Union Republic is the Supreme Soviet of the Union Republic.

Article 58. The Supreme Soviet of a Union Republic is elected by the citizens of the Republic for a term of four years.

The basis of representation is established by the Constitution of the Union Republic.

Article 59. The Supreme Soviet of a Union Republic is the sole legislative organ of the Republic.

Article 60. The Supreme Soviet of a Union Republic:

a. adopts the Constitution of the Republic and amends it in conformity with Article 16 of the Constitution of the USSR;

b. confirms the Constitutions of the Autonomous Republics included in its territory, and establishes the boundaries of their territory;

c. approves the economic plan and budget of the Republic;

d. exercises the right of amnesty and pardon of citizens sentenced by courts of the Union Republic;

e. establishes the representation of the Union Republic in its international relations;

f. determines the manner of organizing the Republic's military formations.

Article 61. The Supreme Soviet of a Union Republic elects the Presidium of the Supreme Soviet of the Union Republic, consisting of the Chairman of the Presidium of the Supreme Soviet of the Union Republic, Vice-Chairmen, a Secretary of the Presidium, and members of the Presidium of the Supreme Soviet of a Union Republic.

The powers of the Supreme Soviet of a Union Republic are defined by the Constitution of the Union Republic.

Article 62. The Supreme Soviet of a Union Republic elects a Chairman and Vice-Chairmen to conduct its sessions.

Article 63. The Supreme Soviet of a Union Republic appoints the Government of the Union Republic, which is the Council of Ministers of the Union Republic.

V. THE ORGANS OF STATE ADMINISTRATION OF THE UNION OF SOVIET SOCIALIST REPUBLICS

Article 64. The highest executive and administrative organ of state power of the Union of Soviet Socialist Republics is the Council of Ministers of the USSR.

Article 65. The Council of Ministers of the USSR is responsible and accountable to the Supreme Soviet of the USSR, and in the intervals between sessions of the Supreme Soviet it is responsible to the Presidium of the Supreme Soviet of the USSR.

Article 66. The Council of Ministers of the USSR issues decisions and orders on the basis and in pursuance of laws in operation, and verifies their execution.

Article 67. Decisions and orders of the Council of Ministers of the USSR are binding throughout the territory of the USSR.

Article 68. The Council of Ministers of the USSR:

a. coordinates and directs the work of the all-Union and Union-Republic Ministries of the USSR, the State Committees of the Council of Ministers of the USSR, and other agencies under its jurisdiction;

b. adopts measures to carry out the economic plan and the state budget, and to strengthen the credit and monetary system;

c. adopts measures for the maintenance of law and order, for the protection of the interests of the state, and for safeguarding the rights of citizens;

d. exercises general direction in the sphere of relations with foreign states;

e. establishes the annual rosters of citizens liable for active military service, and directs the general organization of the Armed Forces of the country;

f. establishes State Committees of the USSR, wherever necessary, and special committees and central administrations under the Council of Ministers of the USSR for economic and cultural affairs and defense.

Article 69. The Council of Ministers of the USSR has the right, with respect to those branches of administration and the economy which come within the jurisdiction of the USSR, to suspend decisions and orders of the Councils of Ministers of the Union Republics and to annul orders and instructions of Ministers of the USSR and also statutory acts of other bodies under its jurisdiction.

Article 70. The Council of Ministers of the USSR is appointed by the Supreme Soviet of the USSR, and consists of:

Chairman of the Council of Ministers of the USSR;
First Vice-Chairmen of the Council of Ministers of the USSR;
Vice-Chairmen of the Council of Ministers of the USSR;
Ministers of the USSR;
Chairman of the State Planning Committee of the Council of Ministers of the USSR;
Chairman of the State Construction Committee of the Council of Ministers of the USSR;
Chairman of the State Committee of the Council of Ministers of the USSR for Material and Technical Supply;
Chairman of the People's Control Committee of the USSR;
Chairman of the State Committee for Labor and Wages of the Council of Ministers of the USSR;
Chairman of the State Committee of the Council of Ministers of the USSR for Science and Technology;
Chairman of the State Committee of the Council of Ministers of the USSR for Prices;
Chairman of the State Committee of the Council of Ministers of the USSR for Standards;
Chairman of the State Committee of the Council of Ministers of the USSR for Vocational Training;
Chairman of the State Committee of the Council of Ministers of the USSR for Television and Radio Broadcasting;
Chairman of the State Committee of the Council of Ministers of the USSR for Cinematography;
Chairman of the State Committee of the Council of Ministers of the USSR for Publishing Houses, Printing, and Book Trade;
Chairman of the State Security Committee under the Council of Ministers of the USSR;
Chairman of the All-Union Board of the Council of Ministers of the USSR for the Supply of Farm Machinery, Fuel, and Fertilizers;
Chairman of the Administrative Board of the State Bank of the USSR;

Director of the Central Statistical Administration under the Council of Ministers of the USSR.

The Council of Ministers of the USSR includes the Chairmen of the Councils of Ministers of the Union Republics ex officio.

Article 71. The Government of the USSR or a Minister of the USSR to whom a question of a member of the Supreme Soviet of the USSR is addressed must give a verbal or written reply in the respective chamber within a period not exceeding three days.

Article 72. The Ministers of the USSR direct the branches of state administration which come within the jurisdiction of the USSR.

Article 73. The Ministers of the USSR, within the limits of the jurisdiction of their respective Ministries, issue orders and instructions on the basis and in pursuance of the laws which are in force, and also of decisions and orders of the Council of Ministers of the USSR, and verify their execution.

Article 74. The Ministries of the USSR are either all-Union or Union-Republic Ministries.

Article 75. The all-Union Ministries direct the branch of state administration entrusted to them throughout the territory of the USSR either directly or through bodies appointed by them.

Article 76. The Union-Republic Ministries, as a rule, direct the branches of state administration entrusted to them through Ministries of the Union Republics having the same designation; they administer directly only a certain limited number of enterprises according to a list approved by the Presidium of the Supreme Soviet of the USSR.

Article 77. The following Ministries are all-Union Ministries:

Ministry of the Aircraft Industry;
Ministry of the Automotive Industry;
Ministry of Foreign Trade;
Ministry of the Gas Industry;
Ministry of Civil Aviation;
Ministry of Machine-Building;
Ministry of Machine-Building for the Light and Food Industries and Household Appliances;
Ministry of the Medical Industry;
Ministry of the Merchant Marine;
Ministry of the Oil-Extracting Industry;
Ministry of the Defense Industry;
Ministry of General Machine-Building;
Ministry of Instrument Manufacture, Automation and Control Systems;
Ministry of Transport;
Ministry of the Radio Industry;
Ministry of Medium Machine-Building;

Ministry of the Tool-Making Industry;

Ministry of Machine-Building for Construction, Roads, and Municipal
  Services;

Ministry of Machine-Building for the Oil and Gas Industry;

Ministry of Shipbuilding;

Ministry of Machine-Building for Tractors and Agricultural Equipment;

Ministry of Transport Construction;

Ministry of Machine-Building for Heavy Industry, Power, and
  Transport;

Ministry of Machine-Building for the Chemical and Oil Industry;

Ministry of the Chemical Industry;

Ministry of the Cellulose and Paper Industry;

Ministry of the Electronics Industry;

Ministry of Electrical Engineering;

Article 78. The following Ministries are Union-Republic Ministries:

Ministry of Higher and Specialized Secondary Education;

Ministry of Geology;

Ministry of Agricultural Deliveries;

Ministry of Public Health;

Ministry of Foreign Affairs;

Ministry of Culture;

Ministry of Light Industry;

Ministry of the Timber and Woodworking Industry;

Ministry of Soil and Water Conservation;

Ministry of Installation and Special Construction;

Ministry of the Meat and Dairy Industry;

Ministry of Oil Refining and Petrochemical Industry;

Ministry of Defense;

Ministry of Internal Affairs;

Ministry of the Food Industry;

Ministry of Industrial Construction;

Ministry of the Building Materials Industry;

Ministry of Public Education;

Ministry of Fisheries;

Ministry of Communications;

Ministry of Rural Construction;

Ministry of Agriculture;

Ministry of Construction;

Ministry of Heavy Industrial Construction;

Ministry of Trade;

Ministry of the Coal Industry;

Ministry of Finance;

Ministry of Nonferrous Metallurgy;
Ministry of Ferrous Metallurgy;
Ministry of Electric Power and Electrification;
Ministry of Justice.

VI. THE ORGANS OF STATE ADMINISTRATION
OF THE UNION REPUBLICS

Article 79. The highest executive and administrative organ of state power of a Union Republic is the Council of Ministers of the Union Republic.

Article 80. The Council of Ministers of a Union Republic is responsible and accountable to the Supreme Soviet of the Union Republic, and in the intervals between sessions of the Supreme Soviet of the Union Republic it is responsible to the Presidium of the Supreme Soviet of the Union Republic.

Article 81. The Council of Ministers of a Union Republic issues decisions and orders on the basis and in pursuance of the laws of the USSR and of the Union Republic, and of the decisions and orders of the Council of Ministers of the USSR, and verifies their execution.

Article 82. The Council of Ministers of a Union Republic has the right to suspend decisions and orders of the Councils of Ministers of its Autonomous Republics, and to annul decisions and orders of the Executive Committees of the Soviets of Working People's Deputies of its territories, provinces, and autonomous regions.

Article 83. The Council of Ministers of a Union Republic is appointed by the Supreme Soviet of the Union Republic, and consists of: the Chairman of the Council of Ministers of the Union Republic; the Vice-Chairmen of the Council of Ministers; the Ministers; the Chairmen of State Committees, Commissions, and the heads of other departments of the Council of Ministers established by the Supreme Soviet of the Union Republic in conformity with the Constitution of the Union Republic.

Article 84. The Ministers of a Union Republic direct the branches of state administration which come within the jurisdiction of the Union Republic.

Article 85. The Ministers of a Union Republic, within the limits of the jurisdiction of their respective Ministries, issue orders and instructions on the basis of and in pursuance of the laws of the USSR and of the Union Republic, of the decisions and orders of the Council of Ministers of the USSR and the Council of Ministers of the Union Republic, and of the orders and instructions of the Union-Republic Ministries of the USSR.

Article 86. The Ministries of a Union Republic are either Union-Republic or Republic Ministries.

Article 87. Each Union-Republic Ministry directs the branch of state administration entrusted to it, and is subordinate both to the Council of Ministers of the Union Republic and to the corresponding Union-Republic Ministry of the USSR.

Article 88. Each Republic Ministry directs the branch of state administration entrusted to it, and is directly subordinate to the Council of Ministers of the Union Republic.

VII. THE HIGHER ORGANS OF STATE POWER OF THE AUTONOMOUS SOVIET SOCIALIST REPUBLICS

Article 89. The highest organ of state power in an Autonomous Republic is the Supreme Soviet of the Autonomous Republic.

Article 90. The Supreme Soviet of an Autonomous Republic is elected by the citizens of the Republic for a term of four years on a basis of representation established by the Constitution of the Autonomous Republic.

Article 91. The Supreme Soviet of an Autonomous Republic is the sole legislative organ of the Autonomous Republic.

Article 92. Each Autonomous Republic has its own Constitution, which takes into account the specific features of the Autonomous Republic, and is drawn up in full conformity with the Constitution of the Union Republic.

Article 93. The Supreme Soviet of an Autonomous Republic elects the Presidium of the Supreme Soviet of the Autonomous Republic and appoints the Council of Ministers of the Autonomous Republic, in accordance with its Constitution.

VIII. THE LOCAL ORGANS OF STATE POWER

Article 94. The organs of state power in territories, provinces, autonomous regions, areas, districts, cities, and rural localities (stanitsas, villages, hamlets, kishlaks, auls) are the Soviets of Working People's Deputies.

Article 95. The Soviets of Working People's Deputies of territories, provinces, autonomous regions, areas, districts, cities and rural localities (stanitsas, villages, hamlets, kishlaks, auls) are elected by the working people of the respective territory, province, autonomous region, area, district, city, or rural locality for a term of two years.

Article 96. The basis of representation for Soviets of Working People's Deputies is established by the Constitutions of the Union Republics.

Article 97. The Soviets of Working People's Deputies direct the work of the organs of administration subordinate to them, ensure the maintenance of the state order, observance of the laws, and protection of the rights of citizens, direct local economic and cultural affairs, and establish the local budget.

Article 98. The Soviets of Working People's Deputies adopt decisions and issue directives within the limits of the rights vested in them by the laws of the USSR and of the Union Republic.

Article 99. The executive and administrative organ of the Soviet of Working People's Deputies of a territory, province, autonomous region, area, district, city, or rural locality is the Executive Committee elected by it, consisting of a Chairman, Vice-Chairmen, a Secretary, and members.

Article 100. The executive and administrative organ of the Soviet of Working People's Deputies of a small locality, in accordance with the Constitution of the Union Republic, is the Chairman, the Vice-Chairman, and Secretary elected by the Soviet of Working People's Deputies.

Article 101. The executive organs of Soviets of Working People's Deputies are directly accountable both to the Soviet of Working People's Deputies which elected them and to the executive organ of the superior Soviet of Working People's Deputies.

IX. THE COURTS AND THE PROCURACY

Article 102. In the USSR justice is administered by the Supreme Court of the USSR, the Supreme Courts of the Union Republics, the courts of the territories, provinces, Autonomous Republics, autonomous regions and areas, special courts of the USSR, and people's courts.

Article 103. In all courts, cases are tried with the participation of people's assessors, except in instances specially provided by law.

Article 104. The Supreme Court of the USSR is the highest judicial organ. The Supreme Court of the USSR is charged with the supervision of the judicial activity of all the judicial bodies of the USSR and of the Union Republics, within the limits established by law.

Article 105. The Supreme Court of the USSR is elected by the Supreme Soviet of the USSR for a term of five years.

The Supreme Court of the' USSR includes the Chairmen of the Supreme Courts of the Union Republics ex officio.

Article 106. The Supreme Courts of the Union Republics are elected by the Supreme Soviets of the Union Republics for a term of five years.

Article 107. The Supreme Courts of the Autonomous Republics are elected by the Supreme Soviets of the Autonomous Republics for a term of five years.

Article 108. The courts of territories, provinces, autonomous regions, and areas are elected by the Soviets of Working People's Deputies of the respective territories, provinces, autonomous regions, and areas for a term of five years.

Article 109. People's judges of district and city people's courts are elected by citizens of the districts and cities on the basis of universal, equal, and direct suffrage by secret ballot for a term of five years.

People's assessors of district and city people's courts are elected at general meetings of industrial, office, and professional workers, of peasants at their place of work or residence, and of military personnel in military units, for a term of two years.

Article 110. Judicial proceedings are conducted in the language of the Union Republic, Autonomous Republic, or autonomous region, persons not knowing this language being guaranteed the opportunity of fully acquainting themselves with the materials of the case through an interpreter, as well as the right to use their own language in court.

Article 111. Cases in all courts of the USSR are heard in public, unless otherwise provided for by law, and the accused is guaranteed the right to defense.

Article 112. Judges are independent and subject only to the law.

Article 113. Supreme supervisory power over the strict execution of the law by all Ministries and institutions subordinate to them, as well as by individual officials and by citizens of the USSR, is vested in the Procurator-General of the USSR.

Article 114. The Procurator-General of the USSR is appointed by the Supreme Soviet of the USSR for a term of seven years.

Article 115. Procurators of Republics, territories, provinces, Autonomous Republics, and autonomous regions are appointed by the Procurator-General of the USSR for a term of five years.

Article 116. Area, district, and city procurators are appointed by the Procurators of the Union Republics, subject to the approval of the Procurator-General of the USSR, for a term of five years.

Article 117. The organs of the Procurator's Office perform their functions independently of all local bodies, being subordinate only to the Procurator-General of the USSR.

X. FUNDAMENTAL RIGHTS AND DUTIES OF CITIZENS

Article 118. Citizens of the USSR have the right to work, that is, the right to guaranteed employment and payment for their work in accordance with its quantity and quality.

The right to work is ensured by the socialist organization of the national economy, the steady growth of the productive forces of Soviet society, the elimination of the possibility of economic crises, and the abolition of unemployment.

Article 119. Citizens of the USSR have the right to rest and leisure.

The right to rest and leisure is ensured by the establishment of a seven-hour day for industrial, office, and professional workers, the reduction of the working day to six hours for certain professions with arduous working conditions, and to four hours in shops where conditions of work are particularly arduous; by the establishment of annual vacations with full pay for industrial, office, and professional workers; and by providing an extensive network of sanatoriums, vacation homes, and clubs at the disposal of the working people.

Article 120. Citizens of the USSR have the right to maintenance in old age, as well as in case of sickness or disability.

This right is ensured by extensive development of social insurance for workers and employees at state expense, by free medical care for the working people, and by provision of an extensive network of health resorts for the use of the working people.

Article 121. Citizens of the USSR have the right to education.

This right is ensured by universal, compulsory eight-year education; by extensive development of secondary general polytechnical education, vocational education, secondary specialized education, and higher education, all based on close ties between the school, real life, and production; by comprehensive development of evening and correspondence education; by free instruction in all schools; by the system of state stipends; by instruction in schools in the native language; and by the organization at enterprises and on state and collective farms of free vocational, technical, and agricultural instruction.

Article 122. Women in the USSR are accorded equal rights with men in all spheres of economic, governmental, cultural, and social-political life.

The possibility of exercising these rights of women is ensured by providing women with the same rights as men to work, payment for work, rest and leisure, social insurance and education, and also by state protection of the interests of mother and child, state aid to mothers of large families and to unmarried mothers, maternity leave with full pay, and the provision of an extensive network of maternity homes, nurseries and kindergartens.

Article 123. Equality of rights of citizens of the USSR, regardless of nationality or race, in all spheres of economic, governmental, cultural, and social-political life is an indefeasible law.

Any direct or indirect restriction of the rights of, or, conversely, the establishment of any direct or indirect privileges for, citizens on account of their race or nationality, as well as any advocacy of racial or national exclusiveness or of hatred or contempt, are punishable by law.

Article 124. In order to ensure citizens freedom of conscience, the church in the USSR is separated from the state, and the school from the church. Freedom of religious worship and freedom of antireligious propaganda are recognized for all citizens.

Article 125. In conformity with the interests of the working people, and in order to strengthen the socialist system, citizens of the USSR are guaranteed by law:

a.   freedom of speech;
b.   freedom of the press;
c.   freedom of assembly and mass meetings;
d.   freedom of street processions and demonstrations.

These rights of citizens are ensured by placing at the disposal of the working people and their organizations printing presses, stocks of paper, public buildings, the streets, communications facilities, and other material requisites for the exercise of these rights.

Article 126.   In conformity with the interests of the working people, and in order to develop the initiative and political activity of the masses of the people, citizens of the USSR are guaranteed the right to unite in mass organizations—trade unions, cooperative associations, youth organizations, sports and defense organizations, cultural, technical and scientific societies; and the most active and politically conscious citizens in the ranks of the working class, working peasants, and working intelligentsia voluntarily unite in the Communist Party of the Soviet Union, which is the vanguard of the working people in their struggle to build communist society, and is the leading core of all organizations of the working people, both governmental and nongovernmental.

Article 127.   Citizens of the USSR are guaranteed inviolability of the person. No person shall be placed under arrest except by decision of a court or with the sanction of a procurator.

Article 128.   The inviolability of the homes of citizens and privacy of correspondence are protected by law.

Article 129.   The USSR affords the right of asylum to foreign citizens persecuted for defending the interests of the working people, for their scholarly activities, or for struggling for national liberation.

Article 130.   It is the duty of every citizen of the USSR to abide by the Constitution of the Union of Soviet Socialist Republics, to observe the laws, to maintain labor discipline, to perform public duties honestly, and to respect the rules of socialist society.

Article 131.   It is the duty of every citizen of the USSR to safeguard and strengthen public, socialist ownership as the sacred and inviolable foundation of the Soviet system, as the source of wealth and might of the homeland, and as the source of the prosperous and cultured life of all working people.

Persons who commit offenses against public, socialist property are enemies of the people.

Article 132.   Universal military obligation is law.

Military service in the Armed Forces of the USSR is the honorable duty of citizens of the USSR.

Article 133. Defense of the fatherland is the sacred duty of every citizen of the USSR. Treason to the homeland—violation of the oath of allegiance, desertion to the enemy, damaging the military might of the state, and espionage—is punished with the full severity of the law as the most heinous of crimes.

XI. THE ELECTORAL SYSTEM

Article 134. Elections of deputies to all Soviets of Working People's Deputies—the Supreme Soviet of the USSR, the Supreme Soviets of the Union Republics, the Soviets of Working People's Deputies of territories and provinces, the Supreme Soviets of the Autonomous Republics, the Soviets of Working People's Deputies of Autonomous Regions, and the area, district, city and rural (stanitsa, village, hamlet, kishlak, aul) Soviets of Working People's Deputies—are elected on the basis of universal, equal and direct suffrage by secret ballot.

Article 135. Elections of deputies are universal: all citizens of the USSR who have attained the age of 18 years, regardless of race or nationality, sex, religion, education, domicile, social origin, property status, or past activities, have the right to vote in elections of deputies, with the exception of persons who have been declared insane and persons deprived of electoral rights by a court.

Every citizen of the USSR who has attained the age of 23 years may be elected as deputy to the Supreme Soviet of the USSR regardless of race, nationality, sex, religion, education, domicile, social origin, property status, or past activities.

Article 136. Elections of deputies are equal: each citizen has one vote; all citizens participate in elections on an equal basis.

Article 137. Women have the right to vote and to be elected on equal terms with men.

Article 138. Citizens serving in the Armed Forces of the USSR have the right to vote and to be elected on equal terms with all other citizens.

Article 139. Elections of deputies are direct: elections of all Soviets of Working People's Deputies, from rural and city Soviets of Working People's Deputies to the Supreme Soviet of the USSR, are carried out directly by citizens by means of direct elections.

Article 140. Voting at elections of deputies is secret.

Article 141. Candidates in elections are nominated by electoral districts.

The right to nominate candidates is secured to nongovernmental organizations and societies of the working people: Communist Party organizations, trade unions, cooperatives, youth organizations, and cultural societies.

Article 142. Every deputy is obligated to report to his electorate on his work and on the work of his Soviet of Working People's Deputies, and he may be recalled at any time by decision of a majority of the electors in a manner established by law.

XII. ARMS, FLAG, CAPITAL

Article 143. The arms of the Union of Soviet Socialist Republics consist of a sickle and hammer against a globe depicted in the rays of the sun and framed by ears of grain, with the inscription in the languages of the Union Republics: "Proletarians of All Countries, Unite!" At the top of the arms is a five-pointed star.

Article 144. The state flag of the Union of Soviet Socialist Republics is of red cloth with the sickle and hammer in the upper corner near the flagstaff and above them a red five-pointed star bordered in gold. The ratio of width to length is 1 to 2.

Article 145. The capital of the Union of Soviet Socialist Republics is the city of Moscow.

XIII. PROCEDURE FOR AMENDING THE CONSTITUTION

Article 146. The Constitution of the USSR may be amended only by a decision of the Supreme Soviet of the USSR adopted by a majority of not less than two thirds of the votes in each of its chambers.

Appendix 2

RULES OF THE COMMUNIST PARTY OF THE SOVIET UNION*

I. PARTY MEMBERS, THEIR DUTIES AND RIGHTS

1. Membership in the CPSU is open to any citizen of the Soviet Union who accepts the Program and the Rules of the Party, takes an active part in communist construction, works in one of the Party organizations, carries out all Party decisions, and pays membership dues.

2. It is the duty of a Party member:

a. To work for the creation of the material and technical basis of communism; to serve as an example of the communist attitude towards labor; to raise labor productivity; to display initiative in all that is new and progressive; to support and propagate advanced methods; to master techniques, to improve his skill; to protect and increase public socialist property, the mainstay of the might and prosperity of the Soviet country;

b. To put Party decisions firmly and steadfastly into effect; to explain the policy of the Party to the masses; to help strengthen and multiply the Party's bonds with the people; to be considerate and attentive to people; to respond promptly to the needs and requirements of the working people;

c. To take an active part in the political life of the country, in the administration of state affairs, and in economic and cultural development; to set an example in the fulfillment of his public duty; to assist in developing and strengthening communist social relations;

---

* Adopted at the 22nd Party Congress in 1961 and amended at the 23rd Congress in 1966 and the 24th Congress in 1971.

d. To master Marxist-Leninist theory, to improve his ideological knowledge, and to contribute to the molding and education of the man of communist society; to combat vigorously all manifestations of bourgeois ideology, remnants of a private-property psychology, religious prejudices, and other survivals of the past; to observe the principles of communist morality, and place public interests above his own;

e. To be an active proponent of the ideas of socialist internationalism and Soviet patriotism among the masses of the working people; to combat survivals of nationalism and chauvinism; to contribute by word and by deed to the consolidation of the friendship of the peoples of the USSR and the fraternal bonds linking the Soviet people with the peoples of the countries of the socialist camp, with the proletarians and other working people in all countries;

f. To strengthen to the utmost the ideological and organizational unity of the Party; to safeguard the Party against the infiltration of people unworthy of the lofty name of Communist; to be truthful and honest with the Party and the people; to display vigilance; to guard Party and state secrets;

g. To develop criticism and self-criticism, boldly lay bare shortcomings and strive for their removal; to combat ostentation, conceit, complacency, and parochial tendencies; to rebuff firmly all attempts at suppressing criticism; to resist all actions injurious to the Party and the state, and to give information about them to Party bodies, up to and including the CC CPSU;

h. To implement undeviatingly the Party's policy with regard to the proper selection of personnel according to their political qualifications and personal qualities; to be uncompromising whenever the Leninist principles of the selection and education of personnel are infringed;

i. To observe Party and state discipline, which is equally binding on all Party members. The Party has one discipline, one law, for all Communists, irrespective of their past services or the positions they occupy;

j. To help, in every possible way, to strengthen the defense capacity of the USSR; to wage an unflagging struggle for peace and friendship among nations.

3. A Party member has the right:

a. To elect and be elected to Party bodies;

b. To discuss freely questions of the Party's policies and practical activities at Party meetings, conferences and congresses, at the meetings of Party committees and in the Party press; to table motions; openly to express and uphold his opinion as long as the Party organization concerned has not adopted a decision;

c. To criticize any Communist, irrespective of the position he holds, at Party meetings, conferences and congresses, and at the plenary meetings of Party committees. Those who commit the offense of suppressing criticism or victimizing anyone for criticism are responsible to and will be penalized by the Party, to the point of explusion from the CPSU;

d. To attend in person all Party meetings and all bureau and committee meetings that discuss his activities or conduct;

e. To address any question, statement or proposal to any Party body, up to and including the CC CPSU, and to demand an answer on the substance of his address.

4. Applicants are admitted to Party membership only individually. Membership of the Party is open to politically conscious and active workers, peasants, and representatives of the intelligentsia, devoted to the communist cause. New members are admitted from among the candidate members who have passed through the established probationary period.

Persons may join the Party on attaining the age of eighteen. Young people up to the age of 23 may join the Party only through the Leninist Young Communist League of the Soviet Union (YCL).

The procedure for the admission of candidate members to full Party membership is as follows:

a. Applicants for Party membership must submit recommendations from three members of the CPSU who have a Party standing of not less than five years and who know the applicants from having worked with them, professionally and socially, for not less than one year.

Note 1. Members of the YCL who join the Party shall submit a recommendation of the district or city committee of the YCL, which is the equivalent of the recommendation of one Party member.

Note 2. Members and alternate members of the CC CPSU shall refrain from giving recommendations.

b. Applications for Party membership are discussed and a decision is taken by the general meeting of the primary Party organization; the decision is considered adopted if voted by no less than two thirds of the Party members at the meeting, and takes effect after endorsement by the district Party committee, or by the city Party committee in cities with no district divisions.

The presence of those who have recommended an applicant for Party membership at the discussion of the application concerned is optional.

c. Citizens of the USSR who formerly belonged to the Communist or Workers' Party of another country are admited to membership of the Communist Party of the Soviet Union in conformity with the rules established by the CC CPSU.

Former members of other parties are admitted to membership of the CPSU in conformity with the regular procedure, except that their admission must be endorsed by a regional or territorial committee or the CC of the Communist Party of a Union Republic.

5. Communists recommending applicants for Party membership are

responsible to Party organizations for the impartiality of their description of the moral qualities and professional and political qualifications of those they recommend.

6. The Party standing of those admitted to membership dates from the day when the general meeting of the primary Party organization decides to accept them as full members.

7. The procedure of registering members and candidate members of the Party, and their transfer from one organization to another is determined by the appropriate instructions of the CC CPSU.

8. If a Party member or candidate member fails to pay membership dues for three months in succession without sufficient reason, the matter shall be discussed by the primary Party organization. If it is revealed as a result that the Party member or candidate member in question has in fact lost contact with the Party organization, he shall be regarded as having ceased to be a member of the Party; the primary Party organization shall pass a decision thereon and submit it to the district or city committee of the Party for endorsement.

9. A Party member or candidate member who fails to fulfill his duties as laid down in the Rules, or commits other offenses, shall be called to account, and may be subjected to the penalty of admonition, reprimand (severe reprimand), or reprimand (severe reprimand) with entry in the registration card. The highest Party penalty is expulsion from the Party.

In the case of minor offenses, measures of Party education and influence should be applied—in the form of comradely criticism, Party censure, warning, or reproof.

When the question of expelling a member from the Party is discussed, the maximum attention must be shown, and the grounds for the charges preferred against him must be thoroughly investigated.

10. The decision to expel a Communist from the Party is made by the general meeting of a primary Party organization. The decision of the primary Party organization expelling a member is regarded as adopted if not less than two thirds of the Party members attending the meeting have voted for it, and takes effect after endorsement by the district or city Party committee.

Until such time as the decision to expel him is endorsed by a district or city Party committee, the Party member or candidate member retains his membership card and is entitled to attend closed Party meetings.

An expelled Party member retains the right to appeal, within the period of two months, to the higher Party bodies, up to and including the CC CPSU.

11. The question of calling a member or alternate member of the CC of the Communist Party of a Union Republic, of a territorial, provincial, area, city, or district Party committee, as well as a member of an

auditing commission, to account before the Party is discussed by primary Party organizations.

Party organizations pass decisions imposing penalties on members or alternate members of the said Party committees, or on members of auditing commissions, in conformity with the regular procedure.

A Party organization which proposes expelling a Communist from the CPSU communicates its proposal to the Party committee of which he is a member. A decision expelling from the Party a member or alternate member of the CC of the Communist Party of a Union Republic or a territorial, provincial, area, city, or district Party committee, or a member of an auditing commission, is taken at the plenary meeting of the committee concerned by a majority of two thirds of the membership.

The decision to expel from the Party a member or alternate member of the Central Committee of the CPSU, or a member of the Central Auditing Commission, is made by the Party Congress, and in the interval between two congresses, by a plenary meeting of the Central Committee, by a majority of two thirds of its members.

12. Should a Party member commit a criminal offense, he shall be expelled from the Party and prosecuted in conformity with the law.

13. Appeals against expulsion from the Party or against the imposition of a penalty, as well as the decisions of Party organizations on expulsion from the Party shall be examined by the appropriate Party bodies within not more than one month from the date of their receipt.

II. CANDIDATE MEMBERS

14. All persons joining the Party must pass through a probationary period as candidate members in order to more thoroughly familiarize themselves with the Program and the Rules of the CPSU and prepare for admission to full membership of the Party. Party organizations must assist candidates to prepare for admission to full membership of the Party, and test their personal qualities.

The period of probationary membership shall be one year.

15. The procedure for the admission of candidate members (individual admission, submission of recommendations, decision of the primary organization as to admission, and its endorsement) is identical with the procedure for the admission of Party members.

16. On the expiration of a candidate member's probationary period the primary Party organization discusses and passes a decision on his admission to full membership. Should a candidate member fail, in the course of his probationary period, to prove his worthiness, and should his personal traits make it evident that he cannot be admitted to membership of the CPSU, the Party organization shall pass a decision rejecting

his admission to membership of the Party; after endorsement of that decision by the district or city Party committee, he shall cease to be considered a candidate member of the CPSU.

17. Candidate members of the Party participate in all the activities of their Party organizations; they shall have a consultative voice at Party meetings. They may not be elected to any leading Party body, nor may they be elected delegates to a Party conference or congress.

18. Candidate members of the CPSU pay membership dues at the same rate as full members.

III.   ORGANIZATIONAL STRUCTURE OF THE PARTY: INNER-PARTY DEMOCRACY

19. The guiding principle of the organizational structure of the Party is democratic centralism, which signifies:

a.   Election of all leading Party bodies, from the lowest to the highest;

b.   Periodic reports of Party bodies to their Party organizations and to higher bodies;

c.   Strict Party discipline and subordination of the minority to the majority;

d.   The decisions of higher bodies are obligatory for lower bodies.

20. The Party is built on the territorial-and-production principle: primary organizations are established wherever Communists are employed, and are associated territorially in district, city, etc., organizations. An organization serving a given area is higher than any Party organization serving part of that area.

21. All Party organizations are autonomous in the decision of local questions, unless their decisions conflict with Party policy.

22. The highest leading body of a Party organization is the general meeting (in the case of primary organizations), conference (in the case of district, city, area, provincial, or territorial organizations), or congress (in the case of the Communist Parties of the Union Republics and the Communist Party of the Soviet Union).

23. The general meeting, conference or congress, elects a bureau or committee which acts as its executive body and directs all the current work of the Party organization.

24. The election of Party bodies shall be effected by secret ballot. In an election, all Party members have the unlimited right to challenge candidates and to criticize them. Each candidate shall be voted upon separately. A candidate is considered elected if more than one half those attending the meeting, conference, or congress have voted for him. At elections of all Party organs—from primary organizations to the Central Committee of the CPSU—the principle of systematic renewal of their staff and continuity of leadership will be observed.

25. A member or alternate member of the CC CPSU must by his entire activity justify the great trust placed in him by the Party. A member or alternate member of the CC CPSU who degrades his honor and dignity may not remain on the Central Committee. The question of the removal of a member or alternate member of the CC CPSU from that body shall be decided by a plenary meeting of the Central Committee by secret ballot. The decision is regarded as adopted if not less than two thirds of the membership of the CC CPSU vote for it.

The question of the removal of a member or alternate member of the CC of the Communist Party of a Union Republic, or of a territorial, provincial, area, city, or district Party committee from the Party body concerned is decided by a plenary meeting of that body. The decision is regarded as adopted if not less than two thirds of the membership of the committee in question vote for it by secret ballot.

A member of the Central Auditing Commission who does not justify the great trust placed in him by the Party shall be removed from that body. This question shall be decided by a meeting of the Central Auditing Commission. The decision is regarded as adopted if not less than two thirds of the membership of the Central Auditing Commission vote by secret ballot for the removal of the member concerned from that body.

The question of the removal of a member from the auditing commission of a republic, territorial, provincial, area, city, or district Party organization shall be decided by a meeting of the appropriate commission according to the procedure established for members and alternate members of Party committees.

26. The free and businesslike discussion of questions of Party policy in individual Party organizations or in the Party as a whole is the inalienable right of every Party member and an important principle of inner-Party democracy. Only on the basis of inner-Party democracy is it possible to develop criticism and self-criticism and to strengthen Party discipline, which must be conscious and not mechanical.

Discussion of controversial or insufficiently clear issues may be held within the framework of individual organizations or the Party as a whole.

Partywide discussion is necessary:

a. If the necessity is recognized by several Party organizations at the provincial or republic level;

b. If there is not a sufficiently solid majority in the Central Committee on major questions of Party policy;

c. If the CC CPSU considers it necessary to consult the Party as a whole on any particular question of policy.

Wide discussion, especially discussion on a countrywide scale, of questions of Party policy must be so held as to ensure for Party members the free expression of their views and preclude attempts to form factional groupings destroying Party unity, attempts to split the Party.

27.   The supreme principle of Party leadership is collective leadership, which is an absolute requisite for the normal functioning of Party organizations, the proper education of cadres, and the promotion of the activity and initiative of Communists. The cult of the individual and the violations of inner-Party democracy resulting from it must not be tolerated in the Party; they are incompatible with the Leninist principles of Party life.

Collective leadership does not exempt individuals in office from personal responsibility for the job entrusted to them.

28.   The Central Committees of the Communist Parties of the Union Republics, and territorial, provincial, area, city, and district Party committees shall systematically inform Party organizations of their work in the intervals between congresses and conferences.

29.   Meetings of the aktiv of district, city, area, provincial, and territorial Party organizations and of the Communist Parties of the Union Republics shall be held to discuss major decisions of the Party and to work out measures for their execution, as well as to examine questions of local significance.

IV.   HIGHER PARTY ORGANS

30.   The supreme organ of the Communist Party of the Soviet Union is the Party Congress. Congresses are convened by the Central Committee at least once in five years. The convocation of a Party Congress and its agenda shall be announced at least six weeks before the Congress. Extraordinary congresses are convened by the Central Committee of the Party on its own initiative or on the demand of not less than one third of the total membership represented at the preceding Party Congress. Extraordinary congresses shall be convened within two months. A congress is considered properly constituted if not less than one half of the total Party membership is represented at it.

The rates of representation at a Party Congress are determined by the Central Committee.

31.   Should the Central Committee of the Party fail to convene an extraordinary congress within the period specified in Article 30, the organizations which demanded it have the right to form an Organizing Committee which shall enjoy the powers of the Central Committee of the Party in respect of the convocation of the extraordinary congress.

32.   The Congress:

a.   Hears and approves the reports of the Central Committee, of the Central Auditing Commission, and of the other central organizations;

b.   Reviews, amends and endorses the Program and the Rules of the Party;

c.   Determines the line of the Party in matters of domestic and foreign policy, and examines and decides the most important questions of communist construction;

d. Elects the Central Committee and the Central Auditing Commission.

33. The number of members to be elected to the Central Committee and to the Central Auditing Commission is determined by the Congress. In the event of vacancies occurring in the Central Committee, they are filled from among the alternate members of the CC CPSU elected by the Congress.

34. Between Congresses, the Central Committee of the Communist Party of the Soviet Union directs the activities of the Party, the local Party bodies, selects and appoints leading functionaries, directs the work of central government bodies and public organizations of working people through the Party groups in them, sets up various Party organs, institutions, and enterprises and directs their activities, appoints the editors of the central newspapers and journals operating under its control, and distributes the funds of the Party budget and controls its execution.

The Central Committee represents the CPSU in its relations with other parties.

35. The CC CPSU shall keep the Party organizations regularly informed of its work.

36. The Central Auditing Commission of the CPSU supervises the expeditious and proper handling of affairs by the central bodies of the Party, and audits the accounts of the treasury and the enterprises of the Central Committee of the CPSU.

37. The CC CPSU shall hold not less than one plenary meeting every six months. Alternate members of the Central Committee shall attend its plenary meetings with the right of consultative voting.

38. The Central Committee of the Communist Party of the Soviet Union elects a Politburo to direct the work of the Party between plenary meetings and a Secretariat to direct current work, chiefly the selection of cadres and the verification of the fulfillment of Party decisions. The Central Committee elects a General Secretary of the CC CPSU.

39. The Central Committee of the Communist Party of the Soviet Union organizes the Party Control Committee of the CC.

The Party Control Committee of the CC CPSU:

a. Verifies the observance of Party discipline by members and candidate members of the CPSU, and takes action against Communists who violate the Program and the Rules of the Party and Party or state discipline, and against violators of Party ethics;

b. Considers appeals against decisions of Central Committees of the Communist Parties of the Union Republics, or of territorial and provincial Party committees, to expel members from the Party or impose Party penalties upon them.

40.   In the period between congresses of the Party, the Central Committee of the CPSU may as necessary convene all-Union Party conferences for discussion of urgent questions of Party policy. The procedure for conducting an all-Union Party conference is determined by the CC CPSU.

V. REPUBLIC, TERRITORIAL, REGIONAL, AREA, CITY, AND DISTRICT ORGANIZATIONS OF THE PARTY

41.   The republic, territorial, provincial, area, city, and district Party organizations and their committees take guidance in their activities from the Program and the Rules of the CPSU, conduct all work for the implementation of Party policy and organize the fulfillment of the directives of the CC CPSU within the republics, territories, regions, areas, cities, and districts concerned.

42.   The basic duties of republic, territorial, provincial, area, city, and district Party organizations, and of their leading bodies, are:

a.   Political and organizational work among the masses; mobilization of the masses for the fulfillment of the tasks of communist construction, for the maximum development of industrial and agricultural production, for the fulfillment and overfulfillment of state plans; solicitude for the steady improvement of the material and cultural standards of the working people;

b.   Organization of ideological work, propaganda of Marxism-Leninism, promotion of the communist awareness of the working people, guidance of the local press, radio and television, and control over the activities of cultural and educational institutions;

c.   Guidance of soviets, trade unions, the YCL, the cooperatives, and other public organizations through the Party groups in them, and increasingly broad enlistment of working people in the activities of these organizations; development of the initiative and activity of the masses as an essential condition for the gradual transition from socialist statehood to public self-government under communism.

Party organizations must not act in place of government, trade union, cooperative, or other public organizations of the working people; they must not allow either the merging of the functions of Party and other bodies or undue parallelism in work;

d.   Selection and appointment of leading personnel, their education in the spirit of communist ideas, honesty, and truthfulness, and a high sense of responsibility to the Party and the people for the work entrusted to them;

e.   Large-scale enlistment of Communists in the conduct of Party activities as nonstaff workers, as a form of civic work;

f. Organization of various institutions and enterprises of the Party within the bounds of their republic, territory, provincial, area, city, or district, and guidance of their activities; distribution of Party funds within the given organization; systematic information of the higher Party body, and accountability to it for their work.

Leading Bodies of Republic, Territorial, and Provincial Party Organizations

43. The highest body of provincial, territorial, and republic Party organizations is the respective provincial or territorial Party conference or the congress of the Communist Party of the Union Republic, and in the intervals between them the provincial committee, territorial committee, or the Central Committee of the Communist Party of the Union Republic.

44. Regular provincial and territorial Party conferences are convened by the respective provincial or territorial committees once every two or three years. Regular congresses of the Communist Parties of the Union Republics are convened by the CC of the Communist Party at least once in every five years. Extraordinary conferences and congresses are convened by decision of regional or territorial committees, or the CC of the Communist Parties of the Union Republics or on the demand of one third of the total membership of the organizations belonging to the regional, territorial or republic Party organization.

The rates of representation at provincial and territorial conferences and at congresses of the Communist Parties of the Union Republics are determined by the respective Party committees.

Provincial and territorial conferences, and congresses of the Communist Parties of the Union Republics hear the reports of the respective provincial or territorial committees, or the Central Committee of the Communist Party of the Union Republic, and of the auditing commission; discuss at their own discretion other matters of Party, economic, and cultural development; and elect the provincial or territorial committee, the Central Committee of the Union Republic, the auditing commission, and the delegates to the Congress of the CPSU.

In the period between congresses of the Communist Parties of the Union Republics, for discussion of important questions for action by the Party organization, the CC of the Communist Party can as necessary convene republic Party conferences. The procedure for conducting republic Party conferences shall be determined by the CC of the Communist Party of the Union Republic.

45. The provincial and territorial committees and the Central Committees of the Communist Parties of the Union Republics elect bureaus, which also include secretaries of the committees. The secretaries must

have a Party standing of not less than five years. The plenary meetings of the committees also confirm the chairmen of Party commissions, heads of departments of these committees, editors of Party newspapers and journals.

Provincial and territorial committees and the Central Committees of the Communist Parties of the Union Republics may set up secretariats to examine current business and verify the execution of decisions.

46. The plenary meetings of provincial and territorial committees and the Central Committees of the Communist Parties of the Union Republics shall be convened at least once every four months.

47. The provincial and territorial committees and the Central Committees of the Communist Parties of the Union Republics direct the area, city and district Party organizations, inspect their work and regularly hear reports of area, city and district Party committees.

Party organizations in Autonomous Republics, and in autonomous and other regions forming part of a territory or a Union Republic, function under the guidance of the respective territorial committees or Central Committees of the Communist Parties of the Union Republics.

Leading Bodies of Area, City, and District (Urban and Rural) Party Organizations

48. The highest body of an area, city, or district Party organization is the area, city, and district Party conference or the general meeting of Communists convened by the area, city, or district committee every two or three years, and the extraordinary conference convened by decision of the respective committee or on the demand of one third of the total membership of the Party organization concerned.

The area, city, or district conference (general meeting) hears reports of the committee and auditing commission, discusses at its own discretion other questions of Party, economic, and cultural development, and elects the area, city, and district committee, the auditing commission and delegates to the regional and territorial conference or the congress of the Communist Party of the Union Republic.

The norms of representation to the area, city, or district conference are established by the respective Party committee.

49. The area, city, or district committee elects a bureau, including the committee secretaries, and confirms the appointment of heads of committee departments and newspaper editors. The secretaries of the area, city, and district committees must have a Party standing of at least three years. The committee secretaries are confirmed by the respective regional or territorial committee, or the Central Committee of the Communist Party of the Union Republic.

50. The area, city, or district committee organizes and confirms the primary Party organizations, directs their work, regularly hears reports concerning the work of Party organizations, and keeps a register of Communists.

51. The plenary meeting of the area, city, or district committee is convened at least once in three months.

52. The area, city, or district committee has nonstaff instructors, sets up standing and ad hoc commissions on various aspects of Party work and uses other ways to draw Communists into the activities of the Party committee on social lines.

VI. PRIMARY PARTY ORGANIZATIONS

53. The Primary Party organizations are the basis of the Party.

Primary Party organizations are formed at the places of work of Party members—in factories, state farms, and other enterprises, collective farms, units of the Soviet Army, offices, educational establishments, etc., wherever there are not less than three Party members. Primary Party organizations may also be organized on the residential principle in villages and at housing administrations.

In individual cases, with the permission of the provincial committee, the territorial committee, or the Central Committee of the Communist Party of a Union Republic, primary party organizations may be established in the framework of several enterprises forming part of a production combine and located, as a rule, on the territory of one district or several urban districts.

54. At enterprises, collective farms, and institutions with over 50 Party members and candidate members, shop, sectional, farm, team, departmental, etc., Party organizations may be formed as units of the general primary Party organizations with the sanction of the district, city or area committee.

Within shop, sectional, etc., organizations, and also within primary Party organizations having less than 50 members and candidate members, Party groups may be formed in the teams and other production units.

55. The highest organ of the primary Party organization is the Party meeting, which is convened at least once a month. In Party organizations having shop organizations, a general Party meeting is conducted at least once every two months.

In large Party organizations with a membership of more than 300 Communists, a general Party meeting is convened when necessary at times fixed by the Party committee or on the demand of a number of shop or departmental Party organizations.

56. For the conduct of current business the primary, shop, or departmental Party organization elects a bureau for the term of one year.

The number of its members is fixed by the Party meeting. Primary, shop and departmental Party organizations with less than 15 Party members do not elect a bureau. Instead, they elect a secretary and deputy secretary of the Party organization.

Secretaries of primary, shop, and departmental Party organizations must have a Party standing of at least one year.

Primary Party organizations with less than 150 Party members shall have, as a rule, no salaried staff released from their regular work.

57. In large factories and offices with more than 300 members and candidate members of the Party, and in exceptional cases in factories and offices with over 100 Communists by virtue of special production conditions and territorial dispersion, subject to the approval of the provincial committee, territorial committee, or Central Committee of the Communist Party of the Union Republic, Party committees may be formed, the shop and departmental Party organizations at these factories and offices being granted the status of primary Party organizations.

The Party organizations of collective and state farms may set up Party committees if they have a minimum of 50 Communists.

In Party organizations with more than 500 Communists, with the permission of the provincial committee, the territorial committee, or the Central Committee of the Communist Party of a Union Republic, Party committees can be formed in large shops, and the rights of a primary Party organization can be extended to Party organizations of production divisions.

The Party committees are elected for a term of two or three years. Their numerical composition is fixed by the general Party meeting or conference.

58. Party committees of primary organizations having more than 1,000 Communists, with the permission of the CC of the Union Republic Communist Party, may be granted the rights of a district Party committee regarding questions of acceptance into Party membership, and of registering regular and candidate members, and of examination of personal cases of Communists.

59. Party committees which have been granted the rights of district Party committees are elected for a two-year term.

In its activities the primary Party organization takes guidance from the Program and the Rules of the CPSU. It conducts its work directly among the working people, rallies them around the Communist Party of the Soviet Union, organizes the masses to carry out the Party policy and to work for the building of communism.

The primary Party organization:

a. Admits new members to the CPSU;

b. Educates Communists in a spirit of loyalty to the Party cause, ideological firmness, and communist ethics;

c. Organizes the study by Communists of Marxist-Leninist theory in close relation with the practice of communist construction and opposes all attempts at revisionist distortions of Marxism-Leninism and its dogmatic interpretation;

d. Supports the vanguard of Communists in the sphere of labor and in the sociopolitical and economic activities of enterprises, collective farms, institutions, educational establishments, etc.;

e. Acts as the organizer of the working people for the performance of the current tasks of communist construction, heads the socialist emulation movement for the fulfillment of state plans and undertakings of the working people, rallies the masses to disclose and make the best use of untapped resources at enterprises and collective farms, and to apply in production on a broad scale the achievements of science, engineering, and the experience of front-rankers; works for the strengthening of labor discipline, the steady increase of labor productivity and improvement of the quality of production, and shows concern for the protection and increase of social wealth at enterprises, state farms, and collective farms;

f. Conducts agitational and propaganda work among the masses, educates them in the communist spirit, helps the working people to acquire proficiency in administering state and social affairs;

g. On the basis of extensive criticism and self-criticism, combats cases of bureaucracy, parochialism, and violations of state discipline, thwarts attempts to deceive the state, acts against negligence, waste, and extravagance at enterprises, collective farms, and offices;

h. Assists the area, city, and district committees in their activities and is accountable to them for its work.

The Party organization must see to it that every Communist should observe in his own life and cultivate among working people the moral principles set forth in the Program of the CPSU, in the moral code of the builder of communism:

Loyalty to the communist cause, love of his own socialist country, and of other socialist countries;

Conscientious labor for the benefit of society, for he who does not work, neither shall he eat;

Concern on everyone's part for the protection and increase of social wealth;

Lofty sense of public duty, intolerance of violations of public interests;

Collectivism and comradely mutual assistance: one for all, and all for one;

Humane relations and mutual respect among people; man is to man a friend, comrade and brother;

Honesty and truthfulness, moral purity, unpretentiousness, and modesty in public and personal life;

Mutual respect in the family circle and concern for the upbringing of children;

Intolerance of injustice, parasitism, dishonesty, careerism, and moneygrubbing;

Friendship and fraternity among all peoples of the USSR, intolerance of national and racial hostility;

Intolerance of the enemies of communism, the enemies of peace and those who oppose the freedom of the peoples;

Fraternal solidarity with the working people of all countries, with all peoples.

60.   Primary Party organizations of enterprises in industry, transportation, communications, construction, material-technical supply, trade, food service, services to the public, collective farms, state farms, and other agricultural enterprises, design organizations, construction bureaus, scientific-research institutes, educational institutions, cultural and health establishments have the right of supervision of administration.

Party organizations in Ministries, State Committees, and other central and local soviet and economic establishments and offices carry on supervision of the work of the apparatus in the fulfillment of directives of the Party and the government and the observance of Soviet laws. They must actively promote improvement of the apparatus, cultivate among the personnel a high sense of responsibility for work entrusted to them, promote state discipline and the better servicing of the population, firmly combat bureaucracy and red tape, inform the appropriate Party bodies in good time about shortcomings in the work of the respective offices and individuals, regardless of what posts the latter may occupy.

VII.   THE PARTY AND THE YCL

61.   The Leninist Young Communist League of the Soviet Union is an independently acting social organization of young people, an active helper and reserve of the Party. The YCL helps the Party educate youth in the communist spirit, draw it into the work of building a new society, train a rising generation of harmoniously developed people who will live and work and administer public affairs under communism.

62.   YCL organizations enjoy the right of broad initiative in discussing and submitting to the appropriate Party organizations questions related to the work of enterprises, collective farms and offices. They must be active agents in the implementation of Party directives in all spheres of communist construction, especially where there are no primary Party organizations.

63.   The YCL conducts its activities under the guidance of the Communist Party of the Soviet Union. The work of the local YCL organiza-

tions is directed and controlled by the appropriate republic, territorial, provincial, area, city, and district Party organizations.

In their communist educational work among youth, local Party bodies and primary Party organizations rely on the support of the YCL organizations, and uphold and promote their useful undertakings.

64.   Members of the YCL who have been admitted into the CPSU cease to belong to the YCL the moment they join the Party, provided they do not hold leading posts in YCL organizations.

VIII.   PARTY ORGANIZATIONS IN THE SOVIET ARMY

65.   Party organizations in the Soviet Army take guidance in their work from the Program and the Rules of the CPSU and operate on the basis of instructions issued by the Central Committee.

The Party organizations of the Soviet Army carry out the policies of the Party in the Armed Forces, rally servicemen around the Communist Party, educate them in the spirit of Marxism-Leninism and boundless loyalty to the socialist homeland, actively further the unity of the army and the people, work for the strengthening of military discipline, rally servicemen to carry out the tasks of military and political training and acquire skill in the use of new technology and weapons, and to perform irreproachably their military duty and the orders and instructions of the command.

66.   The guidance of Party work in the Armed Forces is exercised by the Central Committee of the CPSU through the Main Political Administration of the Soviet Army and Navy, which functions as a department of the CC CPSU.

The chiefs of the political administrations of military areas and fleets, and chiefs of the political administrations of armies must be Party members of five years' standing, and the chiefs of political departments of military formations must be Party members of three years' standing.

67.   The Party organizations and political bodies of the Soviet Army maintain close contact with local Party committees, and keep them informed about political work in the military units. The secretaries of military Party organizations and chiefs of political bodies participate in the work of local Party committees.

IX.   PARTY GROUPS IN NON-PARTY ORGANIZATIONS

68.   At congresses, conferences, and meetings and in the elective bodies of soviets, trade unions, cooperatives, and other mass organizations of the working people having at least three Party members, Party groups are formed for the purpose of strengthening the influence of the Party

in every way and carrying out Party policy among non-Party people, strengthening Party and state discipline, combating bureaucracy, and verifying the fulfillment of Party and government directives.

69.   The Party groups are subordinate to the appropriate Party bodies: the Central Committee of the Communist Party of the Soviet Union, the Central Committees of the Communist Parties of the Union Republics, territorial, provincial, area, city, or district Party committees.

In all matters the groups must strictly and unswervingly abide by decisions of the leading Party bodies.

X.   PARTY FUNDS

70.   The funds of the Party and its organizations are derived from membership dues, income from Party enterprises, and other revenue.

71.   The monthly membership dues for Party members and candidate members are as follows:

	Dues per Month	
Monthly Earnings	*Kopeks*	*Percent*
Up to 50 rubles	10	
From 51 to 100 rubles		0.5
From 101 to 150 rubles		1.0
From 151 to 200 rubles		1.5
From 201 to 250 rubles		2.0
From 251 to 300 rubles		2.5
Over 300 rubles		3.0

72.   An entrance fee of 2 percent of monthly earnings is paid on admission to the Party as a candidate member.

Appendix 3

Succession to Leading Posts
(July 1973)

Position	Name	Start of Service	End of Service
Chairman, Council of Ministers*	Vladimir I. Lenin	Nov. 1917	Jan. 1924
	Alexei I. Rykov	Feb. 1924	Dec. 1930
	Vyacheslav M. Molotov	Dec. 1930	May 1941
	Iosif V. Stalin	May 1941	March 1953
	Georgi M. Malenkov	March 1953	Feb. 1955
	Nikolai A. Bulganin	Feb. 1955	March 1958
	Nikita S. Khrushchev	March 1958	Oct. 1964
	Alexei N. Kosygin	Oct. 1964	present
Chairman, Presidium of the Supreme Soviet†	Yakov M. Sverdlov	Nov. 1917	March 1919
	Mikhail M. Kalinin	March 1919	March 1946
	Nikolai M. Shvernik	March 1946	March 1953
	Kliment Ye. Voroshilov	March 1953	May 1960
	Leonid I. Brezhnev	May 1960	July 1964
	Anastas I. Mikoyan	July 1964	Dec. 1965
	Nikolai V. Podgorny	Dec. 1965	present
General Secretary of the Communist Party‡	Iosif V. Stalin	March 1922	March 1953
	Nikita S. Khrushchev	Sept. 1953	Oct. 1964
	Leonid I. Brezhnev	Oct. 1964	present

*Lenin, technically, was Chairman of the RSFSR Council of People's Commissars, his successors until 1946, chairmen of the USSR Council of People's Commissars, and thereafter chairmen of the USSR Council of Ministers.

†Until 1924, these were chairmen of the All-Russian Central Executive Committee; thereafter, until 1936, chairmen of the USSR Central Executive Committee; and, after 1936, chairmen of the Presidium of the Supreme Soviet.

‡Khrushchev in 1953 adopted the title of First Secretary. At the 23rd Party Congress in 1966, the designation of General Secretary was restored.

Appendix 4

Dates of Party Congresses

Designation of Party	Number of Congress	Time and Place*
All-Russian Social Democratic Labor Party	First	Minsk, March 1898
	Second	Brussels and London, July–August 1903
	Third	London, April–May 1905
	Fourth	Stockholm, April–May 1906
	Fifth	London, May–June 1907
All-Russian Social Democratic Labor Party (Bolsheviks)	Sixth	Petrograd, July–August 1917
All-Russian Communist Party (Bolsheviks)	Seventh	Petrograd, March 1918
	Eighth	Moscow, March 1919
	Ninth	March–April 1920
	Tenth	March 1921
	11th	March–April 1922
	12th	April 1923
	13th	May 1924
All-Union Communist Party (Bolsheviks)	14th	December 1925
	15th	December 1927
	16th	June–July 1930
	17th	January–February 1934
	18th	March 1939
Communist Party of the Soviet Union	19th	October 1952
	20th	February 1956
	21st	January–February 1959
	22nd	October 1961
	23rd	March–April 1966
	24th	March–April 1971

*All Congresses from 1919 on were in Moscow.

Index

INDEX